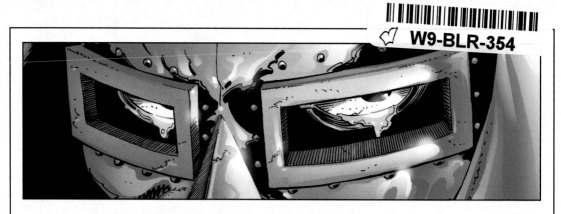

dominated news headlines in the 1980s and 1990s. With an HIV-positive baby girl at the heart of the story, Northstar forcefully makes a point that, hard as it may be to believe, many failed to grasp back in 1992: "AIDS is not a disease restricted to homosexuals, as much as it seems, at times, the rest of the world wishes that were so!"

The influence of AIDS could be seen in the deadly and, for a long time, incurable Legacy virus plaguing mutantkind in the early 1990s — and the sense of powerlessness in the face of such a disease is conveyed in *Uncanny X-Men #303* (August 1993). Colossus' sister Illyana Rasputin succumbs to the virus, and a grief-stricken Jubilee and her teammates must deal with the anguish of her final hours and ultimate passing. Even the mightiest of Marvel's heroes is not immune to the impact of AIDS, as shown in *Incredible Hulk #420* (August 1994), where Bruce Banner's old friend Jim Wilson, suffering from the disease, pleads with the Hulk to attempt to save his life with what would amount to a reckless transfusion of gamma-irradiated blood.

A very different tragedy changed the world around us on September 11, 2001 — the terrorist attacks on America that claimed almost 3,000 lives. New York City is home to Marvel Comics — and to many of our characters — so an atrocity that struck so close to home could not be ignored. The *Amazing Spider-Man* creative team, J. Michael Straczynski and John Romita Jr., interrupted their highly successful run to present a deeply personal reaction in the form of *Amazing Spider-Man #36* (December 2001). The standalone story depicts Spider-Man and other costumed adventurers standing side-by-side with the real-life heroes of New York — the firefighters, police officers and relief workers — dealing with the aftermath of

disaster. And as the country came to terms with a new threat that could strike on America's shores, its fictional champion wrestled with the implications in *Captain America #1* (June 2002), by John Ney Rieber and John Cassaday. Just as he had against Nazis and Communists in earlier eras, Cap joins the fight against terror — while striving to uphold the values and ideals of his divided homeland.

In 2009, Peter Parker joined the media hordes covering the inauguration of Barack Obama as America's first African American president — and, naturally, Spider-Man is called into action to hail the new chief in *Amazing Spider-Man #583* (March 2009). "History in the making," as Peter's inner monologue acknowledges. Then-Editor in Chief Joe Quesada said at the time: "When we heard that President-Elect Obama is a collector of Spider-Man comics, we knew that these two historic figures had to meet in our comics' Marvel Universe." Thanks in part to a media frenzy, the comic went to five printings, selling more than 350,000 copies.

Astonishing X-Men #51 (August 2012) is another comic that illustrates the remarkable social change that can take place in the real world while relatively few years pass in "Marvel time." Here, we reconnect with Northstar for his wedding to boyfriend Kyle Jinadu — the first same-sex marriage in mainstream comics. "When gay marriage became legal in New York State, it raised obvious questions since most of our heroes reside in New York State," then-Editor in Chief Axel Alonso told *Rolling Stone* magazine. "Our comics are always best when they respond to and reflect developments in the real world. We've been doing that for decades, and this is just the latest expression of that."

Few modern characters illustrate that ethos more than Kamala Khan, the new Ms. Marvel, who quickly joined the ranks of comic book headline-makers when it was announced that this young Muslim hero was going to star in her own series. She has established herself as one of Marvel's most popular characters — a shining celebration of its legacy — and so it is fitting that, during the high-profile election campaign of 2016, she should enter the conversation in the pages of *Ms. Marvel #13* (January 2017). Kamala stands up for democracy in her native Jersey City, imploring her community — and in turn, her readers — to get out and vote.

And finally, Kamala and the fellow heroes of her generation, the Champions, must deal with one of today's most pressing and depressing issues: gun violence in schools. *Champions #24* (November 2018) focuses on events following a shooting at Brooklyn Visions Academy, where Miles Morales, the young Spider-Man, studies. Writer Jim Zub explained: "Marvel strives to depict the 'world outside your window,' and this just became too big a topic to ignore."

Indeed, these topics — and other real-life problems, controversies and threats — simply cannot be ignored in the pages of Marvel Comics. Just as our readers confront them each day, so too must our heroes — and they'll continue to do exactly that for the next 80 years.

JESS HARROLD IS A BRITISH WRITER AND JOURNALIST SPECIALIZING IN PROPERTY LAW AND SUPER HEROES, THOUGH NOT USUALLY BOTH AT THE SAME TIME. HE HAS WORKED FOR MARVEL FOR MORE THAN A DECADE, CONTRIBUTING EXTENSIVELY TO *MARVEL SPOTLIGHT* AS WELL AS OTHER MAGAZINES AND BOOKS. ON THE RETURN OF *STAR WARS* TO THE HOUSE OF IDEAS, HARROLD WROTE THE CELEBRATORY ART COLLECTIONS *STAR WARS: THE MARVEL COVERS* AND *STAR WARS: A NEW HOPE — THE 40TH ANNIVERSARY*. HIS BOOKS ALSO INCLUDE *THE A-Z OF MARVEL MONSTERS* AND *THE ART OF WAR OF THE REALMS*.

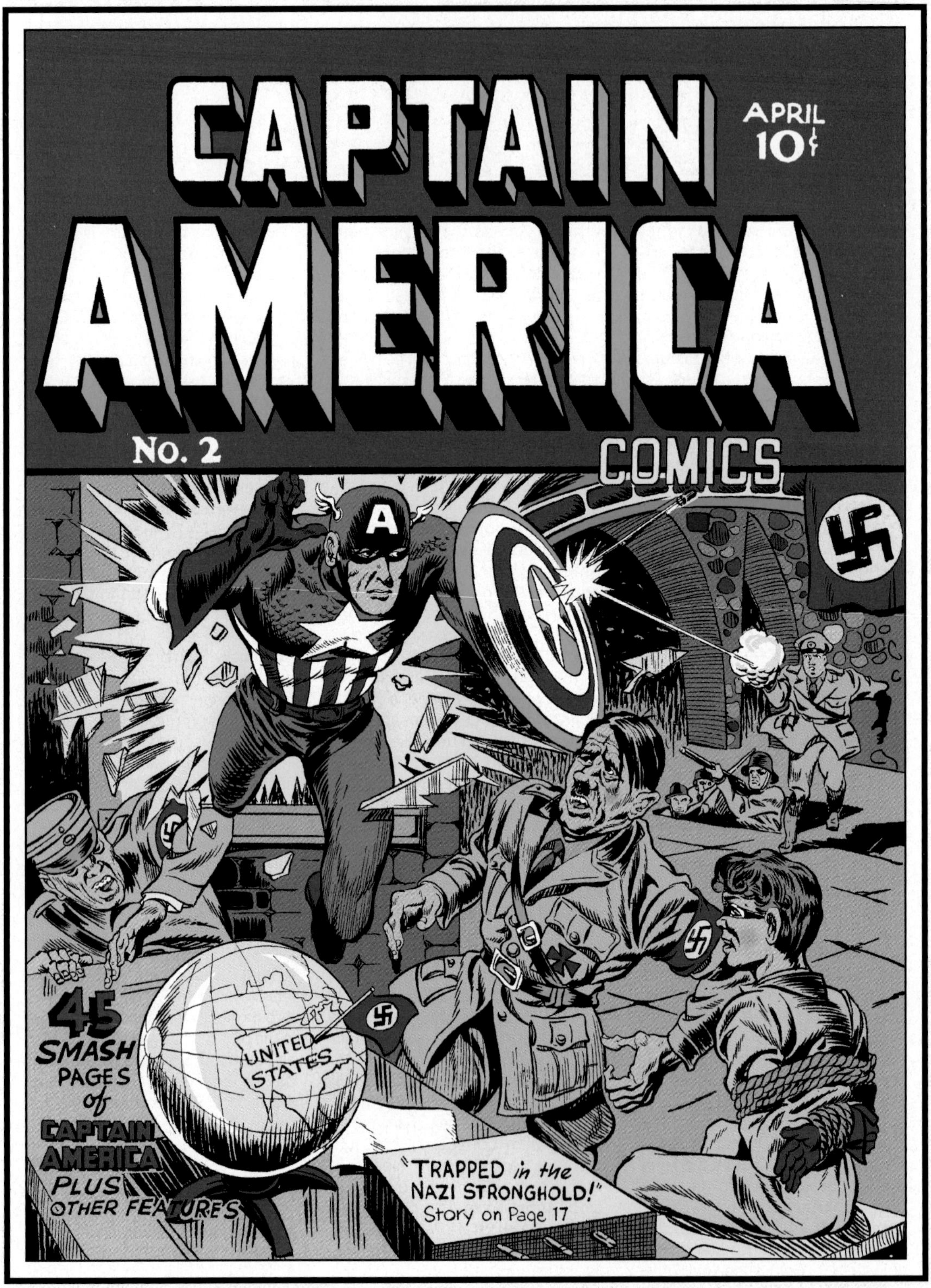

CAPTAIN AMERICA
APRIL
10¢
No. 2
COMICS
UNITED STATES
45 SMASH PAGES of CAPTAIN AMERICA PLUS OTHER FEATURES
"TRAPPED in the NAZI STRONGHOLD!"
Story on Page 17

MARVEL COMICS

THE WORLD OUTSIDE YOUR WINDOW

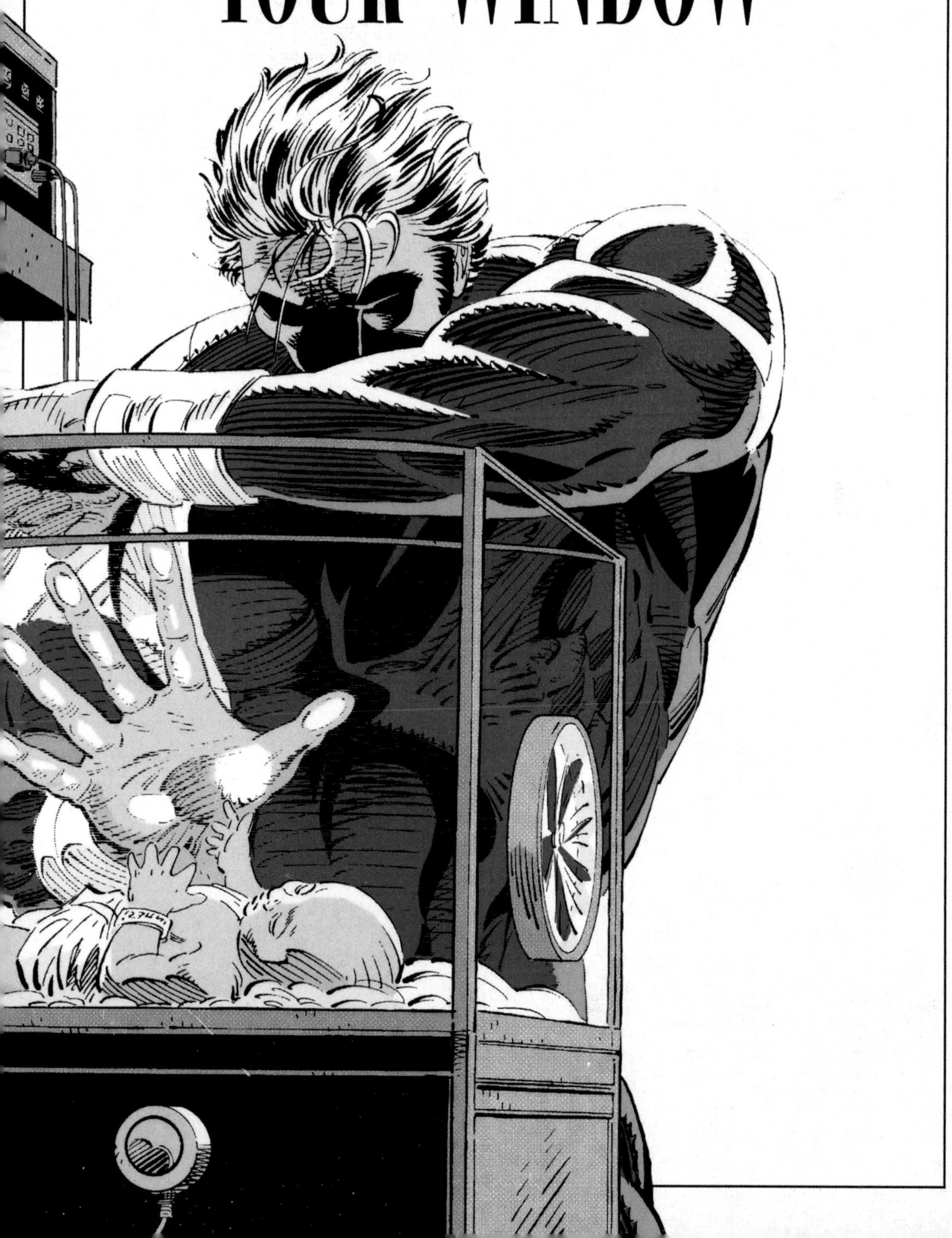

CAPTAIN AMERICA COMICS #2
APRIL 1941

JOE SIMON
WITH **JACK KIRBY**
WRITERS

JACK KIRBY &
REED CRANDALL
PENCILERS

REED CRANDALL
& CO.
INKERS

JOE SIMON
EDITOR

AMAZING SPIDER-MAN #97
JUNE 1971

STAN LEE
WRITER & EDITOR

GIL KANE
PENCILER

FRANK GIACOIA
INKER

SAM ROSEN
LETTERER

HOWARD THE DUCK #8
JANUARY 1977

STEVE GERBER
WRITER

GENE COLAN
PENCILER

STEVE LEIALOHA
INKER

JANICE COHEN
COLORIST

IRVING WATANABE
LETTERER

ARCHIE GOODWIN
EDITOR

IRON MAN #128
NOVEMBER 1979

DAVID MICHELINIE
CO-PLOTTER & SCRIPTER

JOHN ROMITA JR.
PENCILER

BOB LAYTON
CO-PLOTTER & INKER

BOB SHAREN
COLORIST

JOHN COSTANZA
LETTERER

JIM SALICRUP
ASSISTANT EDITOR

ROGER STERN
EDITOR

NEW MUTANTS #45
NOVEMBER 1986

CHRIS CLAREMONT
WRITER

BUTCH GUICE
PENCILER

KYLE BAKER
INKER

GLYNIS OLIVER
COLORIST

LOIS BUHALIS &
TOM ORZECHOWSKI
LETTERERS

TERRY KAVANAGH
ASSISTANT EDITOR

ANN NOCENTI
EDITOR

ALPHA FLIGHT #106
MARCH 1992

SCOTT LOBDELL
WRITER

MARK PACELLA
PENCILER

DAN PANOSIAN
INKER

BOB SHAREN
COLORIST

JANICE CHIANG
LETTERER

CHRIS COOPER
ASSISTANT EDITOR

BOBBIE CHASE
EDITOR

UNCANNY X-MEN #303
AUGUST 1993

SCOTT LOBDELL
WRITER

RICHARD BENNETT
PENCILER

RICHARD BENNETT
& DAN GREEN
INKERS

JOE ROSAS
COLORIST

CHRIS ELIOPOULOS
LETTERER

LISA PATRICK
ASSISTANT EDITOR

BOB HARRAS
EDITOR

INCREDIBLE HULK #420
AUGUST 1994

PETER DAVID
WRITER

GARY FRANK
PENCILER

CAM SMITH
INKER

GLYNIS OLIVER
COLORIST

JOE ROSEN
LETTERER

JAMES FELDER
ASSISTANT EDITOR

BOBBIE CHASE
EDITOR

AMAZING SPIDER-MAN #36
DECEMBER 2001

J. MICHAEL STRACZYNSKI
WRITER

JOHN ROMITA JR.
PENCILER

SCOTT HANNA
INKER

AVALON's DAN KEMP
COLORIST

RICHARD STARKINGS
& COMICRAFT's
WES ABBOTT
LETTERER

JOHN MIESEGAES
ASSISTANT EDITOR

AXEL ALONSO
EDITOR

MARVEL COMICS

THE WORLD OUTSIDE YOUR WINDOW

CAPTAIN AMERICA #1
JUNE 2002

JOHN NEY RIEBER
WRITER

JOHN CASSADAY
ARTIST

DAVE STEWART
COLORIST

RICHARD STARKINGS & COMICRAFT's WES ABBOTT
LETTERER

KELLY LAMY
ASSOCIATE MANAGING EDITOR

NANCI DAKESIAN
MANAGING EDITOR

STUART MOORE
EDITOR

AMAZING SPIDER-MAN #583
MARCH 2009

ZEB WELLS
WRITER

TODD NAUCK
ARTIST

FRANK D'ARMATA WITH **DEAN WHITE**
COLORISTS

JARED K. FLETCHER
LETTERER

TOM BRENNAN
ASSISTANT EDITOR

STEPHEN WACKER
EDITOR

ASTONISHING X-MEN #51
AUGUST 2012

MARJORIE LIU
WRITER

MIKE PERKINS
PENCILER

MIKE PERKINS WITH **ANDREW HENNESSY**
INKERS

ANDY TROY, JIM CHARALAMPIDIS & RACHELLE ROSENBERG
COLORISTS

VC's JOE CARAMAGNA, CORY PETIT & CLAYTON COWLES
LETTERERS

DANIEL KETCHUM
ASSOCIATE EDITOR

JEANINE SCHAEFER
EDITOR

NICK LOWE
GROUP EDITOR

MS. MARVEL #13
JANUARY 2017

G. WILLOW WILSON
WRITER

MIRKA ANDOLFO
ARTIST

IAN HERRING
COLORIST

VC's JOE CARAMAGNA
LETTERER

CHARLES BEACHAM
ASSISTANT EDITOR

SANA AMANAT
EDITOR

CHAMPIONS #24
NOVEMBER 2018

JIM ZUB
WRITER

SEAN IZAAKSE
ARTIST

MARCIO MENYZ & ERICK ARCINIEGA
COLORISTS

VC's CLAYTON COWLES
LETTERER

ALANNA SMITH
ASSOCIATE EDITOR

TOM BREVOORT
EDITOR

STÉPHANE ROUX
FRONT COVER ARTIST

MARK D. BEAZLEY
COLLECTION EDITOR

MAIA LOY
ASSISTANT MANAGING EDITOR

LISA MONTALBANO
ASSISTANT MANAGING EDITOR

JOE HOCHSTEIN
ASSOCIATE MANAGER, DIGITAL ASSETS

CORY SEDLMEIER
MASTERWORKS EDITOR

JENNIFER GRÜNWALD
SENIOR EDITOR, SPECIAL PROJECTS

JEFF YOUNGQUIST
VP PRODUCTION & SPECIAL PROJECTS

JEPH YORK
RESEARCH & LAYOUT

JOE FRONTIRRE
PRODUCTION

JAY BOWEN
BOOK DESIGNER

DAVID GABRIEL
SVP PRINT, SALES & MARKETING

C.B. CEBULSKI
EDITOR IN CHIEF

MARVEL COMICS: THE WORLD OUTSIDE YOUR WINDOW. Contains material originally published in magazine form as AMAZING SPIDER-MAN (1963) #97, HOWARD THE DUCK (1976) #8, IRON MAN (1968) #128, NEW MUTANTS (1983) #45, ALPHA FLIGHT (1983) #106, UNCANNY X-MEN (1981) #303, INCREDIBLE HULK (1968) #420, AMAZING SPIDER-MAN (1999) #36 and #583, CAPTAIN AMERICA (2002) #1, ASTONISHING X-MEN (2004) #51, MS. MARVEL (2015) #13, CHAMPIONS (2016) #24, and CAPTAIN AMERICA COMICS #2. First printing 2020. ISBN 978-1-302-92353-2. Published by MARVEL WORLDWIDE, INC., a subsidiary of MARVEL ENTERTAINMENT, LLC. OFFICE OF PUBLICATION: 1290 Avenue of the Americas, New York, NY 10104. © 2020 MARVEL No similarity between any of the names, characters, persons, and/or institutions in this magazine with those of any living or dead person or institution is intended, and any such similarity which may exist is purely coincidental. **Printed in the U.S.A.** KEVIN FEIGE, Chief Creative Officer; DAN BUCKLEY, President, Marvel Entertainment; JOHN NEE, Publisher; JOE QUESADA, EVP & Creative Director; TOM BREVOORT, SVP of Publishing; DAVID BOGART, Associate Publisher & SVP of Talent Affairs; Publishing & Partnership; DAVID GABRIEL, VP of Print & Digital Publishing; JEFF YOUNGQUIST, VP of Production & Special Projects; DAN CARR, Executive Director of Publishing Technology; ALEX MORALES, Director of Publishing Operations; DAN EDINGTON, Managing Editor; SUSAN CRESPI, Production Manager; STAN LEE, Chairman Emeritus. For information regarding advertising in Marvel Comics or on Marvel.com, please contact Vit DeBellis, Custom Solutions & Integrated Advertising Manager, at vdebellis@marvel.com, please call 888-511-5480. **Manufactured between 7/3/2020 and 8/4/2020 by LSC COMMUNICATIONS INC., KENDALLVILLE, IN, USA.**

10 9 8 7 6 5 4 3 2 1

INTRODUCTION

BY JESS HARROLD

In 1986, as part of the celebration of the 25th anniversary of *Fantastic Four #1*, Marvel Comics introduced the New Universe, a fresh comic book line heralded as "the world outside your window." Then-Editor in Chief Jim Shooter sought to honor the creative legacies of "revolutionaries" like Stan Lee, Jack Kirby and Steve Ditko, who had imbued their colorful, costumed characters with "human, real-life problems" like nothing seen before in comics. After all, the Marvel Universe has resembled and reflected that world outside the windows of its readers from day one — long before anyone ever even referred to it as the "Marvel Universe"…or even to the publisher as Marvel Comics. It has done so now for a remarkable 80 years. In this volume, we draw together stories from across the decades — from the early 1940s to the end of 2018 — that exemplify the enduring connection between Marvel's heroes and the lives of those who follow their adventures each month.

Journey with us back to 1941, when the stories of early Timely Comics icons like the Sub-Mariner and the android Human Torch took place against the backdrop of World War II. Of course, Captain America was no exception, and our chosen tale, "Trapped in the Nazi Stronghold," from *Captain America Comics #2* (April 1941), features Cap and Bucky going into action against two of the most notorious figures of the age — Adolf Hitler and Hermann Göring. And, remarkably, this was published months before the U.S.A. officially entered the war — attracting some controversy at the time. For Captain America co-creators Joe Simon and Jack Kirby, the rising threat of the Nazis directly inspired their Sentinel of Liberty. As Simon once said: "World events gave us the perfect comic book villain, Adolf Hitler…so we decided to create the perfect hero who would be his foil."

Flashing forward a few decades to 1971, we join another Marvel icon who, perhaps more than any other, battles real-world struggles as challenging as any super-powered foe. We are talking, of course, of Peter Parker, the amazing Spider-Man — Stan Lee and Steve Ditko's "everyman" hero, whose overwhelming sense of responsibility as Spidey so often comes at a cost to his personal life. Rarely is this inner conflict more pronounced than in *Amazing Spider-Man #97* (June 1971), illustrated by Gil Kane, where Spider-Man is locked in conflict with his archenemy, Norman Osborn, A.K.A. the Green Goblin, just as Osborn's son Harry — Peter's best friend — succumbs to his inner demons and seeks solace in pills. Stan Lee, the book's writer and Marvel's editor in chief at the time, had received a letter from the Department of Health, Education and Welfare seeking to take advantage of Marvel's influence on young readers to feature a story warning kids about the dangerous effects of drug addiction. Stan was happy to help out, but at the time, the Comics Code Authority would not allow mention of drugs in a comic book story. So Stan and Marvel's publisher Martin Goodman made the brave — and unprecedented — decision to publish their three-part story without the CCA seal on its covers. As Stan saw it, "We would do more harm to the country by not running the story than by running it."

Speaking of harm to the country, how about Howard the Duck for president? Writer Steve Gerber's offbeat fowl "waddles blindly into the world of harsh political reality" in the pages of *Howard the Duck #8* (January 1977), as a candidate in the first election following President Richard Nixon's 1974 resignation in the wake of the Watergate scandal. In the real world, Jimmy Carter triumphed over Nixon's successor, Gerald Ford — but Marvel offered

1976's voters an irascible third-party candidate: Howard. It's a fine example of the kind of satire that Gerber, and his characters, excels at. As Howard puts it: "'Why a duck?' you ask! I say, why not a duck? You've had turkeys running this country for 200 years!"

As the 1970s came to an end, David Michelinie, Bob Layton and John Romita Jr. delivered a character-redefining run on *Iron Man*, which brought a very believable vulnerability to the Invincible Avenger. *Iron Man #128* (November 1979) — "Demon in a Bottle" — is one of the most famous Marvel comic books ever printed, as a Tony Stark who has become used to drowning his sorrows seeks to overcome his alcohol addiction. The issue reminds us that "a hero is, above all, a man…a man subject to pressures and responsibilities far beyond those of his peers. Such is a burden that must take its toll, eventually, from even the most valiant warrior."

Our journey through Marvel history passes through the 1980s with *New Mutants #45* (November 1986), a poignant tale that illustrates the plight of these young X-Men in training to fight for a world that hates and fears them. Marvel's mutants have always served as an allegory for prejudice in the real world, and in this story, written by legendary *X-Men* writer Chris Claremont, the psychological impact that prejudice can have on a bullied youth is powerfully explored, as Kitty Pryde and her fellow classmates must deal with the aftermath of a teen suicide.

Another form of prejudice — homophobia — is confronted in *Alpha Flight #106* (March 1992), a comic that made international headlines when it featured Northstar as the first Marvel super hero to come out as gay. The story, written by Scott Lobdell, is also pioneering for tackling the AIDS epidemic that

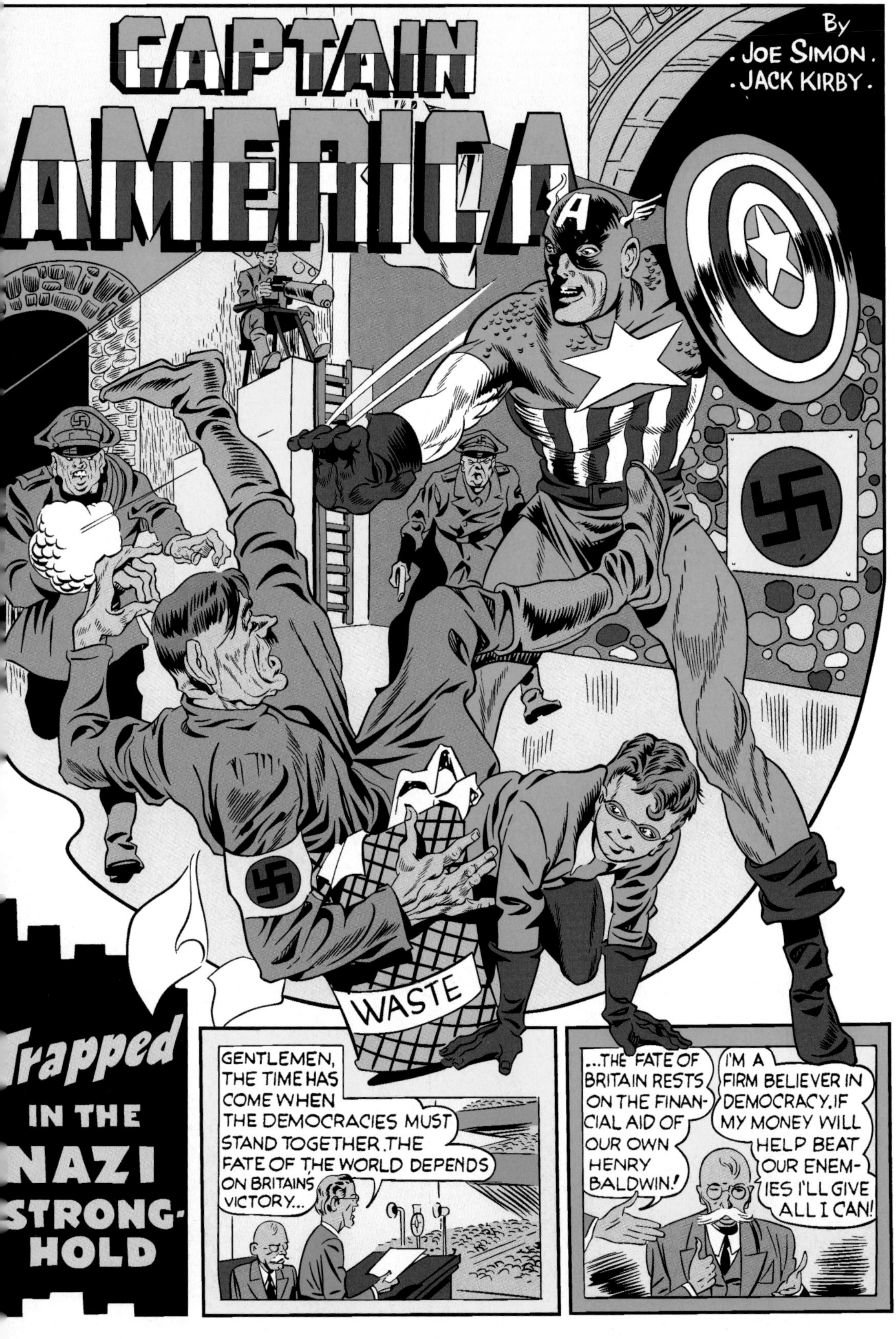
CAPTAIN AMERICA
By
• JOE SIMON •
• JACK KIRBY •
WASTE
Trapped IN THE NAZI STRONG-HOLD
GENTLEMEN, THE TIME HAS COME WHEN THE DEMOCRACIES MUST STAND TOGETHER. THE FATE OF THE WORLD DEPENDS ON BRITAIN'S VICTORY...
...THE FATE OF BRITAIN RESTS ON THE FINAN-CIAL AID OF OUR OWN HENRY BALDWIN!
I'M A FIRM BELIEVER IN DEMOCRACY. IF MY MONEY WILL HELP BEAT OUR ENEM-IES I'LL GIVE ALL I CAN!

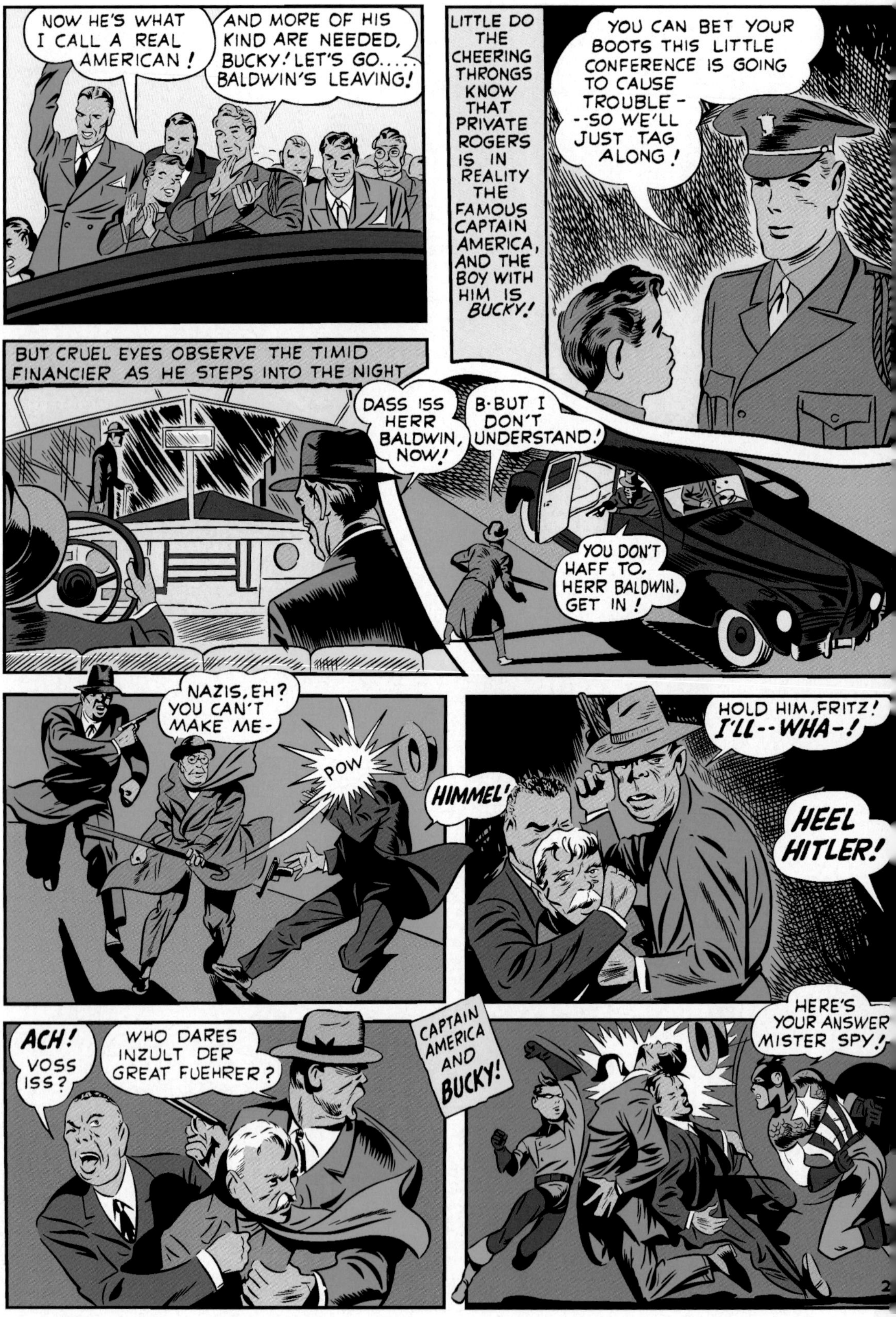
NOW HE'S WHAT I CALL A REAL AMERICAN!
AND MORE OF HIS KIND ARE NEEDED, BUCKY! LET'S GO..... BALDWIN'S LEAVING!
LITTLE DO THE CHEERING THRONGS KNOW THAT PRIVATE ROGERS IS IN REALITY THE FAMOUS CAPTAIN AMERICA, AND THE BOY WITH HIM IS BUCKY!
YOU CAN BET YOUR BOOTS THIS LITTLE CONFERENCE IS GOING TO CAUSE TROUBLE - - SO WE'LL JUST TAG ALONG!
BUT CRUEL EYES OBSERVE THE TIMID FINANCIER AS HE STEPS INTO THE NIGHT
DASS ISS HERR BALDWIN, NOW!
B-BUT I DON'T UNDERSTAND!
YOU DON'T HAFF TO, HERR BALDWIN. GET IN!
NAZIS, EH? YOU CAN'T MAKE ME-
POW
HOLD HIM, FRITZ! I'LL--WHA-!
HIMMEL!
HEEL HITLER!
ACH! VOSS ISS?
WHO DARES INZULT DER GREAT FUEHRER?
CAPTAIN AMERICA AND BUCKY!
HERE'S YOUR ANSWER MISTER SPY!

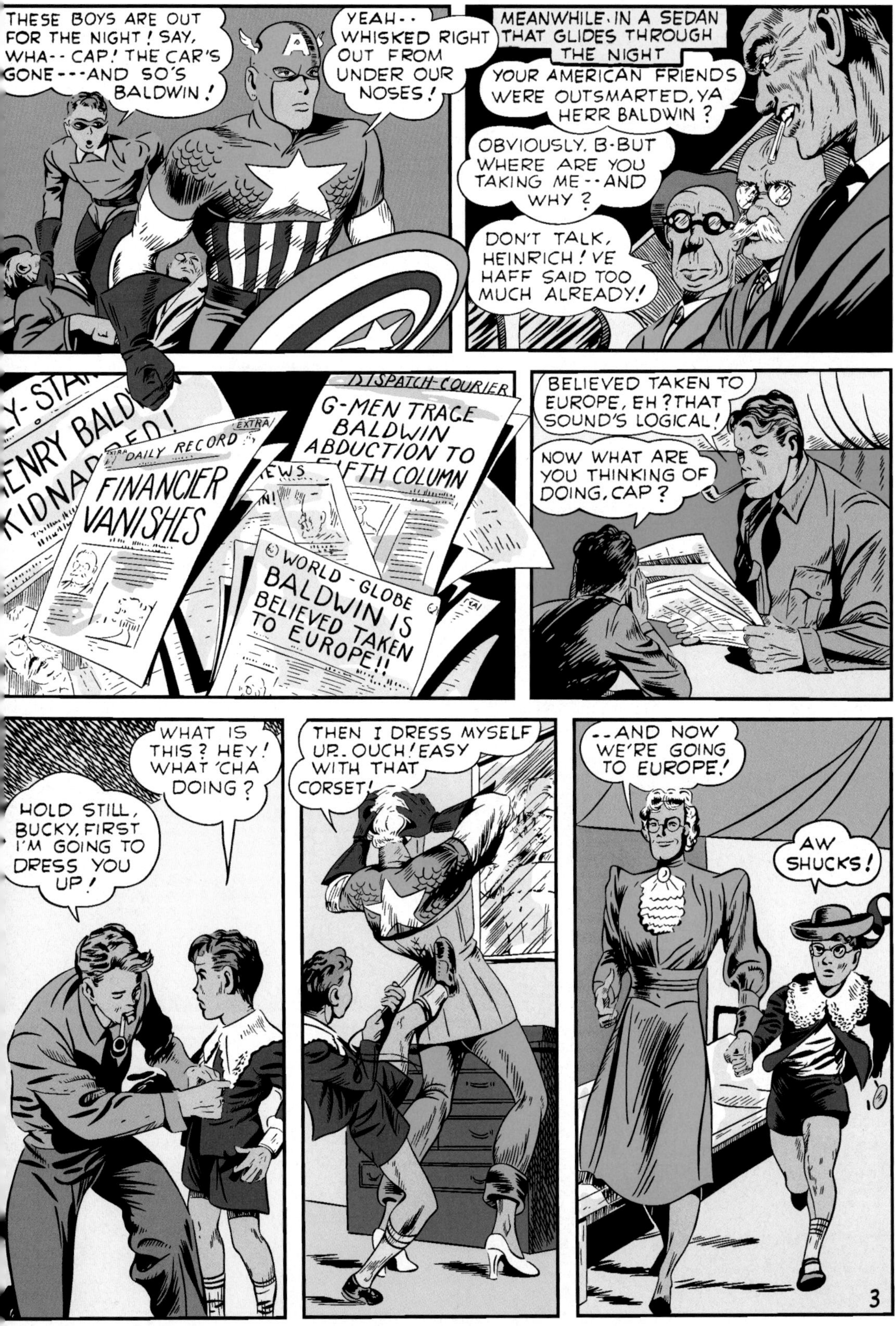
THESE BOYS ARE OUT FOR THE NIGHT! SAY, WHA-- CAP! THE CAR'S GONE---AND SO'S BALDWIN!
YEAH-- WHISKED RIGHT OUT FROM UNDER OUR NOSES!
MEANWHILE IN A SEDAN THAT GLIDES THROUGH THE NIGHT
YOUR AMERICAN FRIENDS WERE OUTSMARTED, YA HERR BALDWIN?
OBVIOUSLY. B-BUT WHERE ARE YOU TAKING ME--AND WHY?
DON'T TALK, HEINRICH! VE HAFF SAID TOO MUCH ALREADY!
HENRY BALD
KIDNAP
DAILY RECORD
FINANCIER VANISHES
DISPATCH-COURIER
G-MEN TRACE BALDWIN ABDUCTION TO FIFTH COLUMN
WORLD-GLOBE
BALDWIN IS BELIEVED TAKEN TO EUROPE!!
BELIEVED TAKEN TO EUROPE, EH? THAT SOUND'S LOGICAL!
NOW WHAT ARE YOU THINKING OF DOING, CAP?
WHAT IS THIS? HEY! WHAT 'CHA DOING?
HOLD STILL, BUCKY, FIRST I'M GOING TO DRESS YOU UP!
THEN I DRESS MYSELF UP.. OUCH! EASY WITH THAT CORSET!
--AND NOW WE'RE GOING TO EUROPE!
AW SHUCKS!
3

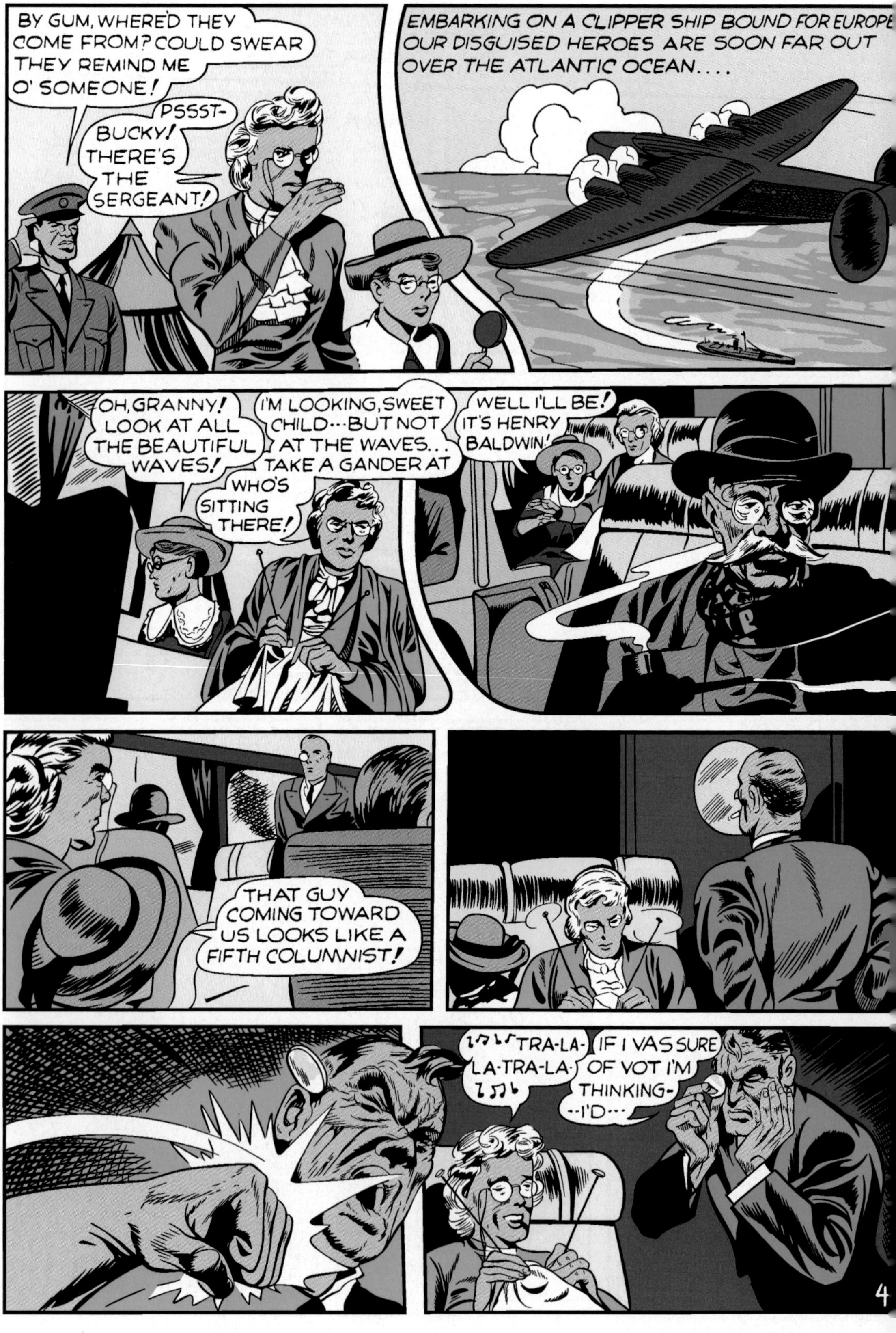
BY GUM, WHERE'D THEY COME FROM? COULD SWEAR THEY REMIND ME O' SOMEONE!
PSSST- BUCKY! THERE'S THE SERGEANT!
EMBARKING ON A CLIPPER SHIP BOUND FOR EUROPE OUR DISGUISED HEROES ARE SOON FAR OUT OVER THE ATLANTIC OCEAN....
OH, GRANNY! LOOK AT ALL THE BEAUTIFUL WAVES!
I'M LOOKING, SWEET CHILD--- BUT NOT AT THE WAVES... TAKE A GANDER AT WHO'S SITTING THERE!
WELL I'LL BE! IT'S HENRY BALDWIN!
THAT GUY COMING TOWARD US LOOKS LIKE A FIFTH COLUMNIST!
TRA-LA-LA-TRA-LA-
IF I VAS SURE OF VOT I'M THINKING- --I'D---
4

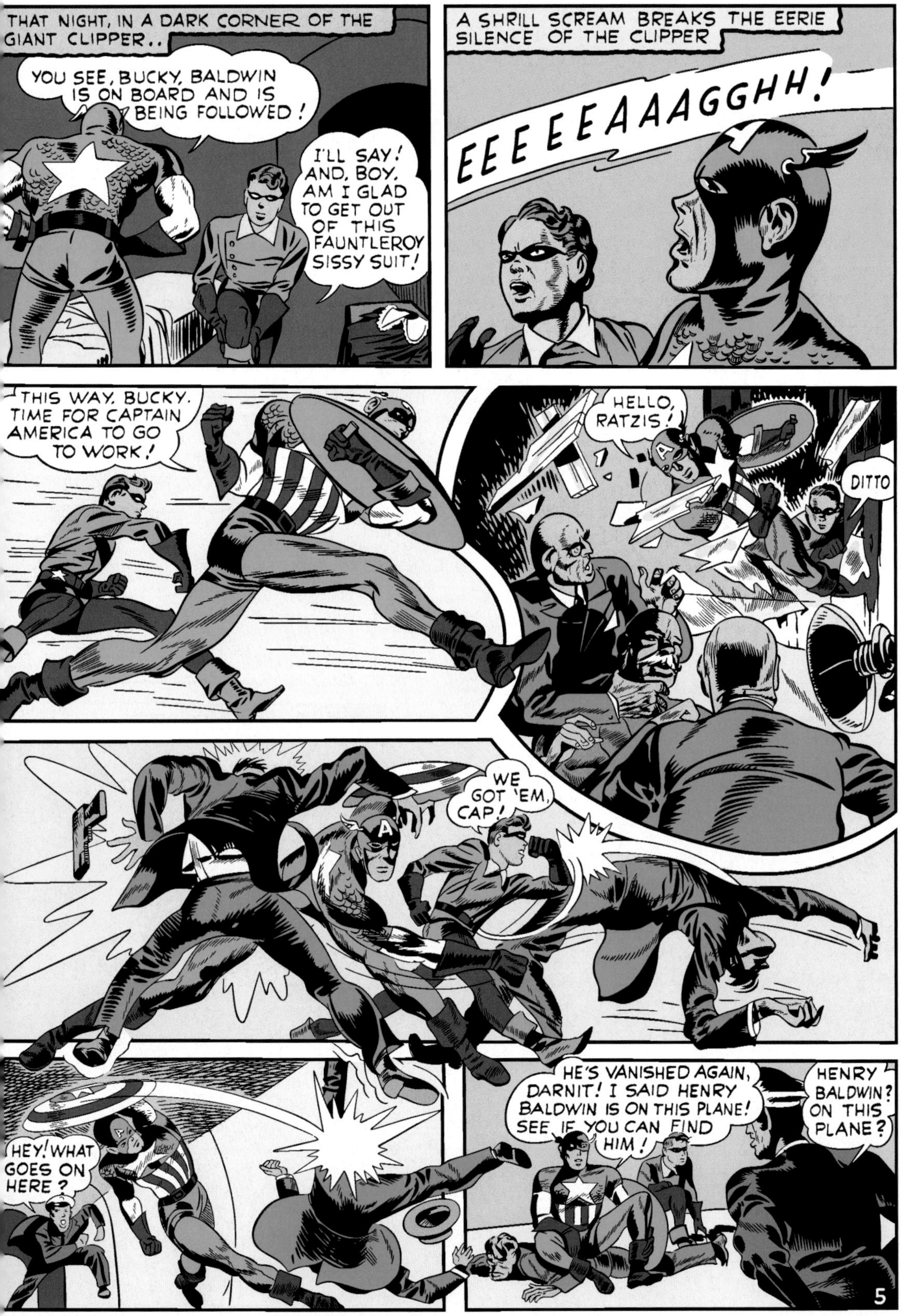
THAT NIGHT, IN A DARK CORNER OF THE GIANT CLIPPER..
YOU SEE, BUCKY, BALDWIN IS ON BOARD AND IS BEING FOLLOWED!
I'LL SAY! AND, BOY, AM I GLAD TO GET OUT OF THIS FAUNTLEROY SISSY SUIT!
A SHRILL SCREAM BREAKS THE EERIE SILENCE OF THE CLIPPER
EEEEEAAAAGGHH!
THIS WAY, BUCKY. TIME FOR CAPTAIN AMERICA TO GO TO WORK!
HELLO, RATZIS!
DITTO
WE GOT 'EM, CAP!
HEY! WHAT GOES ON HERE?
HE'S VANISHED AGAIN, DARNIT! I SAID HENRY BALDWIN IS ON THIS PLANE! SEE IF YOU CAN FIND HIM!
HENRY BALDWIN? ON THIS PLANE?
5

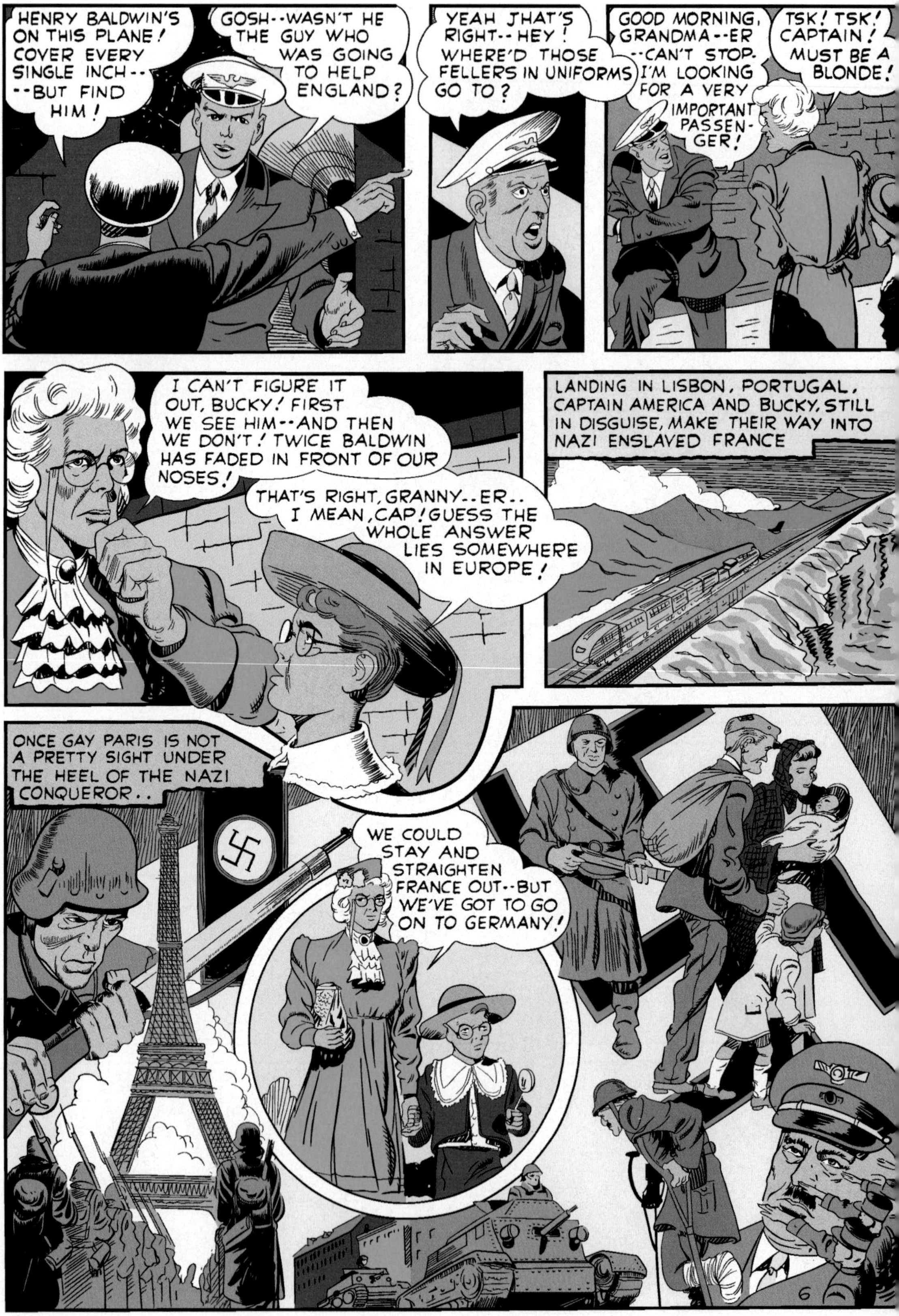
HENRY BALDWIN'S ON THIS PLANE! COVER EVERY SINGLE INCH-- --BUT FIND HIM!
GOSH--WASN'T HE THE GUY WHO WAS GOING TO HELP ENGLAND?
YEAH JHAT'S RIGHT--HEY! WHERE'D THOSE FELLERS IN UNIFORMS GO TO?
GOOD MORNING, GRANDMA--ER --CAN'T STOP. I'M LOOKING FOR A VERY IMPORTANT PASSENGER!
TSK! TSK! CAPTAIN! MUST BE A BLONDE!
I CAN'T FIGURE IT OUT, BUCKY! FIRST WE SEE HIM--AND THEN WE DON'T! TWICE BALDWIN HAS FADED IN FRONT OF OUR NOSES!
THAT'S RIGHT, GRANNY--ER.. I MEAN, CAP! GUESS THE WHOLE ANSWER LIES SOMEWHERE IN EUROPE!
LANDING IN LISBON, PORTUGAL, CAPTAIN AMERICA AND BUCKY, STILL IN DISGUISE, MAKE THEIR WAY INTO NAZI ENSLAVED FRANCE
ONCE GAY PARIS IS NOT A PRETTY SIGHT UNDER THE HEEL OF THE NAZI CONQUEROR..
WE COULD STAY AND STRAIGHTEN FRANCE OUT--BUT WE'VE GOT TO GO ON TO GERMANY!
6

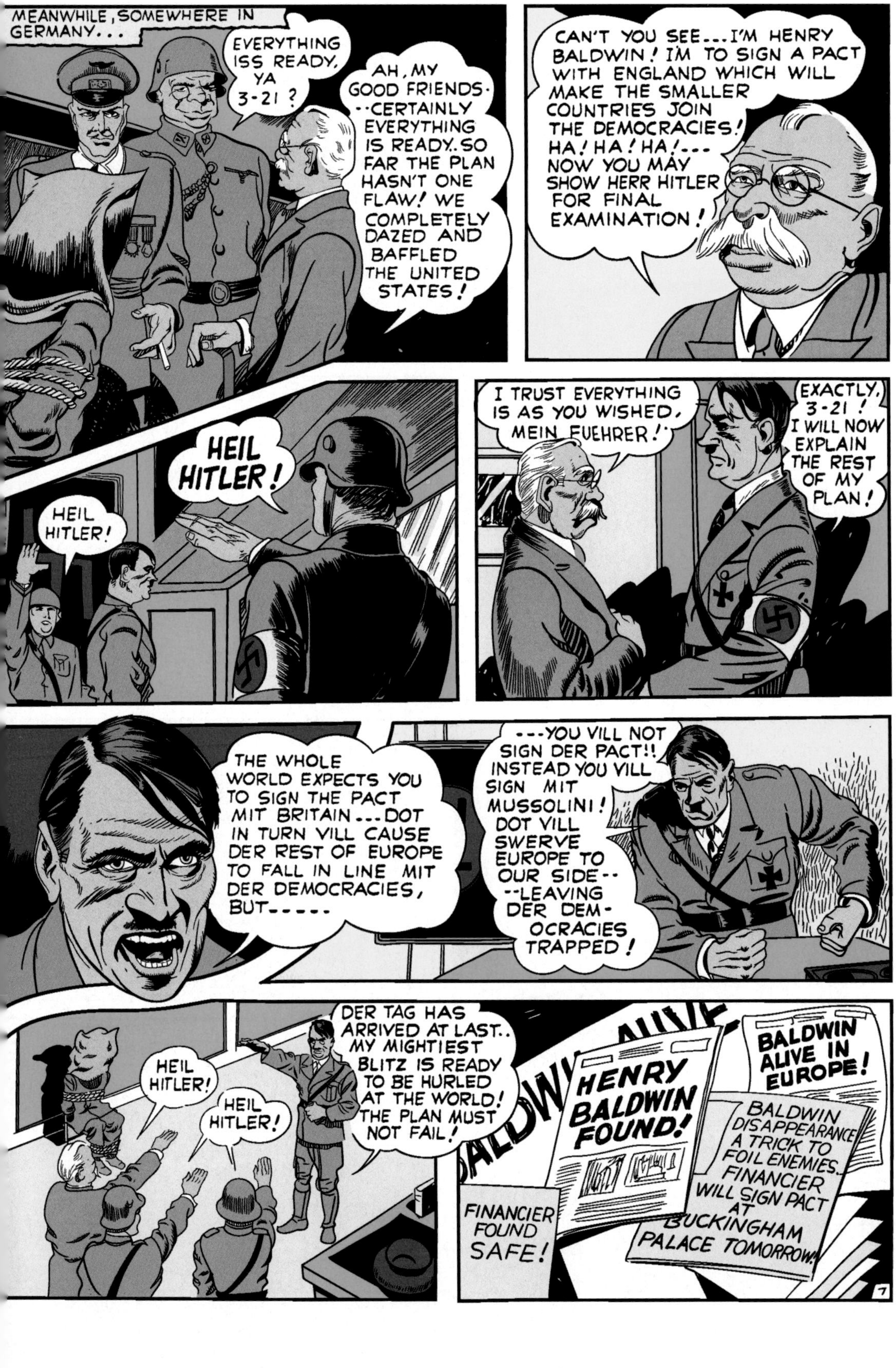
MEANWHILE, SOMEWHERE IN GERMANY...
EVERYTHING ISS READY, YA 3-21 ?
AH, MY GOOD FRIENDS. --CERTAINLY EVERYTHING IS READY.. SO FAR THE PLAN HASN'T ONE FLAW! WE COMPLETELY DAZED AND BAFFLED THE UNITED STATES!
CAN'T YOU SEE...I'M HENRY BALDWIN! I'M TO SIGN A PACT WITH ENGLAND WHICH WILL MAKE THE SMALLER COUNTRIES JOIN THE DEMOCRACIES! HA! HA! HA!... NOW YOU MAY SHOW HERR HITLER FOR FINAL EXAMINATION!
HEIL HITLER!
HEIL HITLER!
I TRUST EVERYTHING IS AS YOU WISHED, MEIN FUEHRER!
EXACTLY, 3-21! I WILL NOW EXPLAIN THE REST OF MY PLAN!
THE WHOLE WORLD EXPECTS YOU TO SIGN THE PACT MIT BRITAIN...DOT IN TURN VILL CAUSE DER REST OF EUROPE TO FALL IN LINE MIT DER DEMOCRACIES, BUT-----
---YOU VILL NOT SIGN DER PACT!! INSTEAD YOU VILL SIGN MIT MUSSOLINI! DOT VILL SWERVE EUROPE TO OUR SIDE-- --LEAVING DER DEMOCRACIES TRAPPED!
HEIL HITLER!
HEIL HITLER!
DER TAG HAS ARRIVED AT LAST.. MY MIGHTIEST BLITZ IS READY TO BE HURLED AT THE WORLD! THE PLAN MUST NOT FAIL!
HENRY BALDWIN FOUND!
BALDWIN ALIVE IN EUROPE!
BALDWIN DISAPPEARANCE A TRICK TO FOIL ENEMIES.. FINANCIER WILL SIGN PACT AT BUCKINGHAM PALACE TOMORROW
FINANCIER FOUND SAFE!
7

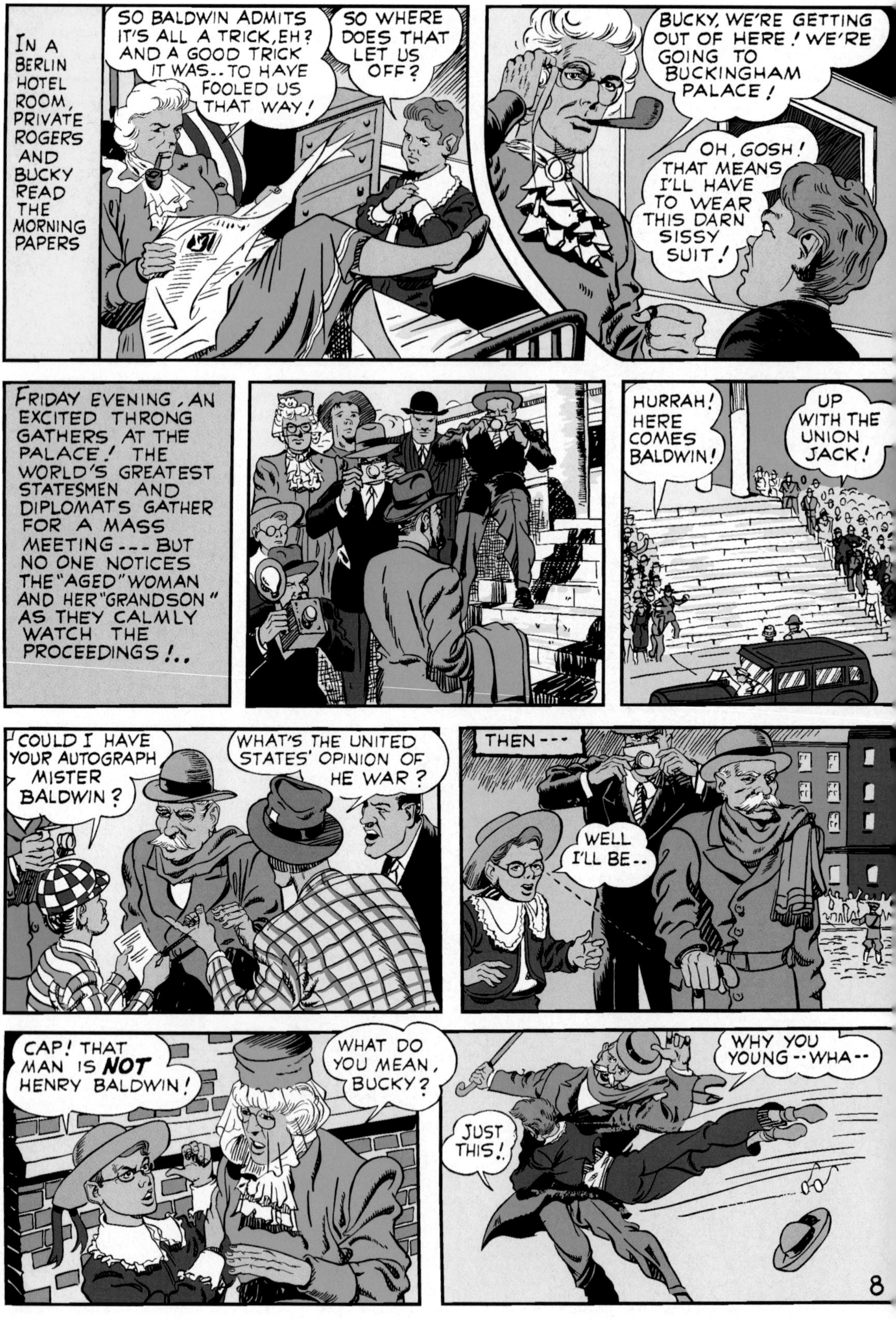
IN A BERLIN HOTEL ROOM, PRIVATE ROGERS AND BUCKY READ THE MORNING PAPERS
SO BALDWIN ADMITS IT'S ALL A TRICK, EH? AND A GOOD TRICK IT WAS.. TO HAVE FOOLED US THAT WAY!
SO WHERE DOES THAT LET US OFF?
BUCKY, WE'RE GETTING OUT OF HERE! WE'RE GOING TO BUCKINGHAM PALACE!
OH, GOSH! THAT MEANS I'LL HAVE TO WEAR THIS DARN SISSY SUIT!
FRIDAY EVENING, AN EXCITED THRONG GATHERS AT THE PALACE! THE WORLD'S GREATEST STATESMEN AND DIPLOMATS GATHER FOR A MASS MEETING --- BUT NO ONE NOTICES THE "AGED" WOMAN AND HER "GRANDSON" AS THEY CALMLY WATCH THE PROCEEDINGS!..
HURRAH! HERE COMES BALDWIN!
UP WITH THE UNION JACK!
COULD I HAVE YOUR AUTOGRAPH MISTER BALDWIN?
WHAT'S THE UNITED STATES' OPINION OF HE WAR?
THEN ---
WELL I'LL BE--
CAP! THAT MAN IS **NOT** HENRY BALDWIN!
WHAT DO YOU MEAN, BUCKY?
WHY YOU YOUNG--WHA--
JUST THIS!
8

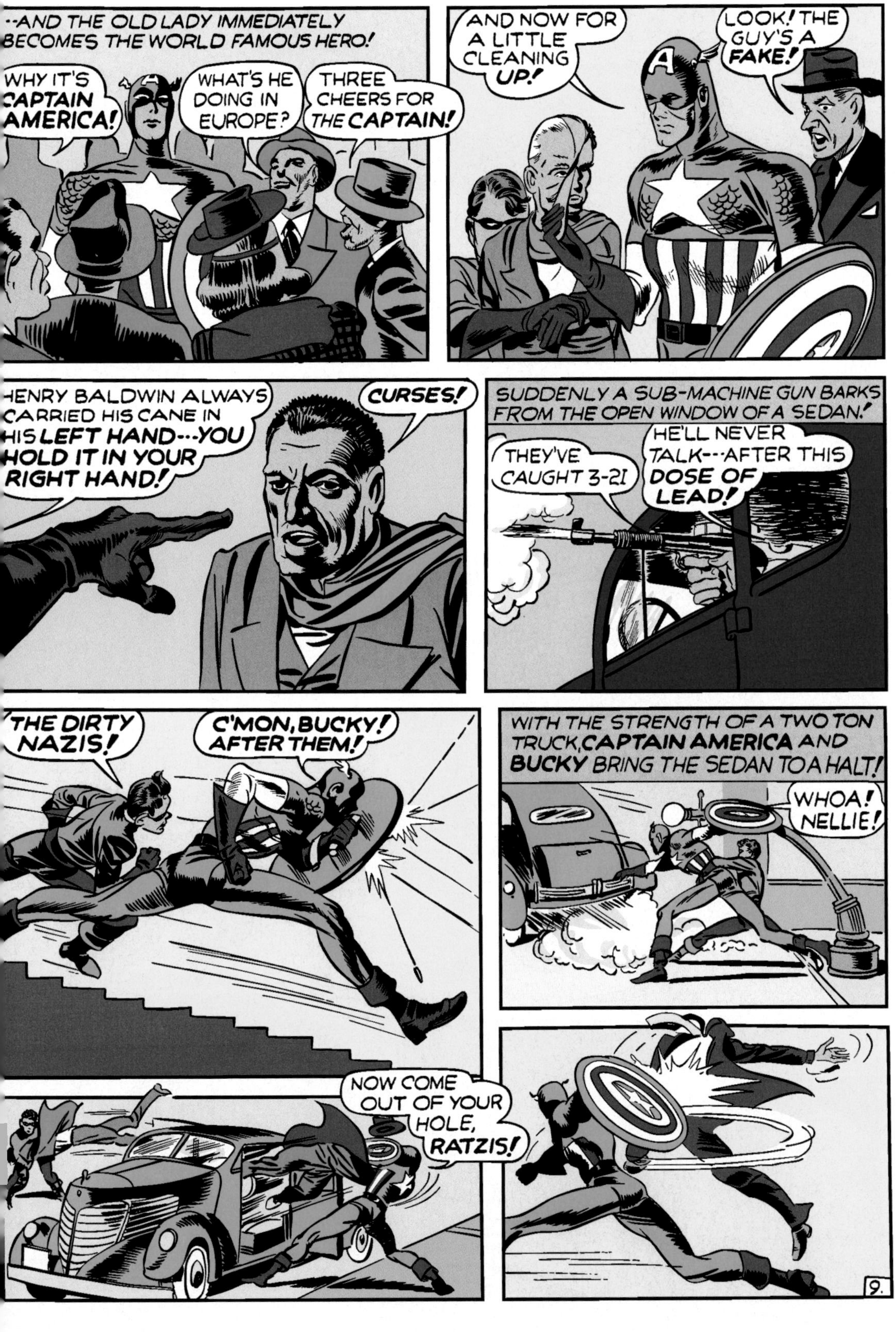

--AND THE OLD LADY IMMEDIATELY BECOMES THE WORLD FAMOUS HERO!
WHY IT'S CAPTAIN AMERICA!
WHAT'S HE DOING IN EUROPE?
THREE CHEERS FOR THE CAPTAIN!
AND NOW FOR A LITTLE CLEANING UP!
LOOK! THE GUY'S A FAKE!
HENRY BALDWIN ALWAYS CARRIED HIS CANE IN HIS LEFT HAND--- YOU HOLD IT IN YOUR RIGHT HAND!
CURSES!
SUDDENLY A SUB-MACHINE GUN BARKS FROM THE OPEN WINDOW OF A SEDAN!
THEY'VE CAUGHT 3-21
HE'LL NEVER TALK---AFTER THIS DOSE OF LEAD!
THE DIRTY NAZIS!
C'MON, BUCKY! AFTER THEM!
WITH THE STRENGTH OF A TWO TON TRUCK, CAPTAIN AMERICA AND BUCKY BRING THE SEDAN TO A HALT!
WHOA! NELLIE!
NOW COME OUT OF YOUR HOLE, RATZIS!
9.

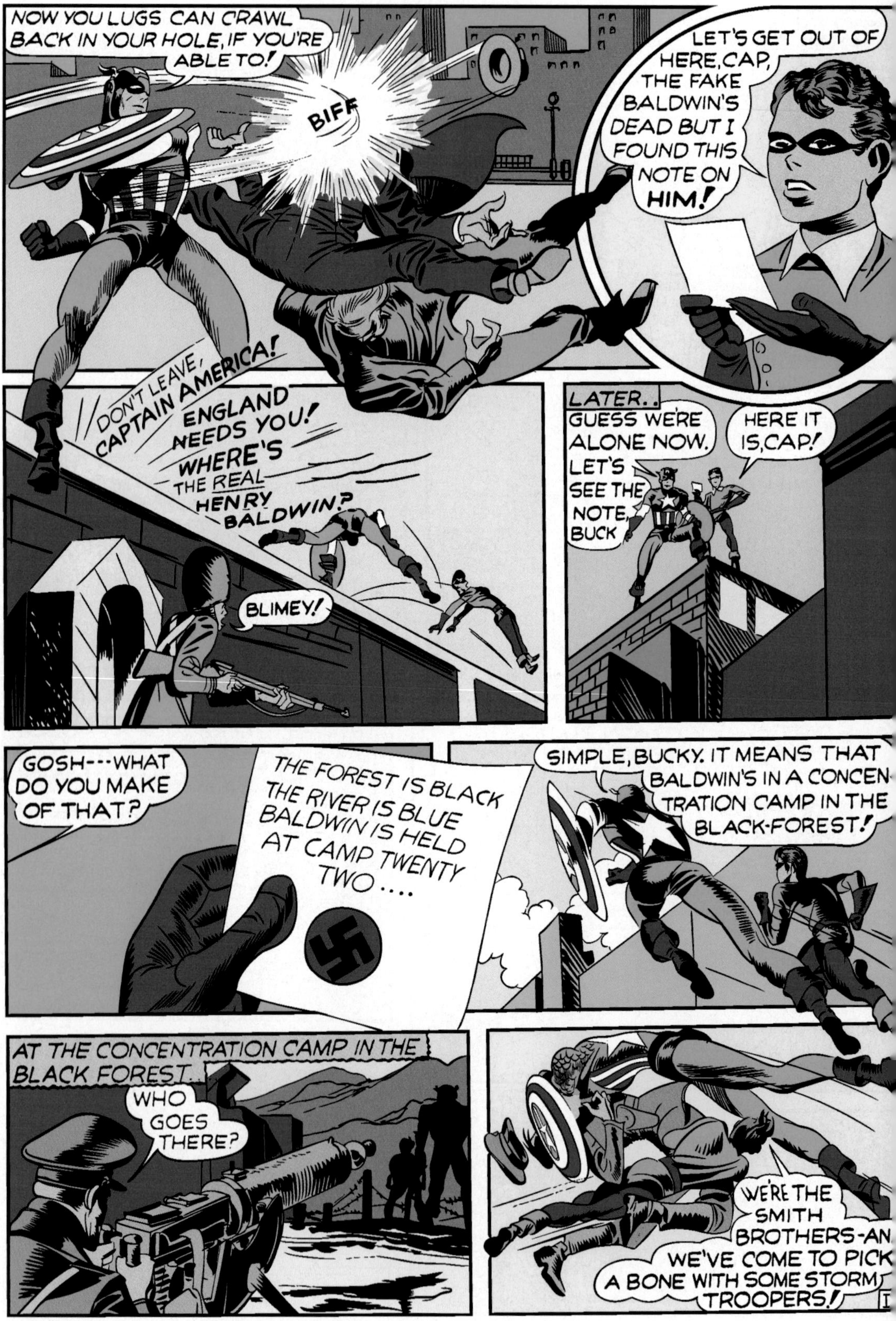
NOW YOU LUGS CAN CRAWL BACK IN YOUR HOLE, IF YOU'RE ABLE TO!
BIFF
LET'S GET OUT OF HERE, CAP, THE FAKE BALDWIN'S DEAD BUT I FOUND THIS NOTE ON HIM!
DON'T LEAVE, CAPTAIN AMERICA! ENGLAND NEEDS YOU! WHERE'S THE REAL HENRY BALDWIN?
BLIMEY!
LATER..
GUESS WE'RE ALONE NOW. LET'S SEE THE NOTE, BUCK
HERE IT IS, CAP!
GOSH---WHAT DO YOU MAKE OF THAT?
THE FOREST IS BLACK THE RIVER IS BLUE BALDWIN IS HELD AT CAMP TWENTY TWO....
SIMPLE, BUCKY. IT MEANS THAT BALDWIN'S IN A CONCEN-TRATION CAMP IN THE BLACK-FOREST!
AT THE CONCENTRATION CAMP IN THE BLACK FOREST..
WHO GOES THERE?
WE'RE THE SMITH BROTHERS-AN WE'VE COME TO PICK A BONE WITH SOME STORM TROOPERS!

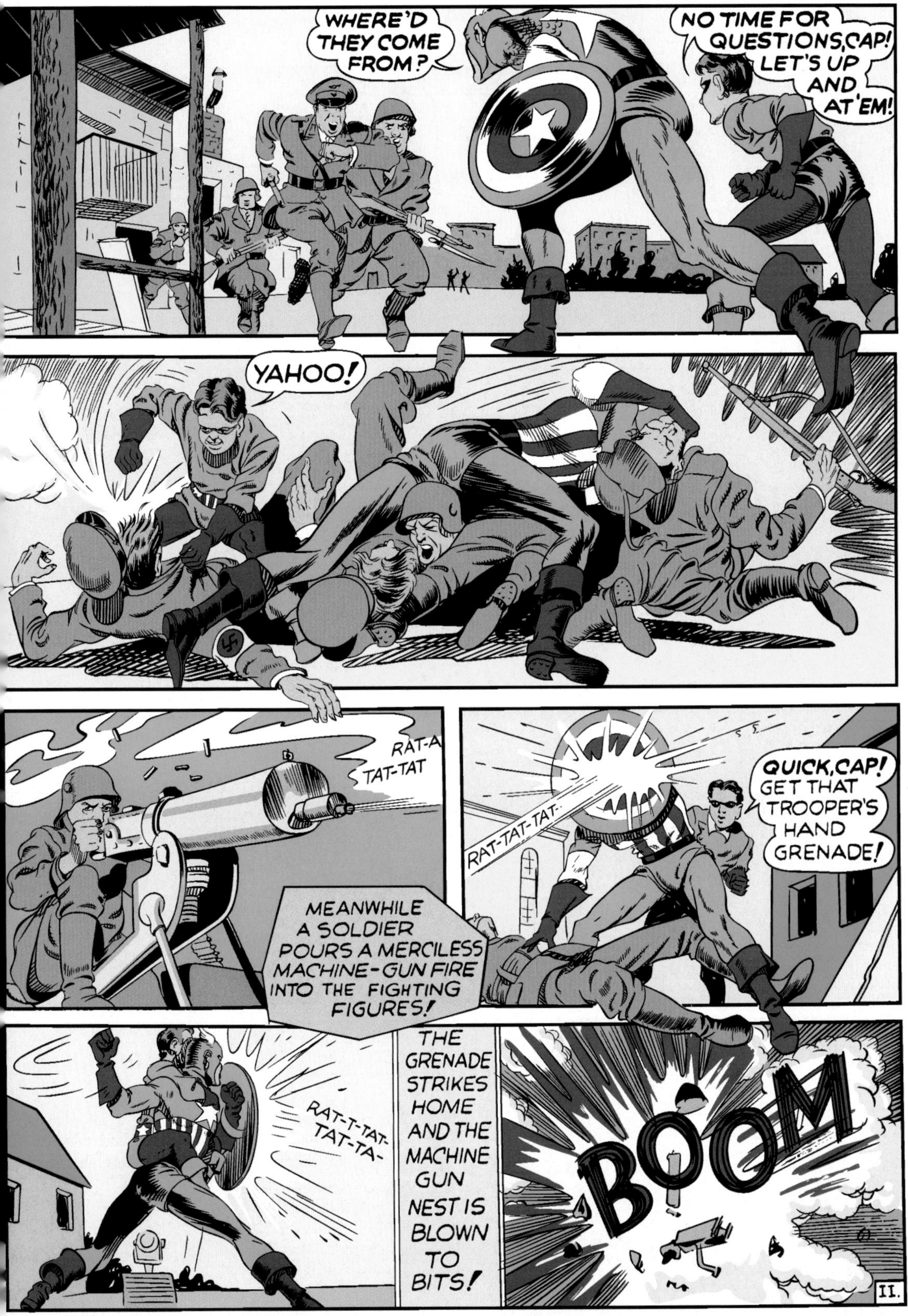
WHERE'D THEY COME FROM?
NO TIME FOR QUESTIONS, CAP! LET'S UP AND AT 'EM!
YAHOO!
RAT-A TAT-TAT
MEANWHILE A SOLDIER POURS A MERCILESS MACHINE-GUN FIRE INTO THE FIGHTING FIGURES!
RAT-TAT-TAT-
QUICK, CAP! GET THAT TROOPER'S HAND GRENADE!
RAT-T-TAT-TAT-TA-
THE GRENADE STRIKES HOME AND THE MACHINE GUN NEST IS BLOWN TO BITS!
BOOM
11.

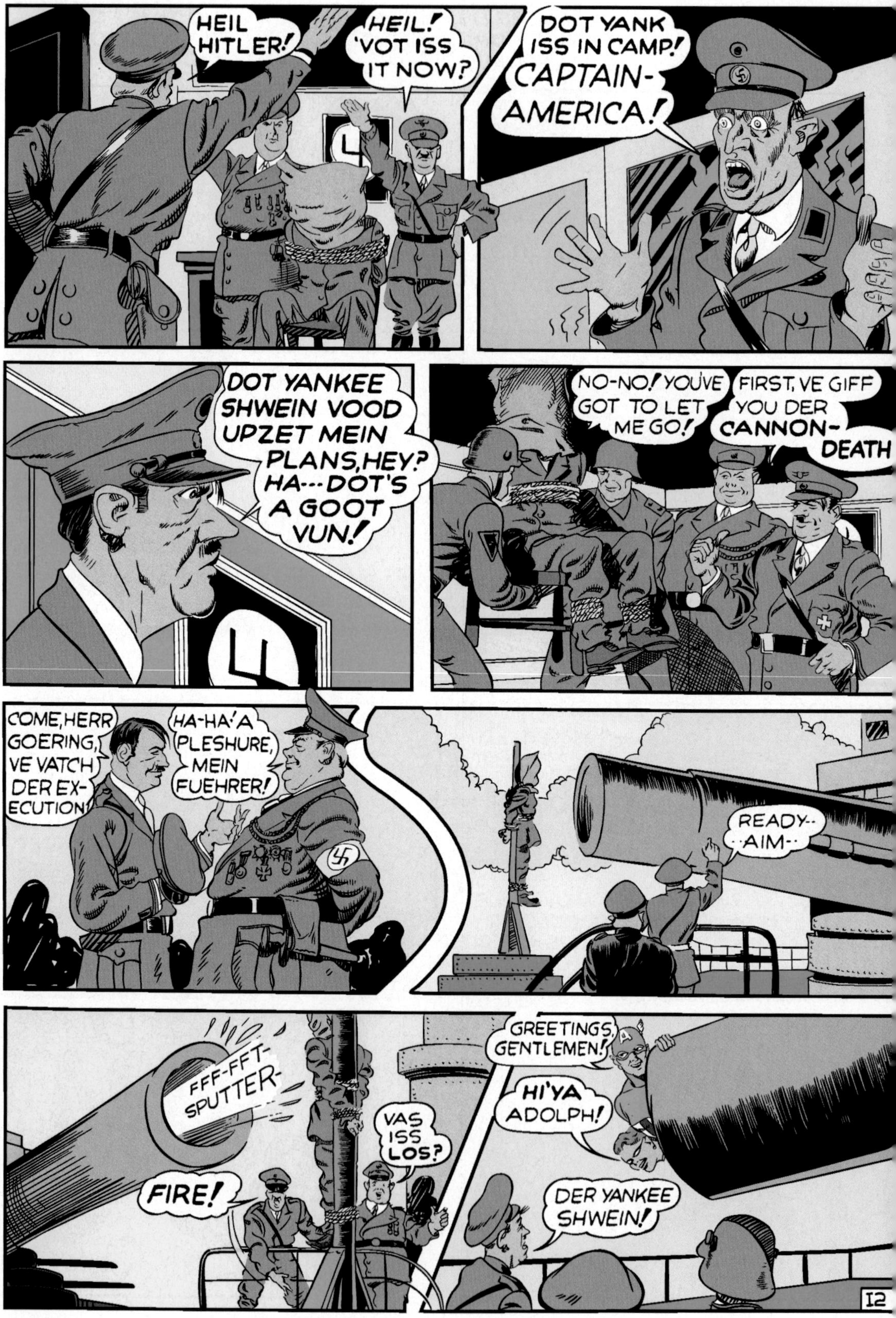
HEIL HITLER!
HEIL! 'VOT ISS IT NOW?
DOT YANK ISS IN CAMP! CAPTAIN-AMERICA!
DOT YANKEE SHWEIN VOOD UPZET MEIN PLANS, HEY? HA---DOT'S A GOOT VUN!
NO-NO! YOU'VE GOT TO LET ME GO!
FIRST, VE GIFF YOU DER CANNON-DEATH
COME, HERR GOERING, VE VATCH DER EX-ECUTION!
HA-HA! A PLESHURE, MEIN FUEHRER!
READY-- --AIM--
FFF-FFT-SPUTTER-
FIRE!
VAS ISS LOS?
GREETINGS, GENTLEMEN!
HI'YA ADOLPH!
DER YANKEE SHWEIN!
12

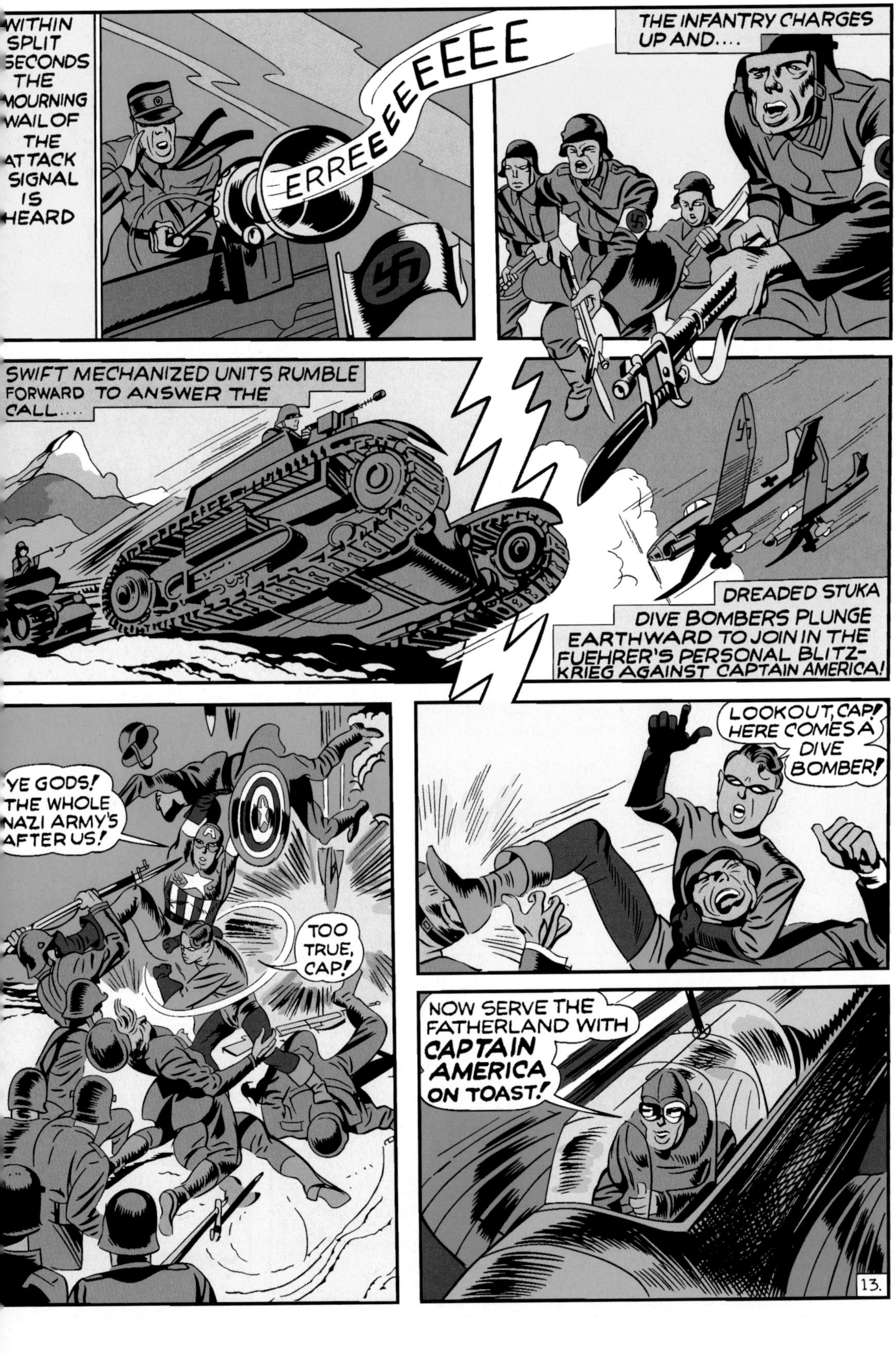
WITHIN SPLIT SECONDS THE MOURNING WAIL OF THE ATTACK SIGNAL IS HEARD
ERREEEEEEEE
THE INFANTRY CHARGES UP AND....
SWIFT MECHANIZED UNITS RUMBLE FORWARD TO ANSWER THE CALL....
DREADED STUKA DIVE BOMBERS PLUNGE EARTHWARD TO JOIN IN THE FUEHRER'S PERSONAL BLITZ-KRIEG AGAINST CAPTAIN AMERICA!
YE GODS! THE WHOLE NAZI ARMY'S AFTER US!
TOO TRUE, CAP!
LOOKOUT, CAP! HERE COMES A DIVE BOMBER!
NOW SERVE THE FATHERLAND WITH CAPTAIN AMERICA ON TOAST!
13.

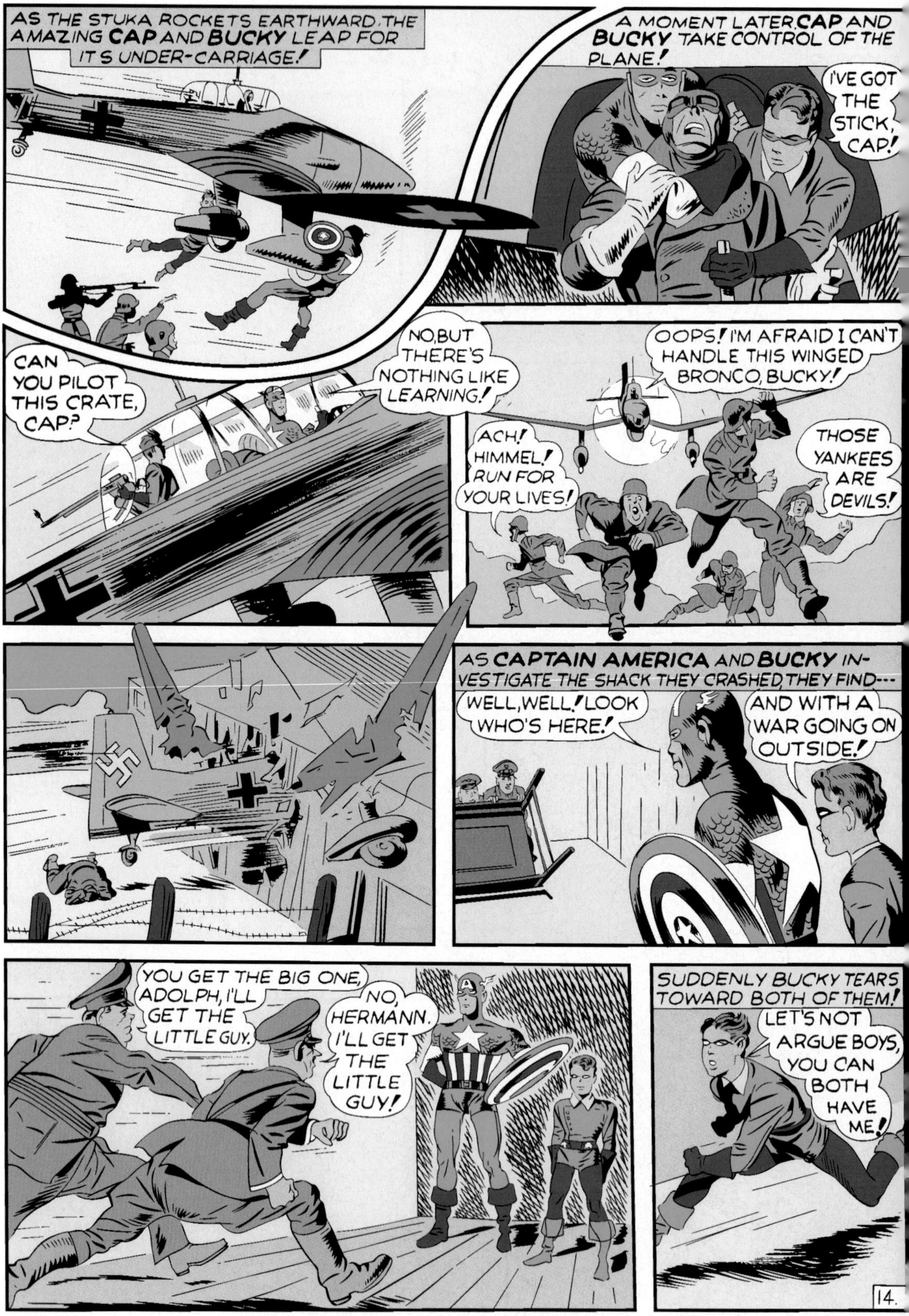

AS THE STUKA ROCKETS EARTHWARD, THE AMAZING CAP AND BUCKY LEAP FOR ITS UNDER-CARRIAGE!
A MOMENT LATER, CAP AND BUCKY TAKE CONTROL OF THE PLANE!
I'VE GOT THE STICK, CAP!
CAN YOU PILOT THIS CRATE, CAP?
NO, BUT THERE'S NOTHING LIKE LEARNING!
OOPS! I'M AFRAID I CAN'T HANDLE THIS WINGED BRONCO, BUCKY!
ACH! HIMMEL! RUN FOR YOUR LIVES!
THOSE YANKEES ARE DEVILS!
AS CAPTAIN AMERICA AND BUCKY INVESTIGATE THE SHACK THEY CRASHED, THEY FIND---
WELL, WELL! LOOK WHO'S HERE!
AND WITH A WAR GOING ON OUTSIDE!
YOU GET THE BIG ONE, ADOLPH, I'LL GET THE LITTLE GUY.
NO, HERMANN. I'LL GET THE LITTLE GUY!
SUDDENLY BUCKY TEARS TOWARD BOTH OF THEM!
LET'S NOT ARGUE BOYS, YOU CAN BOTH HAVE ME!
14.

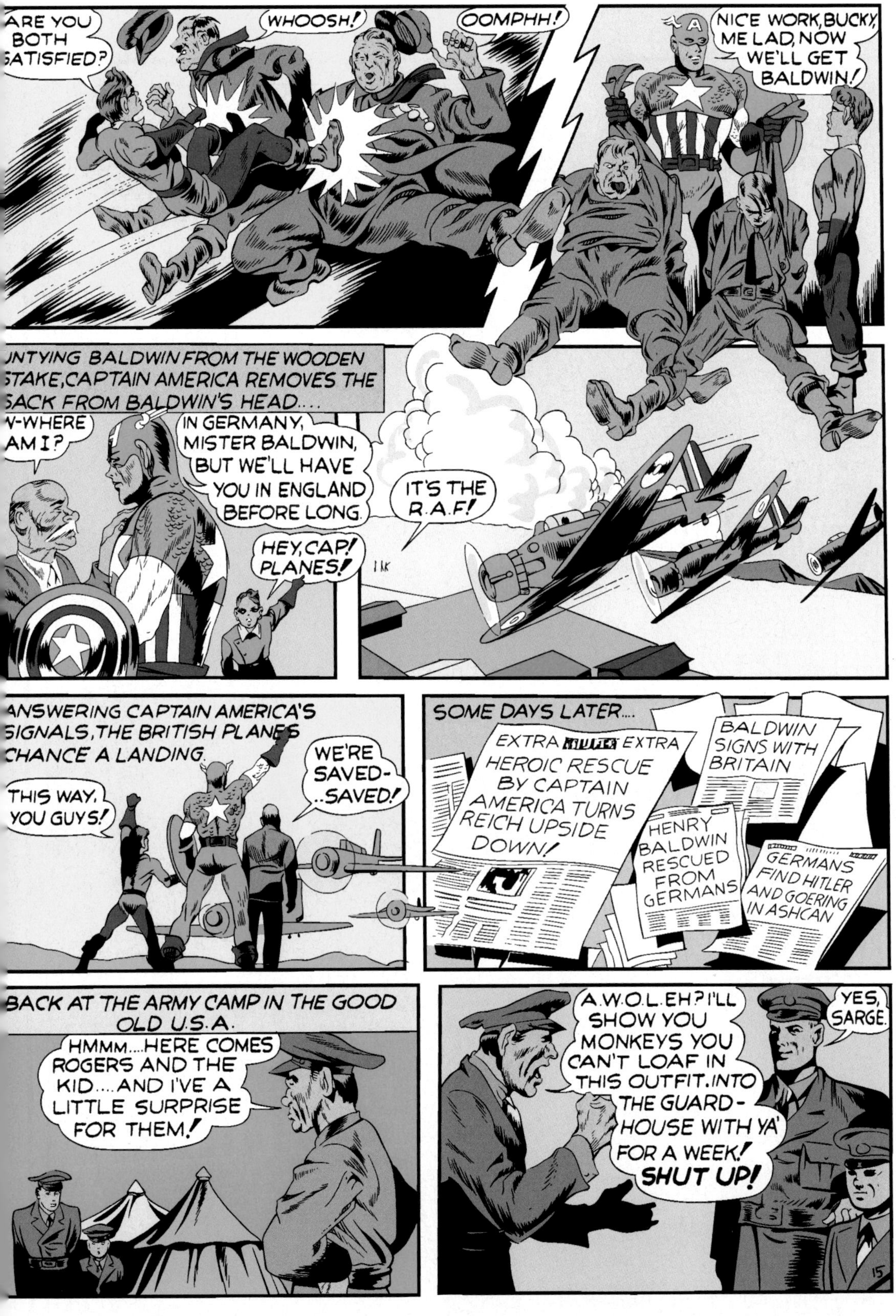
ARE YOU BOTH SATISFIED?
WHOOSH!
OOMPHH!
NICE WORK, BUCKY, ME LAD, NOW WE'LL GET BALDWIN!
UNTYING BALDWIN FROM THE WOODEN STAKE, CAPTAIN AMERICA REMOVES THE SACK FROM BALDWIN'S HEAD...
W-WHERE AM I?
IN GERMANY, MISTER BALDWIN, BUT WE'LL HAVE YOU IN ENGLAND BEFORE LONG.
HEY, CAP! PLANES!
IT'S THE R.A.F!
ANSWERING CAPTAIN AMERICA'S SIGNALS, THE BRITISH PLANES CHANCE A LANDING.
THIS WAY, YOU GUYS!
WE'RE SAVED- ..SAVED!
SOME DAYS LATER....
EXTRA EXTRA
HEROIC RESCUE BY CAPTAIN AMERICA TURNS REICH UPSIDE DOWN!
BALDWIN SIGNS WITH BRITAIN
HENRY BALDWIN RESCUED FROM GERMANS
GERMANS FIND HITLER AND GOERING IN ASHCAN
BACK AT THE ARMY CAMP IN THE GOOD OLD U.S.A.
HMMM....HERE COMES ROGERS AND THE KID....AND I'VE A LITTLE SURPRISE FOR THEM!
A.W.O.L. EH? I'LL SHOW YOU MONKEYS YOU CAN'T LOAF IN THIS OUTFIT. INTO THE GUARD-HOUSE WITH YA' FOR A WEEK! SHUT UP!
YES, SARGE.
15

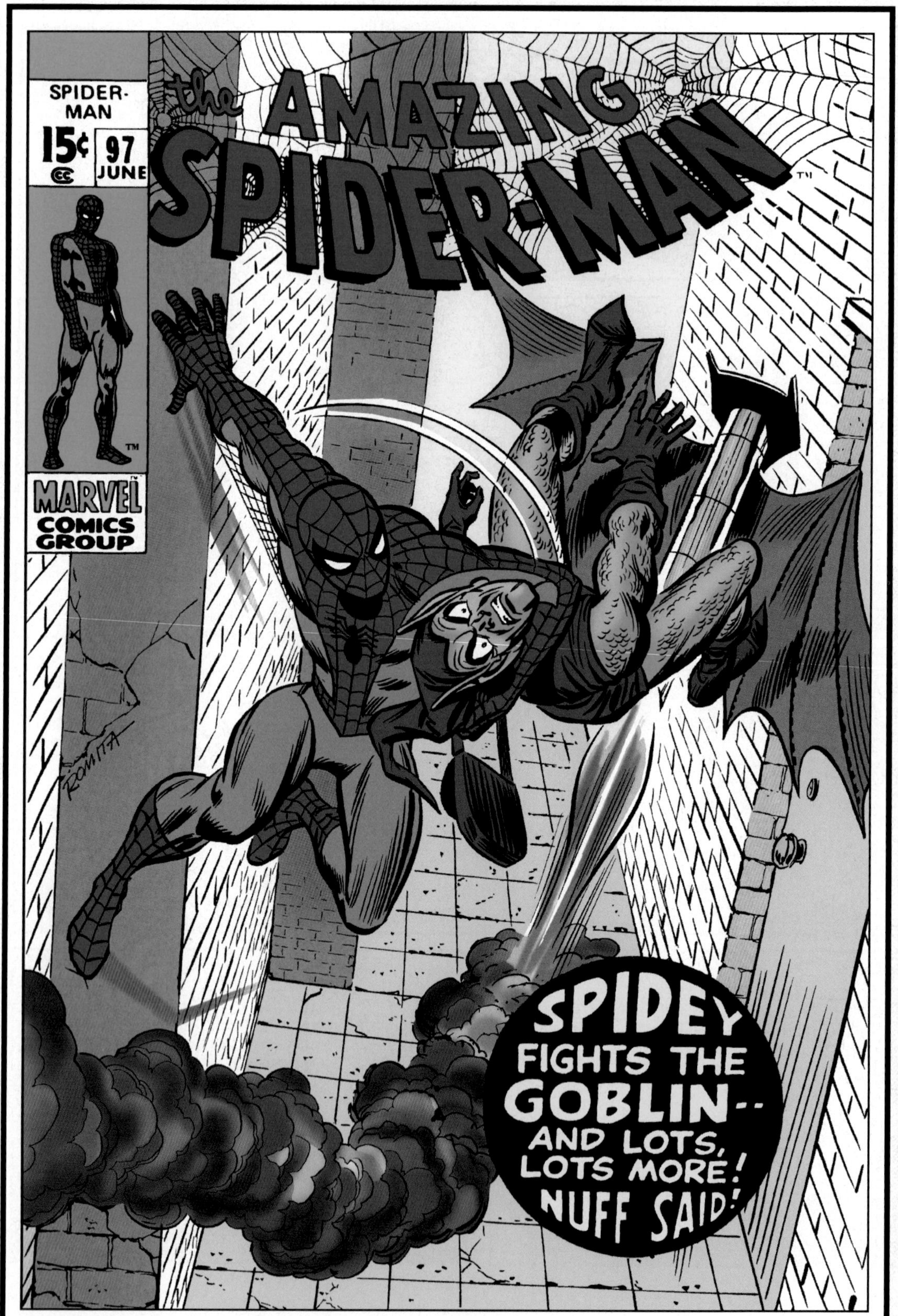

SPIDER-MAN
15¢
97
JUNE
the AMAZING SPIDER-MAN
MARVEL COMICS GROUP
ROMITA
SPIDEY FIGHTS THE GOBLIN-- AND LOTS, LOTS MORE! NUFF SAID!

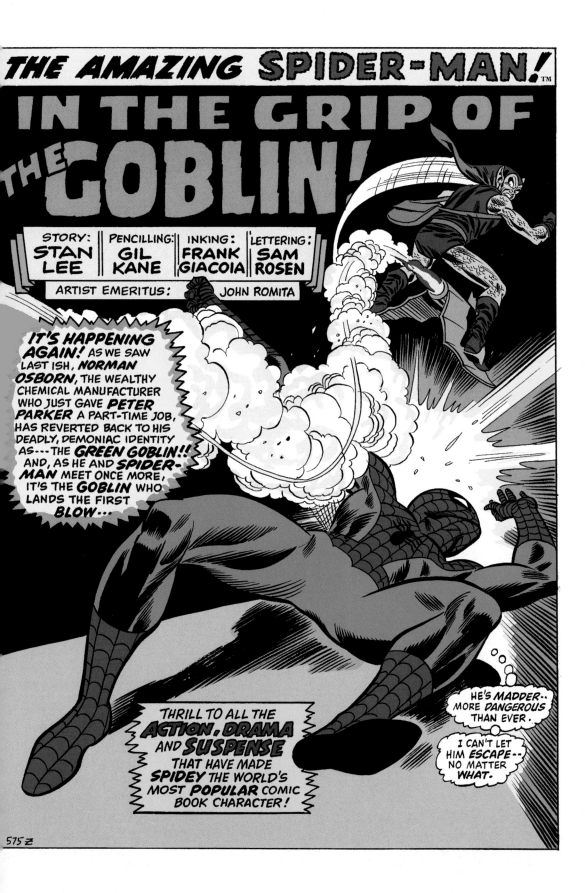

THE AMAZING SPIDER-MAN!™

IN THE GRIP OF THE GOBLIN!

STORY: **STAN LEE** | PENCILLING: **GIL KANE** | INKING: **FRANK GIACOIA** | LETTERING: **SAM ROSEN**

ARTIST EMERITUS: **JOHN ROMITA**

IT'S HAPPENING AGAIN! AS WE SAW LAST ISH, **NORMAN OSBORN**, THE WEALTHY CHEMICAL MANUFACTURER WHO JUST GAVE **PETER PARKER** A PART-TIME JOB, HAS REVERTED BACK TO HIS DEADLY, DEMONIAC IDENTITY AS--- THE **GREEN GOBLIN!!** AND, AS HE AND **SPIDER-MAN** MEET ONCE MORE, IT'S THE **GOBLIN** WHO LANDS THE FIRST **BLOW**...

THRILL TO ALL THE **ACTION, DRAMA** AND **SUSPENSE** THAT HAVE MADE **SPIDEY** THE WORLD'S MOST **POPULAR** COMIC BOOK CHARACTER!

HE'S **MADDER**-- MORE **DANGEROUS** THAN EVER.

I CAN'T LET HIM **ESCAPE**-- NO MATTER **WHAT**.

575Ƶ

23

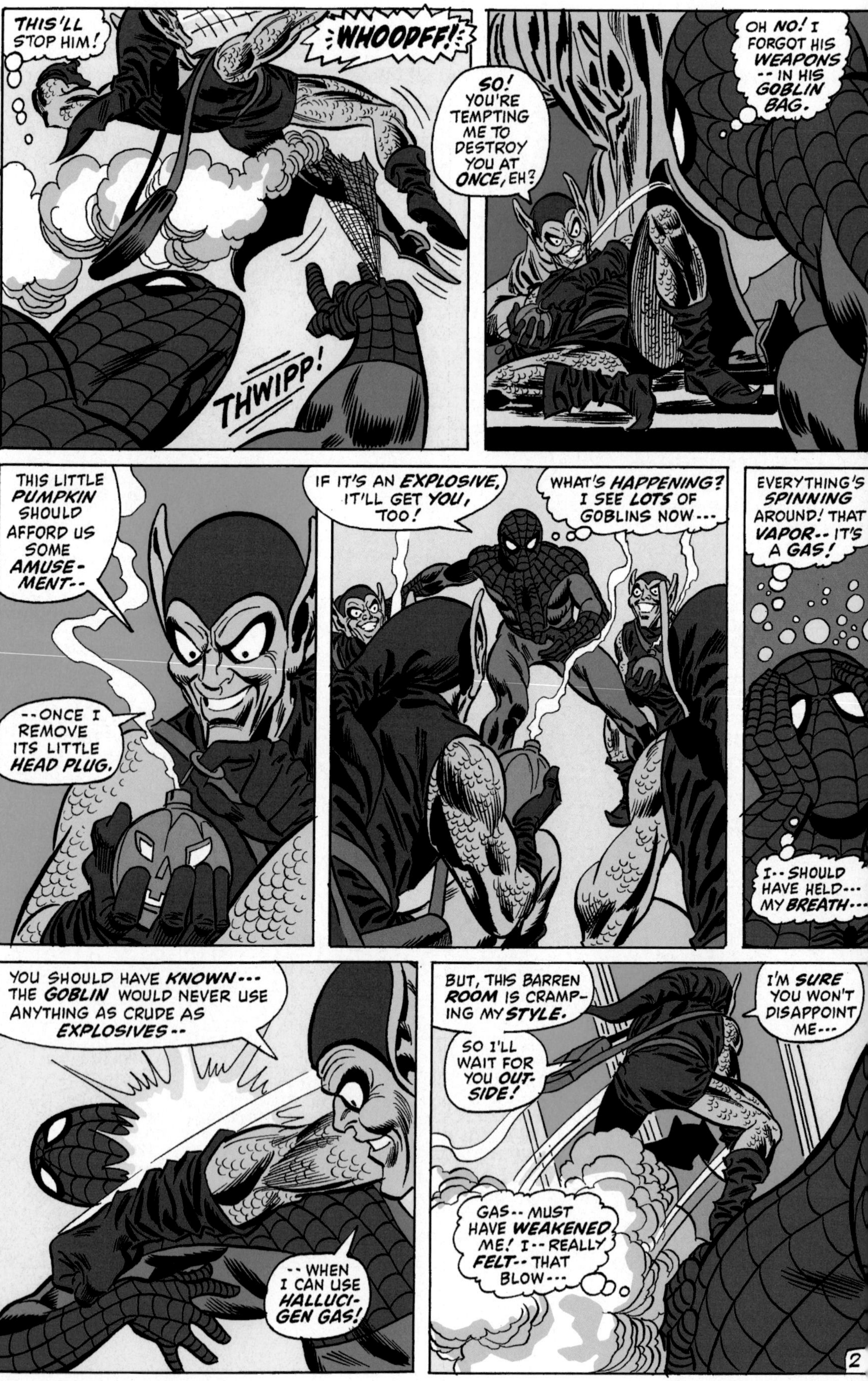
THIS'LL STOP HIM!
WHOODFF!
THWIPP!
SO! YOU'RE TEMPTING ME TO DESTROY YOU AT ONCE, EH?
OH NO! I FORGOT HIS WEAPONS -- IN HIS GOBLIN BAG.
THIS LITTLE PUMPKIN SHOULD AFFORD US SOME AMUSE-MENT--
--ONCE I REMOVE ITS LITTLE HEAD PLUG.
IF IT'S AN EXPLOSIVE, IT'LL GET YOU, TOO!
WHAT'S HAPPENING? I SEE LOTS OF GOBLINS NOW---
EVERYTHING'S SPINNING AROUND! THAT VAPOR-- IT'S A GAS!
I-- SHOULD HAVE HELD--- MY BREATH---
YOU SHOULD HAVE KNOWN--- THE GOBLIN WOULD NEVER USE ANYTHING AS CRUDE AS EXPLOSIVES--
-- WHEN I CAN USE HALLUCI-GEN GAS!
BUT, THIS BARREN ROOM IS CRAMP-ING MY STYLE.
SO I'LL WAIT FOR YOU OUT-SIDE!
I'M SURE YOU WON'T DISAPPOINT ME---
GAS-- MUST HAVE WEAKENED ME! I-- REALLY FELT-- THAT BLOW---
2

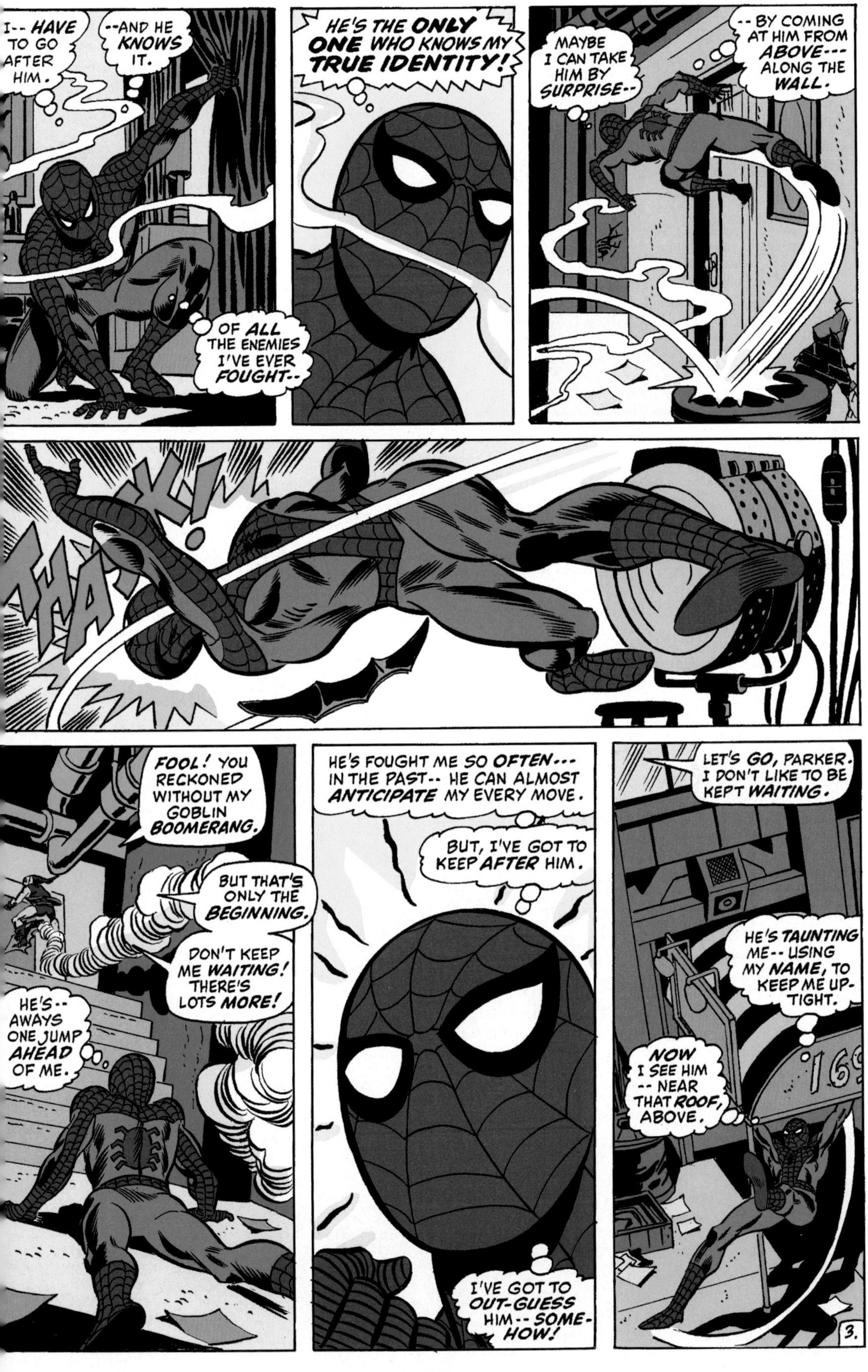

I-- HAVE TO GO AFTER HIM.
--AND HE KNOWS IT.
OF ALL THE ENEMIES I'VE EVER FOUGHT--
HE'S THE ONLY ONE WHO KNOWS MY TRUE IDENTITY!
MAYBE I CAN TAKE HIM BY SURPRISE--
--BY COMING AT HIM FROM ABOVE--- ALONG THE WALL.
FOOL! YOU RECKONED WITHOUT MY GOBLIN BOOMERANG.
BUT THAT'S ONLY THE BEGINNING.
DON'T KEEP ME WAITING! THERE'S LOTS MORE!
HE'S-- AWAYS ONE JUMP AHEAD OF ME.
HE'S FOUGHT ME SO OFTEN--- IN THE PAST-- HE CAN ALMOST ANTICIPATE MY EVERY MOVE.
BUT, I'VE GOT TO KEEP AFTER HIM.
I'VE GOT TO OUT-GUESS HIM--SOME-HOW!
LET'S GO, PARKER. I DON'T LIKE TO BE KEPT WAITING.
HE'S TAUNTING ME-- USING MY NAME, TO KEEP ME UP-TIGHT.
NOW I SEE HIM -- NEAR THAT ROOF, ABOVE.
3.

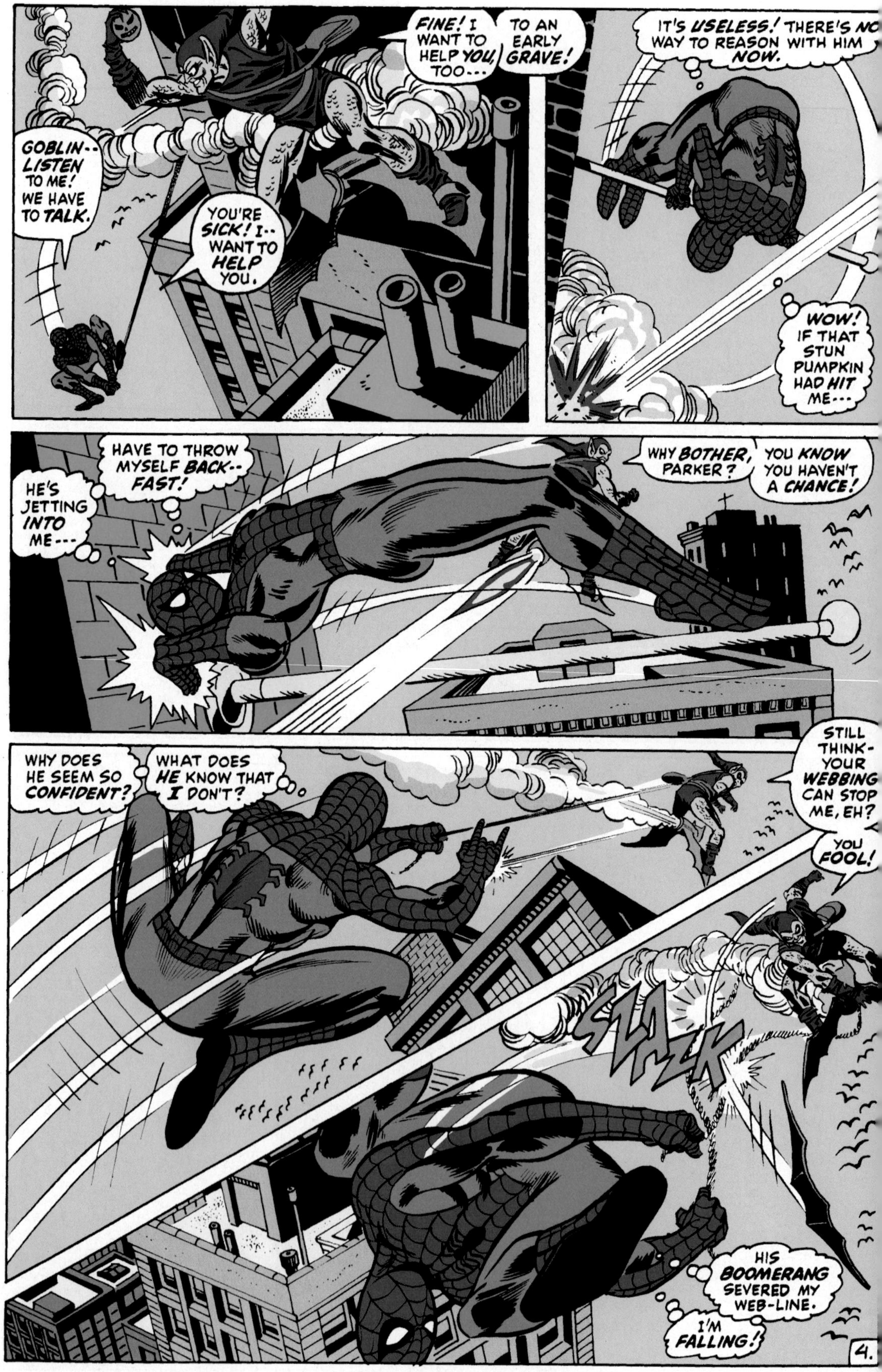
GOBLIN-- LISTEN TO ME! WE HAVE TO TALK.
YOU'RE SICK! I-- WANT TO HELP YOU.
FINE! I WANT TO HELP YOU, TOO...
TO AN EARLY GRAVE!
IT'S USELESS! THERE'S NO WAY TO REASON WITH HIM NOW.
WOW! IF THAT STUN PUMPKIN HAD HIT ME---
HE'S JETTING INTO ME---
HAVE TO THROW MYSELF BACK-- FAST!
WHY BOTHER, PARKER?
YOU KNOW YOU HAVEN'T A CHANCE!
WHY DOES HE SEEM SO CONFIDENT?
WHAT DOES HE KNOW THAT I DON'T?
STILL THINK-YOUR WEBBING CAN STOP ME, EH?
YOU FOOL!
SLAK
HIS BOOMERANG SEVERED MY WEB-LINE.
I'M FALLING!
4.

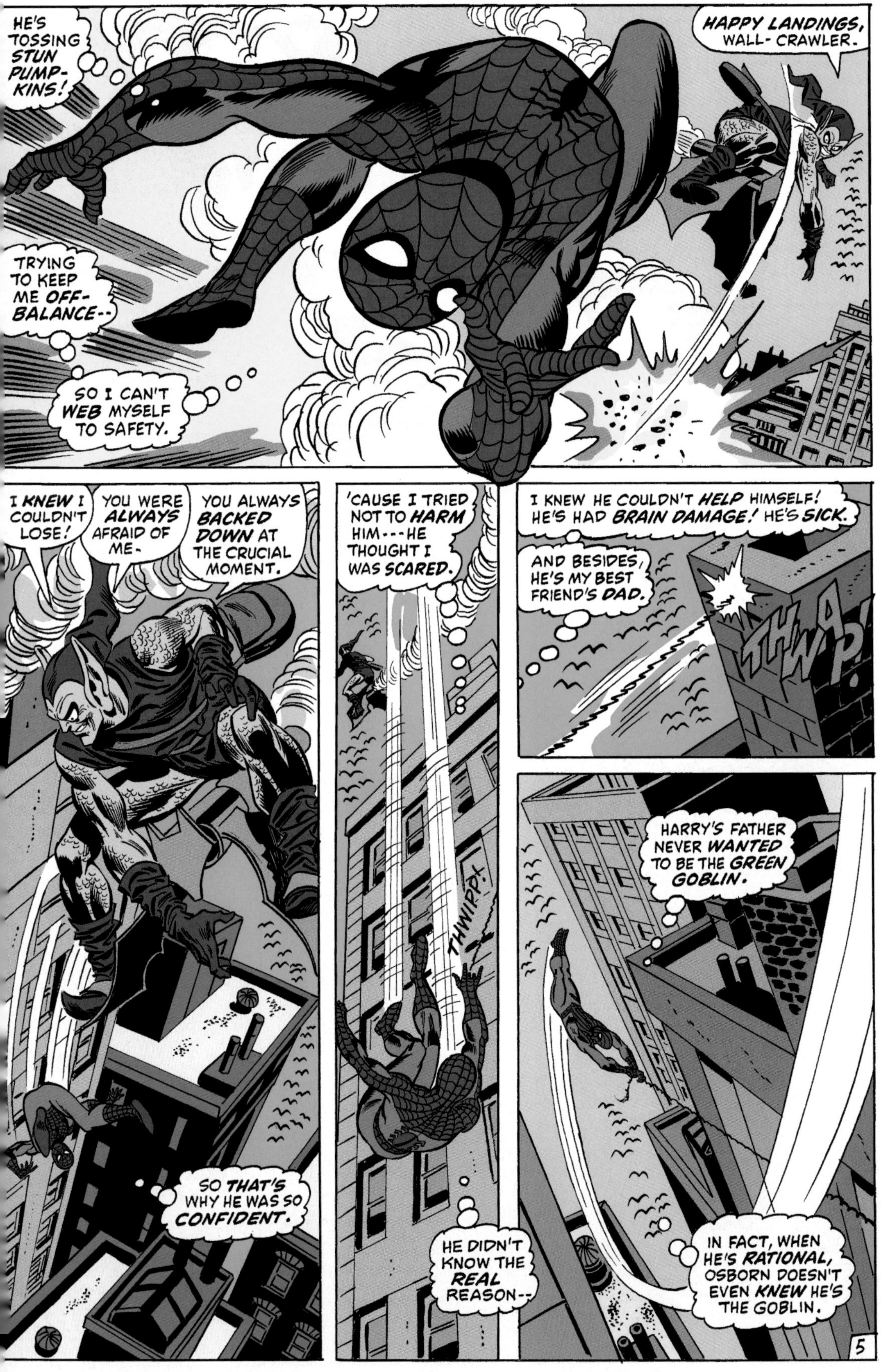
HE'S TOSSING STUN PUMPKINS!
TRYING TO KEEP ME OFF-BALANCE--
SO I CAN'T WEB MYSELF TO SAFETY.
HAPPY LANDINGS, WALL-CRAWLER.
I KNEW I COULDN'T LOSE!
YOU WERE ALWAYS AFRAID OF ME.
YOU ALWAYS BACKED DOWN AT THE CRUCIAL MOMENT.
SO THAT'S WHY HE WAS SO CONFIDENT.
'CAUSE I TRIED NOT TO HARM HIM---HE THOUGHT I WAS SCARED.
THWIPP!
HE DIDN'T KNOW THE REAL REASON--
I KNEW HE COULDN'T HELP HIMSELF! HE'S HAD BRAIN DAMAGE! HE'S SICK.
AND BESIDES, HE'S MY BEST FRIEND'S DAD.
THWAP!
HARRY'S FATHER NEVER WANTED TO BE THE GREEN GOBLIN.
IN FACT, WHEN HE'S RATIONAL, OSBORN DOESN'T EVEN KNEW HE'S THE GOBLIN.
5

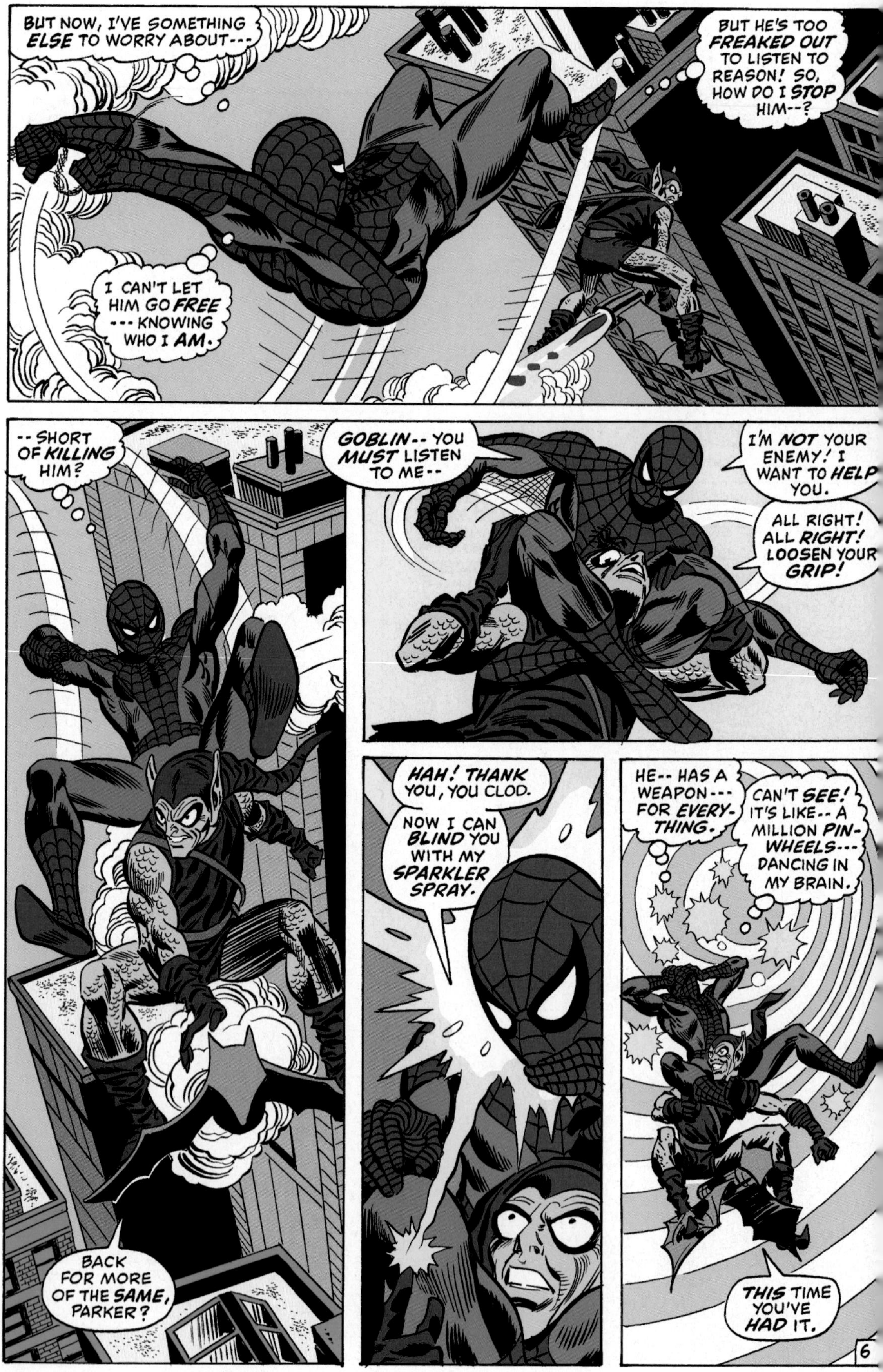
BUT NOW, I'VE SOMETHING ELSE TO WORRY ABOUT---
BUT HE'S TOO FREAKED OUT TO LISTEN TO REASON! SO, HOW DO I STOP HIM--?
I CAN'T LET HIM GO FREE --- KNOWING WHO I AM.
-- SHORT OF KILLING HIM?
BACK FOR MORE OF THE SAME, PARKER?
GOBLIN-- YOU MUST LISTEN TO ME--
I'M NOT YOUR ENEMY! I WANT TO HELP YOU.
ALL RIGHT! ALL RIGHT! LOOSEN YOUR GRIP!
HAH! THANK YOU, YOU CLOD.
NOW I CAN BLIND YOU WITH MY SPARKLER SPRAY.
HE-- HAS A WEAPON --- FOR EVERY-THING.
CAN'T SEE! IT'S LIKE-- A MILLION PIN-WHEELS--- DANCING IN MY BRAIN.
THIS TIME YOU'VE HAD IT.
6

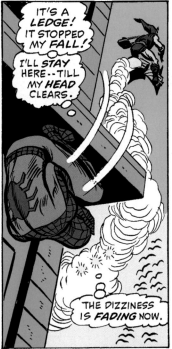

CAN'T FOCUS MY *THOUGHTS*.

WHERE AM I? WHAT--

I-- CAUGHT ON TO SOMETHING--

IT'S A *LEDGE!* IT STOPPED MY *FALL!*

I'LL *STAY* HERE--TILL MY *HEAD* CLEARS.

THE DIZZINESS IS *FADING* NOW.

HE'S *GONE!* MUST HAVE FALLEN TO HIS *DEATH!* AND GOOD *RIDDANCE.*

HIS ACCURSED *GRIP* ALMOST *FINISHED* ME JUST THEN.

BUT NOW I'M FREE TO FOLLOW MY *DESTINY!*

WITH *SPIDER-MAN* BEATEN, THE GOBLIN IS *SUPREME.*

HE'S TOO *FAR* AWAY-- CAN'T REACH HIM WITH MY *WEBBING.*

AND HE'S TRAVELING TOO *FAST* FOR ME TO *CATCH* HIM.

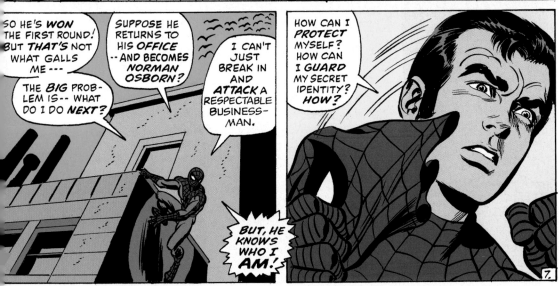

SO HE'S *WON* THE FIRST ROUND! BUT *THAT'S* NOT WHAT GALLS ME ---

THE *BIG* PROBLEM IS -- WHAT DO I DO *NEXT?*

SUPPOSE HE RETURNS TO HIS *OFFICE* --AND BECOMES *NORMAN OSBORN?*

I CAN'T JUST *BREAK* IN AND *ATTACK* A *RESPECTABLE* BUSINESSMAN.

HOW CAN I *PROTECT* MYSELF? HOW CAN I *GUARD* MY SECRET IDENTITY? *HOW?*

BUT, HE KNOWS WHO I *AM!*

7.

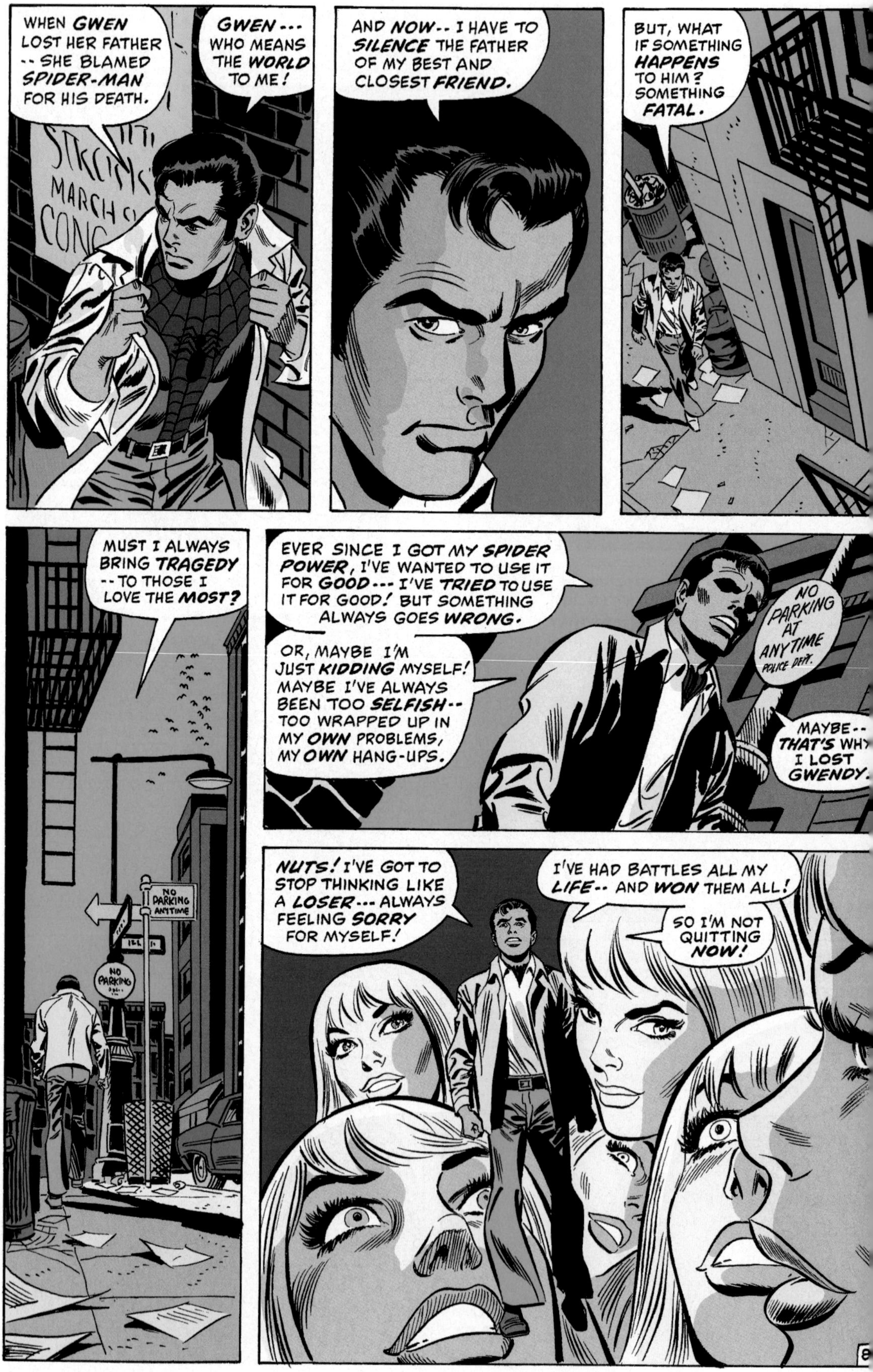
WHEN GWEN LOST HER FATHER -- SHE BLAMED SPIDER-MAN FOR HIS DEATH.
GWEN--- WHO MEANS THE WORLD TO ME!
AND NOW-- I HAVE TO SILENCE THE FATHER OF MY BEST AND CLOSEST FRIEND.
BUT, WHAT IF SOMETHING HAPPENS TO HIM? SOMETHING FATAL.
MUST I ALWAYS BRING TRAGEDY -- TO THOSE I LOVE THE MOST?
NO PARKING ANYTIME
NO PARKING
EVER SINCE I GOT MY SPIDER POWER, I'VE WANTED TO USE IT FOR GOOD--- I'VE TRIED TO USE IT FOR GOOD! BUT SOMETHING ALWAYS GOES WRONG.
OR, MAYBE I'M JUST KIDDING MYSELF! MAYBE I'VE ALWAYS BEEN TOO SELFISH-- TOO WRAPPED UP IN MY OWN PROBLEMS, MY OWN HANG-UPS.
NO PARKING AT ANYTIME POLICE DEPT.
MAYBE-- THAT'S WHY I LOST GWENDY.
NUTS! I'VE GOT TO STOP THINKING LIKE A LOSER--- ALWAYS FEELING SORRY FOR MYSELF!
I'VE HAD BATTLES ALL MY LIFE-- AND WON THEM ALL!
SO I'M NOT QUITTING NOW!
8

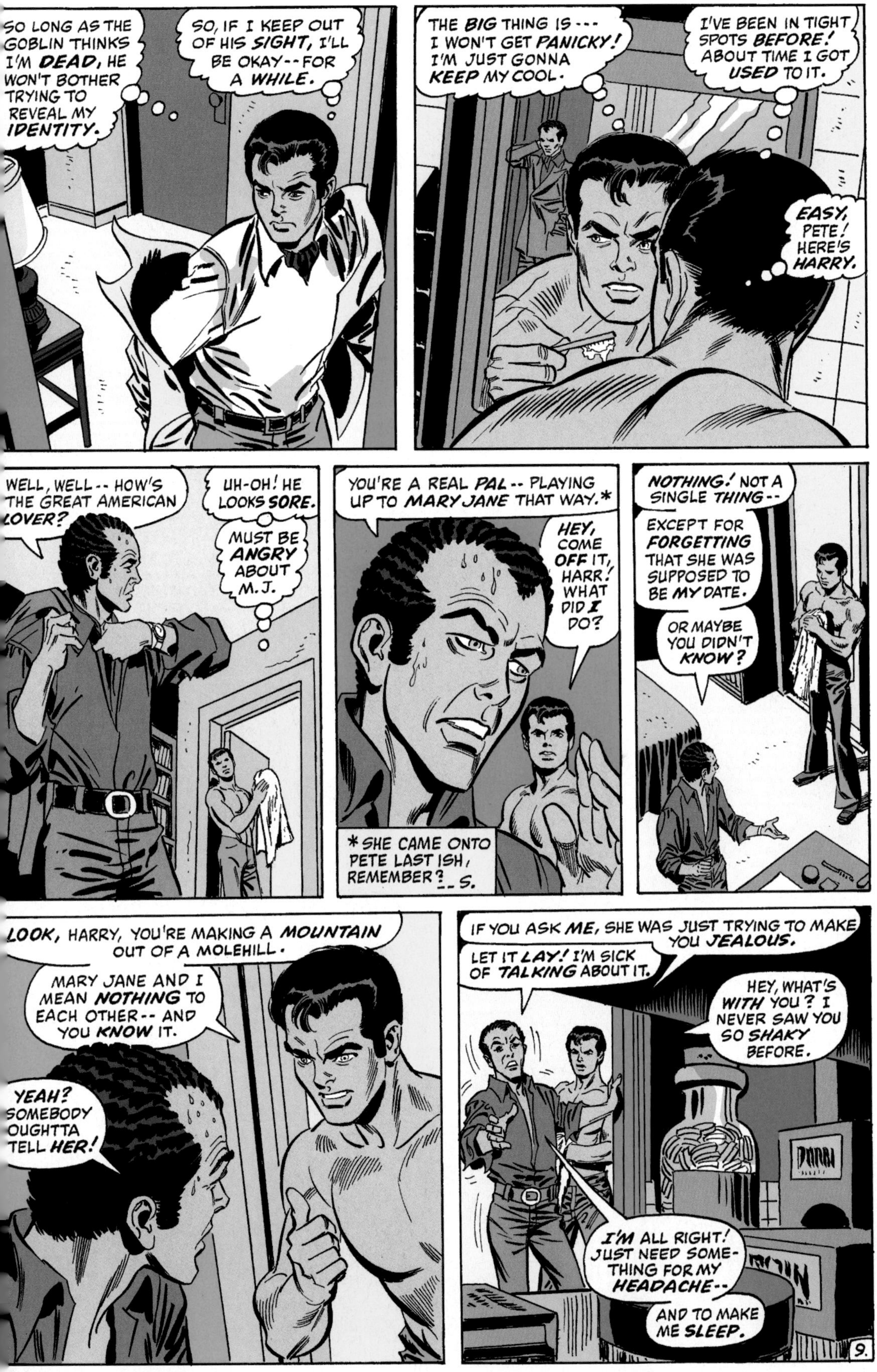

SO LONG AS THE GOBLIN THINKS I'M DEAD, HE WON'T BOTHER TRYING TO REVEAL MY IDENTITY.
SO, IF I KEEP OUT OF HIS SIGHT, I'LL BE OKAY-- FOR A WHILE.
THE BIG THING IS--- I WON'T GET PANICKY! I'M JUST GONNA KEEP MY COOL.
I'VE BEEN IN TIGHT SPOTS BEFORE! ABOUT TIME I GOT USED TO IT.
EASY, PETE! HERE'S HARRY.
WELL, WELL-- HOW'S THE GREAT AMERICAN LOVER?
UH-OH! HE LOOKS SORE.
MUST BE ANGRY ABOUT M.J.
YOU'RE A REAL PAL-- PLAYING UP TO MARY JANE THAT WAY.*
HEY, COME OFF IT, HARR! WHAT DID I DO?
*SHE CAME ONTO PETE LAST ISH, REMEMBER?--S.
NOTHING! NOT A SINGLE THING--
EXCEPT FOR FORGETTING THAT SHE WAS SUPPOSED TO BE MY DATE.
OR MAYBE YOU DIDN'T KNOW?
LOOK, HARRY, YOU'RE MAKING A MOUNTAIN OUT OF A MOLEHILL.
MARY JANE AND I MEAN NOTHING TO EACH OTHER-- AND YOU KNOW IT.
YEAH? SOMEBODY OUGHTTA TELL HER!
IF YOU ASK ME, SHE WAS JUST TRYING TO MAKE YOU JEALOUS.
LET IT LAY! I'M SICK OF TALKING ABOUT IT.
HEY, WHAT'S WITH YOU? I NEVER SAW YOU SO SHAKY BEFORE.
I'M ALL RIGHT! JUST NEED SOMETHING FOR MY HEADACHE--
AND TO MAKE ME SLEEP.
9.

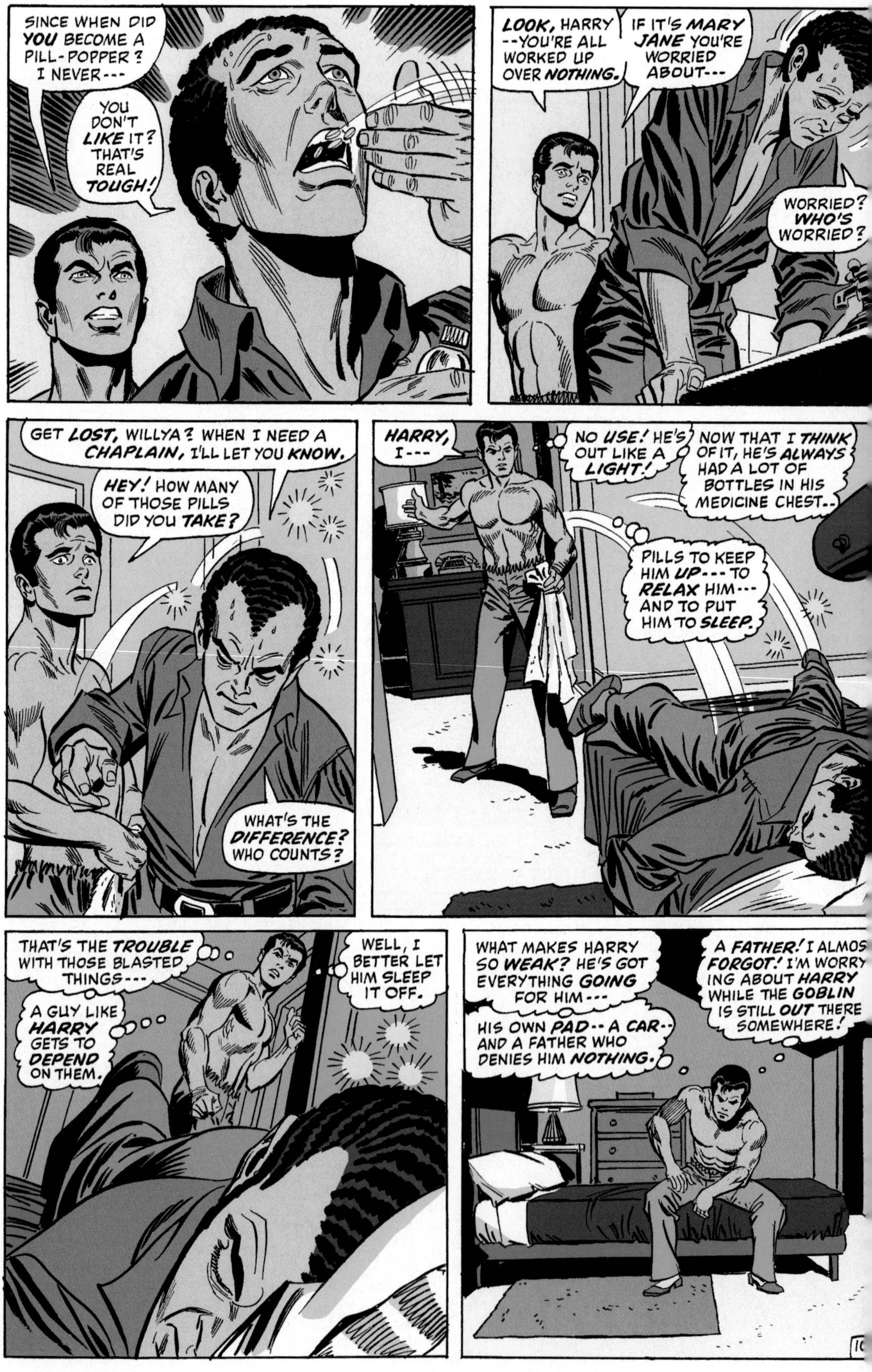

SINCE WHEN DID YOU BECOME A PILL-POPPER? I NEVER---
YOU DON'T LIKE IT? THAT'S REAL TOUGH!
LOOK, HARRY --YOU'RE ALL WORKED UP OVER NOTHING.
IF IT'S MARY JANE YOU'RE WORRIED ABOUT---
WORRIED? WHO'S WORRIED?
GET LOST, WILLYA? WHEN I NEED A CHAPLAIN, I'LL LET YOU KNOW.
HEY! HOW MANY OF THOSE PILLS DID YOU TAKE?
WHAT'S THE DIFFERENCE? WHO COUNTS?
HARRY, I---
NO USE! HE'S OUT LIKE A LIGHT!
NOW THAT I THINK OF IT, HE'S ALWAYS HAD A LOT OF BOTTLES IN HIS MEDICINE CHEST..
PILLS TO KEEP HIM UP--- TO RELAX HIM--- AND TO PUT HIM TO SLEEP.
THAT'S THE TROUBLE WITH THOSE BLASTED THINGS---
A GUY LIKE HARRY GETS TO DEPEND ON THEM.
WELL, I BETTER LET HIM SLEEP IT OFF.
WHAT MAKES HARRY SO WEAK? HE'S GOT EVERYTHING GOING FOR HIM---
HIS OWN PAD-- A CAR-- AND A FATHER WHO DENIES HIM NOTHING.
A FATHER! I ALMOS FORGOT! I'M WORRY ING ABOUT HARRY WHILE THE GOBLIN IS STILL OUT THERE SOMEWHERE!

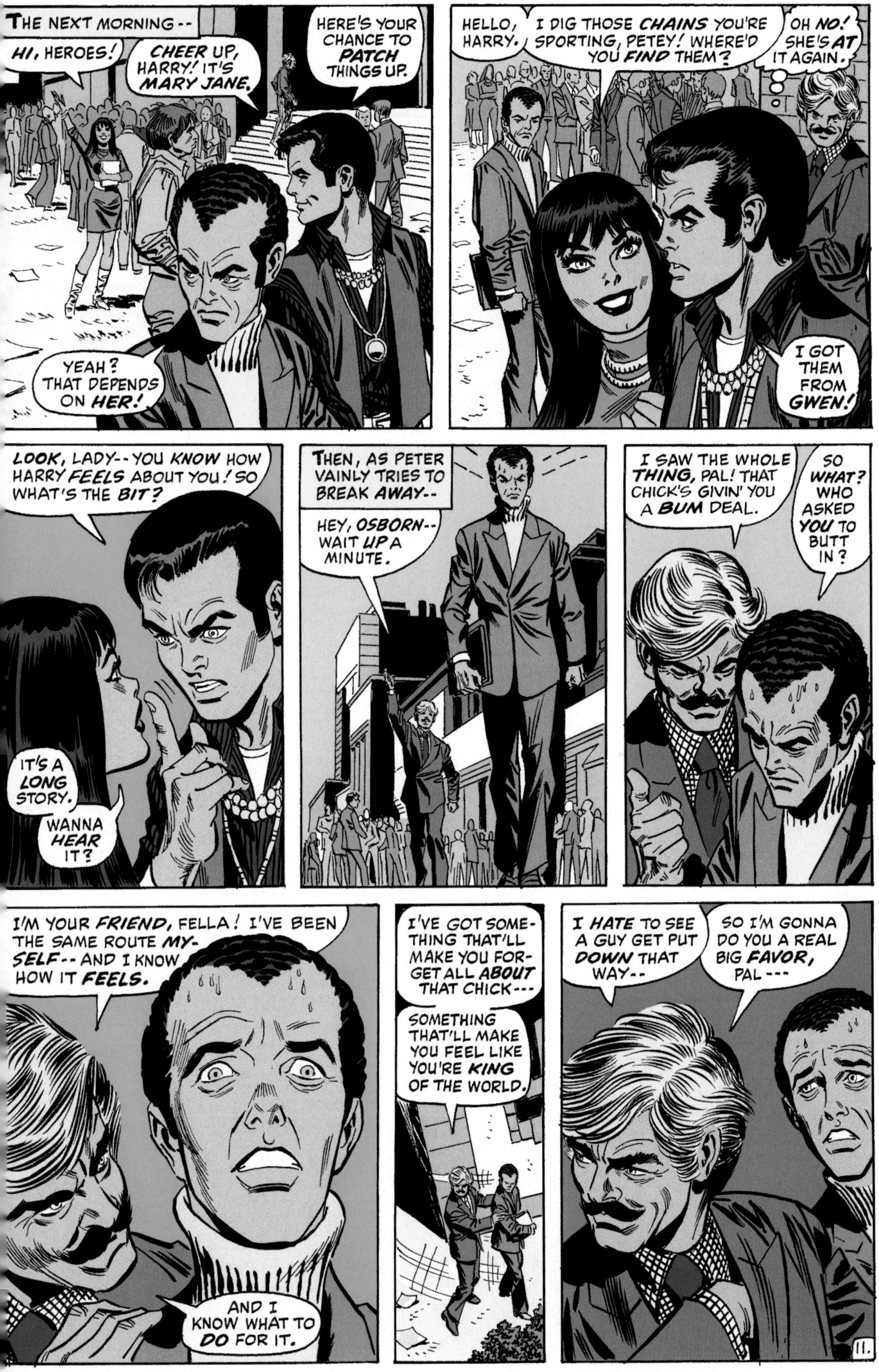
THE NEXT MORNING --
HI, HEROES!
CHEER UP, HARRY! IT'S MARY JANE.
HERE'S YOUR CHANCE TO PATCH THINGS UP.
YEAH? THAT DEPENDS ON HER!
HELLO, HARRY.
I DIG THOSE CHAINS YOU'RE SPORTING, PETEY! WHERE'D YOU FIND THEM?
OH NO! SHE'S AT IT AGAIN.
I GOT THEM FROM GWEN!
LOOK, LADY-- YOU KNOW HOW HARRY FEELS ABOUT YOU! SO WHAT'S THE BIT?
IT'S A LONG STORY.
WANNA HEAR IT?
THEN, AS PETER VAINLY TRIES TO BREAK AWAY--
HEY, OSBORN-- WAIT UP A MINUTE.
I SAW THE WHOLE THING, PAL! THAT CHICK'S GIVIN' YOU A BUM DEAL.
SO WHAT? WHO ASKED YOU TO BUTT IN?
I'M YOUR FRIEND, FELLA! I'VE BEEN THE SAME ROUTE MY-SELF-- AND I KNOW HOW IT FEELS.
AND I KNOW WHAT TO DO FOR IT.
I'VE GOT SOME-THING THAT'LL MAKE YOU FOR-GET ALL ABOUT THAT CHICK---
SOMETHING THAT'LL MAKE YOU FEEL LIKE YOU'RE KING OF THE WORLD.
I HATE TO SEE A GUY GET PUT DOWN THAT WAY--
SO I'M GONNA DO YOU A REAL BIG FAVOR, PAL---
11.

THIS STUFF IS REAL *NEW*-- AND IT AIN'T EASY TO *COME* BY--

BUT, FOR A GUY WHO CAN *USE* 'EM, LIKE *YOU*...

LEMME *SEE!* WHAT *ARE* THOSE THINGS?

DON'T TAKE *MY* WORD FOR IT, OSBORN! JUST *TRY* A FEW-- AND *NOTHING'S* GONNA BOTHER YOU.

IT'LL BE WORTH *ANY-THING*-- TO GET HER OUT OF MY *MIND!*

12

SURE, KID --SURE! I *KNOW* HOW YOU FEEL.

EVERYONE'S GOT A MILLION *HANG-UPS* NOWADAYS.

THAT'S WHY THIS STUFF I GOT IS JUST WHAT THE DOCTOR *ORDERED.*

SO HOW *ABOUT* IT?

OKAY, OKAY.

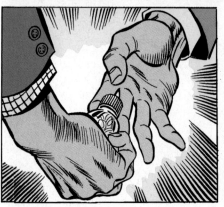

NICE DOING *BUSINESS* WITH YOU, OSBORN! SEE YOU *AGAIN.*

OH *NO!* THIS IS THE *FIRST* TIME-- AND THE *LAST.*

I'M NOT GETTING HOOKED.

YEAH-- THAT'S WHAT THEY *SAY.*

13

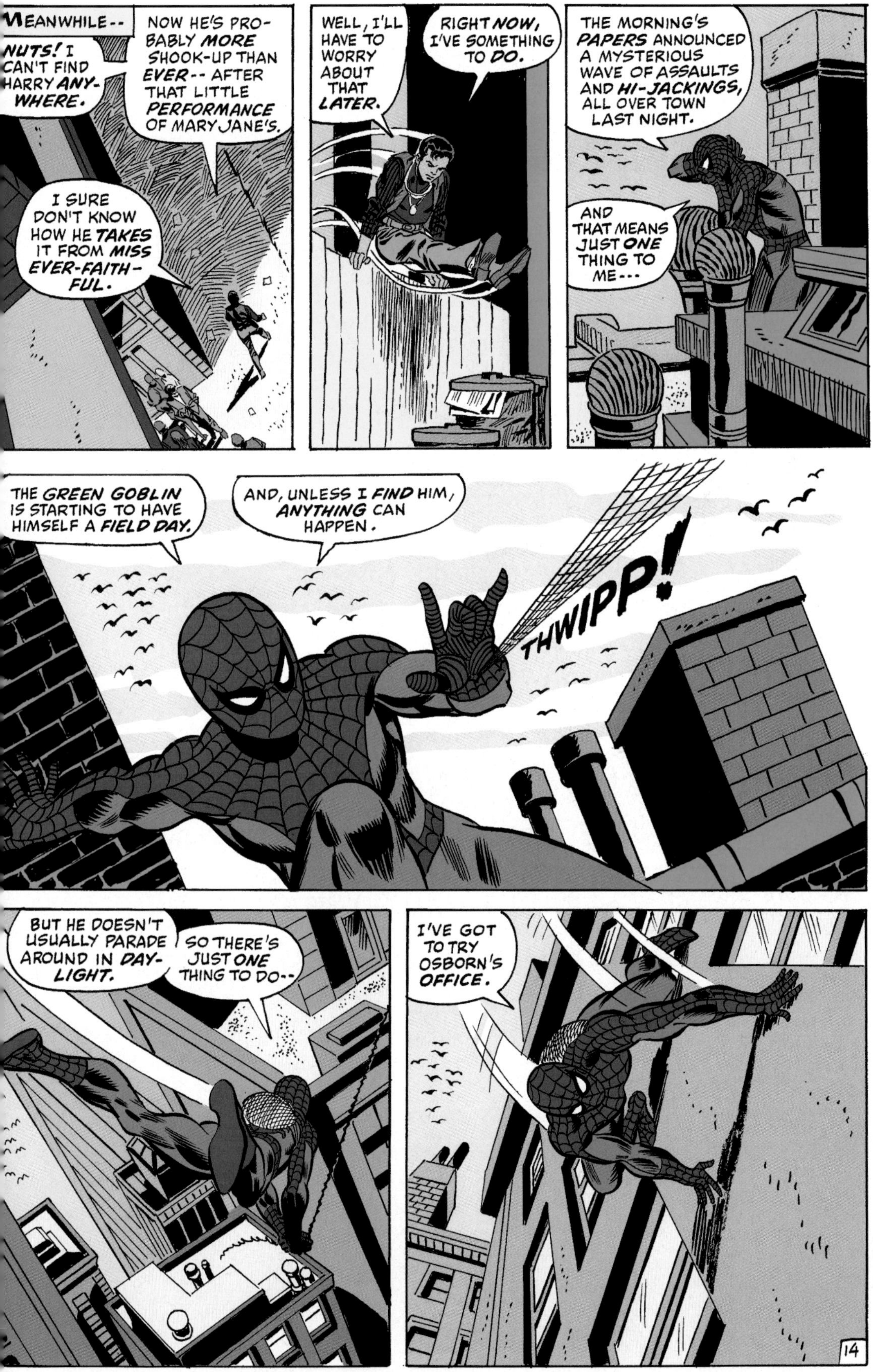
MEANWHILE--
NUTS! I CAN'T FIND HARRY ANYWHERE.
NOW HE'S PROBABLY MORE SHOOK-UP THAN EVER-- AFTER THAT LITTLE PERFORMANCE OF MARY JANE'S.
I SURE DON'T KNOW HOW HE TAKES IT FROM MISS EVER-FAITHFUL.
WELL, I'LL HAVE TO WORRY ABOUT THAT LATER.
RIGHT NOW, I'VE SOMETHING TO DO.
THE MORNING'S PAPERS ANNOUNCED A MYSTERIOUS WAVE OF ASSAULTS AND HI-JACKINGS, ALL OVER TOWN LAST NIGHT.
AND THAT MEANS JUST ONE THING TO ME---
THE GREEN GOBLIN IS STARTING TO HAVE HIMSELF A FIELD DAY.
AND, UNLESS I FIND HIM, ANYTHING CAN HAPPEN.
THWIPP!
BUT HE DOESN'T USUALLY PARADE AROUND IN DAYLIGHT.
SO THERE'S JUST ONE THING TO DO--
I'VE GOT TO TRY OSBORN'S OFFICE.
14

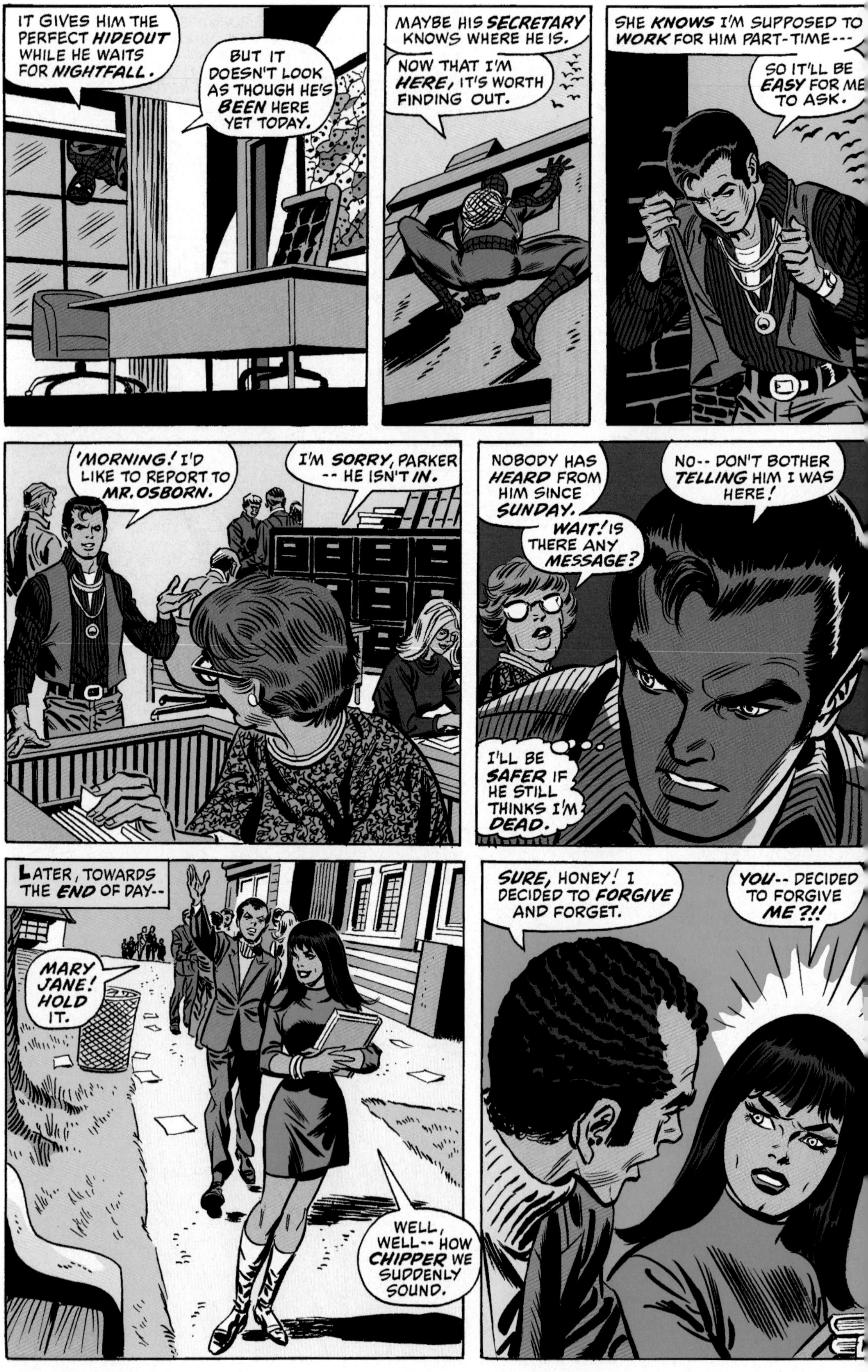

IT GIVES HIM THE PERFECT HIDEOUT WHILE HE WAITS FOR NIGHTFALL.
BUT IT DOESN'T LOOK AS THOUGH HE'S BEEN HERE YET TODAY.
MAYBE HIS SECRETARY KNOWS WHERE HE IS.
NOW THAT I'M HERE, IT'S WORTH FINDING OUT.
SHE KNOWS I'M SUPPOSED TO WORK FOR HIM PART-TIME---
SO IT'LL BE EASY FOR ME TO ASK.
'MORNING! I'D LIKE TO REPORT TO MR. OSBORN.
I'M SORRY, PARKER -- HE ISN'T IN.
NOBODY HAS HEARD FROM HIM SINCE SUNDAY.
WAIT! IS THERE ANY MESSAGE?
NO-- DON'T BOTHER TELLING HIM I WAS HERE!
I'LL BE SAFER IF HE STILL THINKS I'M DEAD.
LATER, TOWARDS THE END OF DAY--
MARY JANE! HOLD IT.
WELL, WELL-- HOW CHIPPER WE SUDDENLY SOUND.
SURE, HONEY! I DECIDED TO FORGIVE AND FORGET.
YOU-- DECIDED TO FORGIVE ME?!!

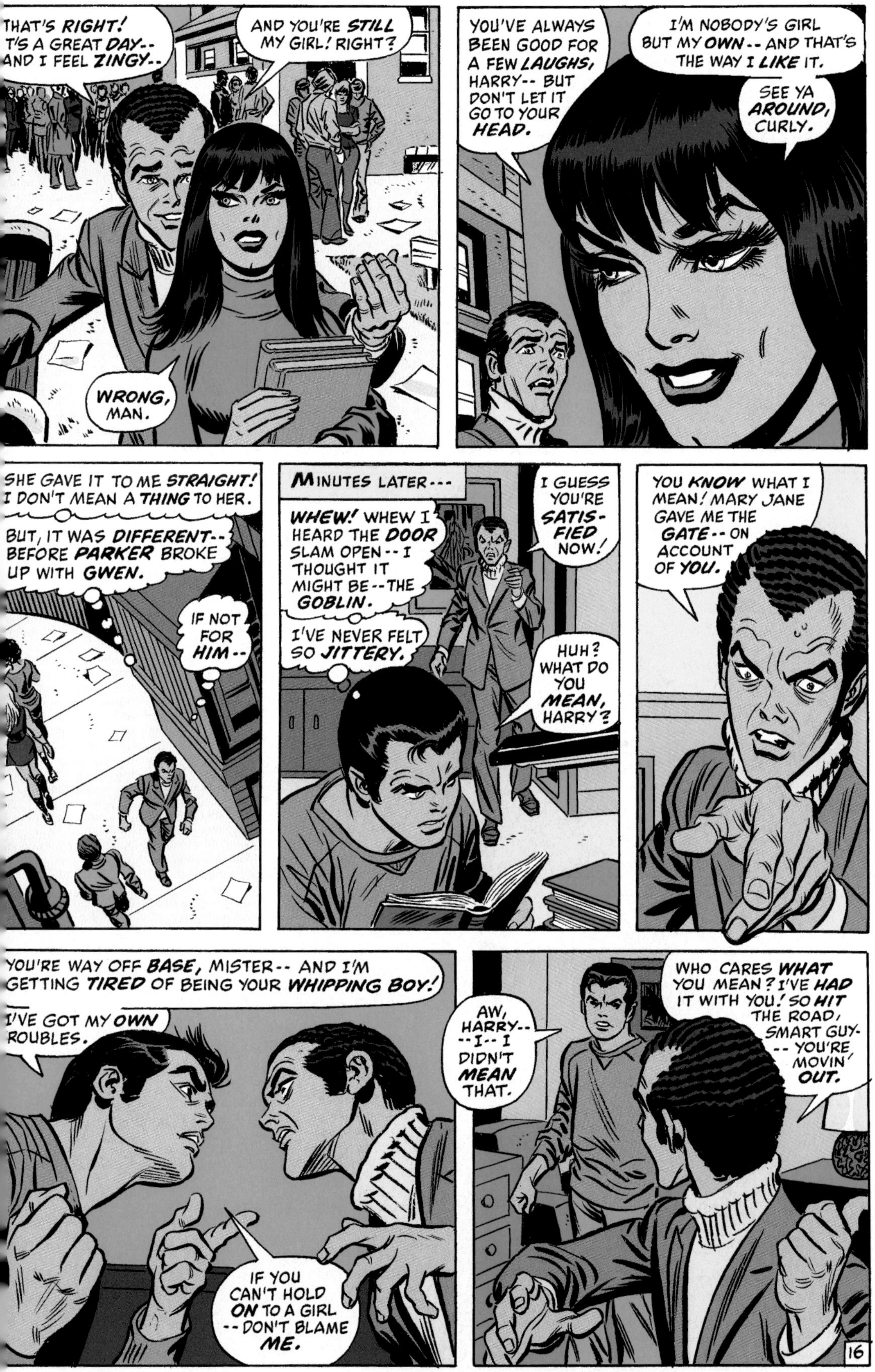
THAT'S RIGHT! IT'S A GREAT DAY-- AND I FEEL ZINGY--
AND YOU'RE STILL MY GIRL! RIGHT?
WRONG, MAN.
YOU'VE ALWAYS BEEN GOOD FOR A FEW LAUGHS, HARRY-- BUT DON'T LET IT GO TO YOUR HEAD.
I'M NOBODY'S GIRL BUT MY OWN -- AND THAT'S THE WAY I LIKE IT.
SEE YA AROUND, CURLY.
SHE GAVE IT TO ME STRAIGHT! I DON'T MEAN A THING TO HER.
BUT, IT WAS DIFFERENT-- BEFORE PARKER BROKE UP WITH GWEN.
IF NOT FOR HIM--
MINUTES LATER---
WHEW! WHEW I HEARD THE DOOR SLAM OPEN -- I THOUGHT IT MIGHT BE -- THE GOBLIN.
I'VE NEVER FELT SO JITTERY.
I GUESS YOU'RE SATIS-FIED NOW!
HUH? WHAT DO YOU MEAN, HARRY?
YOU KNOW WHAT I MEAN! MARY JANE GAVE ME THE GATE -- ON ACCOUNT OF YOU.
YOU'RE WAY OFF BASE, MISTER -- AND I'M GETTING TIRED OF BEING YOUR WHIPPING BOY!
I'VE GOT MY OWN TROUBLES.
IF YOU CAN'T HOLD ON TO A GIRL -- DON'T BLAME ME.
AW, HARRY-- --I-- I DIDN'T MEAN THAT.
WHO CARES WHAT YOU MEAN? I'VE HAD IT WITH YOU! SO HIT THE ROAD, SMART GUY- -- YOU'RE MOVIN' OUT.
16

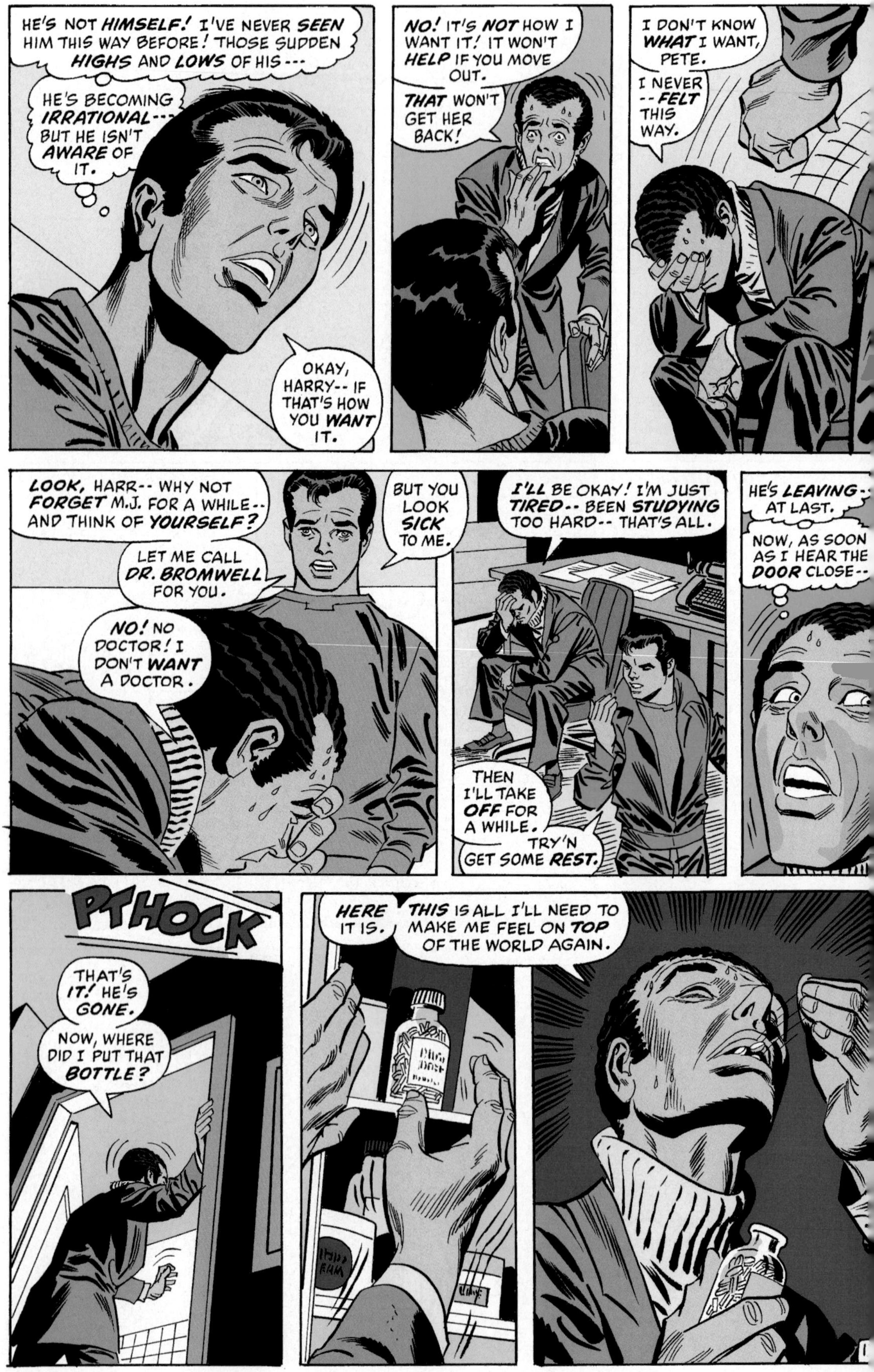

HE'S NOT HIMSELF! I'VE NEVER SEEN HIM THIS WAY BEFORE! THOSE SUDDEN HIGHS AND LOWS OF HIS---
HE'S BECOMING IRRATIONAL--- BUT HE ISN'T AWARE OF IT.
OKAY, HARRY-- IF THAT'S HOW YOU WANT IT.
NO! IT'S NOT HOW I WANT IT! IT WON'T HELP IF YOU MOVE OUT.
THAT WON'T GET HER BACK!
I DON'T KNOW WHAT I WANT, PETE.
I NEVER --FELT THIS WAY.
LOOK, HARR-- WHY NOT FORGET M.J. FOR A WHILE-- AND THINK OF YOURSELF?
LET ME CALL DR. BROMWELL FOR YOU.
NO! NO DOCTOR! I DON'T WANT A DOCTOR.
BUT YOU LOOK SICK TO ME.
I'LL BE OKAY! I'M JUST TIRED-- BEEN STUDYING TOO HARD-- THAT'S ALL.
THEN I'LL TAKE OFF FOR A WHILE.
TRY'N GET SOME REST.
HE'S LEAVING-- AT LAST.
NOW, AS SOON AS I HEAR THE DOOR CLOSE--
PTHOCK
THAT'S IT! HE'S GONE.
NOW, WHERE DID I PUT THAT BOTTLE?
HERE IT IS.
THIS IS ALL I'LL NEED TO MAKE ME FEEL ON TOP OF THE WORLD AGAIN.

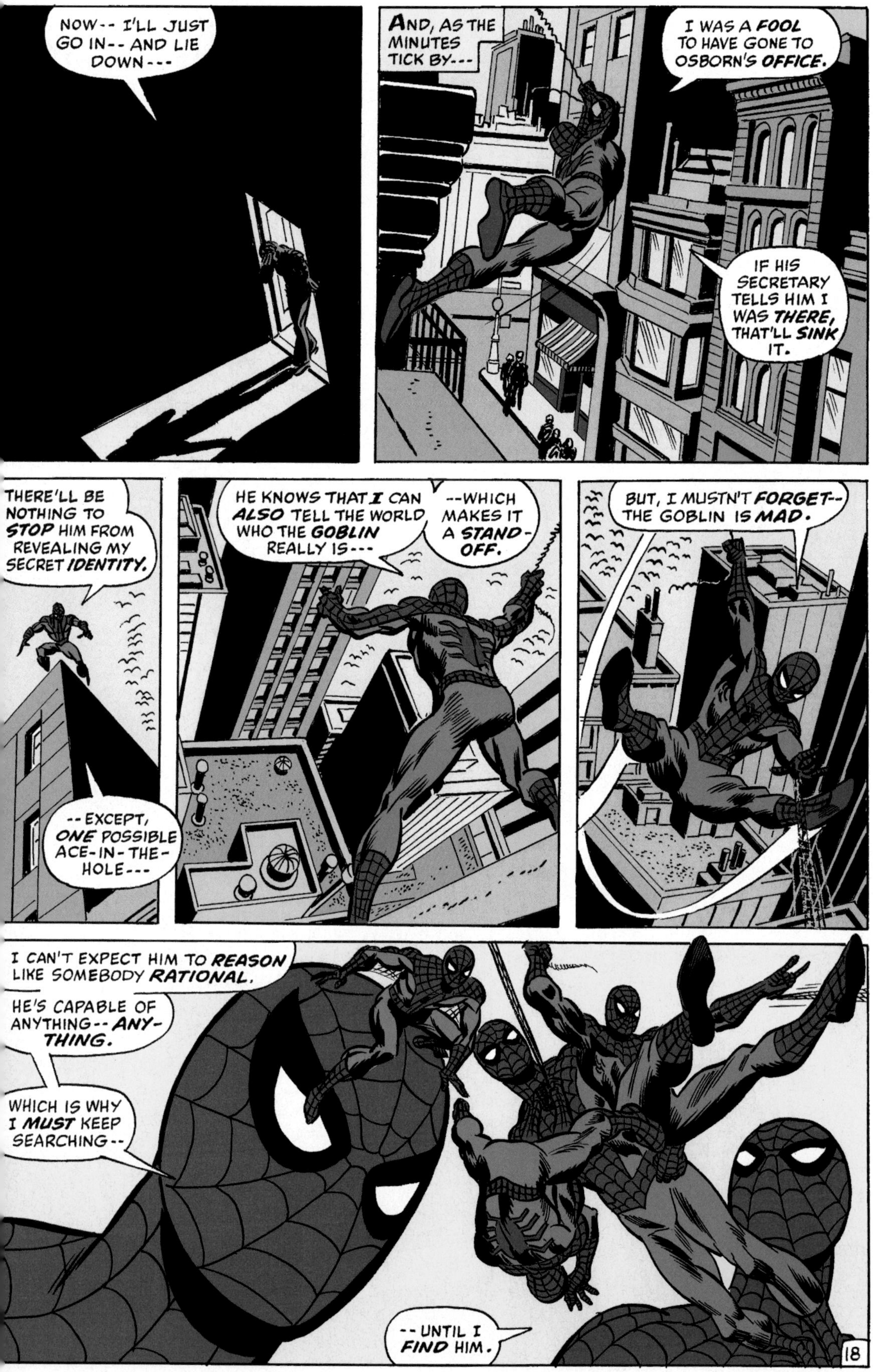
NOW-- I'LL JUST GO IN-- AND LIE DOWN---
AND, AS THE MINUTES TICK BY---
I WAS A FOOL TO HAVE GONE TO OSBORN'S OFFICE.
IF HIS SECRETARY TELLS HIM I WAS THERE, THAT'LL SINK IT.
THERE'LL BE NOTHING TO STOP HIM FROM REVEALING MY SECRET IDENTITY.
--EXCEPT, ONE POSSIBLE ACE-IN-THE-HOLE---
HE KNOWS THAT I CAN ALSO TELL THE WORLD WHO THE GOBLIN REALLY IS---
--WHICH MAKES IT A STAND-OFF.
BUT, I MUSTN'T FORGET-- THE GOBLIN IS MAD.
I CAN'T EXPECT HIM TO REASON LIKE SOMEBODY RATIONAL.
HE'S CAPABLE OF ANYTHING-- ANY-THING.
WHICH IS WHY I MUST KEEP SEARCHING--
--UNTIL I FIND HIM.
18

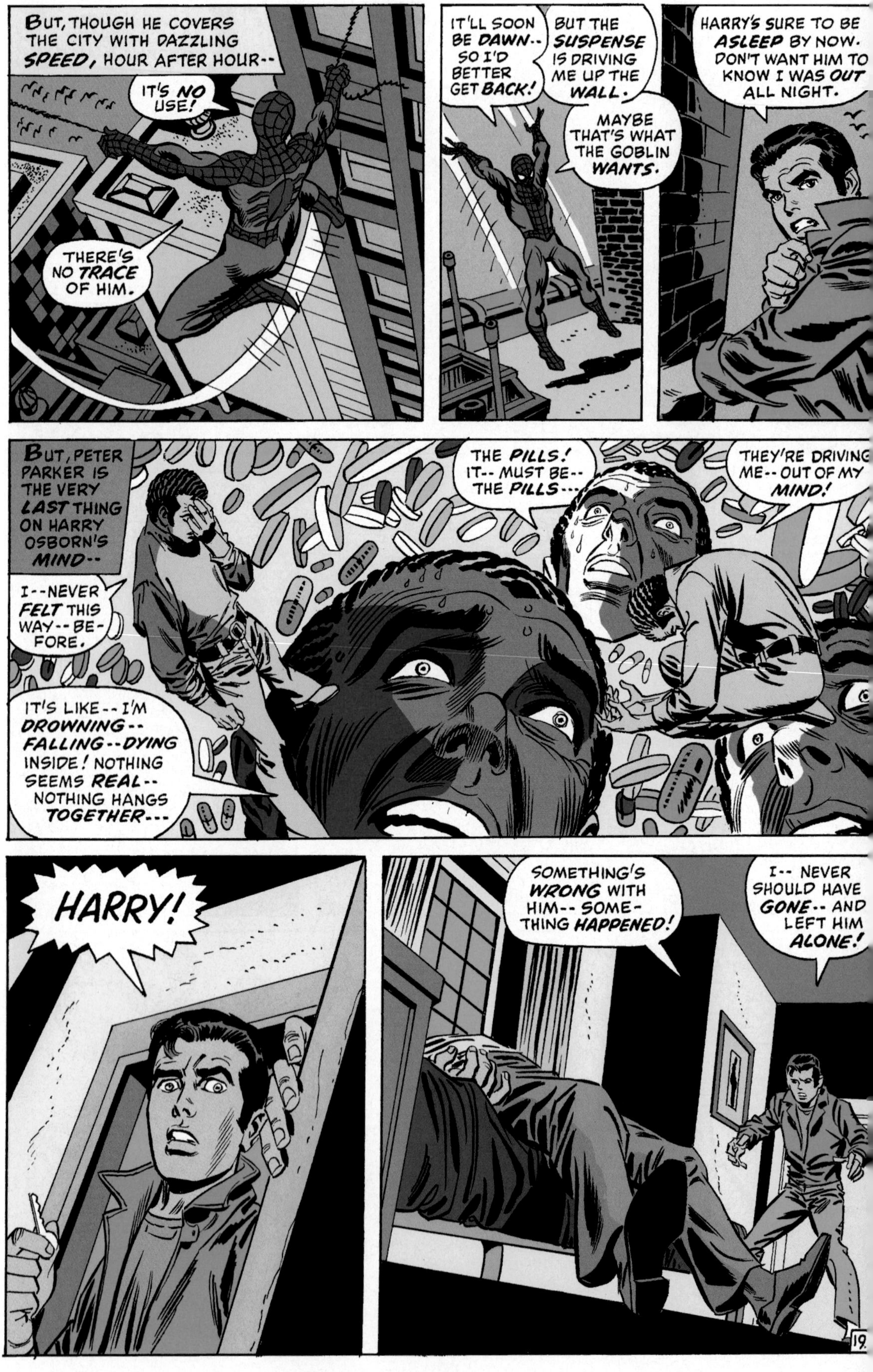

BUT, THOUGH HE COVERS THE CITY WITH DAZZLING SPEED, HOUR AFTER HOUR--
IT'S NO USE!
THERE'S NO TRACE OF HIM.
IT'LL SOON BE DAWN-- SO I'D BETTER GET BACK!
BUT THE SUSPENSE IS DRIVING ME UP THE WALL.
MAYBE THAT'S WHAT THE GOBLIN WANTS.
HARRY'S SURE TO BE ASLEEP BY NOW. DON'T WANT HIM TO KNOW I WAS OUT ALL NIGHT.
BUT, PETER PARKER IS THE VERY LAST THING ON HARRY OSBORN'S MIND--
I--NEVER FELT THIS WAY-- BE-FORE.
IT'S LIKE-- I'M DROWNING-- FALLING--DYING INSIDE! NOTHING SEEMS REAL-- NOTHING HANGS TOGETHER---
THE PILLS! IT-- MUST BE-- THE PILLS---
THEY'RE DRIVING ME-- OUT OF MY MIND!
HARRY!
SOMETHING'S WRONG WITH HIM-- SOME-THING HAPPENED!
I-- NEVER SHOULD HAVE GONE-- AND LEFT HIM ALONE!
19

HARRY! SNAP OUT OF IT! WAKE UP, DO YOU HEAR ME? WAKE UP!
PETE-- HELP ME! I-- I'M SICK---
SURE, HARRY! DON'T WORRY, PAL-- I'LL CALL THE DOC.
THAT LAUGH--
HAHAHAHAHAHAHAHAHAHA
OUTSIDE THE WINDOW.
IT-- IT SOUNDS LIKE---
THE GOBLIN!
DID YOU THINK I WOULDN'T FIND YOU, PARKER?
DID YOU EXPECT THE GREEN GOBLIN TO LET SPIDER-MAN LIVE?
NEXT ISSUE: THE GOBLIN'S POWER!
20

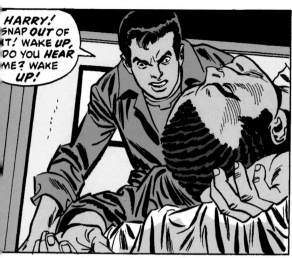

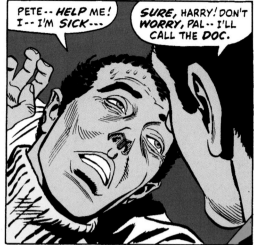

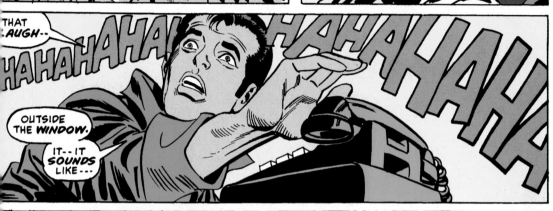

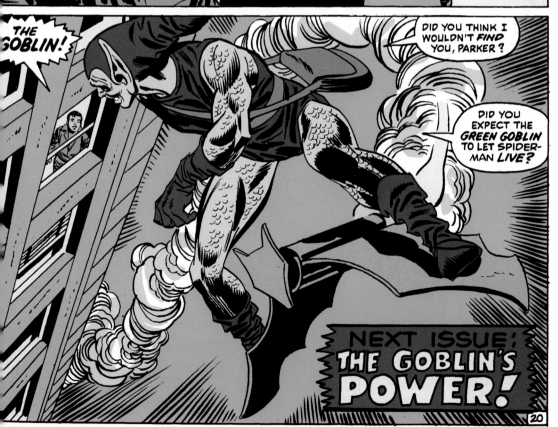

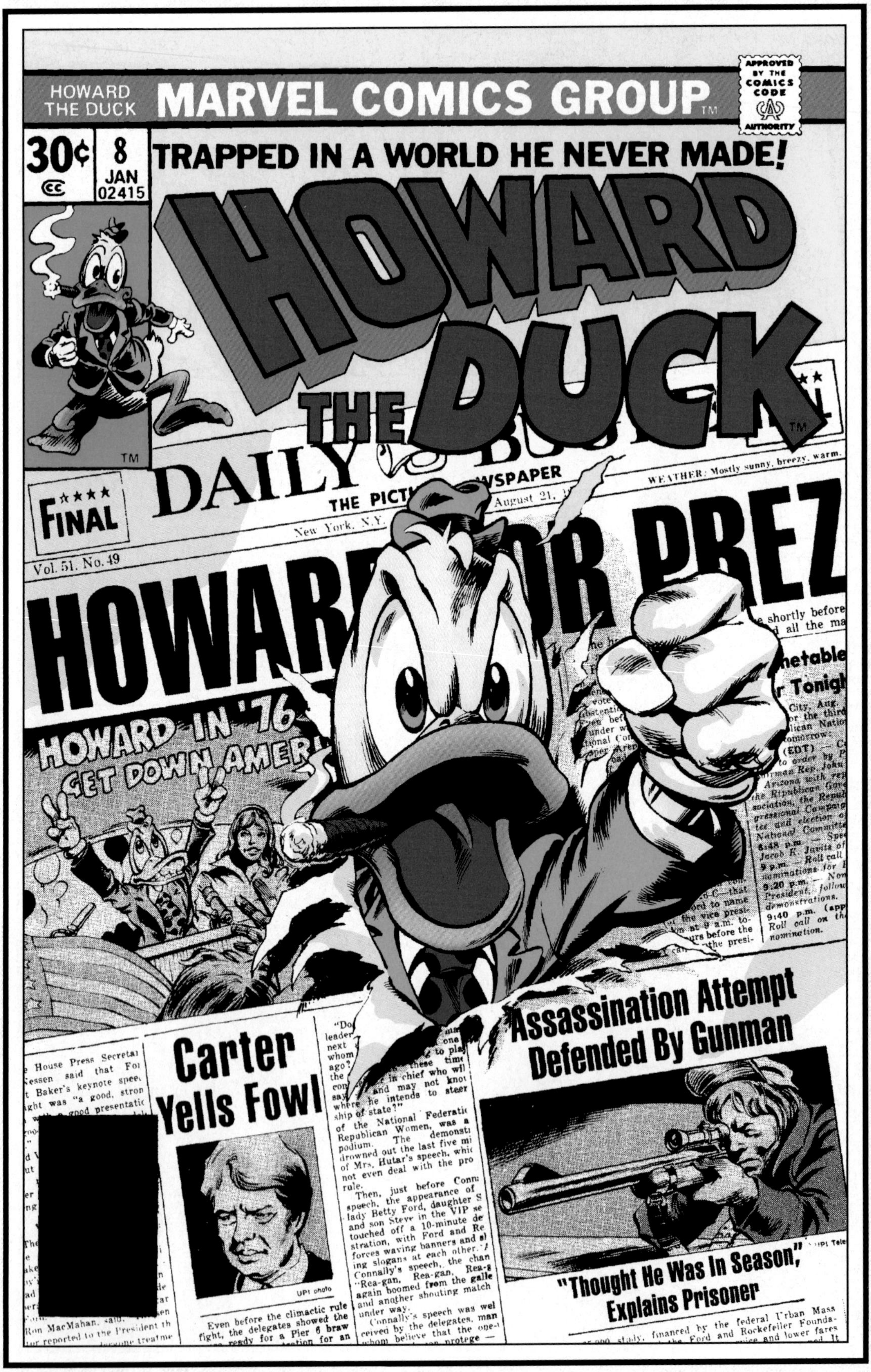

HOWARD THE DUCK
MARVEL COMICS GROUP
APPROVED BY THE COMICS CODE AUTHORITY
30¢
8 JAN 02415
TRAPPED IN A WORLD HE NEVER MADE!
HOWARD THE DUCK
FINAL
Vol. 51. No. 49
WEATHER: Mostly sunny, breezy, warm.
HOWARD IN '76
Carter Yells Fowl
Assassination Attempt Defended By Gunman
"Thought He Was In Season," Explains Prisoner
[redacted]

From the time of his hatching, he was...different. A potentially brilliant scholar who dreaded the structured environment of school, he educated himself in the streets, taking whatever work was available, formulating his philosophy of self from what he learned of the world about him. And then the Cosmic Axis shifted...and that world *changed.* Suddenly, he was stranded in a universe he could not fathom. Without warning, he became a strange fowl in an even stranger land.

Stan Lee PRESENTS: HOWARD THE DUCK! TM

STEVE GERBER * GENE COLAN * STEVE LEIALOHA * I. WATANABE * JAN COHEN * ARCHIE GOODWIN
WRITER * ARTIST * INKER * LETTERER * COLORIST * EDITOR

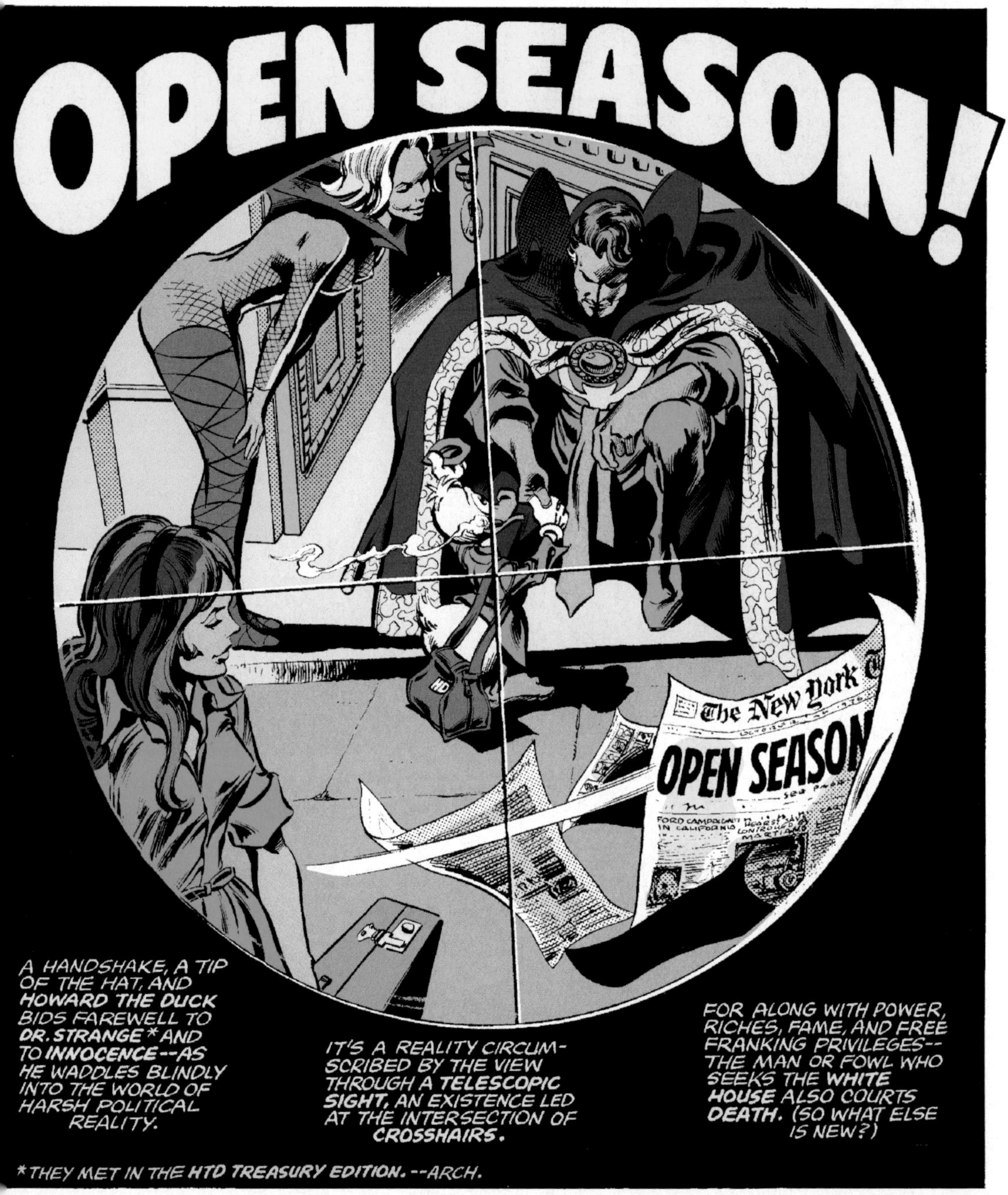

OPEN SEASON!
The New York T
OPEN SEASON
HD
A HANDSHAKE, A TIP OF THE HAT, AND HOWARD THE DUCK BIDS FAREWELL TO DR. STRANGE* AND TO INNOCENCE--AS HE WADDLES BLINDLY INTO THE WORLD OF HARSH POLITICAL REALITY.
IT'S A REALITY CIRCUM-SCRIBED BY THE VIEW THROUGH A TELESCOPIC SIGHT, AN EXISTENCE LED AT THE INTERSECTION OF CROSSHAIRS.
FOR ALONG WITH POWER, RICHES, FAME, AND FREE FRANKING PRIVILEGES--THE MAN OR FOWL WHO SEEKS THE WHITE HOUSE ALSO COURTS DEATH. (SO WHAT ELSE IS NEW?)
*THEY MET IN THE HTD TREASURY EDITION. --ARCH.

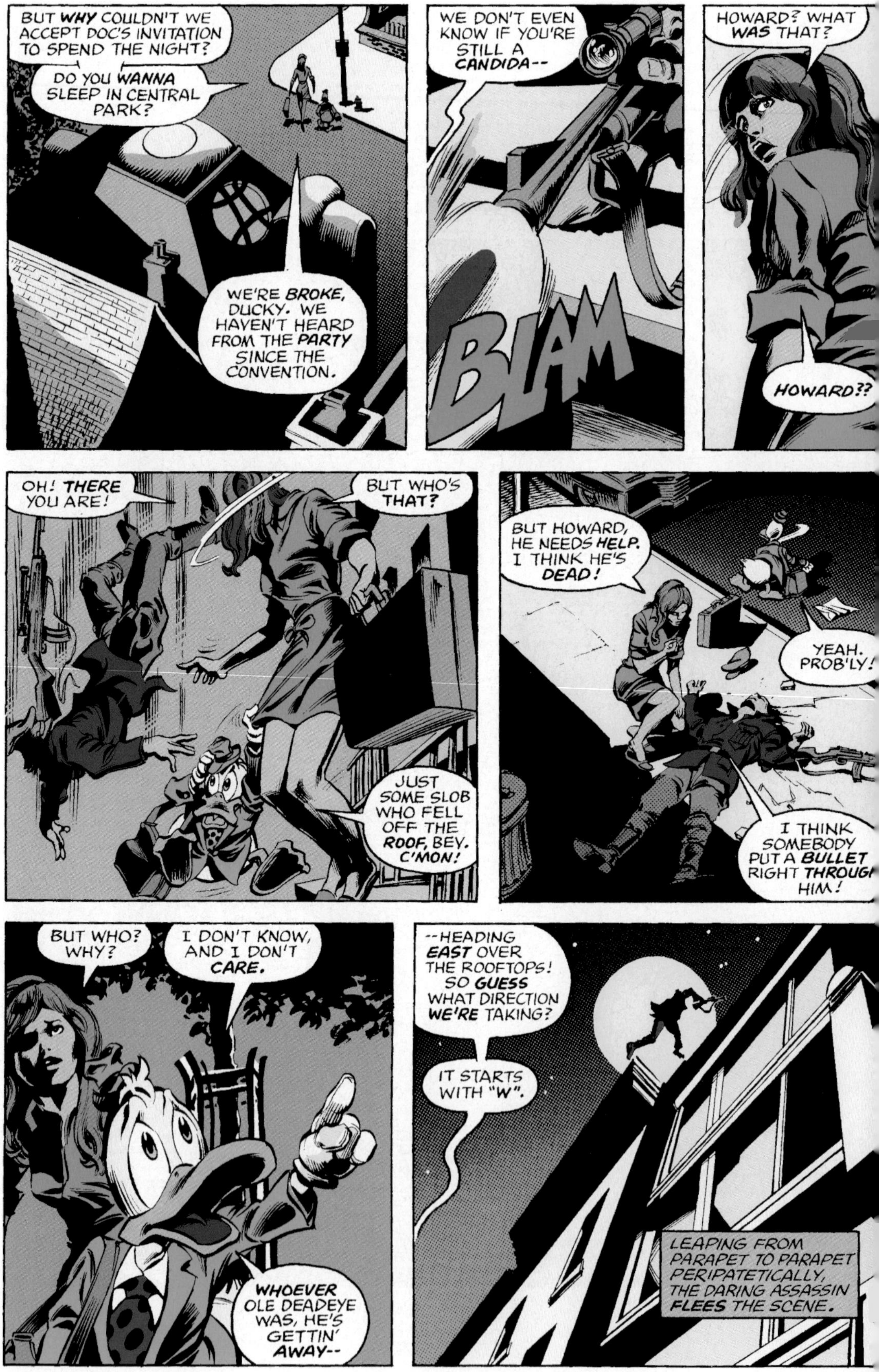
BUT WHY COULDN'T WE ACCEPT DOC'S INVITATION TO SPEND THE NIGHT?
DO YOU WANNA SLEEP IN CENTRAL PARK?
WE'RE BROKE, DUCKY. WE HAVEN'T HEARD FROM THE PARTY SINCE THE CONVENTION.
WE DON'T EVEN KNOW IF YOU'RE STILL A CANDIDA--
BLAM
HOWARD? WHAT WAS THAT?
HOWARD??
OH! THERE YOU ARE!
BUT WHO'S THAT?
JUST SOME SLOB WHO FELL OFF THE ROOF, BEY. C'MON!
BUT HOWARD, HE NEEDS HELP. I THINK HE'S DEAD!
YEAH. PROB'LY!
I THINK SOMEBODY PUT A BULLET RIGHT THROUG
HIM!
BUT WHO? WHY?
I DON'T KNOW, AND I DON'T CARE.
WHOEVER OLE DEADEYE WAS, HE'S GETTIN' AWAY--
--HEADING EAST OVER THE ROOFTOPS! SO GUESS WHAT DIRECTION WE'RE TAKING?
IT STARTS WITH "W".
LEAPING FROM PARAPET TO PARAPET PERIPATETICALLY, THE DARING ASSASSIN FLEES THE SCENE.

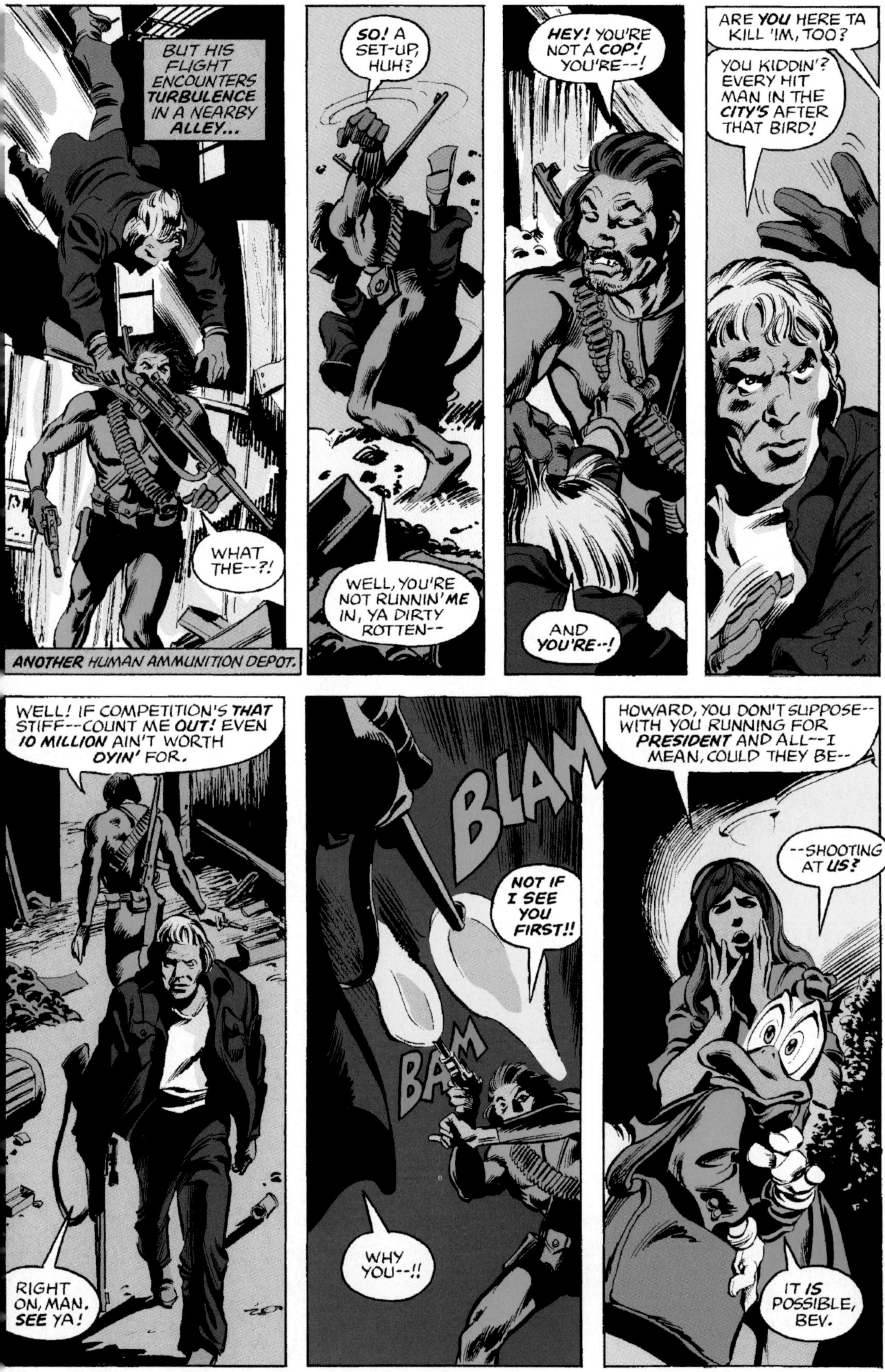

BUT HIS FLIGHT ENCOUNTERS TURBULENCE IN A NEARBY ALLEY...
WHAT THE--?!
ANOTHER HUMAN AMMUNITION DEPOT.
SO! A SET-UP, HUH?
WELL, YOU'RE NOT RUNNIN' ME IN, YA DIRTY ROTTEN--
HEY! YOU'RE NOT A COP! YOU'RE--!
AND YOU'RE--!
ARE YOU HERE TA KILL 'IM, TOO?
YOU KIDDIN'? EVERY HIT MAN IN THE CITY'S AFTER THAT BIRD!
WELL! IF COMPETITION'S THAT STIFF--COUNT ME OUT! EVEN 10 MILLION AIN'T WORTH OYIN' FOR.
RIGHT ON, MAN. SEE YA!
BLAM
NOT IF I SEE YOU FIRST!!
BAM
WHY YOU--!!
HOWARD, YOU DON'T SUPPOSE--WITH YOU RUNNING FOR PRESIDENT AND ALL--I MEAN, COULD THEY BE--
--SHOOTING AT US?
IT IS POSSIBLE, BEV.

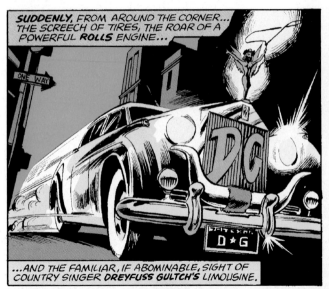

SUDDENLY, FROM AROUND THE CORNER... THE SCREECH OF TIRES, THE ROAR OF A POWERFUL *ROLLS* ENGINE...

ONE WAY

...AND THE FAMILIAR, IF ABOMINABLE, SIGHT OF COUNTRY SINGER *DREYFUSS GULTCH'S* LIMOUSINE.

HURRY, Y'ALL! MUH BULLET-PROOF GLASS WILL *PROTECT* YA!

IT'S BEEN *TESTED* BY NORTH CAROLINA WOMEN!

SCRREE EE CH

THE DOOR SLAMS SHUT... AND CHRISTOPHER STREET BECOMES A *WAR ZONE!* ASSASSINS WHO MIGHT OTHERWISE HAVE WAITED THEIR *TURNS* EMERGE, GUNS BLAZING, FROM EVERY NOOK, CRANNY AND *MANHOLE!*

WHERE'D YA' ALL RUN *OFF* TO, HOWIE? IT AIN'T *SAFE* FOR YA TO TO BE WALKIN' THE STREETS!

BRRRP PINNNG

POW POW

BAM

YEAH. I GATHERED. GOT ANY SPARE HYPOTHESES *WHY?*

SHORE. I KNOW WHY! IT'S THEM WILD-EYED POLITICAL *PROMISES* YOU BEEN MAKIN'!

WHAT PROMISES?! I HAVEN'T--

NAW, BUT YOUR AD *AGENCY* HAS. C'MON. THEIR OFFICE IS RIGHT UPSTAIRS.

IT'S TIME YOU *MET* 'EM.

YEAH. I'D SAY SO.

WOW. HEY, DUCKY, I'M IMPRESSED.

I USED TO THINK *I* WAS ALL THINGS TO ALL MEN...BUT EVEN IN MY *DEVIL-MAY-CARE* DAYS, I COULDN'T BEAT *THIS*!

...OWARD-PRE...

STAND UP, AMERICA— VOTE HOWARD THE DUCK IN '76

VO... FOR PRESID...

I DON'T BELIEVE IT.

HOWARD FOR PRESIDENT

WHOSE WARPED MIND IS *RESPONSIBLE* FOR THIS HOKUM?

G.Q. STUDLEY HIMSELF ENGINEERED THE CAMPAIGN, HOWIE. HE'S *FAMOUS* FOR--

G.Q. STUDLEY ASSOC.

--HUCKSTERISM, PROBABLY. I WANNA *TALK* TO THIS GUY!

HOWEVER...

I'M *SO* SORRY.

HE'S IN *CONFERENCE* JUST NOW...ABOUT THE *DUCK* CAMPAIGN. WON'T YOU TAKE A SEAT?

⸸WAAAUGH⸸ LADY, *I'M* THE BLASTED DUCK!!

I'M THE CANDIDATE! I WANT SOME *SAY* IN WHAT I *SAY*, Y'KNOW?

GIMME THAT SWITCH-BOARD!!

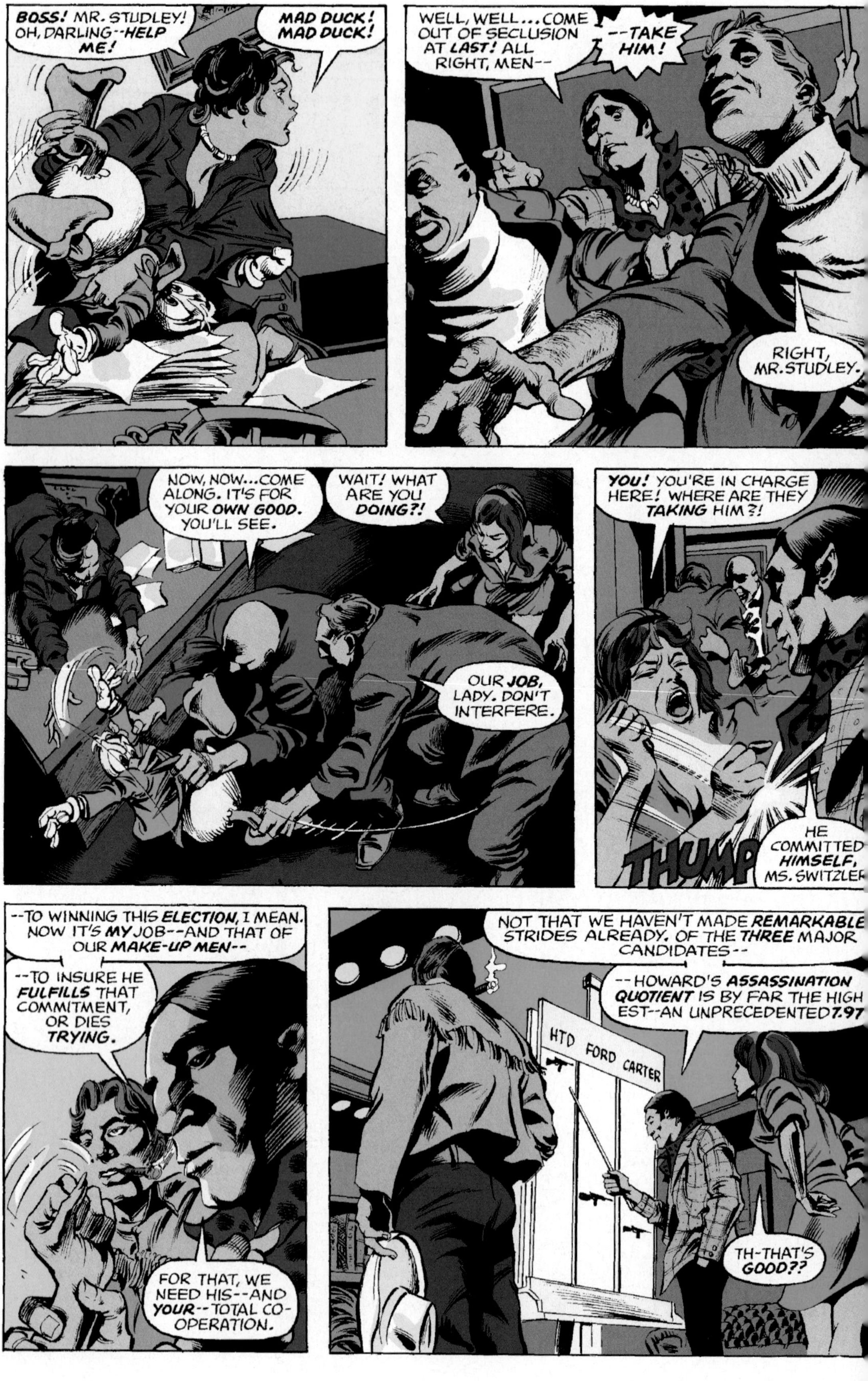
BOSS! MR. STUDLEY! OH, DARLING--HELP ME!
MAD DUCK! MAD DUCK!
WELL, WELL...COME OUT OF SECLUSION AT LAST! ALL RIGHT, MEN--
--TAKE HIM!
RIGHT, MR. STUDLEY.
NOW, NOW...COME ALONG. IT'S FOR YOUR OWN GOOD. YOU'LL SEE.
WAIT! WHAT ARE YOU DOING?!
OUR JOB, LADY. DON'T INTERFERE.
YOU! YOU'RE IN CHARGE HERE! WHERE ARE THEY TAKING HIM?!
THUMP
HE COMMITTED HIMSELF, MS. SWITZLER
--TO WINNING THIS ELECTION, I MEAN. NOW IT'S MY JOB--AND THAT OF OUR MAKE-UP MEN--
--TO INSURE HE FULFILLS THAT COMMITMENT, OR DIES TRYING.
FOR THAT, WE NEED HIS--AND YOUR--TOTAL CO-OPERATION.
NOT THAT WE HAVEN'T MADE REMARKABLE STRIDES ALREADY. OF THE THREE MAJOR CANDIDATES--
--HOWARD'S ASSASSINATION QUOTIENT IS BY FAR THE HIGHEST--AN UNPRECEDENTED 7.97
HTD FORD CARTER
TH-THAT'S GOOD??

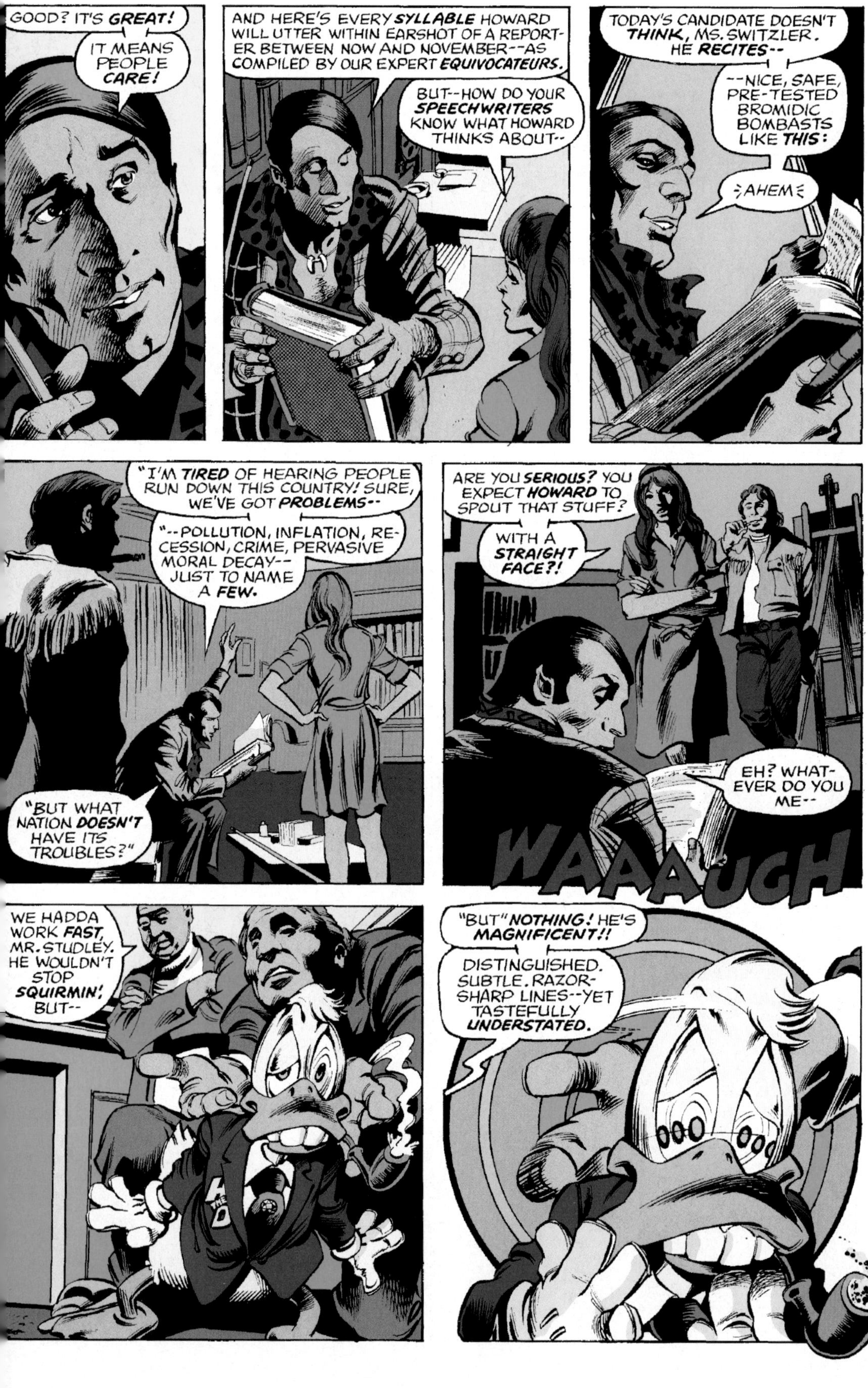
GOOD? IT'S GREAT!
IT MEANS PEOPLE CARE!
AND HERE'S EVERY SYLLABLE HOWARD WILL UTTER WITHIN EARSHOT OF A REPORTER BETWEEN NOW AND NOVEMBER--AS COMPILED BY OUR EXPERT EQUIVOCATEURS.
BUT--HOW DO YOUR SPEECHWRITERS KNOW WHAT HOWARD THINKS ABOUT--
TODAY'S CANDIDATE DOESN'T THINK, MS. SWITZLER. HE RECITES--
--NICE, SAFE, PRE-TESTED BROMIDIC BOMBASTS LIKE THIS:
AHEM
"I'M TIRED OF HEARING PEOPLE RUN DOWN THIS COUNTRY! SURE, WE'VE GOT PROBLEMS--
"--POLLUTION, INFLATION, RECESSION, CRIME, PERVASIVE MORAL DECAY--JUST TO NAME A FEW.
"BUT WHAT NATION DOESN'T HAVE ITS TROUBLES?"
ARE YOU SERIOUS? YOU EXPECT HOWARD TO SPOUT THAT STUFF?
WITH A STRAIGHT FACE?!
EH? WHATEVER DO YOU ME--
WAAAUGH
WE HADDA WORK FAST, MR. STUDLEY. HE WOULDN'T STOP SQUIRMIN'! BUT--
"BUT" NOTHING! HE'S MAGNIFICENT!!
DISTINGUISHED. SUBTLE. RAZOR-SHARP LINES--YET TASTEFULLY UNDERSTATED.

AND EXUDING UNMISTAKABLE *SEX APPEAL!* AND LORD A'MIGHTY, THAT *WINNING SMILE!!*

YEAH? WELL, IF YA *LIKE* IT SO MUCH--

CHOMP

--YA CAN KEEP IT, YA POMPOUS, PRESUMPTUOUS, PLASTICIZED FASHION PLATE!

STOP!!

YOU'RE COMMITTING POLITICAL *SUICIDE!*

YOU CAN'T *WADDLE* OUT ON US! WHO'LL *PACKAGE* YOU?!

YOU'RE A THIRD-PARTY CANDIDATE AND A *DUCK!*

YOU EXPECT TO SURMOUNT THOSE IMAGE PROBLEMS *ALONE?!*

NYAAH

JUST *WATCH* ME, LAUGHING BOY!

OUTSIDE...

YOU FIGGER *EVERY* CANDIDATE GOES THRU THIS DEBASE-MENT?

NAH. BY THE TIME MOST OF 'EM GET *THIS* FAR, HUMILIATING COMPROMISE COMES *EASY.*

WHAT *ARE* YOU GONNA DO ABOUT AN *AD REP*, THOUGH?

WE'LL PICK OUR *OWN*--THE SCIENTIFIC WAY!

AT *RANDOM*-- FROM THE *YELLOW PAGES!*

TELEPH

AH-HA!

NOW *THAT'S* OUR KINDA PEOPLE!

WELL...*YOUR* KIND, ANYWAY.

MAD GENIUS ASSO ATES

AVENUE ROOM 806

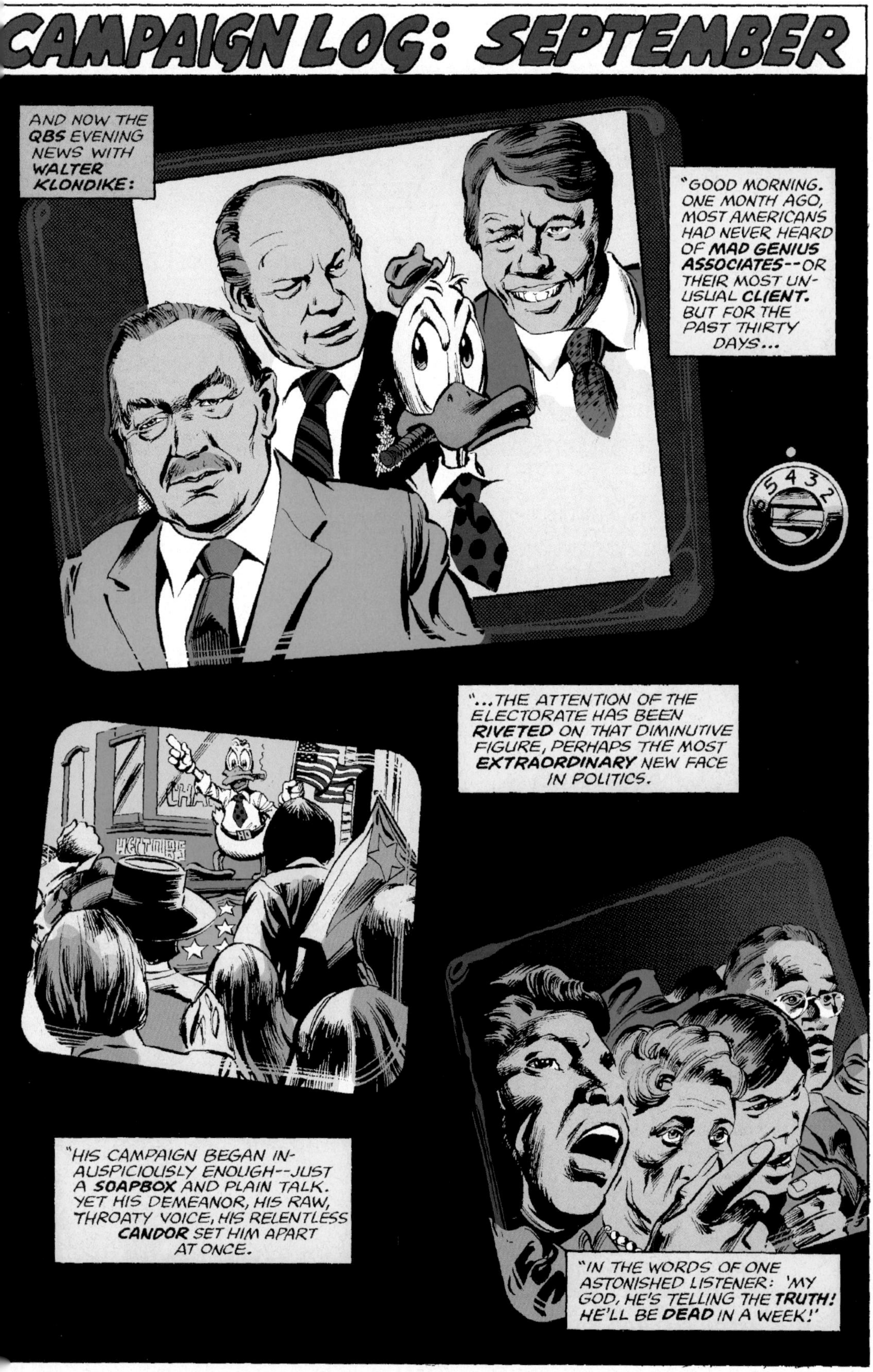
CAMPAIGN LOG: SEPTEMBER
AND NOW THE QBS EVENING NEWS WITH WALTER KLONDIKE:
"GOOD MORNING. ONE MONTH AGO, MOST AMERICANS HAD NEVER HEARD OF MAD GENIUS ASSOCIATES--OR THEIR MOST UN-USUAL CLIENT. BUT FOR THE PAST THIRTY DAYS...
"...THE ATTENTION OF THE ELECTORATE HAS BEEN RIVETED ON THAT DIMINUTIVE FIGURE, PERHAPS THE MOST EXTRAORDINARY NEW FACE IN POLITICS.
"HIS CAMPAIGN BEGAN IN-AUSPICIOUSLY ENOUGH--JUST A SOAPBOX AND PLAIN TALK. YET HIS DEMEANOR, HIS RAW, THROATY VOICE, HIS RELENTLESS CANDOR SET HIM APART AT ONCE.
"IN THE WORDS OF ONE ASTONISHED LISTENER: 'MY GOD, HE'S TELLING THE TRUTH! HE'LL BE DEAD IN A WEEK!'

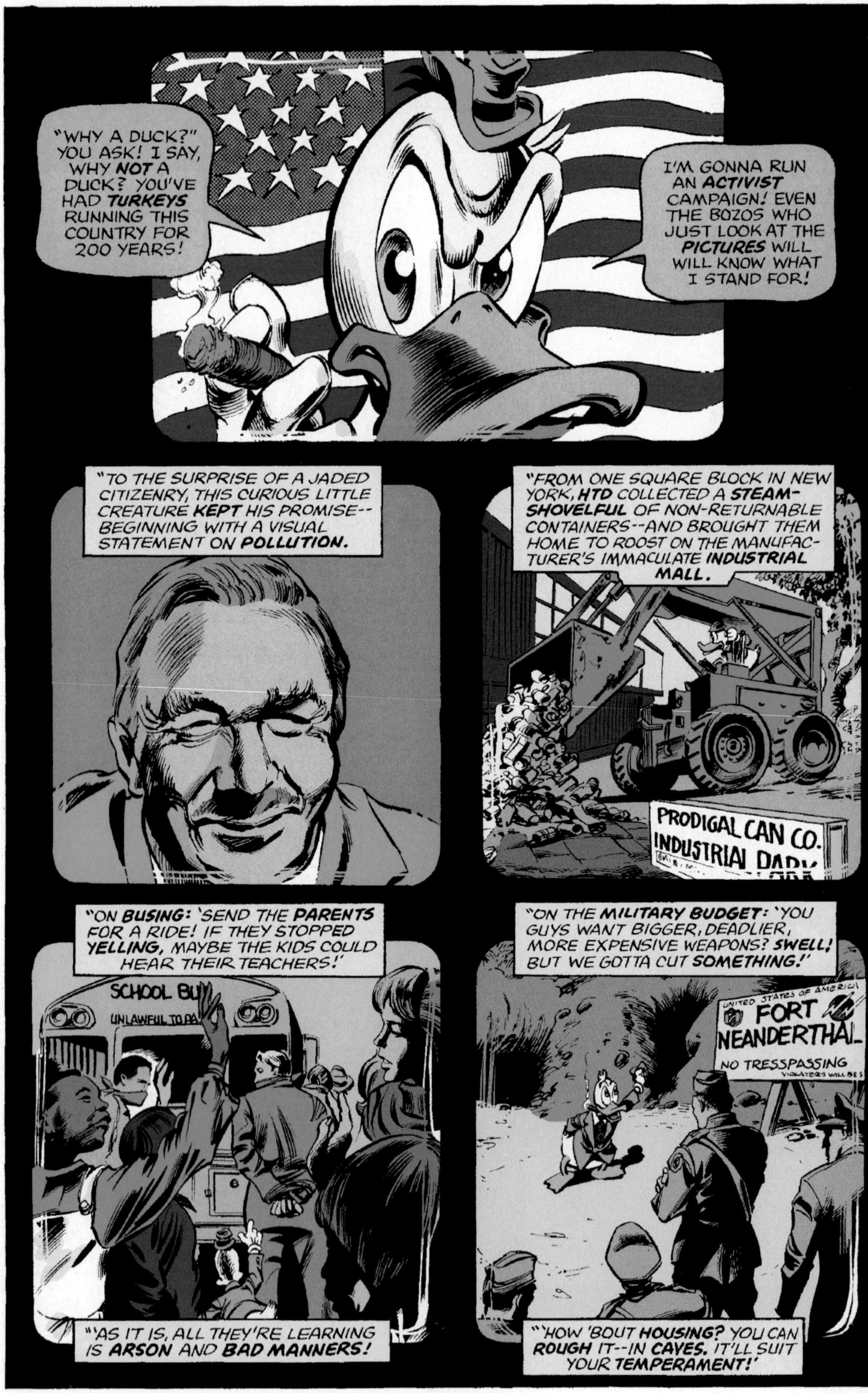
"WHY A DUCK?" YOU ASK! I SAY, WHY NOT A DUCK? YOU'VE HAD TURKEYS RUNNING THIS COUNTRY FOR 200 YEARS!
I'M GONNA RUN AN ACTIVIST CAMPAIGN! EVEN THE BOZOS WHO JUST LOOK AT THE PICTURES WILL WILL KNOW WHAT I STAND FOR!
"TO THE SURPRISE OF A JADED CITIZENRY, THIS CURIOUS LITTLE CREATURE KEPT HIS PROMISE--BEGINNING WITH A VISUAL STATEMENT ON POLLUTION.
"FROM ONE SQUARE BLOCK IN NEW YORK, HTD COLLECTED A STEAM-SHOVELFUL OF NON-RETURNABLE CONTAINERS--AND BROUGHT THEM HOME TO ROOST ON THE MANUFACTURER'S IMMACULATE INDUSTRIAL MALL.
PRODIGAL CAN CO. INDUSTRIAL PARK
"ON BUSING: 'SEND THE PARENTS FOR A RIDE! IF THEY STOPPED YELLING, MAYBE THE KIDS COULD HEAR THEIR TEACHERS!'
SCHOOL BU
"'AS IT IS, ALL THEY'RE LEARNING IS ARSON AND BAD MANNERS!
"ON THE MILITARY BUDGET: 'YOU GUYS WANT BIGGER, DEADLIER, MORE EXPENSIVE WEAPONS? SWELL! BUT WE GOTTA CUT SOMETHING!'
UNITED STATES OF AMERICA
FORT NEANDERTHAL
NO TRESSPASSING
"'HOW 'BOUT HOUSING? YOU CAN ROUGH IT--IN CAVES. IT'LL SUIT YOUR TEMPERAMENT!'

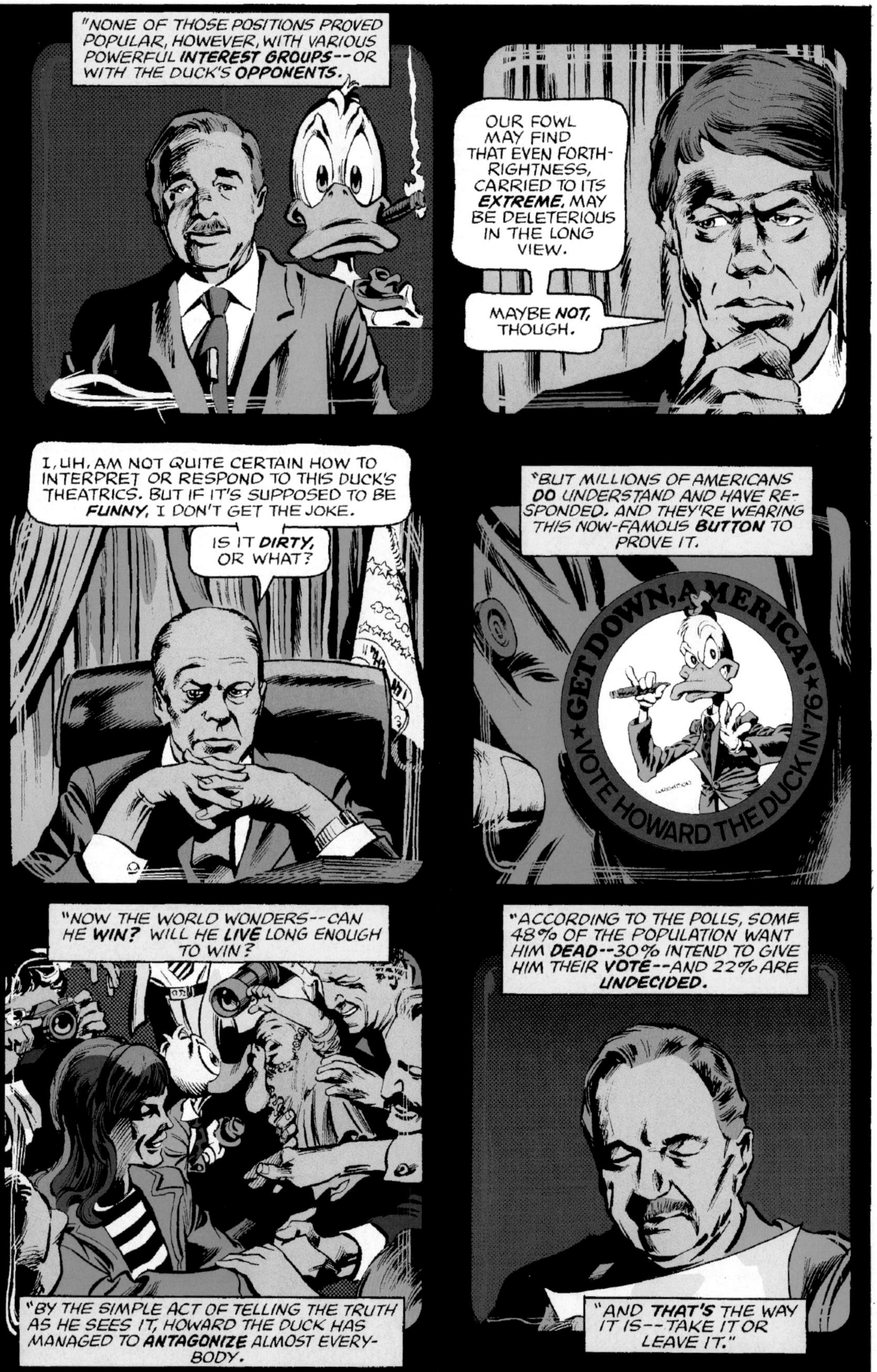

"NONE OF THOSE POSITIONS PROVED POPULAR, HOWEVER, WITH VARIOUS POWERFUL INTEREST GROUPS--OR WITH THE DUCK'S OPPONENTS.
OUR FOWL MAY FIND THAT EVEN FORTH-RIGHTNESS, CARRIED TO ITS EXTREME, MAY BE DELETERIOUS IN THE LONG VIEW.
MAYBE NOT, THOUGH.
I, UH, AM NOT QUITE CERTAIN HOW TO INTERPRET OR RESPOND TO THIS DUCK'S THEATRICS. BUT IF IT'S SUPPOSED TO BE FUNNY, I DON'T GET THE JOKE.
IS IT DIRTY, OR WHAT?
"BUT MILLIONS OF AMERICANS DO UNDERSTAND AND HAVE RE-SPONDED. AND THEY'RE WEARING THIS NOW-FAMOUS BUTTON TO PROVE IT.
GET DOWN, AMERICA!
VOTE HOWARD THE DUCK IN '76
"NOW THE WORLD WONDERS--CAN HE WIN? WILL HE LIVE LONG ENOUGH TO WIN?
"BY THE SIMPLE ACT OF TELLING THE TRUTH AS HE SEES IT, HOWARD THE DUCK HAS MANAGED TO ANTAGONIZE ALMOST EVERY-BODY.
"ACCORDING TO THE POLLS, SOME 48% OF THE POPULATION WANT HIM DEAD--30% INTEND TO GIVE HIM THEIR VOTE--AND 22% ARE UNDECIDED.
"AND THAT'S THE WAY IT IS--TAKE IT OR LEAVE IT."

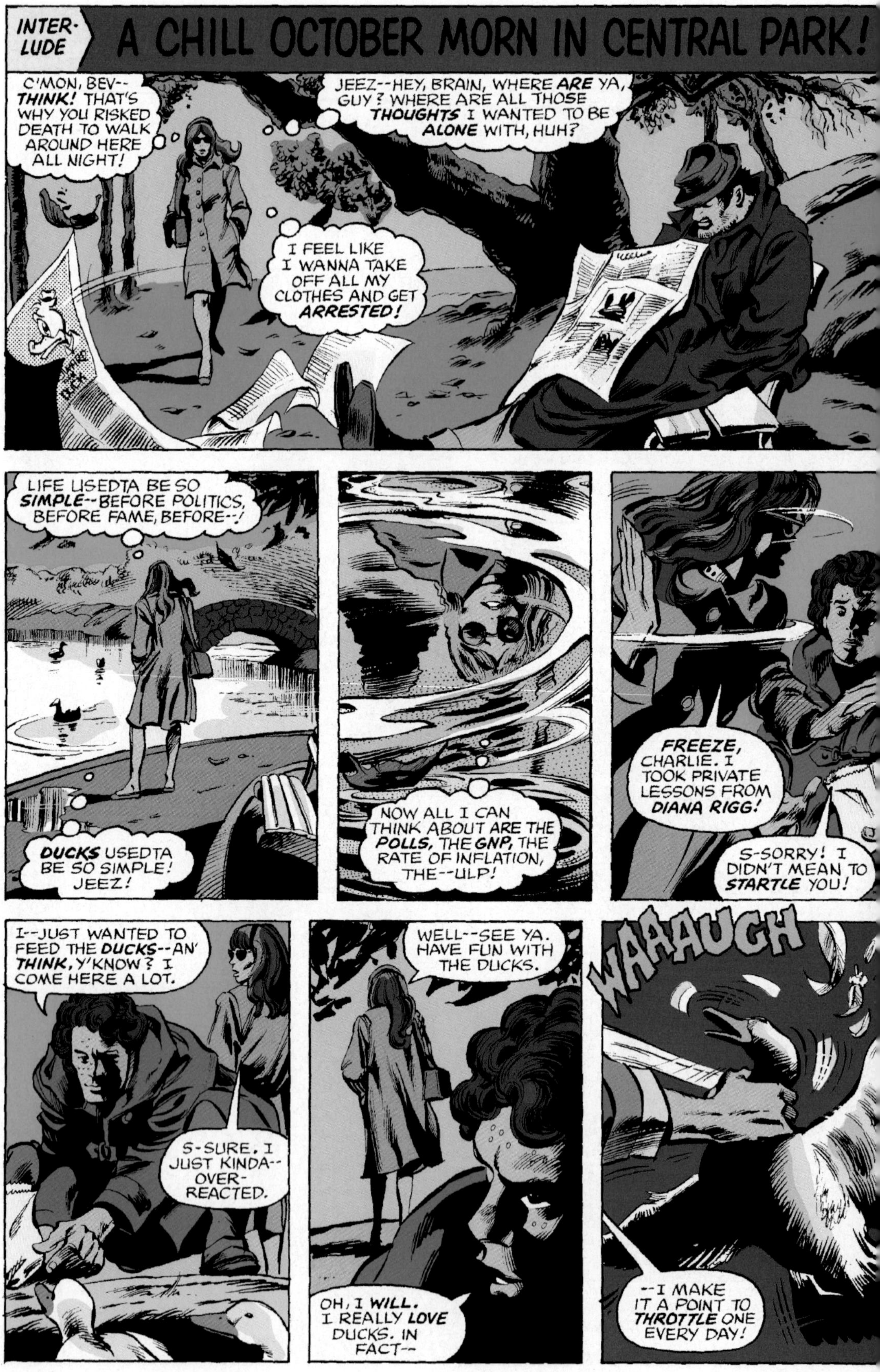
INTER-LUDE
A CHILL OCTOBER MORN IN CENTRAL PARK!
C'MON, BEV-- THINK! THAT'S WHY YOU RISKED DEATH TO WALK AROUND HERE ALL NIGHT!
JEEZ--HEY, BRAIN, WHERE ARE YA, GUY? WHERE ARE ALL THOSE THOUGHTS I WANTED TO BE ALONE WITH, HUH?
I FEEL LIKE I WANNA TAKE OFF ALL MY CLOTHES AND GET ARRESTED!
LIFE USEDTA BE SO SIMPLE--BEFORE POLITICS, BEFORE FAME, BEFORE--!
DUCKS USEDTA BE SO SIMPLE! JEEZ!
NOW ALL I CAN THINK ABOUT ARE THE POLLS, THE GNP, THE RATE OF INFLATION, THE--ULP!
FREEZE, CHARLIE. I TOOK PRIVATE LESSONS FROM DIANA RIGG!
S-SORRY! I DIDN'T MEAN TO STARTLE YOU!
I--JUST WANTED TO FEED THE DUCKS--AN' THINK, Y'KNOW? I COME HERE A LOT.
S-SURE. I JUST KINDA--OVER-REACTED.
WELL--SEE YA. HAVE FUN WITH THE DUCKS.
OH, I WILL. I REALLY LOVE DUCKS. IN FACT--
WAAAUGH
--I MAKE IT A POINT TO THROTTLE ONE EVERY DAY!

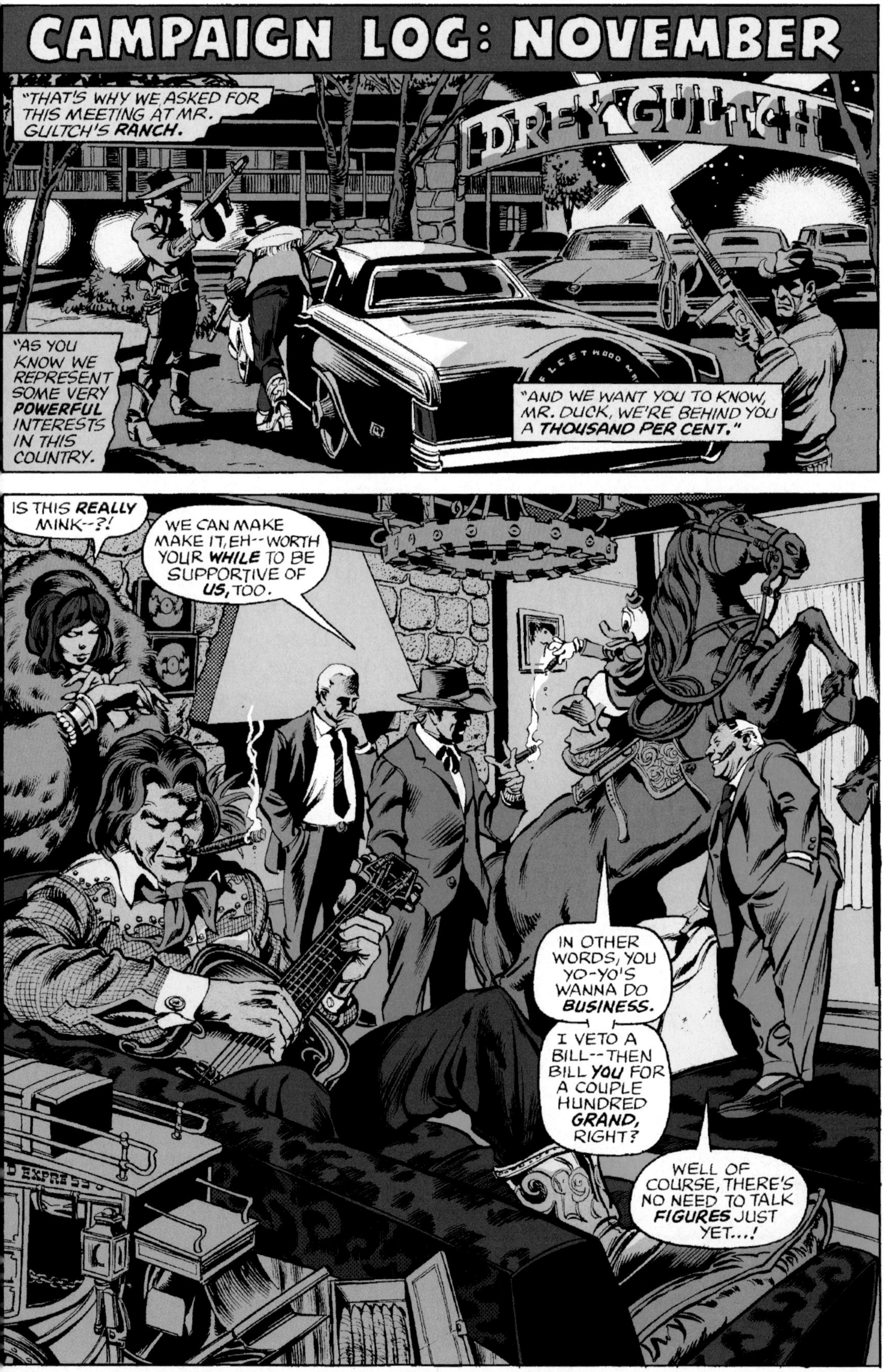
CAMPAIGN LOG: NOVEMBER
"THAT'S WHY WE ASKED FOR THIS MEETING AT MR. GULTCH'S RANCH.
DREYGULTCH
"AS YOU KNOW WE REPRESENT SOME VERY POWERFUL INTERESTS IN THIS COUNTRY.
"AND WE WANT YOU TO KNOW, MR. DUCK, WE'RE BEHIND YOU A THOUSAND PER CENT."
IS THIS REALLY MINK--?!
WE CAN MAKE MAKE IT, EH--WORTH YOUR WHILE TO BE SUPPORTIVE OF US, TOO.
IN OTHER WORDS, YOU YO-YO'S WANNA DO BUSINESS.
I VETO A BILL--THEN BILL YOU FOR A COUPLE HUNDRED GRAND, RIGHT?
WELL OF COURSE, THERE'S NO NEED TO TALK FIGURES JUST YET...!

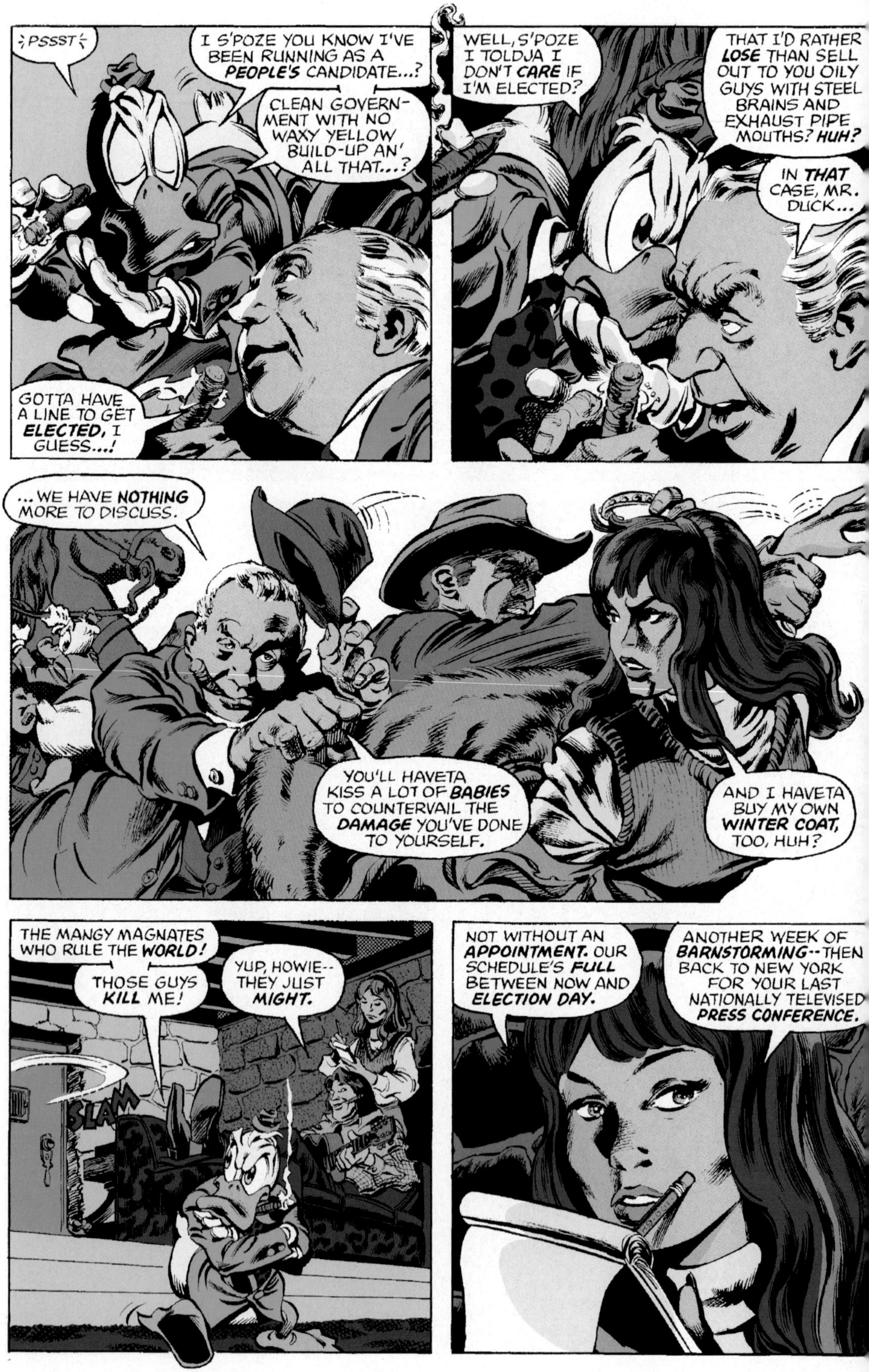

PSSST
I S'POZE YOU KNOW I'VE BEEN RUNNING AS A PEOPLE'S CANDIDATE...?
CLEAN GOVERNMENT WITH NO WAXY YELLOW BUILD-UP AN' ALL THAT...?
GOTTA HAVE A LINE TO GET ELECTED, I GUESS...!
WELL, S'POZE I TOLDJA I DON'T CARE IF I'M ELECTED?
THAT I'D RATHER LOSE THAN SELL OUT TO YOU OILY GUYS WITH STEEL BRAINS AND EXHAUST PIPE MOUTHS? HUH?
IN THAT CASE, MR. DUCK...
...WE HAVE NOTHING MORE TO DISCUSS.
YOU'LL HAVETA KISS A LOT OF BABIES TO COUNTERVAIL THE DAMAGE YOU'VE DONE TO YOURSELF.
AND I HAVETA BUY MY OWN WINTER COAT, TOO, HUH?
THE MANGY MAGNATES WHO RULE THE WORLD!
THOSE GUYS KILL ME!
YUP, HOWIE-- THEY JUST MIGHT.
SLAM
NOT WITHOUT AN APPOINTMENT. OUR SCHEDULE'S FULL BETWEEN NOW AND ELECTION DAY.
ANOTHER WEEK OF BARNSTORMING--THEN BACK TO NEW YORK FOR YOUR LAST NATIONALLY TELEVISED PRESS CONFERENCE.

PARTIAL TRANSCRIPT OF NATIONALLY TELEVISED PRESS CONFERENCE:
Hotel Rykrisp, New York City, November 1, 1976

HOWARD: Ladies an' germs, I'll keep my opening smart remarks brief. I didn't particularly wanna be president of this coast-to-coast funny farm you hairless apes have set up. When they asked me to run, I'd just been hit on the head an' didn't really understand what I was agreein' to. But I've reached the conclusion that most o' the American public is in the same condition most o' the time, so just maybe I'm the ideal candidate. You meatbrains willingly subject yourselves to more abuse, physical and psychological, than any nation in history! You allow your eyes and lungs to be eaten away by pollution. You fill your digestive tracts with chemicals. Your ears are barraged by the sounds of jackhammer progress. All this while politicians and Madison Avenue bang away at your minds. You all wanna be happy an' secure, yet you open yourselves to the constant tension an' pressure of a society that claims to be free, but refuses to let you make a move without first filing forms in triplicate. You wonder why you got violence? Why your young are either dissident, empty-headed, or drugged into a stupor? It's because you've fashioned an emotionally and intellectually sterile culture, that's why! If an individual is unwilling to spend his life in the plodding pursuit of possessions, there's nothing for 'im to *do!* The United States is one big dateless Saturday night! If I'm elected, I'm gonna inject a little *life* back into you anesthetized Americans! For four years, this country's gonna get down an' boogie, see?! Okay!
Now anybody got any brilliant questions?

(Stunned silence, interrupted only by an occasional nervous cough; then...)

RAMSEY KLEP (Devil's Tongue, N.M., *Daily Lick)*: Mr. Duck, which do you favor— conditional amnesty or a blanket pardon for Vietnam draft evaders?

HOWARD: Neither. I favor education.

KLEP: Beg pardon?

HOWARD: Look, as nearly as I can tell, everybody is still reacting on this question with his gut, not his head. It's still "my country right or wrong" versus "make love not war". I figure the answer is a debate, on television, between proponents of each position. The government would buy time on all three networks and the yelling could go on for days. Then, the country could decide in a national referendum, based on each individual's judgment of the facts. Revolutionary, huh? Next!

DUNSTAN QUOBROX (Lima, OH., *Daily Bean*): What's your opinion of the recent Washington scandals? Should elected officials be held accountable for their private morality?

HOWARD: Nah. As long as the taxpayers aren't financin' their little romps, senators an' congressmen deserve to have a little fun. Heck, we oughtta be heartened to know some o' those old prunes have still got it in 'em.

SAM QUENTIN (Dubious, NJ, *Daily Dunno)*; How do you feel, sir, about violence in movies, television programs, and comic books?

HOWARD: I'm all for it.

QUENTIN: What?

HOWARD: As long as it's never presented as cathartic—as a release, as a solution. A kid oughtta know what he's gettin' into if he's contemplatin' stabbing or shootin' somebody. It's messy. The blood gets all over the floor. It smells bad. It's ugly to look at. I think violence should be presented honestly—as disgustingly and offensively as possible. There's no such thing as tasteful violence.

(Beverly Switzler leaps up on the table, does a little dance, blows a whistle, and chirps "Th-th-that's all, folks!" into a microphone. The auditorium explodes in applause, and the press conference concludes.)

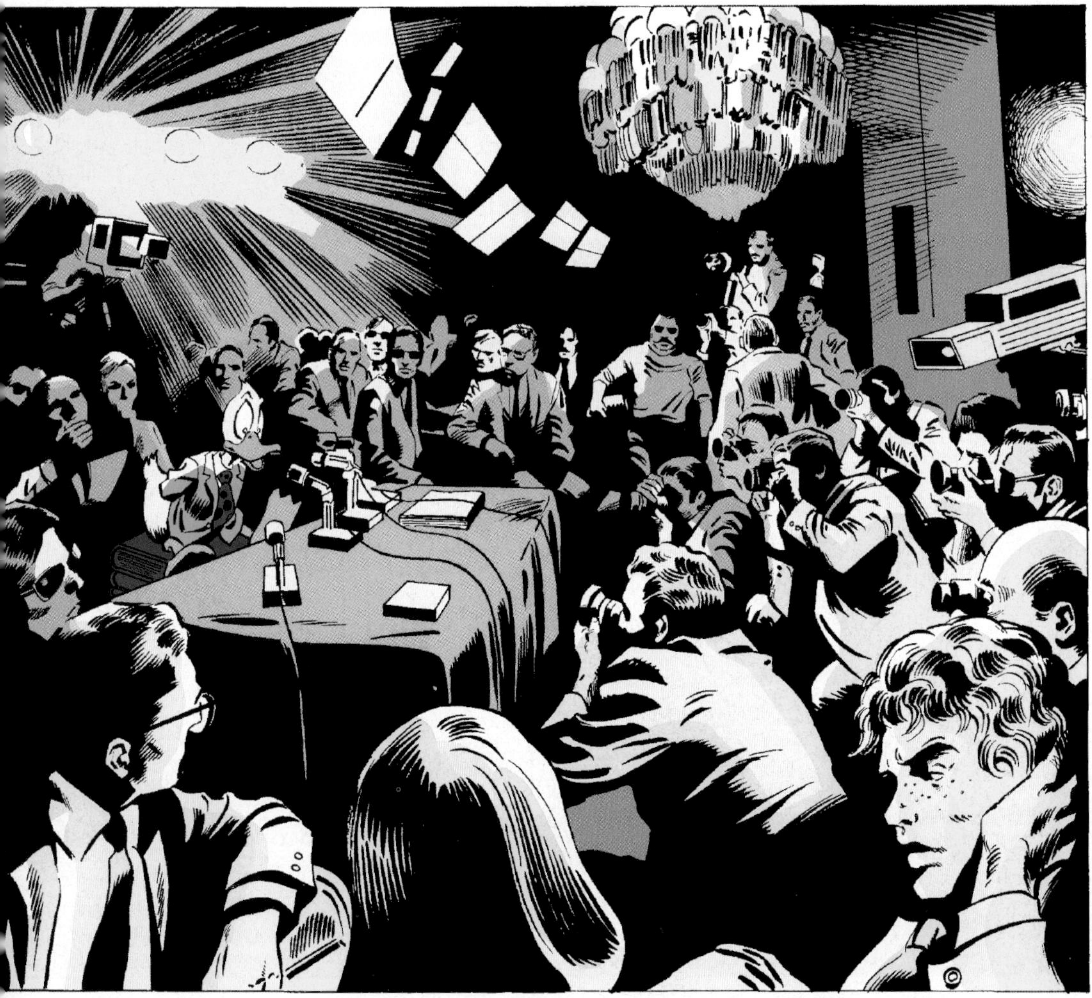

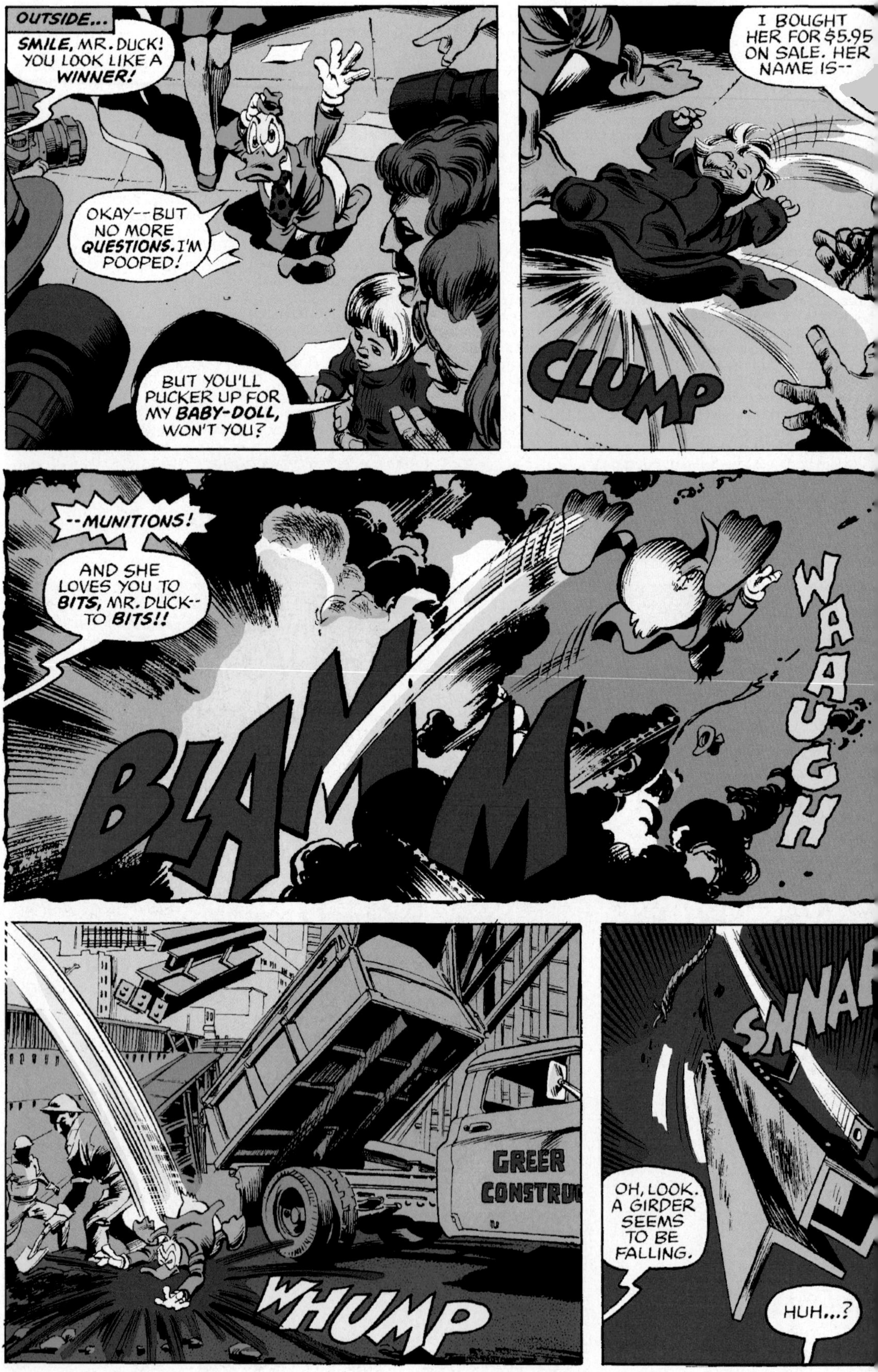
OUTSIDE...
SMILE, MR. DUCK! YOU LOOK LIKE A WINNER!
OKAY--BUT NO MORE QUESTIONS. I'M POOPED!
BUT YOU'LL PUCKER UP FOR MY BABY-DOLL, WON'T YOU?
I BOUGHT HER FOR $5.95 ON SALE. HER NAME IS--
CLUMP
--MUNITIONS!
AND SHE LOVES YOU TO BITS, MR. DUCK-- TO BITS!!
BLAMM
WAAUGH
GREER CONSTRUC
WHUMP
SNNAP
OH, LOOK. A GIRDER SEEMS TO BE FALLING.
HUH...?

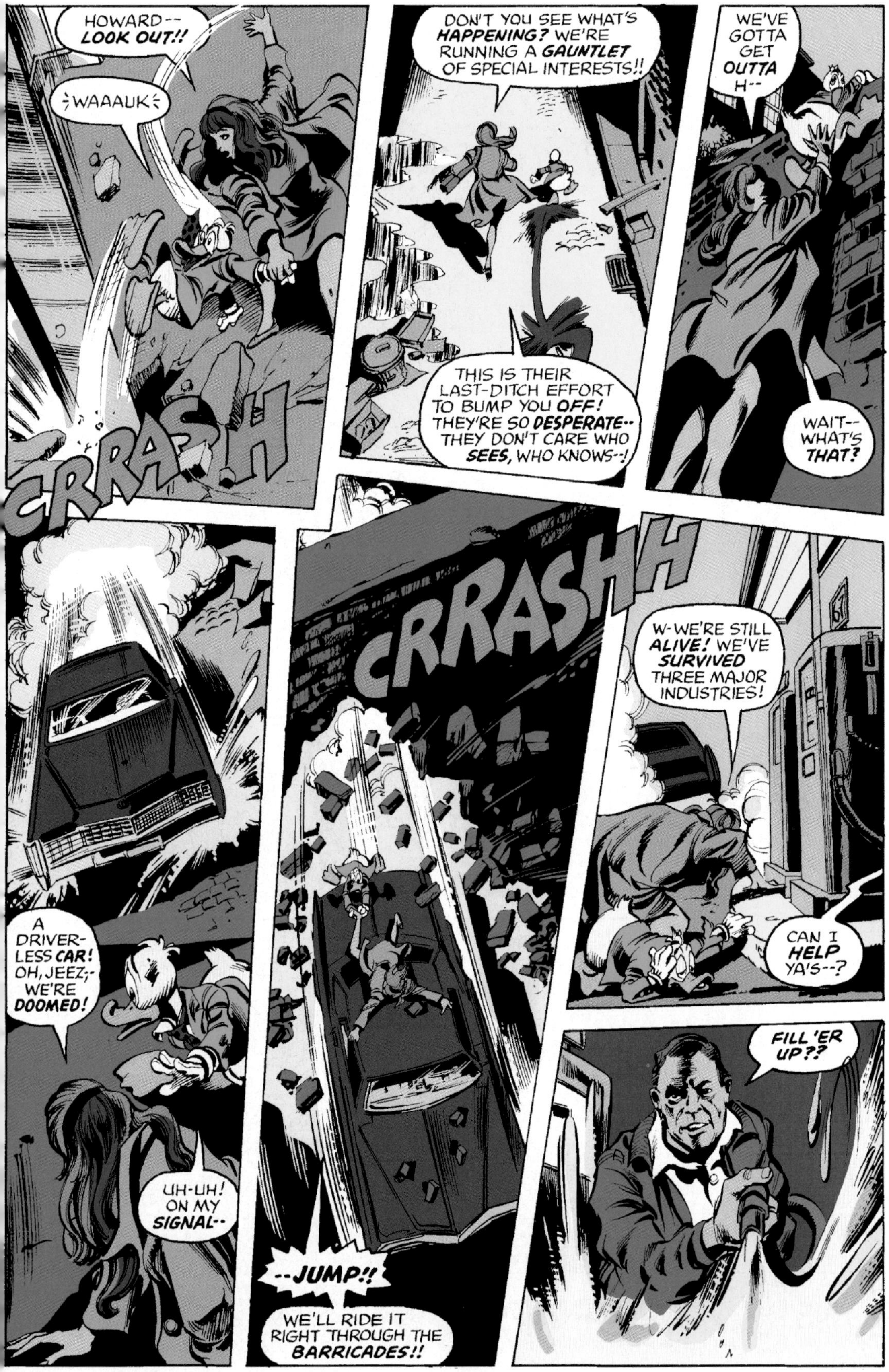
HOWARD-- LOOK OUT!!
WAAAUK
CRRASH
DON'T YOU SEE WHAT'S HAPPENING? WE'RE RUNNING A GAUNTLET OF SPECIAL INTERESTS!!
THIS IS THEIR LAST-DITCH EFFORT TO BUMP YOU OFF! THEY'RE SO DESPERATE-- THEY DON'T CARE WHO SEES, WHO KNOWS--!
WE'VE GOTTA GET OUTTA H--
WAIT-- WHAT'S THAT?
A DRIVER-LESS CAR! OH, JEEZ; WE'RE DOOMED!
UH-UH! ON MY SIGNAL--
CRRASHH
--JUMP!!
WE'LL RIDE IT RIGHT THROUGH THE BARRICADES!!
W-WE'RE STILL ALIVE! WE'VE SURVIVED THREE MAJOR INDUSTRIES!
CAN I HELP YA'S--?
FILL 'ER UP??

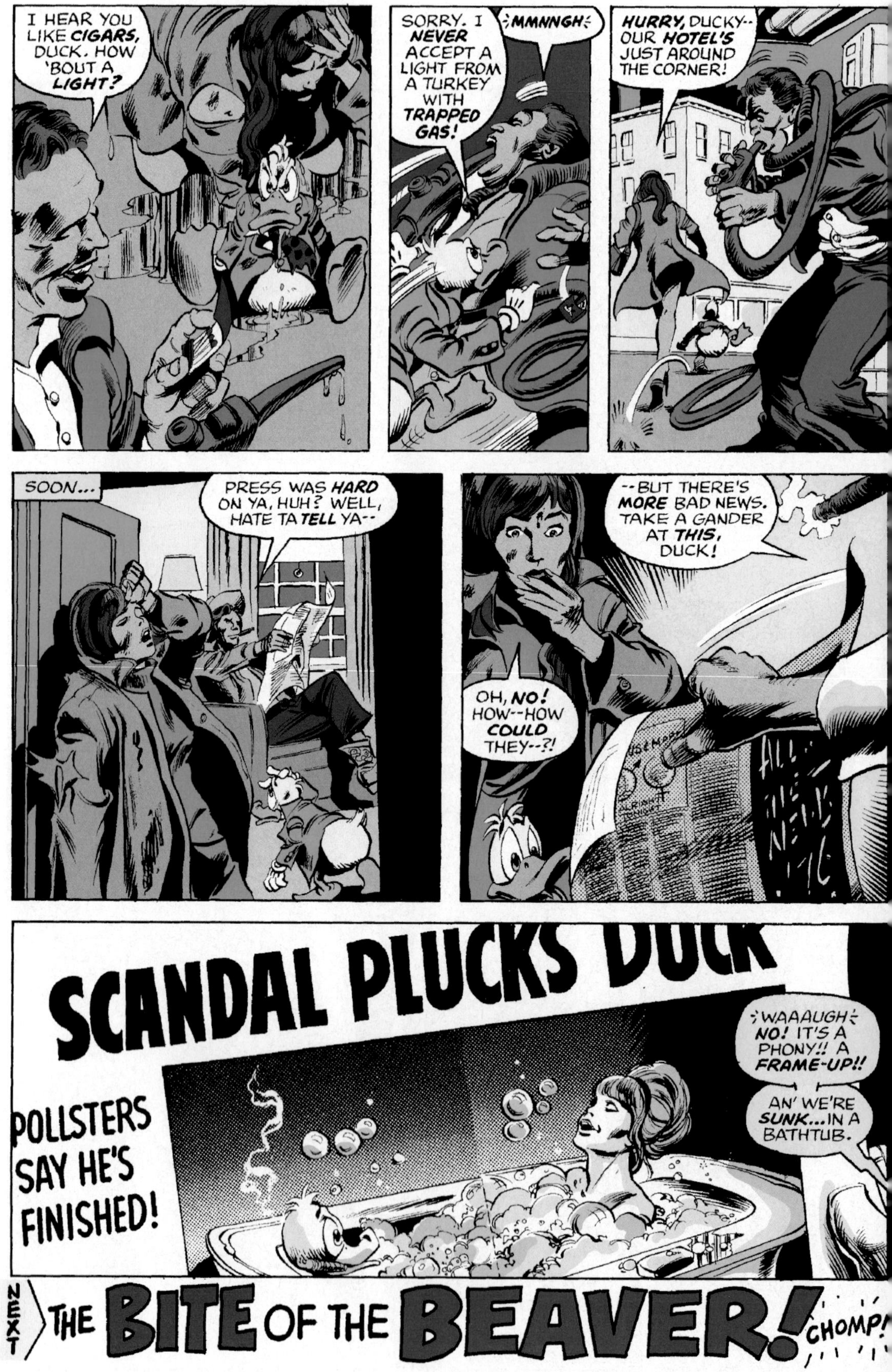
I HEAR YOU LIKE CIGARS, DUCK. HOW 'BOUT A LIGHT?
SORRY. I NEVER ACCEPT A LIGHT FROM A TURKEY WITH TRAPPED GAS!
MMNNGH
HURRY, DUCKY-- OUR HOTEL'S JUST AROUND THE CORNER!
SOON...
PRESS WAS HARD ON YA, HUH? WELL, HATE TA TELL YA--
--BUT THERE'S MORE BAD NEWS. TAKE A GANDER AT THIS, DUCK!
OH, NO! HOW--HOW COULD THEY--?!
SCANDAL PLUCKS DUCK
POLLSTERS SAY HE'S FINISHED!
WAAAUGH NO! IT'S A PHONY!! A FRAME-UP!!
AN' WE'RE SUNK...IN A BATHTUB.
NEXT
THE BITE OF THE BEAVER!
CHOMP!

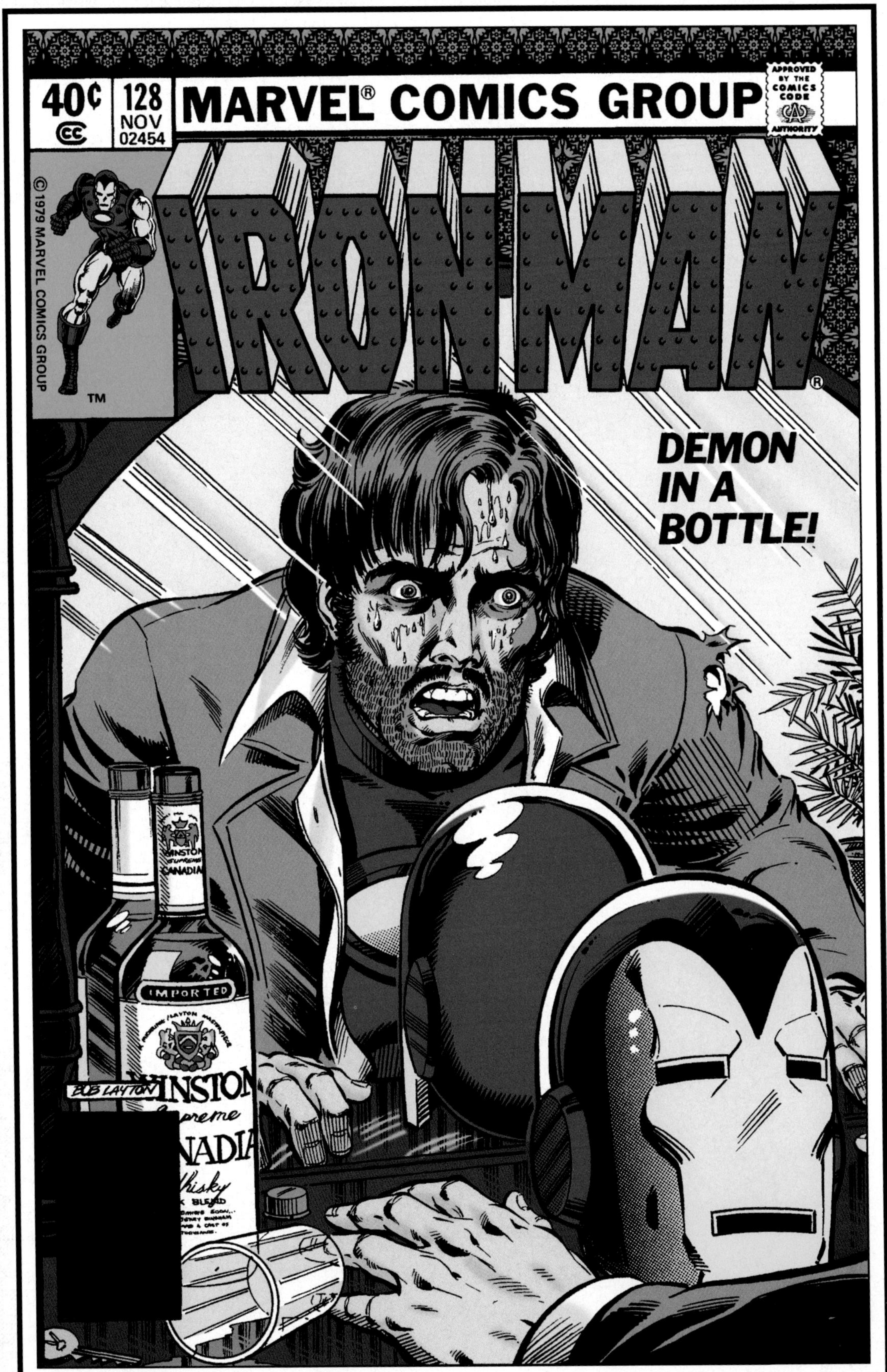

40¢
128
NOV
02454
MARVEL® COMICS GROUP
APPROVED BY THE COMICS CODE AUTHORITY
© 1979 MARVEL COMICS GROUP
TM
IRON MAN®
DEMON IN A BOTTLE!
IMPORTED
BOB LAYTON

When millionaire industrialist *Tony Stark*, inventor extraordinaire, garbs himself in solar-charged, steel-mesh *armor* he becomes the world's greatest human fighting machine...

STAN LEE PRESENTS: THE INVINCIBLE IRON MAN ®

DAVID MICHELINIE writer/plot	JOHN ROMITA JR. pencil art	BOB LAYTON finished art/plot	JOHN COSTANZA letters	BOB SHAREN colors	ROGER STERN editor	JIM SHOOTER editor-in-chief

BY DEFINITION, A HERO IS A MAN WHO BATTLES AGAINST OVERWHELMING ODDS FOR A CAUSE, AN IDEAL, OR FOR THE LIVES OF INNOCENTS. THE CAUSE AND IDEAL MAY VARY WITH THE MORNING HEADLINES-WHILE THE INNOCENTS, IN TODAY'S WORLD OF MUDDY MORALITY, MAY ULTIMATELY PROVE TO BE THE GUILTY.

WHICH LEAVES BUT ONE CONSTANT IN THE DEFINITION: THAT A HERO IS, ABOVE ALL, A MAN...

...A MAN SUBJECT TO PRESSURES AND RESPONSIBILITIES FAR BEYOND THOSE OF HIS PEERS. SUCH IS A BURDEN THAT MUST TAKE ITS TOLL, EVENTUALLY, FROM EVEN THE MOST VALIANT WARRIOR.

AND IT IS THEN THAT THE TEST OF A *TRUE* HERO BEGINS.

IRON MAN, OL' BUDDY, I THOUGHT I KNEW YOU. BUT I DON'T.

I DON'T KNOW YOU AT ALL...

Demon in a Bottle

LG555

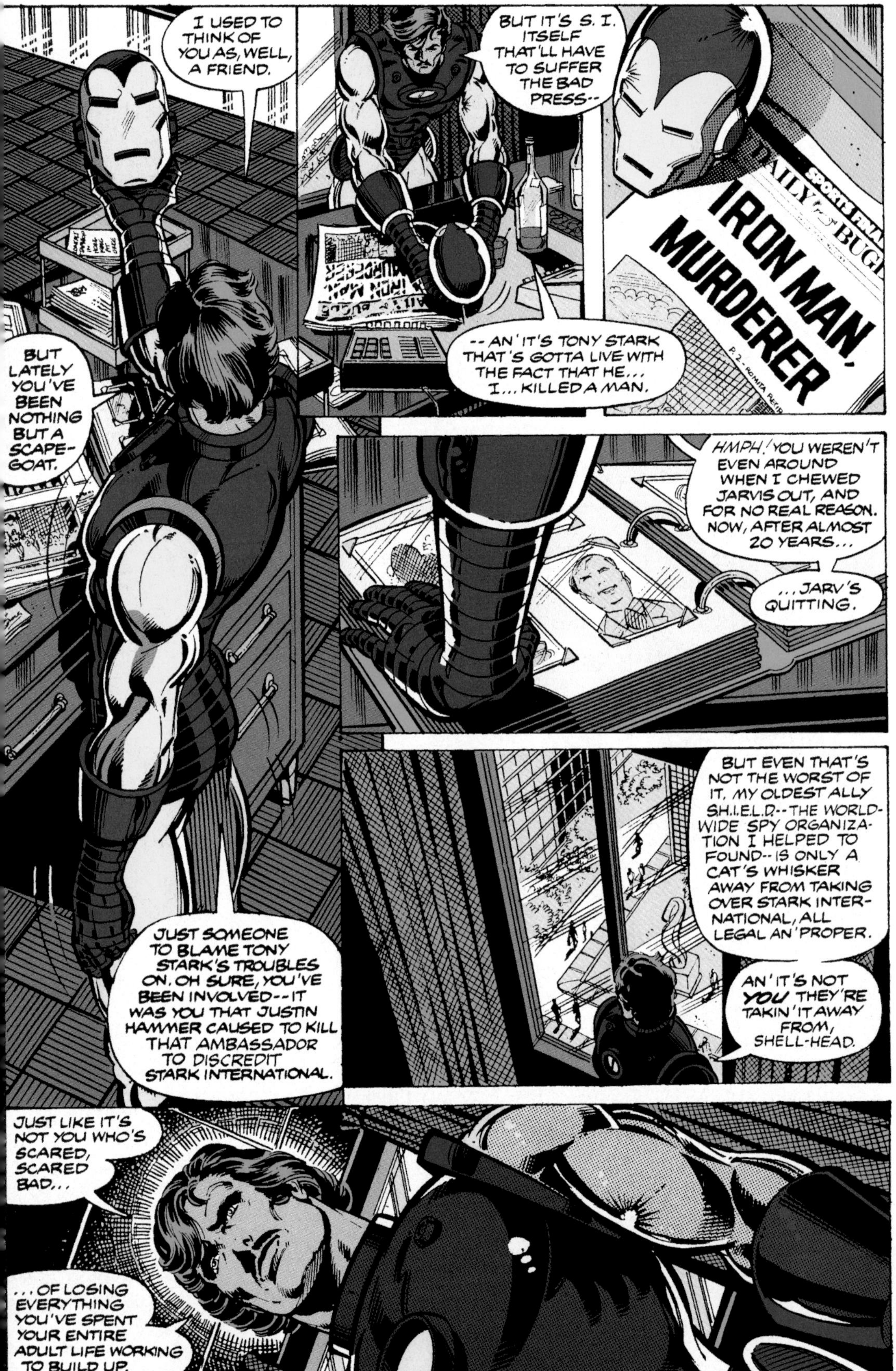
I USED TO THINK OF YOU AS, WELL, A FRIEND.
BUT IT'S S. I. ITSELF THAT'LL HAVE TO SUFFER THE BAD PRESS--
--AN' IT'S TONY STARK THAT'S GOTTA LIVE WITH THE FACT THAT HE... I... KILLED A MAN.
DAILY BUGLE
SPORTS FINAL
IRON MAN, MURDERER
BUT LATELY YOU'VE BEEN NOTHING BUT A SCAPE-GOAT.
HMPH! YOU WEREN'T EVEN AROUND WHEN I CHEWED JARVIS OUT, AND FOR NO REAL REASON. NOW, AFTER ALMOST 20 YEARS...
...JARV'S QUITTING.
BUT EVEN THAT'S NOT THE WORST OF IT. MY OLDEST ALLY SH.I.E.L.D.--THE WORLD-WIDE SPY ORGANIZA-TION I HELPED TO FOUND--IS ONLY A CAT'S WHISKER AWAY FROM TAKING OVER STARK INTER-NATIONAL, ALL LEGAL AN' PROPER.
JUST SOMEONE TO BLAME TONY STARK'S TROUBLES ON. OH SURE, YOU'VE BEEN INVOLVED--IT WAS YOU THAT JUSTIN HAMMER CAUSED TO KILL THAT AMBASSADOR TO DISCREDIT STARK INTERNATIONAL.
AN' IT'S NOT YOU THEY'RE TAKIN' IT AWAY FROM, SHELL-HEAD.
JUST LIKE IT'S NOT YOU WHO'S SCARED, SCARED BAD...
...OF LOSING EVERYTHING YOU'VE SPENT YOUR ENTIRE ADULT LIFE WORKING TO BUILD UP.

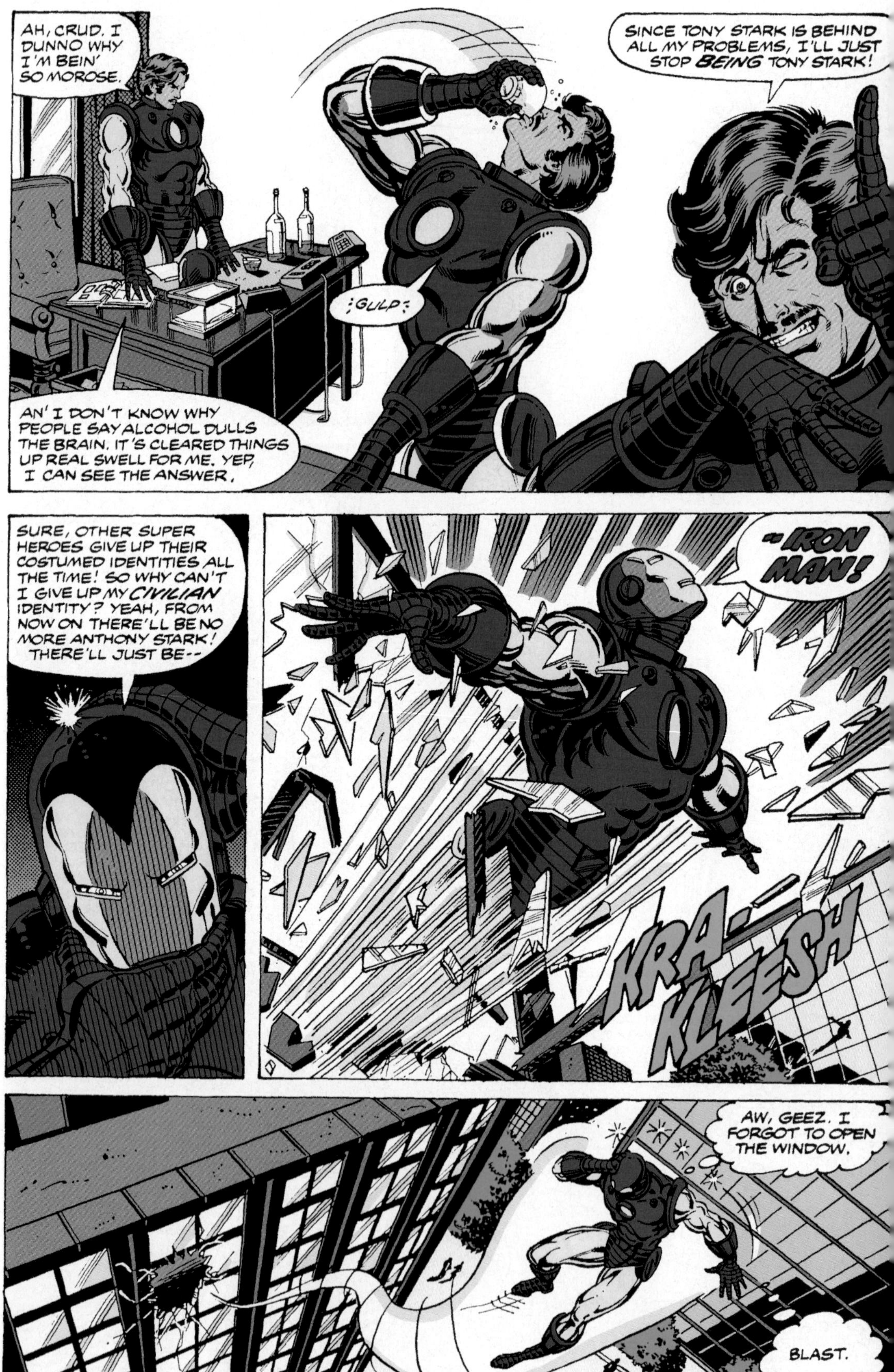
AH, CRUD. I DUNNO WHY I'M BEIN' SO MOROSE.
AN' I DON'T KNOW WHY PEOPLE SAY ALCOHOL DULLS THE BRAIN. IT'S CLEARED THINGS UP REAL SWELL FOR ME. YEP, I CAN SEE THE ANSWER.
GULP
SINCE TONY STARK IS BEHIND ALL MY PROBLEMS, I'LL JUST STOP BEING TONY STARK!
SURE, OTHER SUPER HEROES GIVE UP THEIR COSTUMED IDENTITIES ALL THE TIME! SO WHY CAN'T I GIVE UP MY CIVILIAN IDENTITY? YEAH, FROM NOW ON THERE'LL BE NO MORE ANTHONY STARK! THERE'LL JUST BE--
--IRON MAN!
KRA-KLEESH
AW, GEEZ. I FORGOT TO OPEN THE WINDOW.
BLAST.

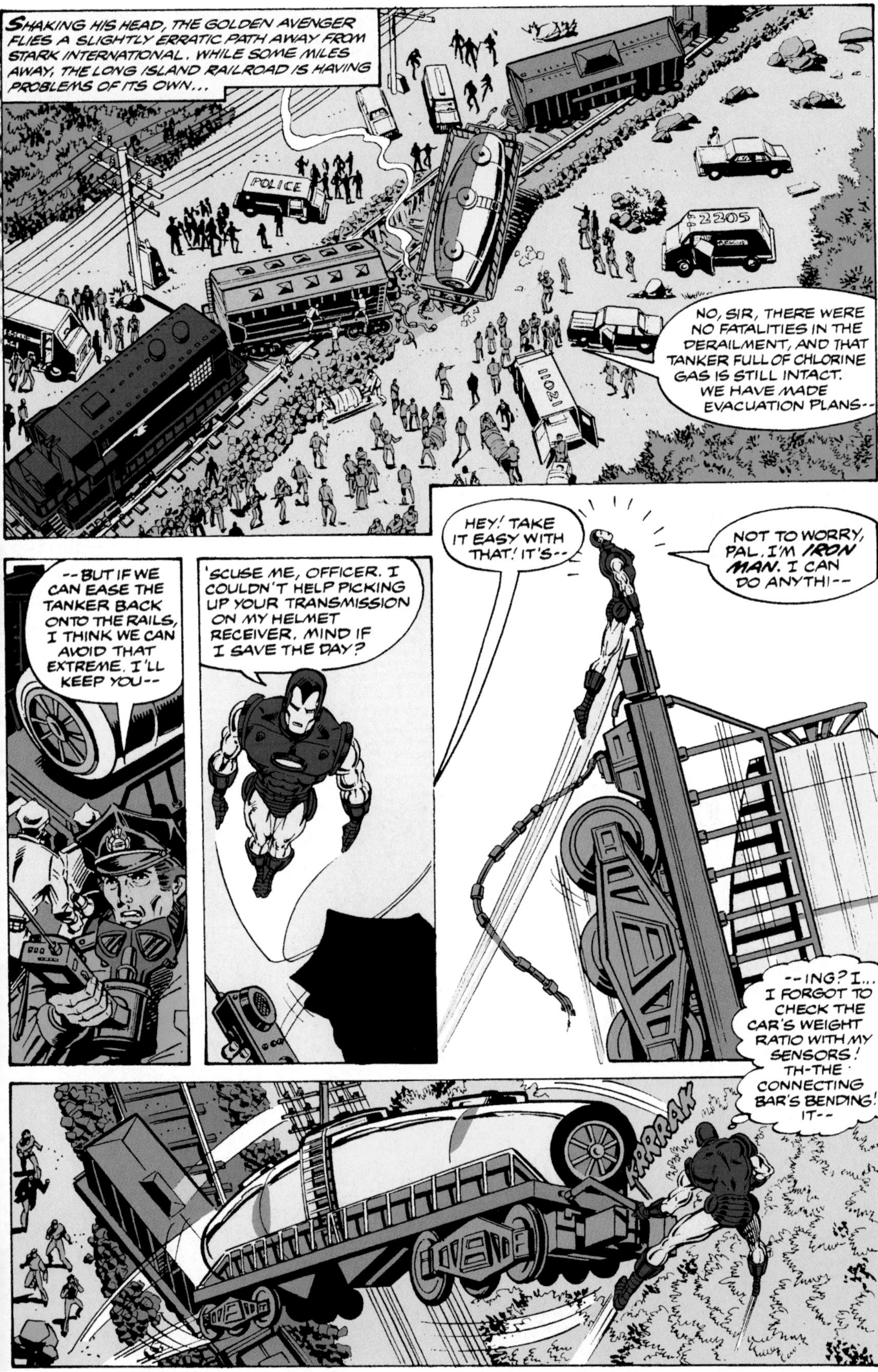

SHAKING HIS HEAD, THE GOLDEN AVENGER FLIES A SLIGHTLY ERRATIC PATH AWAY FROM STARK INTERNATIONAL. WHILE SOME MILES AWAY, THE LONG ISLAND RAILROAD IS HAVING PROBLEMS OF ITS OWN...
POLICE
2205
NO, SIR, THERE WERE NO FATALITIES IN THE DERAILMENT, AND THAT TANKER FULL OF CHLORINE GAS IS STILL INTACT. WE HAVE MADE EVACUATION PLANS--
--BUT IF WE CAN EASE THE TANKER BACK ONTO THE RAILS, I THINK WE CAN AVOID THAT EXTREME. I'LL KEEP YOU--
'SCUSE ME, OFFICER. I COULDN'T HELP PICKING UP YOUR TRANSMISSION ON MY HELMET RECEIVER. MIND IF I SAVE THE DAY?
HEY! TAKE IT EASY WITH THAT! IT'S--
NOT TO WORRY, PAL. I'M IRON MAN. I CAN DO ANYTHI--
--ING? I... I FORGOT TO CHECK THE CAR'S WEIGHT RATIO WITH MY SENSORS! TH-THE CONNECTING BAR'S BENDING! IT--
KRRRAK

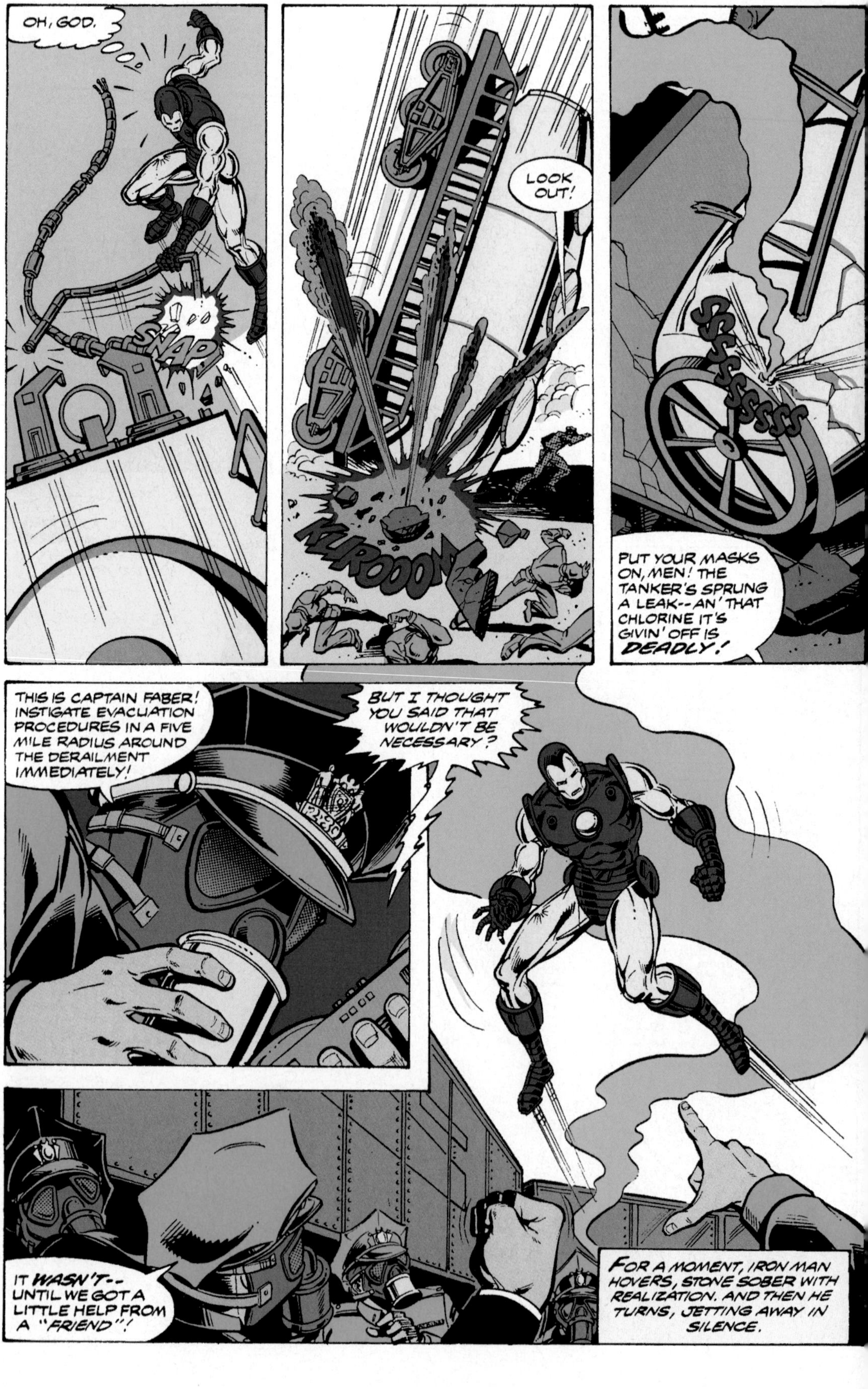
OH, GOD.
SNAP
LOOK OUT!
KUROOOM
SSSSSSSSS
PUT YOUR MASKS ON, MEN! THE TANKER'S SPRUNG A LEAK--AN' THAT CHLORINE IT'S GIVIN' OFF IS DEADLY!
THIS IS CAPTAIN FABER! INSTIGATE EVACUATION PROCEDURES IN A FIVE MILE RADIUS AROUND THE DERAILMENT IMMEDIATELY!
BUT I THOUGHT YOU SAID THAT WOULDN'T BE NECESSARY?
IT WASN'T-- UNTIL WE GOT A LITTLE HELP FROM A "FRIEND"!
FOR A MOMENT, IRON MAN HOVERS, STONE SOBER WITH REALIZATION. AND THEN HE TURNS, JETTING AWAY IN SILENCE.

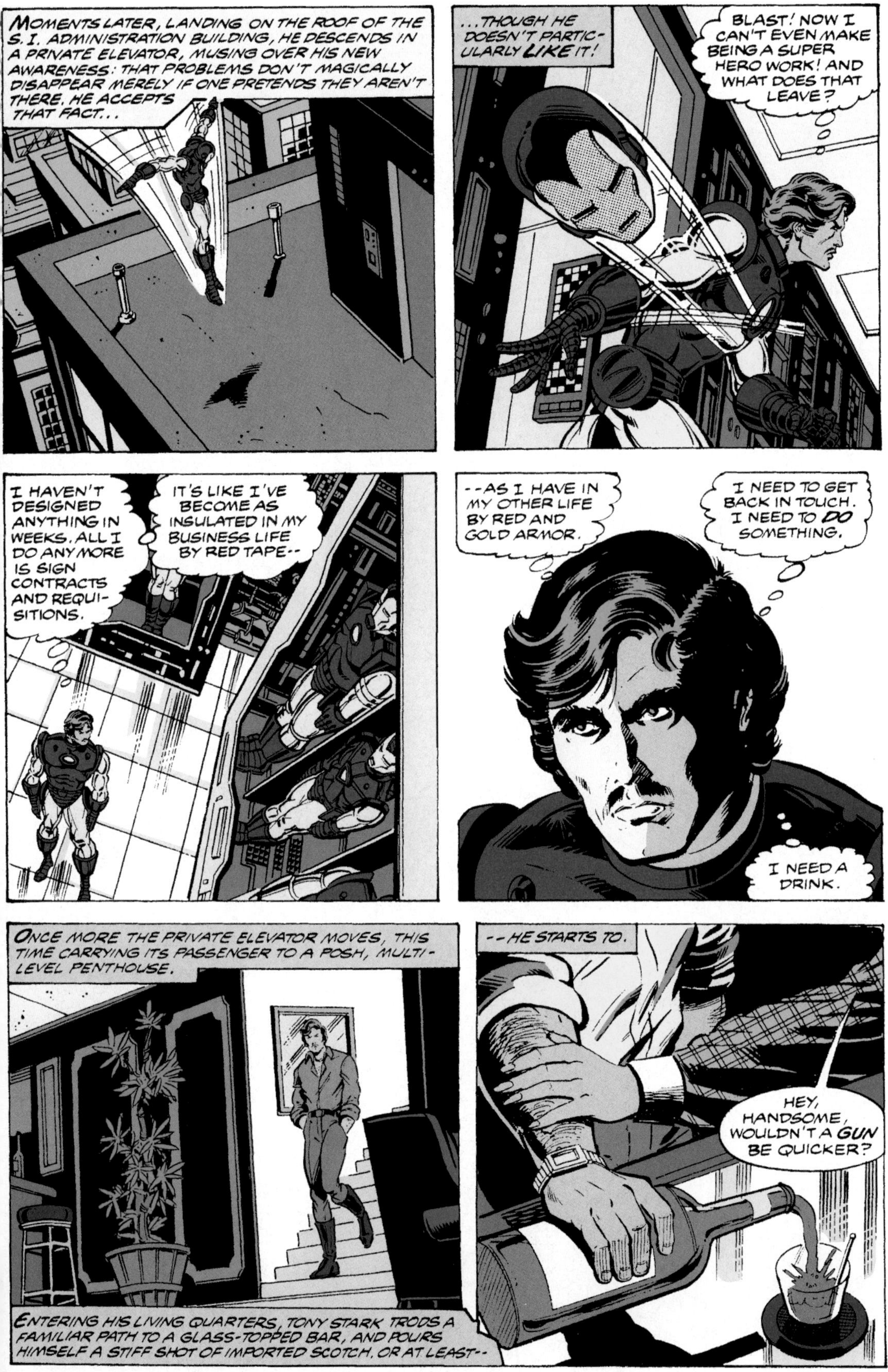

MOMENTS LATER, LANDING ON THE ROOF OF THE S. I. ADMINISTRATION BUILDING, HE DESCENDS IN A PRIVATE ELEVATOR, MUSING OVER HIS NEW AWARENESS: THAT PROBLEMS DON'T MAGICALLY DISAPPEAR MERELY IF ONE PRETENDS THEY AREN'T THERE. HE ACCEPTS THAT FACT...
...THOUGH HE DOESN'T PARTICULARLY LIKE IT!
BLAST! NOW I CAN'T EVEN MAKE BEING A SUPER HERO WORK! AND WHAT DOES THAT LEAVE?
I HAVEN'T DESIGNED ANYTHING IN WEEKS. ALL I DO ANYMORE IS SIGN CONTRACTS AND REQUISITIONS.
IT'S LIKE I'VE BECOME AS INSULATED IN MY BUSINESS LIFE BY RED TAPE--
--AS I HAVE IN MY OTHER LIFE BY RED AND GOLD ARMOR.
I NEED TO GET BACK IN TOUCH. I NEED TO DO SOMETHING.
I NEED A DRINK.
ONCE MORE THE PRIVATE ELEVATOR MOVES, THIS TIME CARRYING ITS PASSENGER TO A POSH, MULTI-LEVEL PENTHOUSE.
ENTERING HIS LIVING QUARTERS, TONY STARK TRODS A FAMILIAR PATH TO A GLASS-TOPPED BAR, AND POURS HIMSELF A STIFF SHOT OF IMPORTED SCOTCH. OR AT LEAST--
--HE STARTS TO.
HEY, HANDSOME, WOULDN'T A GUN BE QUICKER?

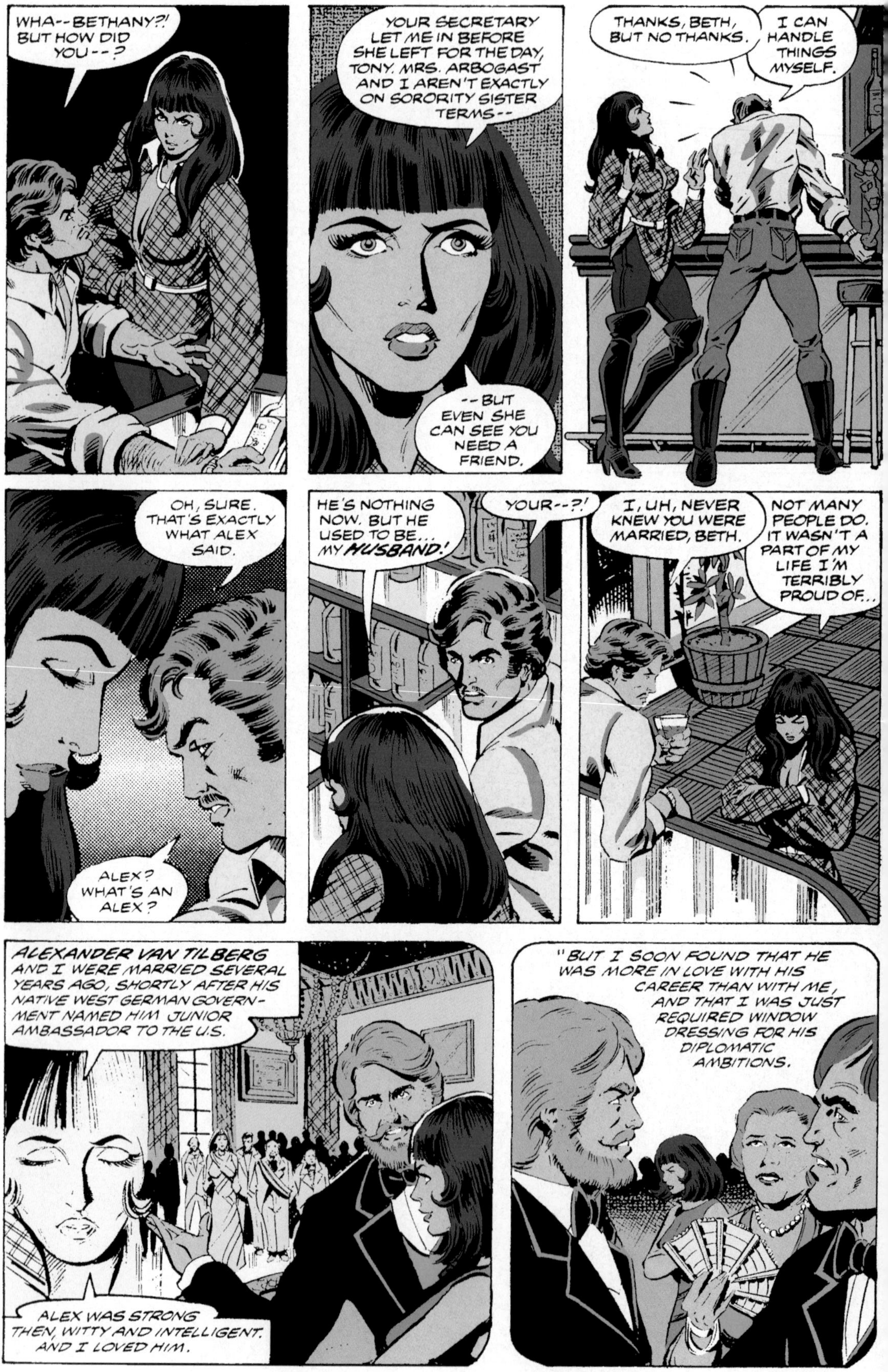
WHA--BETHANY?! BUT HOW DID YOU--?
YOUR SECRETARY LET ME IN BEFORE SHE LEFT FOR THE DAY, TONY. MRS. ARBOGAST AND I AREN'T EXACTLY ON SORORITY SISTER TERMS--
--BUT EVEN SHE CAN SEE YOU NEED A FRIEND.
THANKS, BETH, BUT NO THANKS.
I CAN HANDLE THINGS MYSELF.
OH, SURE. THAT'S EXACTLY WHAT ALEX SAID.
ALEX? WHAT'S AN ALEX?
HE'S NOTHING NOW. BUT HE USED TO BE... MY HUSBAND!
YOUR--?!
I, UH, NEVER KNEW YOU WERE MARRIED, BETH.
NOT MANY PEOPLE DO. IT WASN'T A PART OF MY LIFE I'M TERRIBLY PROUD OF...
ALEXANDER VAN TILBERG AND I WERE MARRIED SEVERAL YEARS AGO, SHORTLY AFTER HIS NATIVE WEST GERMAN GOVERNMENT NAMED HIM JUNIOR AMBASSADOR TO THE U.S.
ALEX WAS STRONG THEN, WITTY AND INTELLIGENT. AND I LOVED HIM.
"BUT I SOON FOUND THAT HE WAS MORE IN LOVE WITH HIS CAREER THAN WITH ME, AND THAT I WAS JUST REQUIRED WINDOW DRESSING FOR HIS DIPLOMATIC AMBITIONS.

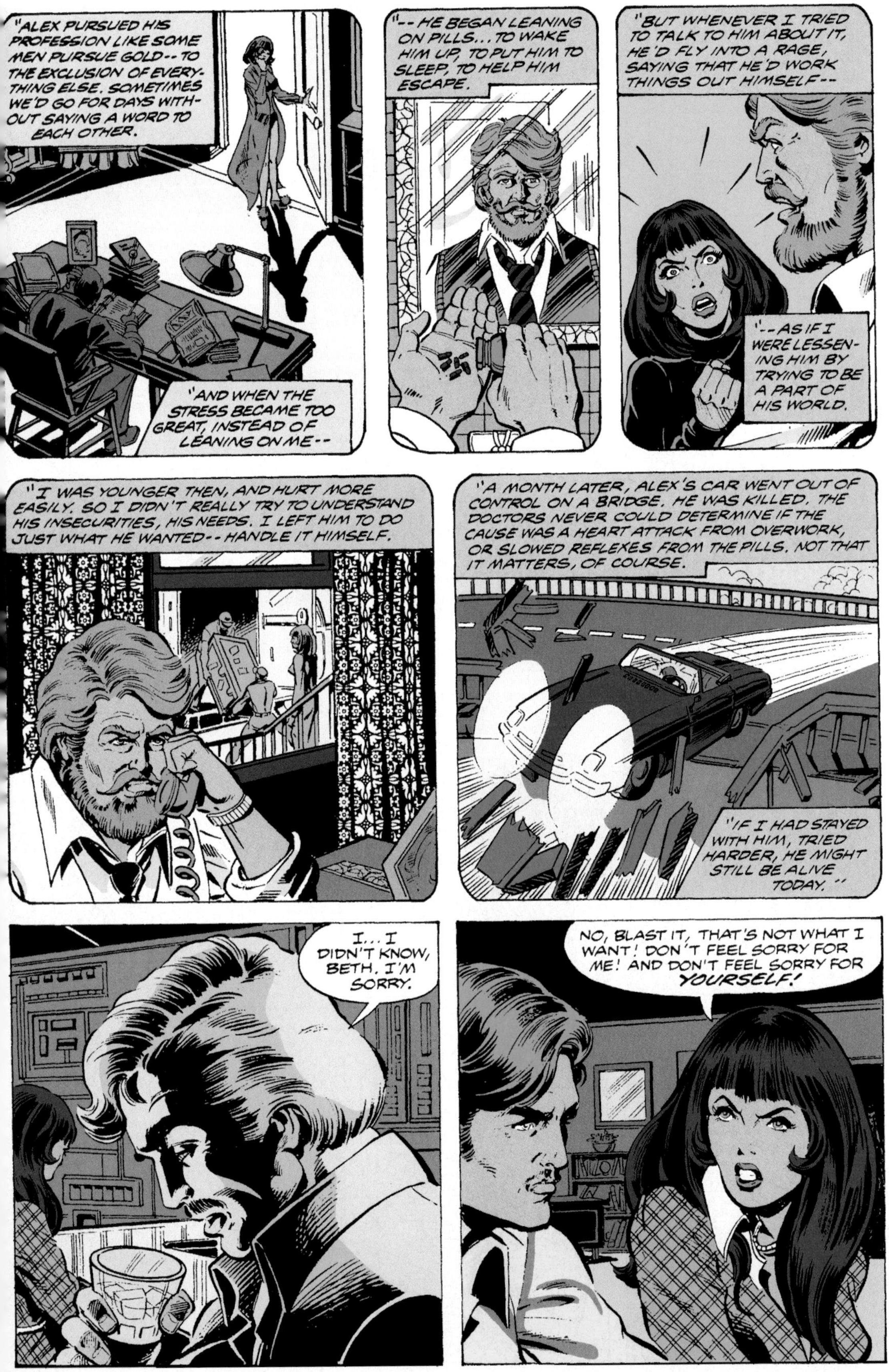
"ALEX PURSUED HIS PROFESSION LIKE SOME MEN PURSUE GOLD-- TO THE EXCLUSION OF EVERYTHING ELSE. SOMETIMES WE'D GO FOR DAYS WITHOUT SAYING A WORD TO EACH OTHER.
"AND WHEN THE STRESS BECAME TOO GREAT, INSTEAD OF LEANING ON ME--
"-- HE BEGAN LEANING ON PILLS... TO WAKE HIM UP, TO PUT HIM TO SLEEP, TO HELP HIM ESCAPE.
"BUT WHENEVER I TRIED TO TALK TO HIM ABOUT IT, HE'D FLY INTO A RAGE, SAYING THAT HE'D WORK THINGS OUT HIMSELF--
"--AS IF I WERE LESSENING HIM BY TRYING TO BE A PART OF HIS WORLD.
"I WAS YOUNGER THEN, AND HURT MORE EASILY. SO I DIDN'T REALLY TRY TO UNDERSTAND HIS INSECURITIES, HIS NEEDS. I LEFT HIM TO DO JUST WHAT HE WANTED-- HANDLE IT HIMSELF.
"A MONTH LATER, ALEX'S CAR WENT OUT OF CONTROL ON A BRIDGE. HE WAS KILLED. THE DOCTORS NEVER COULD DETERMINE IF THE CAUSE WAS A HEART ATTACK FROM OVERWORK, OR SLOWED REFLEXES FROM THE PILLS. NOT THAT IT MATTERS, OF COURSE.
"IF I HAD STAYED WITH HIM, TRIED HARDER, HE MIGHT STILL BE ALIVE TODAY."
I... I DIDN'T KNOW, BETH. I'M SORRY.
NO, BLAST IT, THAT'S NOT WHAT I WANT! DON'T FEEL SORRY FOR ME! AND DON'T FEEL SORRY FOR YOURSELF!

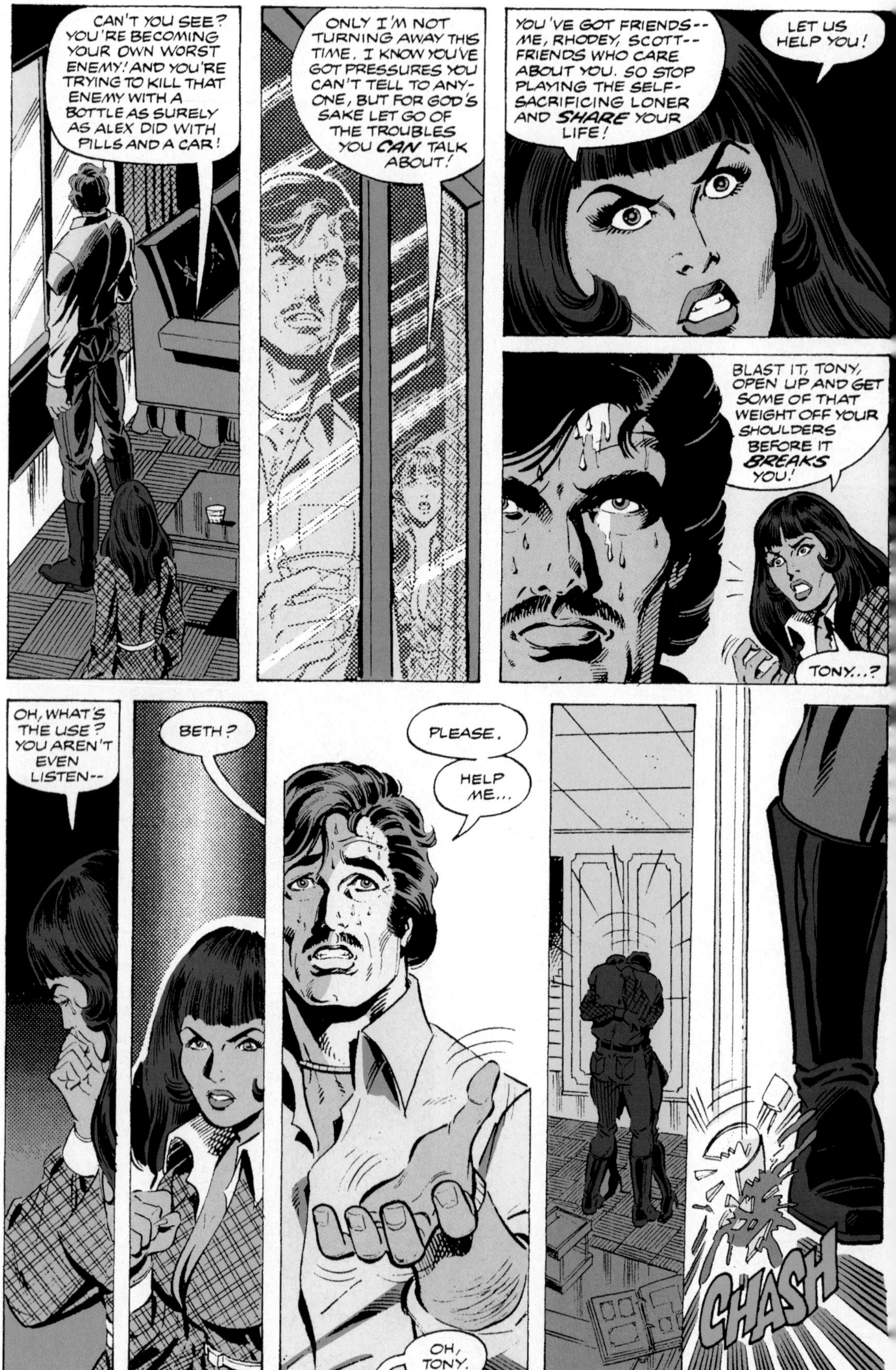
CAN'T YOU SEE? YOU'RE BECOMING YOUR OWN WORST ENEMY! AND YOU'RE TRYING TO KILL THAT ENEMY WITH A BOTTLE AS SURELY AS ALEX DID WITH PILLS AND A CAR!
ONLY I'M NOT TURNING AWAY THIS TIME. I KNOW YOU'VE GOT PRESSURES YOU CAN'T TELL TO ANYONE, BUT FOR GOD'S SAKE LET GO OF THE TROUBLES YOU CAN TALK ABOUT!
YOU'VE GOT FRIENDS-- ME, RHODEY, SCOTT-- FRIENDS WHO CARE ABOUT YOU. SO STOP PLAYING THE SELF-SACRIFICING LONER AND SHARE YOUR LIFE!
LET US HELP YOU!
BLAST IT, TONY, OPEN UP AND GET SOME OF THAT WEIGHT OFF YOUR SHOULDERS BEFORE IT BREAKS YOU!
TONY...?
OH, WHAT'S THE USE? YOU AREN'T EVEN LISTEN--
BETH?
PLEASE.
HELP ME...
OH, TONY.
CHASH

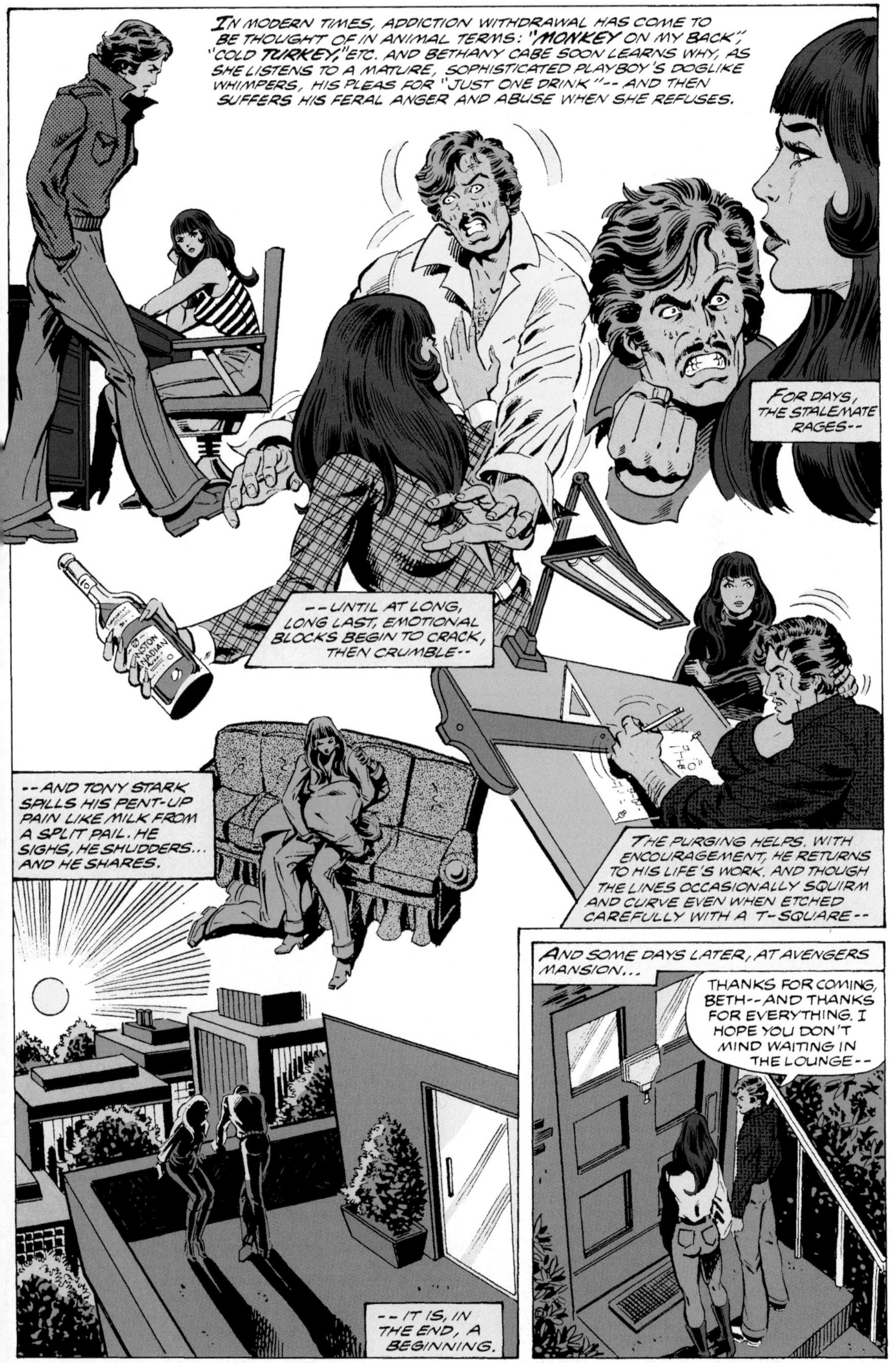

IN MODERN TIMES, ADDICTION WITHDRAWAL HAS COME TO BE THOUGHT OF IN ANIMAL TERMS: "MONKEY ON MY BACK", "COLD TURKEY," ETC. AND BETHANY CABE SOON LEARNS WHY, AS SHE LISTENS TO A MATURE, SOPHISTICATED PLAYBOY'S DOGLIKE WHIMPERS, HIS PLEAS FOR "JUST ONE DRINK"-- AND THEN SUFFERS HIS FERAL ANGER AND ABUSE WHEN SHE REFUSES.
FOR DAYS, THE STALEMATE RAGES--
--UNTIL AT LONG, LONG LAST, EMOTIONAL BLOCKS BEGIN TO CRACK, THEN CRUMBLE--
--AND TONY STARK SPILLS HIS PENT-UP PAIN LIKE MILK FROM A SPLIT PAIL. HE SIGHS, HE SHUDDERS... AND HE SHARES.
THE PURGING HELPS. WITH ENCOURAGEMENT, HE RETURNS TO HIS LIFE'S WORK. AND THOUGH THE LINES OCCASIONALLY SQUIRM AND CURVE EVEN WHEN ETCHED CAREFULLY WITH A T-SQUARE--
--IT IS, IN THE END, A BEGINNING.
AND SOME DAYS LATER, AT AVENGERS MANSION...
THANKS FOR COMING, BETH--AND THANKS FOR EVERYTHING. I HOPE YOU DON'T MIND WAITING IN THE LOUNGE--

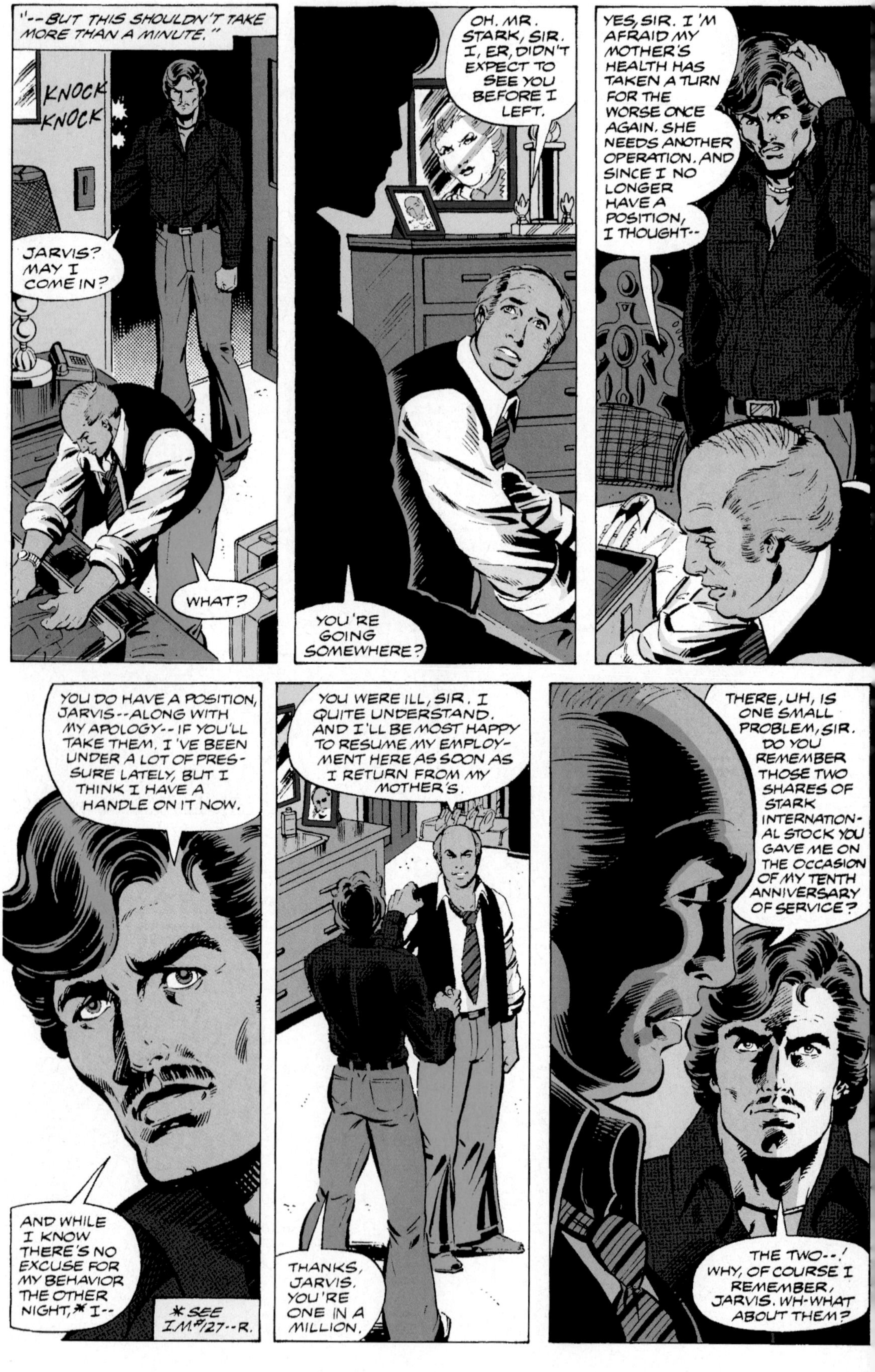
"--BUT THIS SHOULDN'T TAKE MORE THAN A MINUTE."
KNOCK KNOCK
JARVIS? MAY I COME IN?
WHAT?
OH. MR. STARK, SIR. I, ER, DIDN'T EXPECT TO SEE YOU BEFORE I LEFT.
YOU'RE GOING SOMEWHERE?
YES, SIR. I'M AFRAID MY MOTHER'S HEALTH HAS TAKEN A TURN FOR THE WORSE ONCE AGAIN. SHE NEEDS ANOTHER OPERATION. AND SINCE I NO LONGER HAVE A POSITION, I THOUGHT--
YOU DO HAVE A POSITION, JARVIS--ALONG WITH MY APOLOGY--IF YOU'LL TAKE THEM. I'VE BEEN UNDER A LOT OF PRESSURE LATELY, BUT I THINK I HAVE A HANDLE ON IT NOW.
AND WHILE I KNOW THERE'S NO EXCUSE FOR MY BEHAVIOR THE OTHER NIGHT,* I--
*SEE I.M.#127--R.
YOU WERE ILL, SIR. I QUITE UNDERSTAND. AND I'LL BE MOST HAPPY TO RESUME MY EMPLOYMENT HERE AS SOON AS I RETURN FROM MY MOTHER'S.
THANKS, JARVIS. YOU'RE ONE IN A MILLION.
THERE, UH, IS ONE SMALL PROBLEM, SIR. DO YOU REMEMBER THOSE TWO SHARES OF STARK INTERNATIONAL STOCK YOU GAVE ME ON THE OCCASION OF MY TENTH ANNIVERSARY OF SERVICE?
THE TWO--! WHY, OF COURSE I REMEMBER, JARVIS. WH-WHAT ABOUT THEM?

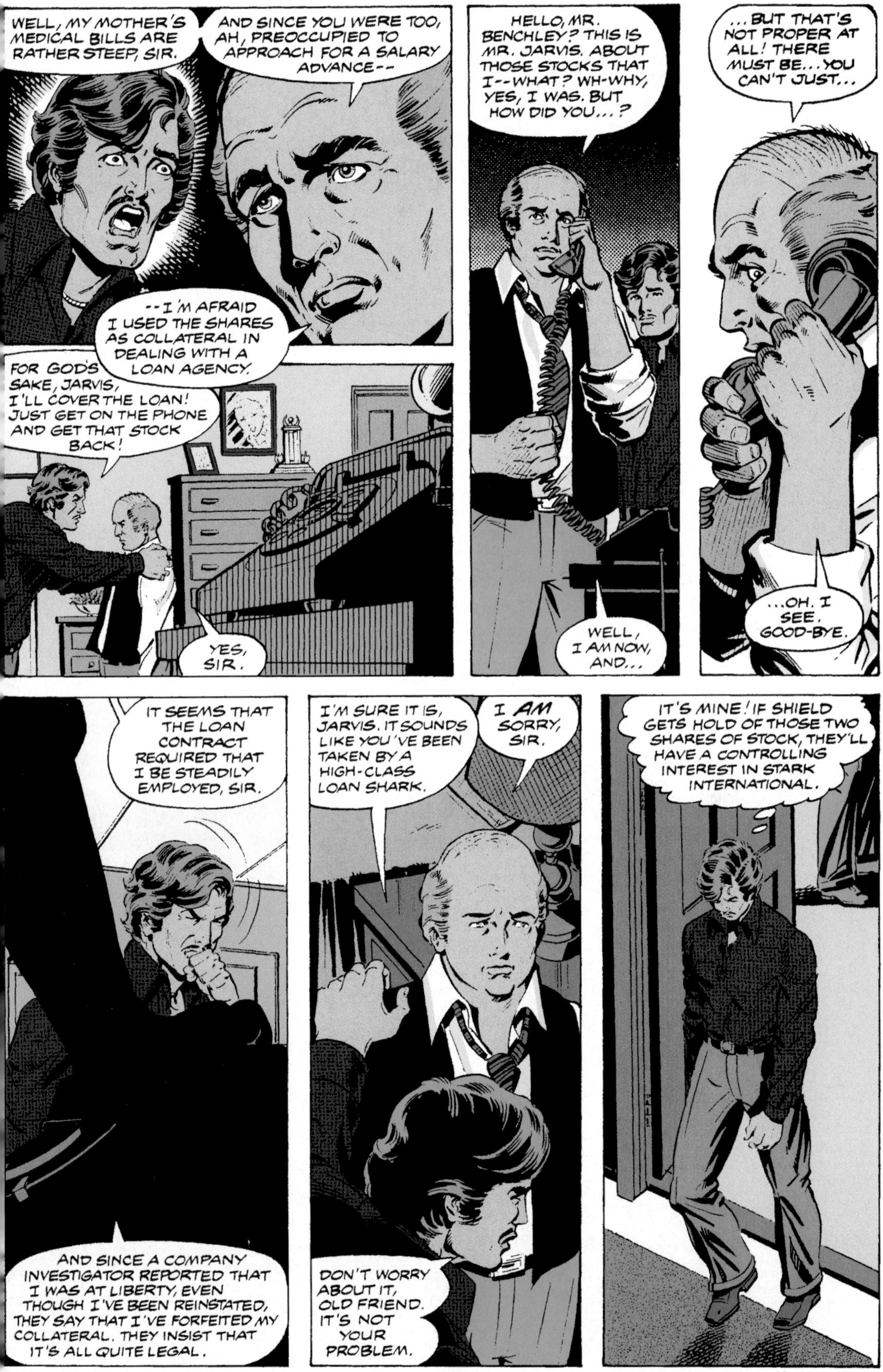
WELL, MY MOTHER'S MEDICAL BILLS ARE RATHER STEEP, SIR.
AND SINCE YOU WERE TOO, AH, PREOCCUPIED TO APPROACH FOR A SALARY ADVANCE--
--I'M AFRAID I USED THE SHARES AS COLLATERAL IN DEALING WITH A LOAN AGENCY.
FOR GOD'S SAKE, JARVIS, I'LL COVER THE LOAN! JUST GET ON THE PHONE AND GET THAT STOCK BACK!
YES, SIR.
HELLO, MR. BENCHLEY? THIS IS MR. JARVIS. ABOUT THOSE STOCKS THAT I--WHAT? WH-WHY, YES, I WAS. BUT HOW DID YOU...?
WELL, I AM NOW, AND...
...BUT THAT'S NOT PROPER AT ALL! THERE MUST BE...YOU CAN'T JUST...
...OH. I SEE. GOOD-BYE.
IT SEEMS THAT THE LOAN CONTRACT REQUIRED THAT I BE STEADILY EMPLOYED, SIR.
AND SINCE A COMPANY INVESTIGATOR REPORTED THAT I WAS AT LIBERTY, EVEN THOUGH I'VE BEEN REINSTATED, THEY SAY THAT I'VE FORFEITED MY COLLATERAL. THEY INSIST THAT IT'S ALL QUITE LEGAL.
I'M SURE IT IS, JARVIS. IT SOUNDS LIKE YOU'VE BEEN TAKEN BY A HIGH-CLASS LOAN SHARK.
I AM SORRY, SIR.
DON'T WORRY ABOUT IT, OLD FRIEND. IT'S NOT YOUR PROBLEM.
IT'S MINE! IF SHIELD GETS HOLD OF THOSE TWO SHARES OF STOCK, THEY'LL HAVE A CONTROLLING INTEREST IN STARK INTERNATIONAL.

THE HALLWAYS OF AVENGERS MANSION ARE QUIET -- BUT THE MAN WHO WALKS THEM IS QUIETER STILL.

FOR HIS NEWFOUND RESOLVE HAS BEEN SHAKEN, AND ONCE MORE HE FEELS NEED.

-- AND GOES INSTEAD TO THE QUARTERS OF THE AVENGERS' CHAIRMAN-IN-ABSENTIA, IRON MAN.

BUT SURPRISINGLY, HE PASSES BY THE ROOM RESERVED FOR ANTHONY STARK, A ROOM THAT HOLDS A GLITTERING BOTTLE BEHIND THE DARK OAK OF A SLIDING DRAWER --

I DON'T NEED THE BOOZE, I DON'T!

I CAN HANDLE THIS ON MY OWN, WITHOUT ANY COUNTERFEIT COURAGE AT ALL!

AND, HONESTLY BELIEVING THAT, TONY STARK THUMBS A PRINT-LOCK MECHANISM TO OPEN A HIDDEN CLOSET --

-- A CLOSET THAT HOLDS A GLITTERING SUIT OF ARMOR BEHIND THE DARK OAK OF A SLIDING DOOR.

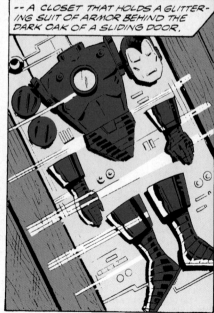

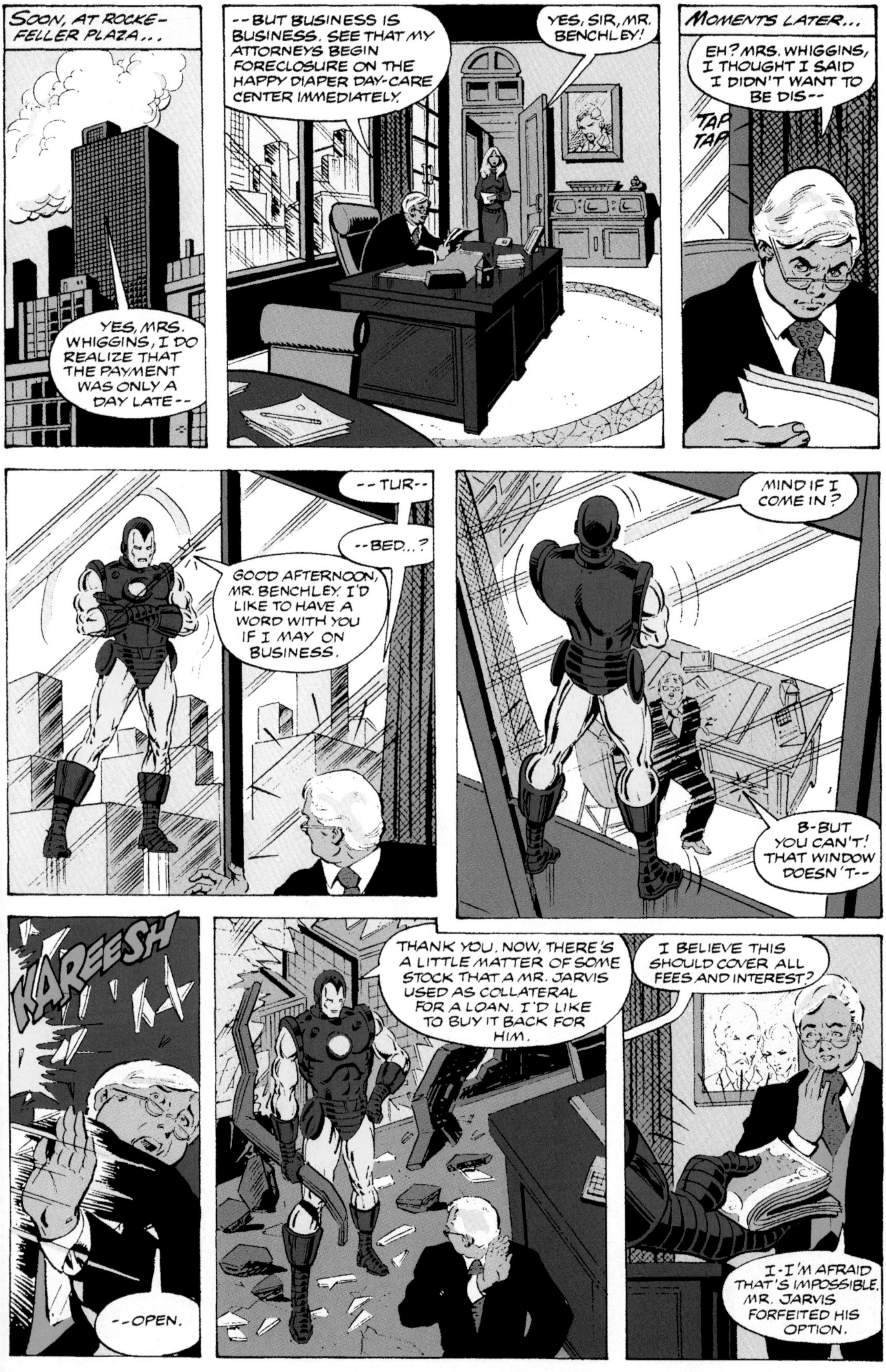
SOON, AT ROCKEFELLER PLAZA...
YES, MRS. WHIGGINS, I DO REALIZE THAT THE PAYMENT WAS ONLY A DAY LATE--
--BUT BUSINESS IS BUSINESS. SEE THAT MY ATTORNEYS BEGIN FORECLOSURE ON THE HAPPY DIAPER DAY-CARE CENTER IMMEDIATELY.
YES, SIR, MR. BENCHLEY!
MOMENTS LATER...
EH? MRS. WHIGGINS, I THOUGHT I SAID I DIDN'T WANT TO BE DIS--
TAP TAP
--TUR--
--BED...?
GOOD AFTERNOON, MR. BENCHLEY. I'D LIKE TO HAVE A WORD WITH YOU IF I MAY ON BUSINESS.
MIND IF I COME IN?
B-BUT YOU CAN'T! THAT WINDOW DOESN'T--
KAREESH
--OPEN.
THANK YOU. NOW, THERE'S A LITTLE MATTER OF SOME STOCK THAT A MR. JARVIS USED AS COLLATERAL FOR A LOAN. I'D LIKE TO BUY IT BACK FOR HIM.
I BELIEVE THIS SHOULD COVER ALL FEES AND INTEREST?
I-I'M AFRAID THAT'S IMPOSSIBLE. MR. JARVIS FORFEITED HIS OPTION.

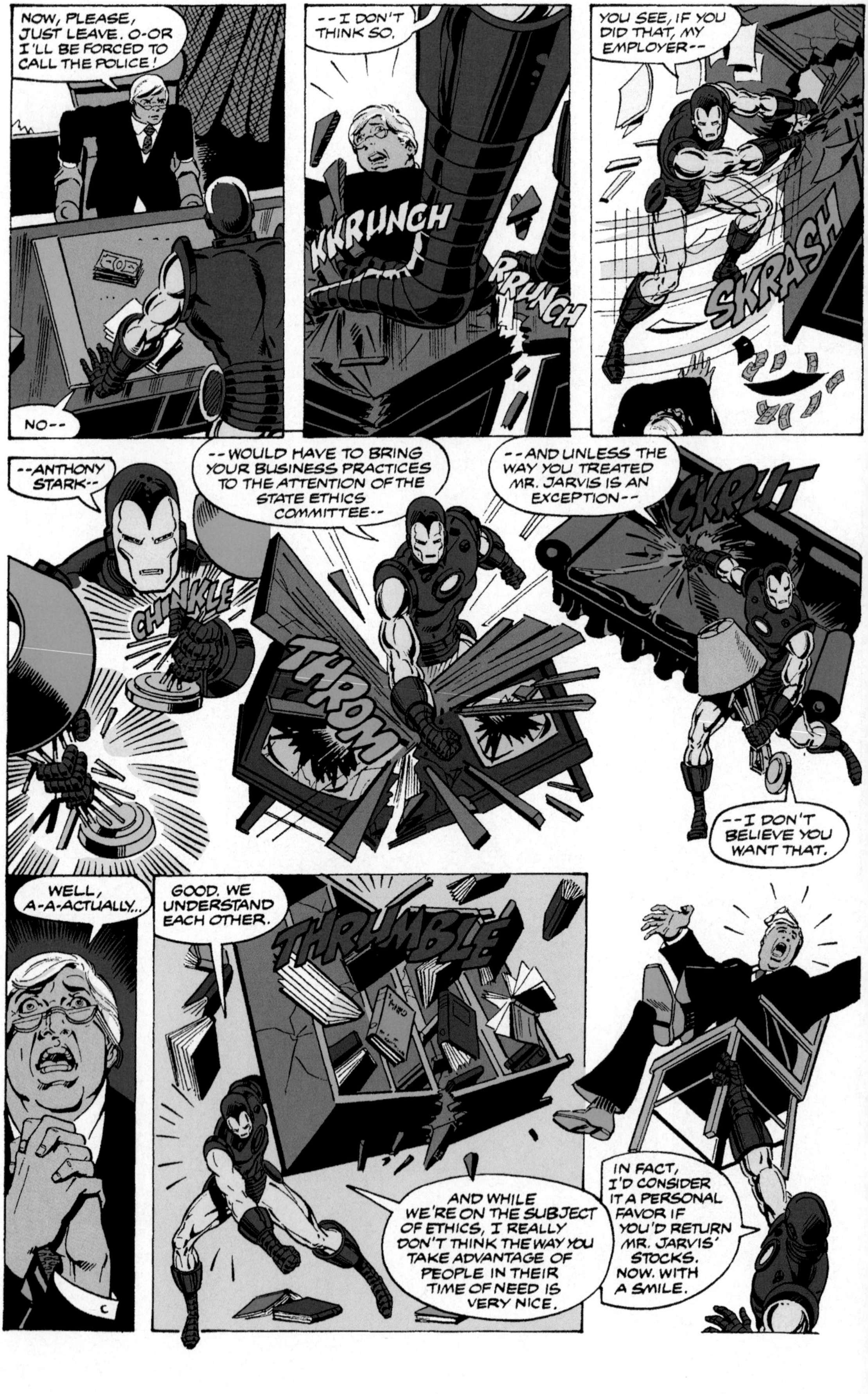

NOW, PLEASE, JUST LEAVE. O-OR I'LL BE FORCED TO CALL THE POLICE!
NO--
--I DON'T THINK SO.
KKRUNCH
RRUNCH
YOU SEE, IF YOU DID THAT, MY EMPLOYER--
SKRASH
--ANTHONY STARK--
CHINKLE
--WOULD HAVE TO BRING YOUR BUSINESS PRACTICES TO THE ATTENTION OF THE STATE ETHICS COMMITTEE--
THROM
--AND UNLESS THE WAY YOU TREATED MR. JARVIS IS AN EXCEPTION--
SKRUT
--I DON'T BELIEVE YOU WANT THAT.
WELL, A-A-ACTUALLY...
GOOD. WE UNDERSTAND EACH OTHER.
THRUMBLE
AND WHILE WE'RE ON THE SUBJECT OF ETHICS, I REALLY DON'T THINK THE WAY YOU TAKE ADVANTAGE OF PEOPLE IN THEIR TIME OF NEED IS VERY NICE.
IN FACT, I'D CONSIDER IT A PERSONAL FAVOR IF YOU'D RETURN MR. JARVIS' STOCKS. NOW. WITH A SMILE.

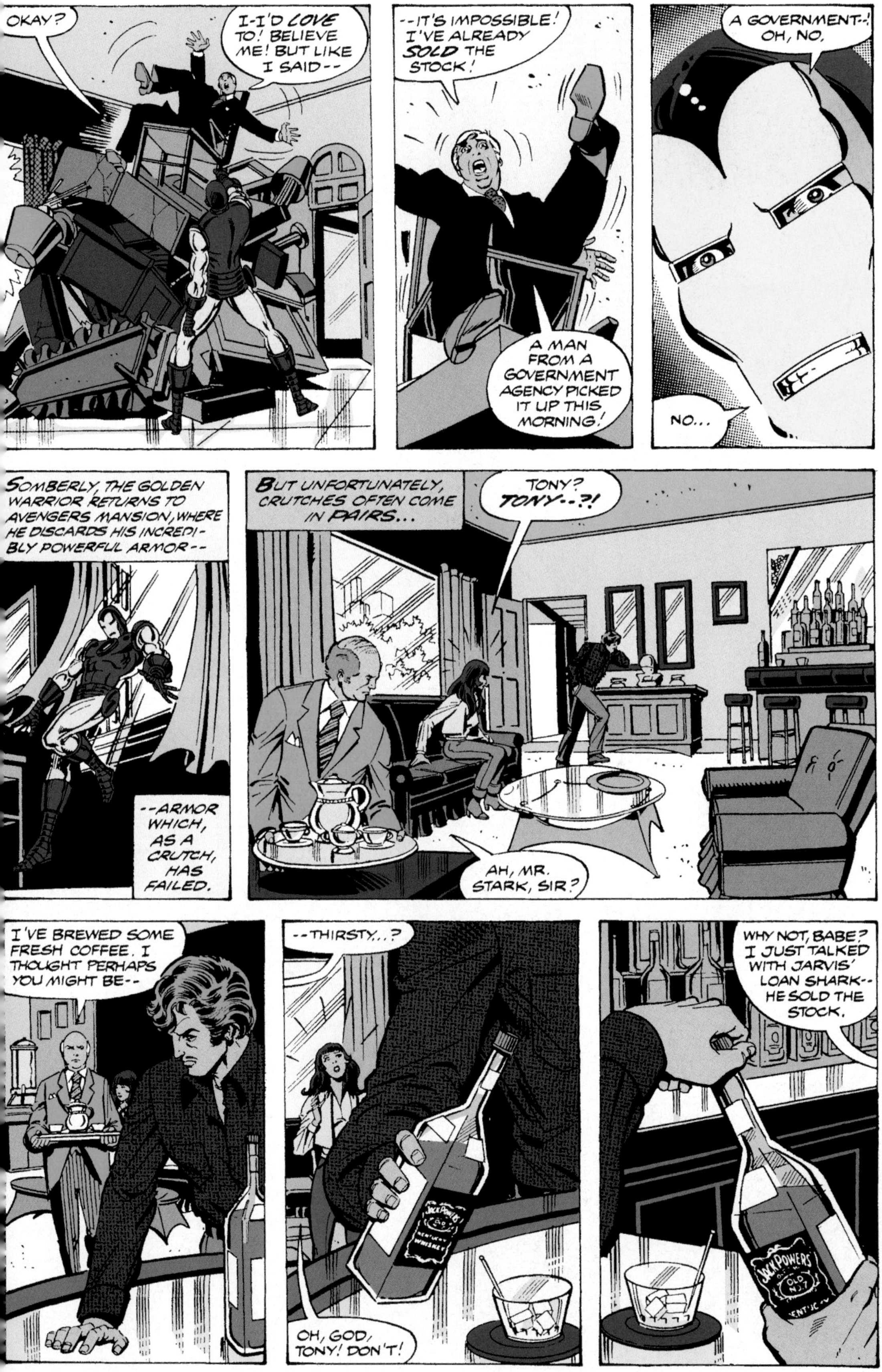

OKAY?
I-I'D LOVE TO! BELIEVE ME! BUT LIKE I SAID--
--IT'S IMPOSSIBLE! I'VE ALREADY SOLD THE STOCK!
A MAN FROM A GOVERNMENT AGENCY PICKED IT UP THIS MORNING!
A GOVERNMENT--! OH, NO,
NO...
SOMBERLY, THE GOLDEN WARRIOR RETURNS TO AVENGERS MANSION, WHERE HE DISCARDS HIS INCREDIBLY POWERFUL ARMOR--
--ARMOR WHICH, AS A CRUTCH, HAS FAILED.
BUT UNFORTUNATELY, CRUTCHES OFTEN COME IN PAIRS...
TONY? TONY--?!
AH, MR. STARK, SIR?
I'VE BREWED SOME FRESH COFFEE. I THOUGHT PERHAPS YOU MIGHT BE--
--THIRSTY...?
OH, GOD, TONY! DON'T!
WHY NOT, BABE? I JUST TALKED WITH JARVIS' LOAN SHARK-- HE SOLD THE STOCK.

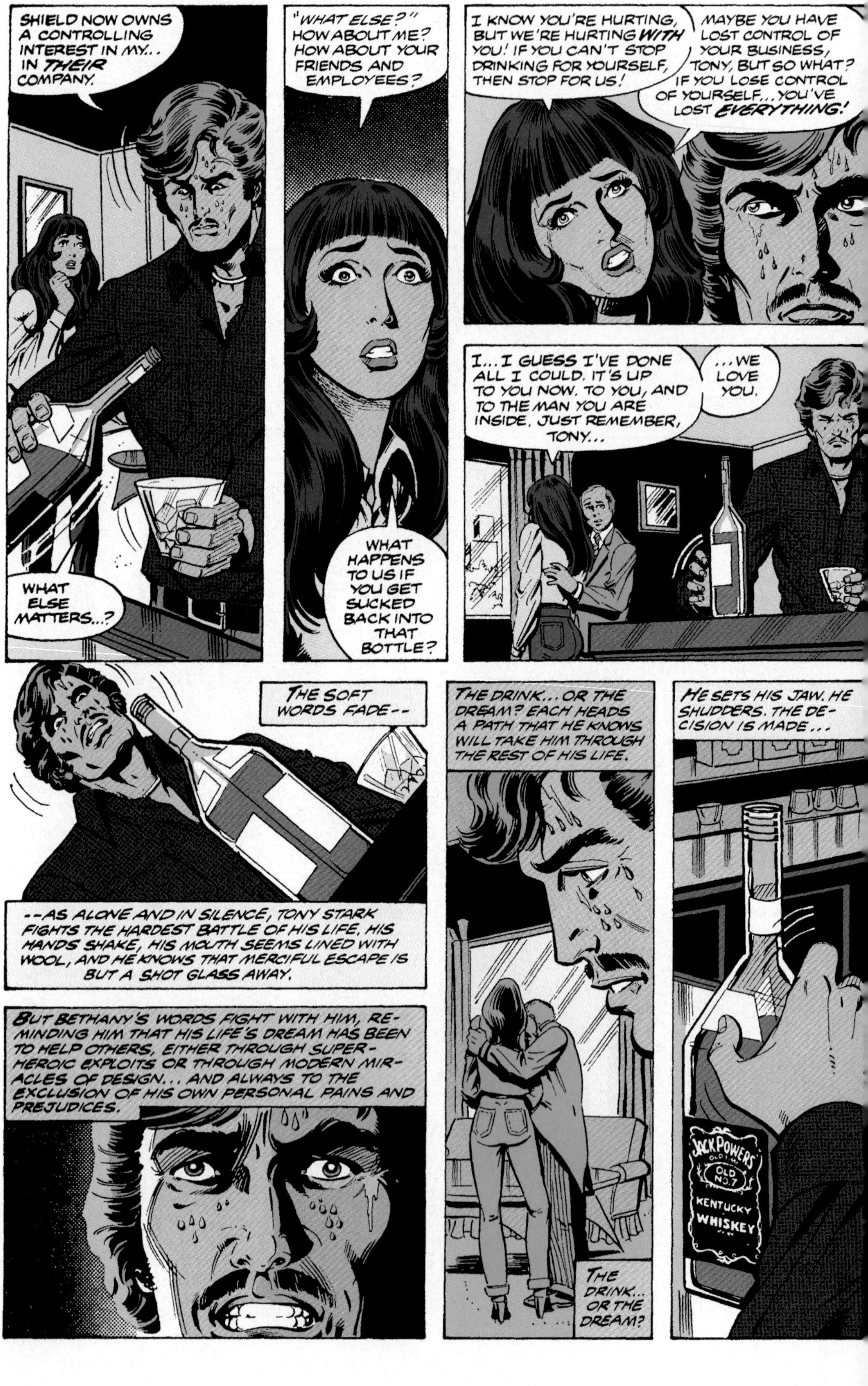
SHIELD NOW OWNS A CONTROLLING INTEREST IN MY... IN THEIR COMPANY.
WHAT ELSE MATTERS...?
"WHAT ELSE?" HOW ABOUT ME? HOW ABOUT YOUR FRIENDS AND EMPLOYEES?
WHAT HAPPENS TO US IF YOU GET SUCKED BACK INTO THAT BOTTLE?
I KNOW YOU'RE HURTING, BUT WE'RE HURTING WITH YOU! IF YOU CAN'T STOP DRINKING FOR YOURSELF, THEN STOP FOR US!
MAYBE YOU HAVE LOST CONTROL OF YOUR BUSINESS, TONY, BUT SO WHAT? IF YOU LOSE CONTROL OF YOURSELF... YOU'VE LOST EVERYTHING!
I... I GUESS I'VE DONE ALL I COULD. IT'S UP TO YOU NOW. TO YOU, AND TO THE MAN YOU ARE INSIDE. JUST REMEMBER, TONY...
...WE LOVE YOU.
THE SOFT WORDS FADE--
--AS ALONE AND IN SILENCE, TONY STARK FIGHTS THE HARDEST BATTLE OF HIS LIFE. HIS HANDS SHAKE, HIS MOUTH SEEMS LINED WITH WOOL, AND HE KNOWS THAT MERCIFUL ESCAPE IS BUT A SHOT GLASS AWAY.
BUT BETHANY'S WORDS FIGHT WITH HIM, REMINDING HIM THAT HIS LIFE'S DREAM HAS BEEN TO HELP OTHERS, EITHER THROUGH SUPER-HEROIC EXPLOITS OR THROUGH MODERN MIRACLES OF DESIGN... AND ALWAYS TO THE EXCLUSION OF HIS OWN PERSONAL PAINS AND PREJUDICES.
THE DRINK... OR THE DREAM? EACH HEADS A PATH THAT HE KNOWS WILL TAKE HIM THROUGH THE REST OF HIS LIFE.
THE DRINK... OR THE DREAM?
HE SETS HIS JAW. HE SHUDDERS. THE DECISION IS MADE...
JACK POWERS
OLD No. 7
KENTUCKY WHISKEY

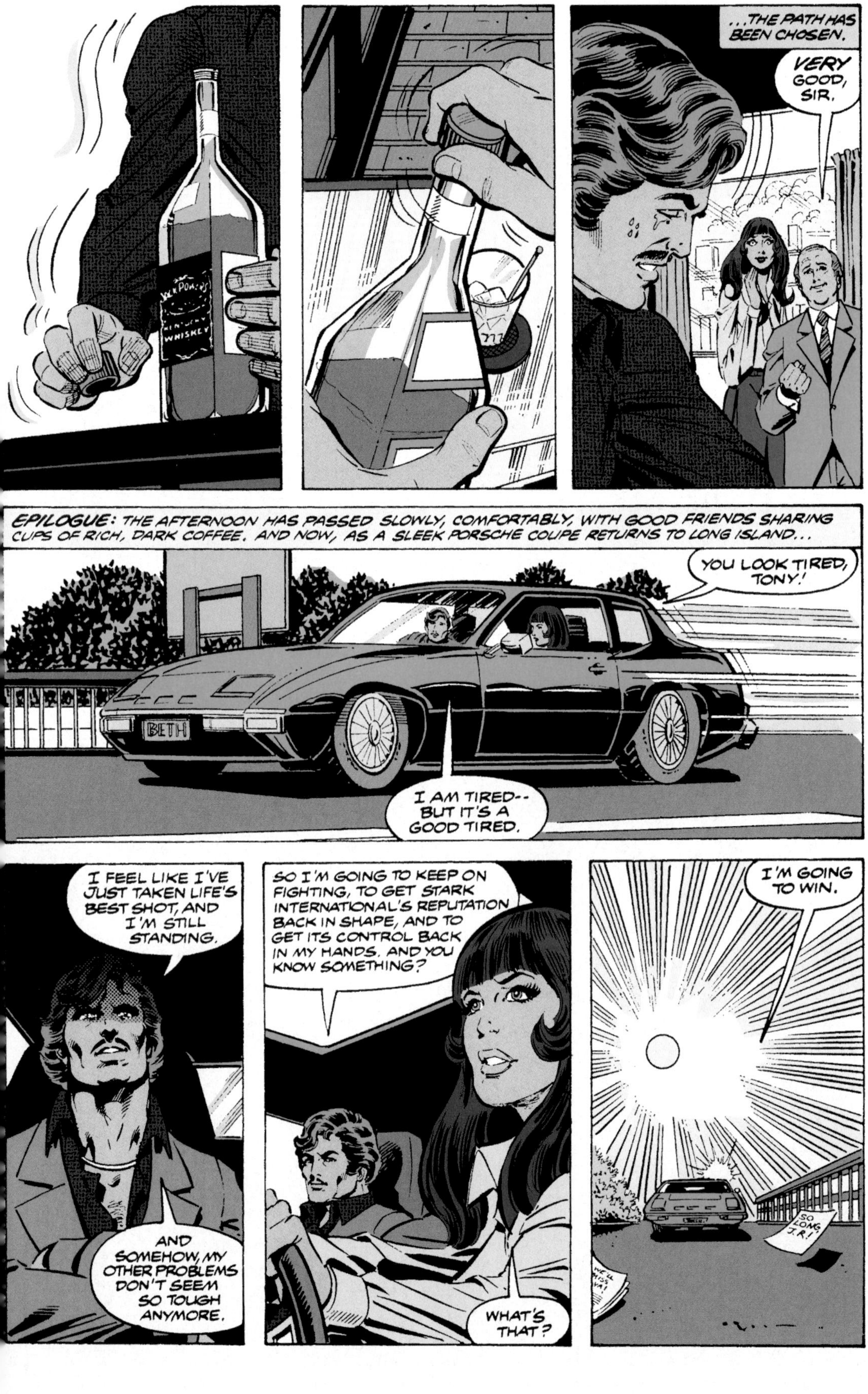

...THE PATH HAS BEEN CHOSEN.
VERY GOOD, SIR.
EPILOGUE: THE AFTERNOON HAS PASSED SLOWLY, COMFORTABLY, WITH GOOD FRIENDS SHARING CUPS OF RICH, DARK COFFEE. AND NOW, AS A SLEEK PORSCHE COUPE RETURNS TO LONG ISLAND...
YOU LOOK TIRED, TONY!
BETH
I AM TIRED-- BUT IT'S A GOOD TIRED.
I FEEL LIKE I'VE JUST TAKEN LIFE'S BEST SHOT, AND I'M STILL STANDING.
AND SOMEHOW, MY OTHER PROBLEMS DON'T SEEM SO TOUGH ANYMORE.
SO I'M GOING TO KEEP ON FIGHTING, TO GET STARK INTERNATIONAL'S REPUTATION BACK IN SHAPE, AND TO GET ITS CONTROL BACK IN MY HANDS. AND YOU KNOW SOMETHING?
WHAT'S THAT?
I'M GOING TO WIN.
SO LONG J.R.!

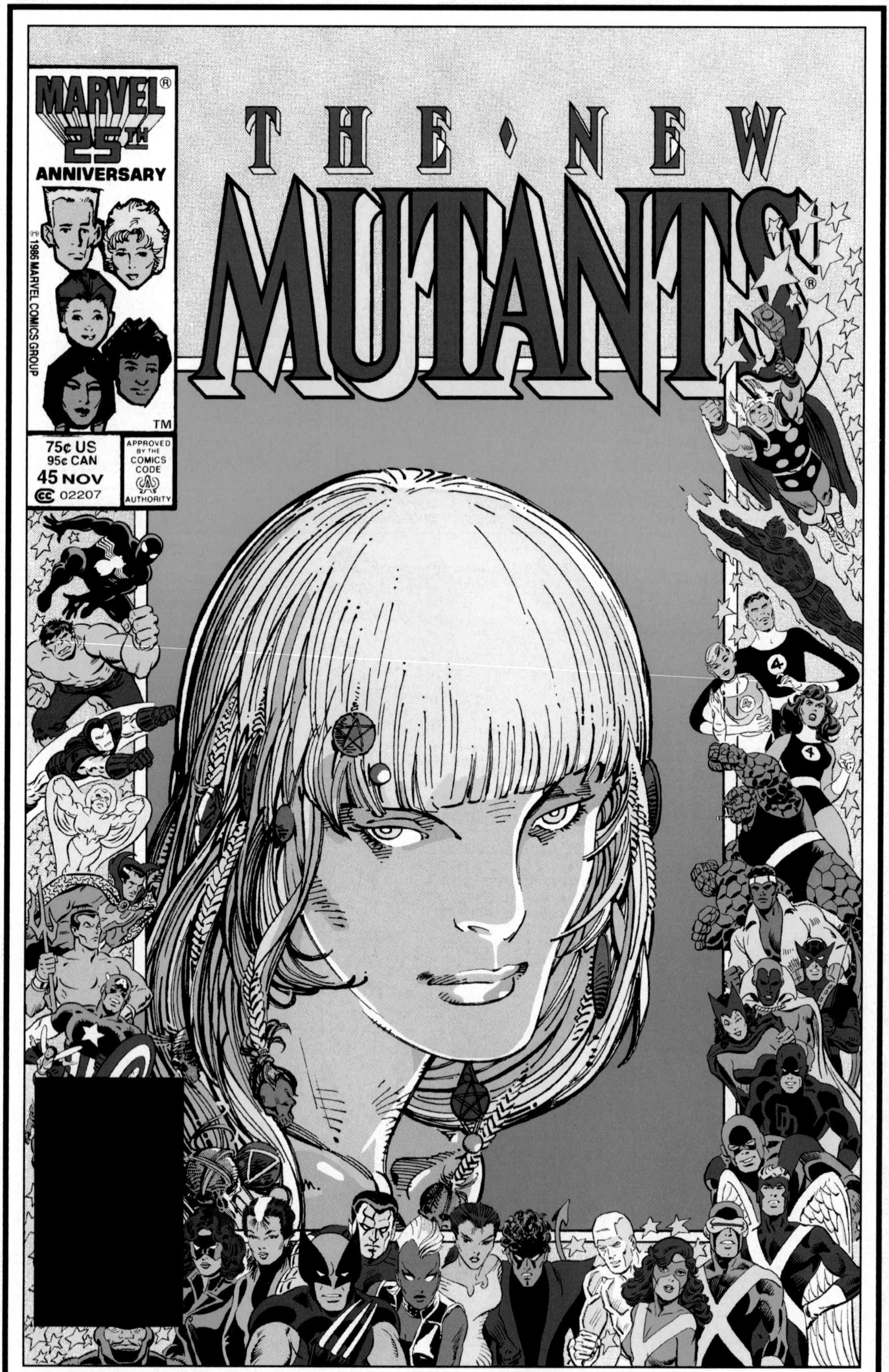
MARVEL®
25TH
ANNIVERSARY
© 1986 MARVEL COMICS GROUP
TM
75¢ US
95¢ CAN
45 NOV
02207
APPROVED BY THE COMICS CODE AUTHORITY
THE NEW
MUTANTS®

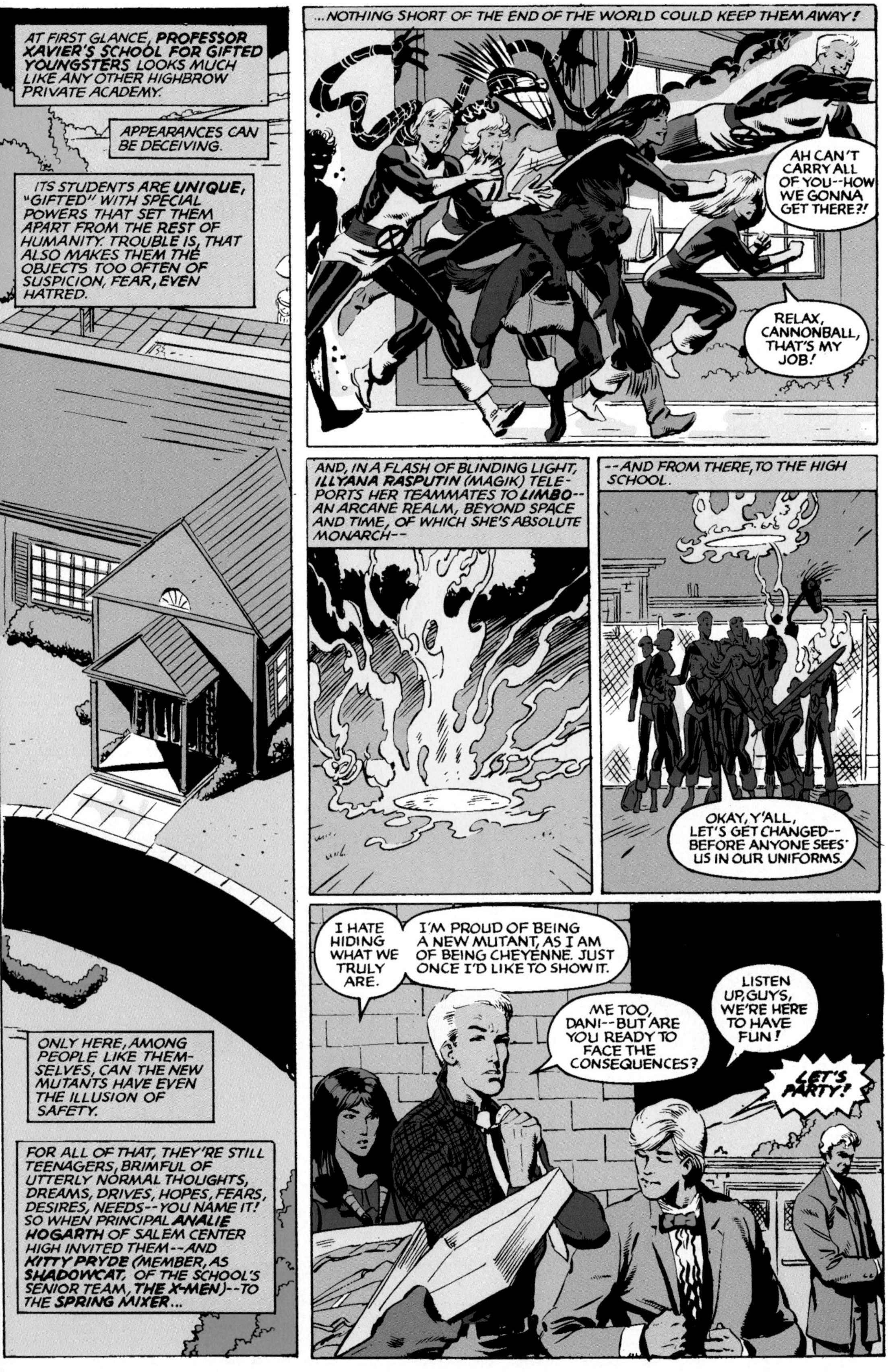
AT FIRST GLANCE, PROFESSOR XAVIER'S SCHOOL FOR GIFTED YOUNGSTERS LOOKS MUCH LIKE ANY OTHER HIGHBROW PRIVATE ACADEMY.
APPEARANCES CAN BE DECEIVING.
ITS STUDENTS ARE UNIQUE, "GIFTED" WITH SPECIAL POWERS THAT SET THEM APART FROM THE REST OF HUMANITY. TROUBLE IS, THAT ALSO MAKES THEM THE OBJECTS TOO OFTEN OF SUSPICION, FEAR, EVEN HATRED.
ONLY HERE, AMONG PEOPLE LIKE THEMSELVES, CAN THE NEW MUTANTS HAVE EVEN THE ILLUSION OF SAFETY.
FOR ALL OF THAT, THEY'RE STILL TEENAGERS, BRIMFUL OF UTTERLY NORMAL THOUGHTS, DREAMS, DRIVES, HOPES, FEARS, DESIRES, NEEDS--YOU NAME IT! SO WHEN PRINCIPAL ANALIE HOGARTH OF SALEM CENTER HIGH INVITED THEM--AND KITTY PRYDE (MEMBER, AS SHADOWCAT, OF THE SCHOOL'S SENIOR TEAM, THE X-MEN)--TO THE SPRING MIXER...
...NOTHING SHORT OF THE END OF THE WORLD COULD KEEP THEM AWAY!
AH CAN'T CARRY ALL OF YOU--HOW WE GONNA GET THERE?!
RELAX, CANNONBALL, THAT'S MY JOB!
AND, IN A FLASH OF BLINDING LIGHT, ILLYANA RASPUTIN (MAGIK) TELEPORTS HER TEAMMATES TO LIMBO-- AN ARCANE REALM, BEYOND SPACE AND TIME, OF WHICH SHE'S ABSOLUTE MONARCH--
--AND FROM THERE, TO THE HIGH SCHOOL.
OKAY, Y'ALL, LET'S GET CHANGED-- BEFORE ANYONE SEES US IN OUR UNIFORMS.
I HATE HIDING WHAT WE TRULY ARE.
I'M PROUD OF BEING A NEW MUTANT, AS I AM OF BEING CHEYENNE. JUST ONCE I'D LIKE TO SHOW IT.
ME TOO, DANI--BUT ARE YOU READY TO FACE THE CONSEQUENCES?
LISTEN UP, GUYS, WE'RE HERE TO HAVE FUN!
LET'S PARTY!

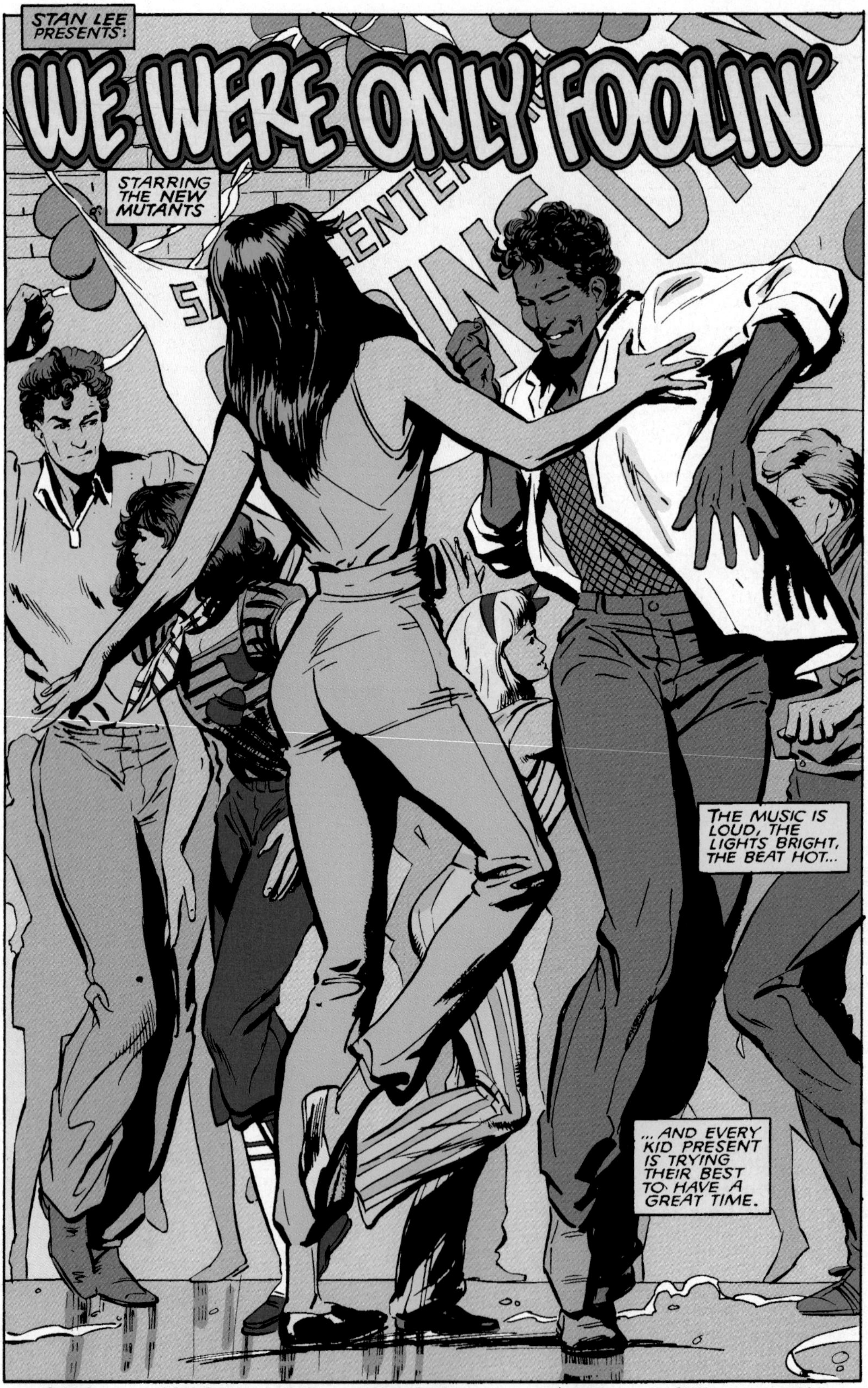
STAN LEE PRESENTS:
WE WERE ONLY FOOLIN'
STARRING THE NEW MUTANTS
THE MUSIC IS LOUD, THE LIGHTS BRIGHT, THE BEAT HOT...
...AND EVERY KID PRESENT IS TRYING THEIR BEST TO HAVE A GREAT TIME.

CHRIS CLAREMONT WRITER · JACKSON GUICE PENCILER · KYLE BAKER INKER · BUHALIS & ORZECHOWSKI LETTERERS · GLYNIS OLIVER COLORIST · ANN NOCENTI EDITOR · JIM SHOOTER EDITOR IN CHIEF

CREATED BY CHRIS CLAREMONT AND BOB McLEOD

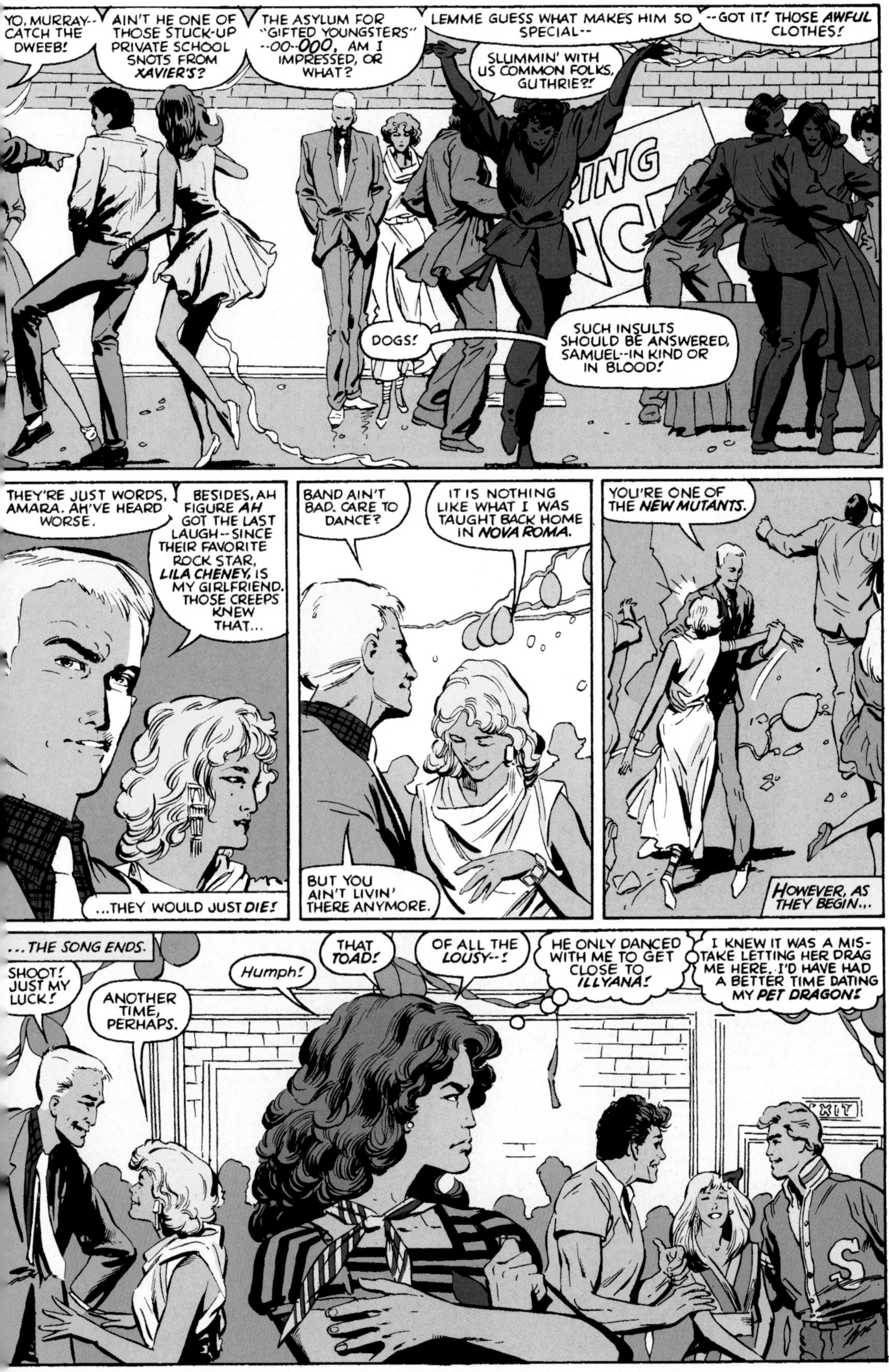

YO, MURRAY--
CATCH THE DWEEB!
AIN'T HE ONE OF THOSE STUCK-UP PRIVATE SCHOOL SNOTS FROM XAVIER'S?
THE ASYLUM FOR "GIFTED YOUNGSTERS" --OO--OOO, AM I IMPRESSED, OR WHAT?
LEMME GUESS WHAT MAKES HIM SO SPECIAL--
--GOT IT! THOSE AWFUL CLOTHES!
SLUMMIN' WITH US COMMON FOLKS, GUTHRIE?!
DOGS!
SUCH INSULTS SHOULD BE ANSWERED, SAMUEL--IN KIND OR IN BLOOD!
THEY'RE JUST WORDS, AMARA. AH'VE HEARD WORSE.
BESIDES, AH FIGURE AH GOT THE LAST LAUGH--SINCE THEIR FAVORITE ROCK STAR, LILA CHENEY, IS MY GIRLFRIEND. THOSE CREEPS KNEW THAT...
...THEY WOULD JUST DIE!
BAND AIN'T BAD. CARE TO DANCE?
IT IS NOTHING LIKE WHAT I WAS TAUGHT BACK HOME IN NOVA ROMA.
BUT YOU AIN'T LIVIN' THERE ANYMORE.
YOU'RE ONE OF THE NEW MUTANTS.
HOWEVER, AS THEY BEGIN...
...THE SONG ENDS.
SHOOT! JUST MY LUCK!
ANOTHER TIME, PERHAPS.
Humph!
THAT TOAD!
OF ALL THE LOUSY--!
HE ONLY DANCED WITH ME TO GET CLOSE TO ILLYANA!
I KNEW IT WAS A MISTAKE LETTING HER DRAG ME HERE. I'D HAVE HAD A BETTER TIME DATING MY PET DRAGON!

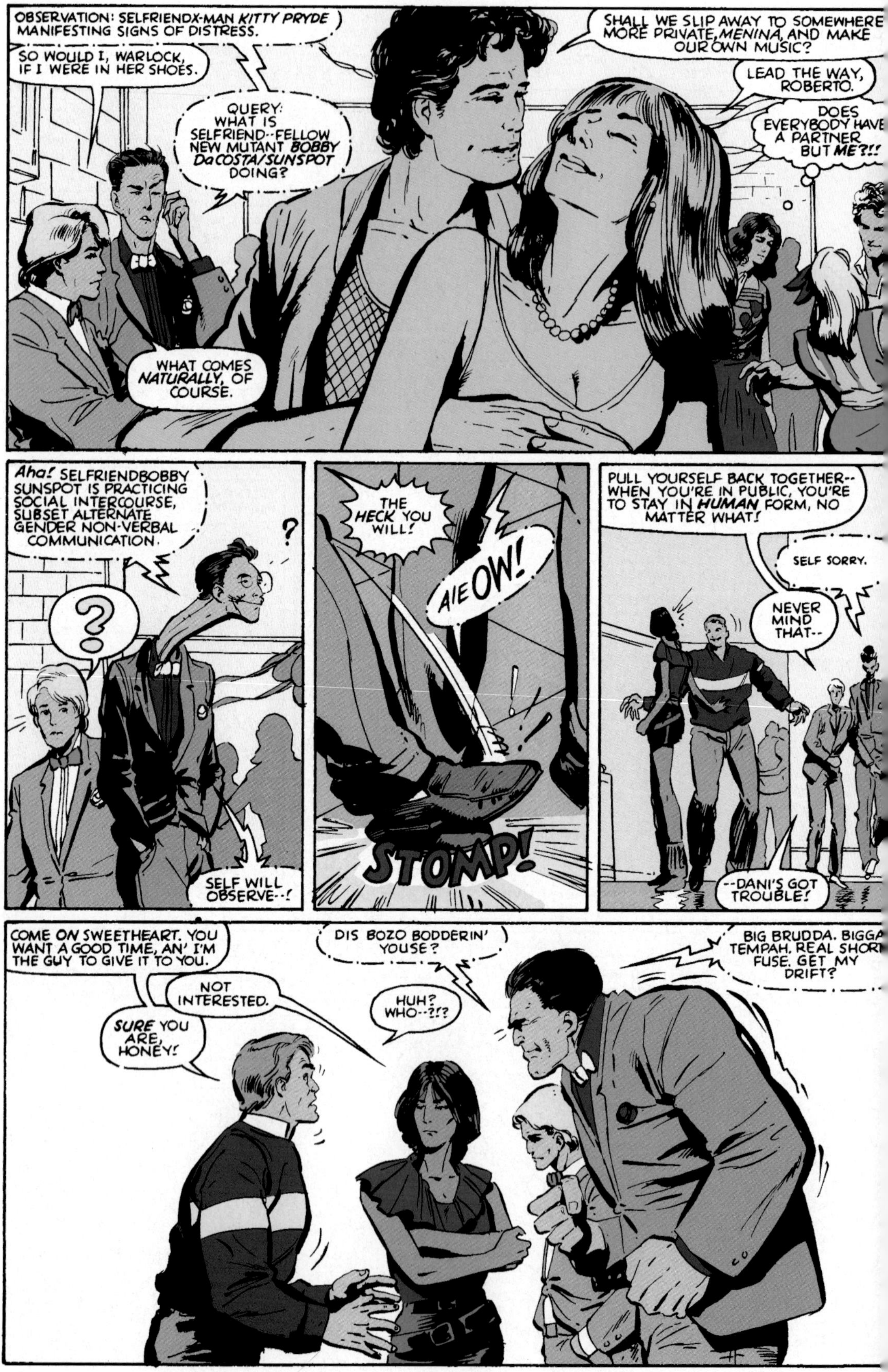
OBSERVATION: SELFRIENDX-MAN KITTY PRYDE MANIFESTING SIGNS OF DISTRESS.
SO WOULD I, WARLOCK, IF I WERE IN HER SHOES.
QUERY: WHAT IS SELFRIEND--FELLOW NEW MUTANT BOBBY DaCOSTA/SUNSPOT DOING?
WHAT COMES NATURALLY, OF COURSE.
SHALL WE SLIP AWAY TO SOMEWHERE MORE PRIVATE, MENINA, AND MAKE OUR OWN MUSIC?
LEAD THE WAY, ROBERTO.
DOES EVERYBODY HAVE A PARTNER BUT ME?!!
Aha! SELFRIENDBOBBY SUNSPOT IS PRACTICING SOCIAL INTERCOURSE, SUBSET ALTERNATE GENDER NON-VERBAL COMMUNICATION.
?
?
SELF WILL OBSERVE--!
THE HECK YOU WILL!
AIEOW!
STOMP!
PULL YOURSELF BACK TOGETHER--WHEN YOU'RE IN PUBLIC, YOU'RE TO STAY IN HUMAN FORM, NO MATTER WHAT!
SELF SORRY.
NEVER MIND THAT--
--DANI'S GOT TROUBLE!
COME ON SWEETHEART. YOU WANT A GOOD TIME, AN' I'M THE GUY TO GIVE IT TO YOU.
NOT INTERESTED.
SURE YOU ARE, HONEY!
DIS BOZO BODDERIN' YOUSE?
HUH? WHO--?!?
BIG BRUDDA. BIGGA TEMPAH. REAL SHORT FUSE. GET MY DRIFT?

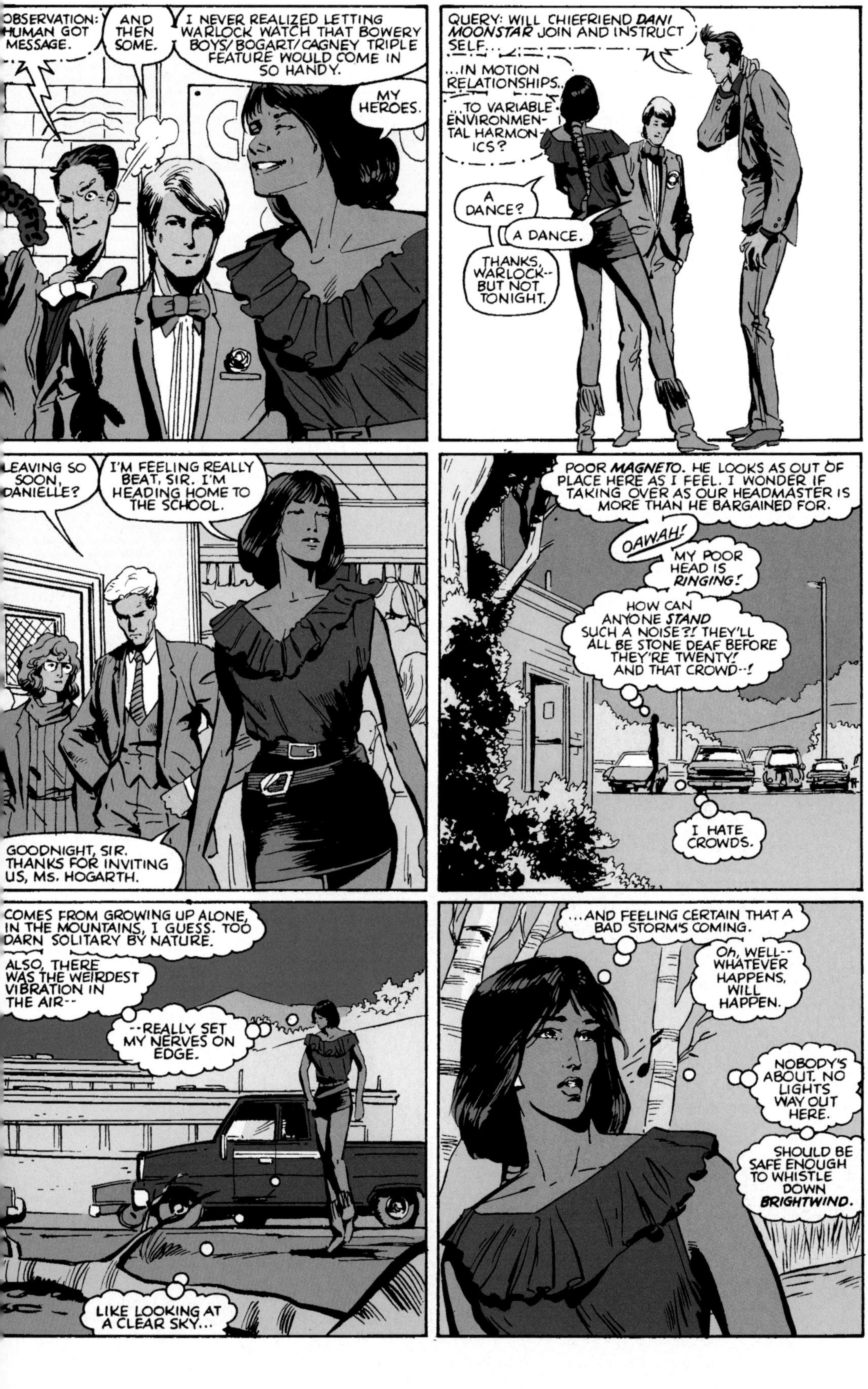
OBSERVATION: HUMAN GOT MESSAGE.
AND THEN SOME.
I NEVER REALIZED LETTING WARLOCK WATCH THAT BOWERY BOYS/BOGART/CAGNEY TRIPLE FEATURE WOULD COME IN SO HANDY.
MY HEROES.
QUERY: WILL CHIEFRIEND DANI MOONSTAR JOIN AND INSTRUCT SELF...
...IN MOTION RELATIONSHIPS...
...TO VARIABLE ENVIRONMENTAL HARMONICS?
A DANCE?
A DANCE.
THANKS, WARLOCK-- BUT NOT TONIGHT.
LEAVING SO SOON, DANIELLE?
I'M FEELING REALLY BEAT, SIR. I'M HEADING HOME TO THE SCHOOL.
GOODNIGHT, SIR. THANKS FOR INVITING US, Ms. HOGARTH.
POOR MAGNETO. HE LOOKS AS OUT OF PLACE HERE AS I FEEL. I WONDER IF TAKING OVER AS OUR HEADMASTER IS MORE THAN HE BARGAINED FOR.
OAWAH!
MY POOR HEAD IS RINGING!
HOW CAN ANYONE STAND SUCH A NOISE?! THEY'LL ALL BE STONE DEAF BEFORE THEY'RE TWENTY! AND THAT CROWD--!
I HATE CROWDS.
COMES FROM GROWING UP ALONE, IN THE MOUNTAINS, I GUESS. TOO DARN SOLITARY BY NATURE.
ALSO, THERE WAS THE WEIRDEST VIBRATION IN THE AIR--
--REALLY SET MY NERVES ON EDGE.
LIKE LOOKING AT A CLEAR SKY...
...AND FEELING CERTAIN THAT A BAD STORM'S COMING.
Oh, WELL-- WHATEVER HAPPENS, WILL HAPPEN.
NOBODY'S ABOUT. NO LIGHTS WAY OUT HERE.
SHOULD BE SAFE ENOUGH TO WHISTLE DOWN BRIGHTWIND.

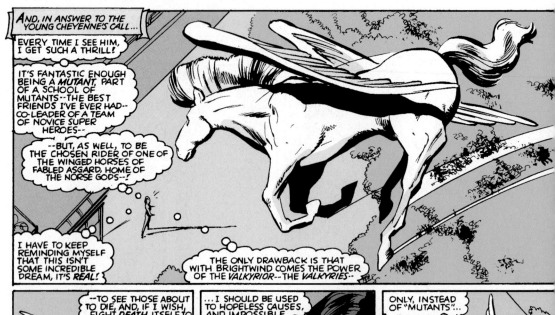

AND, IN ANSWER TO THE YOUNG CHEYENNE'S CALL...

EVERY TIME I SEE HIM, I GET SUCH A THRILL!

IT'S FANTASTIC ENOUGH BEING A *MUTANT*, PART OF A SCHOOL OF MUTANTS--THE BEST FRIENDS I'VE EVER HAD-- CO-LEADER OF A TEAM OF NOVICE SUPER HEROES--

--BUT, AS WELL, TO BE THE *CHOSEN RIDER* OF ONE OF THE *WINGED HORSES* OF FABLED ASGARD, HOME OF THE NORSE GODS--!

I HAVE TO KEEP REMINDING MYSELF THAT THIS ISN'T SOME INCREDIBLE DREAM, IT'S *REAL*!

THE ONLY DRAWBACK IS THAT WITH BRIGHTWIND COMES THE POWER OF THE *VALKYRIOR*--THE *VALKYRIES*--

--TO SEE THOSE ABOUT TO DIE, AND, IF I WISH, FIGHT *DEATH* ITSELF TO SAVE THEM.

HECK, WITH MY ANCESTRY...

...I SHOULD BE USED TO HOPELESS CAUSES, AND IMPOSSIBLE ODDS.

WHAT'S THAT?!

X-FACTOR
WE TAKE CARE OF MUTANTS THE OLD FASHIONED WAY-- *PERMANENTLY!!*

CUTE.

I SAW BUMPER STICKERS LIKE THAT IN COLORADO.

ONLY, INSTEAD OF "MUTANTS"...

...THEY SAID "*REDSKINS*."

SOME THINGS-- SOME ATTITUDES-- NEVER CHANGE.

WOW.

OH, WOW!

THAT GIRL!

THAT HORSE!!

I DON'T BELIEVE MY *EYES*!

DOES IT MEAN...

...SHE'S LIKE *ME*?!?

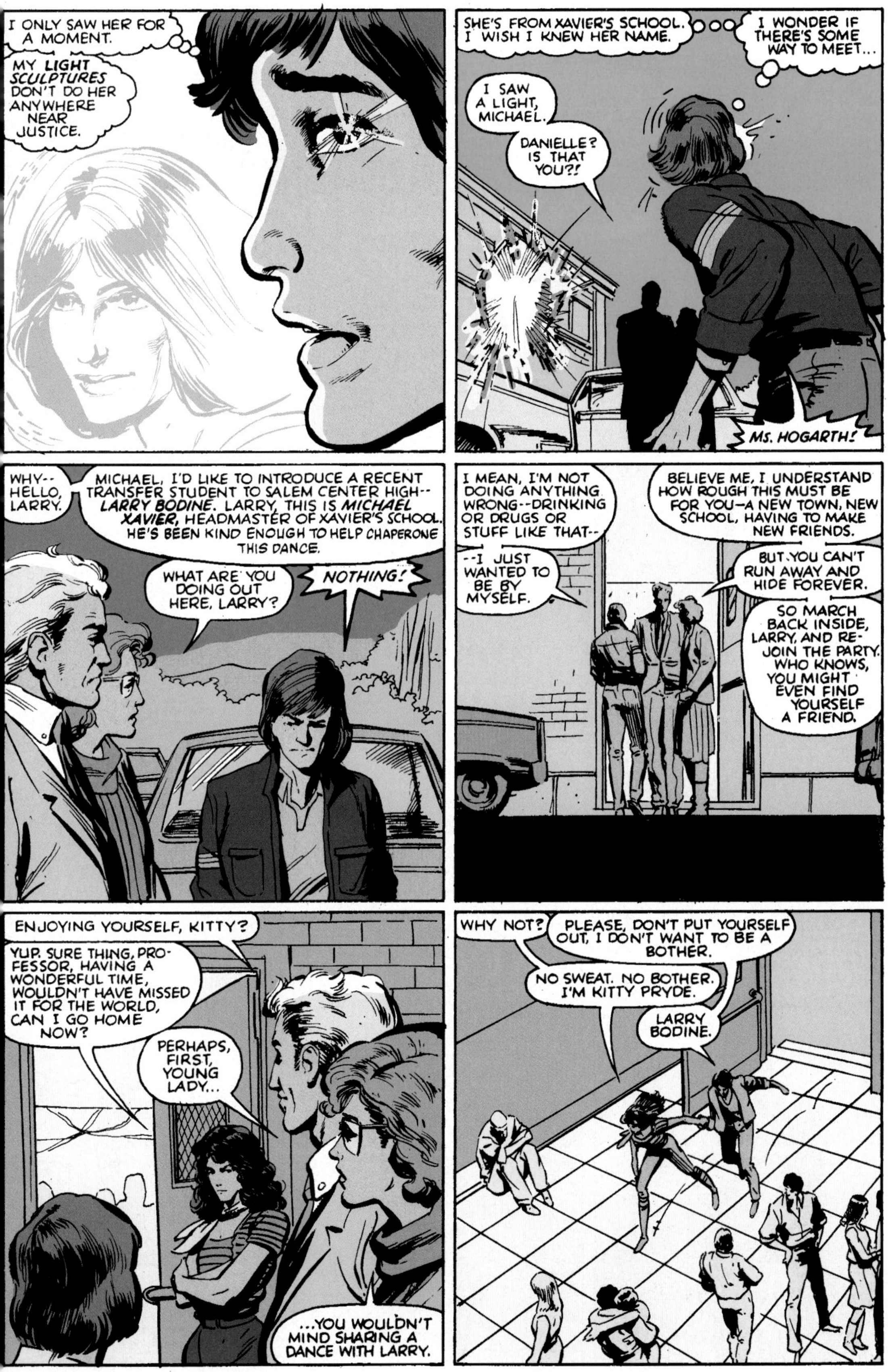

I ONLY SAW HER FOR A MOMENT.
MY LIGHT SCULPTURES DON'T DO HER ANYWHERE NEAR JUSTICE.
SHE'S FROM XAVIER'S SCHOOL. I WISH I KNEW HER NAME.
I WONDER IF THERE'S SOME WAY TO MEET...
I SAW A LIGHT, MICHAEL.
DANIELLE? IS THAT YOU?!
MS. HOGARTH!
WHY--HELLO, LARRY.
MICHAEL, I'D LIKE TO INTRODUCE A RECENT TRANSFER STUDENT TO SALEM CENTER HIGH--LARRY BODINE. LARRY, THIS IS MICHAEL XAVIER, HEADMASTER OF XAVIER'S SCHOOL. HE'S BEEN KIND ENOUGH TO HELP CHAPERONE THIS DANCE.
WHAT ARE YOU DOING OUT HERE, LARRY?
NOTHING!
I MEAN, I'M NOT DOING ANYTHING WRONG--DRINKING OR DRUGS OR STUFF LIKE THAT--
--I JUST WANTED TO BE BY MYSELF.
BELIEVE ME, I UNDERSTAND HOW ROUGH THIS MUST BE FOR YOU—A NEW TOWN, NEW SCHOOL, HAVING TO MAKE NEW FRIENDS.
BUT YOU CAN'T RUN AWAY AND HIDE FOREVER.
SO MARCH BACK INSIDE, LARRY, AND RE-JOIN THE PARTY. WHO KNOWS, YOU MIGHT EVEN FIND YOURSELF A FRIEND.
ENJOYING YOURSELF, KITTY?
YUP. SURE THING, PROFESSOR, HAVING A WONDERFUL TIME, WOULDN'T HAVE MISSED IT FOR THE WORLD, CAN I GO HOME NOW?
PERHAPS, FIRST, YOUNG LADY...
...YOU WOULDN'T MIND SHARING A DANCE WITH LARRY.
WHY NOT?
PLEASE, DON'T PUT YOURSELF OUT, I DON'T WANT TO BE A BOTHER.
NO SWEAT. NO BOTHER. I'M KITTY PRYDE.
LARRY BODINE.

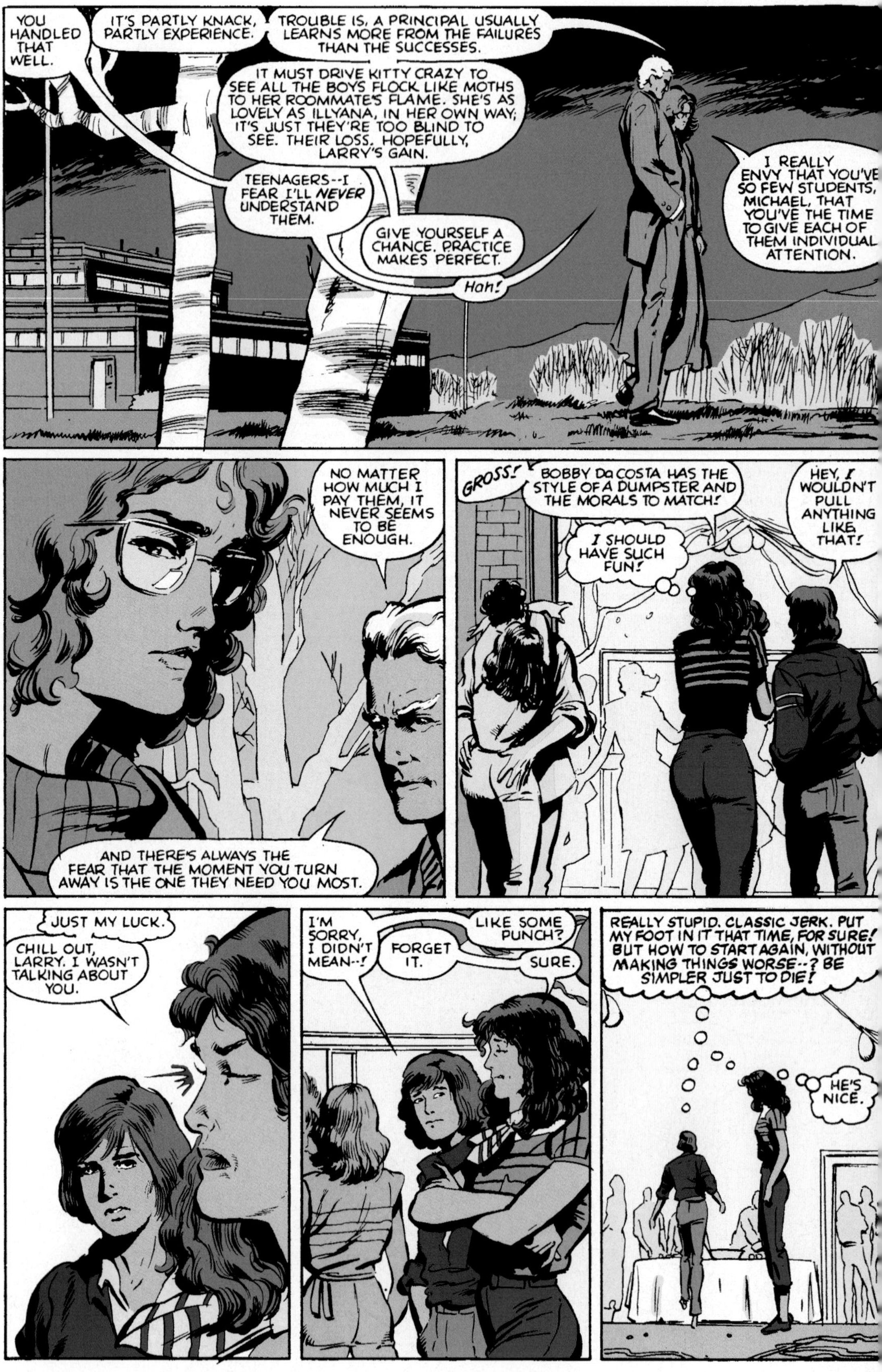

YOU HANDLED THAT WELL.
IT'S PARTLY KNACK, PARTLY EXPERIENCE.
TROUBLE IS, A PRINCIPAL USUALLY LEARNS MORE FROM THE FAILURES THAN THE SUCCESSES.
IT MUST DRIVE KITTY CRAZY TO SEE ALL THE BOYS FLOCK LIKE MOTHS TO HER ROOMMATE'S FLAME. SHE'S AS LOVELY AS ILLYANA, IN HER OWN WAY; IT'S JUST THEY'RE TOO BLIND TO SEE. THEIR LOSS. HOPEFULLY, LARRY'S GAIN.
TEENAGERS--I FEAR I'LL NEVER UNDERSTAND THEM.
GIVE YOURSELF A CHANCE. PRACTICE MAKES PERFECT.
Hah!
I REALLY ENVY THAT YOU'VE SO FEW STUDENTS, MICHAEL, THAT YOU'VE THE TIME TO GIVE EACH OF THEM INDIVIDUAL ATTENTION.
NO MATTER HOW MUCH I PAY THEM, IT NEVER SEEMS TO BE ENOUGH.
AND THERE'S ALWAYS THE FEAR THAT THE MOMENT YOU TURN AWAY IS THE ONE THEY NEED YOU MOST.
GROSS!
BOBBY Da COSTA HAS THE STYLE OF A DUMPSTER AND THE MORALS TO MATCH!
I SHOULD HAVE SUCH FUN!
HEY, I WOULDN'T PULL ANYTHING LIKE THAT!
JUST MY LUCK.
CHILL OUT, LARRY. I WASN'T TALKING ABOUT YOU.
I'M SORRY, I DIDN'T MEAN--!
LIKE SOME PUNCH?
FORGET IT.
SURE.
REALLY STUPID. CLASSIC JERK. PUT MY FOOT IN IT THAT TIME, FOR SURE! BUT HOW TO START AGAIN, WITHOUT MAKING THINGS WORSE--? BE SIMPLER JUST TO DIE!
HE'S NICE.

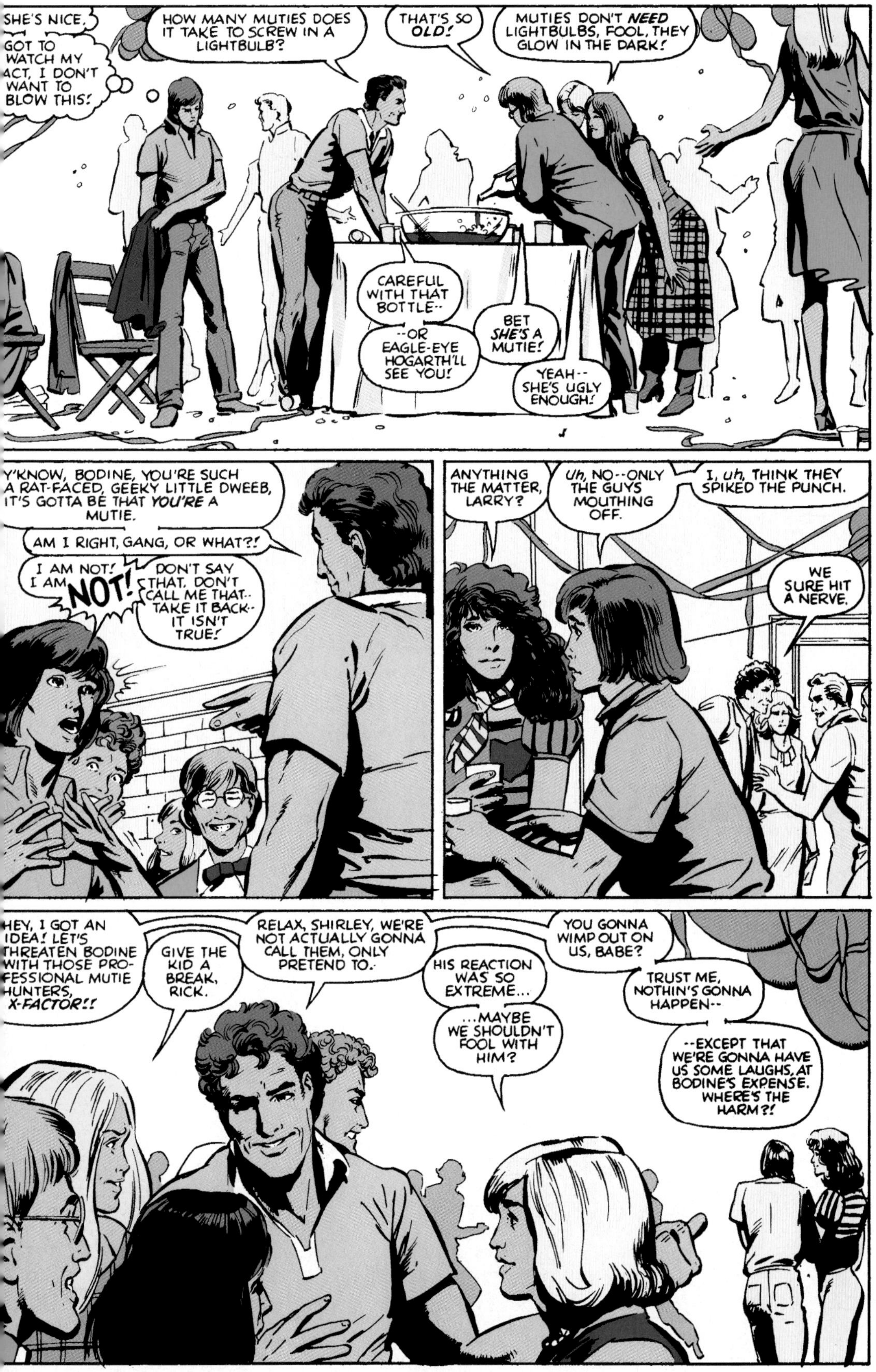
SHE'S NICE.
GOT TO WATCH MY ACT, I DON'T WANT TO BLOW THIS!
HOW MANY MUTIES DOES IT TAKE TO SCREW IN A LIGHTBULB?
THAT'S SO OLD!
MUTIES DON'T NEED LIGHTBULBS, FOOL, THEY GLOW IN THE DARK!
CAREFUL WITH THAT BOTTLE--
--OR EAGLE-EYE HOGARTH'LL SEE YOU!
BET SHE'S A MUTIE!
YEAH--SHE'S UGLY ENOUGH!
Y'KNOW, BODINE, YOU'RE SUCH A RAT-FACED, GEEKY LITTLE DWEEB, IT'S GOTTA BE THAT YOU'RE A MUTIE.
AM I RIGHT, GANG, OR WHAT?!
I AM NOT! I AM NOT!
DON'T SAY THAT. DON'T CALL ME THAT.. TAKE IT BACK.. IT ISN'T TRUE!
ANYTHING THE MATTER, LARRY?
Uh, NO--ONLY THE GUYS MOUTHING OFF.
I, uh, THINK THEY SPIKED THE PUNCH.
WE SURE HIT A NERVE.
HEY, I GOT AN IDEA! LET'S THREATEN BODINE WITH THOSE PROFESSIONAL MUTIE HUNTERS, X-FACTOR!!
GIVE THE KID A BREAK, RICK.
RELAX, SHIRLEY, WE'RE NOT ACTUALLY GONNA CALL THEM, ONLY PRETEND TO..
HIS REACTION WAS SO EXTREME...
...MAYBE WE SHOULDN'T FOOL WITH HIM?
YOU GONNA WIMP OUT ON US, BABE?
TRUST ME, NOTHIN'S GONNA HAPPEN--
--EXCEPT THAT WE'RE GONNA HAVE US SOME LAUGHS, AT BODINE'S EXPENSE. WHERE'S THE HARM?!

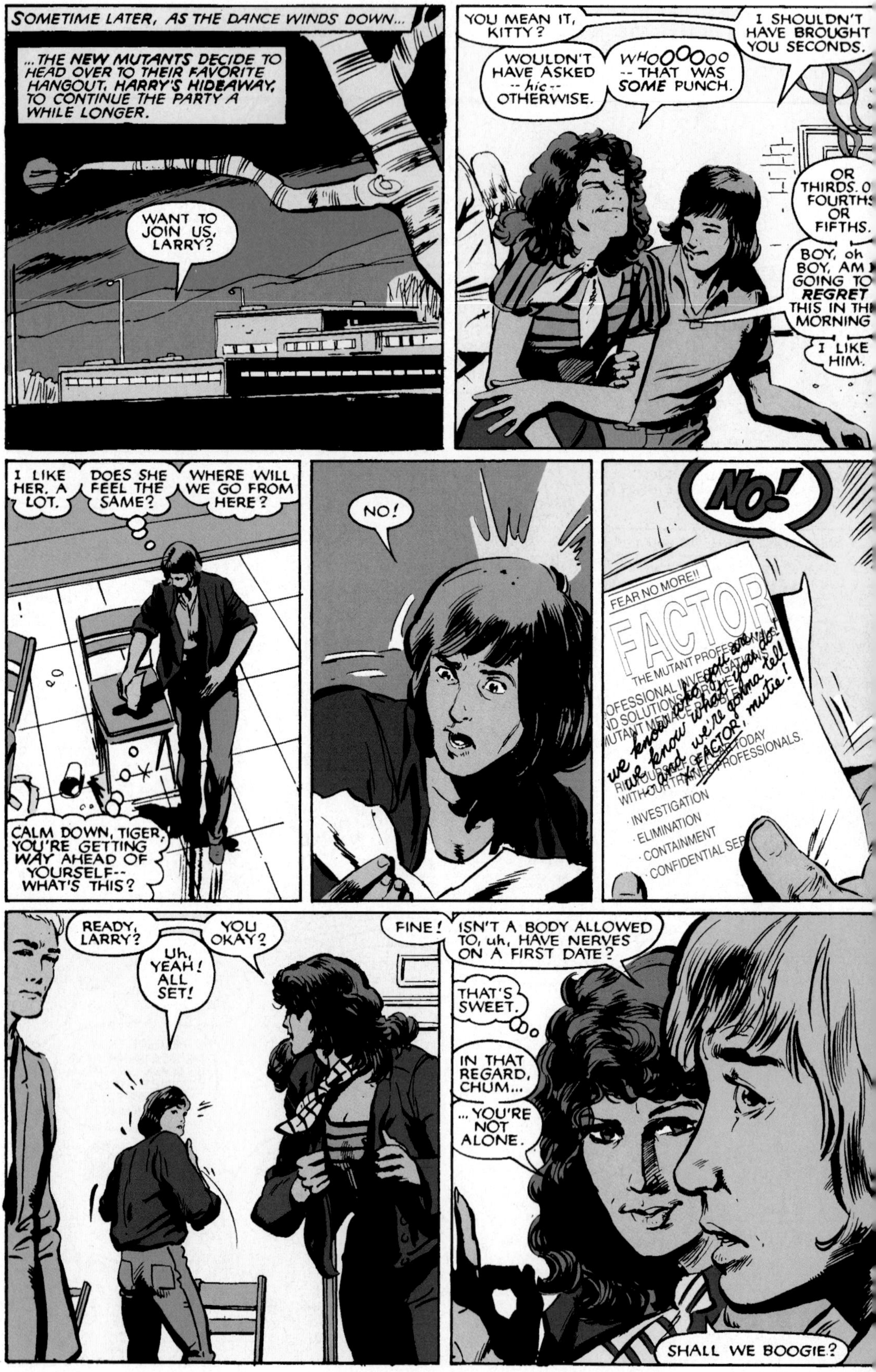
SOMETIME LATER, AS THE DANCE WINDS DOWN...
...THE NEW MUTANTS DECIDE TO HEAD OVER TO THEIR FAVORITE HANGOUT, HARRY'S HIDEAWAY, TO CONTINUE THE PARTY A WHILE LONGER.
WANT TO JOIN US, LARRY?
YOU MEAN IT, KITTY?
WOULDN'T HAVE ASKED -- hic -- OTHERWISE.
WHOOOOOO -- THAT WAS SOME PUNCH.
I SHOULDN'T HAVE BROUGHT YOU SECONDS.
OR THIRDS. O FOURTHS OR FIFTHS.
BOY, oh BOY, AM GOING TO REGRET THIS IN TH MORNING
I LIKE HIM.
I LIKE HER. A LOT.
DOES SHE FEEL THE SAME?
WHERE WILL WE GO FROM HERE?
CALM DOWN, TIGER, YOU'RE GETTING WAY AHEAD OF YOURSELF-- WHAT'S THIS?
NO!
NO!
FEAR NO MORE!!
FACTOR
THE MUTANT PROFESSIONALS
we know who you are
we know what you do!
and we're gonna tell
X-FACTOR, mutie!
INVESTIGATION
ELIMINATION
CONTAINMENT
READY, LARRY?
YOU OKAY?
Uh, YEAH! ALL SET!
FINE!
ISN'T A BODY ALLOWED TO, uh, HAVE NERVES ON A FIRST DATE?
THAT'S SWEET.
IN THAT REGARD, CHUM...
...YOU'RE NOT ALONE.
SHALL WE BOOGIE?

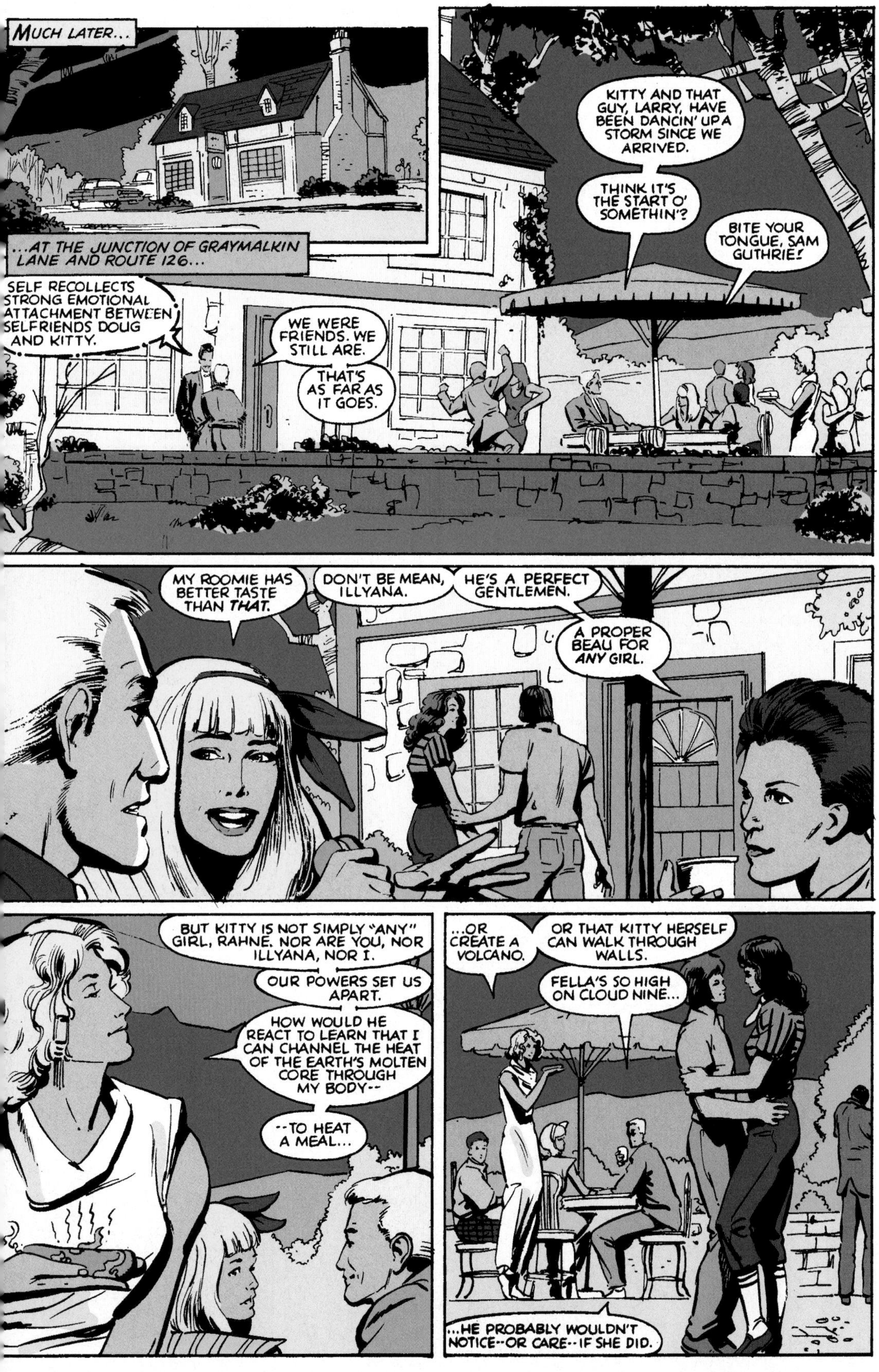
MUCH LATER...
...AT THE JUNCTION OF GRAYMALKIN LANE AND ROUTE 126...
KITTY AND THAT GUY, LARRY, HAVE BEEN DANCIN' UP A STORM SINCE WE ARRIVED.
THINK IT'S THE START O' SOMETHIN'?
BITE YOUR TONGUE, SAM GUTHRIE!
SELF RECOLLECTS STRONG EMOTIONAL ATTACHMENT BETWEEN SELFRIENDS DOUG AND KITTY.
WE WERE FRIENDS. WE STILL ARE.
THAT'S AS FAR AS IT GOES.
MY ROOMIE HAS BETTER TASTE THAN THAT.
DON'T BE MEAN, ILLYANA.
HE'S A PERFECT GENTLEMEN.
A PROPER BEAU FOR ANY GIRL.
BUT KITTY IS NOT SIMPLY "ANY" GIRL, RAHNE. NOR ARE YOU, NOR ILLYANA, NOR I.
OUR POWERS SET US APART.
HOW WOULD HE REACT TO LEARN THAT I CAN CHANNEL THE HEAT OF THE EARTH'S MOLTEN CORE THROUGH MY BODY--
--TO HEAT A MEAL...
...OR CREATE A VOLCANO.
OR THAT KITTY HERSELF CAN WALK THROUGH WALLS.
FELLA'S SO HIGH ON CLOUD NINE...
...HE PROBABLY WOULDN'T NOTICE--OR CARE--IF SHE DID.

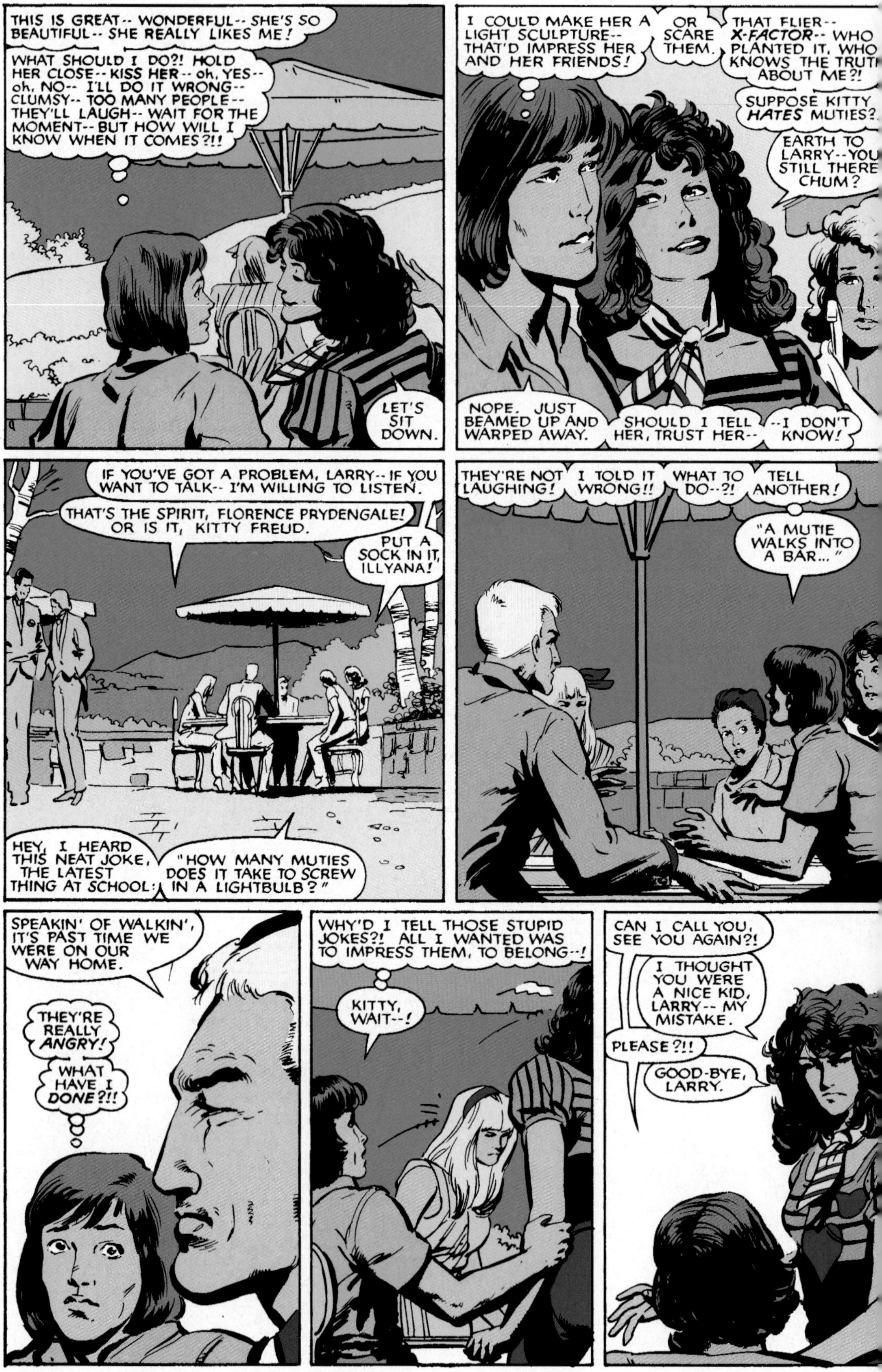
THIS IS GREAT-- WONDERFUL-- SHE'S SO BEAUTIFUL-- SHE REALLY LIKES ME!
WHAT SHOULD I DO?! HOLD HER CLOSE--KISS HER-- oh, YES-- oh, NO-- I'LL DO IT WRONG-- CLUMSY-- TOO MANY PEOPLE-- THEY'LL LAUGH-- WAIT FOR THE MOMENT-- BUT HOW WILL I KNOW WHEN IT COMES?!!
LET'S SIT DOWN.
I COULD MAKE HER A LIGHT SCULPTURE-- THAT'D IMPRESS HER AND HER FRIENDS!
OR SCARE THEM.
THAT FLIER-- X-FACTOR-- WHO PLANTED IT, WHO KNOWS THE TRUTH ABOUT ME?!
SUPPOSE KITTY HATES MUTIES?
EARTH TO LARRY--YOU STILL THERE CHUM?
NOPE. JUST BEAMED UP AND WARPED AWAY.
SHOULD I TELL HER, TRUST HER--
--I DON'T KNOW!
IF YOU'VE GOT A PROBLEM, LARRY-- IF YOU WANT TO TALK-- I'M WILLING TO LISTEN.
THAT'S THE SPIRIT, FLORENCE PRYDENGALE! OR IS IT, KITTY FREUD.
PUT A SOCK IN IT, ILLYANA!
HEY, I HEARD THIS NEAT JOKE, THE LATEST THING AT SCHOOL:
"HOW MANY MUTIES DOES IT TAKE TO SCREW IN A LIGHTBULB?"
THEY'RE NOT LAUGHING!
I TOLD IT WRONG!!
WHAT TO DO--?!
TELL ANOTHER!
"A MUTIE WALKS INTO A BAR..."
SPEAKIN' OF WALKIN', IT'S PAST TIME WE WERE ON OUR WAY HOME.
THEY'RE REALLY ANGRY!
WHAT HAVE I DONE?!!
WHY'D I TELL THOSE STUPID JOKES?! ALL I WANTED WAS TO IMPRESS THEM, TO BELONG--!
KITTY, WAIT--!
CAN I CALL YOU, SEE YOU AGAIN?!
I THOUGHT YOU WERE A NICE KID, LARRY-- MY MISTAKE.
PLEASE?!!
GOOD-BYE, LARRY.

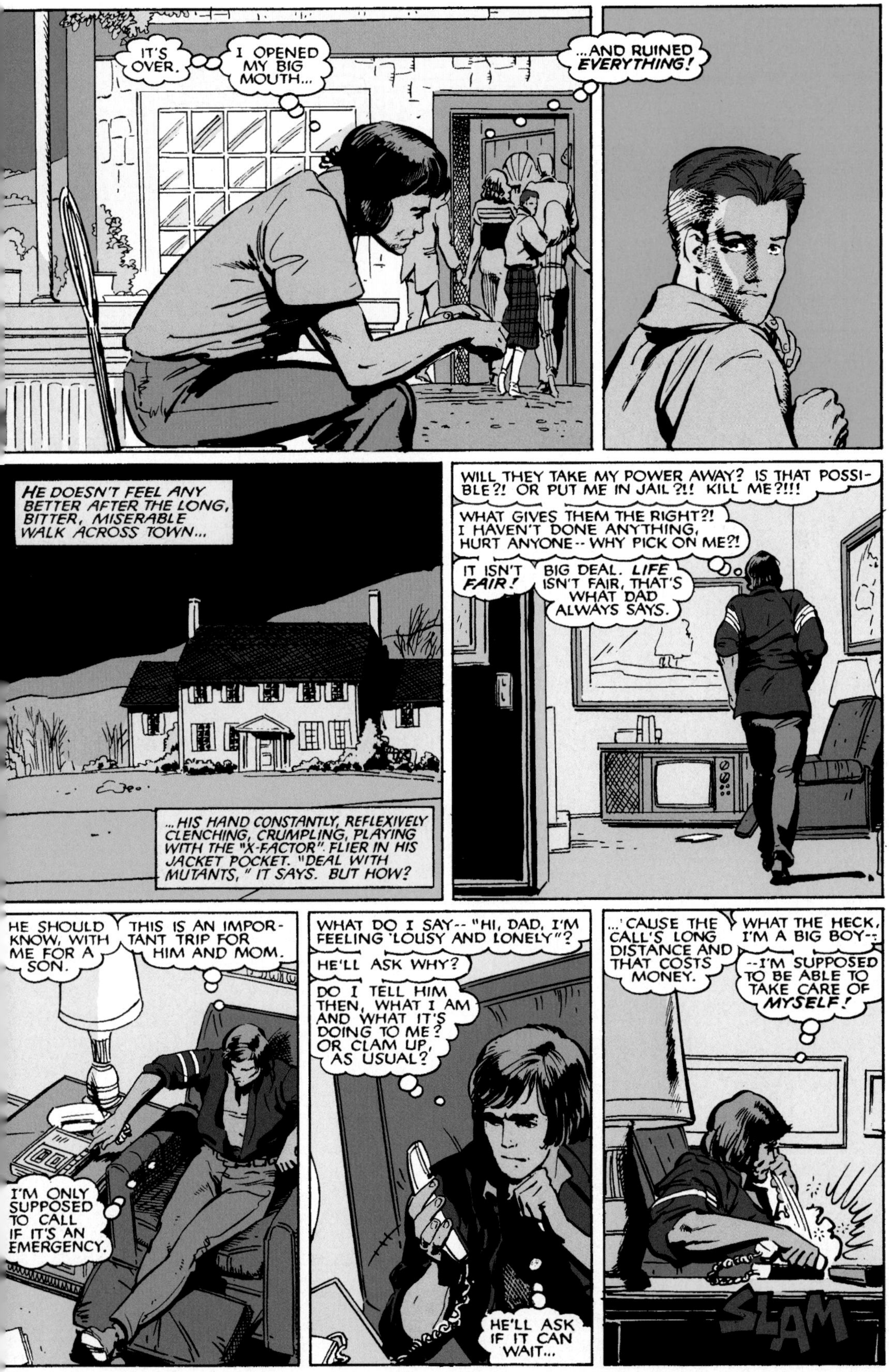
IT'S OVER.
I OPENED MY BIG MOUTH...
...AND RUINED EVERYTHING!
HE DOESN'T FEEL ANY BETTER AFTER THE LONG, BITTER, MISERABLE WALK ACROSS TOWN...
...HIS HAND CONSTANTLY, REFLEXIVELY CLENCHING, CRUMPLING, PLAYING WITH THE "X-FACTOR" FLIER IN HIS JACKET POCKET. "DEAL WITH MUTANTS," IT SAYS. BUT HOW?
WILL THEY TAKE MY POWER AWAY? IS THAT POSSIBLE?! OR PUT ME IN JAIL?!! KILL ME?!!!
WHAT GIVES THEM THE RIGHT?! I HAVEN'T DONE ANYTHING, HURT ANYONE-- WHY PICK ON ME?!
IT ISN'T FAIR!
BIG DEAL. LIFE ISN'T FAIR, THAT'S WHAT DAD ALWAYS SAYS.
HE SHOULD KNOW, WITH ME FOR A SON.
THIS IS AN IMPORTANT TRIP FOR HIM AND MOM.
I'M ONLY SUPPOSED TO CALL IF IT'S AN EMERGENCY.
WHAT DO I SAY-- "HI, DAD, I'M FEELING 'LOUSY AND LONELY"?
HE'LL ASK WHY?
DO I TELL HIM THEN, WHAT I AM AND WHAT IT'S DOING TO ME? OR CLAM UP, AS USUAL?
HE'LL ASK IF IT CAN WAIT...
...'CAUSE THE CALL'S LONG DISTANCE AND THAT COSTS MONEY.
WHAT THE HECK, I'M A BIG BOY--
--I'M SUPPOSED TO BE ABLE TO TAKE CARE OF MYSELF!
SLAM

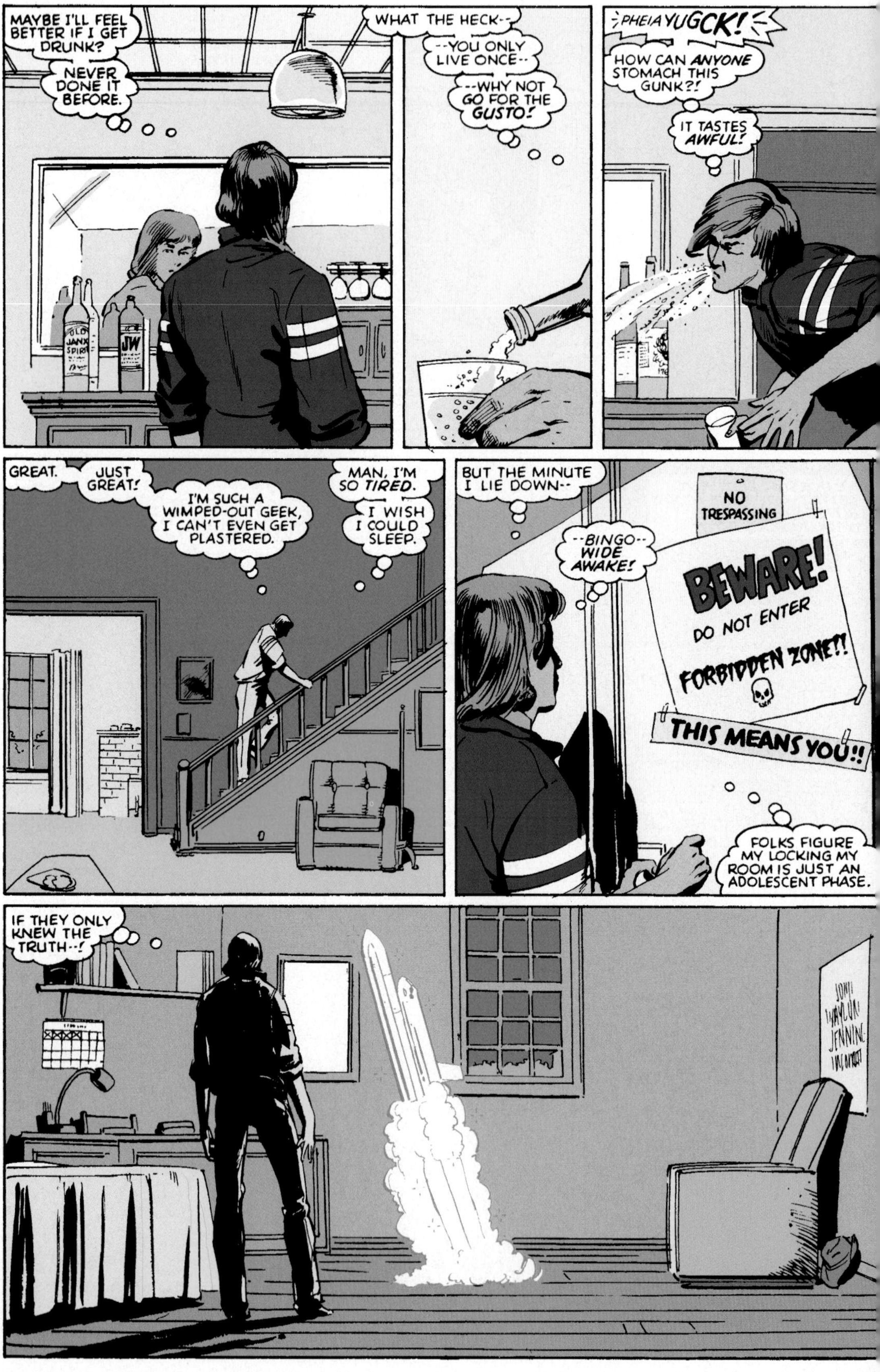

MAYBE I'LL FEEL BETTER IF I GET DRUNK?
NEVER DONE IT BEFORE.
OLD JANX SPIRIT
JW
WHAT THE HECK--
--YOU ONLY LIVE ONCE--
--WHY NOT GO FOR THE GUSTO!
PHEIA YUGCK!
HOW CAN ANYONE STOMACH THIS GUNK?!
IT TASTES AWFUL!
GREAT.
JUST GREAT!
I'M SUCH A WIMPED-OUT GEEK, I CAN'T EVEN GET PLASTERED.
MAN, I'M SO TIRED.
I WISH I COULD SLEEP.
BUT THE MINUTE I LIE DOWN--
--BINGO--WIDE AWAKE!
NO TRESPASSING
BEWARE!
DO NOT ENTER
FORBIDDEN ZONE!!
THIS MEANS YOU!!
FOLKS FIGURE MY LOCKING MY ROOM IS JUST AN ADOLESCENT PHASE.
IF THEY ONLY KNEW THE TRUTH--!

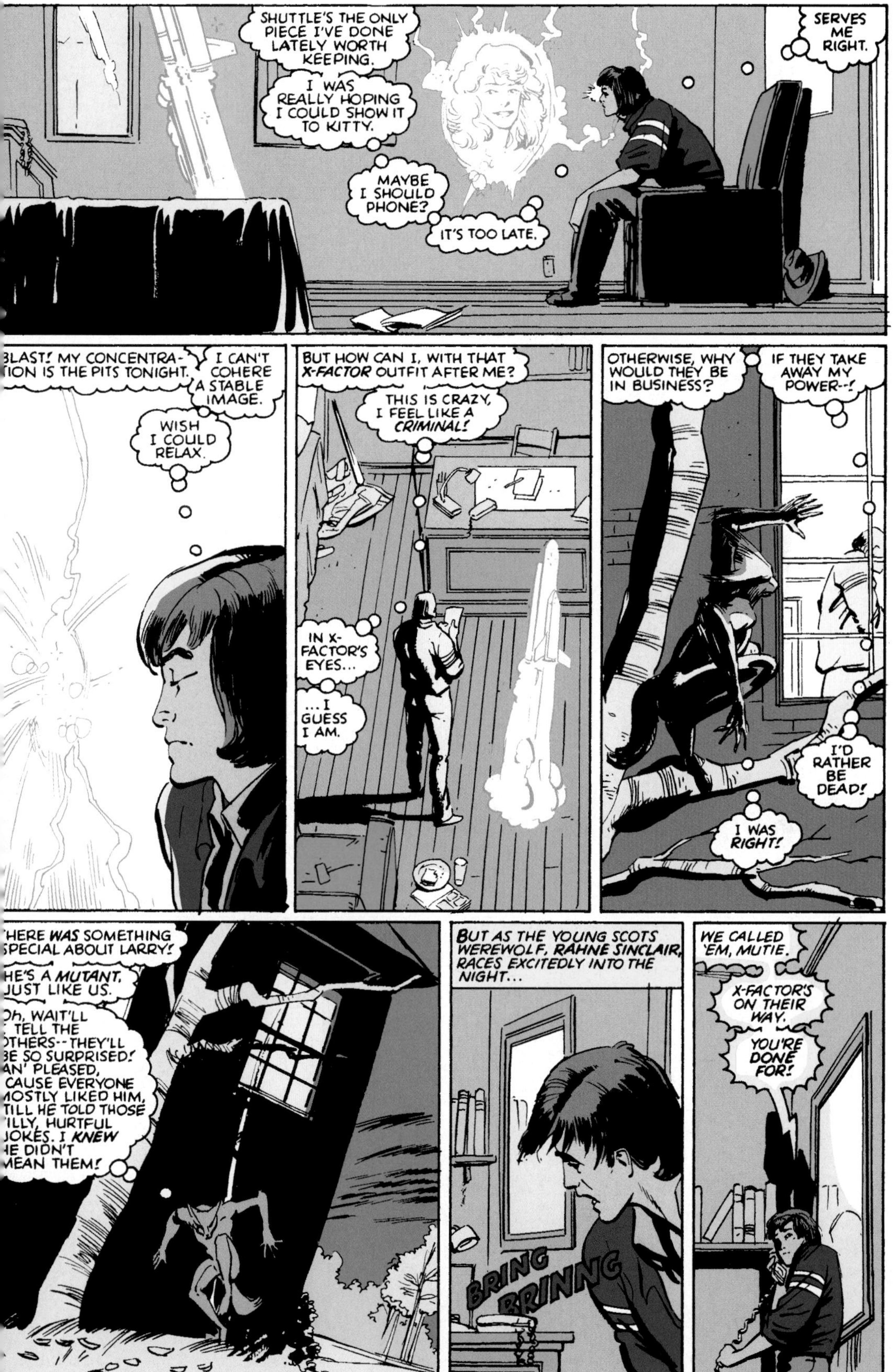
SHUTTLE'S THE ONLY PIECE I'VE DONE LATELY WORTH KEEPING.
I WAS REALLY HOPING I COULD SHOW IT TO KITTY.
MAYBE I SHOULD PHONE?
IT'S TOO LATE.
SERVES ME RIGHT.
BLAST! MY CONCENTRATION IS THE PITS TONIGHT.
I CAN'T COHERE A STABLE IMAGE.
WISH I COULD RELAX.
BUT HOW CAN I, WITH THAT X-FACTOR OUTFIT AFTER ME?
THIS IS CRAZY, I FEEL LIKE A CRIMINAL!
IN X-FACTOR'S EYES...
...I GUESS I AM.
OTHERWISE, WHY WOULD THEY BE IN BUSINESS?
IF THEY TAKE AWAY MY POWER--!
I'D RATHER BE DEAD!
I WAS RIGHT!
HERE WAS SOMETHING SPECIAL ABOUT LARRY!
HE'S A MUTANT, JUST LIKE US.
OH, WAIT'LL I TELL THE OTHERS--THEY'LL BE SO SURPRISED! AN' PLEASED, 'CAUSE EVERYONE MOSTLY LIKED HIM, TILL HE TOLD THOSE SILLY, HURTFUL JOKES. I KNEW HE DIDN'T MEAN THEM!
BUT AS THE YOUNG SCOTS WEREWOLF, RAHNE SINCLAIR, RACES EXCITEDLY INTO THE NIGHT...
BRING BRINNG
WE CALLED 'EM, MUTIE.
X-FACTOR'S ON THEIR WAY.
YOU'RE DONE FOR!

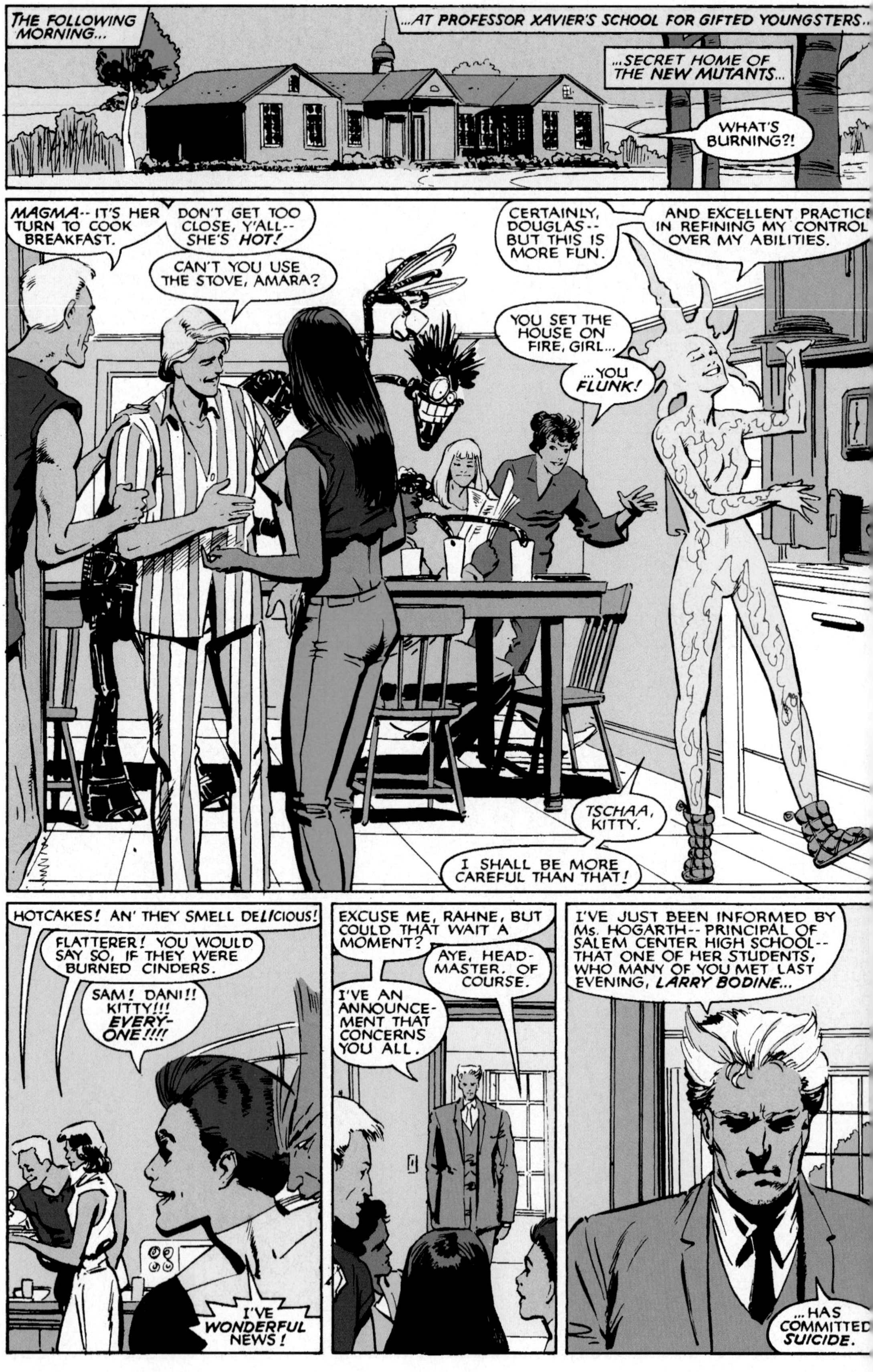

THE FOLLOWING MORNING...
...AT PROFESSOR XAVIER'S SCHOOL FOR GIFTED YOUNGSTERS...
...SECRET HOME OF THE NEW MUTANTS...
WHAT'S BURNING?!
MAGMA-- IT'S HER TURN TO COOK BREAKFAST.
DON'T GET TOO CLOSE, Y'ALL-- SHE'S HOT!
CAN'T YOU USE THE STOVE, AMARA?
CERTAINLY, DOUGLAS-- BUT THIS IS MORE FUN.
AND EXCELLENT PRACTICE IN REFINING MY CONTROL OVER MY ABILITIES.
YOU SET THE HOUSE ON FIRE, GIRL...
...YOU FLUNK!
TSCHAA, KITTY.
I SHALL BE MORE CAREFUL THAN THAT!
HOTCAKES! AN' THEY SMELL DELICIOUS!
FLATTERER! YOU WOULD SAY SO, IF THEY WERE BURNED CINDERS.
SAM! DANI!! KITTY!!! EVERY-ONE!!!!
I'VE WONDERFUL NEWS!
EXCUSE ME, RAHNE, BUT COULD THAT WAIT A MOMENT?
AYE, HEAD-MASTER. OF COURSE.
I'VE AN ANNOUNCE-MENT THAT CONCERNS YOU ALL.
I'VE JUST BEEN INFORMED BY Ms. HOGARTH-- PRINCIPAL OF SALEM CENTER HIGH SCHOOL-- THAT ONE OF HER STUDENTS, WHO MANY OF YOU MET LAST EVENING, LARRY BODINE...
...HAS COMMITTED SUICIDE.

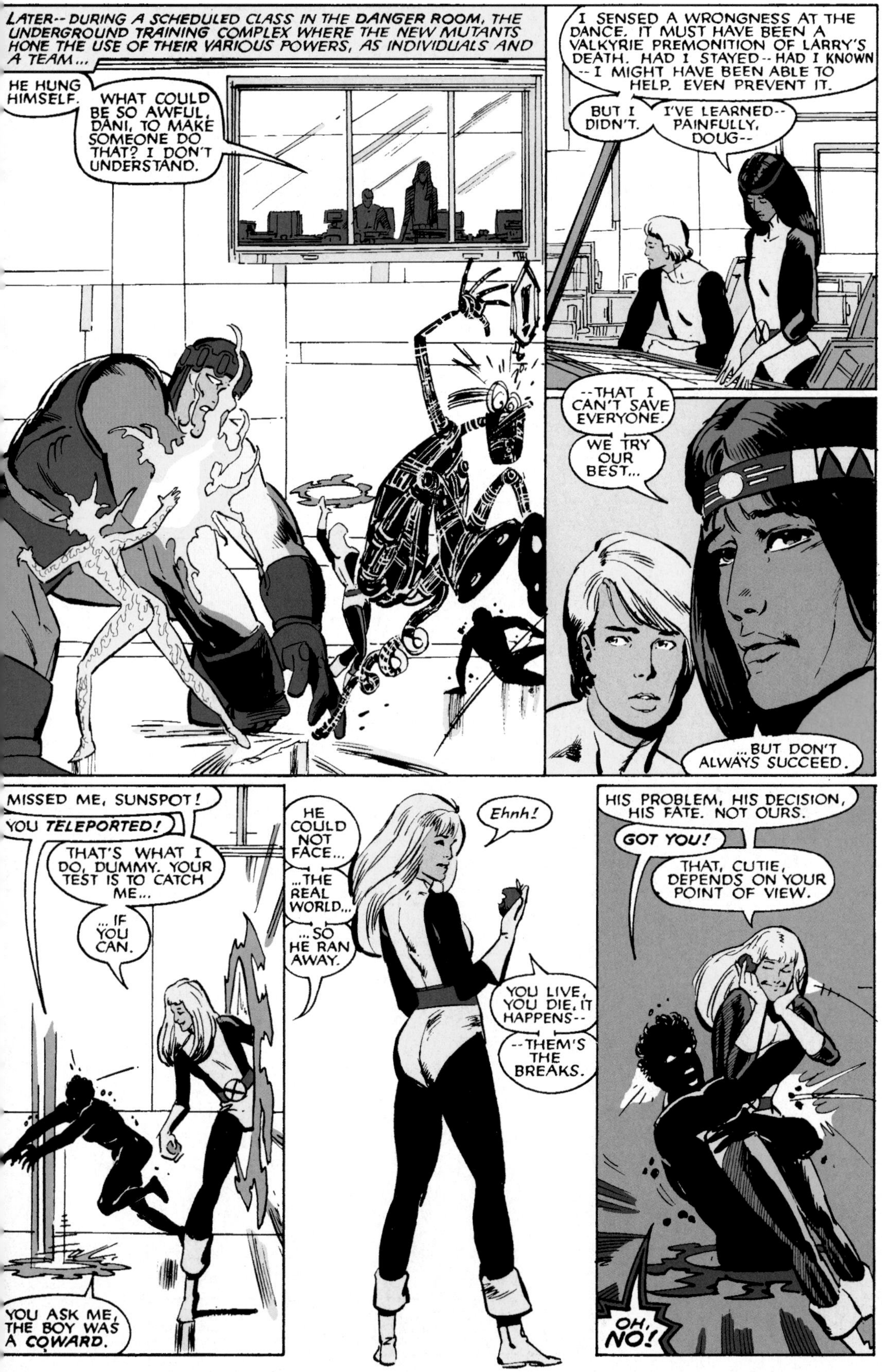

LATER-- DURING A SCHEDULED CLASS IN THE DANGER ROOM, THE UNDERGROUND TRAINING COMPLEX WHERE THE NEW MUTANTS HONE THE USE OF THEIR VARIOUS POWERS, AS INDIVIDUALS AND A TEAM...
HE HUNG HIMSELF.
WHAT COULD BE SO AWFUL, DANI, TO MAKE SOMEONE DO THAT? I DON'T UNDERSTAND.
I SENSED A WRONGNESS AT THE DANCE. IT MUST HAVE BEEN A VALKYRIE PREMONITION OF LARRY'S DEATH. HAD I STAYED--HAD I KNOWN--I MIGHT HAVE BEEN ABLE TO HELP. EVEN PREVENT IT.
BUT I DIDN'T.
I'VE LEARNED-- PAINFULLY, DOUG--
--THAT I CAN'T SAVE EVERYONE.
WE TRY OUR BEST...
...BUT DON'T ALWAYS SUCCEED.
MISSED ME, SUNSPOT!
YOU TELEPORTED!
THAT'S WHAT I DO, DUMMY. YOUR TEST IS TO CATCH ME...
...IF YOU CAN.
YOU ASK ME, THE BOY WAS A COWARD.
HE COULD NOT FACE...
...THE REAL WORLD...
...SO HE RAN AWAY.
Ehnh!
YOU LIVE, YOU DIE, IT HAPPENS--
--THEM'S THE BREAKS.
HIS PROBLEM, HIS DECISION, HIS FATE. NOT OURS.
GOT YOU!
THAT, CUTIE, DEPENDS ON YOUR POINT OF VIEW.
OH, NO!

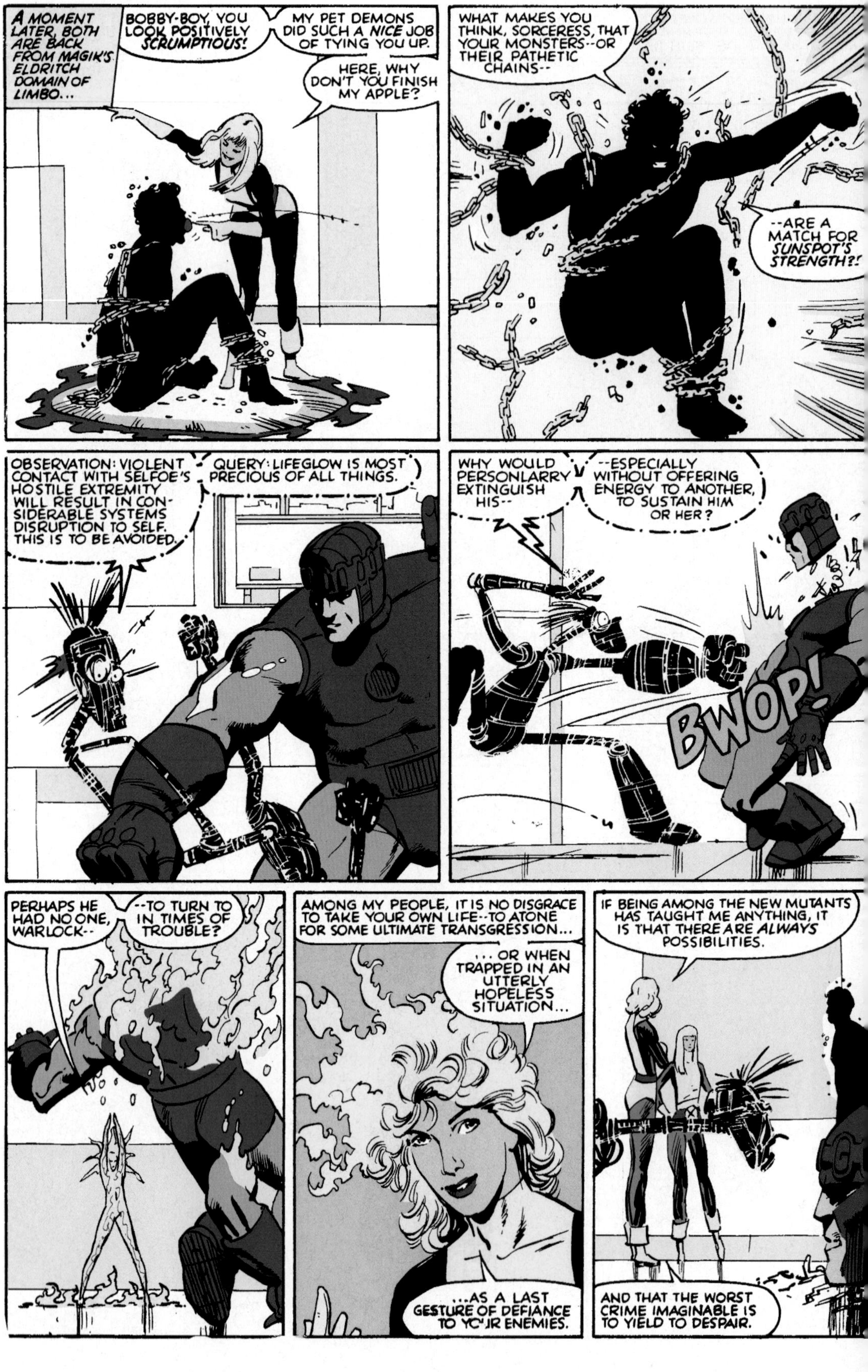

A MOMENT LATER, BOTH ARE BACK FROM MAGIK'S ELDRITCH DOMAIN OF LIMBO...
BOBBY-BOY, YOU LOOK POSITIVELY SCRUMPTIOUS!
MY PET DEMONS DID SUCH A NICE JOB OF TYING YOU UP.
HERE, WHY DON'T YOU FINISH MY APPLE?
WHAT MAKES YOU THINK, SORCERESS, THAT YOUR MONSTERS--OR THEIR PATHETIC CHAINS--
--ARE A MATCH FOR SUNSPOT'S STRENGTH?!
OBSERVATION: VIOLENT CONTACT WITH SELFOE'S HOSTILE EXTREMITY WILL RESULT IN CONSIDERABLE SYSTEMS DISRUPTION TO SELF. THIS IS TO BE AVOIDED.
QUERY: LIFEGLOW IS MOST PRECIOUS OF ALL THINGS.
WHY WOULD PERSONLARRY EXTINGUISH HIS--
--ESPECIALLY WITHOUT OFFERING ENERGY TO ANOTHER, TO SUSTAIN HIM OR HER?
BWOP!
PERHAPS HE HAD NO ONE, WARLOCK--
--TO TURN TO IN TIMES OF TROUBLE?
AMONG MY PEOPLE, IT IS NO DISGRACE TO TAKE YOUR OWN LIFE--TO ATONE FOR SOME ULTIMATE TRANSGRESSION...
...OR WHEN TRAPPED IN AN UTTERLY HOPELESS SITUATION...
...AS A LAST GESTURE OF DEFIANCE TO YOUR ENEMIES.
IF BEING AMONG THE NEW MUTANTS HAS TAUGHT ME ANYTHING, IT IS THAT THERE ARE ALWAYS POSSIBILITIES.
AND THAT THE WORST CRIME IMAGINABLE IS TO YIELD TO DESPAIR.

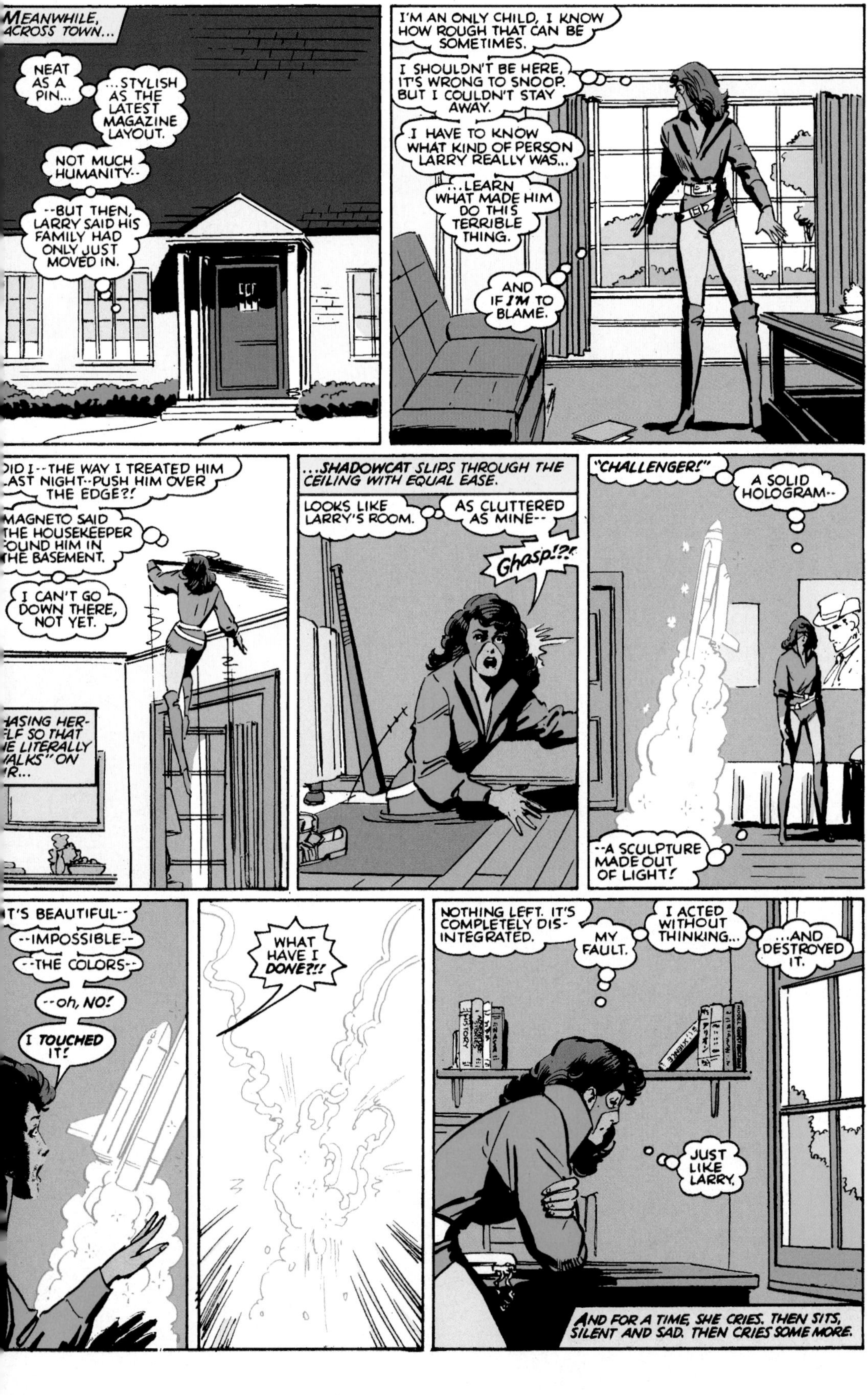
MEANWHILE, ACROSS TOWN...
NEAT AS A PIN...
...STYLISH AS THE LATEST MAGAZINE LAYOUT.
NOT MUCH HUMANITY--
--BUT THEN, LARRY SAID HIS FAMILY HAD ONLY JUST MOVED IN.
I'M AN ONLY CHILD, I KNOW HOW ROUGH THAT CAN BE SOMETIMES.
I SHOULDN'T BE HERE, IT'S WRONG TO SNOOP. BUT I COULDN'T STAY AWAY.
I HAVE TO KNOW WHAT KIND OF PERSON LARRY REALLY WAS...
...LEARN WHAT MADE HIM DO THIS TERRIBLE THING.
AND IF I'M TO BLAME.
DID I--THE WAY I TREATED HIM LAST NIGHT--PUSH HIM OVER THE EDGE?!
MAGNETO SAID THE HOUSEKEEPER FOUND HIM IN THE BASEMENT.
I CAN'T GO DOWN THERE, NOT YET.
HASING HER- ELF SO THAT HE LITERALLY WALKS" ON R...
...SHADOWCAT SLIPS THROUGH THE CEILING WITH EQUAL EASE.
LOOKS LIKE LARRY'S ROOM.
AS CLUTTERED AS MINE--
Ghasp!?!
"CHALLENGER!"
A SOLID HOLOGRAM--
--A SCULPTURE MADE OUT OF LIGHT!
IT'S BEAUTIFUL--
--IMPOSSIBLE--
--THE COLORS--
--oh, NO!
I TOUCHED IT!
WHAT HAVE I DONE?!!
NOTHING LEFT. IT'S COMPLETELY DIS- INTEGRATED.
MY FAULT.
I ACTED WITHOUT THINKING...
...AND DESTROYED IT.
JUST LIKE LARRY.
AND FOR A TIME, SHE CRIES. THEN SITS, SILENT AND SAD. THEN CRIES SOME MORE.

UNTIL... WHAT'S THIS?

SOME SORT OF AD FLIER-- OUTFIT CALLED "X-FACTOR". ARE THEY FOR *REAL?!*

THERE'S WRITING ON THE BACK.

"THEY'RE COMING TO GET ME! WHERE CAN I GO? WHAT CAN I DO? WHAT'S THE POINT IF I CAN'T CREATE?"

"WHY DO THEY HATE ME WHAT HAVE I DONE?!"

"I'M ALONE. NOTHING LEFT. NO WAY OUT."

"I'M SORRY."

OH, LARRY!

I'M SORRY, TOO.

YOU WERE A MUTANT, LIKE US. BUT WE NEVER KNEW.

I DID. I FOLLOWED HIM HOME LAST NIGHT.

WOLFSBANE--?!

HE SEEMED SO SAD AND HURT.

WHAT HE SAID TO US WAS STUPID AND CRUEL, BUT I SENSED HE HAD A GOOD HEART. I MEANT TO TELL YOU ALL, BUT EVERYONE WAS IN BED WHEN I RE- TURNED HOME AND I FELL ASLEEP, AND IN THE MORNING IT WAS TOO LATE.

IT'S NOT YOUR FAULT.

HE WAS SCARED. BOXED IN.

IF ANYONE'S RESPONSIBLE, IT'S THE PEOPLE WHO SENT HIM THIS.

YOU SAW HIS WORK, RAHNE. IMAGINE WHAT HE COULD HAVE DONE...

ALL THAT BEAUTY-- LOST FOREVER.

WHAT A WASTE.

SNIF SNIF

THE SPALEENS' SCENTS ARE ON THIS PAPER. I'LL FIND THEM AND-- BY THE HOLY ROOD--

--I'LL MAKE THEM *PAY!*

SHE HOWLS.

...POURING HER HEART INTO A SONG OF PAIN AND LOSS--AND *VENGEANCE.*

ARRRAOOOOOOOARRRAOOOOOOOOO

WHAT--?!

JIM, LET'S GO AWAY, I CAN'T--!

WE MUST, MARY

BUT MY BABY--!

TELL ME THIS IS A DREAM, JIM! PLEASE, DEAR LORD, LET LARRY BE ALL RIGHT!

I WISH I COULD, MARY.

BUT OUR SON IS DEAD.

100

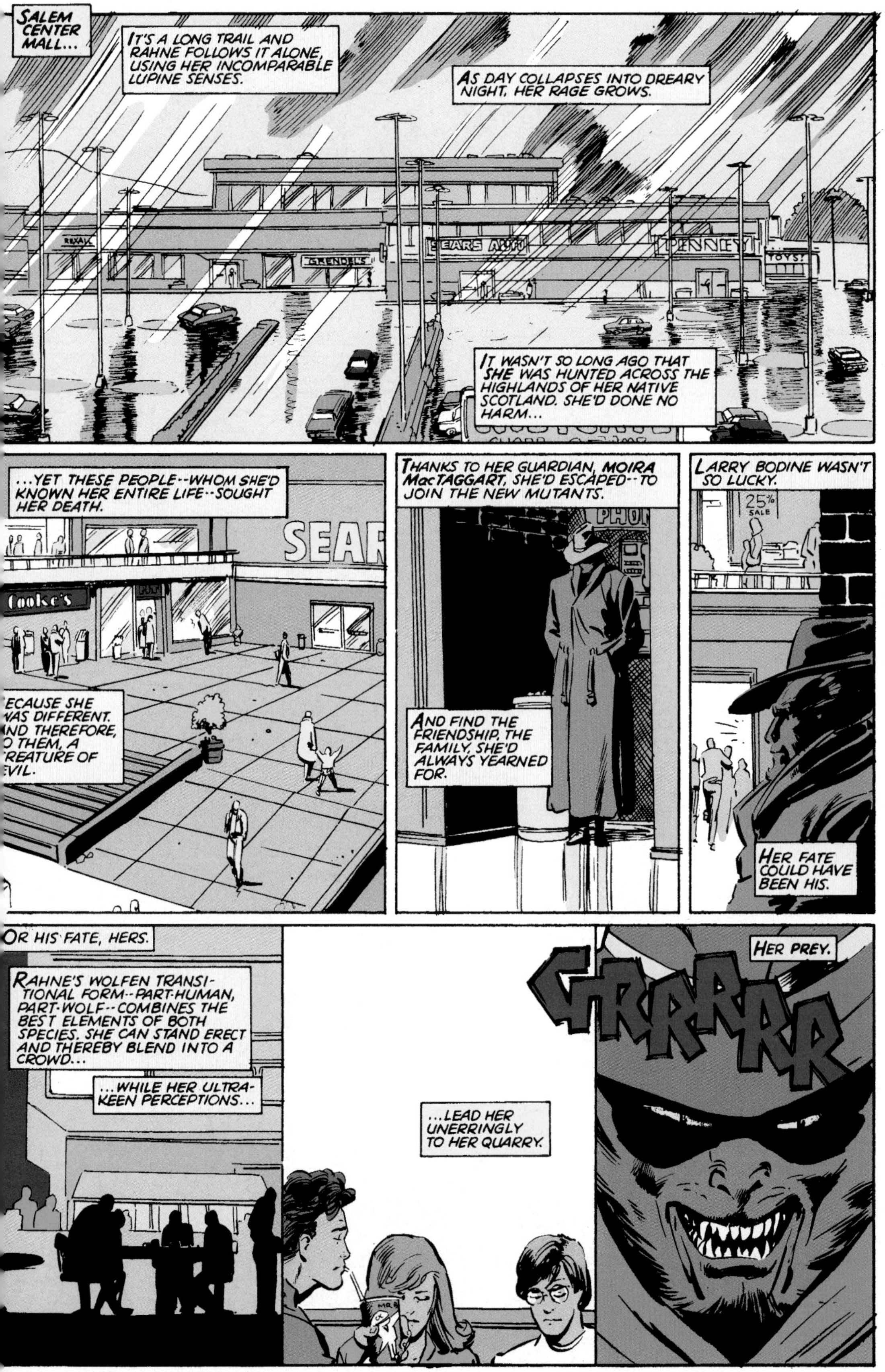
SALEM CENTER MALL...
IT'S A LONG TRAIL AND RAHNE FOLLOWS IT ALONE, USING HER INCOMPARABLE LUPINE SENSES.
AS DAY COLLAPSES INTO DREARY NIGHT, HER RAGE GROWS.
REXALL
GRENDEL'S
SEARS AUTO
PENNEY
TOYS!
IT WASN'T SO LONG AGO THAT SHE WAS HUNTED ACROSS THE HIGHLANDS OF HER NATIVE SCOTLAND. SHE'D DONE NO HARM...
...YET THESE PEOPLE--WHOM SHE'D KNOWN HER ENTIRE LIFE--SOUGHT HER DEATH.
SEAR
Cooke's
ECAUSE SHE VAS DIFFERENT. ND THEREFORE, O THEM, A REATURE OF VIL.
THANKS TO HER GUARDIAN, MOIRA MacTAGGART, SHE'D ESCAPED--TO JOIN THE NEW MUTANTS.
PHON
AND FIND THE FRIENDSHIP, THE FAMILY, SHE'D ALWAYS YEARNED FOR.
LARRY BODINE WASN'T SO LUCKY.
25% SALE
HER FATE COULD HAVE BEEN HIS.
OR HIS FATE, HERS.
RAHNE'S WOLFEN TRANSI-TIONAL FORM--PART-HUMAN, PART-WOLF--COMBINES THE BEST ELEMENTS OF BOTH SPECIES. SHE CAN STAND ERECT AND THEREBY BLEND INTO A CROWD...
...WHILE HER ULTRA-KEEN PERCEPTIONS...
...LEAD HER UNERRINGLY TO HER QUARRY.
HER PREY.
GRRRRR

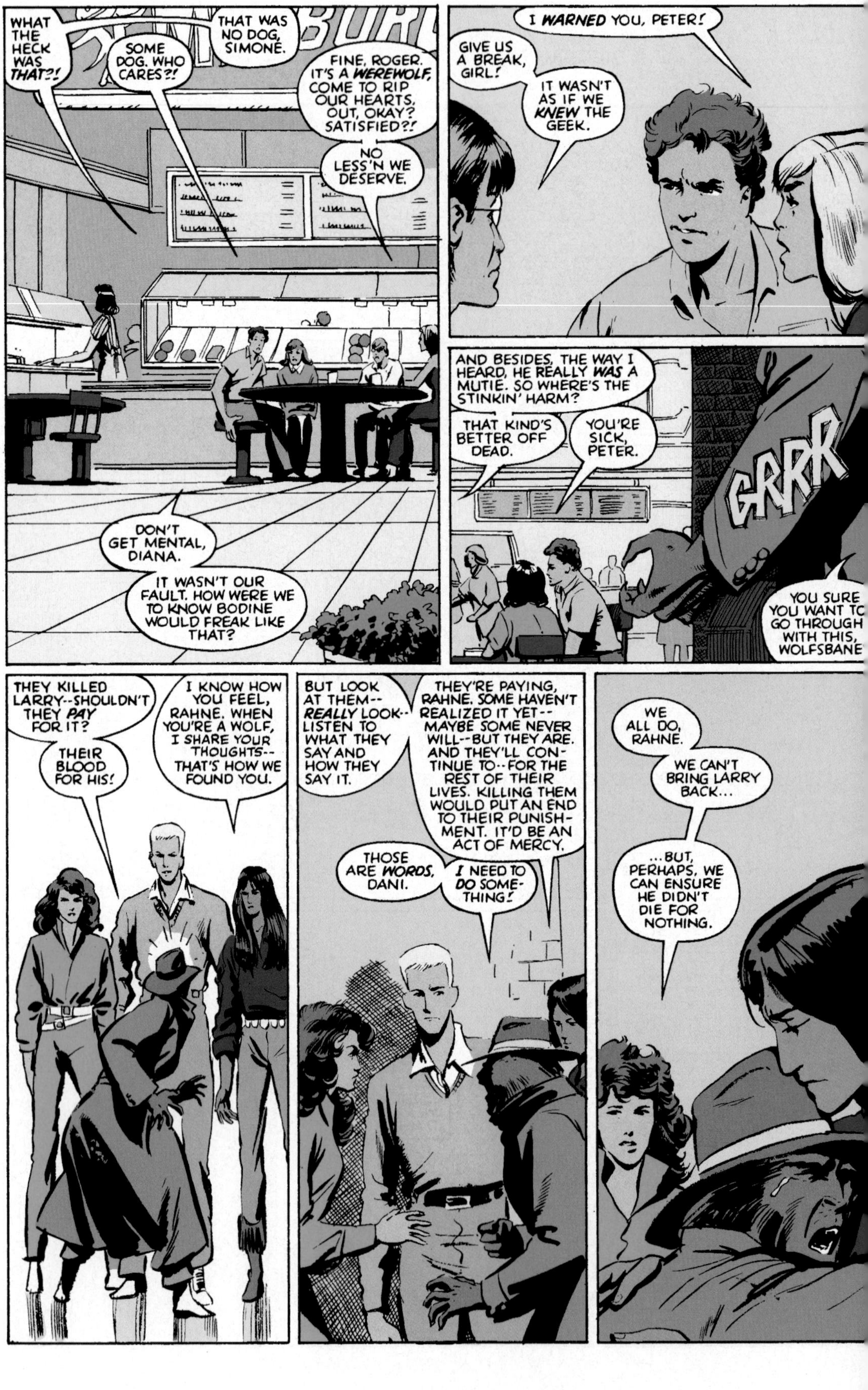
WHAT THE HECK WAS THAT?!
SOME DOG. WHO CARES?!
THAT WAS NO DOG, SIMONE.
FINE, ROGER. IT'S A WEREWOLF, COME TO RIP OUR HEARTS OUT, OKAY? SATISFIED?!
NO LESS'N WE DESERVE.
DON'T GET MENTAL, DIANA.
IT WASN'T OUR FAULT. HOW WERE WE TO KNOW BODINE WOULD FREAK LIKE THAT?
I WARNED YOU, PETER!
GIVE US A BREAK, GIRL!
IT WASN'T AS IF WE KNEW THE GEEK.
AND BESIDES, THE WAY I HEARD, HE REALLY WAS A MUTIE. SO WHERE'S THE STINKIN' HARM?
THAT KIND'S BETTER OFF DEAD.
YOU'RE SICK, PETER.
GRRR
YOU SURE YOU WANT TO GO THROUGH WITH THIS, WOLFSBANE
THEY KILLED LARRY--SHOULDN'T THEY PAY FOR IT?
THEIR BLOOD FOR HIS!
I KNOW HOW YOU FEEL, RAHNE. WHEN YOU'RE A WOLF, I SHARE YOUR THOUGHTS--THAT'S HOW WE FOUND YOU.
BUT LOOK AT THEM--REALLY LOOK--LISTEN TO WHAT THEY SAY AND HOW THEY SAY IT.
THEY'RE PAYING, RAHNE. SOME HAVEN'T REALIZED IT YET--MAYBE SOME NEVER WILL--BUT THEY ARE. AND THEY'LL CONTINUE TO--FOR THE REST OF THEIR LIVES. KILLING THEM WOULD PUT AN END TO THEIR PUNISHMENT. IT'D BE AN ACT OF MERCY.
THOSE ARE WORDS, DANI.
I NEED TO DO SOMETHING!
WE ALL DO, RAHNE.
WE CAN'T BRING LARRY BACK...
...BUT, PERHAPS, WE CAN ENSURE HE DIDN'T DIE FOR NOTHING.

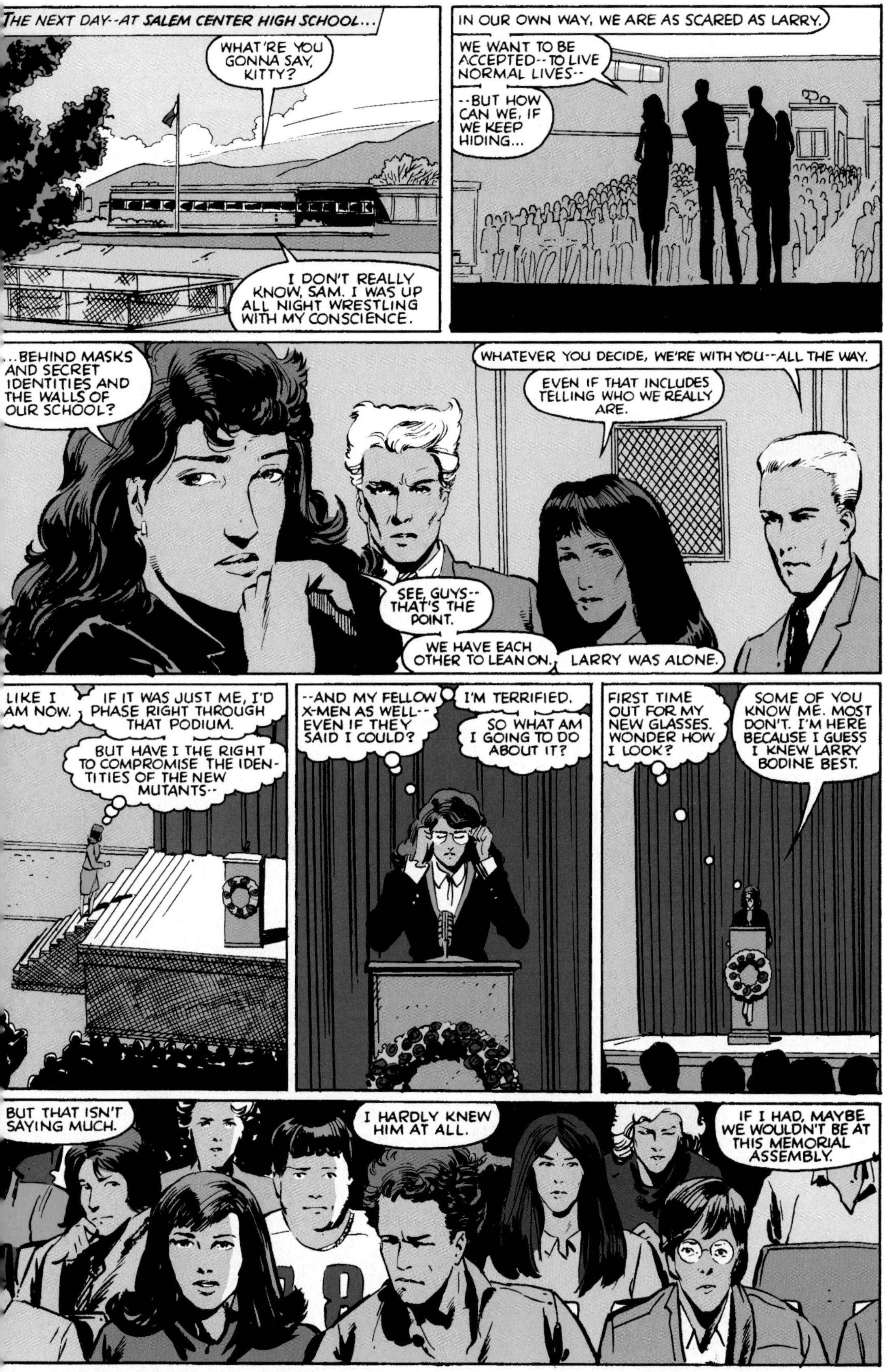
THE NEXT DAY--AT SALEM CENTER HIGH SCHOOL...
WHAT'RE YOU GONNA SAY, KITTY?
I DON'T REALLY KNOW, SAM. I WAS UP ALL NIGHT WRESTLING WITH MY CONSCIENCE.
IN OUR OWN WAY, WE ARE AS SCARED AS LARRY.
WE WANT TO BE ACCEPTED--TO LIVE NORMAL LIVES--
--BUT HOW CAN WE, IF WE KEEP HIDING...
...BEHIND MASKS AND SECRET IDENTITIES AND THE WALLS OF OUR SCHOOL?
WHATEVER YOU DECIDE, WE'RE WITH YOU--ALL THE WAY.
EVEN IF THAT INCLUDES TELLING WHO WE REALLY ARE.
SEE, GUYS--THAT'S THE POINT.
WE HAVE EACH OTHER TO LEAN ON.
LARRY WAS ALONE.
LIKE I AM NOW.
IF IT WAS JUST ME, I'D PHASE RIGHT THROUGH THAT PODIUM.
BUT HAVE I THE RIGHT TO COMPROMISE THE IDENTITIES OF THE NEW MUTANTS--
--AND MY FELLOW X-MEN AS WELL--EVEN IF THEY SAID I COULD?
I'M TERRIFIED.
SO WHAT AM I GOING TO DO ABOUT IT?
FIRST TIME OUT FOR MY NEW GLASSES. WONDER HOW I LOOK?
SOME OF YOU KNOW ME. MOST DON'T. I'M HERE BECAUSE I GUESS I KNEW LARRY BODINE BEST.
BUT THAT ISN'T SAYING MUCH.
I HARDLY KNEW HIM AT ALL.
IF I HAD, MAYBE WE WOULDN'T BE AT THIS MEMORIAL ASSEMBLY.

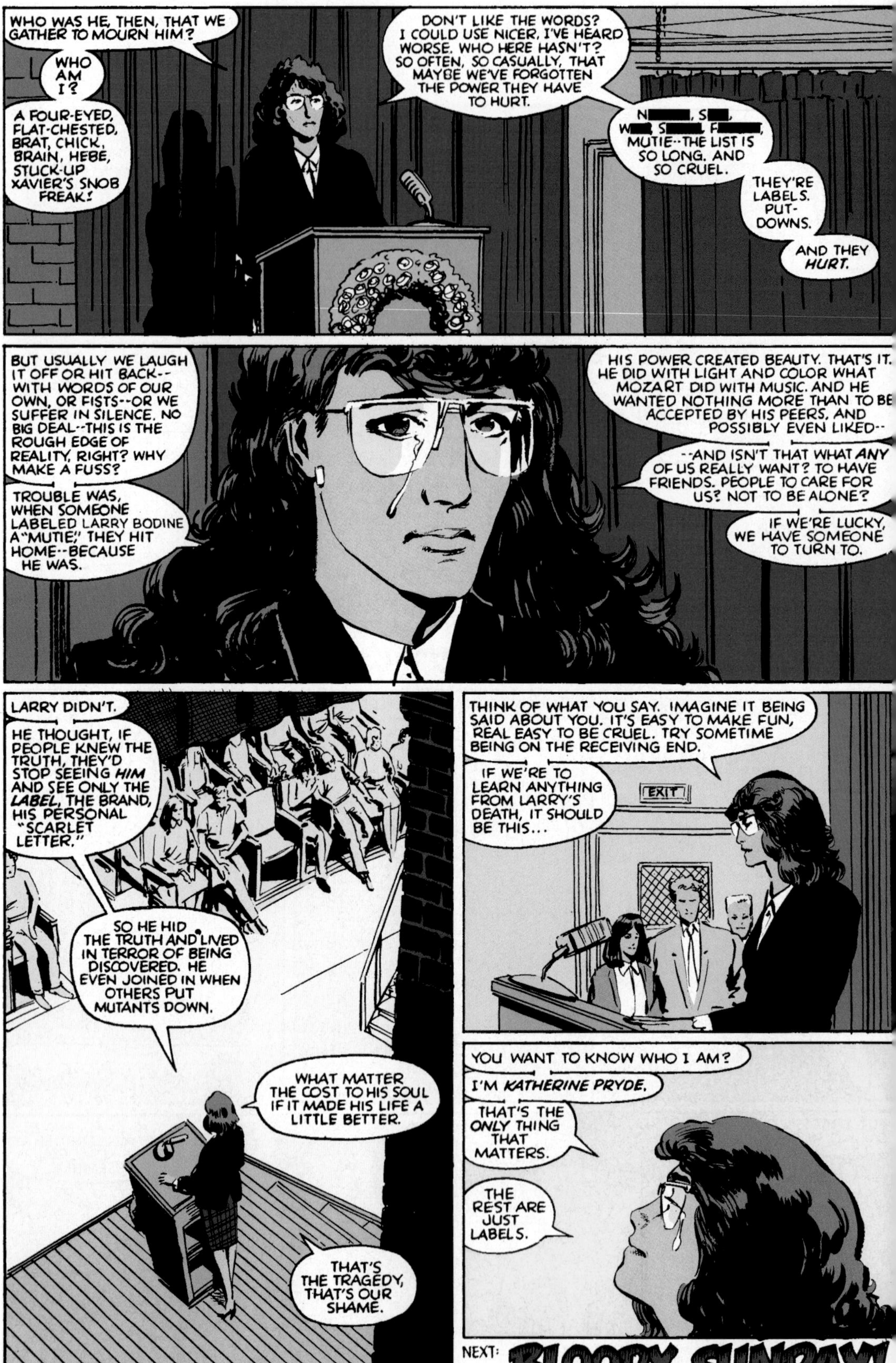

WHO WAS HE, THEN, THAT WE GATHER TO MOURN HIM?
WHO AM I?
A FOUR-EYED, FLAT-CHESTED, BRAT, CHICK, BRAIN, HEBE, STUCK-UP XAVIER'S SNOB FREAK!
DON'T LIKE THE WORDS? I COULD USE NICER. I'VE HEARD WORSE. WHO HERE HASN'T? SO OFTEN, SO CASUALLY, THAT MAYBE WE'VE FORGOTTEN THE POWER THEY HAVE TO HURT.
N[redacted], S[redacted], W[redacted], S[redacted], F[redacted], MUTIE--THE LIST IS SO LONG. AND SO CRUEL.
THEY'RE LABELS. PUT-DOWNS.
AND THEY *HURT.*
BUT USUALLY WE LAUGH IT OFF OR HIT BACK--WITH WORDS OF OUR OWN, OR FISTS--OR WE SUFFER IN SILENCE. NO BIG DEAL--THIS IS THE ROUGH EDGE OF REALITY, RIGHT? WHY MAKE A FUSS?
TROUBLE WAS, WHEN SOMEONE LABELED LARRY BODINE A "MUTIE," THEY HIT HOME--BECAUSE HE WAS.
HIS POWER CREATED BEAUTY. THAT'S IT. HE DID WITH LIGHT AND COLOR WHAT MOZART DID WITH MUSIC. AND HE WANTED NOTHING MORE THAN TO BE ACCEPTED BY HIS PEERS, AND POSSIBLY EVEN LIKED--
--AND ISN'T THAT WHAT *ANY* OF US REALLY WANT? TO HAVE FRIENDS. PEOPLE TO CARE FOR US? NOT TO BE ALONE?
IF WE'RE LUCKY, WE HAVE SOMEONE TO TURN TO.
LARRY DIDN'T.
HE THOUGHT, IF PEOPLE KNEW THE TRUTH, THEY'D STOP SEEING *HIM* AND SEE ONLY THE *LABEL*, THE BRAND, HIS PERSONAL "SCARLET LETTER."
SO HE HID THE TRUTH AND LIVED IN TERROR OF BEING DISCOVERED. HE EVEN JOINED IN WHEN OTHERS PUT MUTANTS DOWN.
WHAT MATTER THE COST TO HIS SOUL IF IT MADE HIS LIFE A LITTLE BETTER.
THAT'S THE TRAGEDY, THAT'S OUR SHAME.
THINK OF WHAT YOU SAY. IMAGINE IT BEING SAID ABOUT YOU. IT'S EASY TO MAKE FUN, REAL EASY TO BE CRUEL. TRY SOMETIME BEING ON THE RECEIVING END.
IF WE'RE TO LEARN ANYTHING FROM LARRY'S DEATH, IT SHOULD BE THIS...
EXIT
YOU WANT TO KNOW WHO I AM?
I'M *KATHERINE PRYDE.*
THAT'S THE *ONLY* THING THAT MATTERS.
THE REST ARE JUST LABELS.
NEXT: BLOODY SUNDAY!

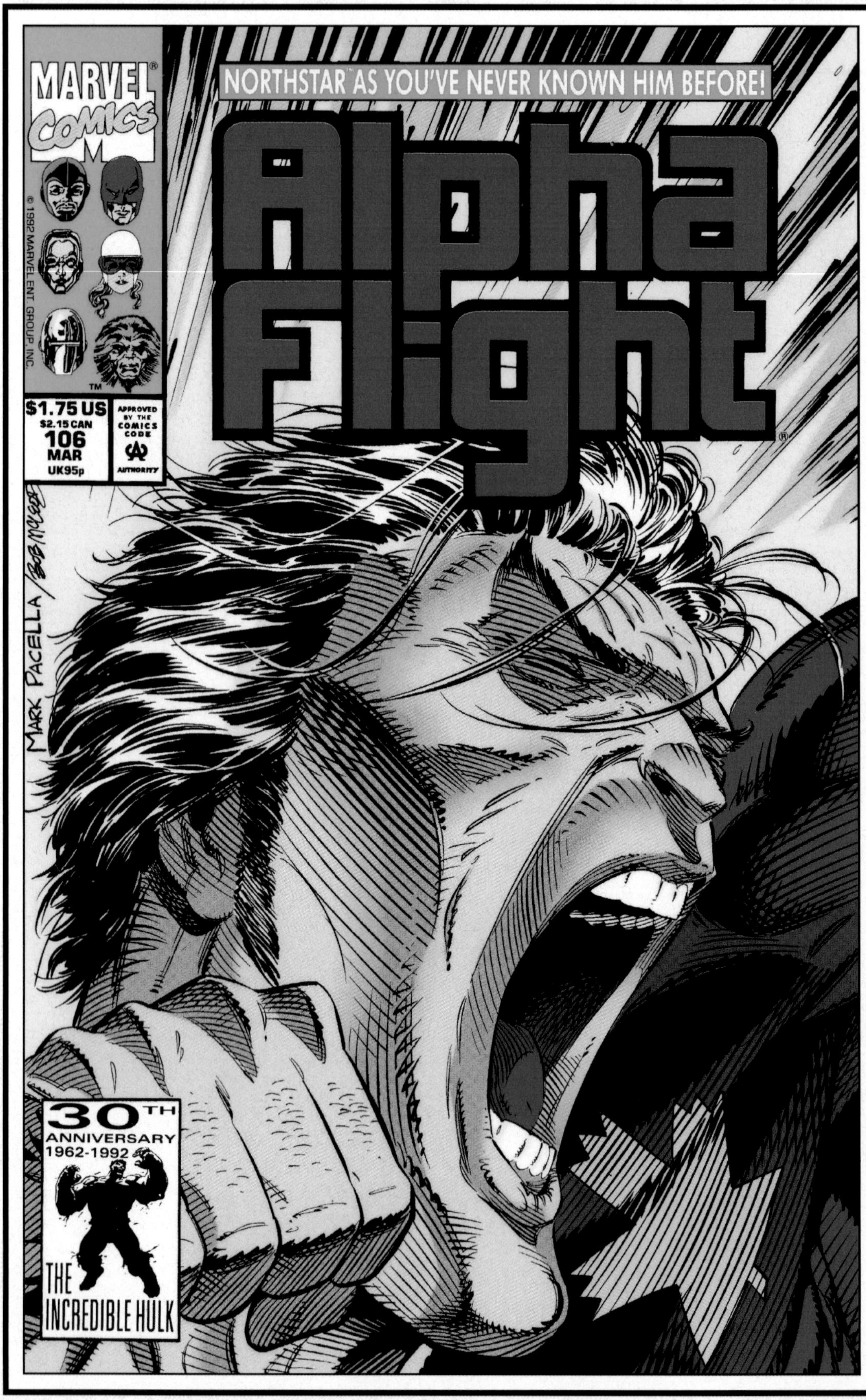

MARVEL COMICS
NORTHSTAR™ AS YOU'VE NEVER KNOWN HIM BEFORE!
Alpha Flight
© 1992 MARVEL ENT. GROUP, INC.
$1.75 US
$2.15 CAN
106
MAR
UK95p
APPROVED BY THE COMICS CODE AUTHORITY
MARK PACELLA
30TH ANNIVERSARY
1962-1992
THE INCREDIBLE HULK

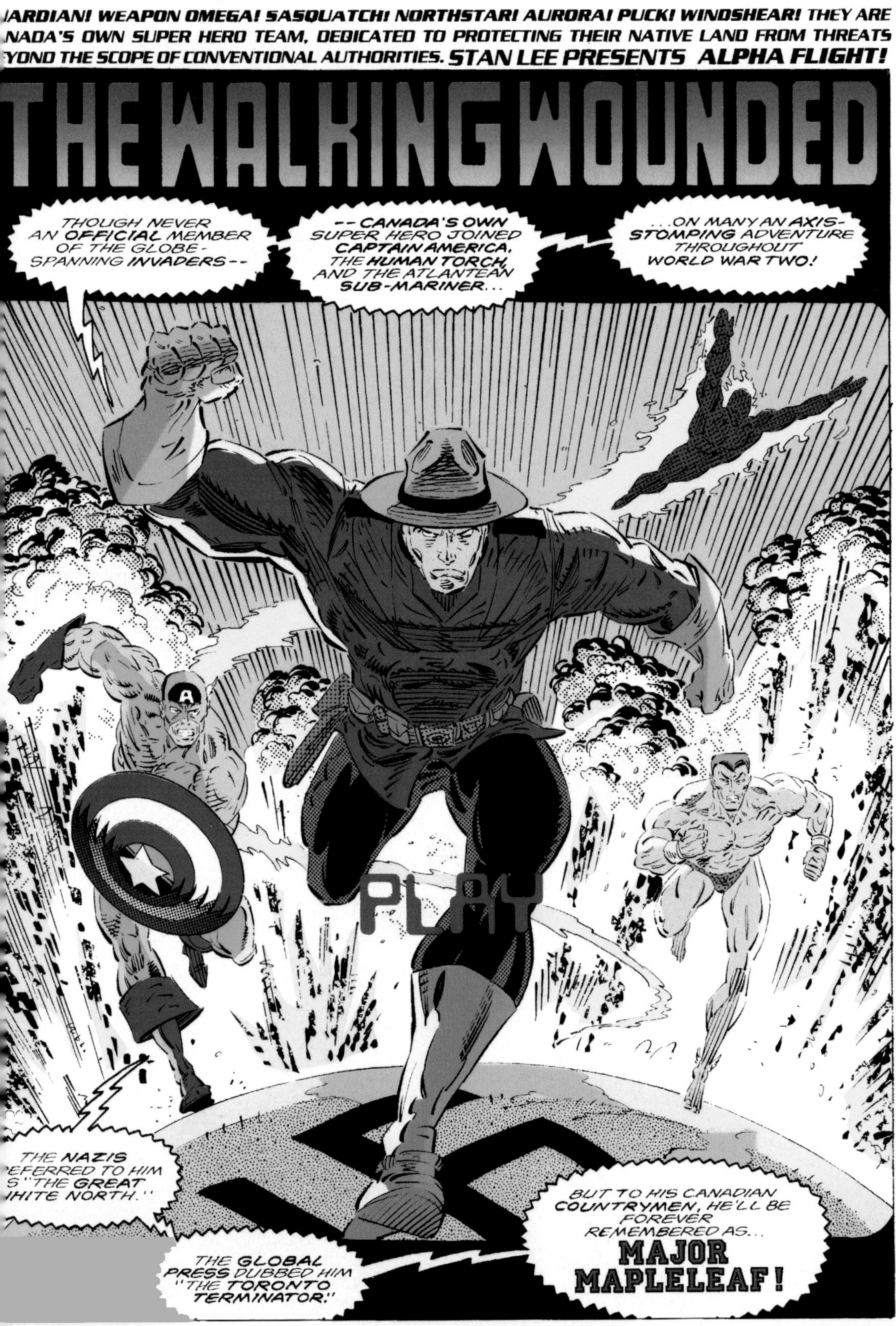
ARDIAN! WEAPON OMEGA! SASQUATCH! NORTHSTAR! AURORA! PUCK! WINDSHEAR! THEY ARE
NADA'S OWN SUPER HERO TEAM, DEDICATED TO PROTECTING THEIR NATIVE LAND FROM THREATS
YOND THE SCOPE OF CONVENTIONAL AUTHORITIES. STAN LEE PRESENTS ALPHA FLIGHT!
THE WALKING WOUNDED
THOUGH NEVER AN OFFICIAL MEMBER OF THE GLOBE-SPANNING INVADERS--
--CANADA'S OWN SUPER HERO JOINED CAPTAIN AMERICA, THE HUMAN TORCH, AND THE ATLANTEAN SUB-MARINER...
...ON MANY AN AXIS-STOMPING ADVENTURE THROUGHOUT WORLD WAR TWO!
THE NAZIS EFERRED TO HIM S "THE GREAT HITE NORTH."
THE GLOBAL PRESS DUBBED HIM "THE TORONTO TERMINATOR."
BUT TO HIS CANADIAN COUNTRYMEN, HE'LL BE FOREVER REMEMBERED AS... MAJOR MAPLELEAF!

NEARLY *FIFTY YEARS* LATER, THE *ORIGIN* OF *OUR* COUNTRY'S *FIRST* SUPER HERO IS STILL A MYSTERY.

THE MOST POPULAR THEORY INVOLVES A *GENETIC EXPERIMENT* WHICH--

KLK

MMMMMMM MMMMM

KLK

--*DEATH O* HIS FAITHFU *SIDEKICK* THE BELOVED

KLK

MMMMMMMMM MM

--*RARELY SEEN* DURING THE FIFTIES, MAJOR MAPLE LEAF WENT *UNDERGROUND* IN HIS CRIME-FIGHTING ENDEAVORS.

THIS RARE FOOTAGE SHOWS HIM BATTLING A *VILLAIN* WHO WOULD LATER CONFRONT THE *FANTASTIC*--

KLK

MMMMMMM

KLK

--*LAST PUBLIC APPEARANC* IN 1963, WHE HE REVEALE HIS *SECRE IDENTITY* AT A PRESS CONFERENC ANNOUNCIN HIS *RETIREMEN*

"SO I CAN DEVOTE MY TIME AND ENERGY TO A *TRULY SUPERHUMAN TASK*...

"...THE *RAISING* OF MY SON, MICHAEL SADLER.

KLK

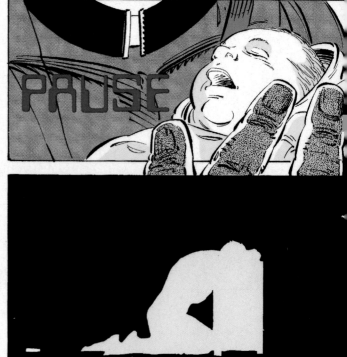

PAUSE

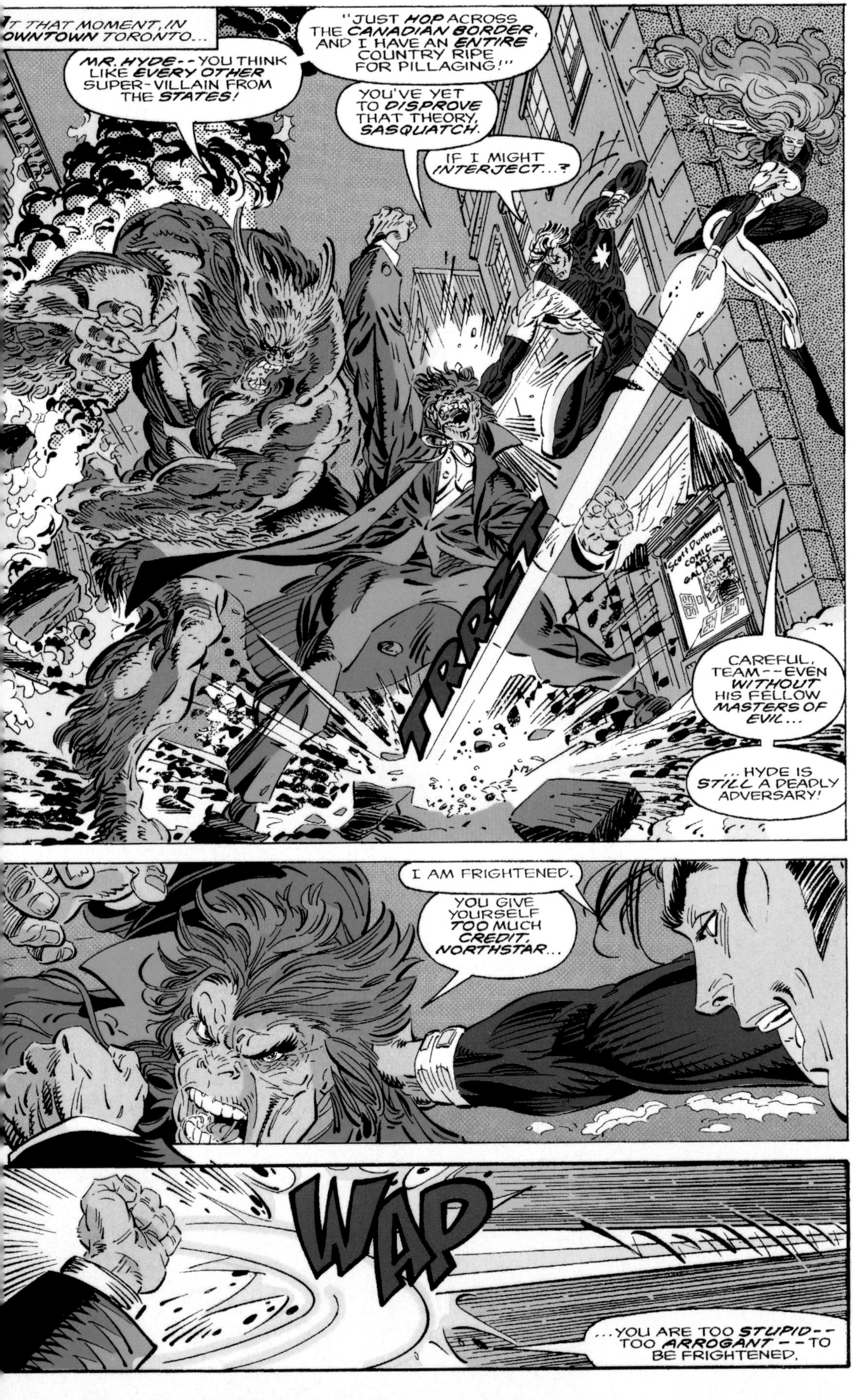
AT THAT MOMENT, IN DOWNTOWN TORONTO...
MR. HYDE--YOU THINK LIKE EVERY OTHER SUPER-VILLAIN FROM THE STATES!
"JUST HOP ACROSS THE CANADIAN BORDER, AND I HAVE AN ENTIRE COUNTRY RIPE FOR PILLAGING!"
YOU'VE YET TO DISPROVE THAT THEORY, SASQUATCH.
IF I MIGHT INTERJECT...?
TRRZZT
Scott Dunbier's COMIC ART GALLERY
CAREFUL, TEAM--EVEN WITHOUT HIS FELLOW MASTERS OF EVIL...
...HYDE IS STILL A DEADLY ADVERSARY!
I AM FRIGHTENED.
YOU GIVE YOURSELF TOO MUCH CREDIT, NORTHSTAR...
WAP
...YOU ARE TOO STUPID--TOO ARROGANT--TO BE FRIGHTENED.

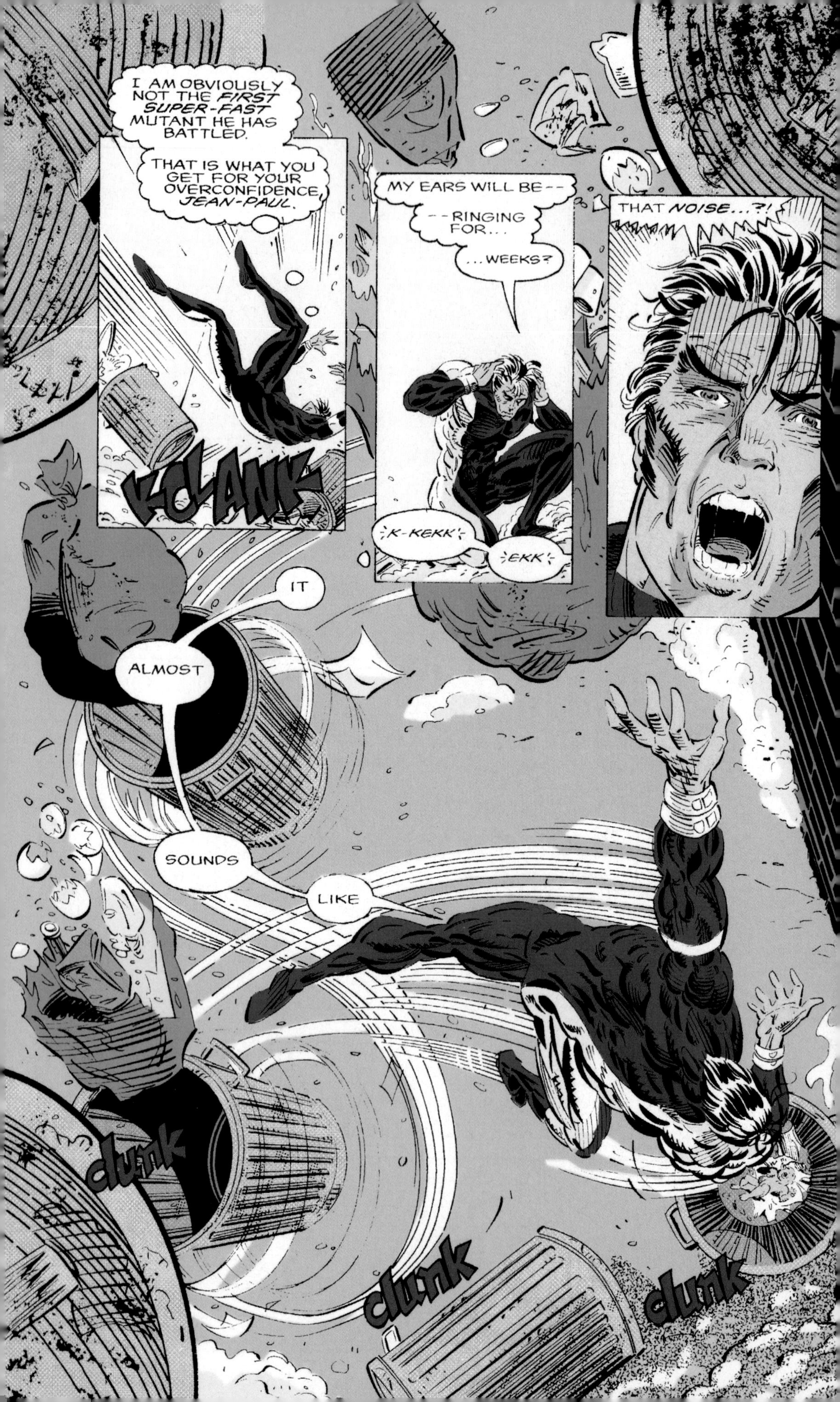

I AM OBVIOUSLY NOT THE *FIRST SUPER-FAST* MUTANT HE HAS BATTLED.
THAT IS WHAT YOU GET FOR YOUR OVERCONFIDENCE, *JEAN-PAUL.*
K-CLANK
MY EARS WILL BE--
--RINGING FOR...
...WEEKS?
K-KEKK
EKK
THAT *NOISE*...?!
IT
ALMOST
SOUNDS
LIKE
clunk
clunk
clunk

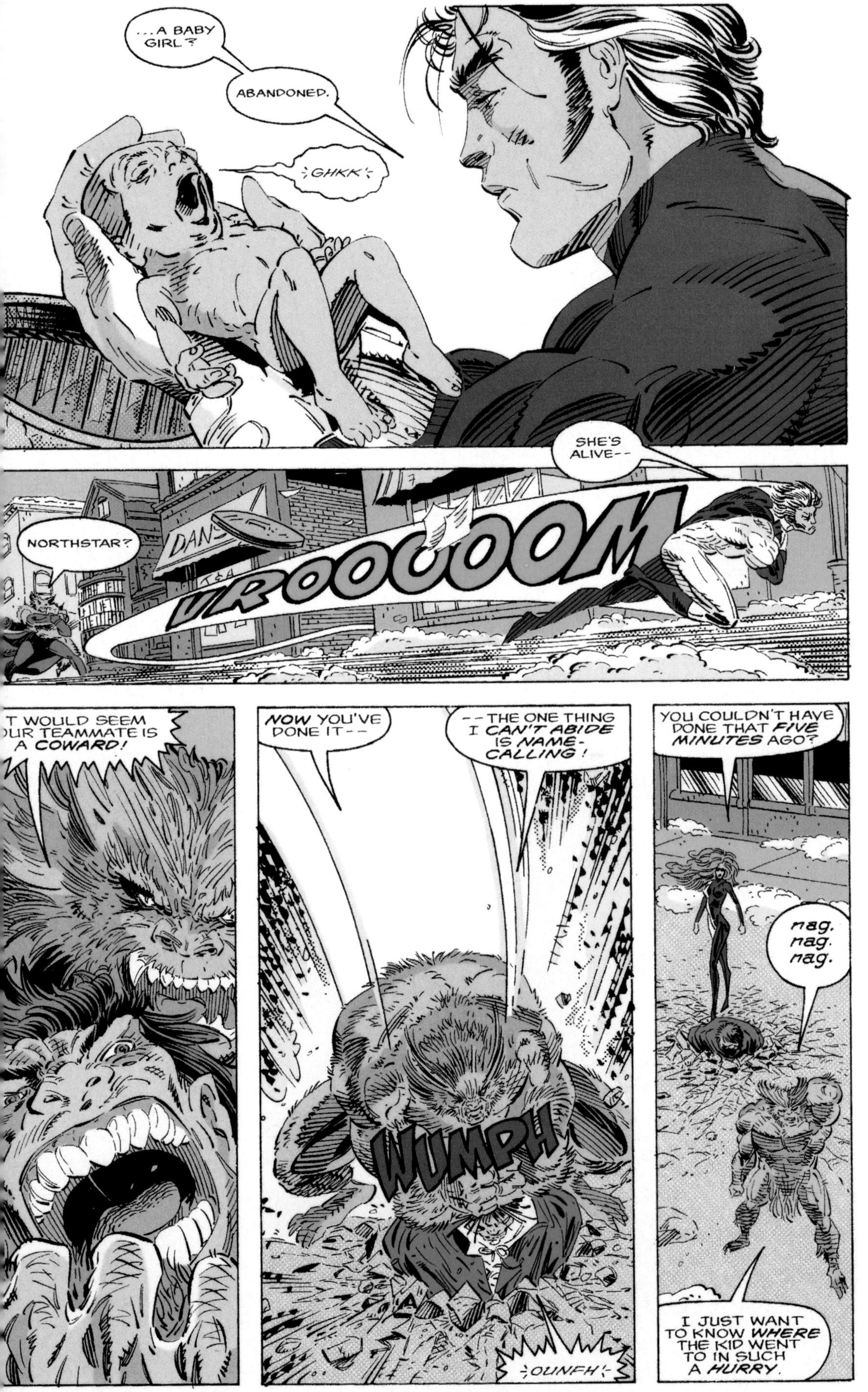
...A BABY GIRL?
ABANDONED.
GHKK
SHE'S ALIVE--
NORTHSTAR?
VROOOOOOM
T WOULD SEEM OUR TEAMMATE IS A COWARD!
NOW YOU'VE DONE IT--
--THE ONE THING I CAN'T ABIDE IS NAME-CALLING!
WUMPH
OUNFH
YOU COULDN'T HAVE DONE THAT FIVE MINUTES AGO?
nag. nag. nag.
I JUST WANT TO KNOW WHERE THE KID WENT TO IN SUCH A HURRY.

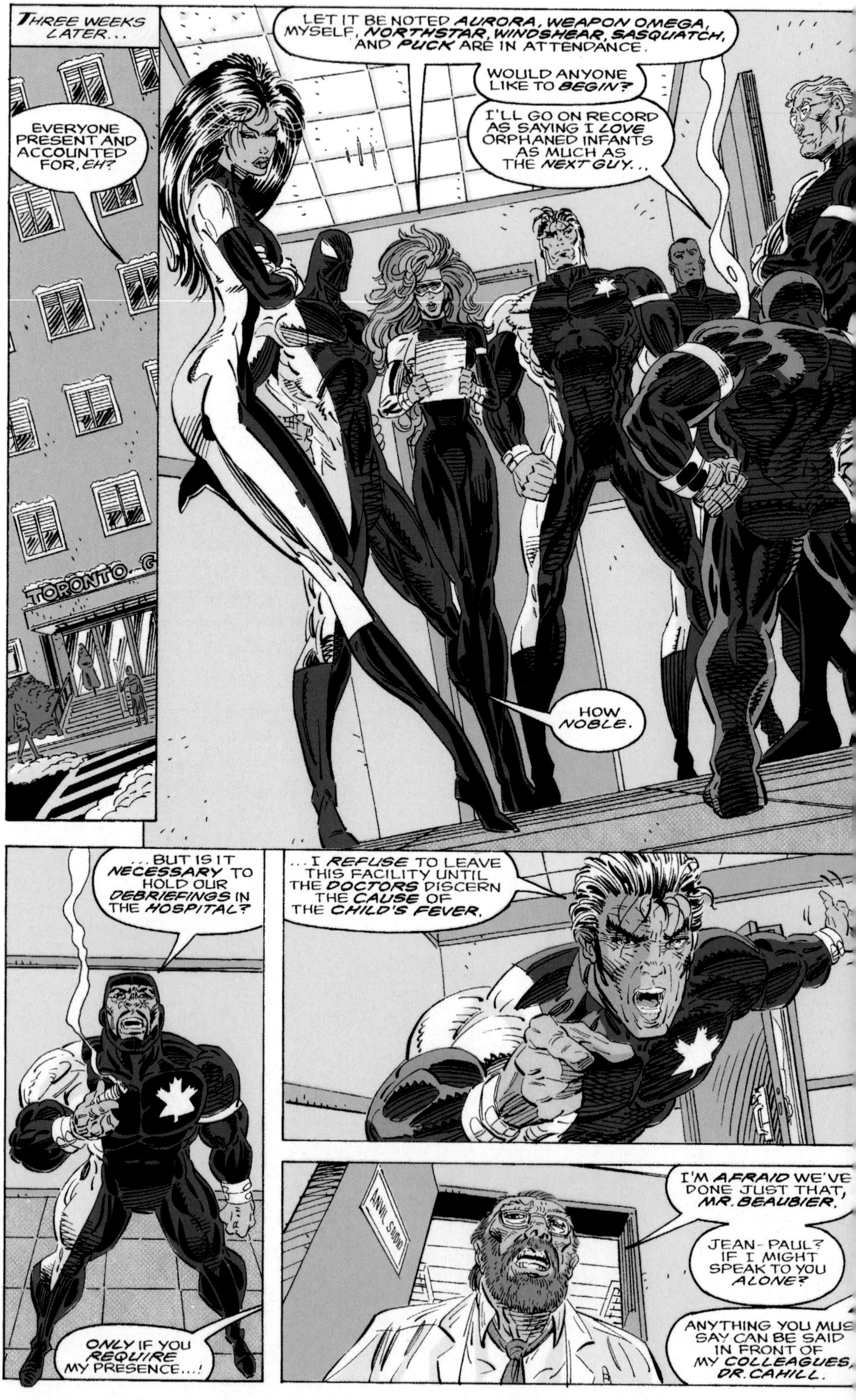
THREE WEEKS LATER...
EVERYONE PRESENT AND ACCOUNTED FOR, EH?
LET IT BE NOTED AURORA, WEAPON OMEGA, MYSELF, NORTHSTAR, WINDSHEAR, SASQUATCH, AND PUCK ARE IN ATTENDANCE.
WOULD ANYONE LIKE TO BEGIN?
I'LL GO ON RECORD AS SAYING I LOVE ORPHANED INFANTS AS MUCH AS THE NEXT GUY...
HOW NOBLE.
TORONTO G
...BUT IS IT NECESSARY TO HOLD OUR DEBRIEFINGS IN THE HOSPITAL?
ONLY IF YOU REQUIRE MY PRESENCE...!
...I REFUSE TO LEAVE THIS FACILITY UNTIL THE DOCTORS DISCERN THE CAUSE OF THE CHILD'S FEVER.
ANVIL STUDIO
I'M AFRAID WE'VE DONE JUST THAT, MR. BEAUBIER.
JEAN-PAUL? IF I MIGHT SPEAK TO YOU ALONE?
ANYTHING YOU MUS SAY CAN BE SAID IN FRONT OF MY COLLEAGUES, DR. CAHILL.

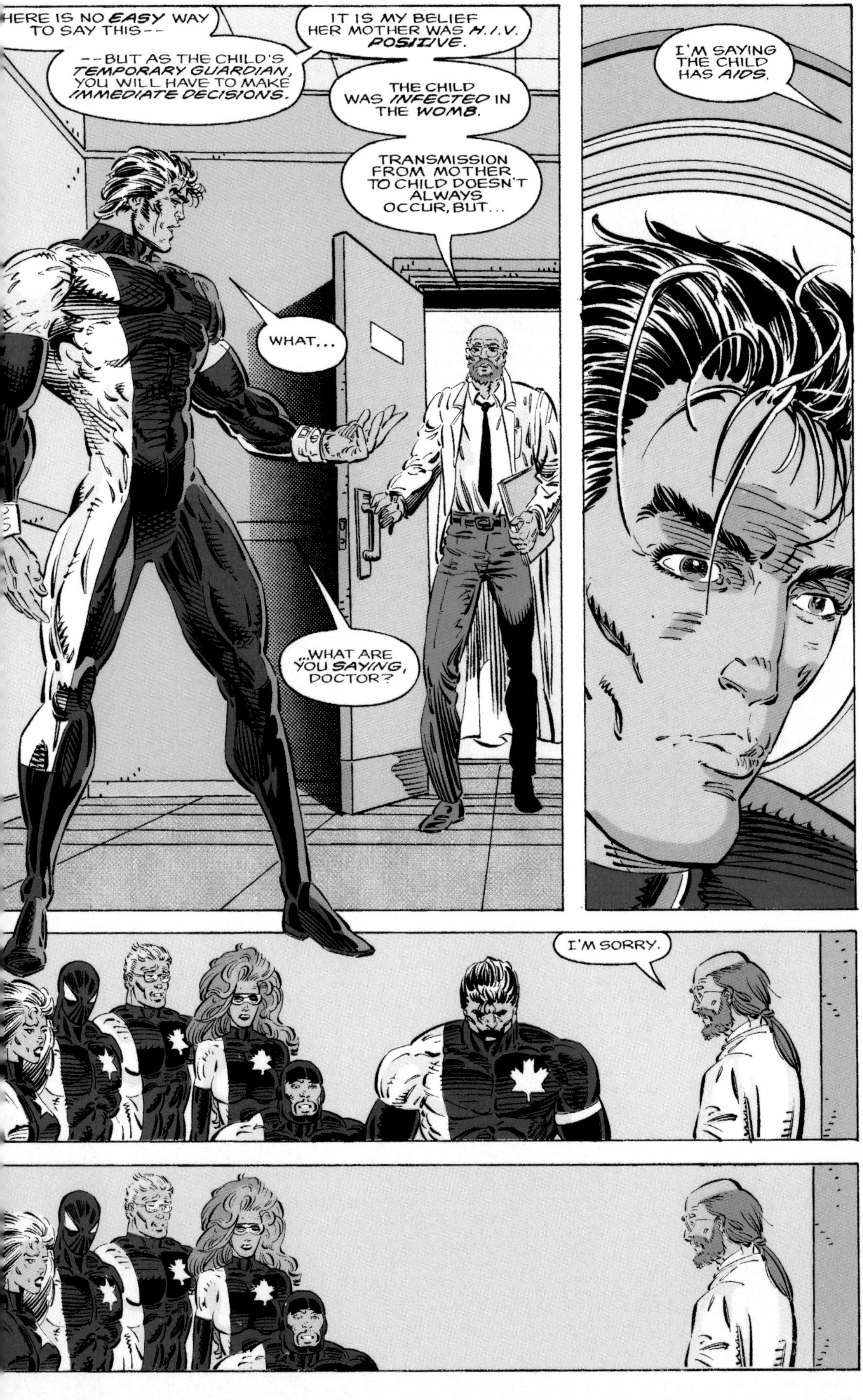

HERE IS NO EASY WAY TO SAY THIS--
--BUT AS THE CHILD'S TEMPORARY GUARDIAN, YOU WILL HAVE TO MAKE IMMEDIATE DECISIONS.
IT IS MY BELIEF HER MOTHER WAS H.I.V. POSITIVE.
THE CHILD WAS INFECTED IN THE WOMB.
TRANSMISSION FROM MOTHER TO CHILD DOESN'T ALWAYS OCCUR, BUT...
WHAT...
...WHAT ARE YOU SAYING, DOCTOR?
I'M SAYING THE CHILD HAS AIDS.
I'M SORRY.

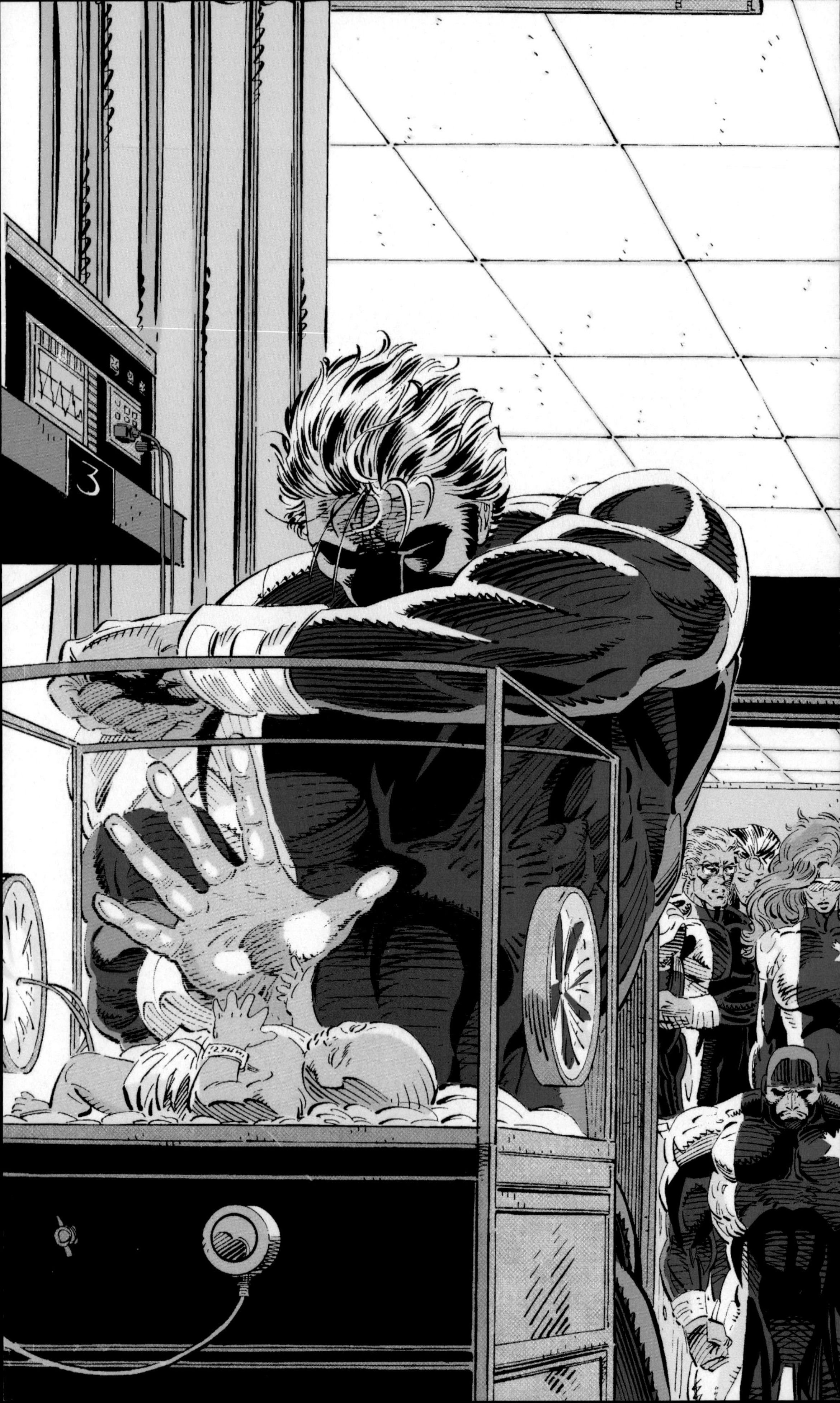
3

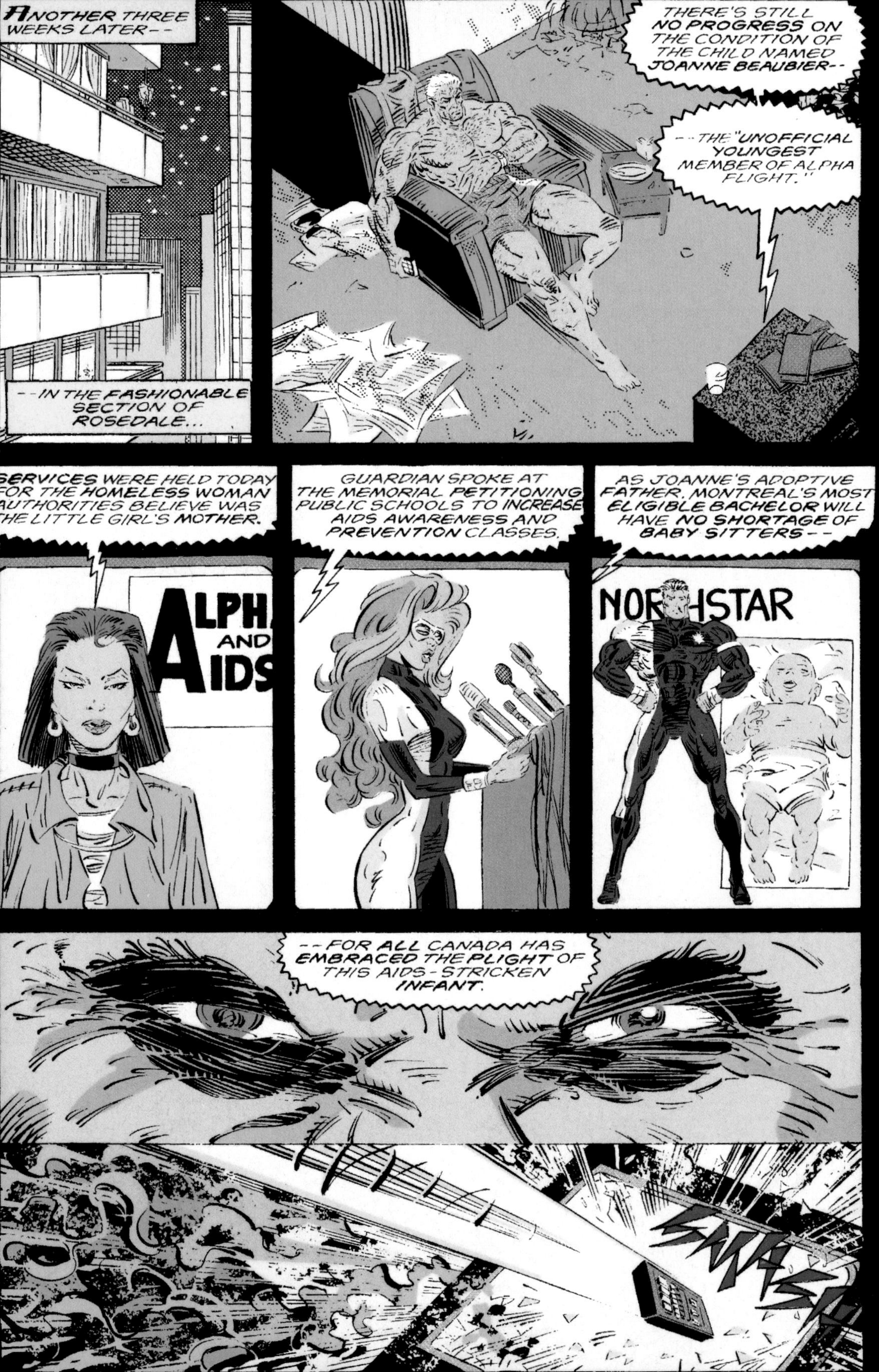

ANOTHER THREE WEEKS LATER--
--IN THE FASHIONABLE SECTION OF ROSEDALE...
THERE'S STILL NO PROGRESS ON THE CONDITION OF THE CHILD NAMED JOANNE BEAUBIER--
--THE "UNOFFICIAL YOUNGEST MEMBER OF ALPHA FLIGHT."
SERVICES WERE HELD TODAY FOR THE HOMELESS WOMAN AUTHORITIES BELIEVE WAS THE LITTLE GIRL'S MOTHER.
ALPH AND AIDS
GUARDIAN SPOKE AT THE MEMORIAL PETITIONING PUBLIC SCHOOLS TO INCREASE AIDS AWARENESS AND PREVENTION CLASSES.
AS JOANNE'S ADOPTIVE FATHER, MONTREAL'S MOST ELIGIBLE BACHELOR WILL HAVE NO SHORTAGE OF BABY SITTERS--
NOR HSTAR
--FOR ALL CANADA HAS EMBRACED THE PLIGHT OF THIS AIDS-STRICKEN INFANT.

THE INTENSIVE CARE WARD OF TORONTO GENERAL...

LOOK, KID--YOU'RE NOT DOING HER *ANY GOOD* BY *EXHAUSTING* YOURSELF.

YOU'RE *RIGHT*, OF COURSE.

YET KNOWING HER CONDITION *WORSENS* EACH DAY--

--EVERY MOMENT I *SPEND* WITH HER IS *PRECIOUS.*

AT LEAST COME GET *SOMETHING* TO EAT.

WE'LL LEAVE THE STUFFED ANIMAL FROM HER *"UNCLE WALTER"* TO *STAND GUARD* UNTIL WE GET BACK.

JEAN-PAUL, I'VE BEEN AROUND FOR A *LOT* OF YEARS-- SEEN A LOT OF *HORRIBLE* THINGS-- BUT *THIS DISEASE...*

A *PLAGUE* FOR OUR *TIMES*, INDEED.

HOW THAT LITTLE BODY FIGHTS ON IS A *MIRACLE.*

LOUNGE

SPEAKING OF BODIES, KID...

...YOU LOOK AS IF YOU HAVEN'T *SLEPT* IN--

BRBOOOM

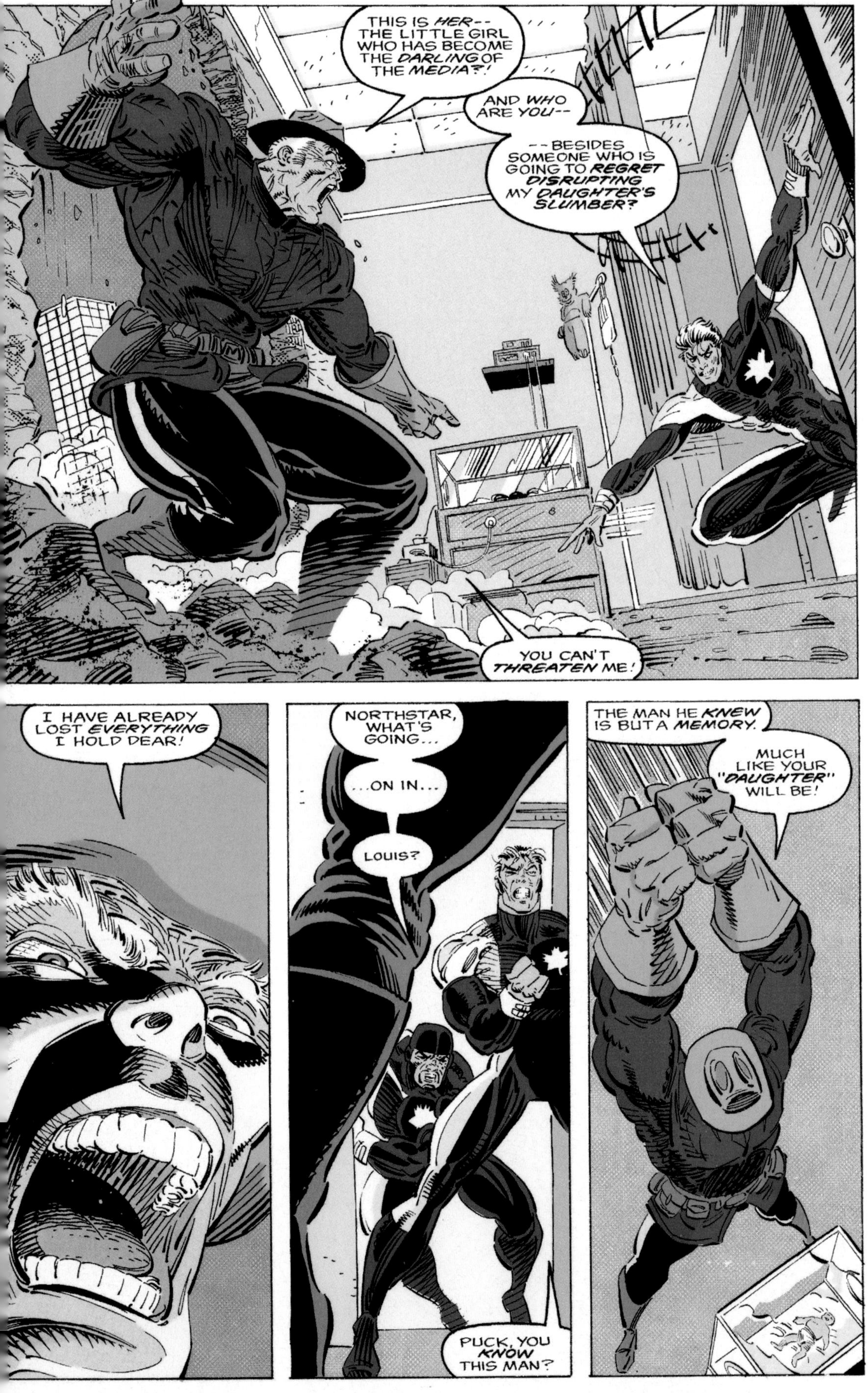

THIS IS HER-- THE LITTLE GIRL WHO HAS BECOME THE DARLING OF THE MEDIA?!
AND WHO ARE YOU--
--BESIDES SOMEONE WHO IS GOING TO REGRET DISRUPTING MY DAUGHTER'S SLUMBER?
YOU CAN'T THREATEN ME!
I HAVE ALREADY LOST EVERYTHING I HOLD DEAR!
NORTHSTAR, WHAT'S GOING...
...ON IN...
LOUIS?
PUCK, YOU KNOW THIS MAN?
THE MAN HE KNEW IS BUT A MEMORY.
MUCH LIKE YOUR "DAUGHTER" WILL BE!

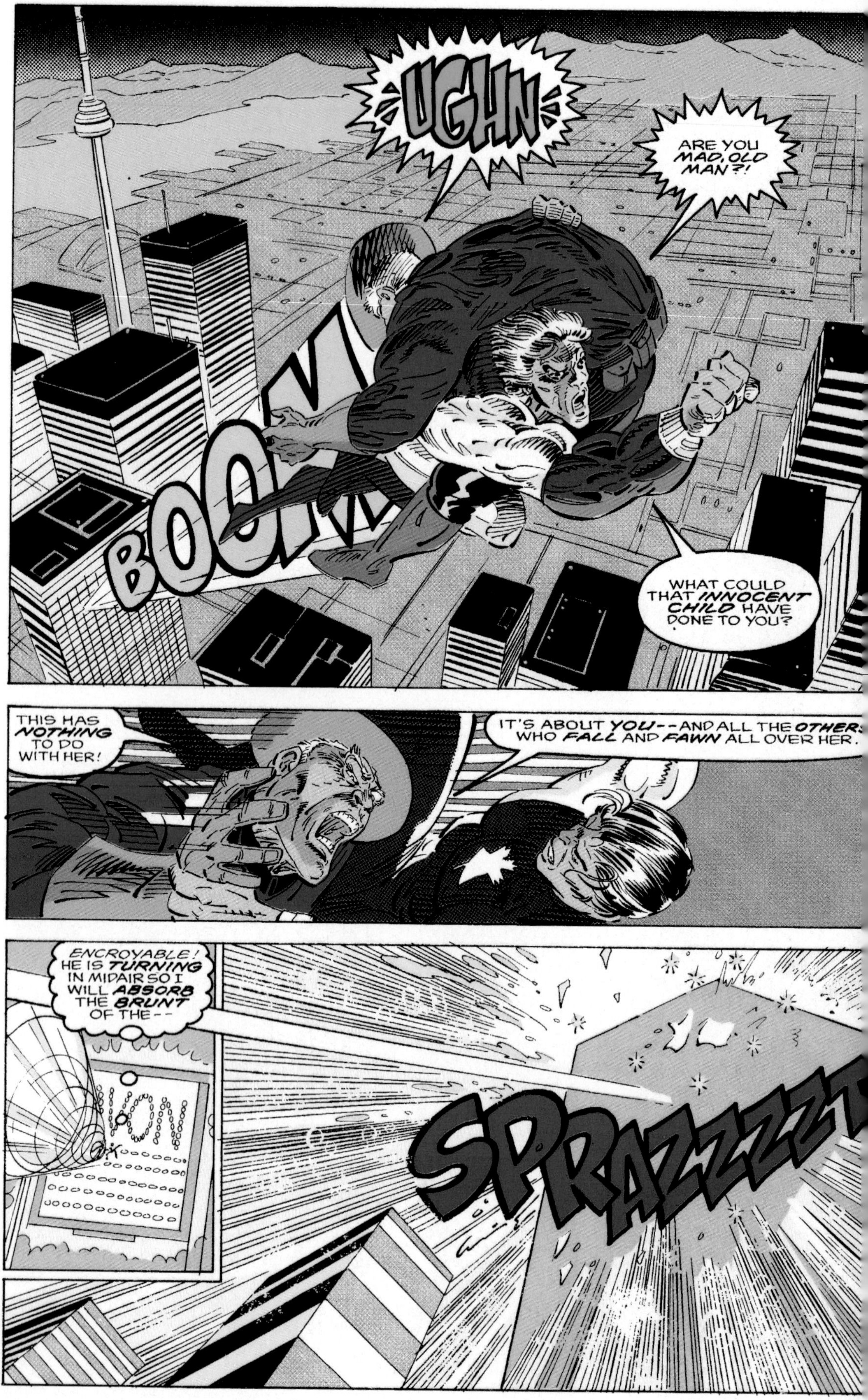
UGHN
ARE YOU MAD, OLD MAN?!
BOOM
WHAT COULD THAT INNOCENT CHILD HAVE DONE TO YOU?
THIS HAS NOTHING TO DO WITH HER!
IT'S ABOUT YOU--AND ALL THE OTHERS WHO FALL AND FAWN ALL OVER HER.
ENCROYABLE! HE IS TURNING IN MIDAIR SO I WILL ABSORB THE BRUNT OF THE--
SPRAZZZZT

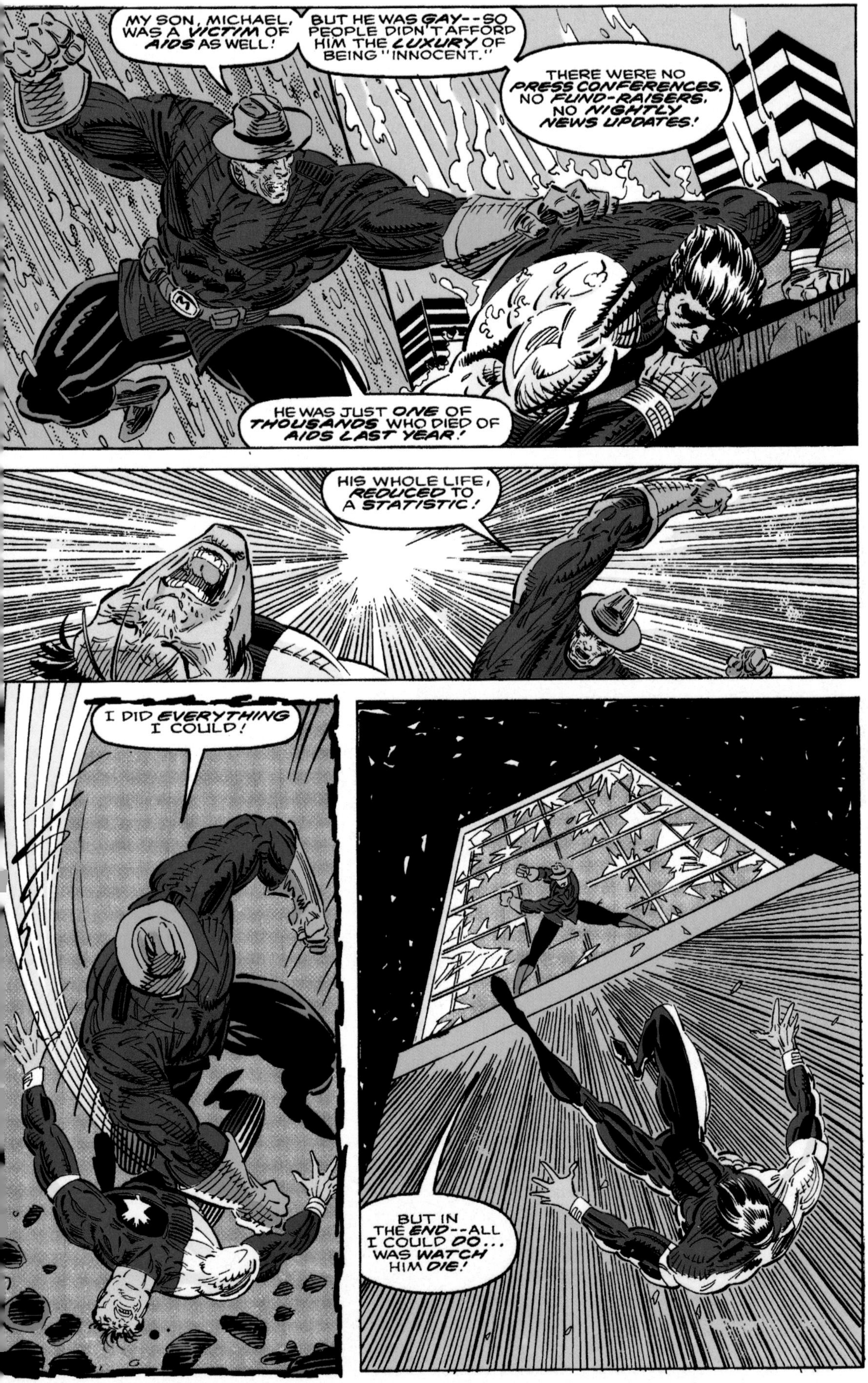
MY SON, MICHAEL, WAS A VICTIM OF AIDS AS WELL!
BUT HE WAS GAY--SO PEOPLE DIDN'T AFFORD HIM THE LUXURY OF BEING "INNOCENT."
THERE WERE NO PRESS CONFERENCES. NO FUND-RAISERS. NO NIGHTLY NEWS UPDATES!
HE WAS JUST ONE OF THOUSANDS WHO DIED OF AIDS LAST YEAR!
HIS WHOLE LIFE, REDUCED TO A STATISTIC!
I DID EVERYTHING I COULD!
BUT IN THE END--ALL I COULD DO... WAS WATCH HIM DIE!

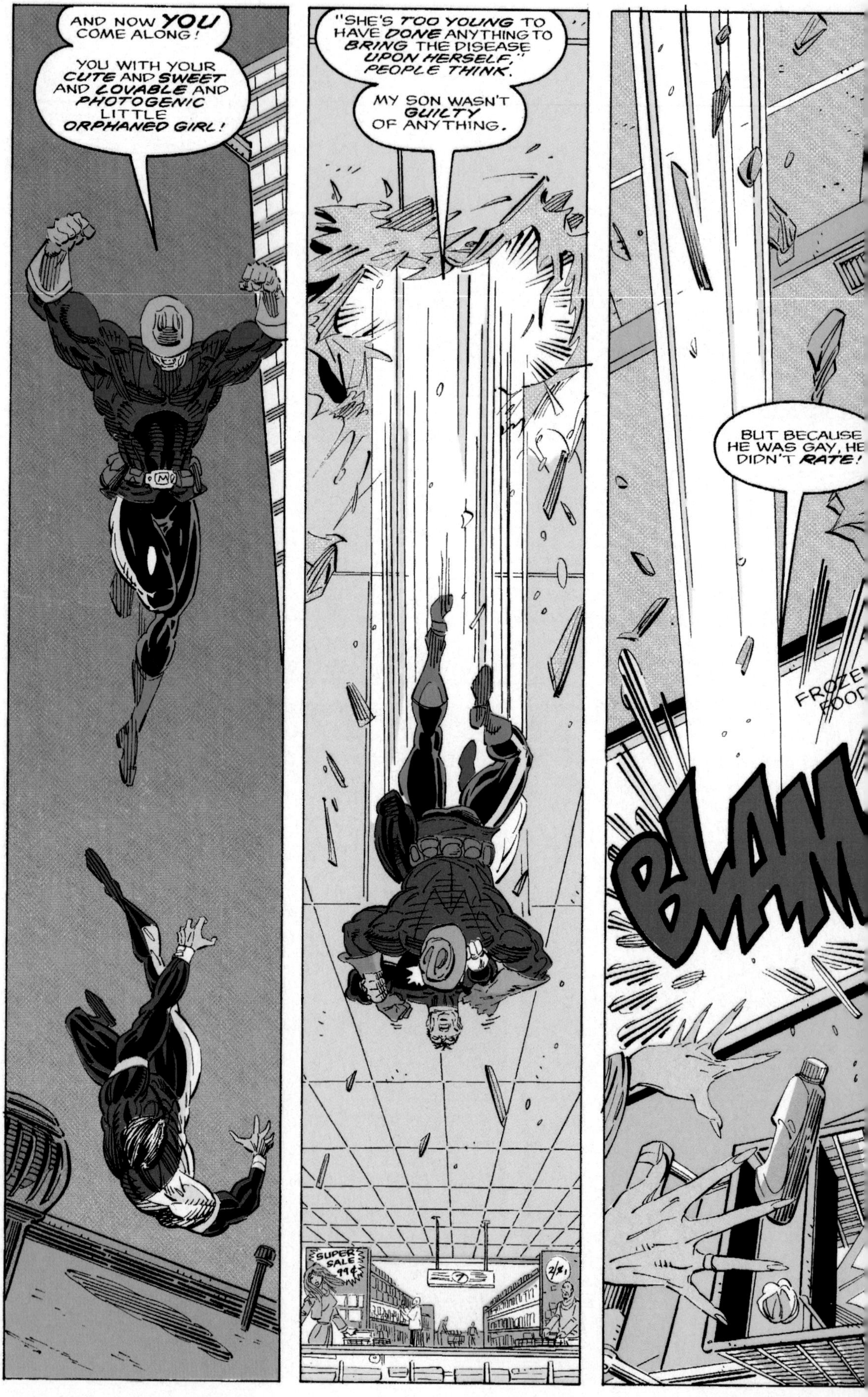
AND NOW YOU COME ALONG!
YOU WITH YOUR CUTE AND SWEET AND LOVABLE AND PHOTOGENIC LITTLE ORPHANED GIRL!
"SHE'S TOO YOUNG TO HAVE DONE ANYTHING TO BRING THE DISEASE UPON HERSELF," PEOPLE THINK.
MY SON WASN'T GUILTY OF ANYTHING.
SUPER SALE 99¢
BUT BECAUSE HE WAS GAY, HE DIDN'T RATE!
BLAM

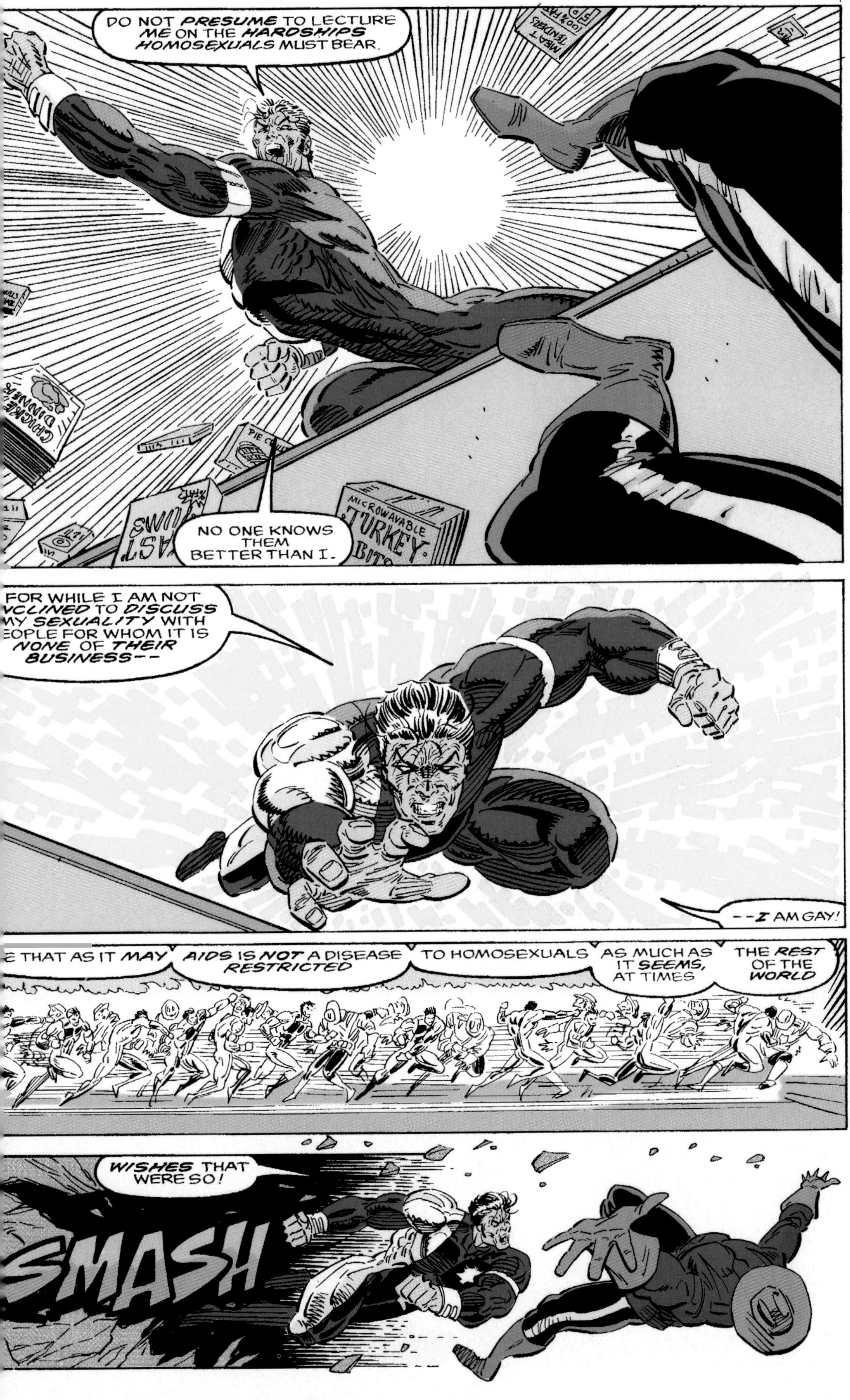

DO NOT PRESUME TO LECTURE ME ON THE HARDSHIPS HOMOSEXUALS MUST BEAR.
MEAT TENDERS 100% FAT
PIE CRUST
MICROWAVABLE TURKEY BITS
NO ONE KNOWS THEM BETTER THAN I.
FOR WHILE I AM NOT NCLINED TO DISCUSS MY SEXUALITY WITH EOPLE FOR WHOM IT IS NONE OF THEIR BUSINESS--
--I AM GAY!
E THAT AS IT MAY
AIDS IS NOT A DISEASE RESTRICTED
TO HOMOSEXUALS
AS MUCH AS IT SEEMS, AT TIMES
THE REST OF THE WORLD
WISHES THAT WERE SO!
SMASH

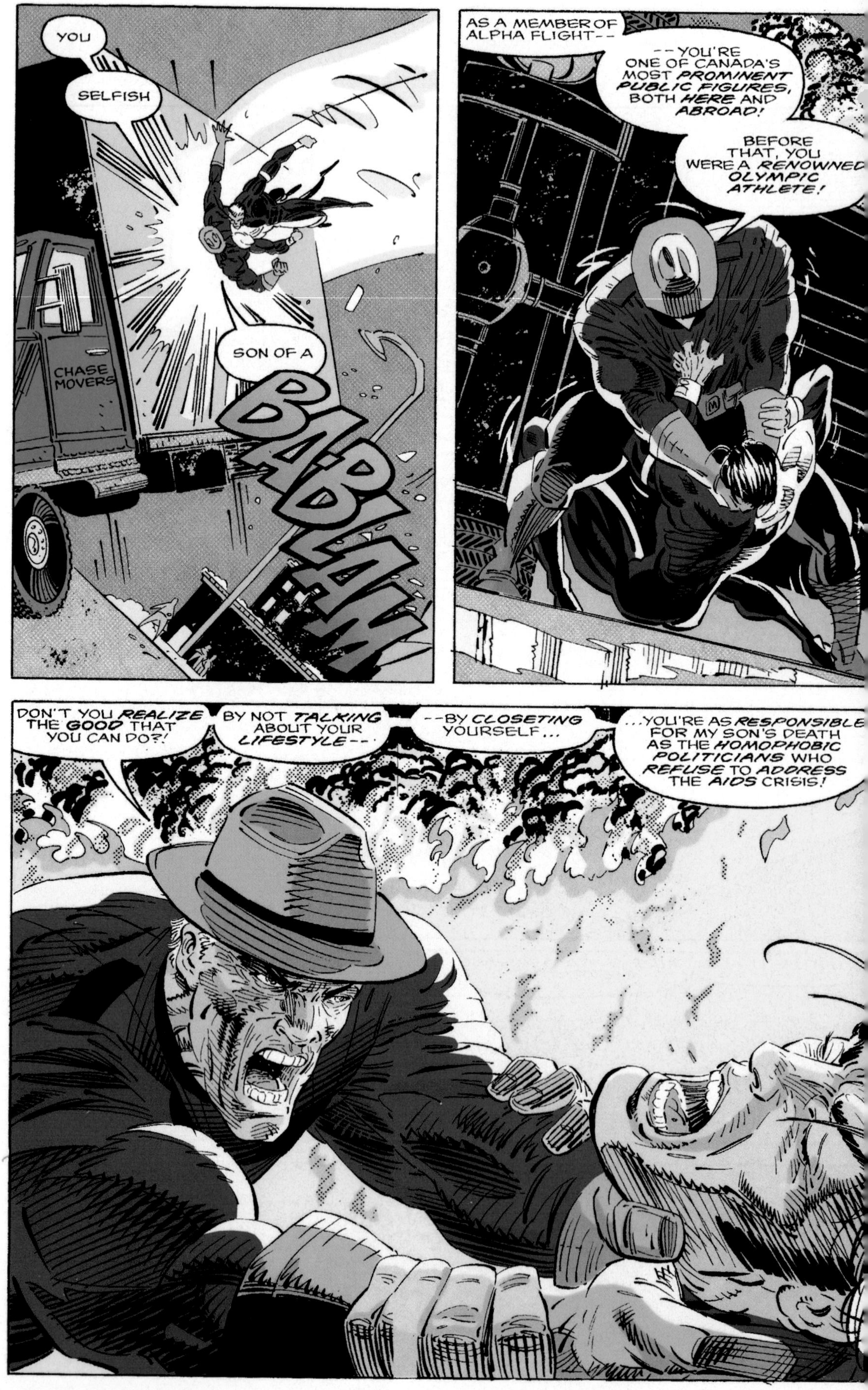
YOU
SELFISH
SON OF A
BABLAM
CHASE MOVERS
AS A MEMBER OF ALPHA FLIGHT--
--YOU'RE ONE OF CANADA'S MOST PROMINENT PUBLIC FIGURES, BOTH HERE AND ABROAD!
BEFORE THAT, YOU WERE A RENOWNED OLYMPIC ATHLETE!
DON'T YOU REALIZE THE GOOD THAT YOU CAN DO?!
BY NOT TALKING ABOUT YOUR LIFESTYLE--
--BY CLOSETING YOURSELF...
...YOU'RE AS RESPONSIBLE FOR MY SON'S DEATH AS THE HOMOPHOBIC POLITICIANS WHO REFUSE TO ADDRESS THE AIDS CRISIS!

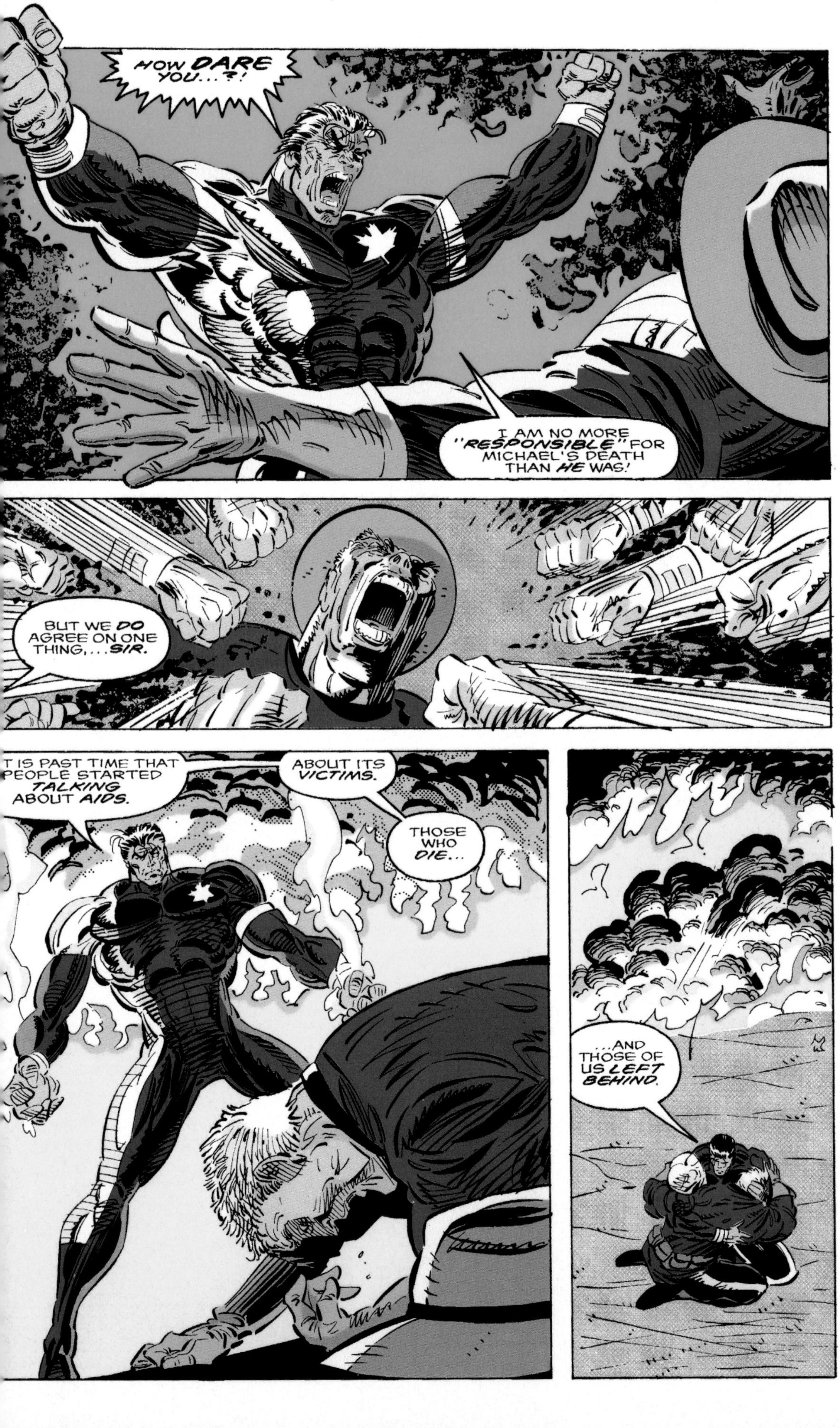

HOW DARE YOU...?!
I AM NO MORE "RESPONSIBLE" FOR MICHAEL'S DEATH THAN HE WAS!
BUT WE DO AGREE ON ONE THING, ...SIR.
T IS PAST TIME THAT PEOPLE STARTED TALKING ABOUT AIDS.
ABOUT ITS VICTIMS.
THOSE WHO DIE...
...AND THOSE OF US LEFT BEHIND.

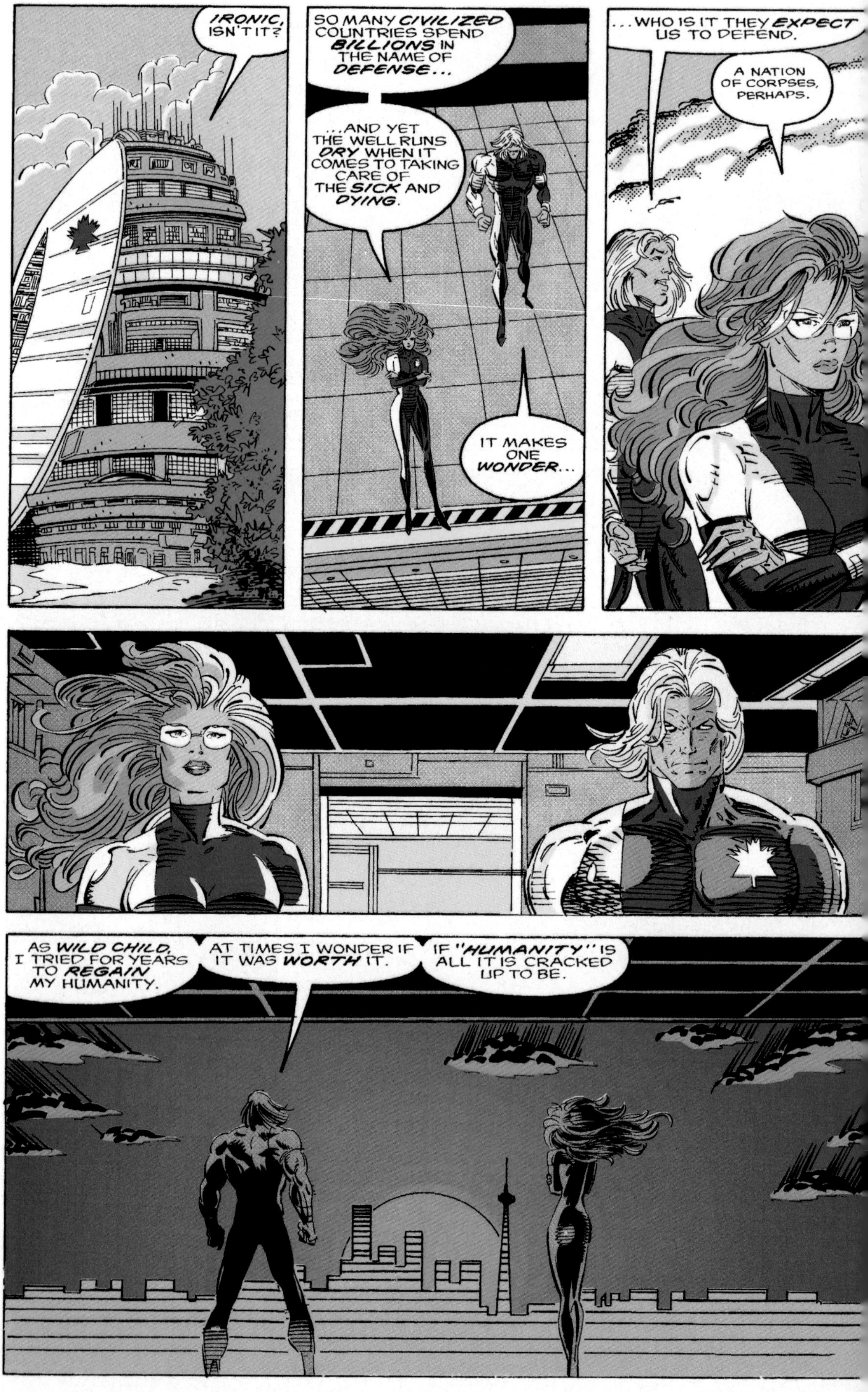
IRONIC, ISN'T IT?
SO MANY CIVILIZED COUNTRIES SPEND BILLIONS IN THE NAME OF DEFENSE...
...AND YET THE WELL RUNS DRY WHEN IT COMES TO TAKING CARE OF THE SICK AND DYING.
IT MAKES ONE WONDER...
...WHO IS IT THEY EXPECT US TO DEFEND.
A NATION OF CORPSES, PERHAPS.
AS WILD CHILD, I TRIED FOR YEARS TO REGAIN MY HUMANITY.
AT TIMES I WONDER IF IT WAS WORTH IT.
IF "HUMANITY" IS ALL IT IS CRACKED UP TO BE.

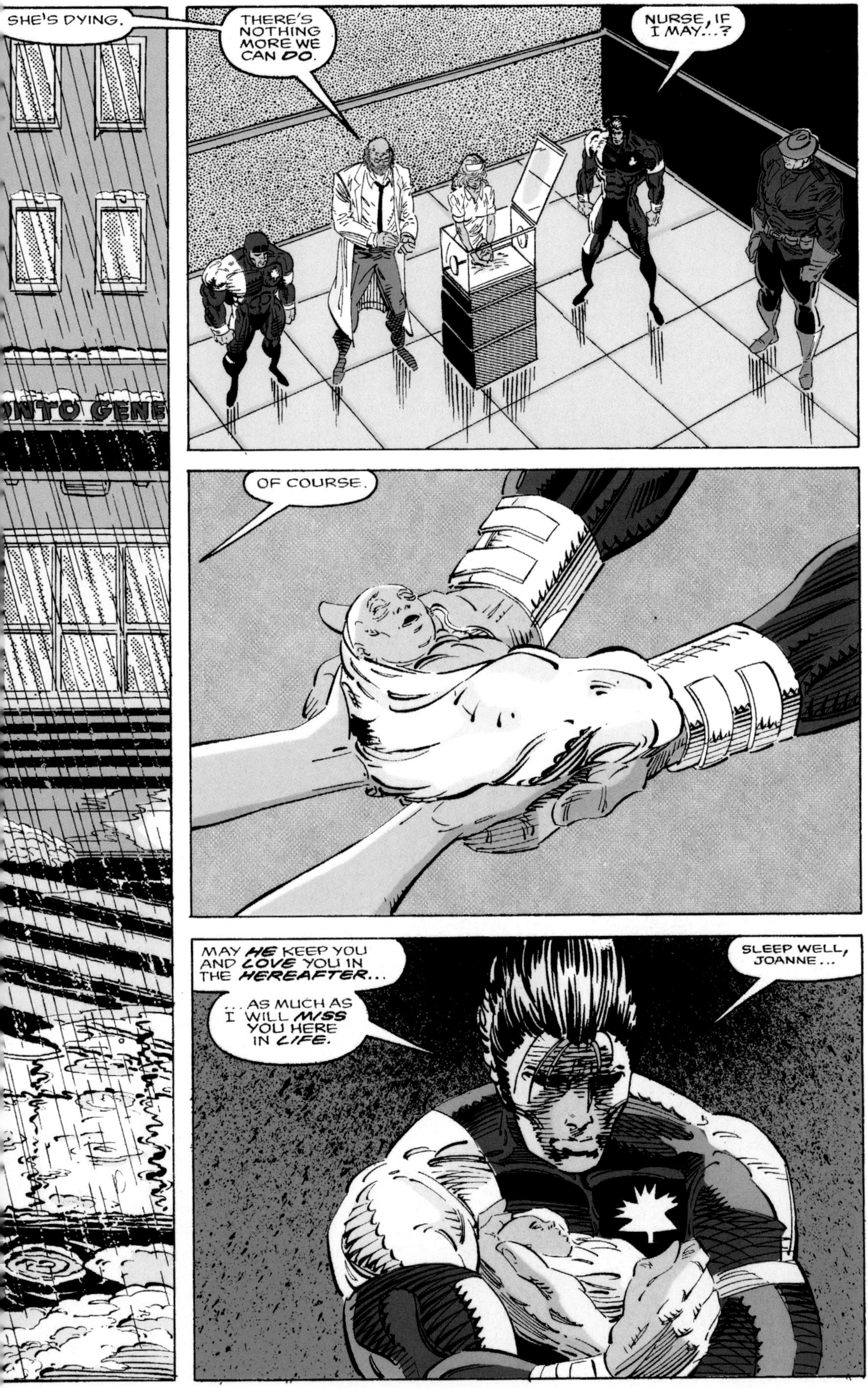
SHE'S DYING.
THERE'S NOTHING MORE WE CAN DO.
NURSE, IF I MAY...?
ONTO GENE
OF COURSE.
MAY HE KEEP YOU AND LOVE YOU IN THE HEREAFTER...
...AS MUCH AS I WILL MISS YOU HERE IN LIFE.
SLEEP WELL, JOANNE...

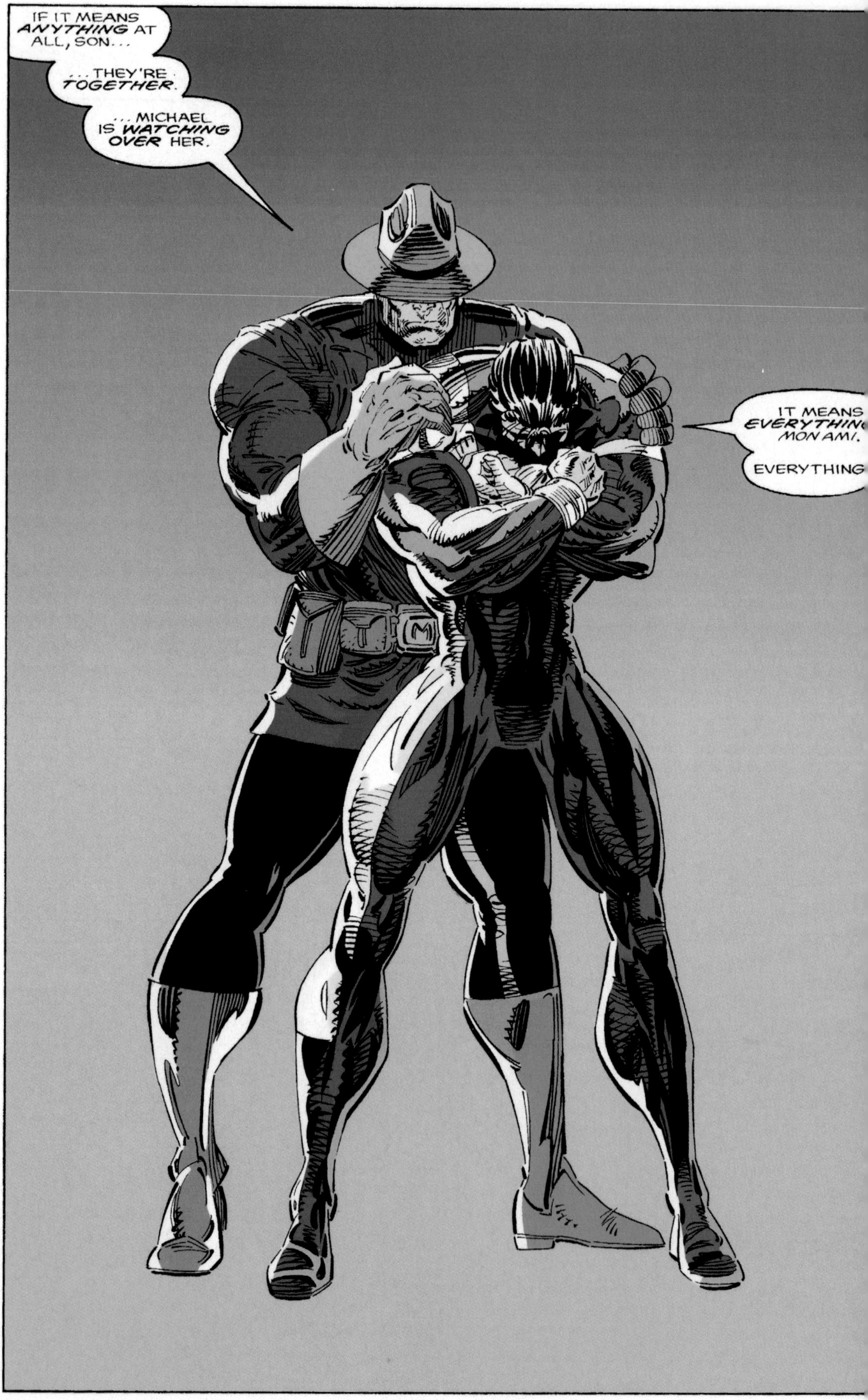
IF IT MEANS ANYTHING AT ALL, SON...
...THEY'RE TOGETHER.
...MICHAEL IS WATCHING OVER HER.
IT MEANS EVERYTHIN MON AMI.
EVERYTHING

HE DAILY MAIL

TUESDAY, JANUARY 21

ALPHA FLIGHT'S NORTHSTAR PROCLAIMS HOMOSEXUALITY

SCOTT LOBDELL
words

MARK PACELLA
pencils

DAN PANOSIAN
inks

JANICE CHIANG
letters

BOB SHAREN
colors

BOBBIE CHASE
edits

TOM DeFALCO
editor-in-chief

"It has been said 'Silence equals Death.' I no longer wish to be that part of the Death that is the AIDS crisis," said Jean-Paul Beaubier, the former Olympic athlete better known as Northstar of Alpha Flight. A day after his adopted daughter Joanne died as a result of complications from AIDS, Beaubier held a press conference where he announced he is gay.

"It is my fervent wish that the expression of my homosexuality will open the doors to conversations

(continued on page A10, column 3)

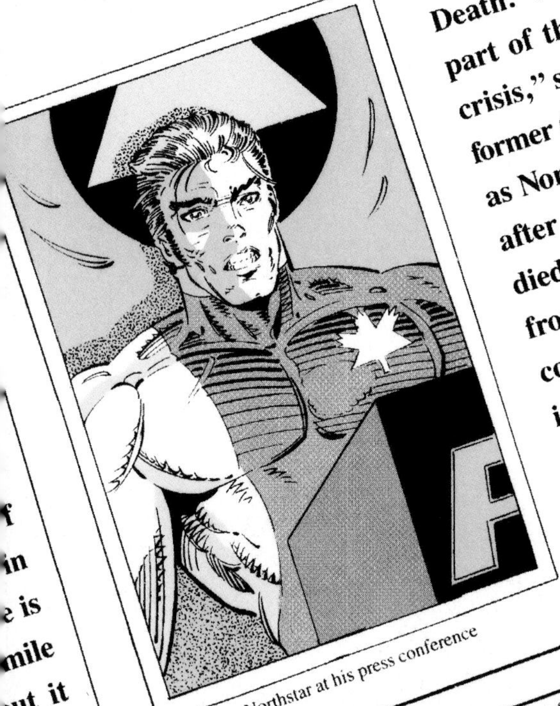

Northstar at his press conference

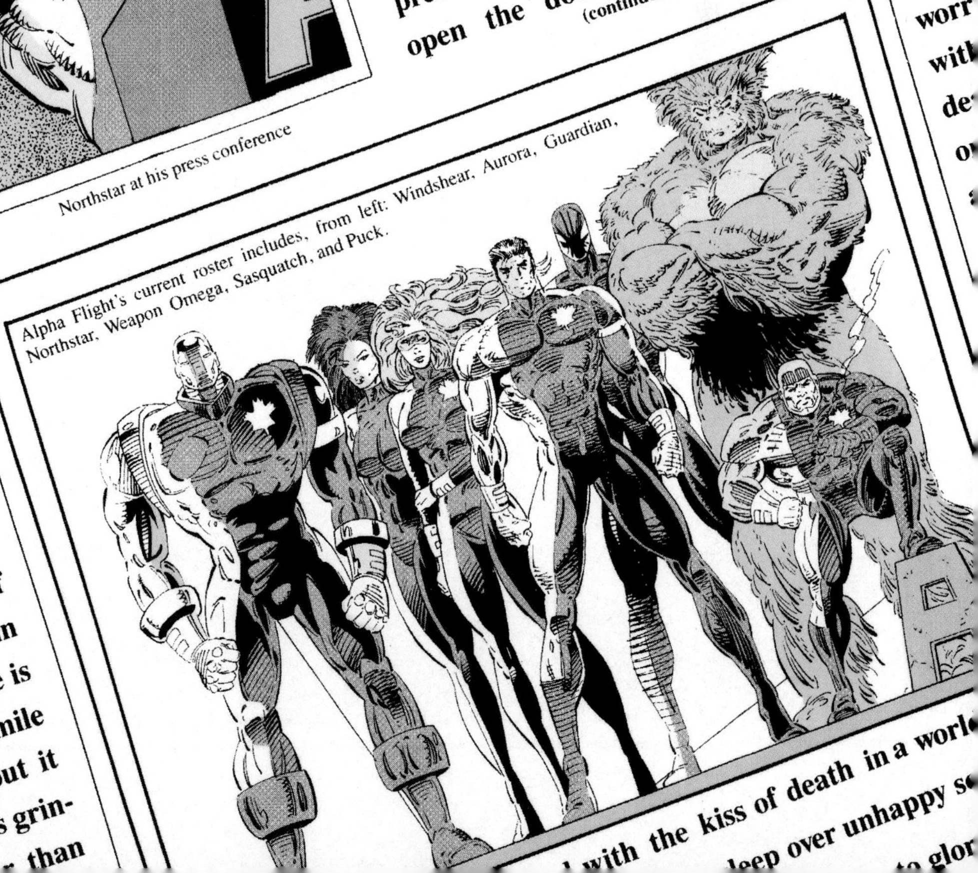

Alpha Flight's current roster includes, from left: Windshear, Aurora, Guardian, Northstar, Weapon Omega, Sasquatch, and Puck.

f
in
e is
mile
out it
s grin-
er than
one mad.
ed swiftly
a man has
o where the
less. Not to
stiny is sealed
or the kiss of
n has to fall in
glory! Patience is
th it can only smile
d those without it
Sometimes grin-
than

Meanw
through
fallen o
black
worr
with
de
o

with the kiss of death in a worl
leep over unhappy s
to glor

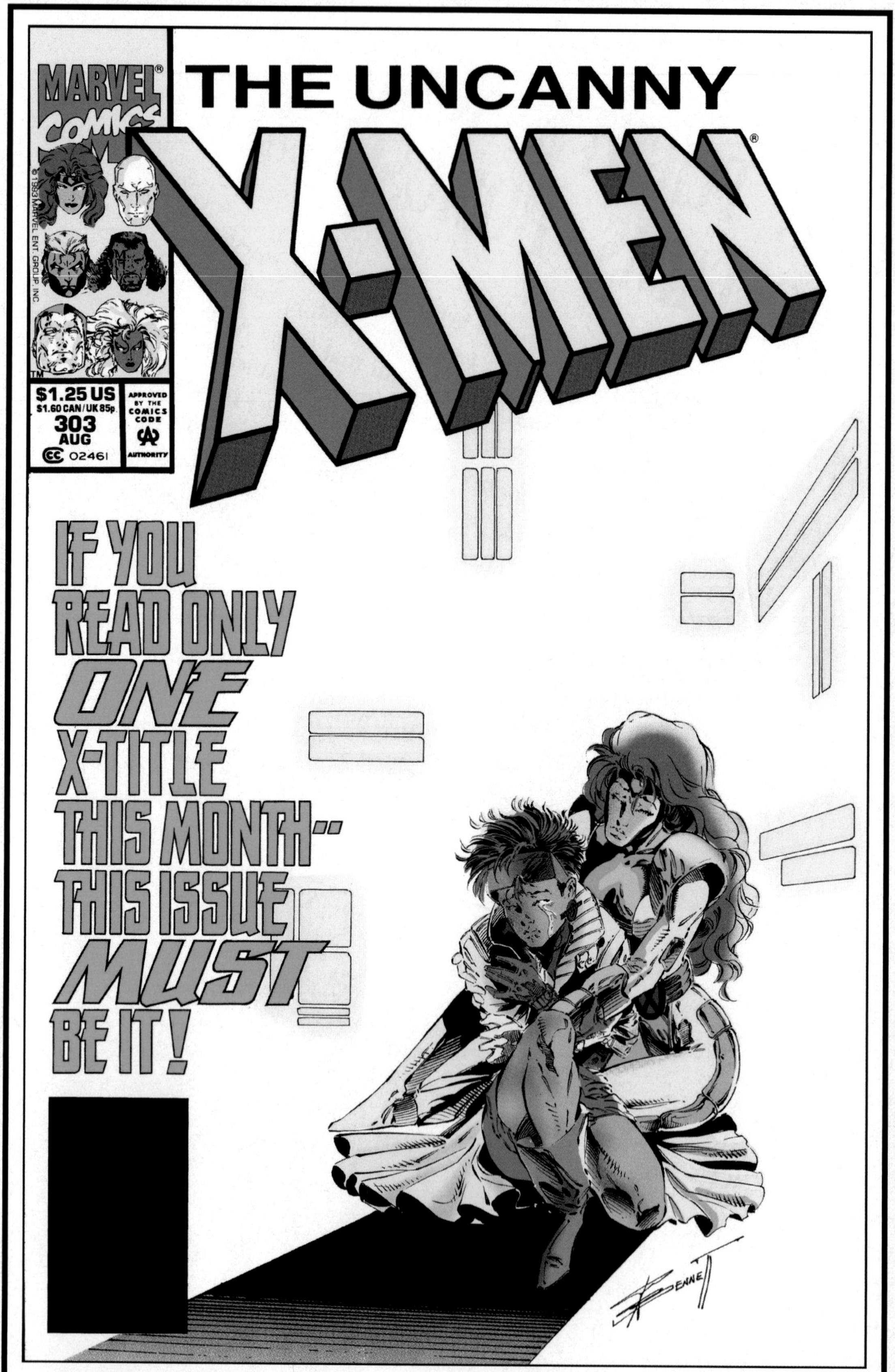

MARVEL COMICS
THE UNCANNY
X-MEN
© 1993 MARVEL ENT. GROUP, INC.
$1.25 US
$1.60 CAN/UK 85p
303
AUG
APPROVED BY THE COMICS CODE AUTHORITY
IF YOU READ ONLY ONE X-TITLE THIS MONTH-- THIS ISSUE MUST BE IT!

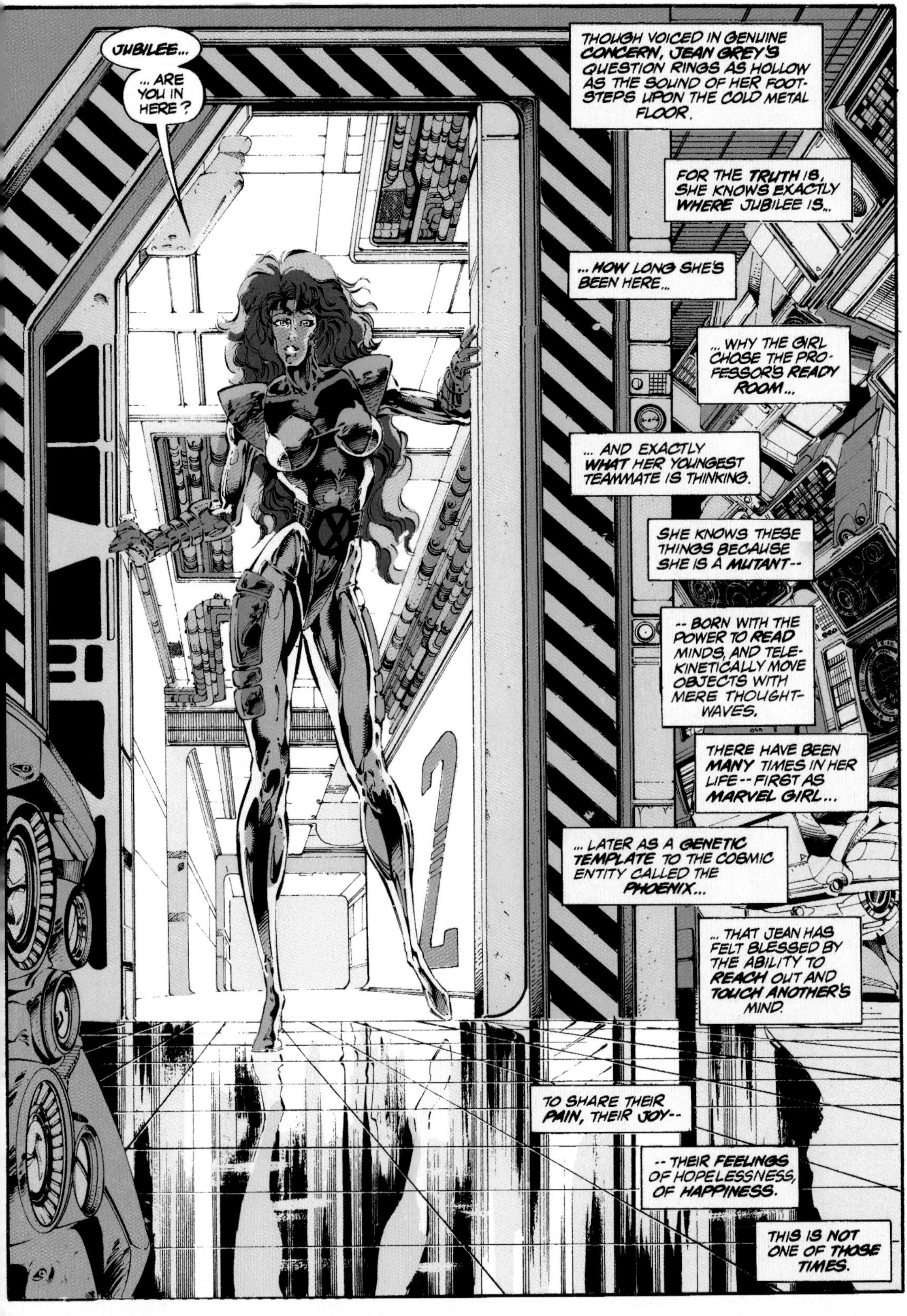
JUBILEE...
... ARE YOU IN HERE?
THOUGH VOICED IN GENUINE CONCERN, JEAN GREY'S QUESTION RINGS AS HOLLOW AS THE SOUND OF HER FOOT-STEPS UPON THE COLD METAL FLOOR.
FOR THE TRUTH IS, SHE KNOWS EXACTLY WHERE JUBILEE IS...
... HOW LONG SHE'S BEEN HERE...
... WHY THE GIRL CHOSE THE PRO-FESSOR'S READY ROOM...
... AND EXACTLY WHAT HER YOUNGEST TEAMMATE IS THINKING.
SHE KNOWS THESE THINGS BECAUSE SHE IS A MUTANT--
-- BORN WITH THE POWER TO READ MINDS, AND TELE-KINETICALLY MOVE OBJECTS WITH MERE THOUGHT-WAVES.
THERE HAVE BEEN MANY TIMES IN HER LIFE -- FIRST AS MARVEL GIRL...
... LATER AS A GENETIC TEMPLATE TO THE COSMIC ENTITY CALLED THE PHOENIX...
... THAT JEAN HAS FELT BLESSED BY THE ABILITY TO REACH OUT AND TOUCH ANOTHER'S MIND.
TO SHARE THEIR PAIN, THEIR JOY--
-- THEIR FEELINGS OF HOPELESSNESS, OF HAPPINESS.
THIS IS NOT ONE OF THOSE TIMES.

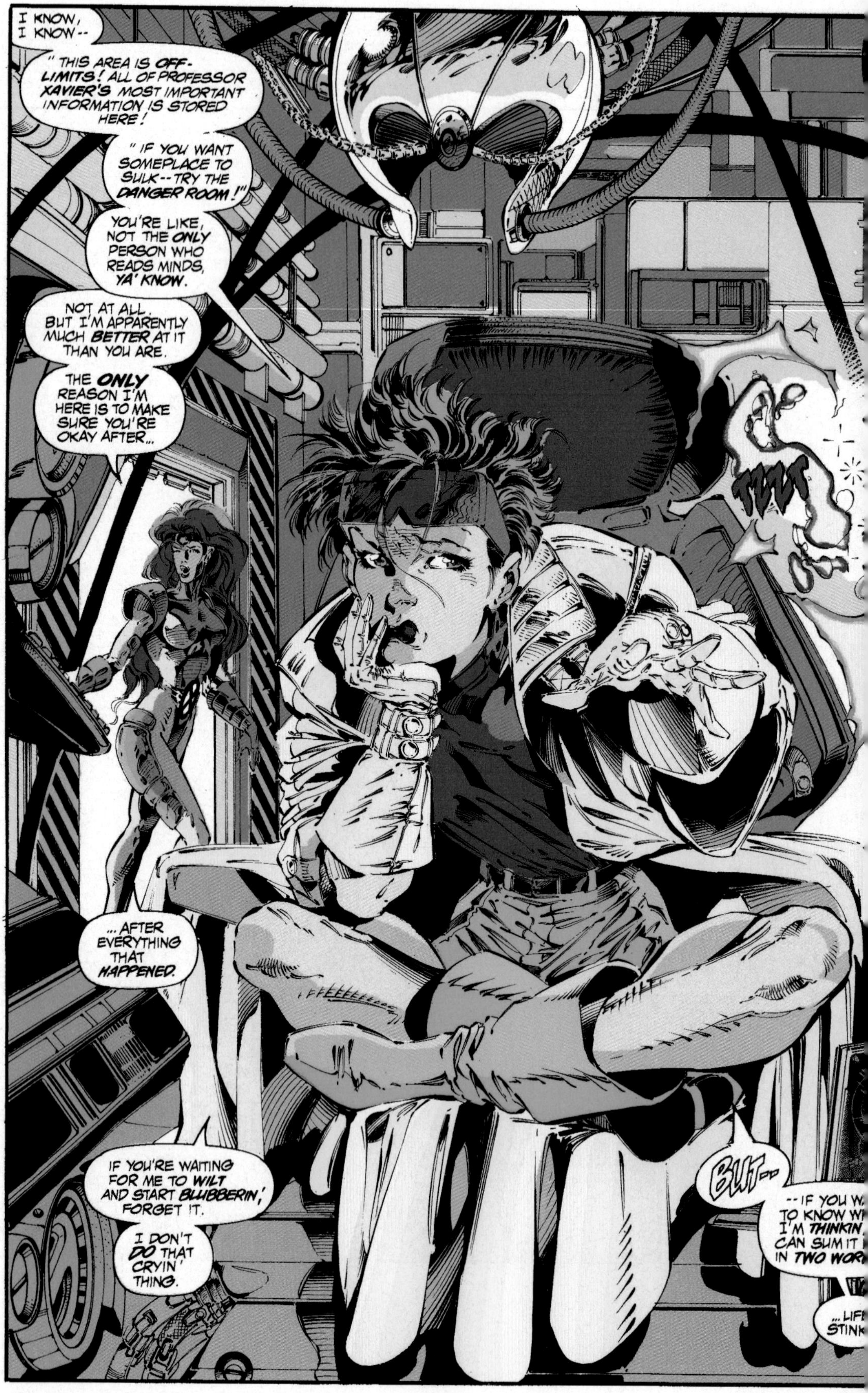

I KNOW, I KNOW--
"THIS AREA IS OFF-LIMITS! ALL OF PROFESSOR XAVIER'S MOST IMPORTANT INFORMATION IS STORED HERE!
"IF YOU WANT SOMEPLACE TO SULK--TRY THE DANGER ROOM!"
YOU'RE LIKE, NOT THE ONLY PERSON WHO READS MINDS, YA' KNOW.
NOT AT ALL. BUT I'M APPARENTLY MUCH BETTER AT IT THAN YOU ARE.
THE ONLY REASON I'M HERE IS TO MAKE SURE YOU'RE OKAY AFTER...
...AFTER EVERYTHING THAT HAPPENED.
TZZZT
IF YOU'RE WAITING FOR ME TO WILT AND START BLUBBERIN', FORGET IT.
I DON'T DO THAT CRYIN' THING.
BUT--

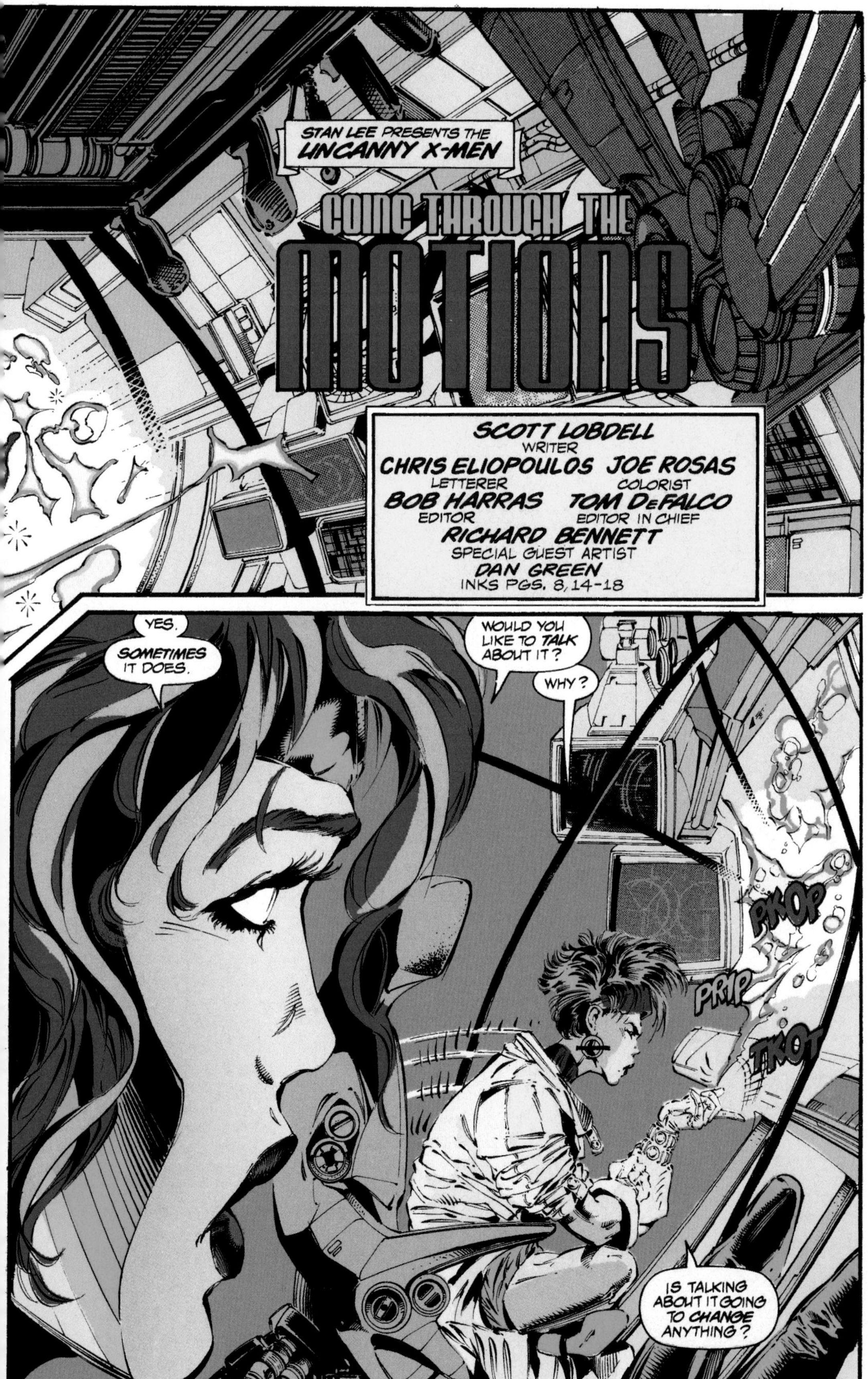
STAN LEE PRESENTS THE UNCANNY X-MEN
GOING THROUGH THE MOTIONS
SCOTT LOBDELL WRITER
CHRIS ELIOPOULOS LETTERER
JOE ROSAS COLORIST
BOB HARRAS EDITOR
TOM DEFALCO EDITOR IN CHIEF
RICHARD BENNETT SPECIAL GUEST ARTIST
DAN GREEN INKS PGS. 8,14-18
YES. SOMETIMES IT DOES.
WOULD YOU LIKE TO TALK ABOUT IT?
WHY?
PKOP
PRIP
TKOT
IS TALKING ABOUT IT GOING TO CHANGE ANYTHING?

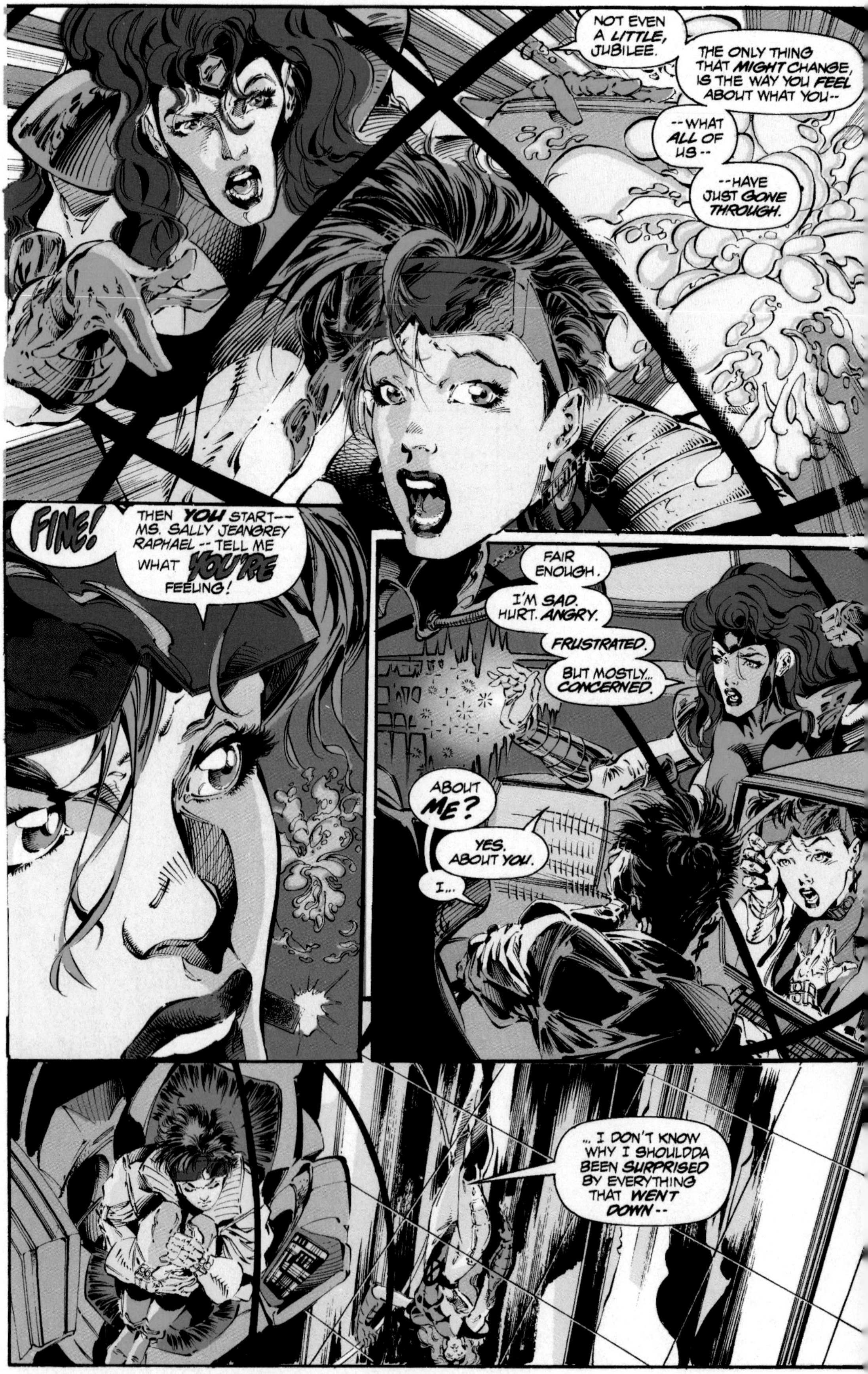
NOT EVEN A LITTLE, JUBILEE.
THE ONLY THING THAT MIGHT CHANGE, IS THE WAY YOU FEEL ABOUT WHAT YOU--
--WHAT ALL OF US--
--HAVE JUST GONE THROUGH.
FINE!
THEN YOU START-- MS. SALLY JEANGREY RAPHAEL -- TELL ME WHAT YOU'RE FEELING!
FAIR ENOUGH.
I'M SAD. HURT. ANGRY.
FRUSTRATED.
BUT MOSTLY... CONCERNED.
ABOUT ME?
YES. ABOUT YOU.
I...
... I DON'T KNOW WHY I SHOULDDA BEEN SURPRISED BY EVERYTHING THAT WENT DOWN--

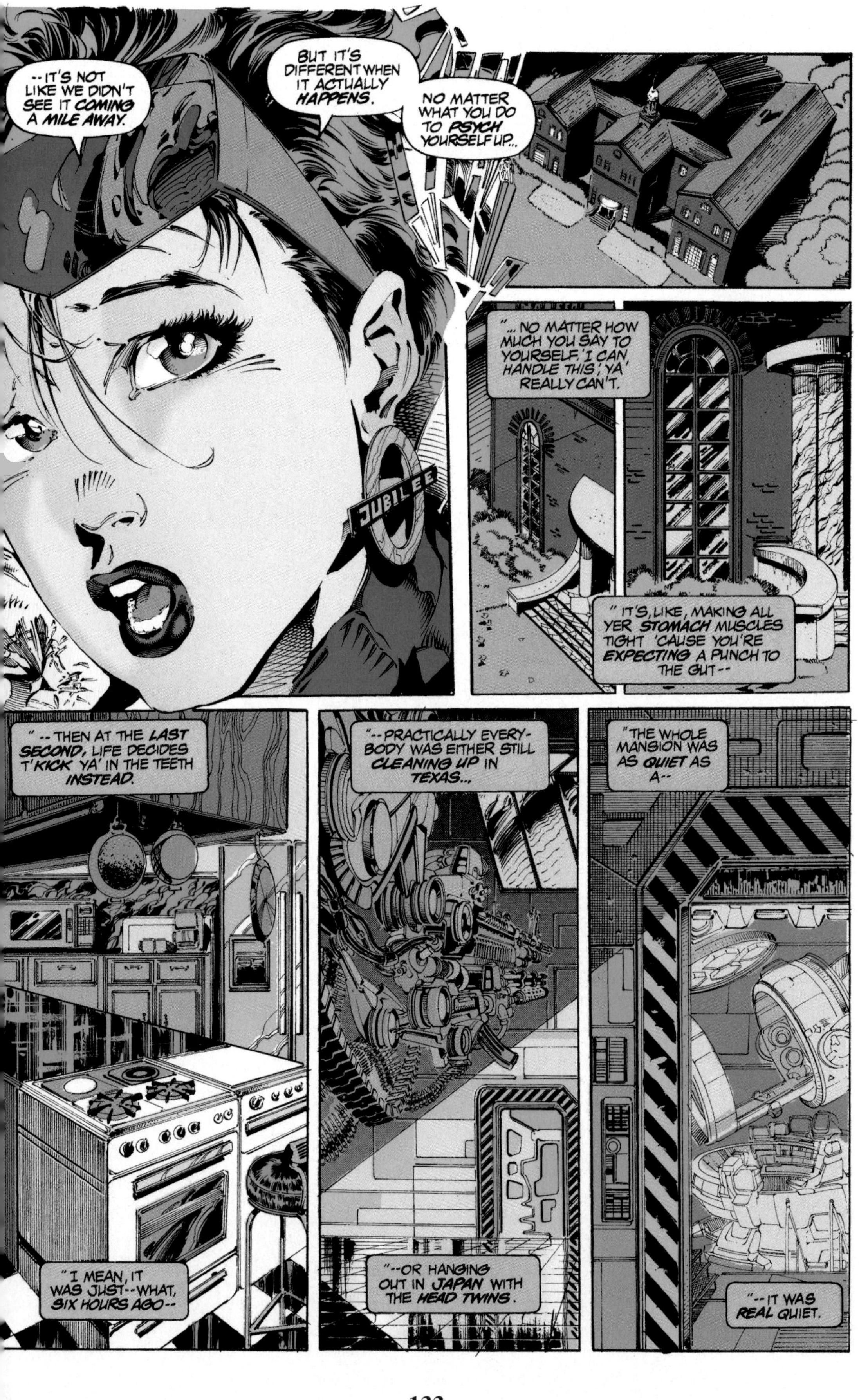
--IT'S NOT LIKE WE DIDN'T SEE IT COMING A MILE AWAY.
BUT IT'S DIFFERENT WHEN IT ACTUALLY HAPPENS.
NO MATTER WHAT YOU DO TO PSYCH YOURSELF UP...
"...NO MATTER HOW MUCH YOU SAY TO YOURSELF, 'I CAN HANDLE THIS,' YA' REALLY CAN'T.
"IT'S, LIKE, MAKING ALL YER STOMACH MUSCLES TIGHT 'CAUSE YOU'RE EXPECTING A PUNCH TO THE GUT--
"--THEN AT THE LAST SECOND, LIFE DECIDES T'KICK YA' IN THE TEETH INSTEAD.
"I MEAN, IT WAS JUST--WHAT, SIX HOURS AGO--
"--PRACTICALLY EVERY-BODY WAS EITHER STILL CLEANING UP IN TEXAS...
"--OR HANGING OUT IN JAPAN WITH THE HEAD TWINS.
"THE WHOLE MANSION WAS AS QUIET AS A--
"--IT WAS REAL QUIET.
JUBILEE

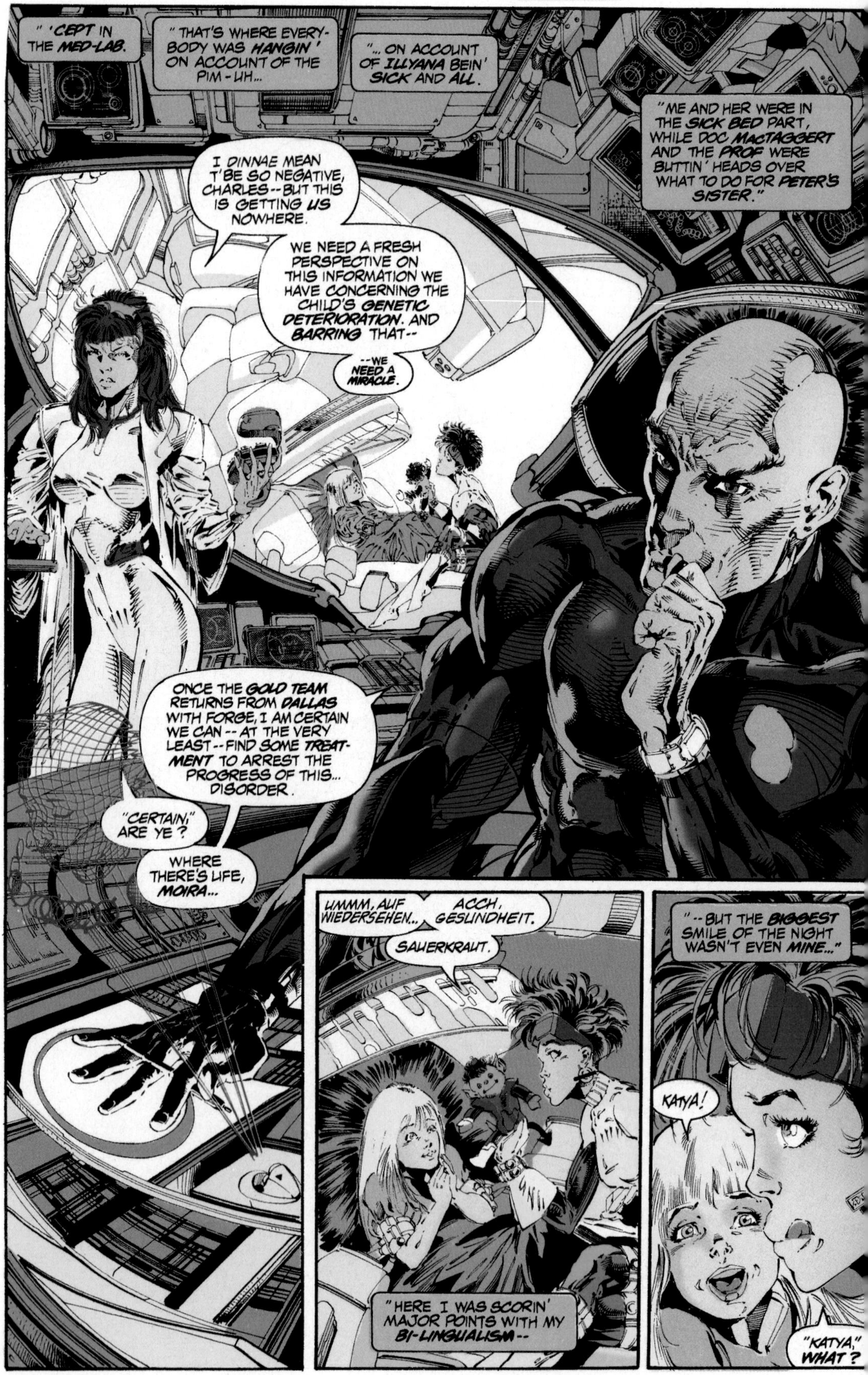
" 'CEPT IN THE MED-LAB.
" THAT'S WHERE EVERY-BODY WAS HANGIN' ON ACCOUNT OF THE PIM-UH...
"... ON ACCOUNT OF ILLYANA BEIN' SICK AND ALL.
"ME AND HER WERE IN THE SICK BED PART, WHILE DOC MACTAGGERT AND THE PROF WERE BUTTIN' HEADS OVER WHAT TO DO FOR PETER'S SISTER."
I DINNAE MEAN T'BE SO NEGATIVE, CHARLES--BUT THIS IS GETTING US NOWHERE.
WE NEED A FRESH PERSPECTIVE ON THIS INFORMATION WE HAVE CONCERNING THE CHILD'S GENETIC DETERIORATION. AND BARRING THAT--
--WE NEED A MIRACLE.
ONCE THE GOLD TEAM RETURNS FROM DALLAS WITH FORGE, I AM CERTAIN WE CAN -- AT THE VERY LEAST--FIND SOME TREATMENT TO ARREST THE PROGRESS OF THIS... DISORDER.
"CERTAIN," ARE YE?
WHERE THERE'S LIFE, MOIRA...
UMMM, AUF WIEDERSEHEN...
ACCH, GESUNDHEIT.
SAUERKRAUT.
"HERE I WAS SCORIN' MAJOR POINTS WITH MY BI-LINGUALISM--
"--BUT THE BIGGEST SMILE OF THE NIGHT WASN'T EVEN MINE..."
KATYA!
"KATYA," WHAT?

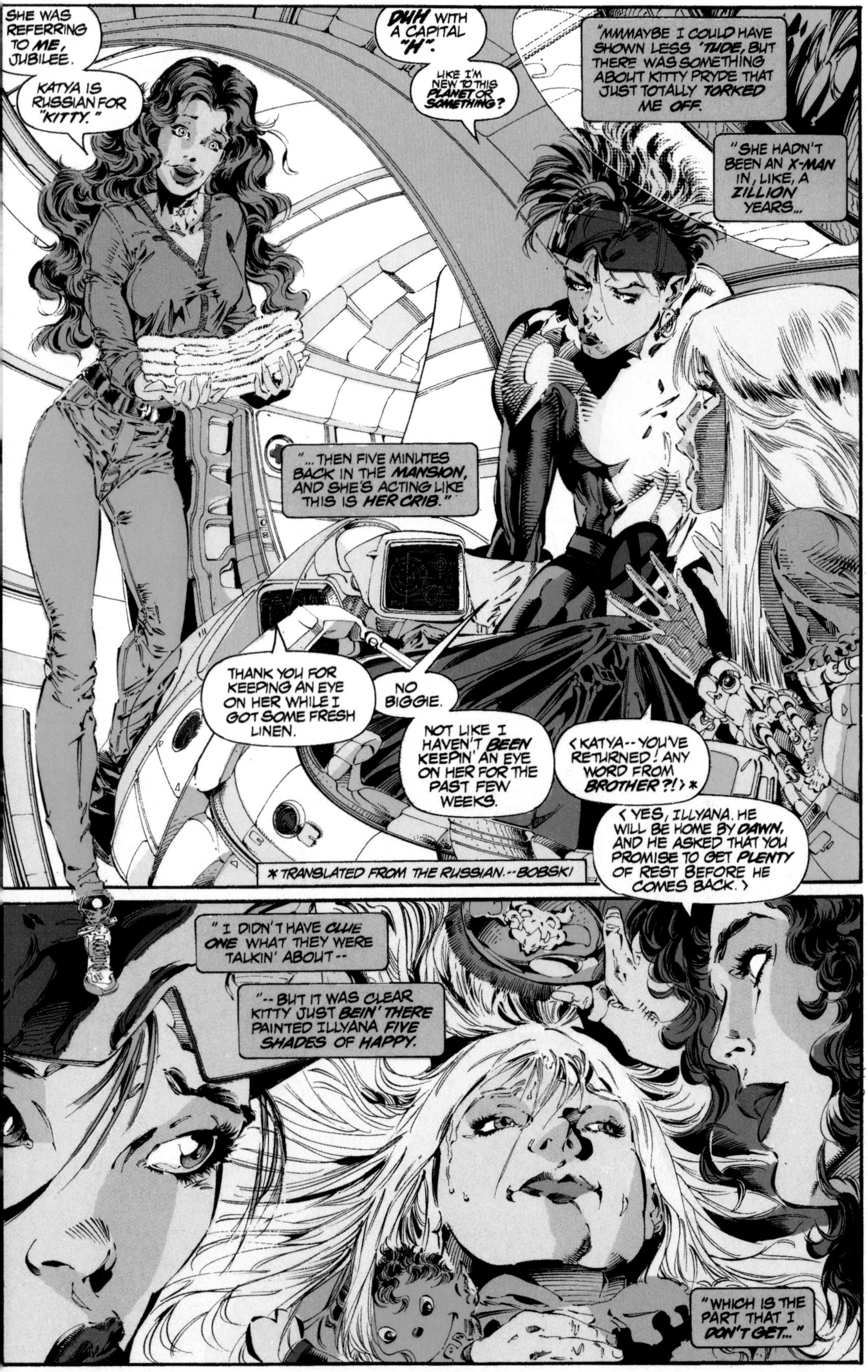
SHE WAS REFERRING TO ME, JUBILEE.
KATYA IS RUSSIAN FOR "KITTY."
DUH WITH A CAPITAL "H".
LIKE I'M NEW TO THIS PLANET OR SOMETHING?
"MMMAYBE I COULD HAVE SHOWN LESS 'TUDE, BUT THERE WAS SOMETHING ABOUT KITTY PRYDE THAT JUST TOTALLY TORKED ME OFF.
"SHE HADN'T BEEN AN X-MAN IN, LIKE, A ZILLION YEARS...
"...THEN FIVE MINUTES BACK IN THE MANSION, AND SHE'S ACTING LIKE THIS IS HER CRIB."
THANK YOU FOR KEEPING AN EYE ON HER WHILE I GOT SOME FRESH LINEN.
NO BIGGIE.
NOT LIKE I HAVEN'T BEEN KEEPIN' AN EYE ON HER FOR THE PAST FEW WEEKS.
<KATYA-- YOU'VE RETURNED! ANY WORD FROM BROTHER?!> *
<YES, ILLYANA. HE WILL BE HOME BY DAWN, AND HE ASKED THAT YOU PROMISE TO GET PLENTY OF REST BEFORE HE COMES BACK.>
* TRANSLATED FROM THE RUSSIAN.--BOBSKI
"I DIDN'T HAVE CLUE ONE WHAT THEY WERE TALKIN' ABOUT--
"--BUT IT WAS CLEAR KITTY JUST BEIN' THERE PAINTED ILLYANA FIVE SHADES OF HAPPY.
"WHICH IS THE PART THAT I DON'T GET..."

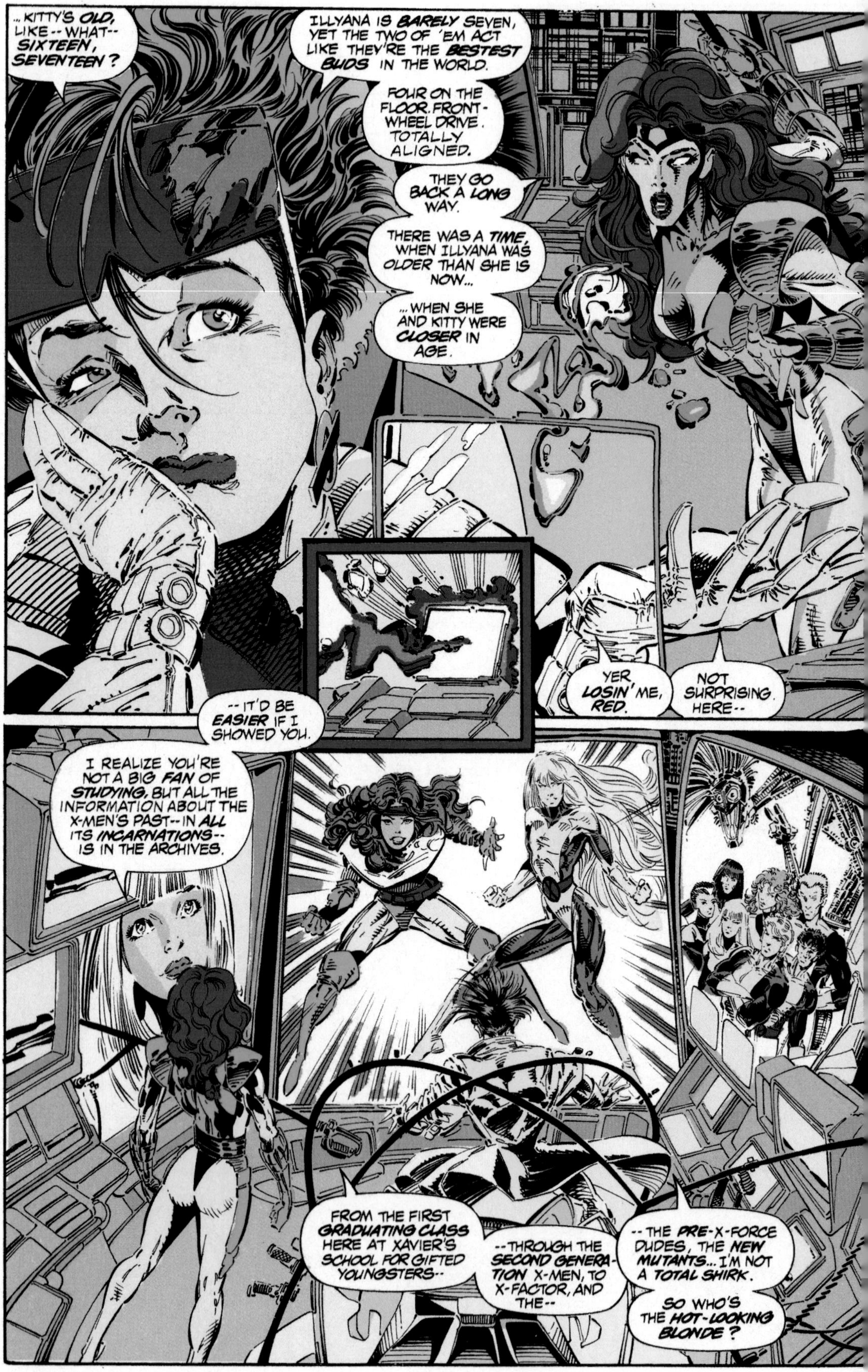
...KITTY'S OLD, LIKE -- WHAT -- SIXTEEN, SEVENTEEN?
ILLYANA IS BARELY SEVEN, YET THE TWO OF 'EM ACT LIKE THEY'RE THE BESTEST BUDS IN THE WORLD.
FOUR ON THE FLOOR. FRONT-WHEEL DRIVE. TOTALLY ALIGNED.
THEY GO BACK A LONG WAY.
THERE WAS A TIME, WHEN ILLYANA WAS OLDER THAN SHE IS NOW...
...WHEN SHE AND KITTY WERE CLOSER IN AGE.
YER LOSIN' ME, RED.
NOT SURPRISING HERE--
-- IT'D BE EASIER IF I SHOWED YOU.
I REALIZE YOU'RE NOT A BIG FAN OF STUDYING, BUT ALL THE INFORMATION ABOUT THE X-MEN'S PAST-- IN ALL ITS INCARNATIONS-- IS IN THE ARCHIVES.
FROM THE FIRST GRADUATING CLASS HERE AT XAVIER'S SCHOOL FOR GIFTED YOUNGSTERS--
--THROUGH THE SECOND GENERATION X-MEN, TO X-FACTOR, AND THE--
-- THE PRE-X-FORCE DUDES, THE NEW MUTANTS... I'M NOT A TOTAL SHIRK.
SO WHO'S THE HOT-LOOKING BLONDE?

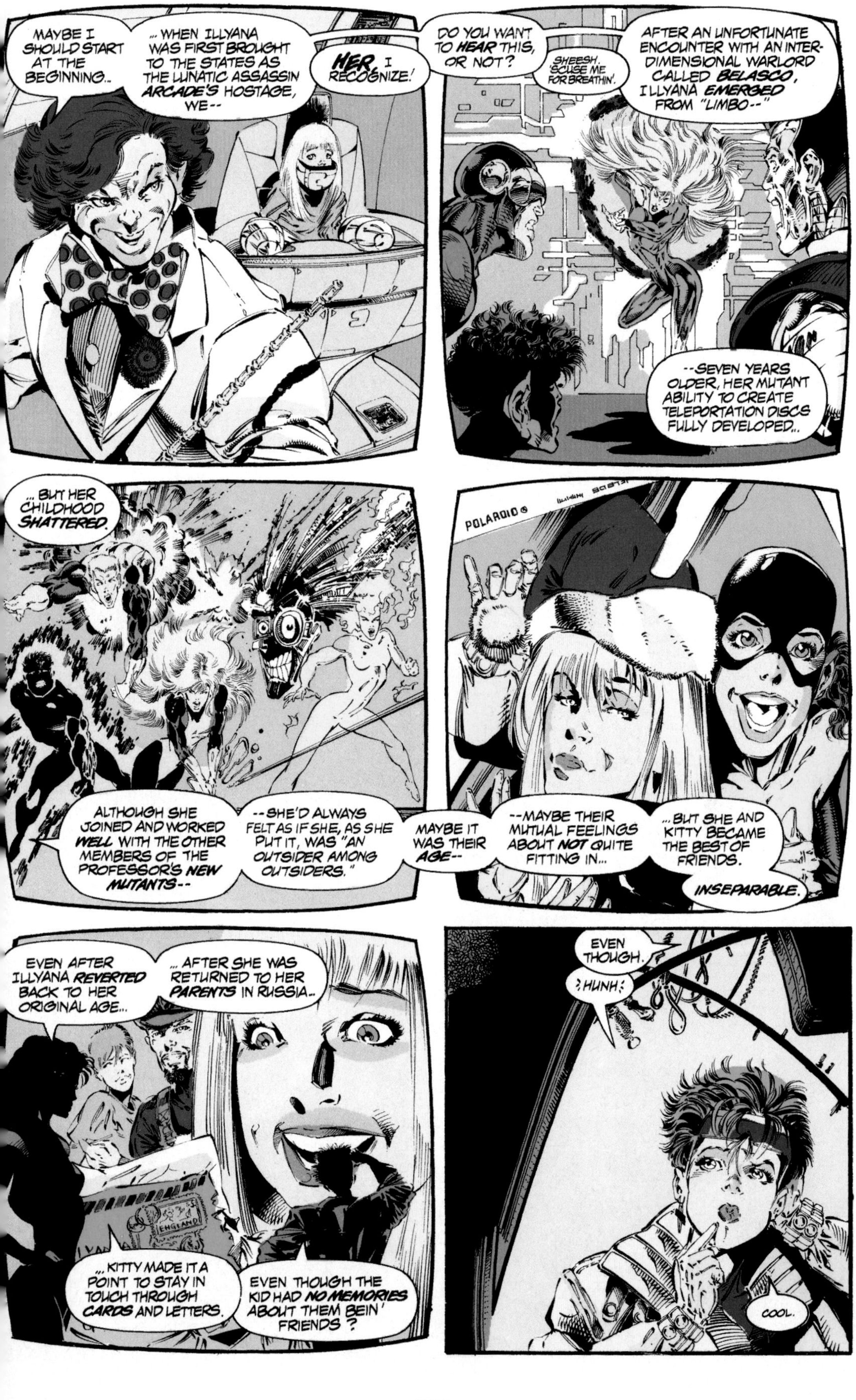
MAYBE I SHOULD START AT THE BEGINNING..
... WHEN ILLYANA WAS FIRST BROUGHT TO THE STATES AS THE LUNATIC ASSASSIN ARCADE'S HOSTAGE, WE--
HER, I RECOGNIZE!
DO YOU WANT TO HEAR THIS, OR NOT?
SHEESH. 'SCUSE ME FOR BREATHIN'.
AFTER AN UNFORTUNATE ENCOUNTER WITH AN INTER-DIMENSIONAL WARLORD CALLED BELASCO, ILLYANA EMERGED FROM "LIMBO--"
--SEVEN YEARS OLDER, HER MUTANT ABILITY TO CREATE TELEPORTATION DISCS FULLY DEVELOPED...
... BUT HER CHILDHOOD SHATTERED.
POLAROID
ALTHOUGH SHE JOINED AND WORKED WELL WITH THE OTHER MEMBERS OF THE PROFESSOR'S NEW MUTANTS--
--SHE'D ALWAYS FELT AS IF SHE, AS SHE PUT IT, WAS "AN OUTSIDER AMONG OUTSIDERS."
MAYBE IT WAS THEIR AGE--
--MAYBE THEIR MUTUAL FEELINGS ABOUT NOT QUITE FITTING IN...
... BUT SHE AND KITTY BECAME THE BEST OF FRIENDS.
INSEPARABLE.
EVEN AFTER ILLYANA REVERTED BACK TO HER ORIGINAL AGE...
... AFTER SHE WAS RETURNED TO HER PARENTS IN RUSSIA...
ENGLAND
... KITTY MADE IT A POINT TO STAY IN TOUCH THROUGH CARDS AND LETTERS.
EVEN THOUGH THE KID HAD NO MEMORIES ABOUT THEM BEIN' FRIENDS?
EVEN THOUGH.
HUNH
COOL.

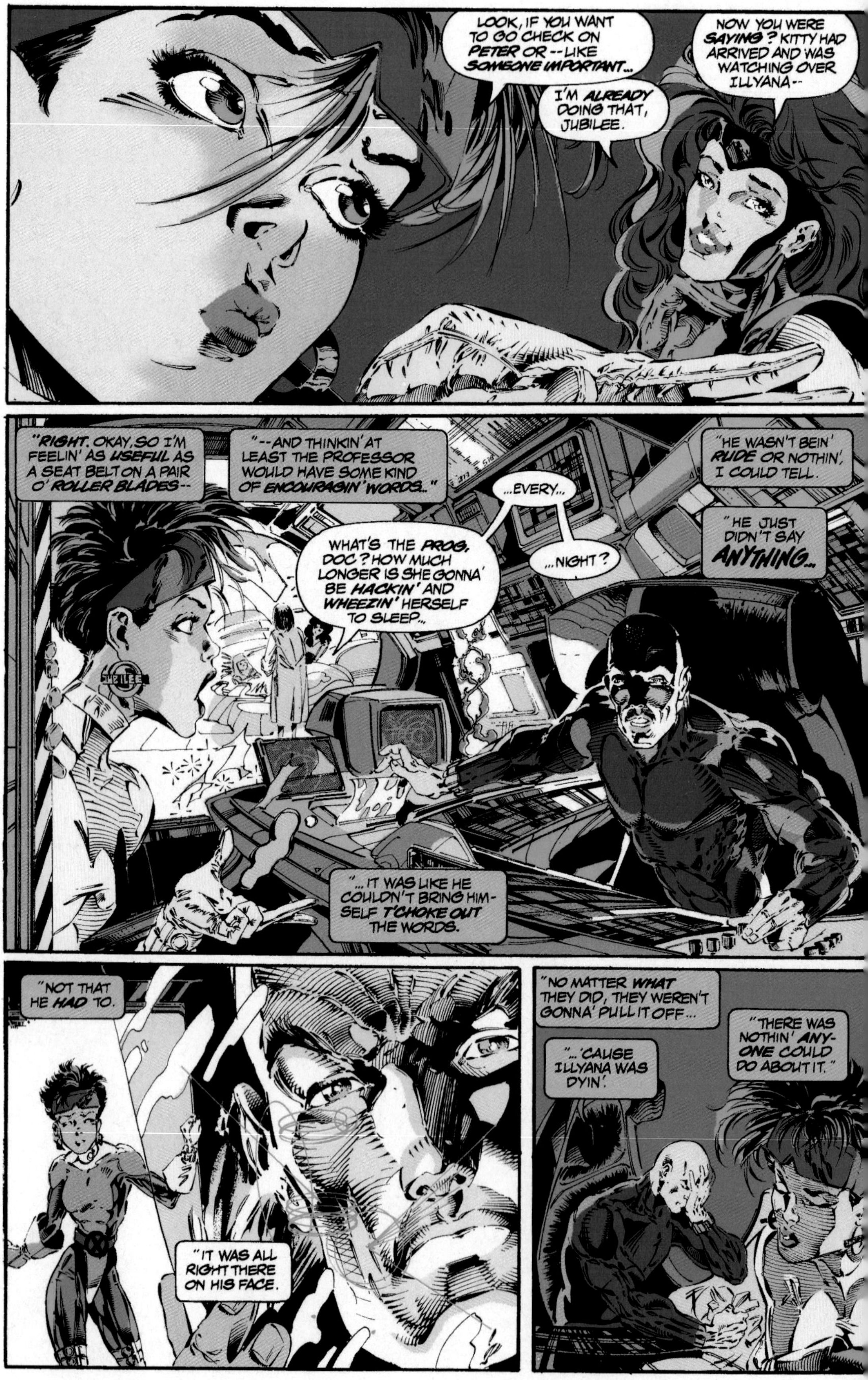
LOOK, IF YOU WANT TO GO CHECK ON PETER OR --LIKE SOMEONE IMPORTANT...
I'M ALREADY DOING THAT, JUBILEE.
NOW YOU WERE SAYING? KITTY HAD ARRIVED AND WAS WATCHING OVER ILLYANA--
"RIGHT. OKAY. SO I'M FEELIN' AS USEFUL AS A SEAT BELT ON A PAIR O' ROLLER BLADES--
"--AND THINKIN' AT LEAST THE PROFESSOR WOULD HAVE SOME KIND OF ENCOURAGIN' WORDS.."
WHAT'S THE PROG, DOC? HOW MUCH LONGER IS SHE GONNA' BE HACKIN' AND WHEEZIN' HERSELF TO SLEEP...
...EVERY...
...NIGHT?
"HE WASN'T BEIN' RUDE OR NOTHIN', I COULD TELL.
"HE JUST DIDN'T SAY ANYTHING...
"... IT WAS LIKE HE COULDN'T BRING HIM-SELF T'CHOKE OUT THE WORDS.
"NOT THAT HE HAD TO.
"IT WAS ALL RIGHT THERE ON HIS FACE.
"NO MATTER WHAT THEY DID, THEY WEREN'T GONNA' PULL IT OFF...
"...'CAUSE ILLYANA WAS DYIN'.
"THERE WAS NOTHIN' ANY-ONE COULD DO ABOUT IT."

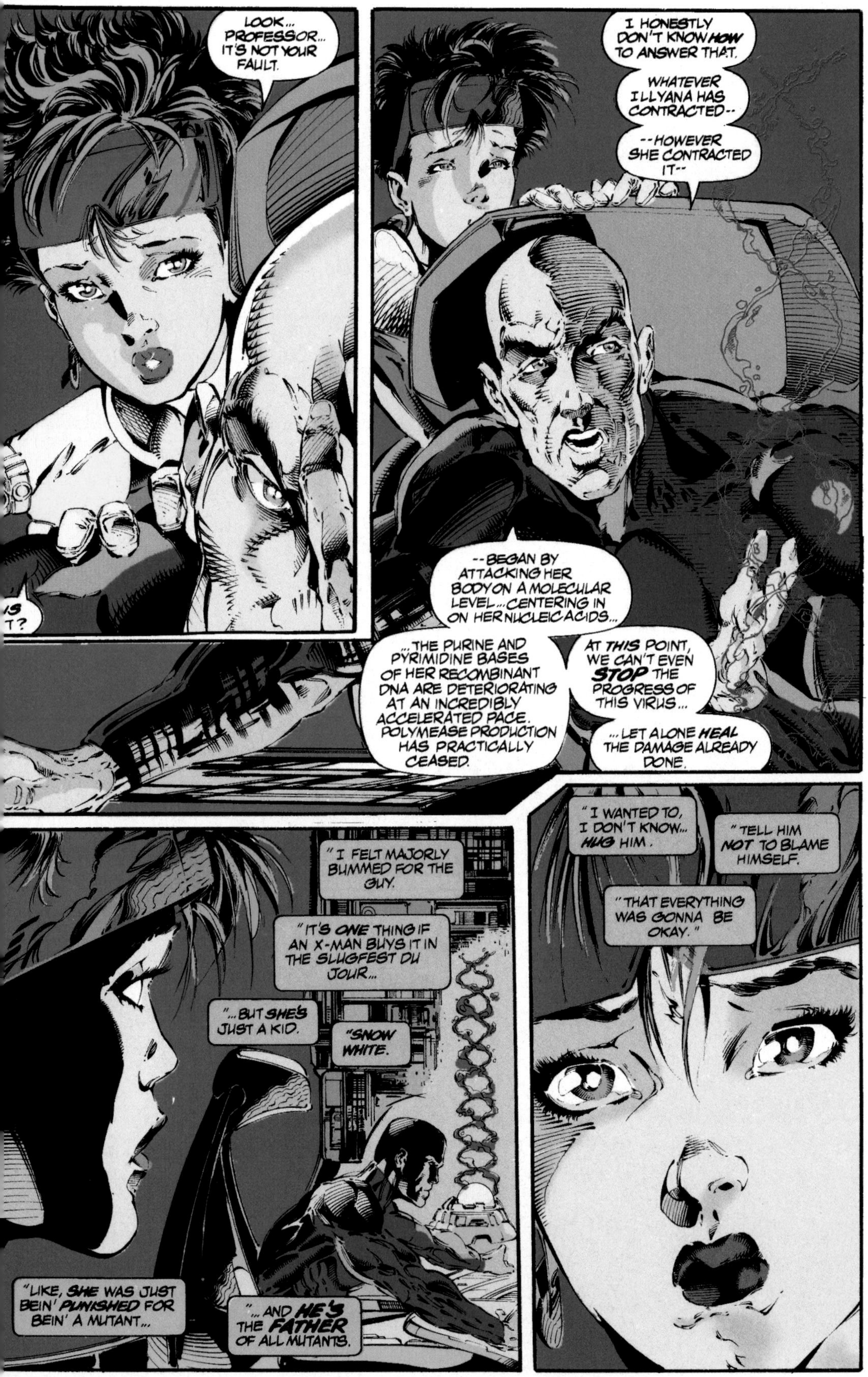
LOOK... PROFESSOR... IT'S NOT YOUR FAULT.
I HONESTLY DON'T KNOW HOW TO ANSWER THAT.
WHATEVER ILLYANA HAS CONTRACTED--
--HOWEVER SHE CONTRACTED IT--
--BEGAN BY ATTACKING HER BODY ON A MOLECULAR LEVEL... CENTERING IN ON HER NUCLEIC ACIDS...
...THE PURINE AND PYRIMIDINE BASES OF HER RECOMBINANT DNA ARE DETERIORATING AT AN INCREDIBLY ACCELERATED PACE. POLYMEASE PRODUCTION HAS PRACTICALLY CEASED.
AT THIS POINT, WE CAN'T EVEN STOP THE PROGRESS OF THIS VIRUS...
...LET ALONE HEAL THE DAMAGE ALREADY DONE.
"I FELT MAJORLY BUMMED FOR THE GUY.
"IT'S ONE THING IF AN X-MAN BUYS IT IN THE SLUGFEST DU JOUR...
"...BUT SHE'S JUST A KID.
"SNOW WHITE.
"LIKE, SHE WAS JUST BEIN' PUNISHED FOR BEIN' A MUTANT...
"...AND HE'S THE FATHER OF ALL MUTANTS.
"I WANTED TO, I DON'T KNOW... HUG HIM.
"TELL HIM NOT TO BLAME HIMSELF.
"THAT EVERYTHING WAS GONNA BE OKAY."

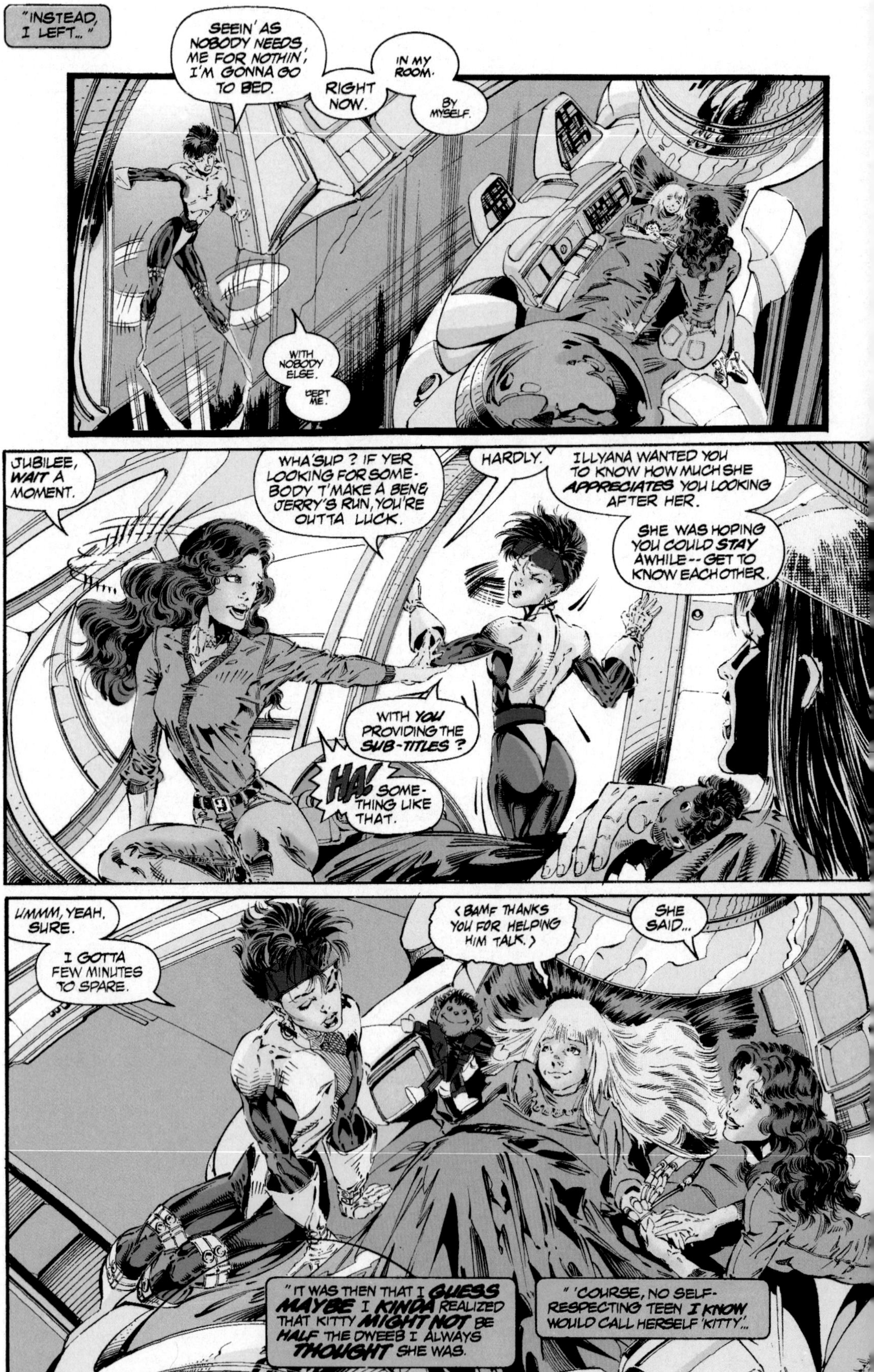
"INSTEAD, I LEFT..."
SEEIN' AS NOBODY NEEDS ME FOR NOTHIN', I'M GONNA GO TO BED.
RIGHT NOW.
IN MY ROOM.
BY MYSELF.
WITH NOBODY ELSE.
'CEPT ME.
JUBILEE, WAIT A MOMENT.
WHA'SUP? IF YER LOOKING FOR SOME-BODY T'MAKE A BEN & JERRY'S RUN, YOU'RE OUTTA LUCK.
HARDLY.
ILLYANA WANTED YOU TO KNOW HOW MUCH SHE APPRECIATES YOU LOOKING AFTER HER.
SHE WAS HOPING YOU COULD STAY AWHILE -- GET TO KNOW EACH OTHER.
WITH YOU PROVIDING THE SUB-TITLES?
HA! SOME-THING LIKE THAT.
UMMM, YEAH, SURE.
I GOTTA FEW MINUTES TO SPARE.
< BAMF THANKS YOU FOR HELPING HIM TALK. >
SHE SAID...
"IT WAS THEN THAT I GUESS MAYBE I KINDA REALIZED THAT KITTY MIGHT NOT BE HALF THE DWEEB I ALWAYS THOUGHT SHE WAS.
"'COURSE, NO SELF-RESPECTING TEEN I KNOW WOULD CALL HERSELF 'KITTY'...

"WHAT WAS IT-- AN HOUR... TWO?

"SITTIN' THERE ON THE BED, YAKKIN' AND WHISPERIN' AND--

"--DON'T EVER TELL ANYBODY THIS, 'CAUSE I'LL DENY IT--

"--AND GIGGLIN'...

"...GAWD, I CAN'T BELIEVE I ACTUALLY GIGGLED!

"EVERYTHING SEEMED, ALMOST FOR A HALF OF A FRACTION OF AN INSTANT, LIKE THAT EVERYTHING WAS 'NORMAL.'

"TRUTH? IT WAS PROBABLY THE FIRST TIME SINCE MY TWELFTH BIRTHDAY, THAT I FELT LESS LIKE A MUTANT...

"...AND MORE LIKE A GIRL.

"AGAIN.

"I KNEW IT COULDN'T LAST."

FITZROY'S INJURIES NECESSITATED HIS RELEASE TO FEDERAL AUTHORITIES, CHARLES.

AND FORGE'S STATUS WITH THE GOVERNMENT HAS DISSUADED THE AUTHORITIES FROM ARRESTING PETER FOR THE ASSAULT. *

*SEE LAST ISSUE. --B.H.

THEN I SHOULD EXPECT YOU HOME BY DAWN?

YES. IT IS TO BE HOPED OUR RETURN WILL CALM PETER...

...HE IS HIGHLY AGITATED...

...AND CONCERNED ABOUT HIS SISTER.

AS ARE WE ALL, ORORO.

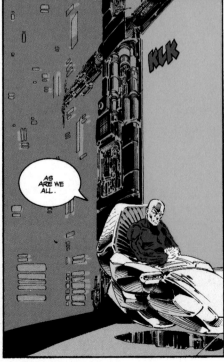

KLK

AS ARE WE ALL.

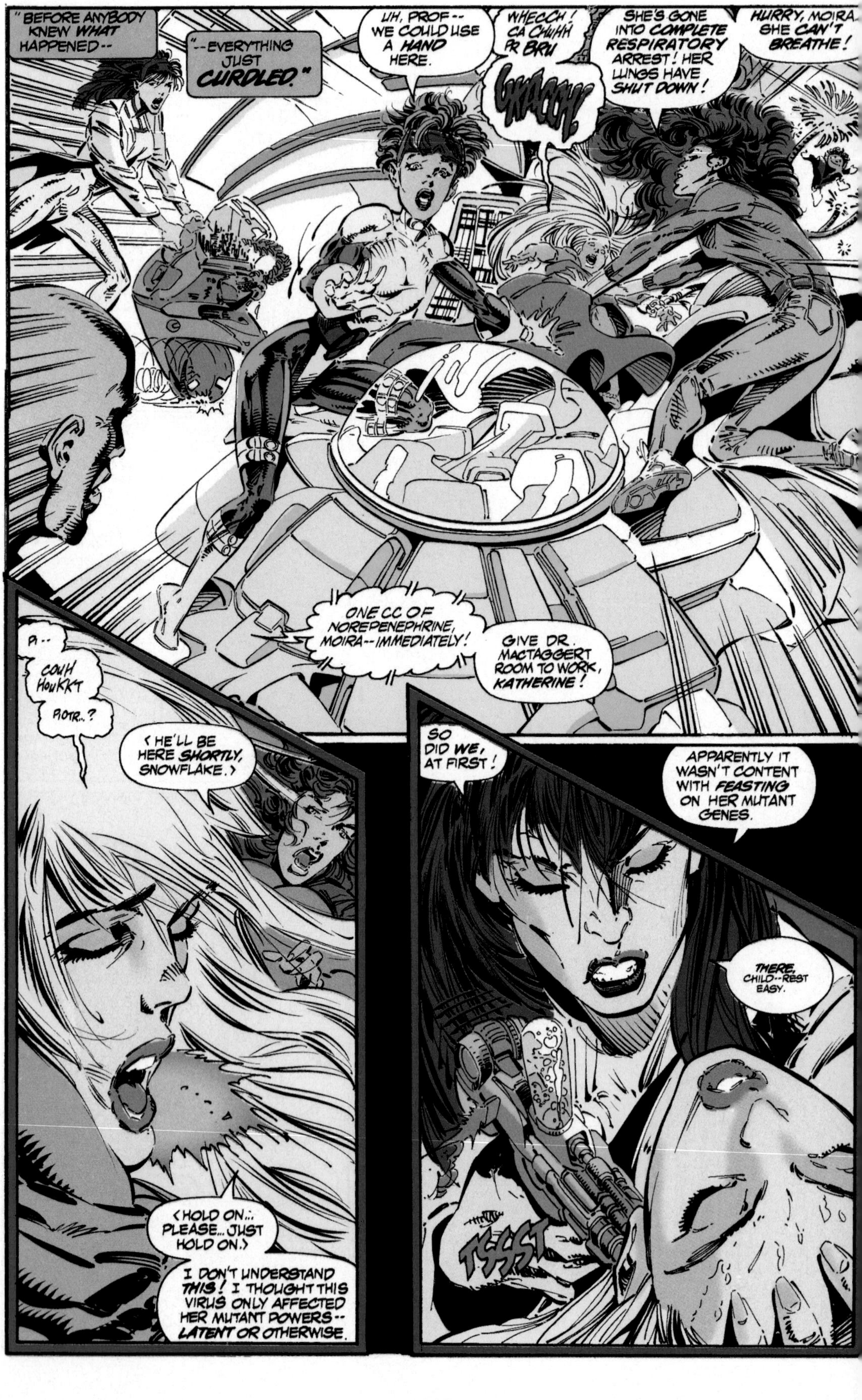

"BEFORE ANYBODY KNEW WHAT HAPPENED--
"--EVERYTHING JUST CURDLED."
UH, PROF-- WE COULD USE A HAND HERE.
WHECCH! CA CHUHH PR BRU
GKACCH!
SHE'S GONE INTO COMPLETE RESPIRATORY ARREST! HER LUNGS HAVE SHUT DOWN!
HURRY, MOIRA. SHE CAN'T BREATHE!
ONE CC OF NOREPENEPHRINE, MOIRA--IMMEDIATELY!
GIVE DR. MACTAGGERT ROOM TO WORK, KATHERINE!
PI--
COUH HOUKKT
PIOTR..?
<HE'LL BE HERE SHORTLY, SNOWFLAKE.>
<HOLD ON... PLEASE... JUST HOLD ON.>
I DON'T UNDERSTAND THIS! I THOUGHT THIS VIRUS ONLY AFFECTED HER MUTANT POWERS--LATENT OR OTHERWISE.
SO DID WE, AT FIRST!
APPARENTLY IT WASN'T CONTENT WITH FEASTING ON HER MUTANT GENES.
THERE, CHILD--REST EASY.
TSSST

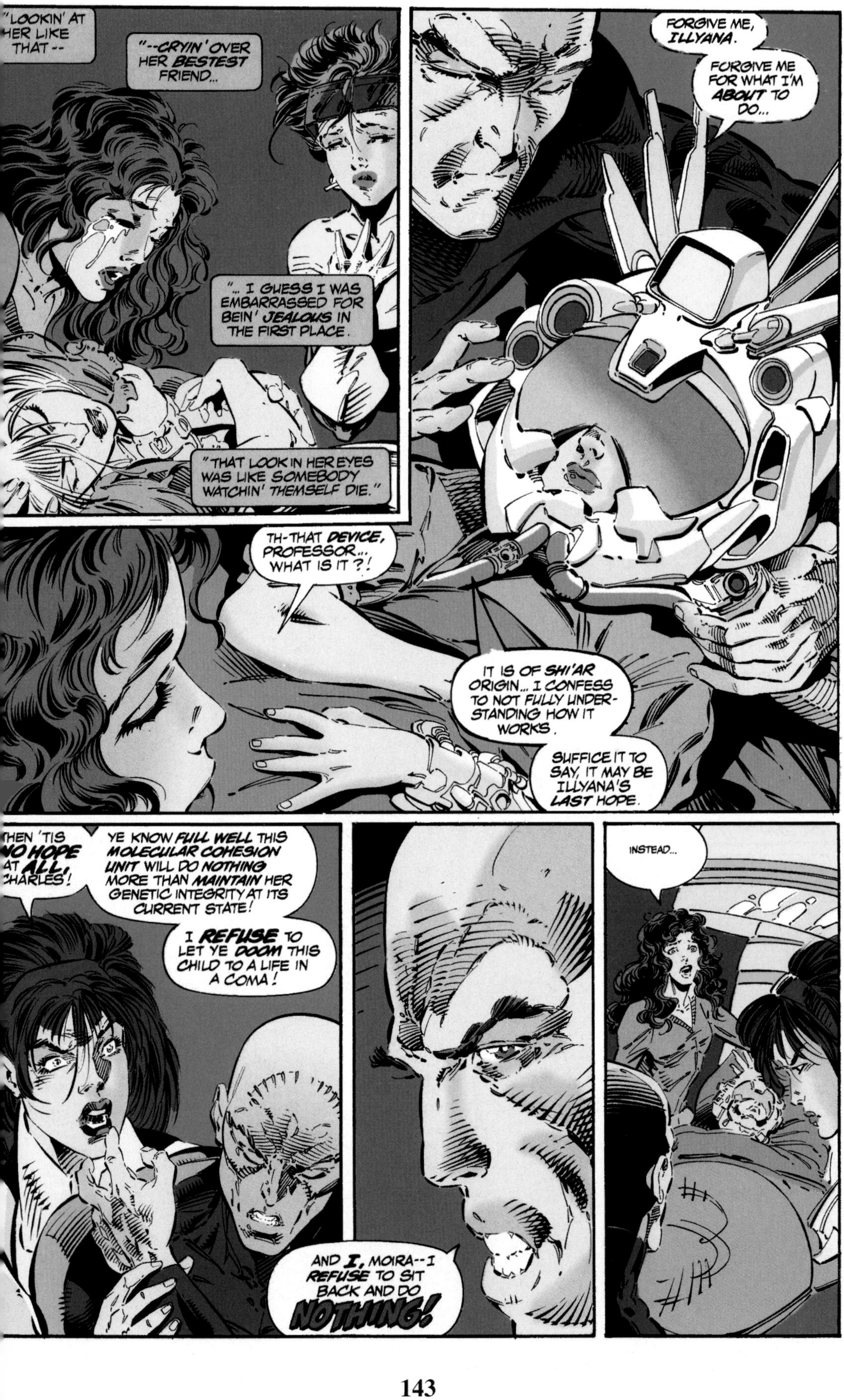
"LOOKIN' AT HER LIKE THAT --
"--CRYIN' OVER HER BESTEST FRIEND...
"... I GUESS I WAS EMBARRASSED FOR BEIN' JEALOUS IN THE FIRST PLACE.
"THAT LOOK IN HER EYES WAS LIKE SOMEBODY WATCHIN' THEMSELF DIE."
FORGIVE ME, ILLYANA.
FORGIVE ME FOR WHAT I'M ABOUT TO DO...
TH-THAT DEVICE, PROFESSOR... WHAT IS IT?!
IT IS OF SHI'AR ORIGIN... I CONFESS TO NOT FULLY UNDER-STANDING HOW IT WORKS.
SUFFICE IT TO SAY, IT MAY BE ILLYANA'S LAST HOPE.
THEN 'TIS NO HOPE AT ALL, CHARLES!
YE KNOW FULL WELL THIS MOLECULAR COHESION UNIT WILL DO NOTHING MORE THAN MAINTAIN HER GENETIC INTEGRITY AT ITS CURRENT STATE!
I REFUSE TO LET YE DOOM THIS CHILD TO A LIFE IN A COMA!
AND I, MOIRA--I REFUSE TO SIT BACK AND DO NOTHING!
INSTEAD...

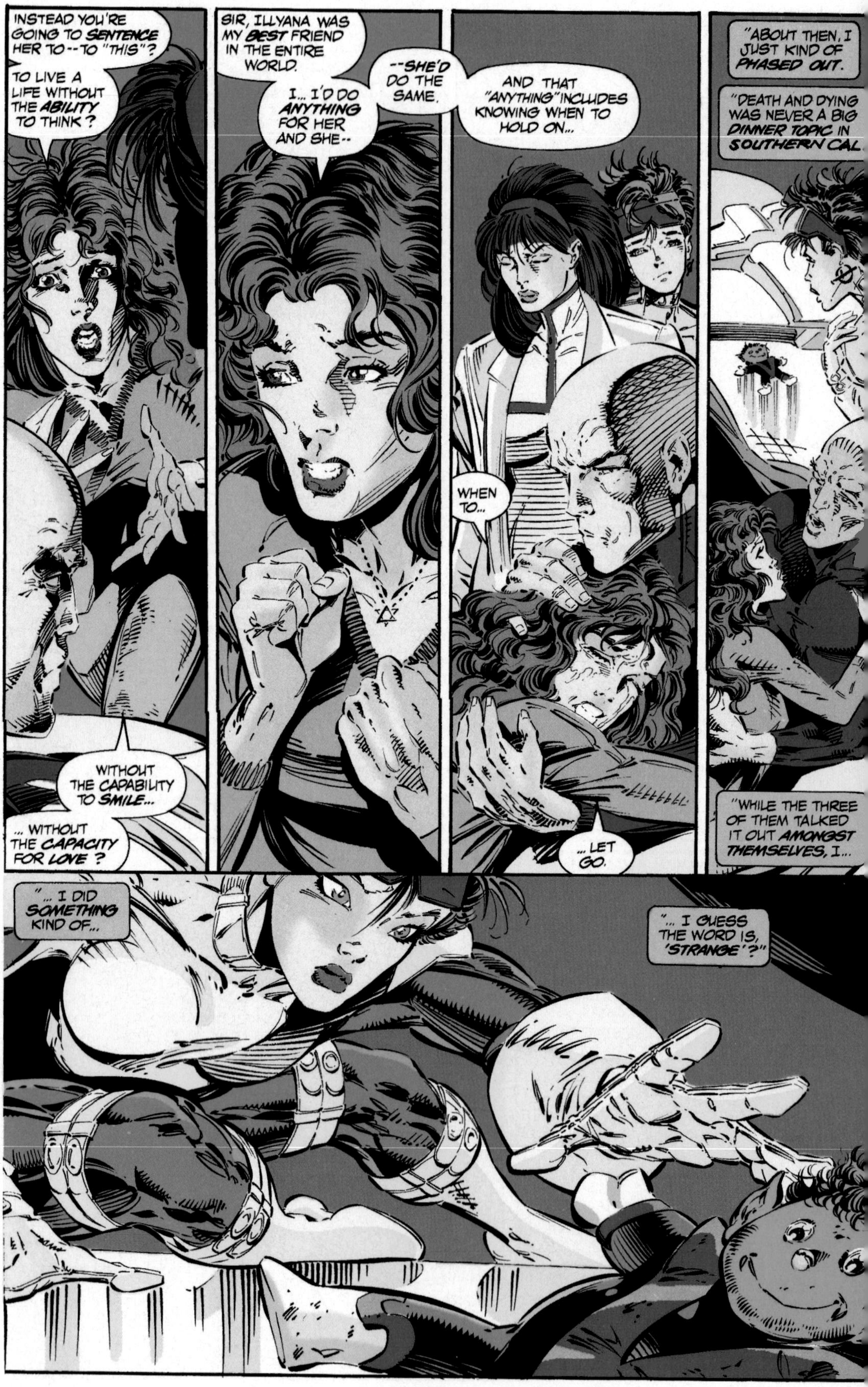

INSTEAD YOU'RE GOING TO SENTENCE HER TO--TO "THIS"?
TO LIVE A LIFE WITHOUT THE ABILITY TO THINK?
WITHOUT THE CAPABILITY TO SMILE...
... WITHOUT THE CAPACITY FOR LOVE?
SIR, ILLYANA WAS MY BEST FRIEND IN THE ENTIRE WORLD.
I... I'D DO ANYTHING FOR HER AND SHE--
--SHE'D DO THE SAME.
AND THAT "ANYTHING" INCLUDES KNOWING WHEN TO HOLD ON...
WHEN TO...
... LET GO.
"ABOUT THEN, I JUST KIND OF PHASED OUT.
"DEATH AND DYING WAS NEVER A BIG DINNER TOPIC IN SOUTHERN CAL.
"WHILE THE THREE OF THEM TALKED IT OUT AMONGST THEMSELVES, I...
"... I DID SOMETHING KIND OF...
"... I GUESS THE WORD IS, 'STRANGE'?"

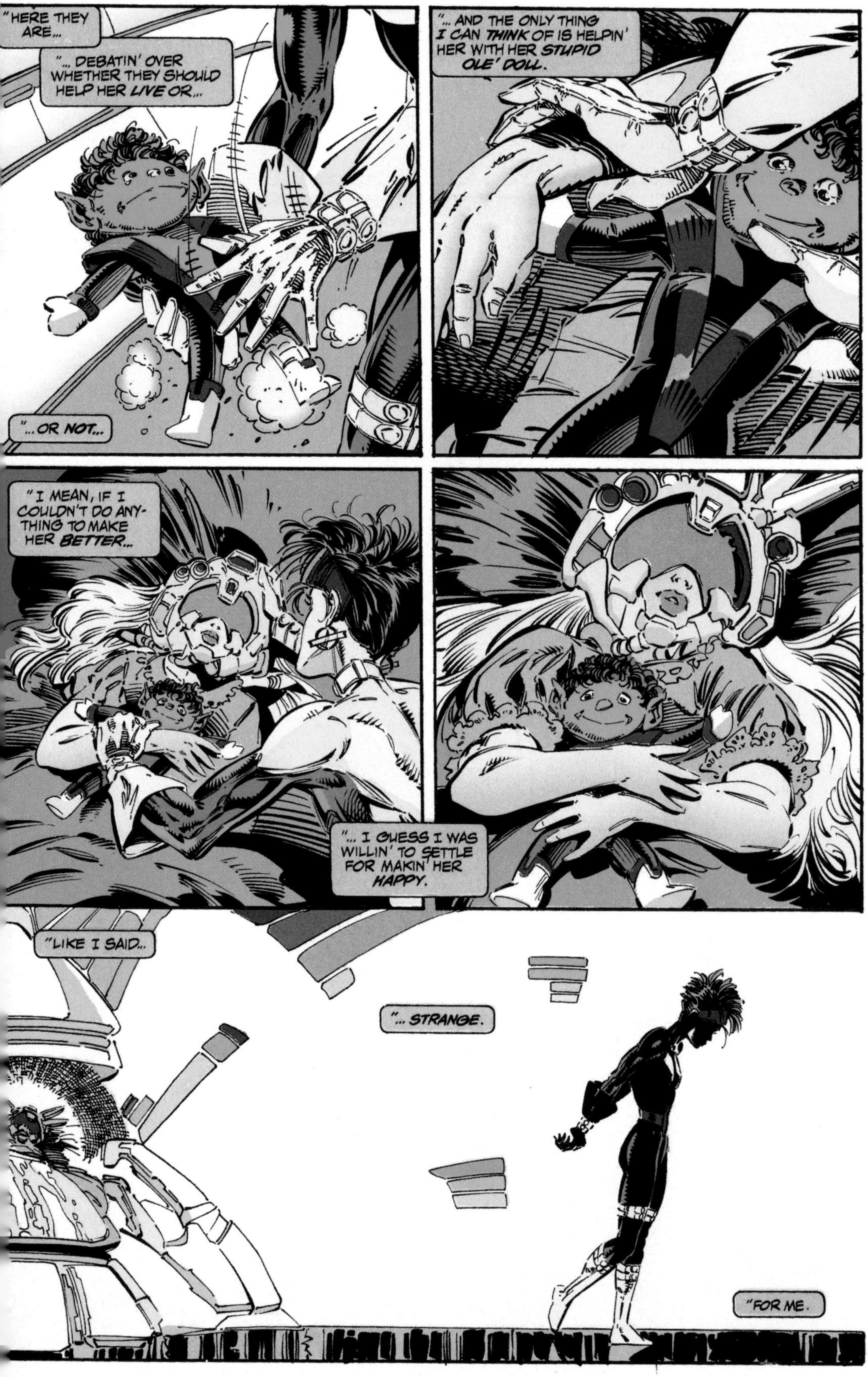
"HERE THEY ARE...
"... DEBATIN' OVER WHETHER THEY SHOULD HELP HER LIVE OR...
"...OR NOT...
"... AND THE ONLY THING I CAN THINK OF IS HELPIN' HER WITH HER STUPID OLE' DOLL.
"I MEAN, IF I COULDN'T DO ANY-THING TO MAKE HER BETTER...
"... I GUESS I WAS WILLIN' TO SETTLE FOR MAKIN' HER HAPPY.
"LIKE I SAID...
"... STRANGE.
"FOR ME.

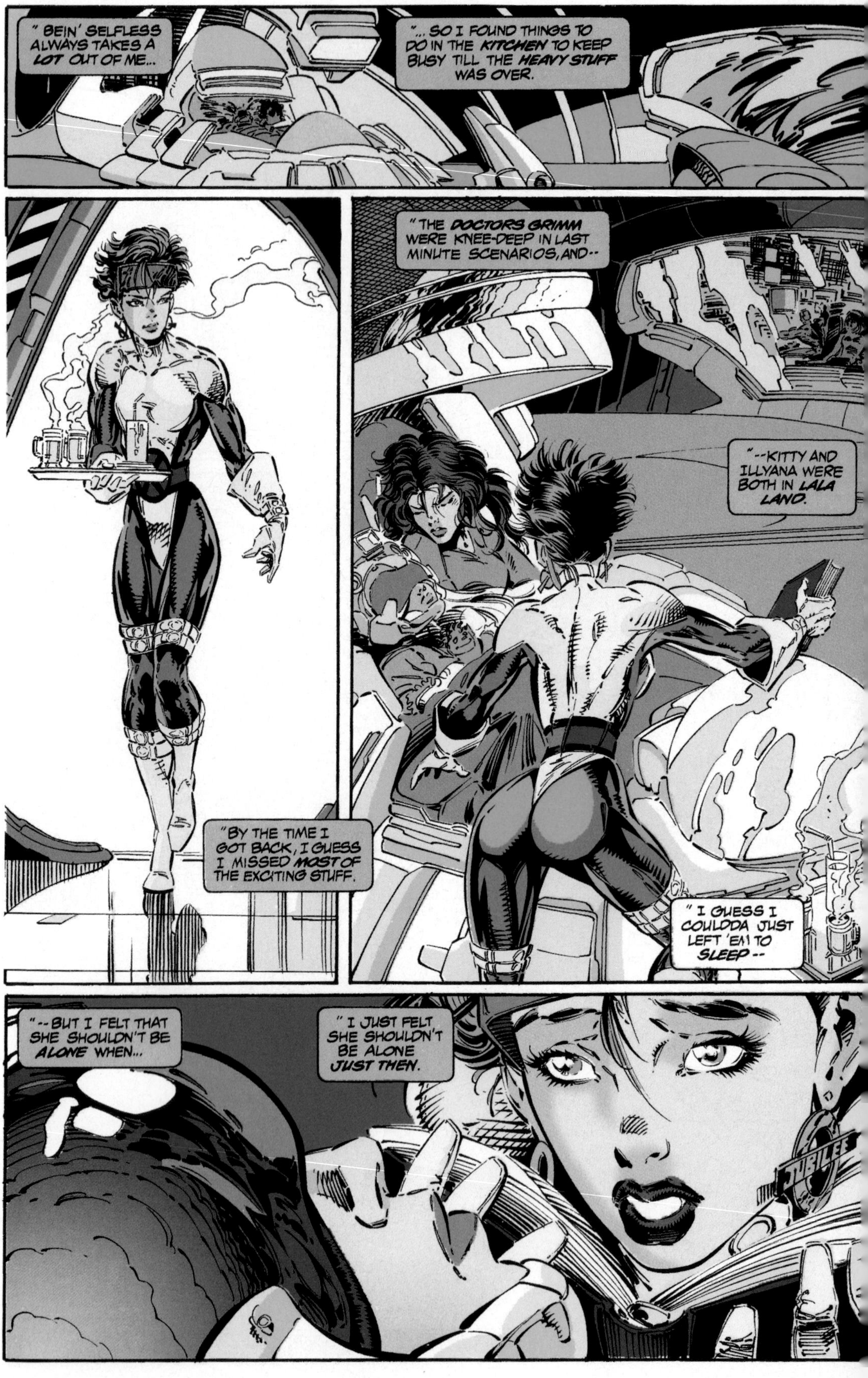

"BEIN' SELFLESS ALWAYS TAKES A LOT OUT OF ME...
"...SO I FOUND THINGS TO DO IN THE KITCHEN TO KEEP BUSY TILL THE HEAVY STUFF WAS OVER.
"BY THE TIME I GOT BACK, I GUESS I MISSED MOST OF THE EXCITING STUFF.
"THE DOCTORS GRIMM WERE KNEE-DEEP IN LAST MINUTE SCENARIOS, AND--
"--KITTY AND ILLYANA WERE BOTH IN LALA LAND.
"I GUESS I COULDDA JUST LEFT 'EM TO SLEEP--
"--BUT I FELT THAT SHE SHOULDN'T BE ALONE WHEN...
"I JUST FELT SHE SHOULDN'T BE ALONE JUST THEN.

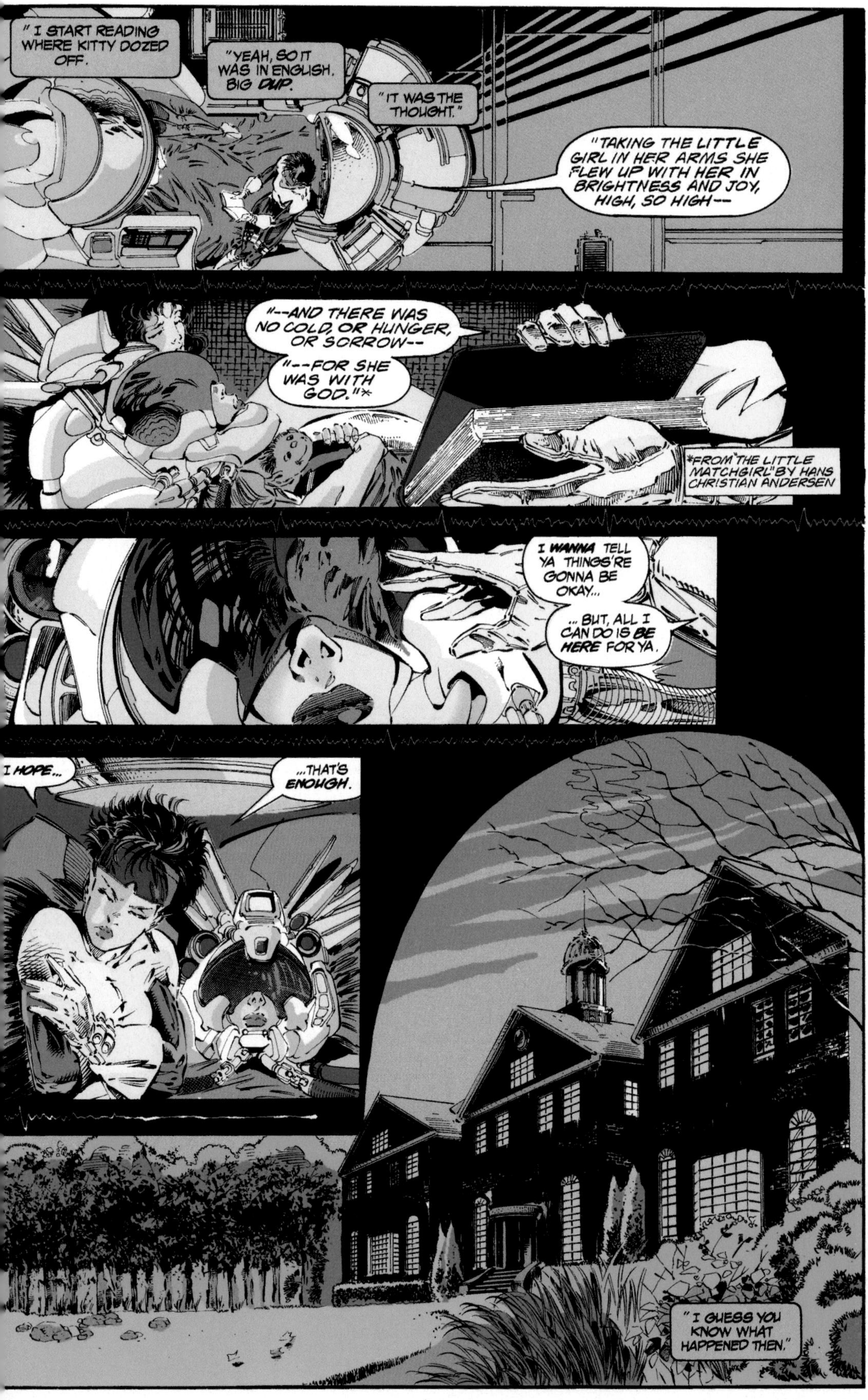

"I START READING WHERE KITTY DOZED OFF.
"YEAH, SO IT WAS IN ENGLISH. BIG DUP.
"IT WAS THE THOUGHT."
"TAKING THE LITTLE GIRL IN HER ARMS SHE FLEW UP WITH HER IN BRIGHTNESS AND JOY, HIGH, SO HIGH--
"--AND THERE WAS NO COLD, OR HUNGER, OR SORROW--
"--FOR SHE WAS WITH GOD."*
*FROM "THE LITTLE MATCHGIRL" BY HANS CHRISTIAN ANDERSEN
I WANNA TELL YA THINGS'RE GONNA BE OKAY...
... BUT, ALL I CAN DO IS BE HERE FOR YA.
I HOPE...
...THAT'S ENOUGH.
"I GUESS YOU KNOW WHAT HAPPENED THEN."

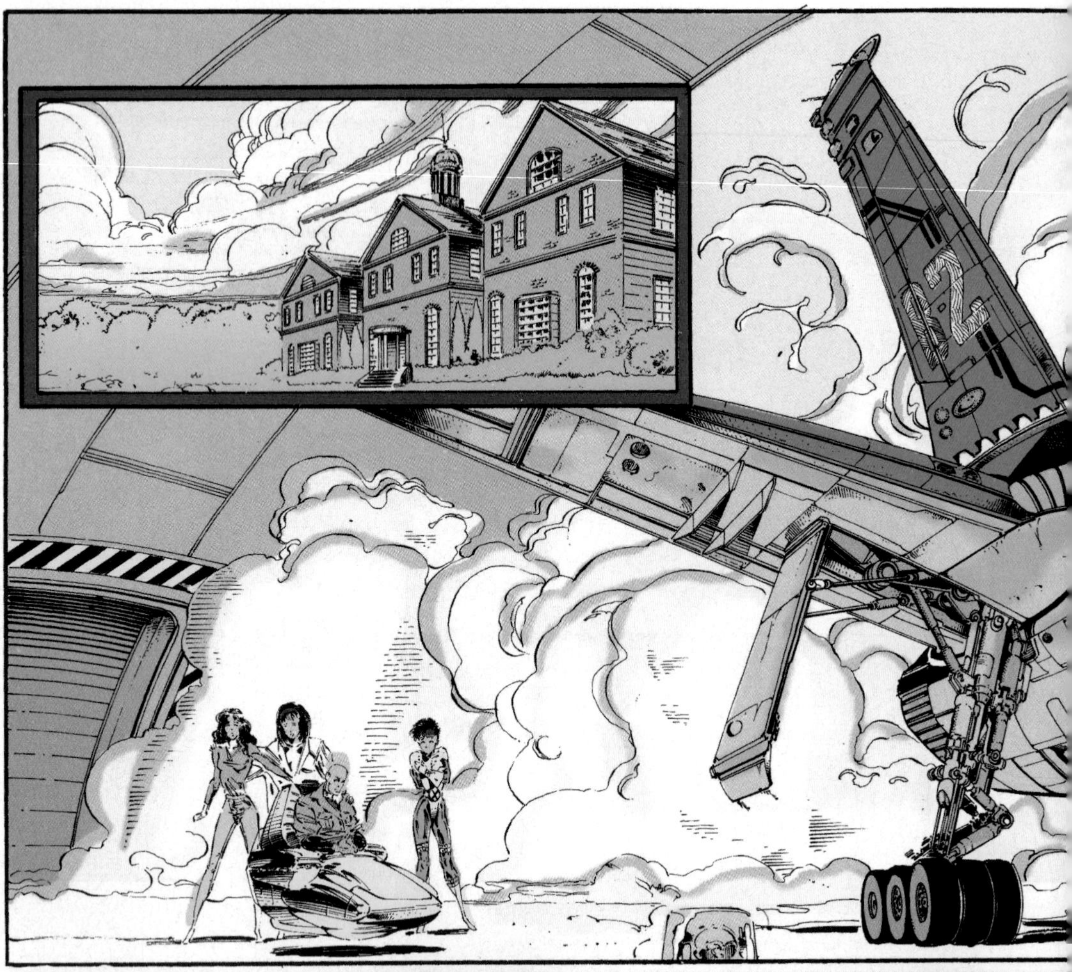

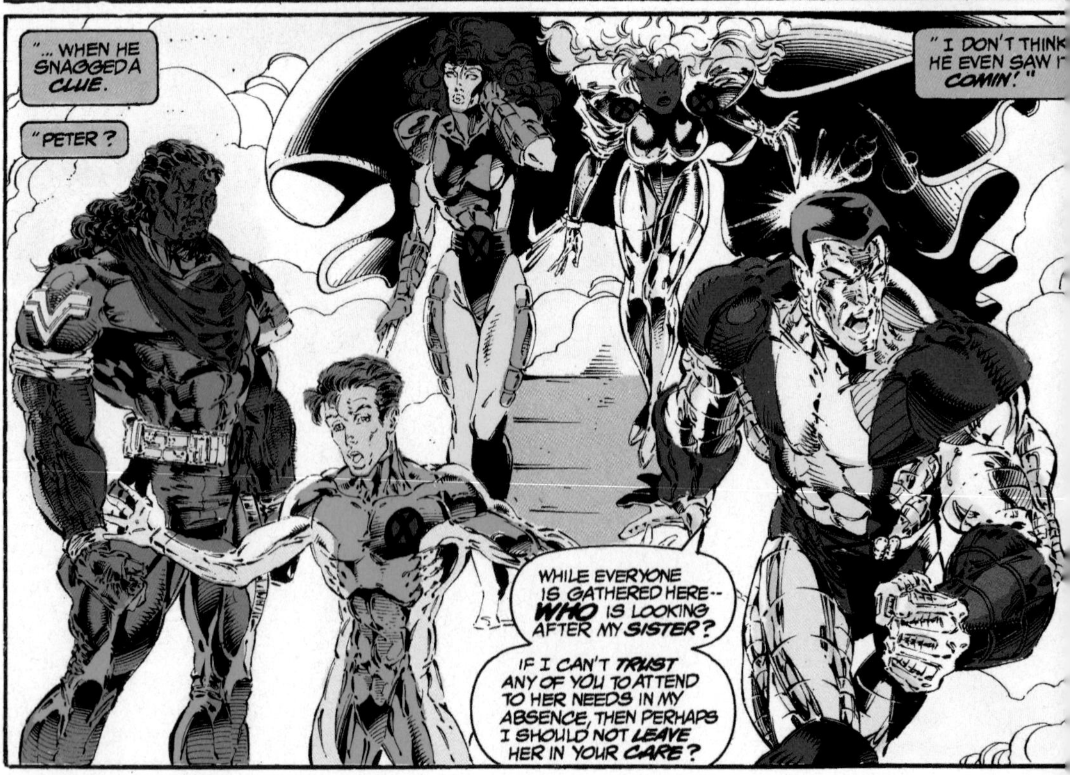
"... WHEN HE SNAGGED A CLUE.
"PETER?
" I DON'T THINK HE EVEN SAW IT COMIN'!"
WHILE EVERYONE IS GATHERED HERE-- WHO IS LOOKING AFTER MY SISTER?
IF I CAN'T TRUST ANY OF YOU TO ATTEND TO HER NEEDS IN MY ABSENCE, THEN PERHAPS I SHOULD NOT LEAVE HER IN YOUR CARE?

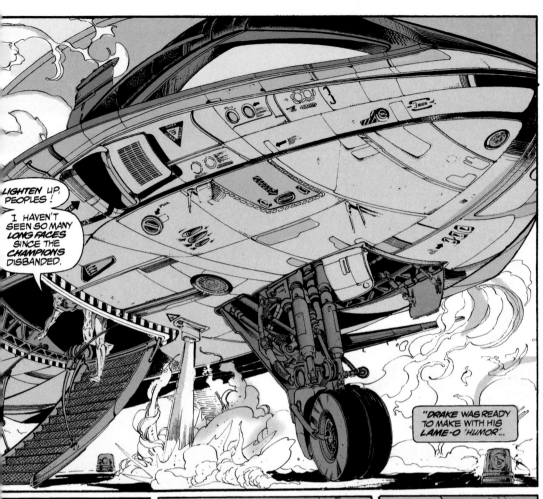

LIGHTEN UP, PEOPLES!

I HAVEN'T SEEN SO MANY *LONG FACES* SINCE THE *CHAMPIONS* DISBANDED.

"DRAKE WAS READY TO MAKE WITH HIS *LAME-O 'HUMOR'*...

PETER?

SON...

...I'M SORRY.

WE...DID *EVERYTHING* WE COULD.

"THE BIG GUY DIDN'T MAKE A *SOUND*.

"NO REACTION AT ALL.

"DIDN'T *SOB*.

"DIDN'T *PUNCH* ANYBODY.

"DIDN'T EVEN TURN AROUND...

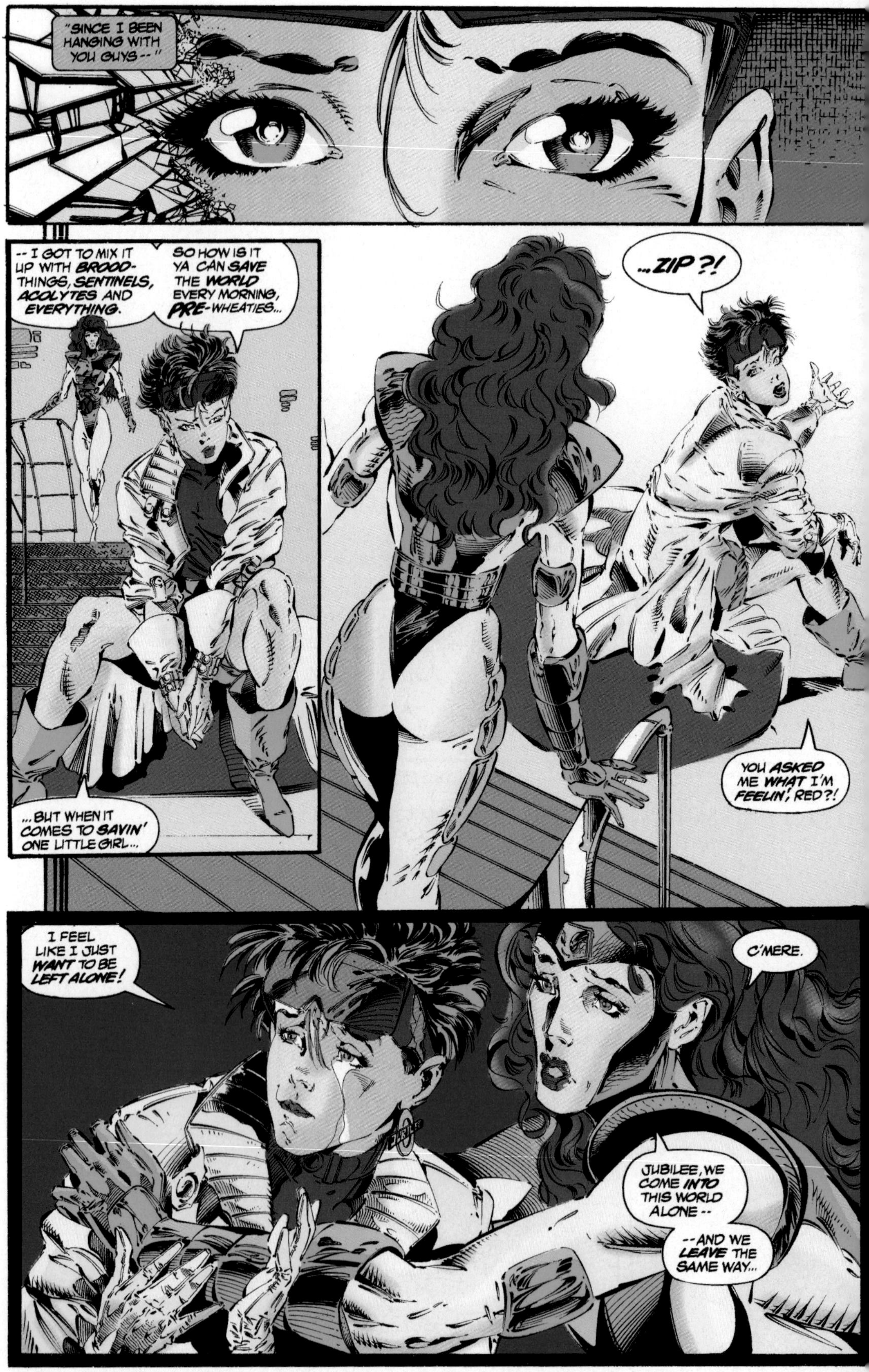
"SINCE I BEEN HANGING WITH YOU GUYS--"
--I GOT TO MIX IT UP WITH BROOD-THINGS, SENTINELS, ACOLYTES AND EVERYTHING.
SO HOW IS IT YA CAN SAVE THE WORLD EVERY MORNING, PRE-WHEATIES...
...BUT WHEN IT COMES TO SAVIN' ONE LITTLE GIRL...
...ZIP?!
YOU ASKED ME WHAT I'M FEELIN', RED?!
I FEEL LIKE I JUST WANT TO BE LEFT ALONE!
C'MERE.
JUBILEE, WE COME INTO THIS WORLD ALONE--
--AND WE LEAVE THE SAME WAY...

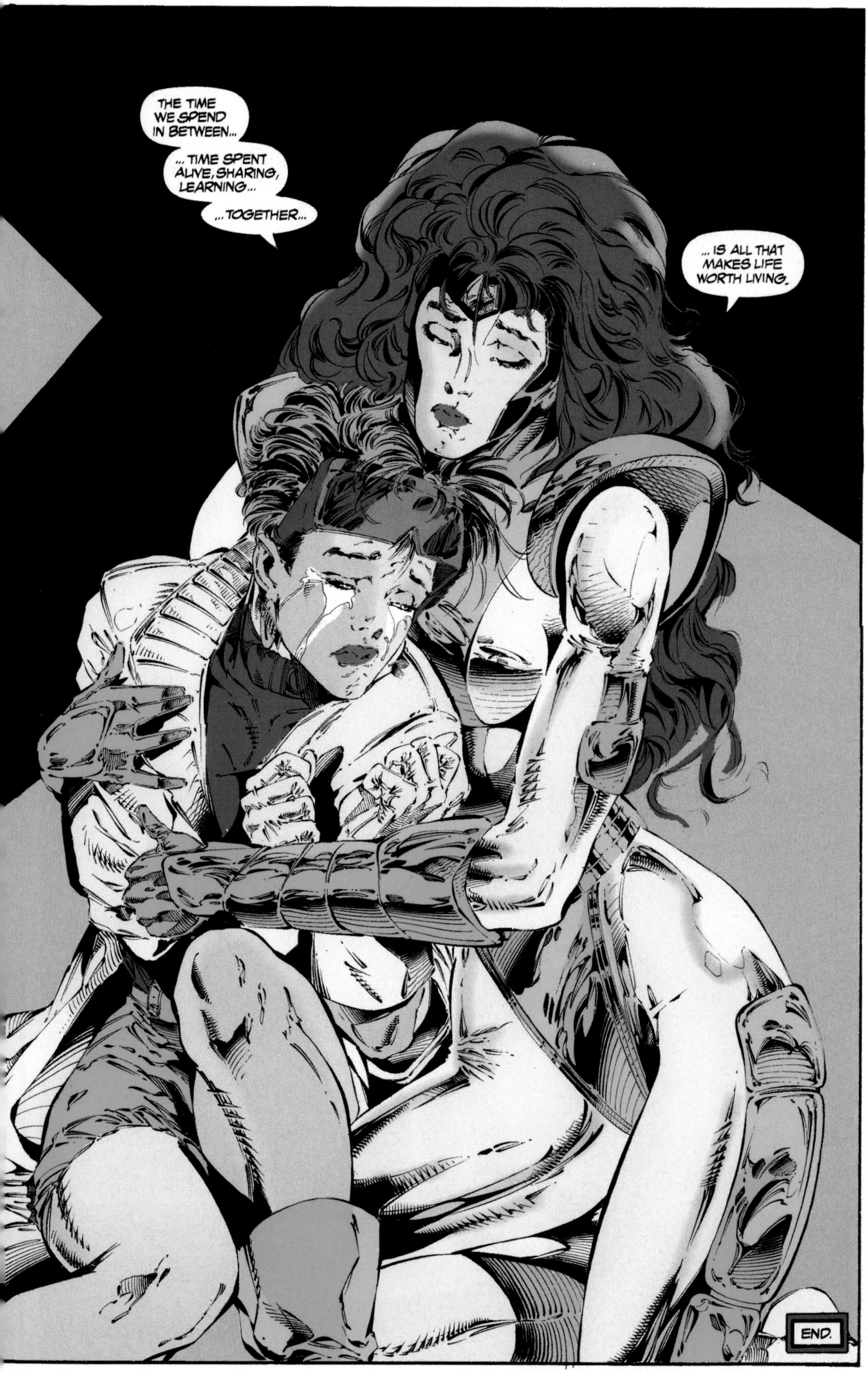
THE TIME WE SPEND IN BETWEEN...
...TIME SPENT ALIVE, SHARING, LEARNING...
...TOGETHER...
...IS ALL THAT MAKES LIFE WORTH LIVING.
END.

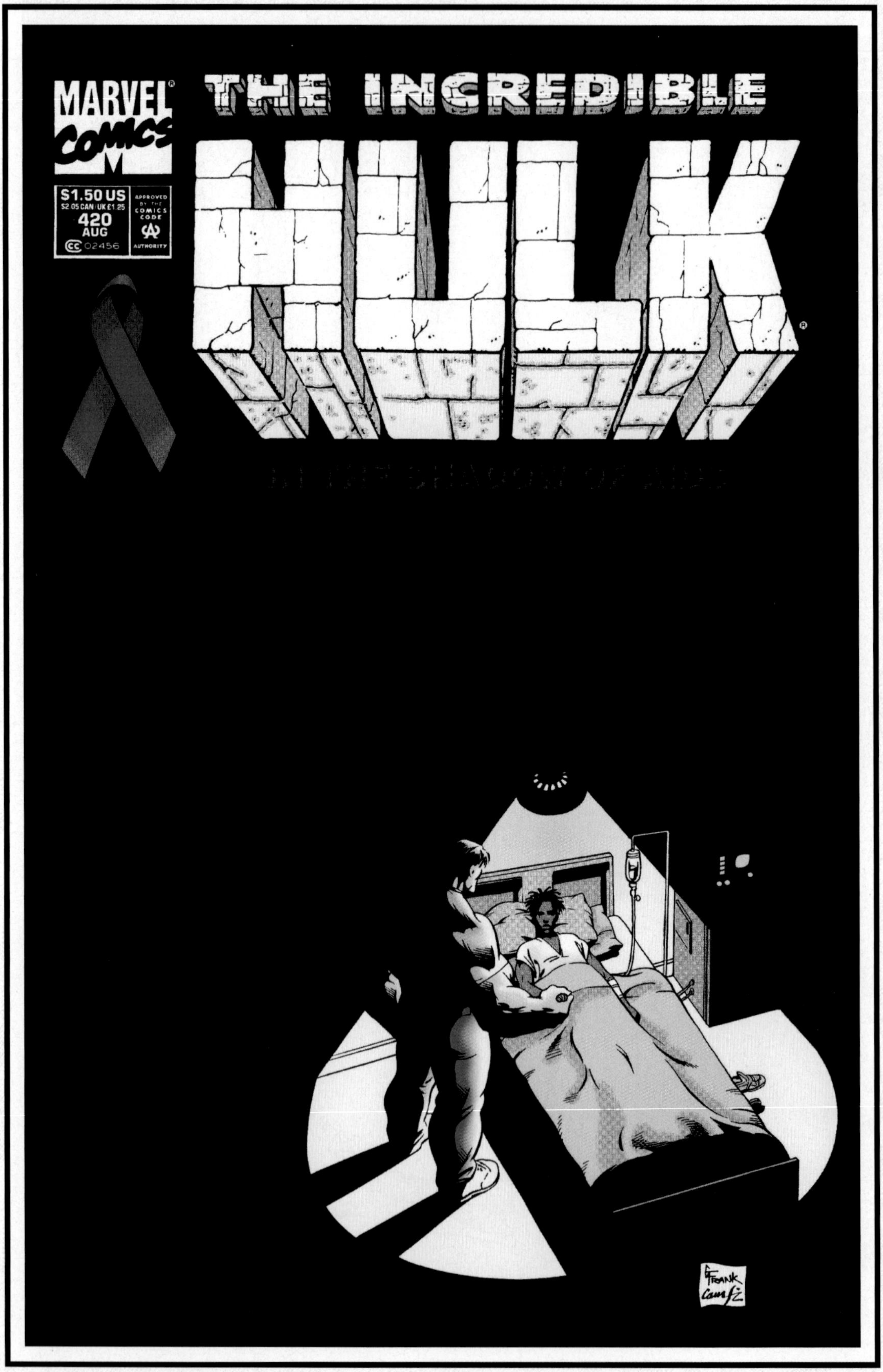
MARVEL COMICS
THE INCREDIBLE
HULK
$1.50 US
$2.05 CAN / UK £1.25
420
AUG
02456
APPROVED BY THE COMICS CODE AUTHORITY

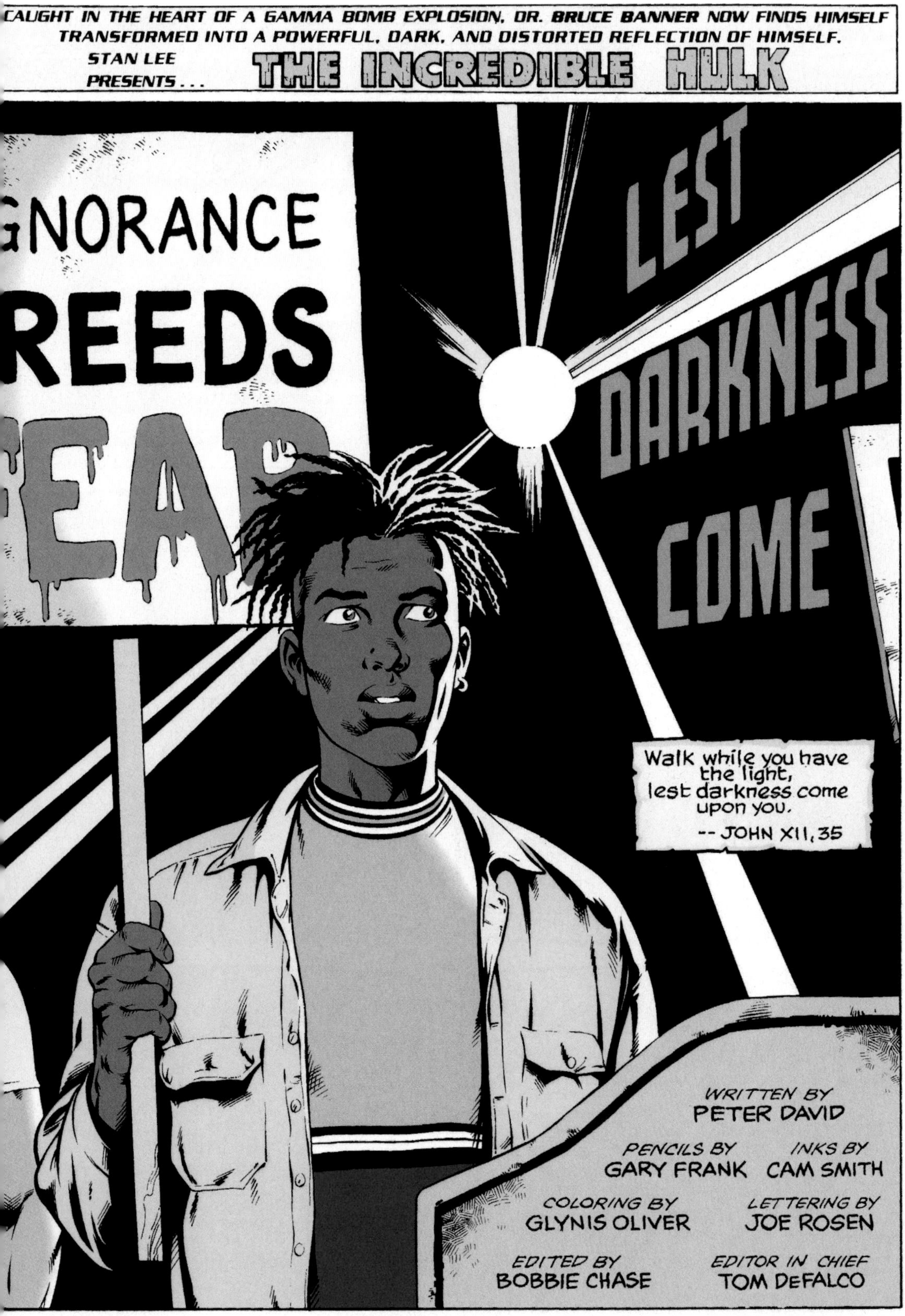
CAUGHT IN THE HEART OF A GAMMA BOMB EXPLOSION, DR. BRUCE BANNER NOW FINDS HIMSELF TRANSFORMED INTO A POWERFUL, DARK, AND DISTORTED REFLECTION OF HIMSELF.
STAN LEE PRESENTS . . .
THE INCREDIBLE HULK
GNORANCE REEDS EAR
LEST DARKNESS COME
Walk while you have the light, lest darkness come upon you. -- JOHN XII, 35
WRITTEN BY PETER DAVID
PENCILS BY GARY FRANK
INKS BY CAM SMITH
COLORING BY GLYNIS OLIVER
LETTERING BY JOE ROSEN
EDITED BY BOBBIE CHASE
EDITOR IN CHIEF TOM DeFALCO

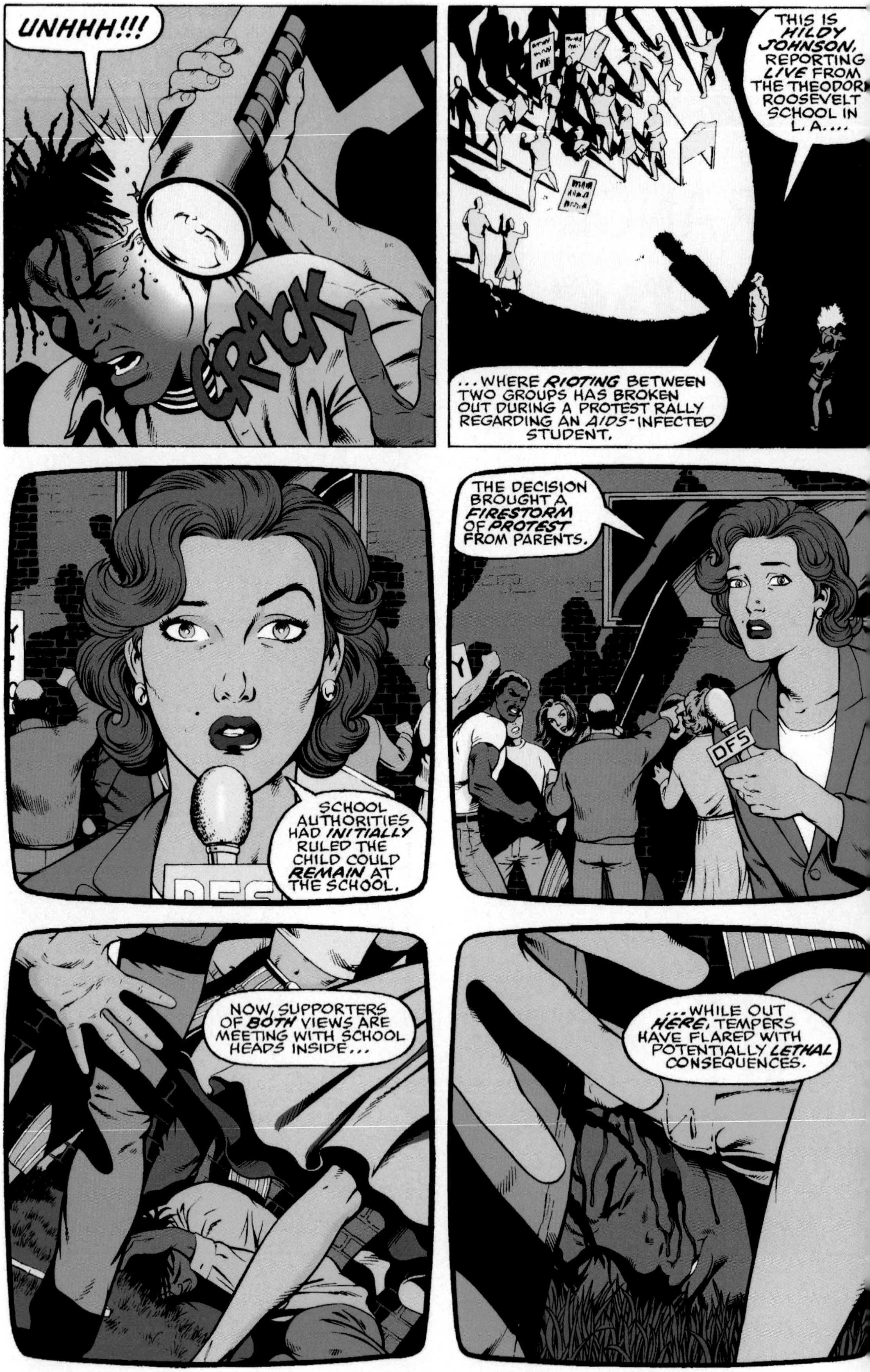
UNHHH!!!
CRACK
THIS IS HILDY JOHNSON, REPORTING LIVE FROM THE THEODOR ROOSEVELT SCHOOL IN L.A....
...WHERE RIOTING BETWEEN TWO GROUPS HAS BROKEN OUT DURING A PROTEST RALLY REGARDING AN AIDS-INFECTED STUDENT.
SCHOOL AUTHORITIES HAD INITIALLY RULED THE CHILD COULD REMAIN AT THE SCHOOL.
THE DECISION BROUGHT A FIRESTORM OF PROTEST FROM PARENTS.
DF5
NOW, SUPPORTERS OF BOTH VIEWS ARE MEETING WITH SCHOOL HEADS INSIDE...
...WHILE OUT HERE, TEMPERS HAVE FLARED WITH POTENTIALLY LETHAL CONSEQUENCES.

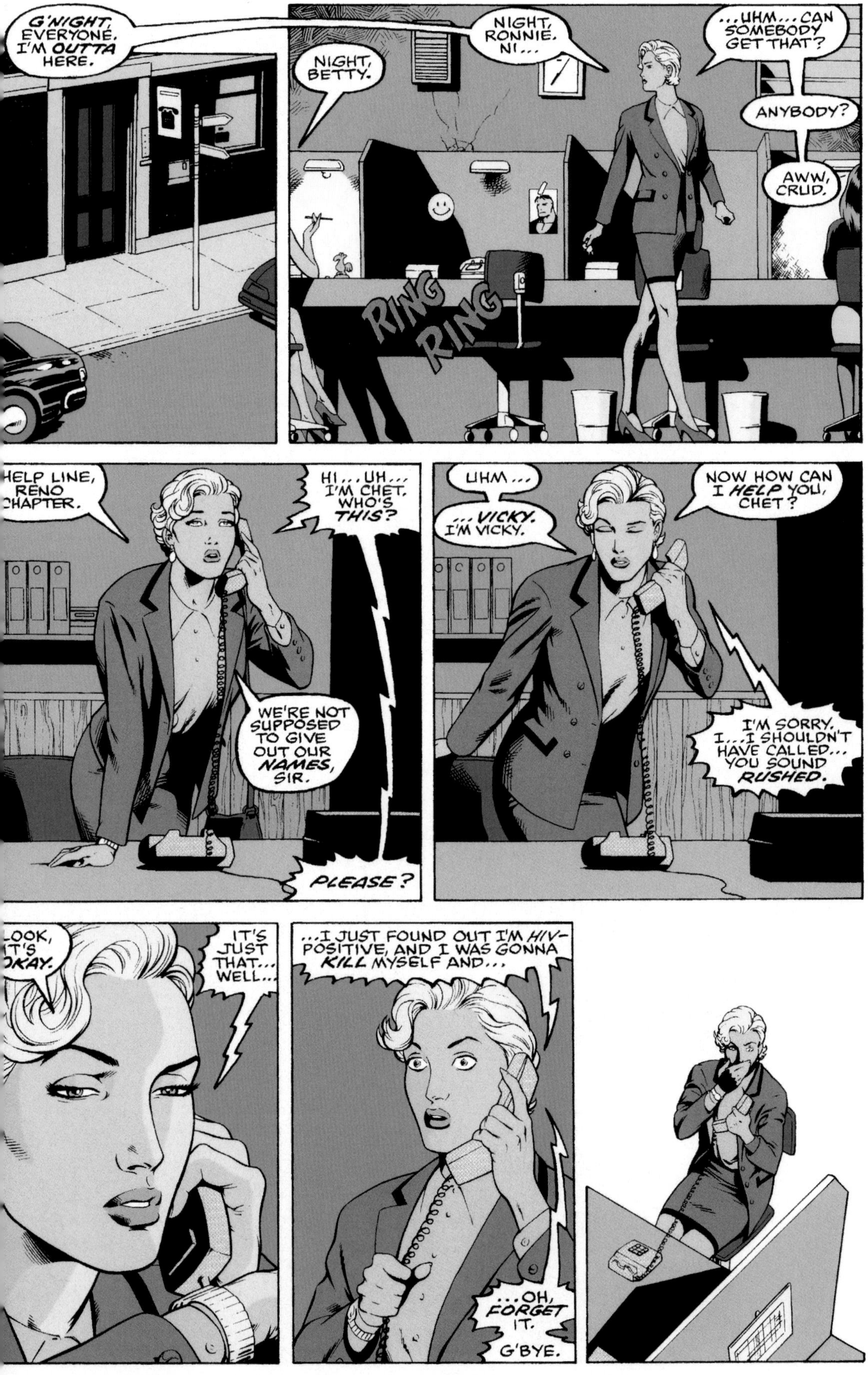

G'NIGHT, EVERYONE. I'M OUTTA HERE.
NIGHT, BETTY.
NIGHT, RONNIE. NI...
...UHM...CAN SOMEBODY GET THAT?
ANYBODY?
AWW, CRUD.
RING RING
HELP LINE, RENO CHAPTER.
HI...UH... I'M CHET. WHO'S THIS?
WE'RE NOT SUPPOSED TO GIVE OUT OUR NAMES, SIR.
PLEASE?
UHM...
...VICKY. I'M VICKY.
NOW HOW CAN I HELP YOU, CHET?
I'M SORRY. I...I SHOULDN'T HAVE CALLED... YOU SOUND RUSHED.
LOOK, IT'S OKAY.
IT'S JUST THAT... WELL...
...I JUST FOUND OUT I'M HIV-POSITIVE, AND I WAS GONNA KILL MYSELF AND...
...OH, FORGET IT.
G'BYE.

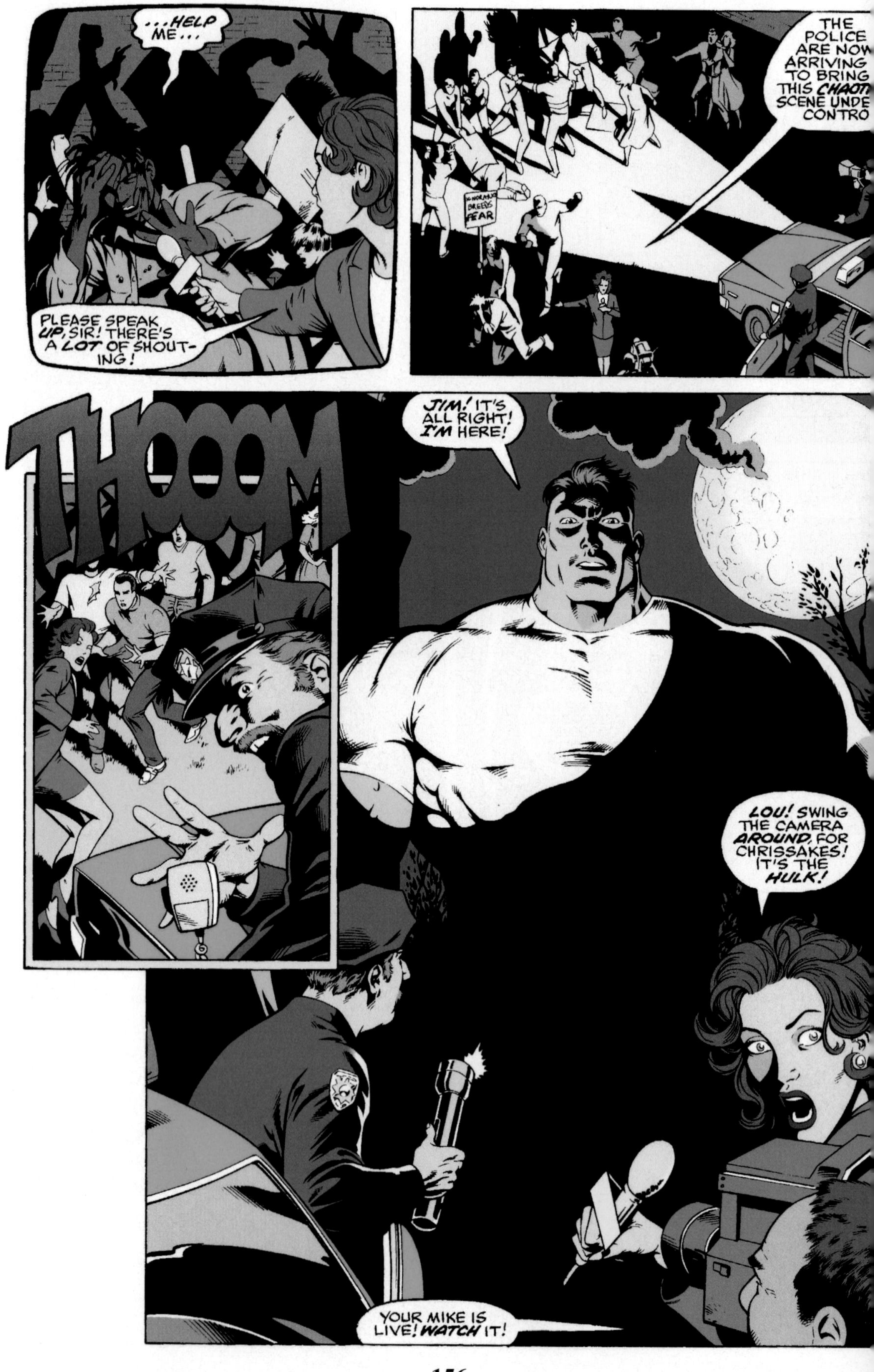
...HELP ME...
PLEASE SPEAK UP, SIR! THERE'S A LOT OF SHOUTING!
THE POLICE ARE NOW ARRIVING TO BRING THIS CHAOTI SCENE UNDE CONTRO
THOOM
JIM! IT'S ALL RIGHT! I'M HERE!
LOU! SWING THE CAMERA AROUND, FOR CHRISSAKES! IT'S THE HULK!
YOUR MIKE IS LIVE! WATCH IT!

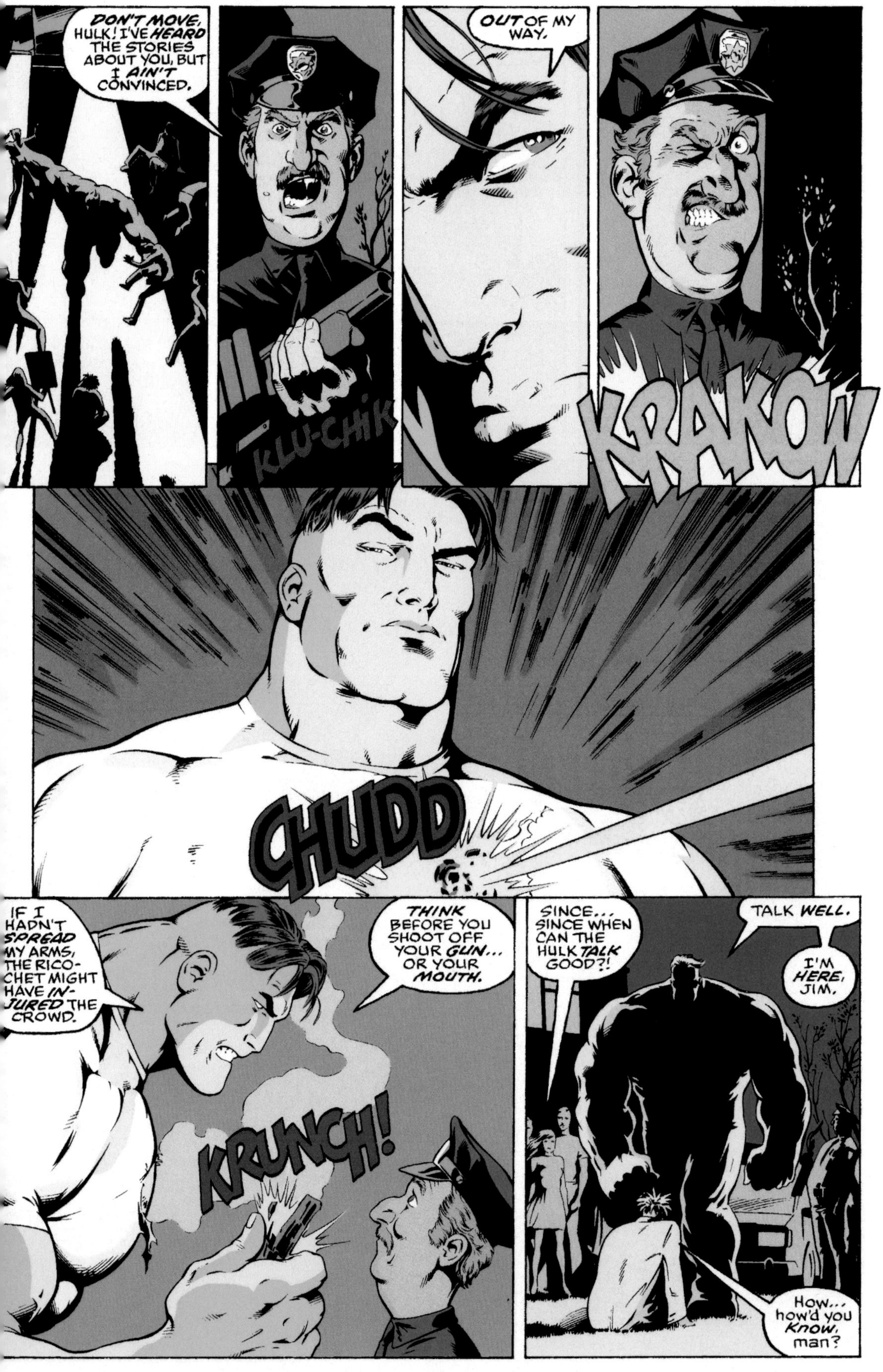
DON'T MOVE, HULK! I'VE HEARD THE STORIES ABOUT YOU, BUT I AIN'T CONVINCED.
KLU-CHIK
OUT OF MY WAY.
KRAKOW
CHUDD
IF I HADN'T SPREAD MY ARMS, THE RICOCHET MIGHT HAVE INJURED THE CROWD.
THINK BEFORE YOU SHOOT OFF YOUR GUN... OR YOUR MOUTH.
KRUNCH!
SINCE... SINCE WHEN CAN THE HULK TALK GOOD?!
TALK WELL.
I'M HERE, JIM.
How... how'd you Know, man?

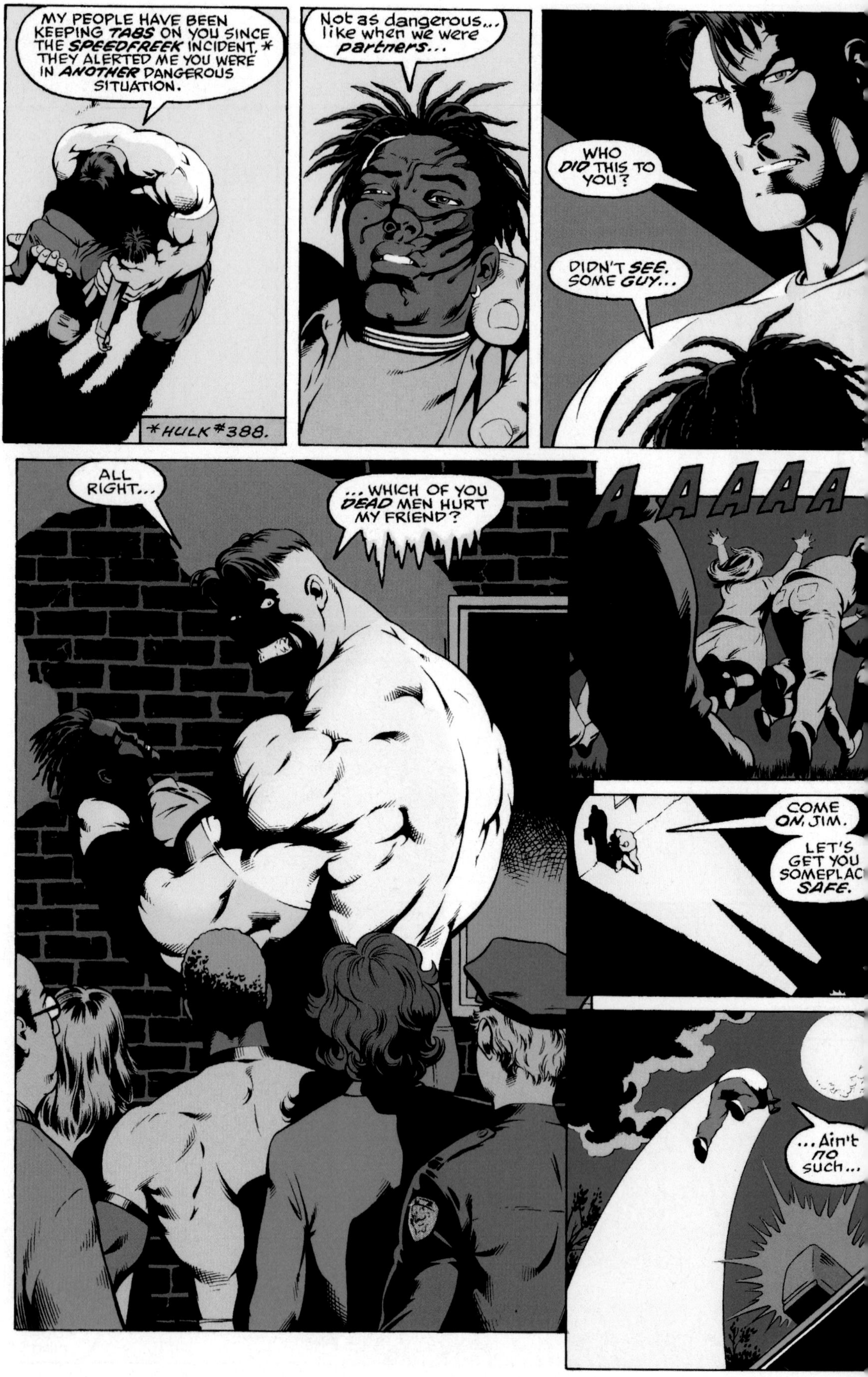
MY PEOPLE HAVE BEEN KEEPING TABS ON YOU SINCE THE SPEEDFREEK INCIDENT.* THEY ALERTED ME YOU WERE IN ANOTHER DANGEROUS SITUATION.
*HULK #388.
Not as dangerous... like when we were partners...
WHO DID THIS TO YOU?
DIDN'T SEE. SOME GUY...
ALL RIGHT...
...WHICH OF YOU DEAD MEN HURT MY FRIEND?
AAAAA
COME ON, JIM.
LET'S GET YOU SOMEPLAC SAFE.
...Ain't no such...

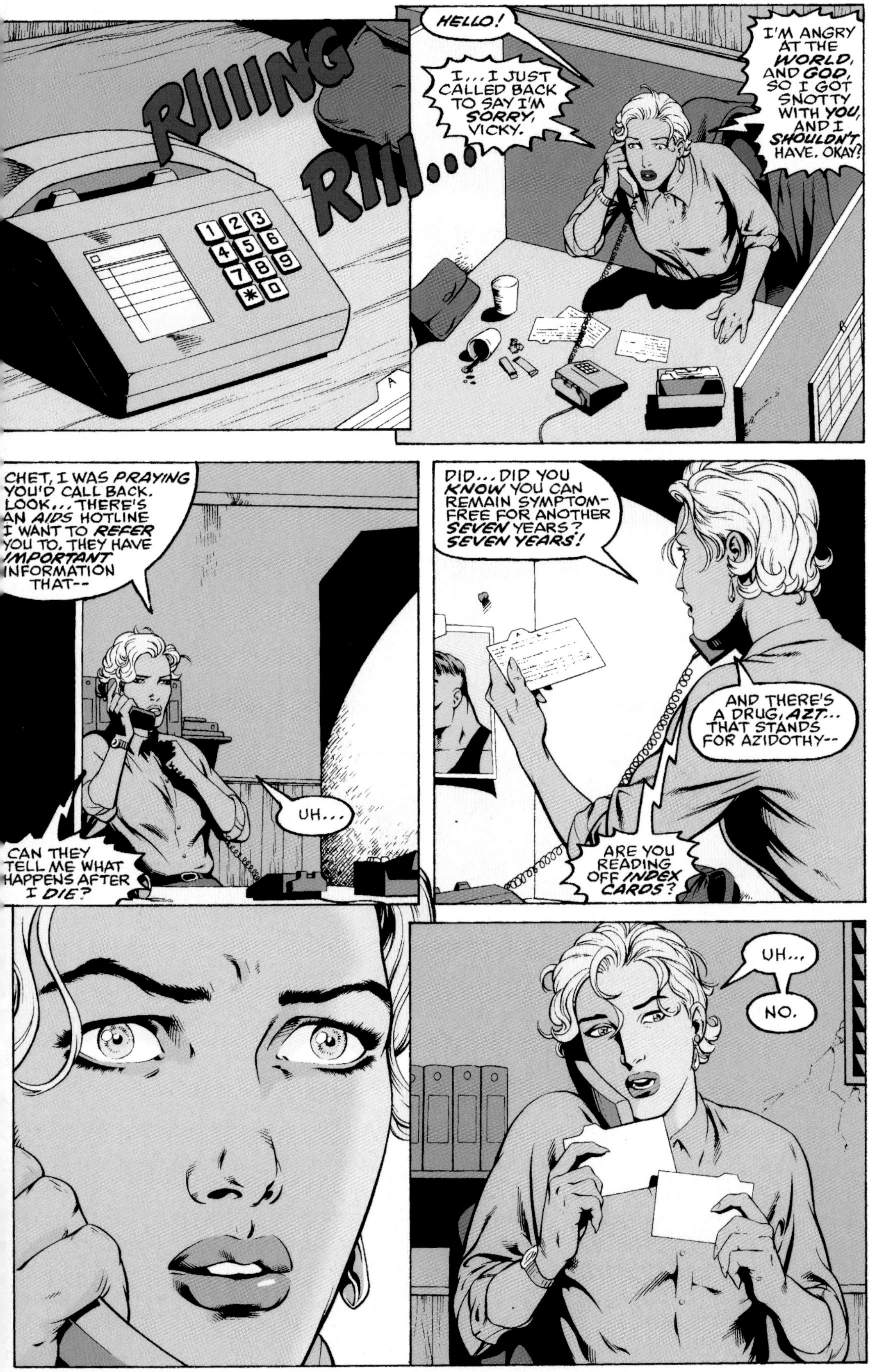
RIIIING
RIII...
HELLO!
I... I JUST CALLED BACK TO SAY I'M SORRY, VICKY.
I'M ANGRY AT THE WORLD, AND GOD, SO I GOT SNOTTY WITH YOU, AND I SHOULDN'T HAVE. OKAY?
CHET, I WAS PRAYING YOU'D CALL BACK. LOOK... THERE'S AN AIDS HOTLINE I WANT TO REFER YOU TO. THEY HAVE IMPORTANT INFORMATION THAT--
UH...
CAN THEY TELL ME WHAT HAPPENS AFTER I DIE?
DID... DID YOU KNOW YOU CAN REMAIN SYMPTOM-FREE FOR ANOTHER SEVEN YEARS? SEVEN YEARS!
AND THERE'S A DRUG, AZT... THAT STANDS FOR AZIDOTHY--
ARE YOU READING OFF INDEX CARDS?
UH...
NO.

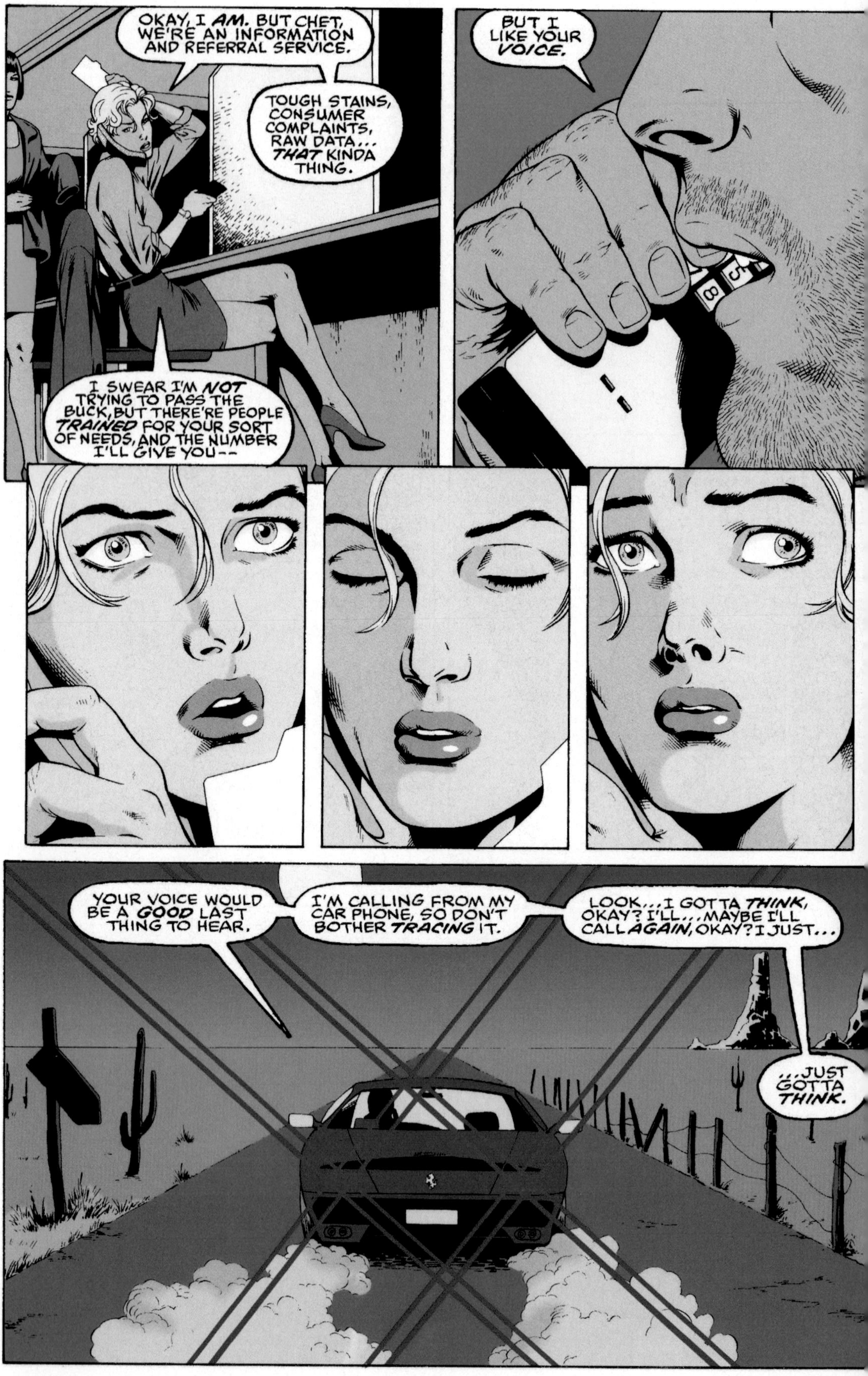

OKAY, I AM. BUT CHET, WE'RE AN INFORMATION AND REFERRAL SERVICE.
TOUGH STAINS, CONSUMER COMPLAINTS, RAW DATA... THAT KINDA THING.
I SWEAR I'M NOT TRYING TO PASS THE BUCK, BUT THERE'RE PEOPLE TRAINED FOR YOUR SORT OF NEEDS, AND THE NUMBER I'LL GIVE YOU--
BUT I LIKE YOUR VOICE.
YOUR VOICE WOULD BE A GOOD LAST THING TO HEAR.
I'M CALLING FROM MY CAR PHONE, SO DON'T BOTHER TRACING IT.
LOOK... I GOTTA THINK, OKAY? I'LL... MAYBE I'LL CALL AGAIN, OKAY? I JUST...
...JUST GOTTA THINK.

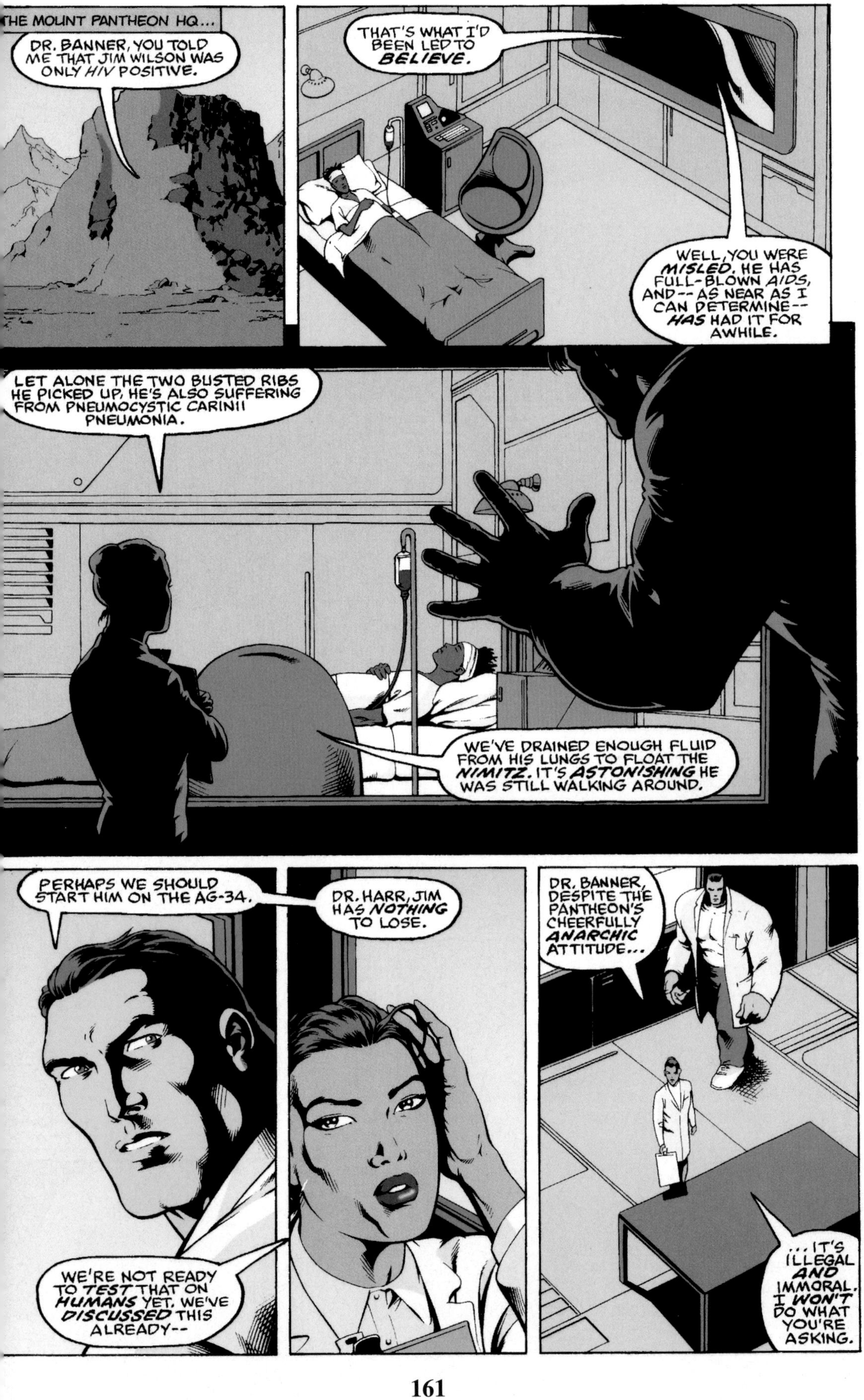
THE MOUNT PANTHEON HQ...
DR. BANNER, YOU TOLD ME THAT JIM WILSON WAS ONLY HIV POSITIVE.
THAT'S WHAT I'D BEEN LED TO BELIEVE.
WELL, YOU WERE MISLED. HE HAS FULL-BLOWN AIDS, AND-- AS NEAR AS I CAN DETERMINE-- HAS HAD IT FOR AWHILE.
LET ALONE THE TWO BUSTED RIBS HE PICKED UP, HE'S ALSO SUFFERING FROM PNEUMOCYSTIC CARINII PNEUMONIA.
WE'VE DRAINED ENOUGH FLUID FROM HIS LUNGS TO FLOAT THE NIMITZ. IT'S ASTONISHING HE WAS STILL WALKING AROUND.
PERHAPS WE SHOULD START HIM ON THE AG-34.
DR. HARR, JIM HAS NOTHING TO LOSE.
WE'RE NOT READY TO TEST THAT ON HUMANS YET. WE'VE DISCUSSED THIS ALREADY--
DR. BANNER, DESPITE THE PANTHEON'S CHEERFULLY ANARCHIC ATTITUDE...
...IT'S ILLEGAL AND IMMORAL. I WON'T DO WHAT YOU'RE ASKING.

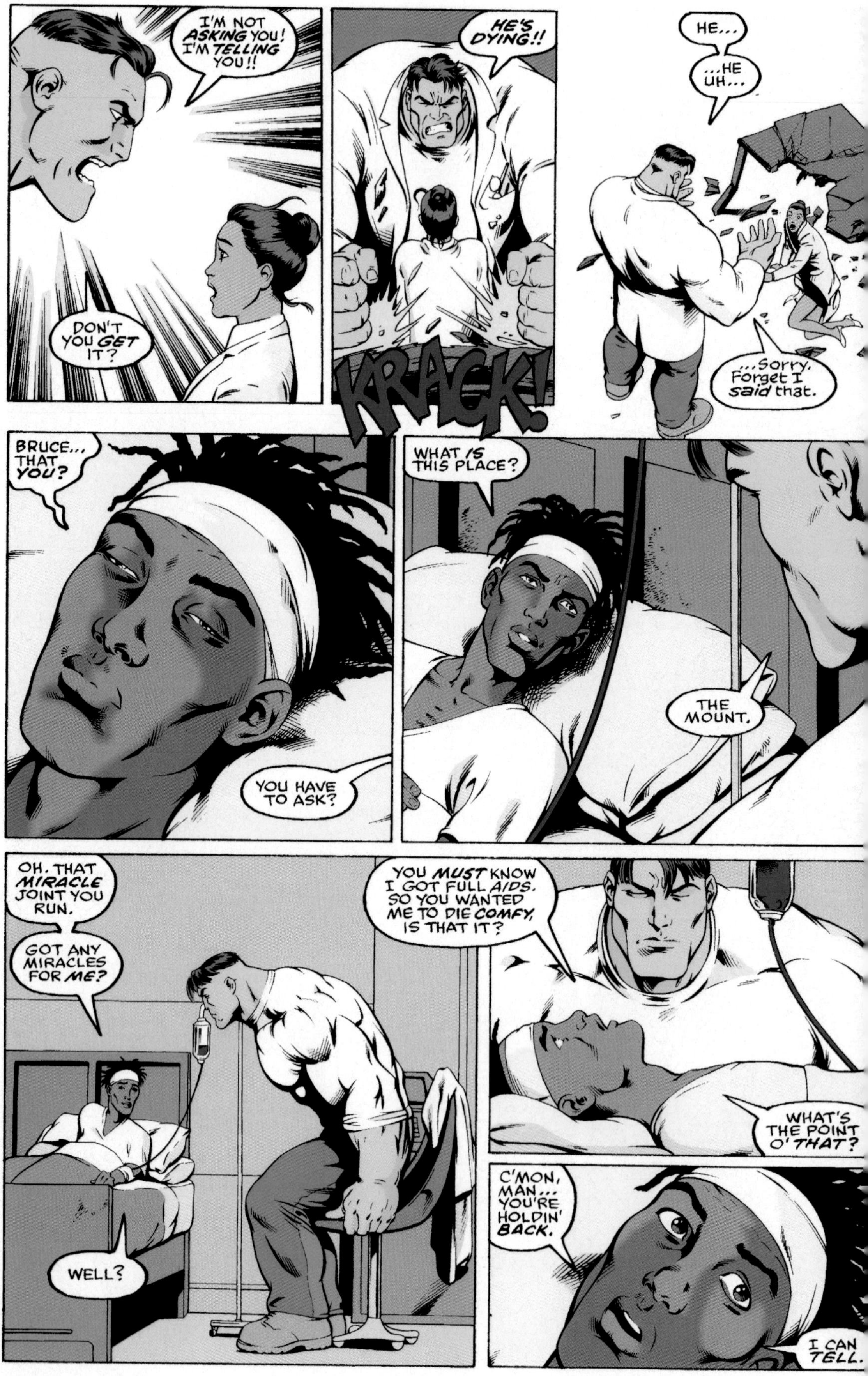
I'M NOT ASKING YOU! I'M TELLING YOU!!
DON'T YOU GET IT?
HE'S DYING!!
KRACK!
HE...
...HE UH...
...Sorry. Forget I said that.
BRUCE... THAT YOU?
YOU HAVE TO ASK?
WHAT IS THIS PLACE?
THE MOUNT.
OH. THAT MIRACLE JOINT YOU RUN.
GOT ANY MIRACLES FOR ME?
WELL?
YOU MUST KNOW I GOT FULL AIDS. SO YOU WANTED ME TO DIE COMFY, IS THAT IT?
WHAT'S THE POINT O' THAT?
C'MON, MAN... YOU'RE HOLDIN' BACK.
I CAN TELL.

DEATH WANTS ME, I'M GOING DOWN *FIGHTIN'*. YOU *MUST* HAVE SOMETHING--

ONLY *EXPERIMENTAL*, JIM, NOT READY FOR HUMANS. I CAN'T CROSS THAT *LINE*.

YOU CAN CROSS *BORDERS* TO MAKE WARS, BUT YOU CAN'T CROSS A LINE TO HELP A FRIEND.

I'M *SORRY*, JIM.

SCREW YOUR "SORRY."

BLOOD TRANS-FUSIONS AREN'T ILLEGAL, ARE THEY?

OF COURSE NOT.

THEN GIMME A TRANSFUSION. *YOUR* BLOOD.

I *CAN'T* DO THAT!

OH YEAH?

WHERE'D *SHE-HULK* COME FROM?

THAT *WAS THEN.*

THIS IS *NOW.*

YOU CAN *HELP* ME! IF YOU *DON'T*, YOU'RE KILLING ME AS MUCH AS THE *VIRUS* IS.

JIM, THAT'S *NOT FAIR.*

YOU'RE TALKIN' TO *ME* ABOUT FAIR?

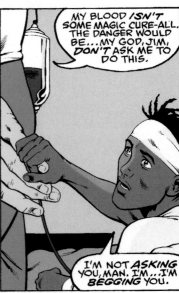

MY BLOOD *ISN'T* SOME MAGIC CURE-ALL. THE DANGER WOULD BE...MY GOD, JIM, *DON'T* ASK ME TO DO THIS.

I'M NOT *ASKING* YOU, MAN. I'M...*I'M BEGGING* YOU.

163

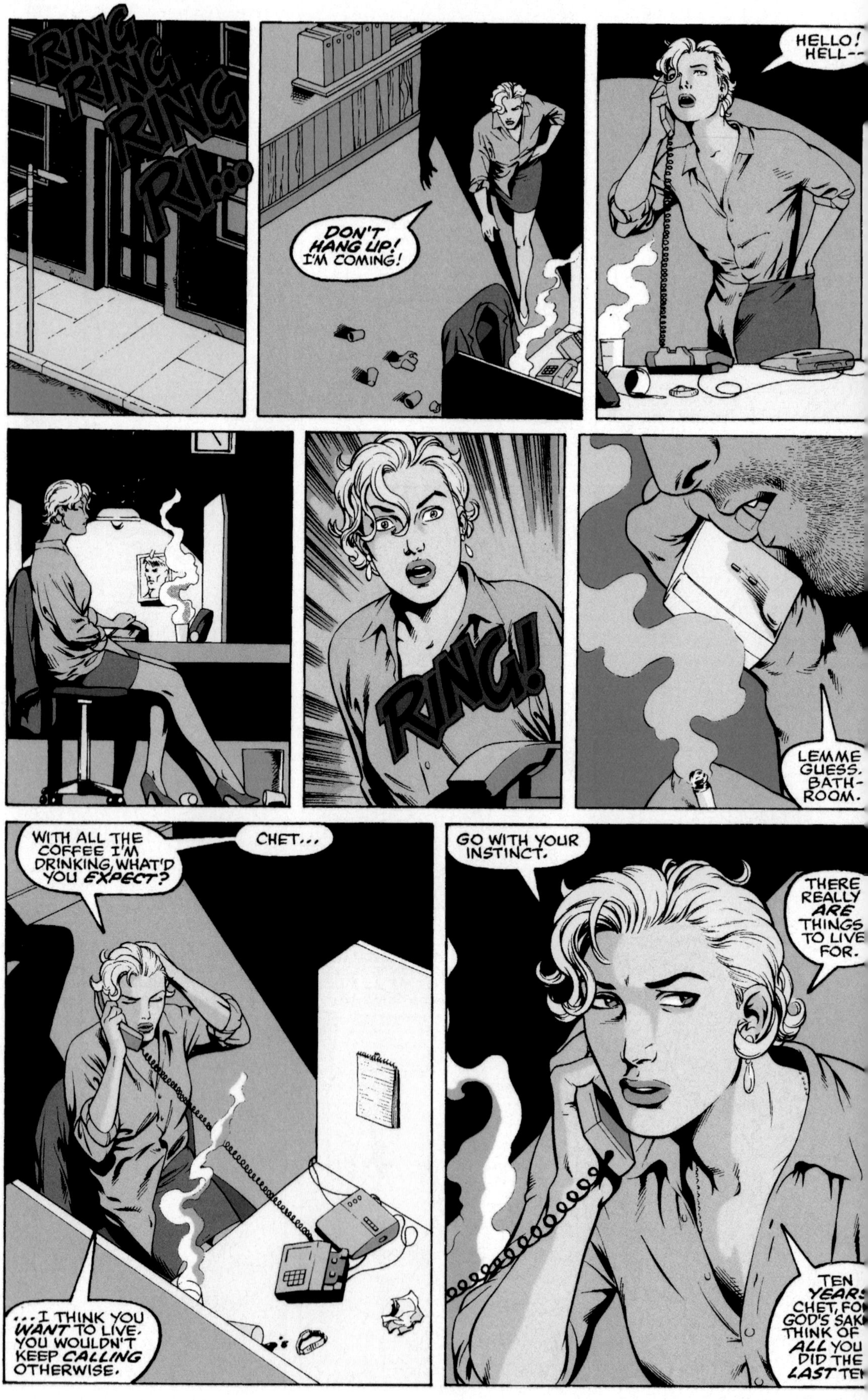

RING RING RING RI...
DON'T HANG UP! I'M COMING!
HELLO! HELL--
RING!
LEMME GUESS. BATH-ROOM.
WITH ALL THE COFFEE I'M DRINKING, WHAT'D YOU EXPECT?
CHET...
...I THINK YOU WANT TO LIVE. YOU WOULDN'T KEEP CALLING OTHERWISE.
GO WITH YOUR INSTINCT.
THERE REALLY ARE THINGS TO LIVE FOR.
TEN YEARS

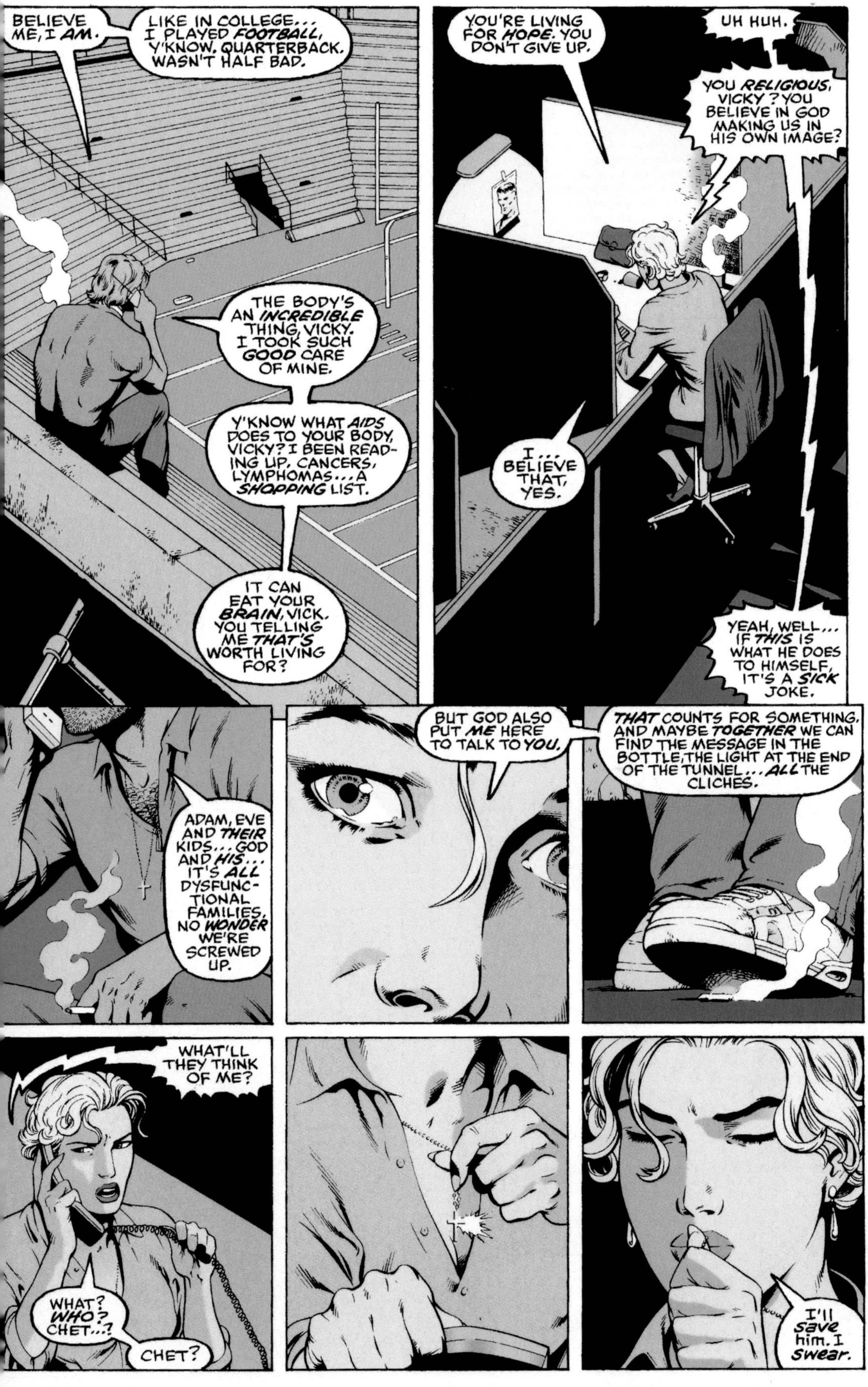

BELIEVE ME, I AM.
LIKE IN COLLEGE... I PLAYED FOOTBALL, Y'KNOW. QUARTERBACK. WASN'T HALF BAD.
THE BODY'S AN INCREDIBLE THING, VICKY. I TOOK SUCH GOOD CARE OF MINE.
Y'KNOW WHAT AIDS DOES TO YOUR BODY, VICKY? I BEEN READING UP. CANCERS, LYMPHOMAS... A SHOPPING LIST.
IT CAN EAT YOUR BRAIN, VICK. YOU TELLING ME THAT'S WORTH LIVING FOR?
YOU'RE LIVING FOR HOPE. YOU DON'T GIVE UP.
UH HUH.
YOU RELIGIOUS, VICKY? YOU BELIEVE IN GOD MAKING US IN HIS OWN IMAGE?
I... BELIEVE THAT, YES.
YEAH, WELL... IF THIS IS WHAT HE DOES TO HIMSELF, IT'S A SICK JOKE.
ADAM, EVE AND THEIR KIDS... GOD AND HIS... IT'S ALL DYSFUNCTIONAL FAMILIES. NO WONDER WE'RE SCREWED UP.
BUT GOD ALSO PUT ME HERE TO TALK TO YOU.
THAT COUNTS FOR SOMETHING. AND MAYBE TOGETHER WE CAN FIND THE MESSAGE IN THE BOTTLE, THE LIGHT AT THE END OF THE TUNNEL... ALL THE CLICHES.
WHAT'LL THEY THINK OF ME?
WHAT? WHO? CHET...?
CHET?
I'll save him. I swear.

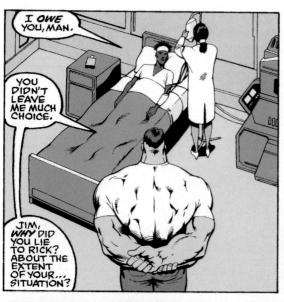

I *OWE* YOU, MAN.

YOU DIDN'T LEAVE ME MUCH CHOICE.

JIM, *WHY* DID YOU LIE TO RICK? ABOUT THE EXTENT OF YOUR... SITUATION?

'CAUSE I DIDN'T THINK HE COULD *HANDLE* IT. THE MOMENT I BROUGHT IT UP, HE TURNED...

WHITE?

EVEN *MORE* THAN USUAL, YEAH. HE ALWAYS *WAS* ONE OF THE *WHITER* WHITE BOYS

EVER HEAR HIM SING *MOTOWN*?

LIKE NAILS ON CHALKBOARD, MAN.

JIM... I WON'T *HEDGE* HERE.

YOU UNDERSTAND THIS IS A LONG SHOT.

I DON'T *CARE*, SO LONG AS IT'S A SHOT.

Y'KNOW WHAT?

WHEN I WAS A KID, THERE WAS THIS OLD MAN LIVED UPSTAIRS... OLD BLUES MAN, NAMED *SMILEY*...

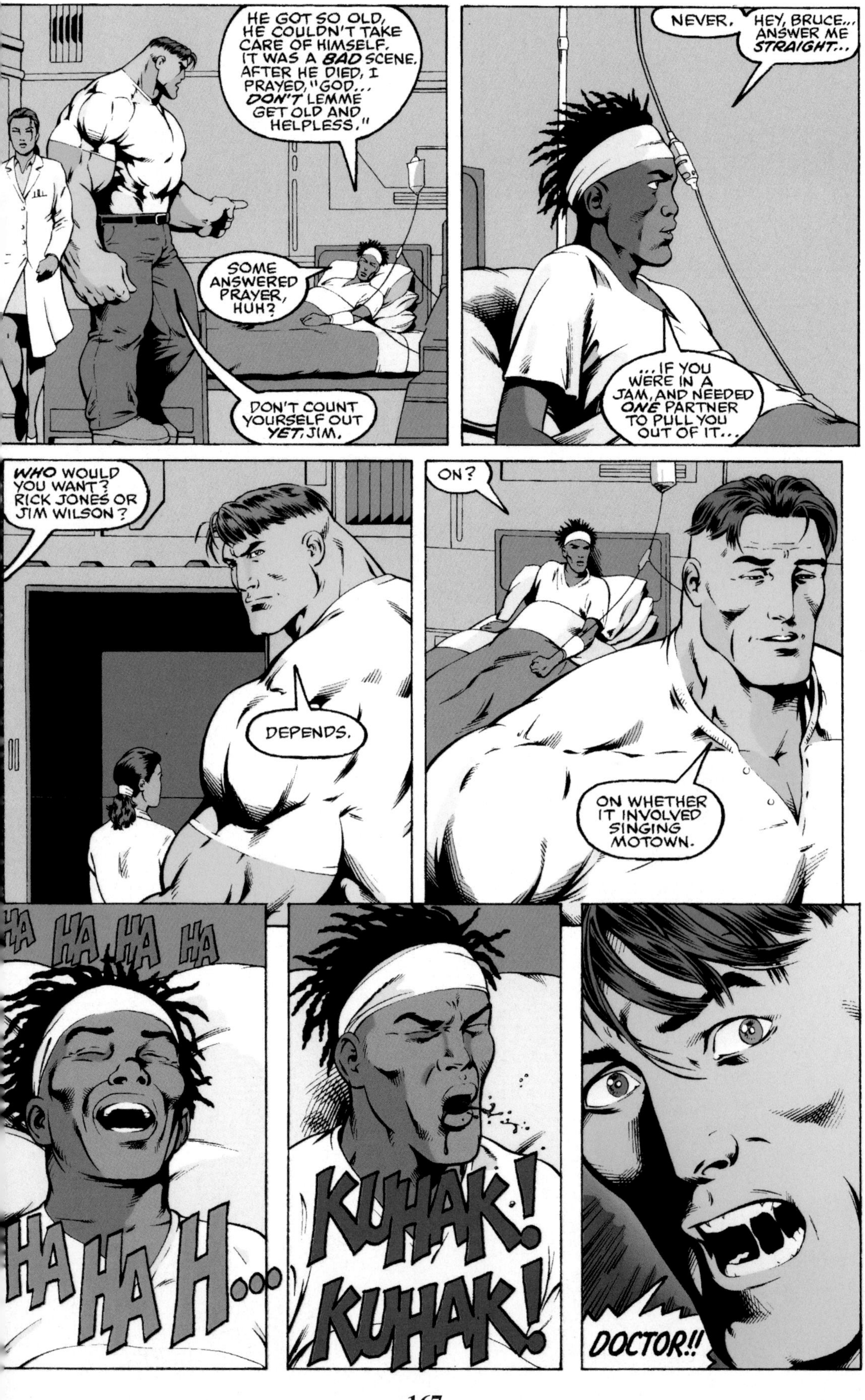
HE GOT SO OLD, HE COULDN'T TAKE CARE OF HIMSELF. IT WAS A BAD SCENE. AFTER HE DIED, I PRAYED, "GOD... DON'T LEMME GET OLD AND HELPLESS."
SOME ANSWERED PRAYER, HUH?
DON'T COUNT YOURSELF OUT YET, JIM.
NEVER.
HEY, BRUCE... ANSWER ME STRAIGHT...
...IF YOU WERE IN A JAM, AND NEEDED ONE PARTNER TO PULL YOU OUT OF IT...
WHO WOULD YOU WANT? RICK JONES OR JIM WILSON?
DEPENDS.
ON?
ON WHETHER IT INVOLVED SINGING MOTOWN.
HA HA HA HA
HA HA HA H...
KUHAK! KUHAK!
DOCTOR!!

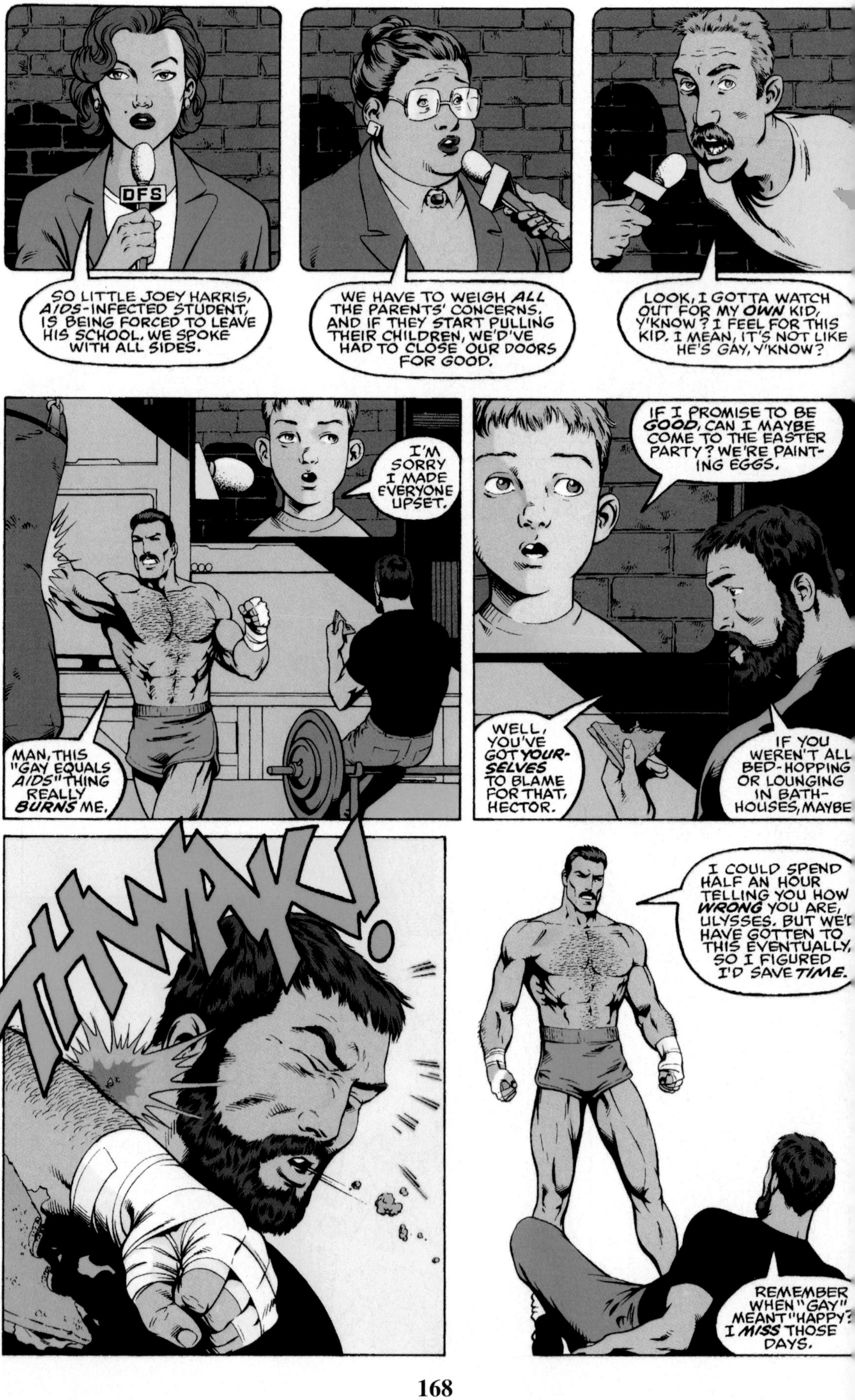
SO LITTLE JOEY HARRIS, AIDS-INFECTED STUDENT, IS BEING FORCED TO LEAVE HIS SCHOOL. WE SPOKE WITH ALL SIDES.
DFS
WE HAVE TO WEIGH ALL THE PARENTS' CONCERNS. AND IF THEY START PULLING THEIR CHILDREN, WE'D'VE HAD TO CLOSE OUR DOORS FOR GOOD.
LOOK, I GOTTA WATCH OUT FOR MY OWN KID, Y'KNOW? I FEEL FOR THIS KID. I MEAN, IT'S NOT LIKE HE'S GAY, Y'KNOW?
I'M SORRY I MADE EVERYONE UPSET.
MAN, THIS "GAY EQUALS AIDS" THING REALLY BURNS ME.
IF I PROMISE TO BE GOOD, CAN I MAYBE COME TO THE EASTER PARTY? WE'RE PAINTING EGGS.
WELL, YOU'VE GOT YOURSELVES TO BLAME FOR THAT, HECTOR.
IF YOU WEREN'T ALL BED-HOPPING OR LOUNGING IN BATH-HOUSES, MAYBE
THWAK!
I COULD SPEND HALF AN HOUR TELLING YOU HOW WRONG YOU ARE, ULYSSES. BUT WE'D HAVE GOTTEN TO THIS EVENTUALLY, SO I FIGURED I'D SAVE TIME.
REMEMBER WHEN "GAY" MEANT "HAPPY"? I MISS THOSE DAYS.

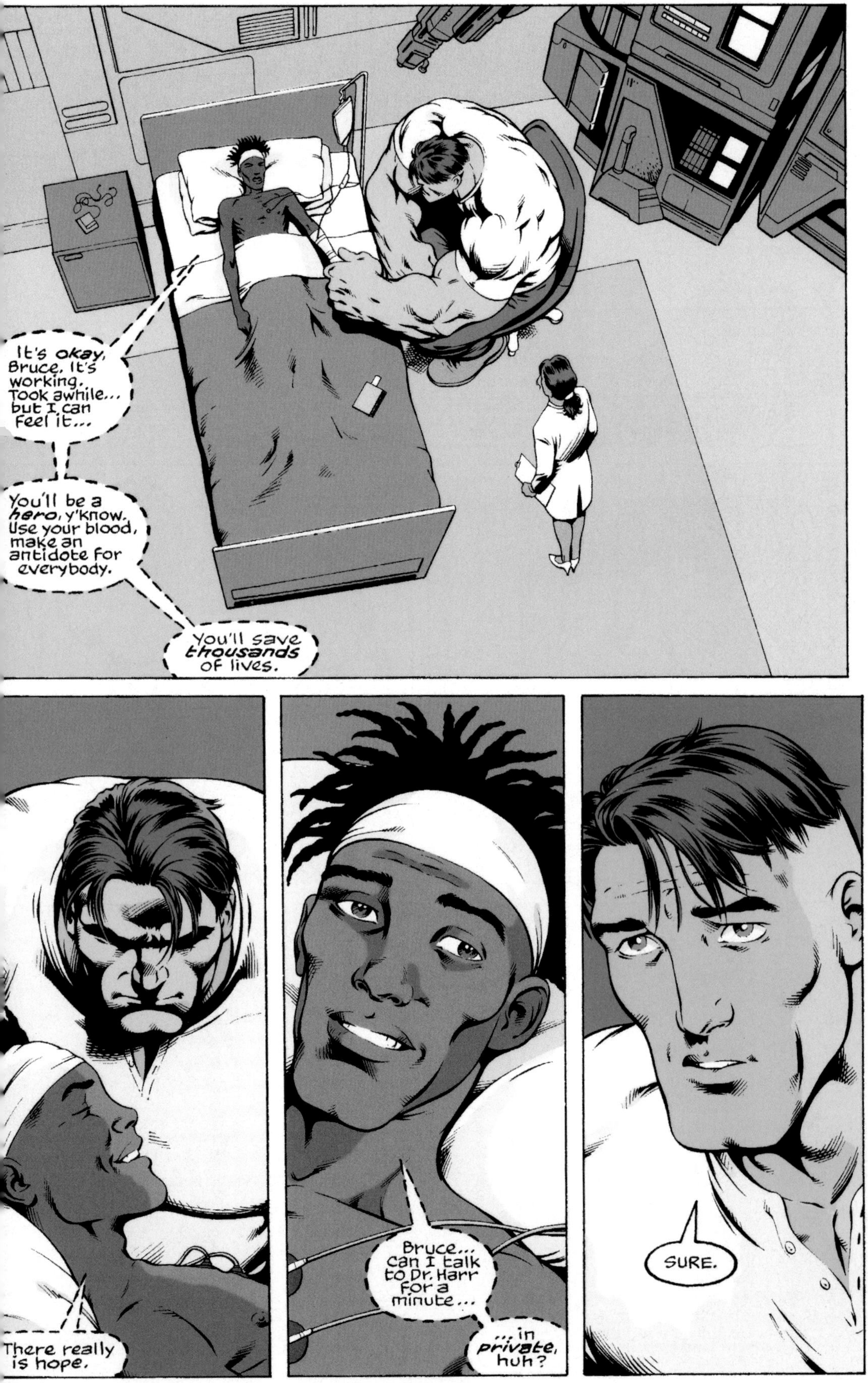
It's okay, Bruce. It's working. Took awhile... but I can feel it...
You'll be a hero, y'know. Use your blood, make an antidote for everybody.
You'll save thousands of lives.
There really is hope.
Bruce... can I talk to Dr. Harr for a minute...
...in private, huh?
SURE.

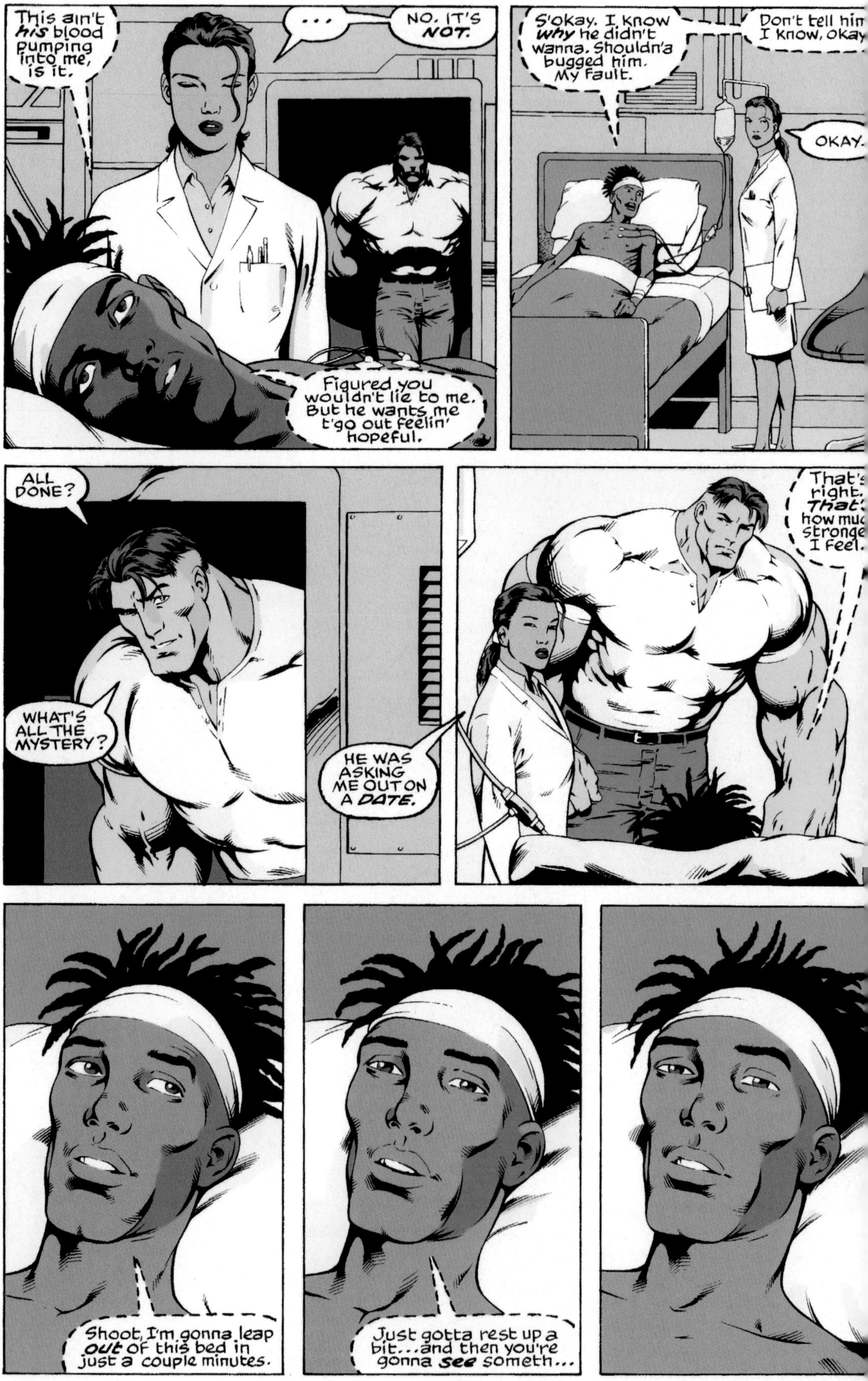
This ain't his blood pumping into me, is it.
...
NO. IT'S NOT.
Figured you wouldn't lie to me. But he wants me t'go out feelin' hopeful.
S'okay. I know why he didn't wanna. Shouldn'a bugged him. My fault.
Don't tell him I know, okay
OKAY.
ALL DONE?
WHAT'S ALL THE MYSTERY?
HE WAS ASKING ME OUT ON A DATE.
That's right. That's how much stronger I feel.
Shoot, I'm gonna leap out of this bed in just a couple minutes.
Just gotta rest up a bit...and then you're gonna see someth...

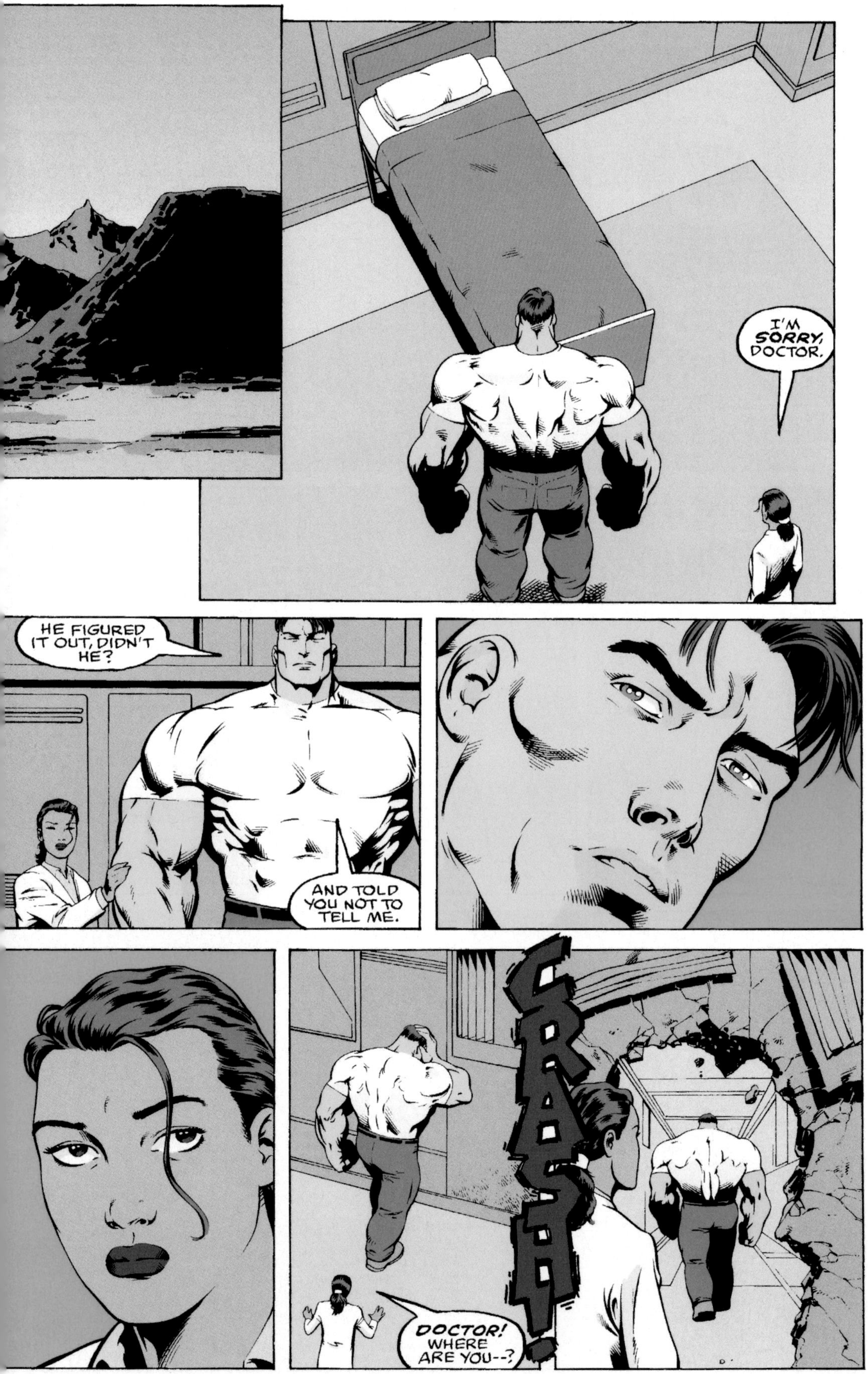
I'M SORRY, DOCTOR.
HE FIGURED IT OUT, DIDN'T HE?
AND TOLD YOU NOT TO TELL ME.
CRASH
DOCTOR! WHERE ARE YOU--?

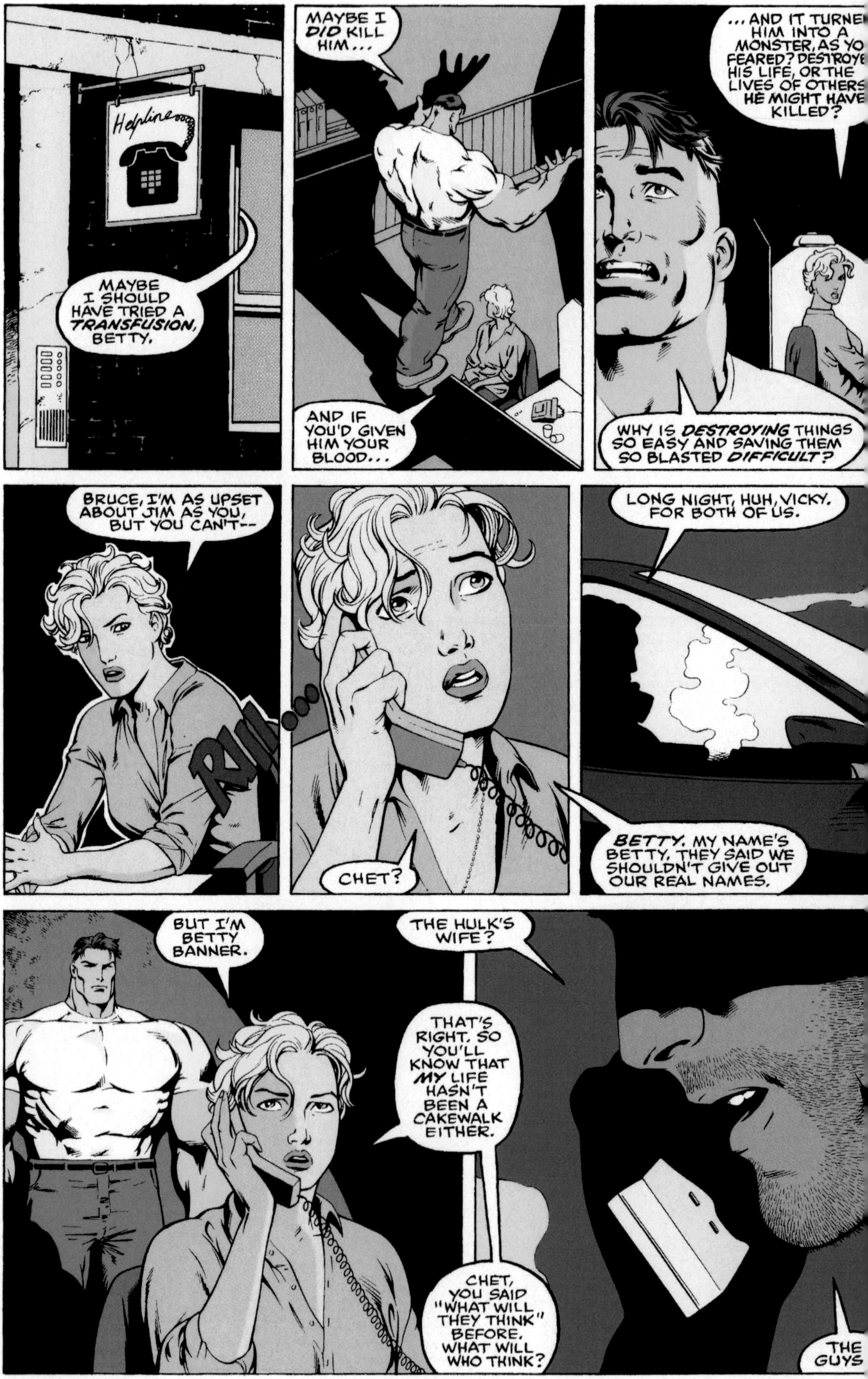
MAYBE I SHOULD HAVE TRIED A TRANSFUSION, BETTY.
MAYBE I DID KILL HIM...
AND IF YOU'D GIVEN HIM YOUR BLOOD...
...AND IT TURNE HIM INTO A MONSTER, AS YO FEARED? DESTROYE HIS LIFE, OR THE LIVES OF OTHERS HE MIGHT HAVE KILLED?
WHY IS DESTROYING THINGS SO EASY AND SAVING THEM SO BLASTED DIFFICULT?
BRUCE, I'M AS UPSET ABOUT JIM AS YOU, BUT YOU CAN'T--
RIII...
CHET?
LONG NIGHT, HUH, VICKY. FOR BOTH OF US.
BETTY. MY NAME'S BETTY. THEY SAID WE SHOULDN'T GIVE OUT OUR REAL NAMES.
BUT I'M BETTY BANNER.
THE HULK'S WIFE?
THAT'S RIGHT. SO YOU'LL KNOW THAT MY LIFE HASN'T BEEN A CAKEWALK EITHER.
CHET, YOU SAID "WHAT WILL THEY THINK" BEFORE. WHAT WILL WHO THINK?
THE GUYS

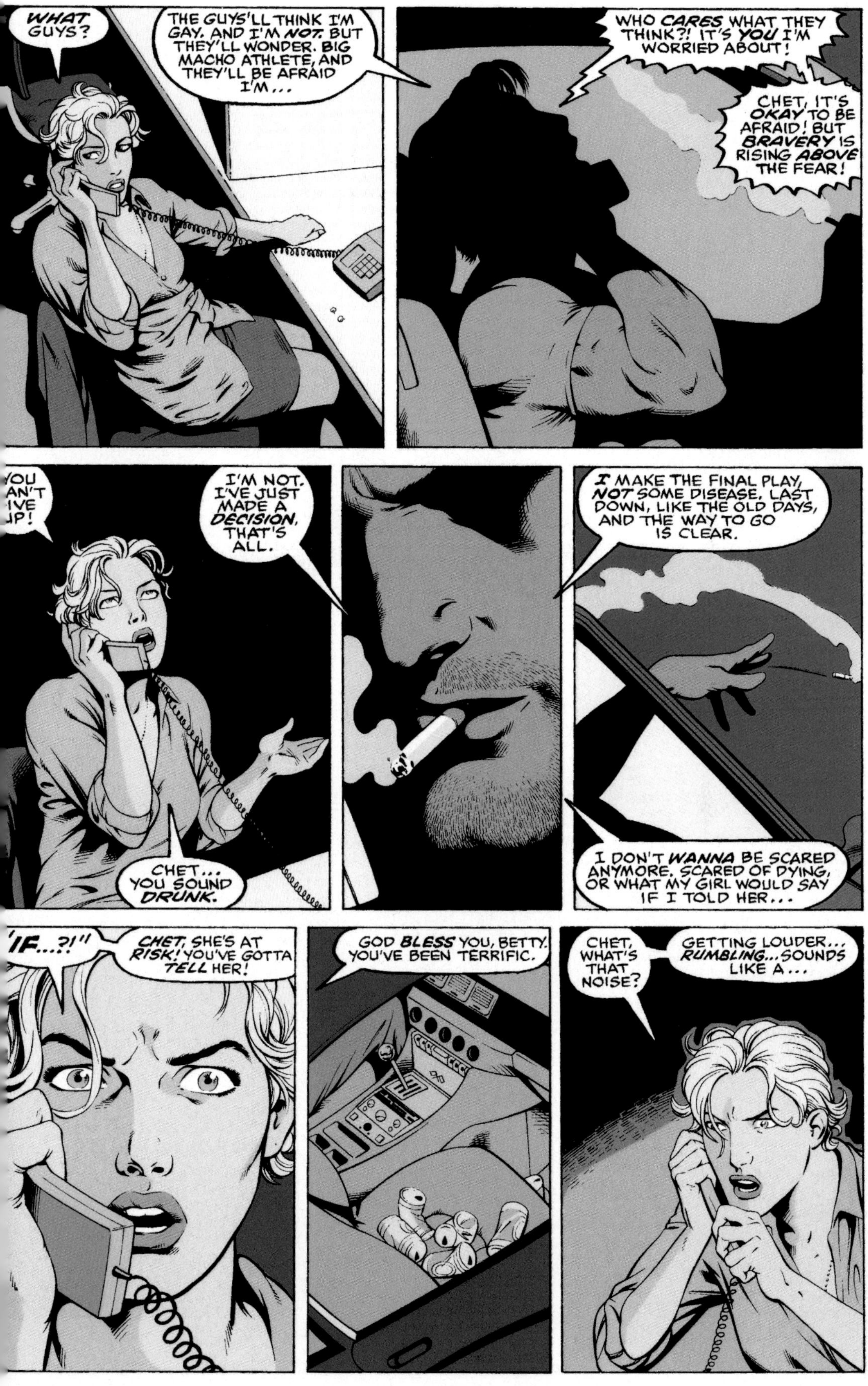
WHAT GUYS?
THE GUYS'LL THINK I'M GAY. AND I'M NOT. BUT THEY'LL WONDER. BIG MACHO ATHLETE, AND THEY'LL BE AFRAID I'M...
WHO CARES WHAT THEY THINK?! IT'S YOU I'M WORRIED ABOUT!
CHET, IT'S OKAY TO BE AFRAID! BUT BRAVERY IS RISING ABOVE THE FEAR!
YOU CAN'T GIVE UP!
I'M NOT. I'VE JUST MADE A DECISION, THAT'S ALL.
I MAKE THE FINAL PLAY, NOT SOME DISEASE. LAST DOWN, LIKE THE OLD DAYS, AND THE WAY TO GO IS CLEAR.
CHET... YOU SOUND DRUNK.
I DON'T WANNA BE SCARED ANYMORE. SCARED OF DYING, OR WHAT MY GIRL WOULD SAY IF I TOLD HER...
"IF...?!"
CHET, SHE'S AT RISK! YOU'VE GOTTA TELL HER!
GOD BLESS YOU, BETTY. YOU'VE BEEN TERRIFIC.
CHET, WHAT'S THAT NOISE?
GETTING LOUDER... RUMBLING... SOUNDS LIKE A...

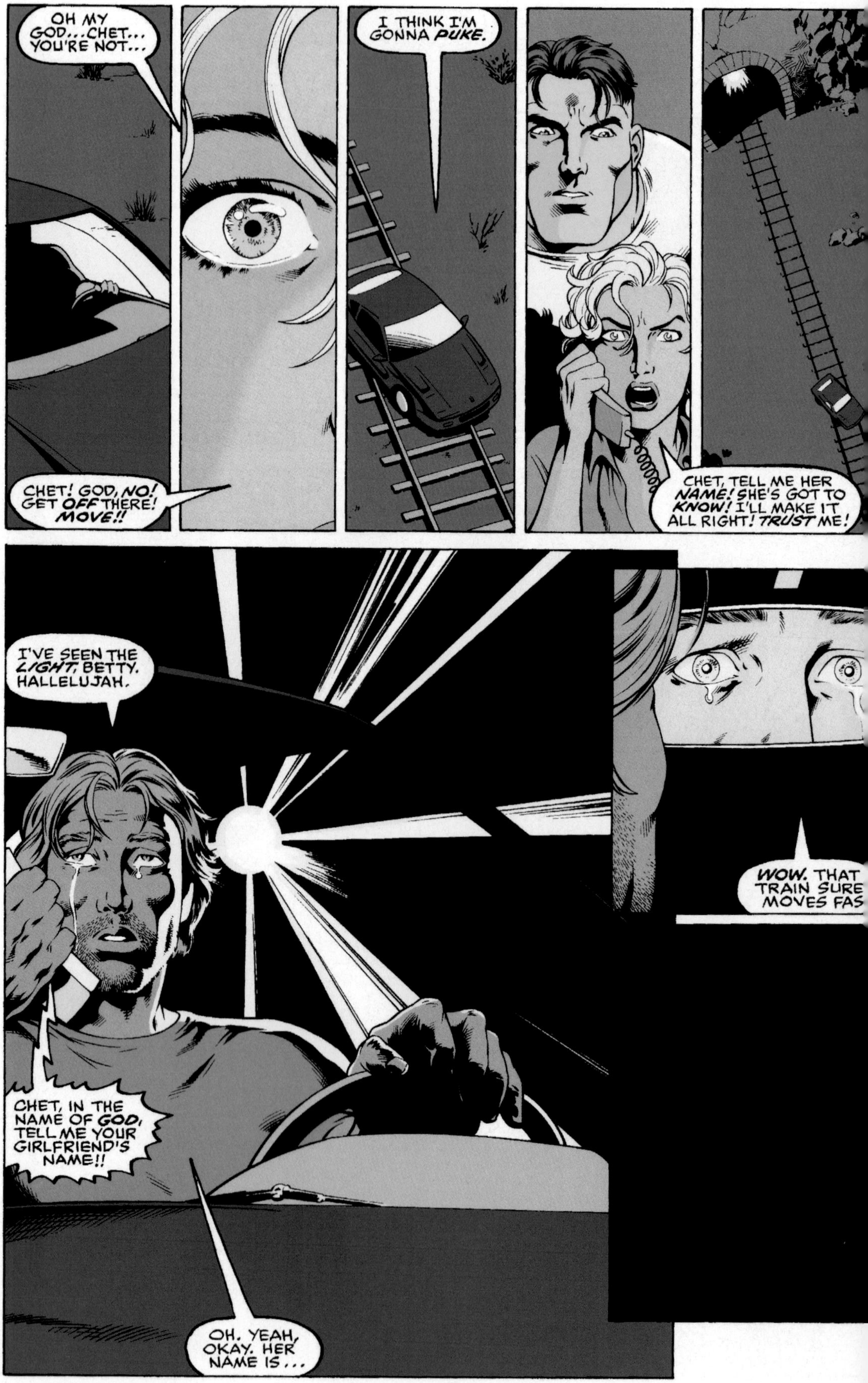

OH MY GOD...CHET... YOU'RE NOT...
CHET! GOD, NO! GET OFF THERE! MOVE!!
I THINK I'M GONNA PUKE.
CHET, TELL ME HER NAME! SHE'S GOT TO KNOW! I'LL MAKE IT ALL RIGHT! TRUST ME!
I'VE SEEN THE LIGHT, BETTY. HALLELUJAH.
WOW. THAT TRAIN SURE MOVES FAS
CHET, IN THE NAME OF GOD, TELL ME YOUR GIRLFRIEND'S NAME!!
OH. YEAH, OKAY. HER NAME IS...

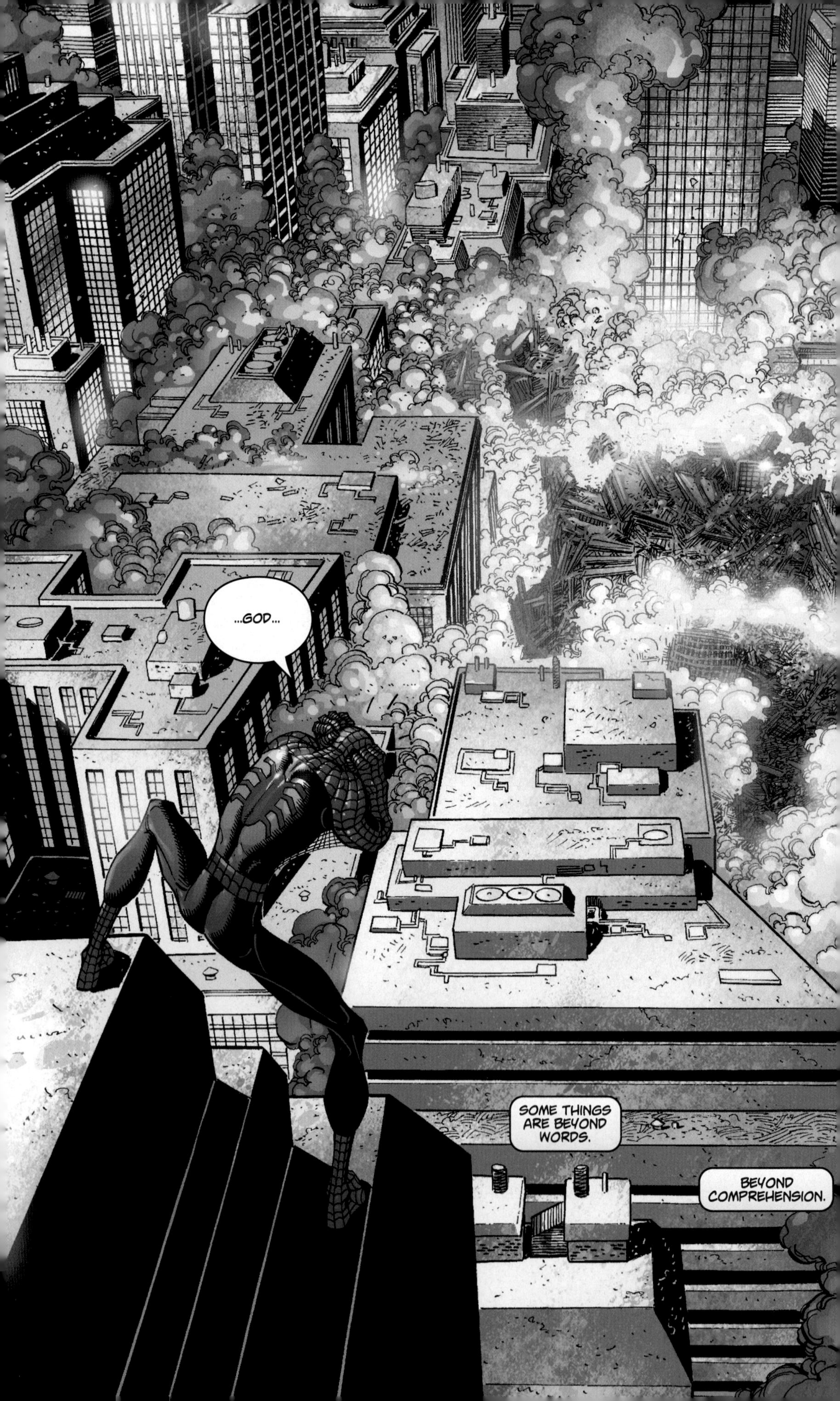
...GOD...
SOME THINGS ARE BEYOND WORDS.
BEYOND COMPREHENSION.

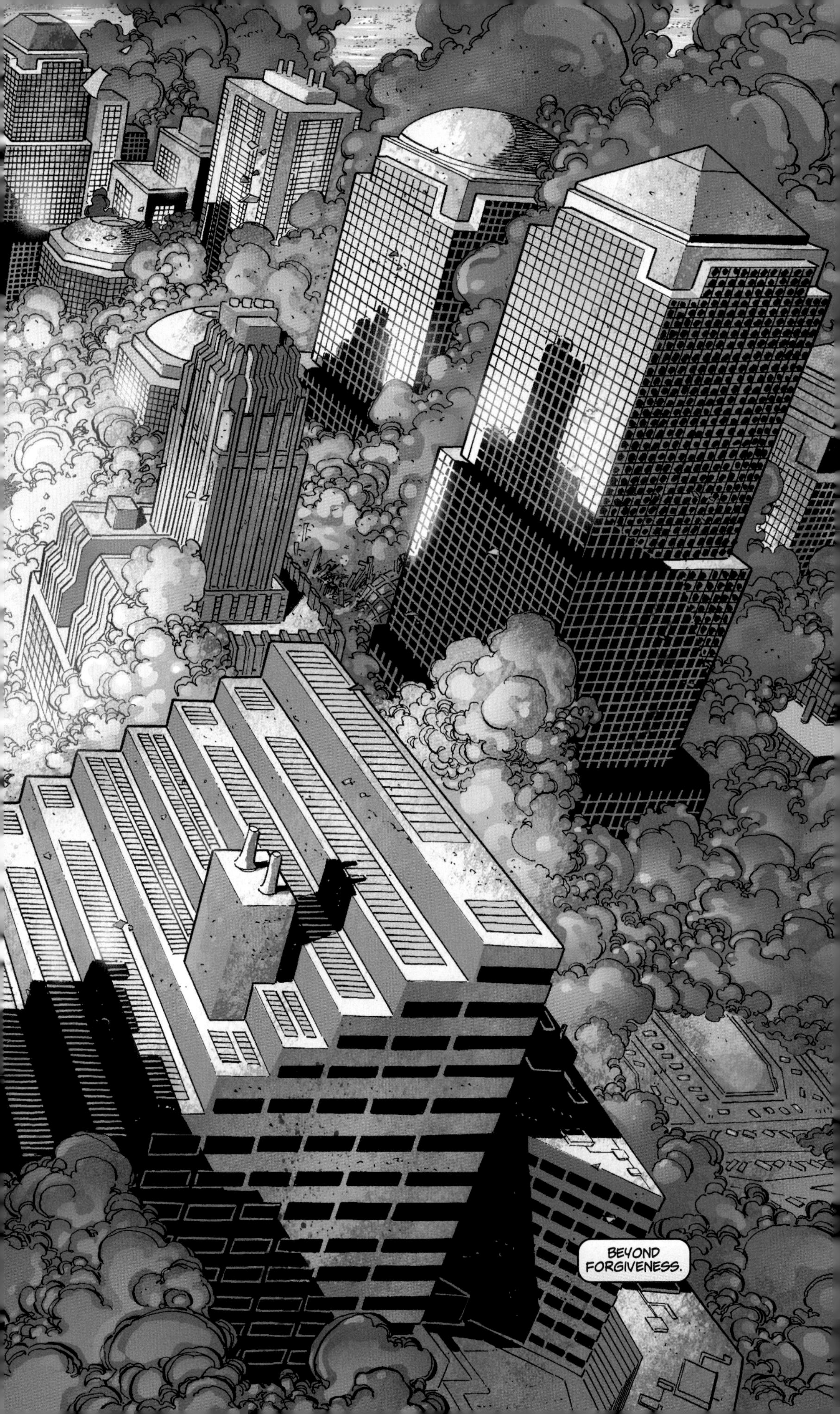
BEYOND FORGIVENESS.

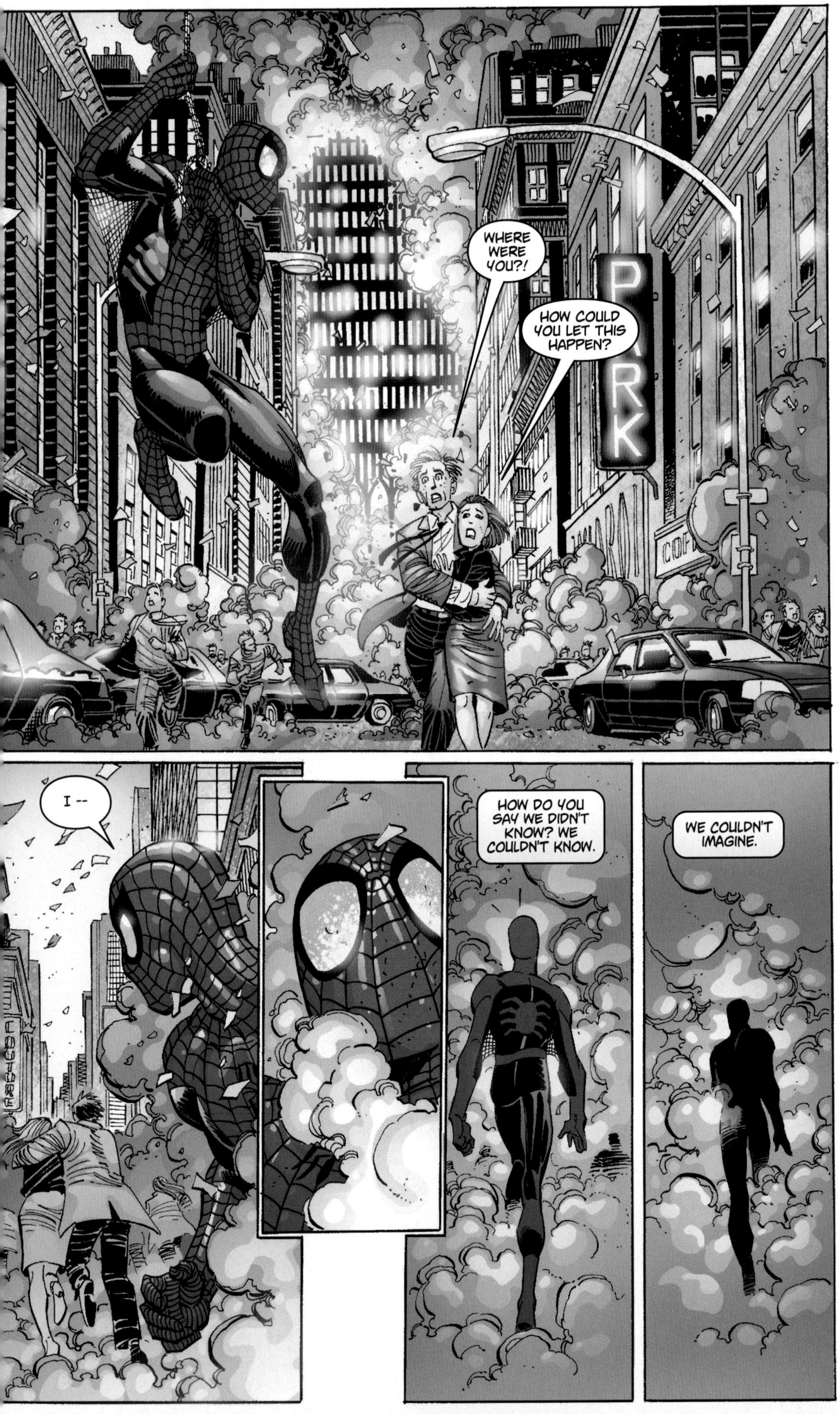
WHERE WERE YOU?!
HOW COULD YOU LET THIS HAPPEN?
PARK
I --
HOW DO YOU SAY WE DIDN'T KNOW? WE COULDN'T KNOW.
WE COULDN'T IMAGINE.

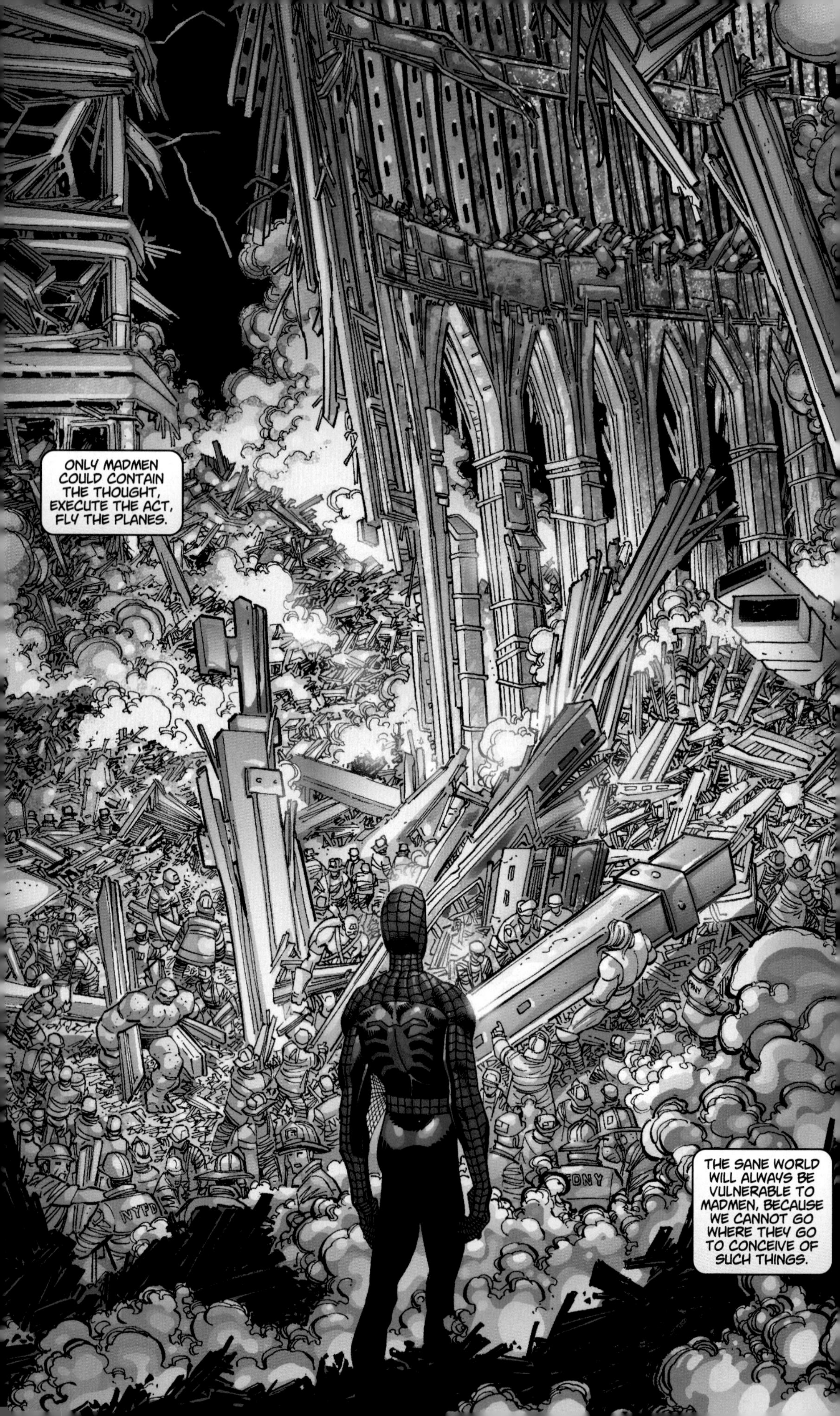
ONLY MADMEN COULD CONTAIN THE THOUGHT, EXECUTE THE ACT, FLY THE PLANES.
THE SANE WORLD WILL ALWAYS BE VULNERABLE TO MADMEN, BECAUSE WE CANNOT GO WHERE THEY GO TO CONCEIVE OF SUCH THINGS.
NYFD
FDNY

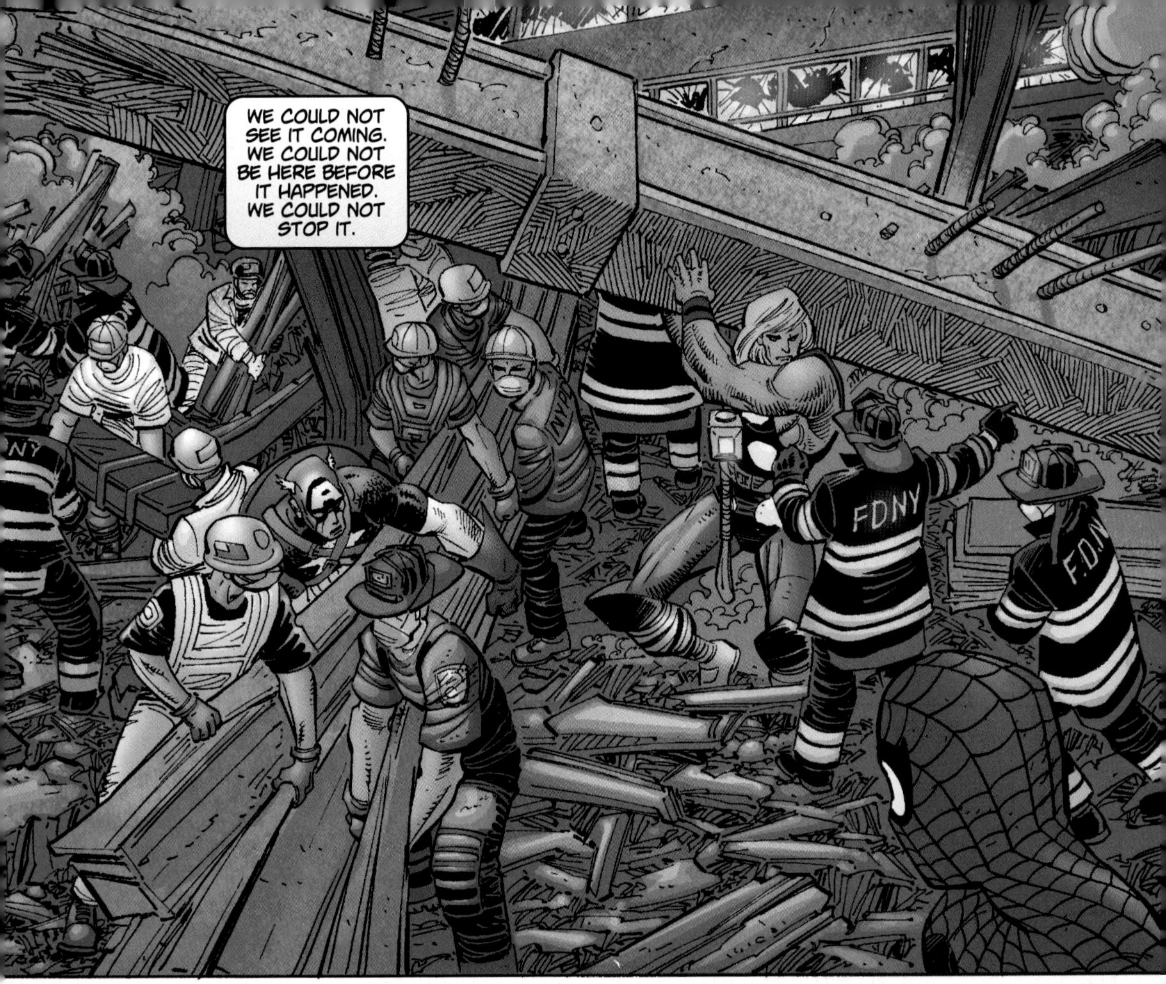
WE COULD NOT SEE IT COMING. WE COULD NOT BE HERE BEFORE IT HAPPENED. WE COULD NOT STOP IT.
FDNY
FDNY
FDNY

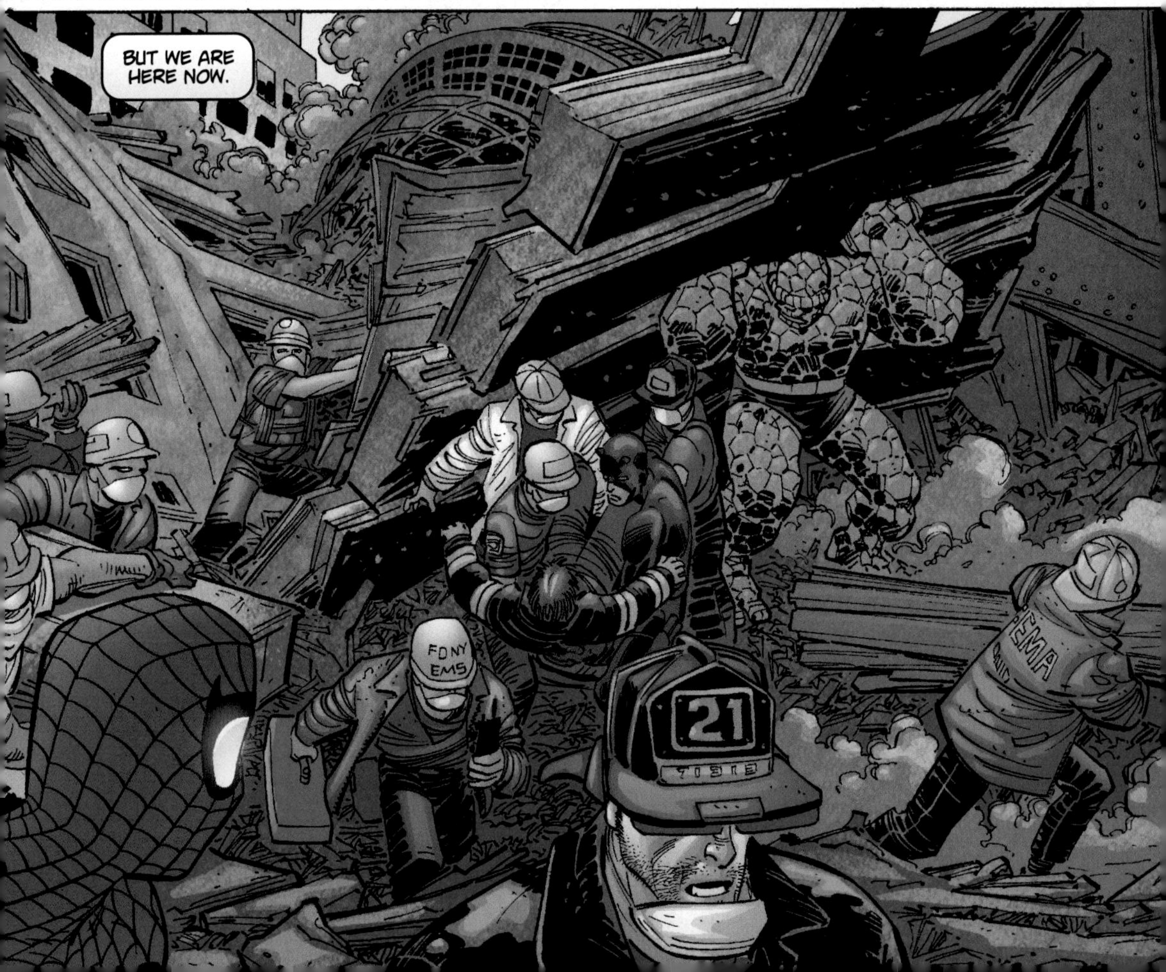
BUT WE ARE HERE NOW.
FDNY EMS
21
FEMA

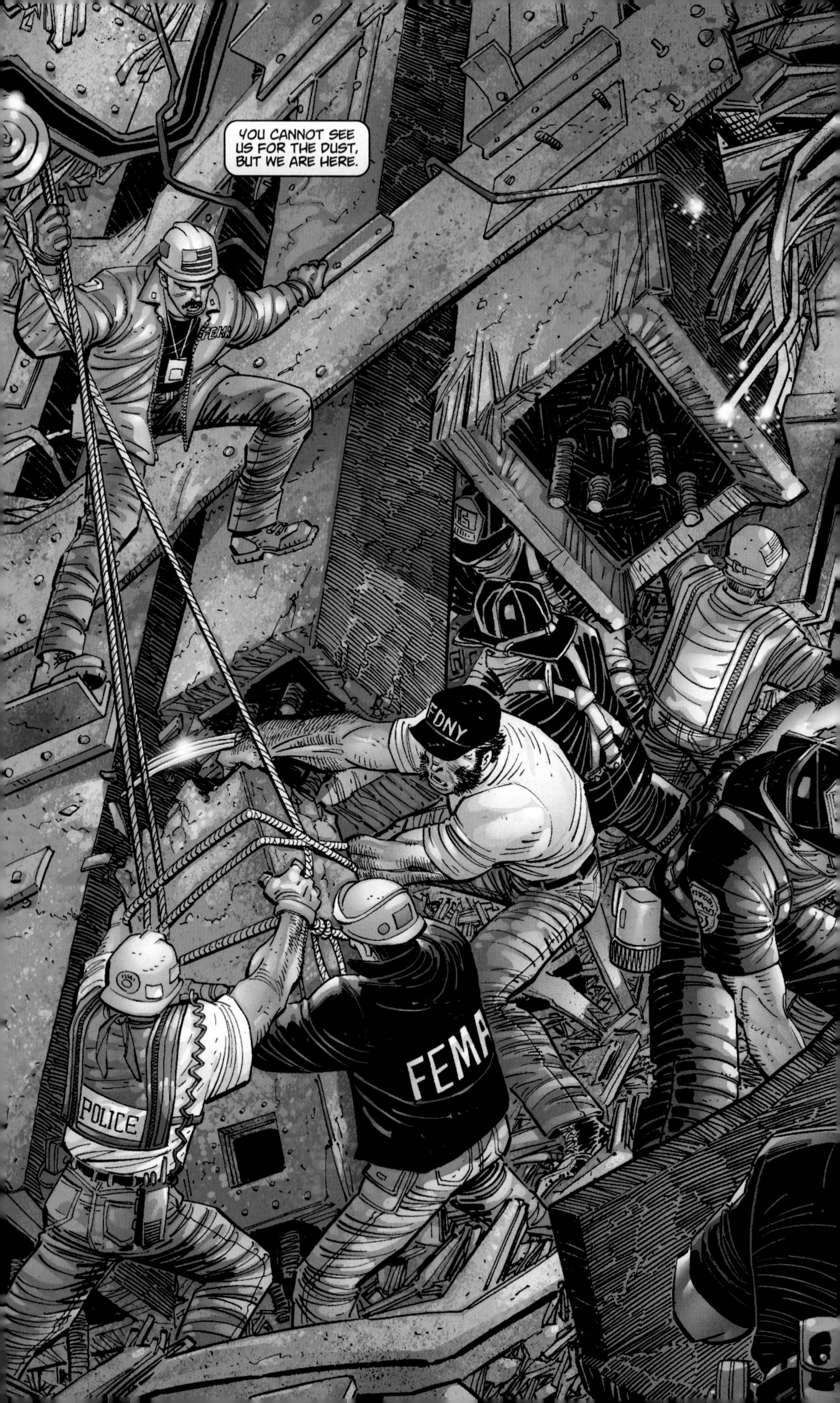
YOU CANNOT SEE US FOR THE DUST, BUT WE ARE HERE.
FEMA
FDNY
FEMA
POLICE

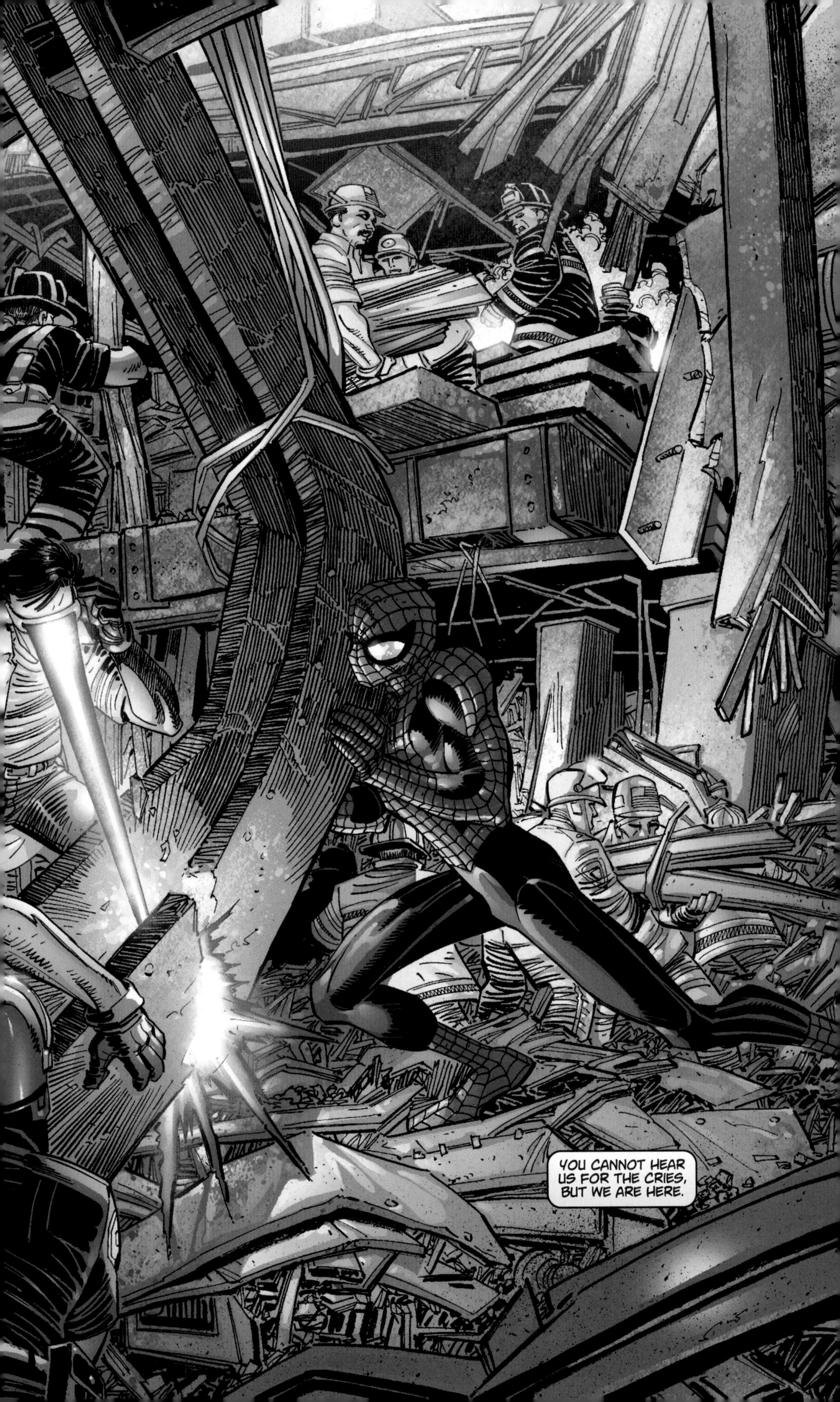
YOU CANNOT HEAR US FOR THE CRIES, BUT WE ARE HERE.

EVEN THOSE WE THOUGHT OUR ENEMIES ARE HERE. BECAUSE SOME THINGS SURPASS RIVALRIES AND BORDERS.

BECAUSE THE STORY OF HUMANITY IS WRITTEN NOT IN TOWERS BUT IN TEARS.

IN THE COMMON COIN OF BLOOD AND BONE.

IN THE VOICE THAT SPEAKS WITHIN EVEN THE WORST OF US, AND SAYS *THIS IS NOT RIGHT.*

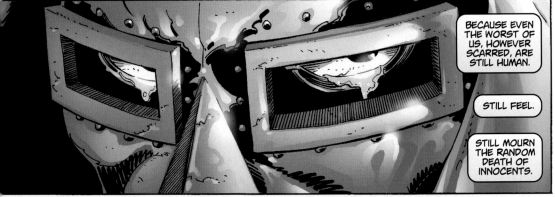

BECAUSE EVEN THE WORST OF US, HOWEVER SCARRED, ARE STILL HUMAN.

STILL FEEL.

STILL MOURN THE RANDOM DEATH OF INNOCENTS.

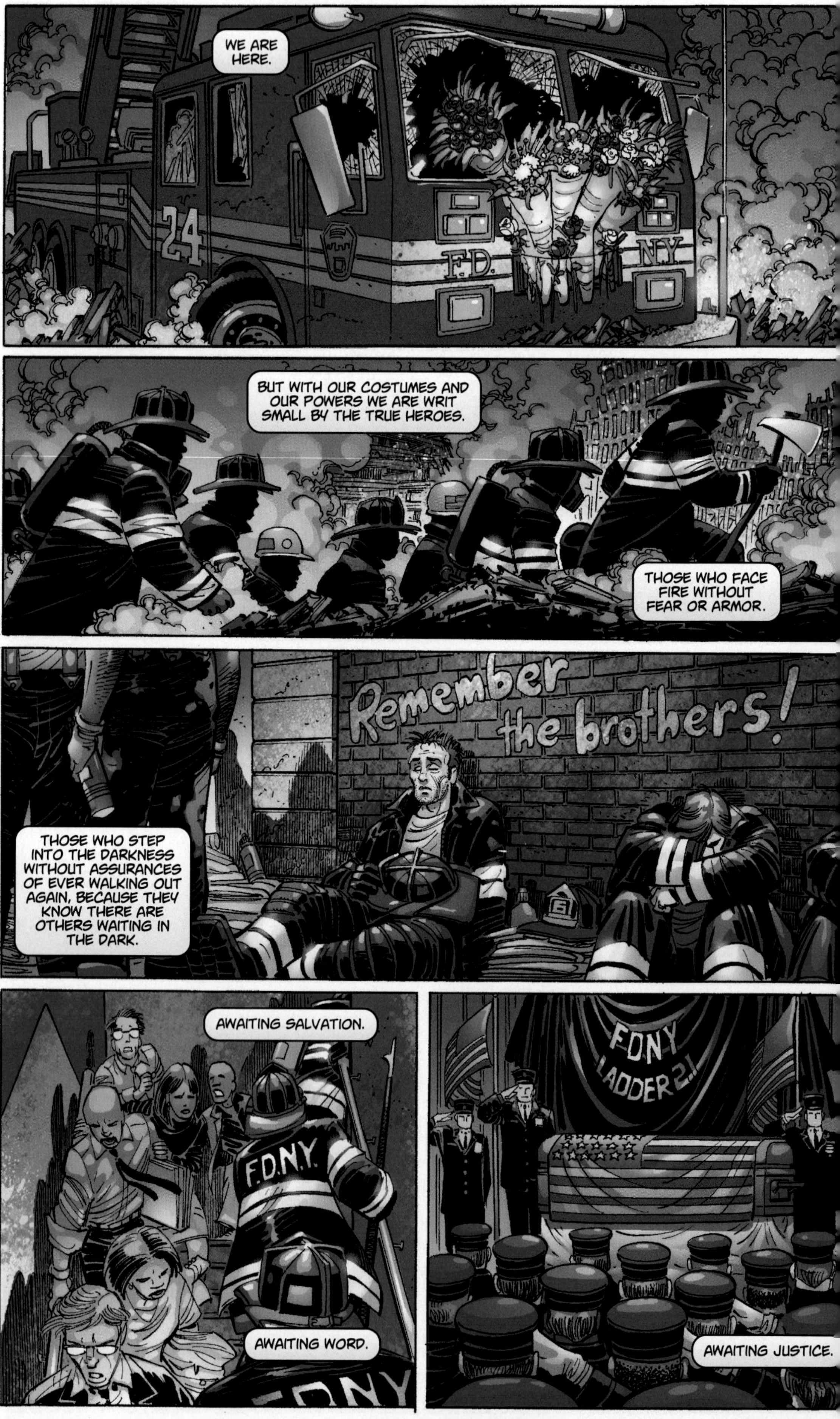
WE ARE HERE.
F.D.
N.Y.
BUT WITH OUR COSTUMES AND OUR POWERS WE ARE WRIT SMALL BY THE TRUE HEROES.
THOSE WHO FACE FIRE WITHOUT FEAR OR ARMOR.
Remember the brothers!
THOSE WHO STEP INTO THE DARKNESS WITHOUT ASSURANCES OF EVER WALKING OUT AGAIN, BECAUSE THEY KNOW THERE ARE OTHERS WAITING IN THE DARK.
AWAITING SALVATION.
F.D.N.Y.
AWAITING WORD.
FDNY LADDER 21
AWAITING JUSTICE.

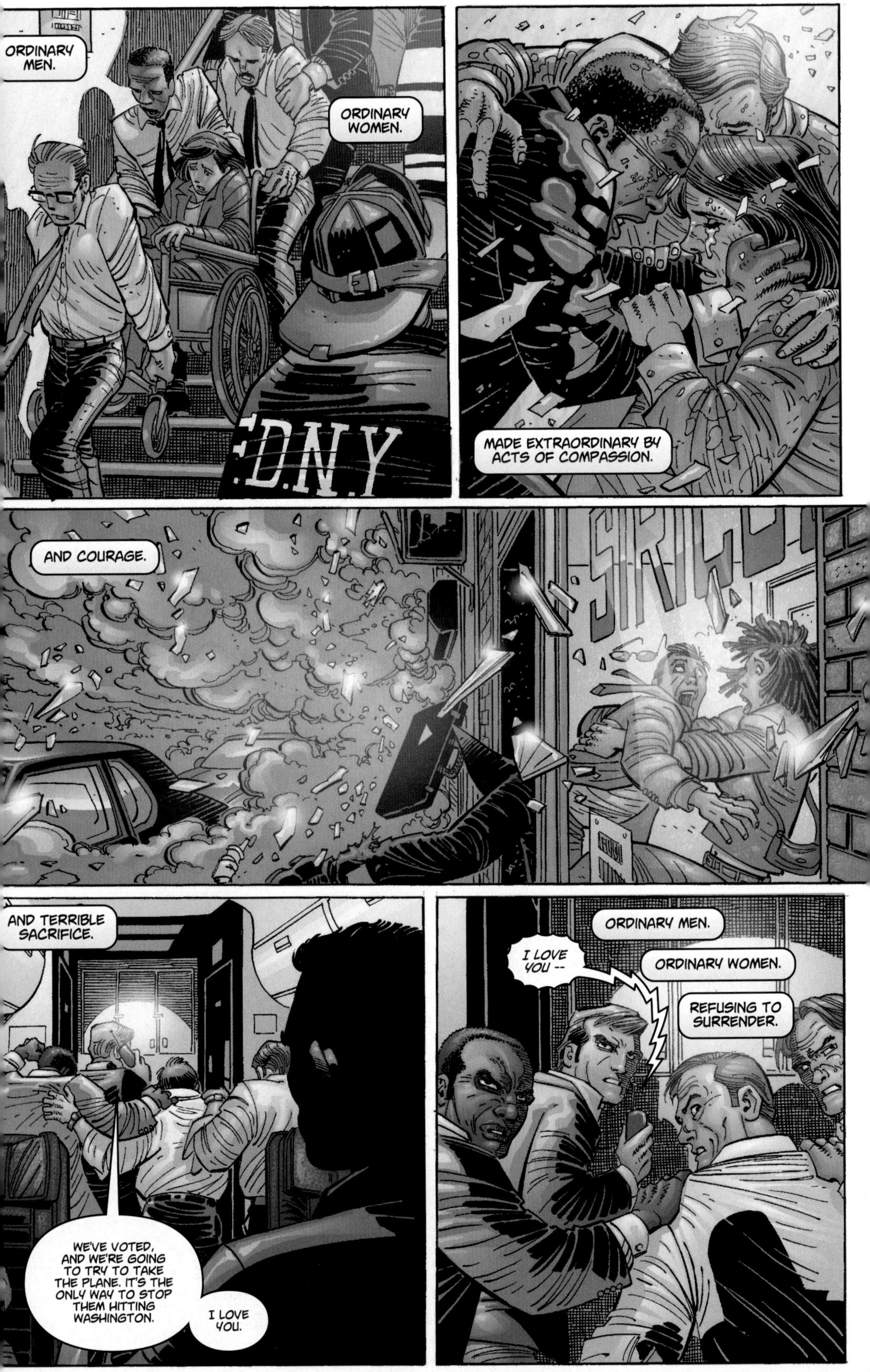
ORDINARY MEN.
ORDINARY WOMEN.
F.D.N.Y
MADE EXTRAORDINARY BY ACTS OF COMPASSION.
AND COURAGE.
AND TERRIBLE SACRIFICE.
WE'VE VOTED, AND WE'RE GOING TO TRY TO TAKE THE PLANE. IT'S THE ONLY WAY TO STOP THEM HITTING WASHINGTON.
I LOVE YOU.
ORDINARY MEN.
I LOVE YOU --
ORDINARY WOMEN.
REFUSING TO SURRENDER.

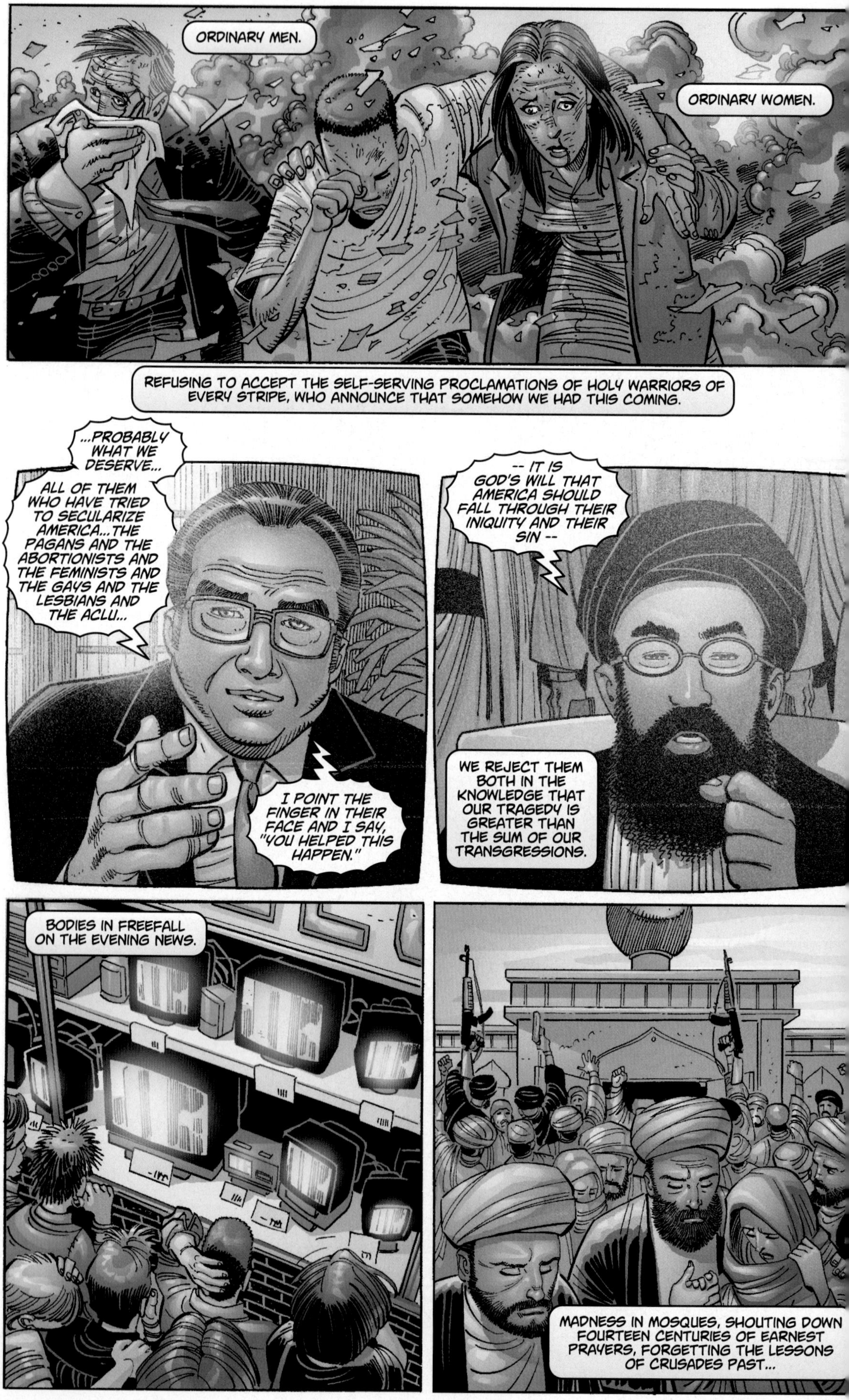
ORDINARY MEN.
ORDINARY WOMEN.
REFUSING TO ACCEPT THE SELF-SERVING PROCLAMATIONS OF HOLY WARRIORS OF EVERY STRIPE, WHO ANNOUNCE THAT SOMEHOW WE HAD THIS COMING.
...PROBABLY WHAT WE DESERVE...
ALL OF THEM WHO HAVE TRIED TO SECULARIZE AMERICA...THE PAGANS AND THE ABORTIONISTS AND THE FEMINISTS AND THE GAYS AND THE LESBIANS AND THE ACLU...
I POINT THE FINGER IN THEIR FACE AND I SAY, "YOU HELPED THIS HAPPEN."
-- IT IS GOD'S WILL THAT AMERICA SHOULD FALL THROUGH THEIR INIQUITY AND THEIR SIN --
WE REJECT THEM BOTH IN THE KNOWLEDGE THAT OUR TRAGEDY IS GREATER THAN THE SUM OF OUR TRANSGRESSIONS.
BODIES IN FREEFALL ON THE EVENING NEWS.
MADNESS IN MOSQUES, SHOUTING DOWN FOURTEEN CENTURIES OF EARNEST PRAYERS, FORGETTING THE LESSONS OF CRUSADES PAST...

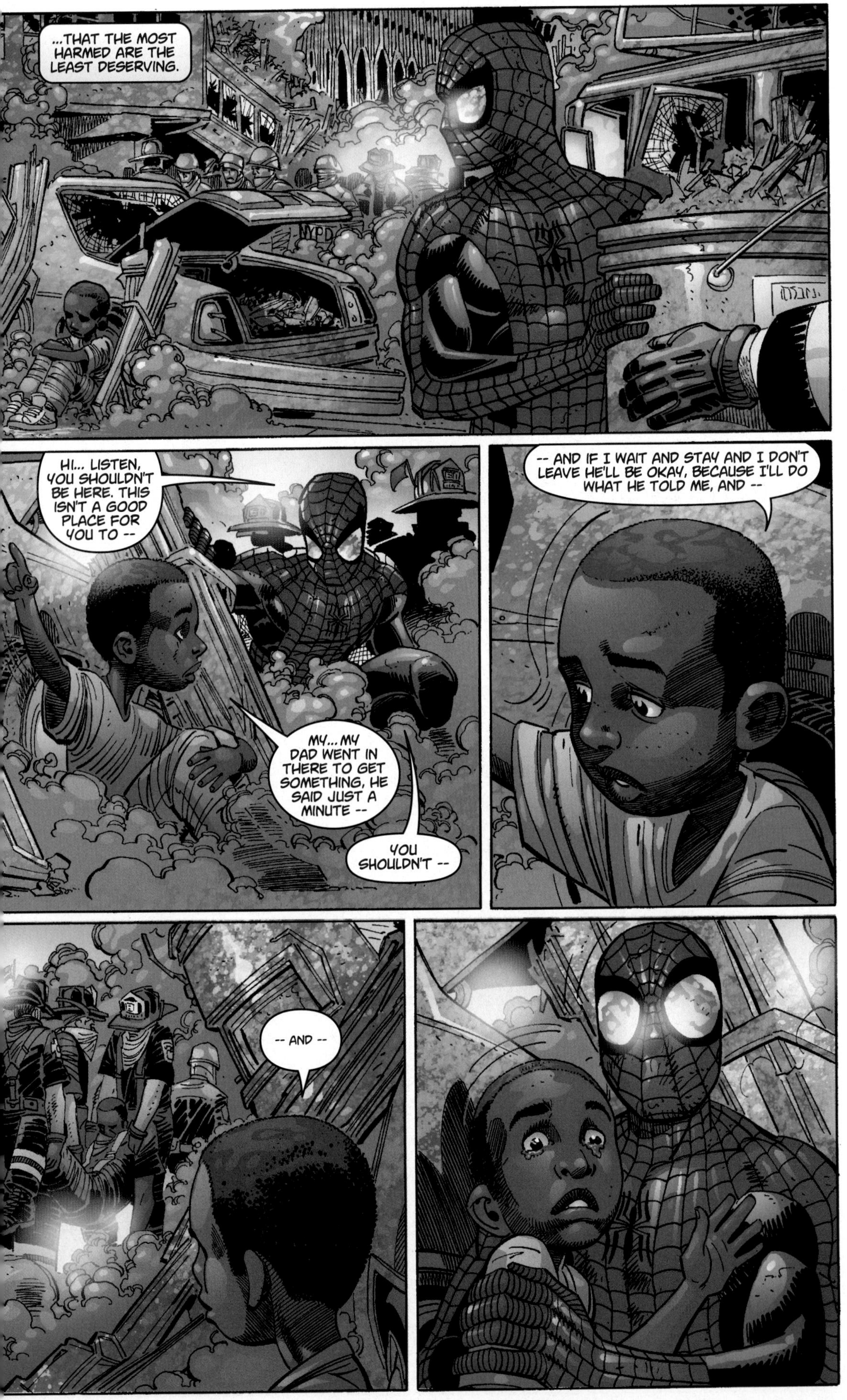
...THAT THE MOST HARMED ARE THE LEAST DESERVING.
NYPD
HI... LISTEN, YOU SHOULDN'T BE HERE. THIS ISN'T A GOOD PLACE FOR YOU TO --
MY... MY DAD WENT IN THERE TO GET SOMETHING, HE SAID JUST A MINUTE --
YOU SHOULDN'T --
-- AND IF I WAIT AND STAY AND I DON'T LEAVE HE'LL BE OKAY, BECAUSE I'LL DO WHAT HE TOLD ME, AND --
-- AND --

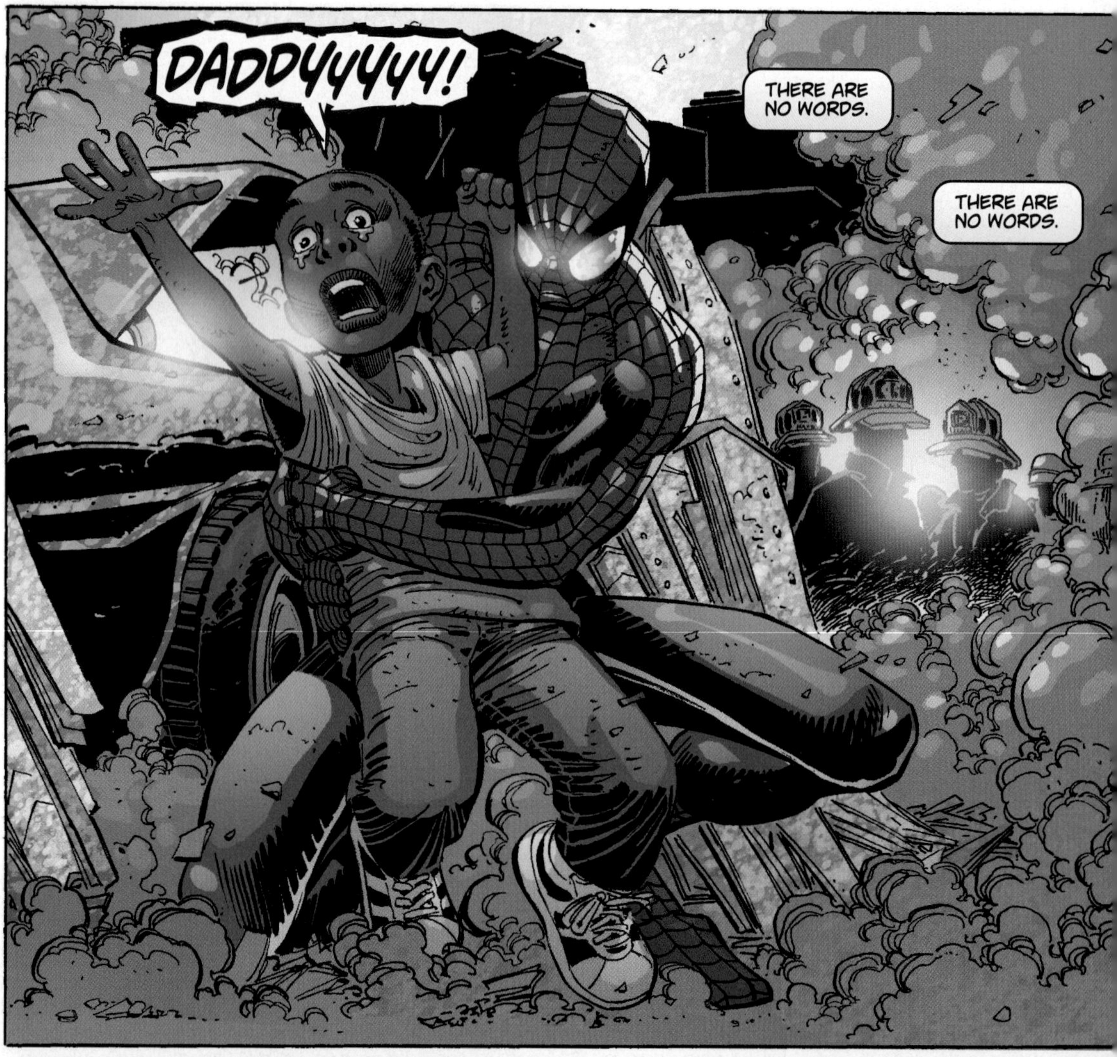
DADDYYYYY!
THERE ARE NO WORDS.
THERE ARE NO WORDS.

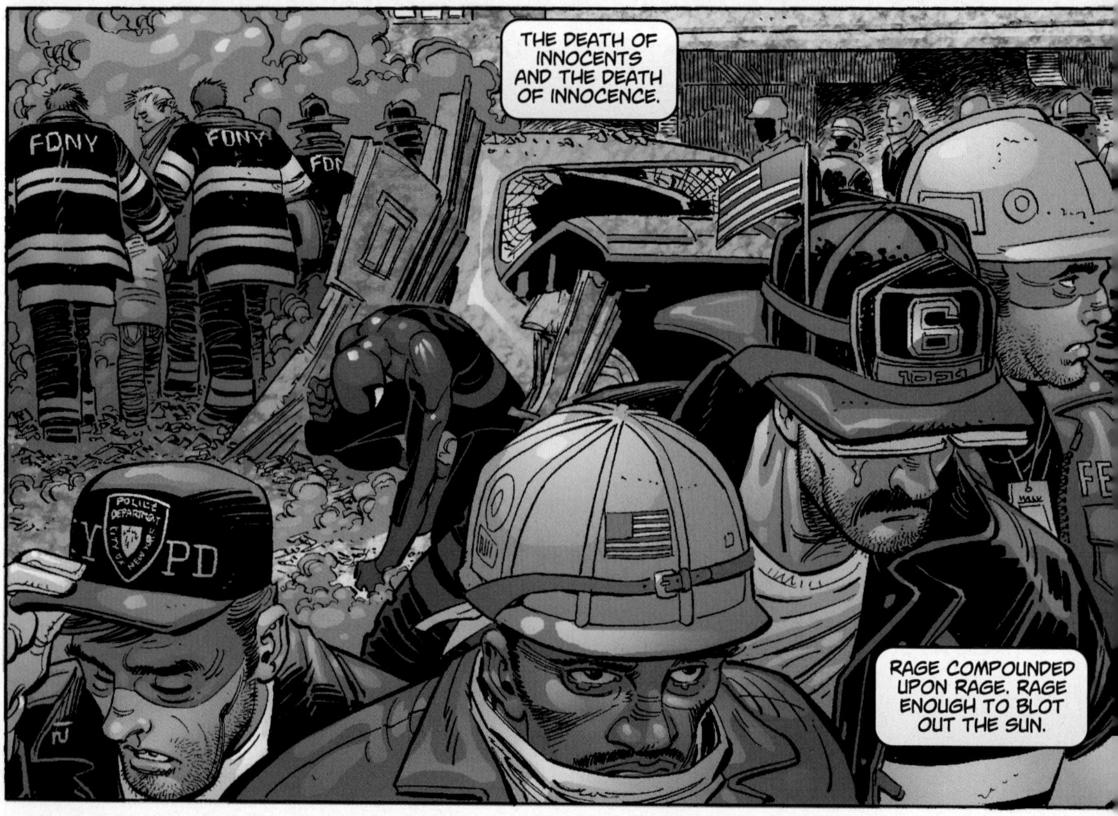
THE DEATH OF INNOCENTS AND THE DEATH OF INNOCENCE.
FDNY
FDNY
YPD
RAGE COMPOUNDED UPON RAGE. RAGE ENOUGH TO BLOT OUT THE SUN.

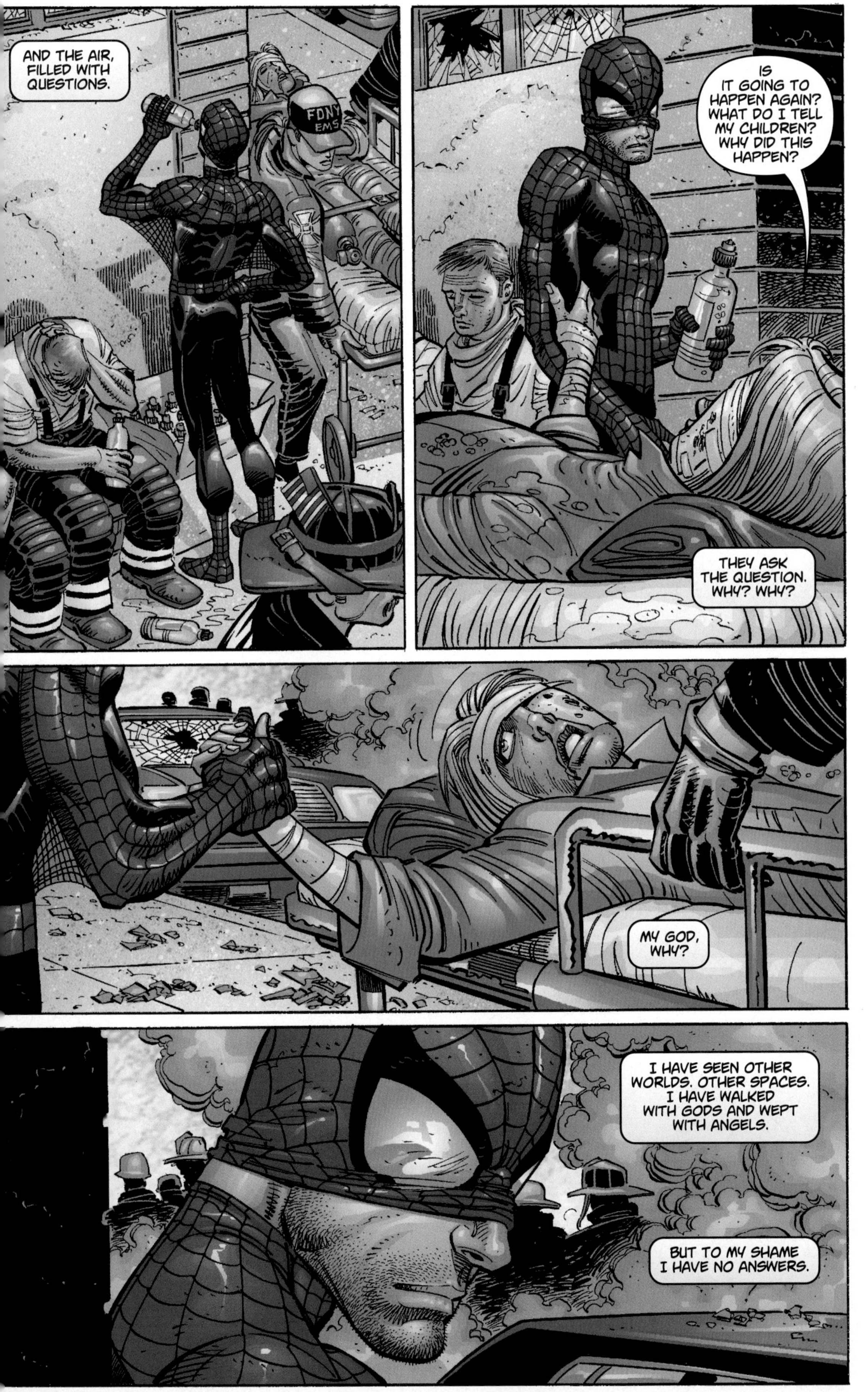
AND THE AIR, FILLED WITH QUESTIONS.
IS IT GOING TO HAPPEN AGAIN? WHAT DO I TELL MY CHILDREN? WHY DID THIS HAPPEN?
THEY ASK THE QUESTION. WHY? WHY?
MY GOD, WHY?
I HAVE SEEN OTHER WORLDS. OTHER SPACES. I HAVE WALKED WITH GODS AND WEPT WITH ANGELS.
BUT TO MY SHAME I HAVE NO ANSWERS.

HE'S THE ONLY ONE WHO COULD KNOW. BECAUSE HE'S BEEN HERE BEFORE.

I WISH I HAD NOT LIVED TO SEE THIS ONCE.

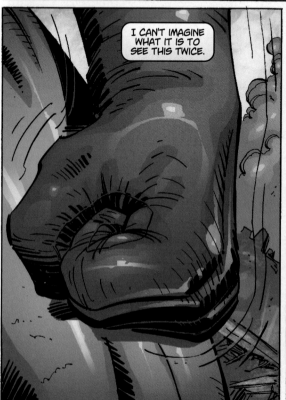

I CAN'T IMAGINE WHAT IT IS TO SEE THIS TWICE.

I JUST CAN'T IMAGINE.

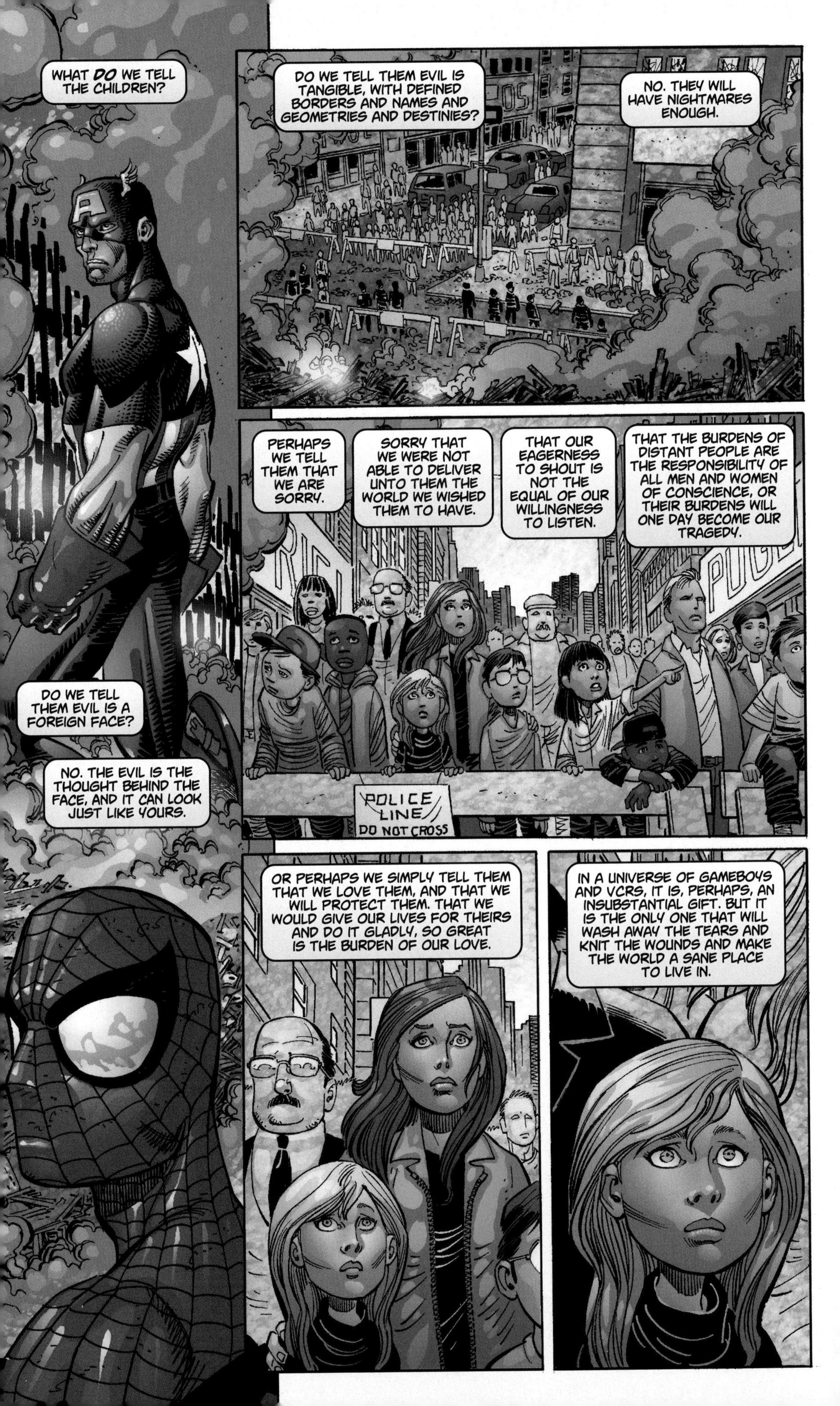
WHAT DO WE TELL THE CHILDREN?
DO WE TELL THEM EVIL IS TANGIBLE, WITH DEFINED BORDERS AND NAMES AND GEOMETRIES AND DESTINIES?
NO. THEY WILL HAVE NIGHTMARES ENOUGH.
DO WE TELL THEM EVIL IS A FOREIGN FACE?
NO. THE EVIL IS THE THOUGHT BEHIND THE FACE, AND IT CAN LOOK JUST LIKE YOURS.
PERHAPS WE TELL THEM THAT WE ARE SORRY.
SORRY THAT WE WERE NOT ABLE TO DELIVER UNTO THEM THE WORLD WE WISHED THEM TO HAVE.
THAT OUR EAGERNESS TO SHOUT IS NOT THE EQUAL OF OUR WILLINGNESS TO LISTEN.
THAT THE BURDENS OF DISTANT PEOPLE ARE THE RESPONSIBILITY OF ALL MEN AND WOMEN OF CONSCIENCE, OR THEIR BURDENS WILL ONE DAY BECOME OUR TRAGEDY.
POLICE LINE DO NOT CROSS
OR PERHAPS WE SIMPLY TELL THEM THAT WE LOVE THEM, AND THAT WE WILL PROTECT THEM. THAT WE WOULD GIVE OUR LIVES FOR THEIRS AND DO IT GLADLY, SO GREAT IS THE BURDEN OF OUR LOVE.
IN A UNIVERSE OF GAMEBOYS AND VCRS, IT IS, PERHAPS, AN INSUBSTANTIAL GIFT. BUT IT IS THE ONLY ONE THAT WILL WASH AWAY THE TEARS AND KNIT THE WOUNDS AND MAKE THE WORLD A SANE PLACE TO LIVE IN.

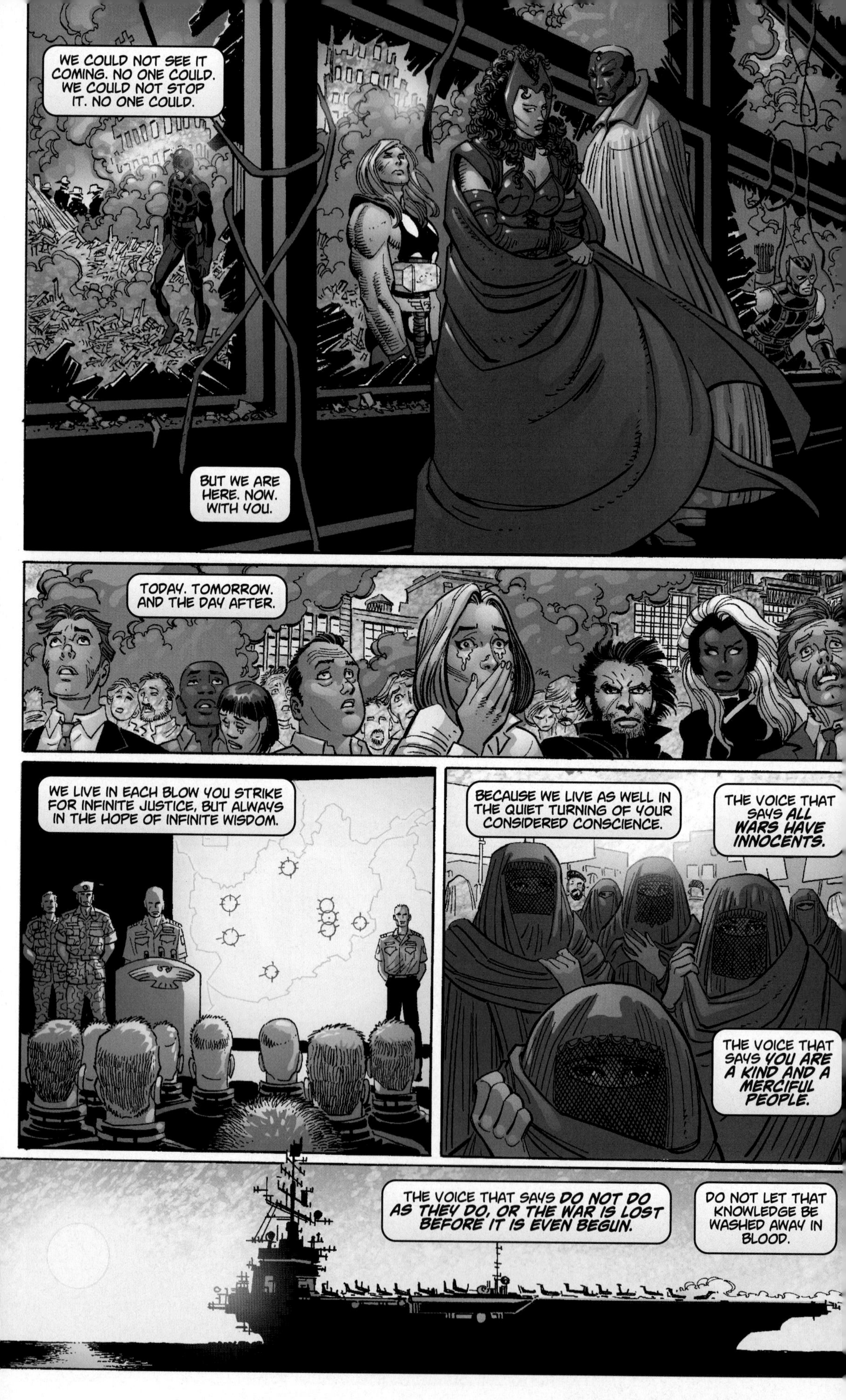

WE COULD NOT SEE IT COMING. NO ONE COULD. WE COULD NOT STOP IT. NO ONE COULD.
BUT WE ARE HERE. NOW. WITH YOU.
TODAY. TOMORROW. AND THE DAY AFTER.
WE LIVE IN EACH BLOW YOU STRIKE FOR INFINITE JUSTICE, BUT ALWAYS IN THE HOPE OF INFINITE WISDOM.
BECAUSE WE LIVE AS WELL IN THE QUIET TURNING OF YOUR CONSIDERED CONSCIENCE.
THE VOICE THAT SAYS *ALL WARS HAVE INNOCENTS.*
THE VOICE THAT SAYS *YOU ARE A KIND AND A MERCIFUL PEOPLE.*
THE VOICE THAT SAYS *DO NOT DO AS THEY DO, OR THE WAR IS LOST BEFORE IT IS EVEN BEGUN.*
DO NOT LET THAT KNOWLEDGE BE WASHED AWAY IN BLOOD.

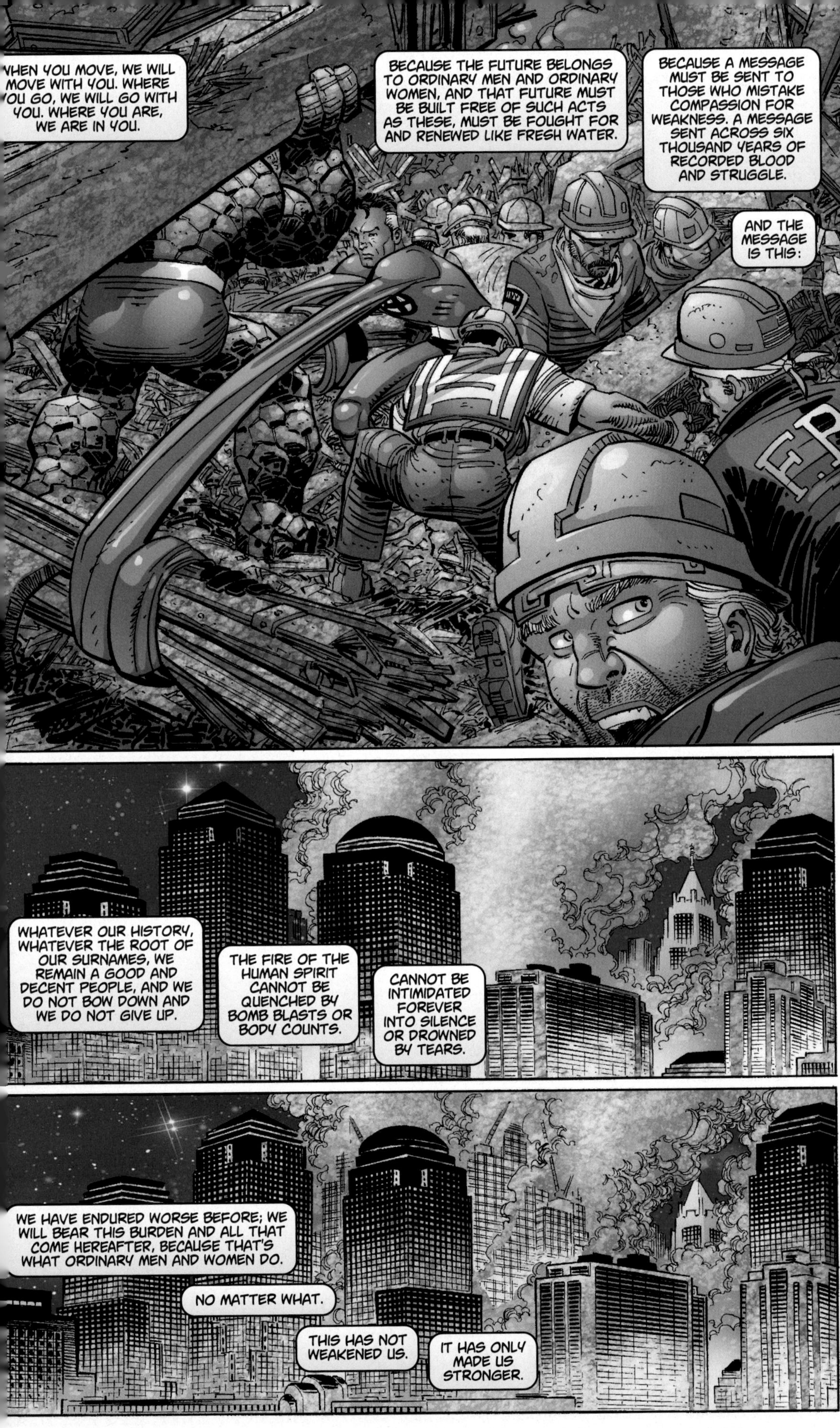

WHEN YOU MOVE, WE WILL MOVE WITH YOU. WHERE YOU GO, WE WILL GO WITH YOU. WHERE YOU ARE, WE ARE IN YOU.
BECAUSE THE FUTURE BELONGS TO ORDINARY MEN AND ORDINARY WOMEN, AND THAT FUTURE MUST BE BUILT FREE OF SUCH ACTS AS THESE, MUST BE FOUGHT FOR AND RENEWED LIKE FRESH WATER.
BECAUSE A MESSAGE MUST BE SENT TO THOSE WHO MISTAKE COMPASSION FOR WEAKNESS. A MESSAGE SENT ACROSS SIX THOUSAND YEARS OF RECORDED BLOOD AND STRUGGLE.
AND THE MESSAGE IS THIS:
F.B.
WHATEVER OUR HISTORY, WHATEVER THE ROOT OF OUR SURNAMES, WE REMAIN A GOOD AND DECENT PEOPLE, AND WE DO NOT BOW DOWN AND WE DO NOT GIVE UP.
THE FIRE OF THE HUMAN SPIRIT CANNOT BE QUENCHED BY BOMB BLASTS OR BODY COUNTS.
CANNOT BE INTIMIDATED FOREVER INTO SILENCE OR DROWNED BY TEARS.
WE HAVE ENDURED WORSE BEFORE; WE WILL BEAR THIS BURDEN AND ALL THAT COME HEREAFTER, BECAUSE THAT'S WHAT ORDINARY MEN AND WOMEN DO.
NO MATTER WHAT.
THIS HAS NOT WEAKENED US.
IT HAS ONLY MADE US STRONGER.

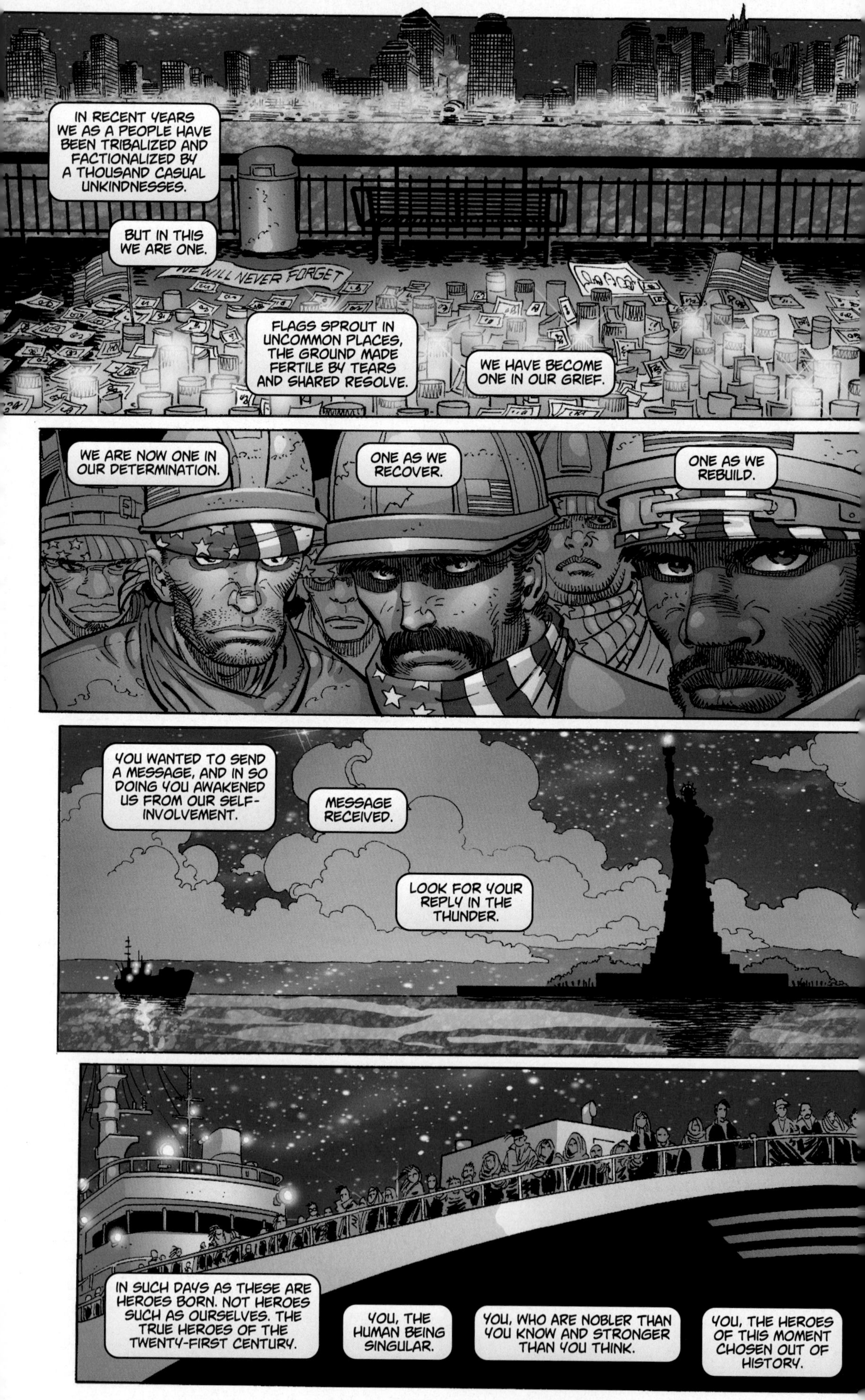
IN RECENT YEARS WE AS A PEOPLE HAVE BEEN TRIBALIZED AND FACTIONALIZED BY A THOUSAND CASUAL UNKINDNESSES.
BUT IN THIS WE ARE ONE.
WE WILL NEVER FORGET
FLAGS SPROUT IN UNCOMMON PLACES, THE GROUND MADE FERTILE BY TEARS AND SHARED RESOLVE.
WE HAVE BECOME ONE IN OUR GRIEF.
WE ARE NOW ONE IN OUR DETERMINATION.
ONE AS WE RECOVER.
ONE AS WE REBUILD.
YOU WANTED TO SEND A MESSAGE, AND IN SO DOING YOU AWAKENED US FROM OUR SELF-INVOLVEMENT.
MESSAGE RECEIVED.
LOOK FOR YOUR REPLY IN THE THUNDER.
IN SUCH DAYS AS THESE ARE HEROES BORN. NOT HEROES SUCH AS OURSELVES. THE TRUE HEROES OF THE TWENTY-FIRST CENTURY.
YOU, THE HUMAN BEING SINGULAR.
YOU, WHO ARE NOBLER THAN YOU KNOW AND STRONGER THAN YOU THINK.
YOU, THE HEROES OF THIS MOMENT CHOSEN OUT OF HISTORY.

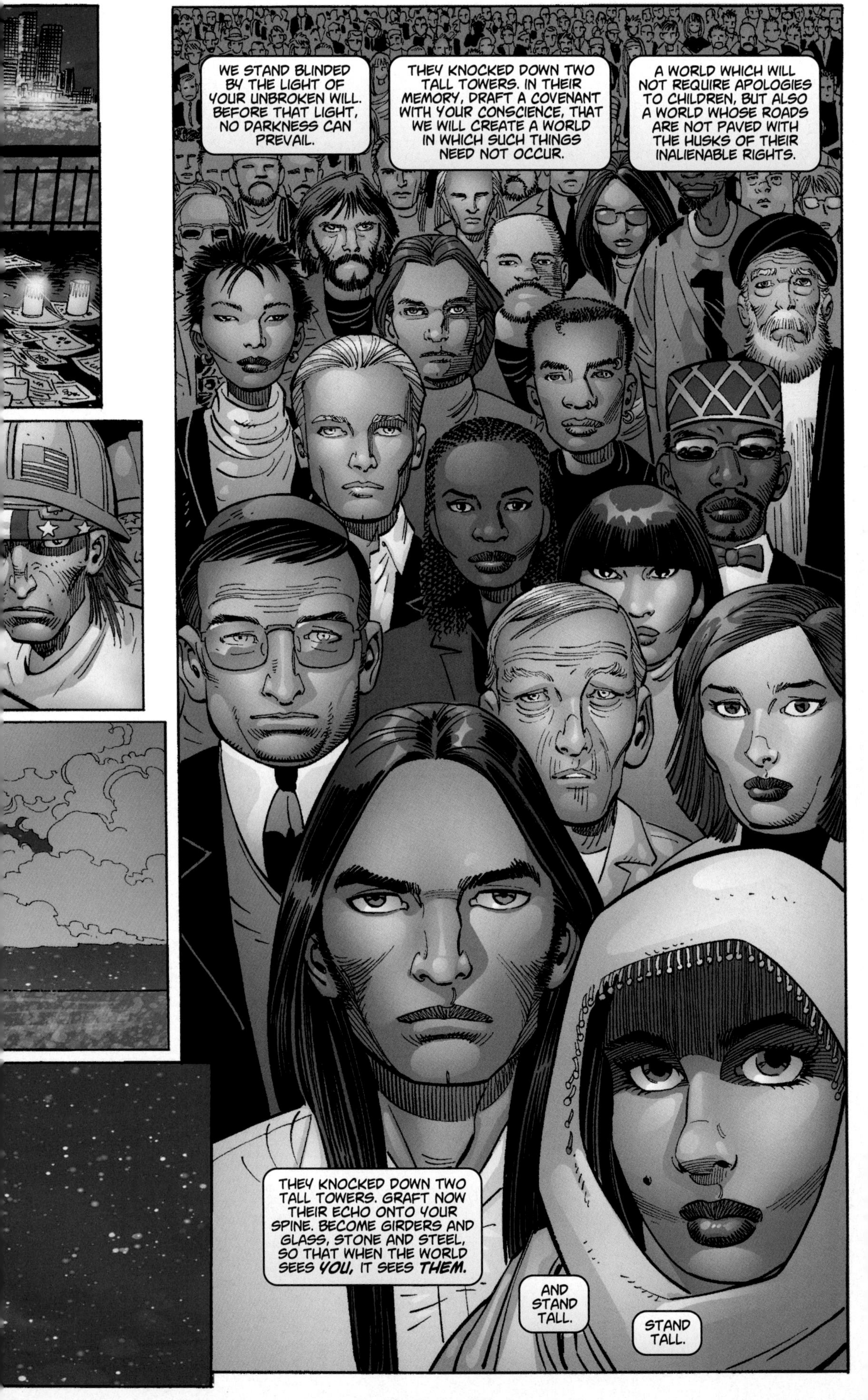
WE STAND BLINDED BY THE LIGHT OF YOUR UNBROKEN WILL. BEFORE THAT LIGHT, NO DARKNESS CAN PREVAIL.
THEY KNOCKED DOWN TWO TALL TOWERS. IN THEIR MEMORY, DRAFT A COVENANT WITH YOUR CONSCIENCE, THAT WE WILL CREATE A WORLD IN WHICH SUCH THINGS NEED NOT OCCUR.
A WORLD WHICH WILL NOT REQUIRE APOLOGIES TO CHILDREN, BUT ALSO A WORLD WHOSE ROADS ARE NOT PAVED WITH THE HUSKS OF THEIR INALIENABLE RIGHTS.
THEY KNOCKED DOWN TWO TALL TOWERS. GRAFT NOW THEIR ECHO ONTO YOUR SPINE. BECOME GIRDERS AND GLASS, STONE AND STEEL, SO THAT WHEN THE WORLD SEES ***YOU,*** IT SEES ***THEM.***
AND STAND TALL.
STAND TALL.

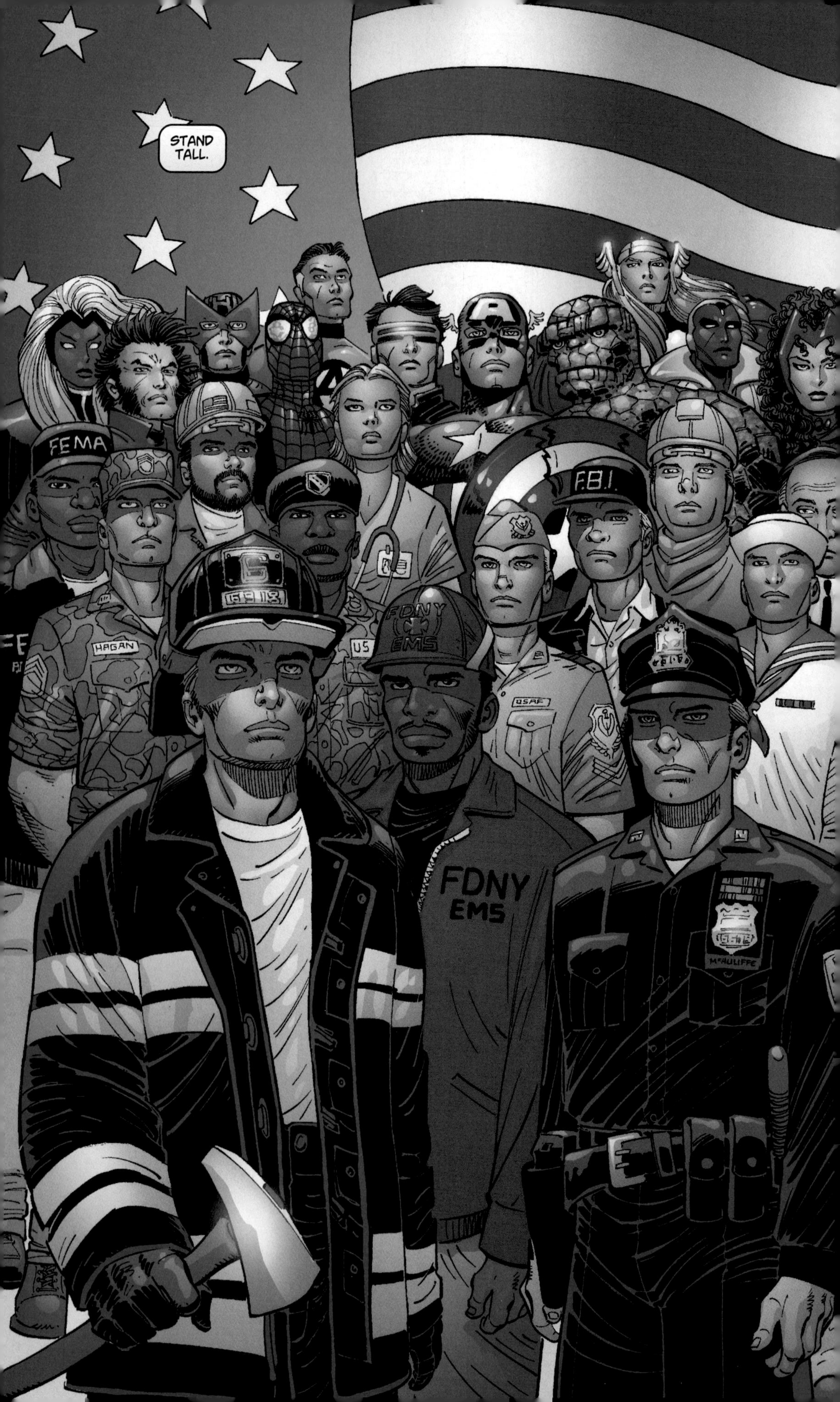
STAND TALL.
FEMA
HAGAN
F.B.I.
FDNY EMS
US
FDNY EMS

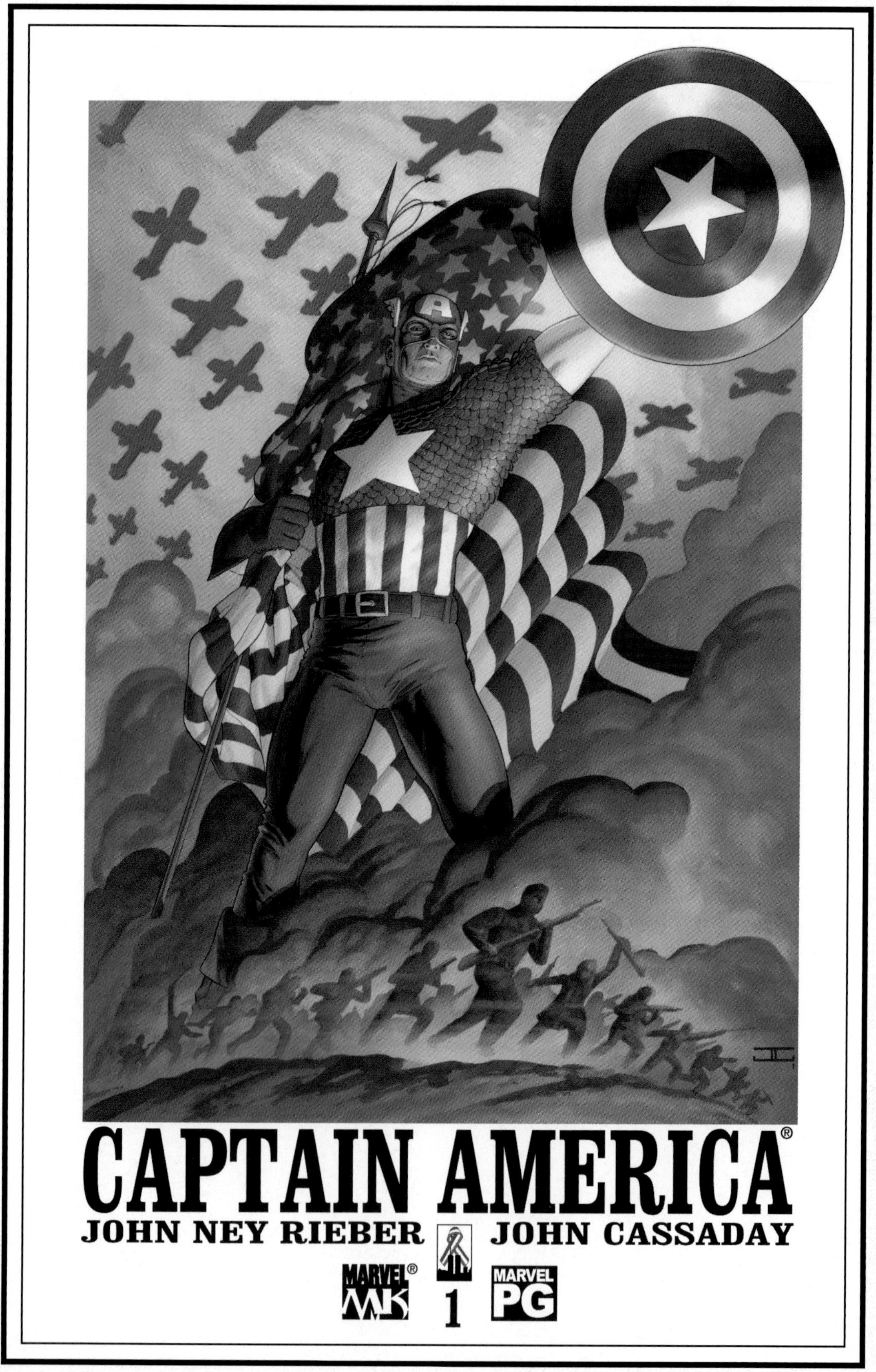
CAPTAIN AMERICA®
JOHN NEY RIEBER
JOHN CASSADAY
MARVEL®
MK
1
MARVEL
PG

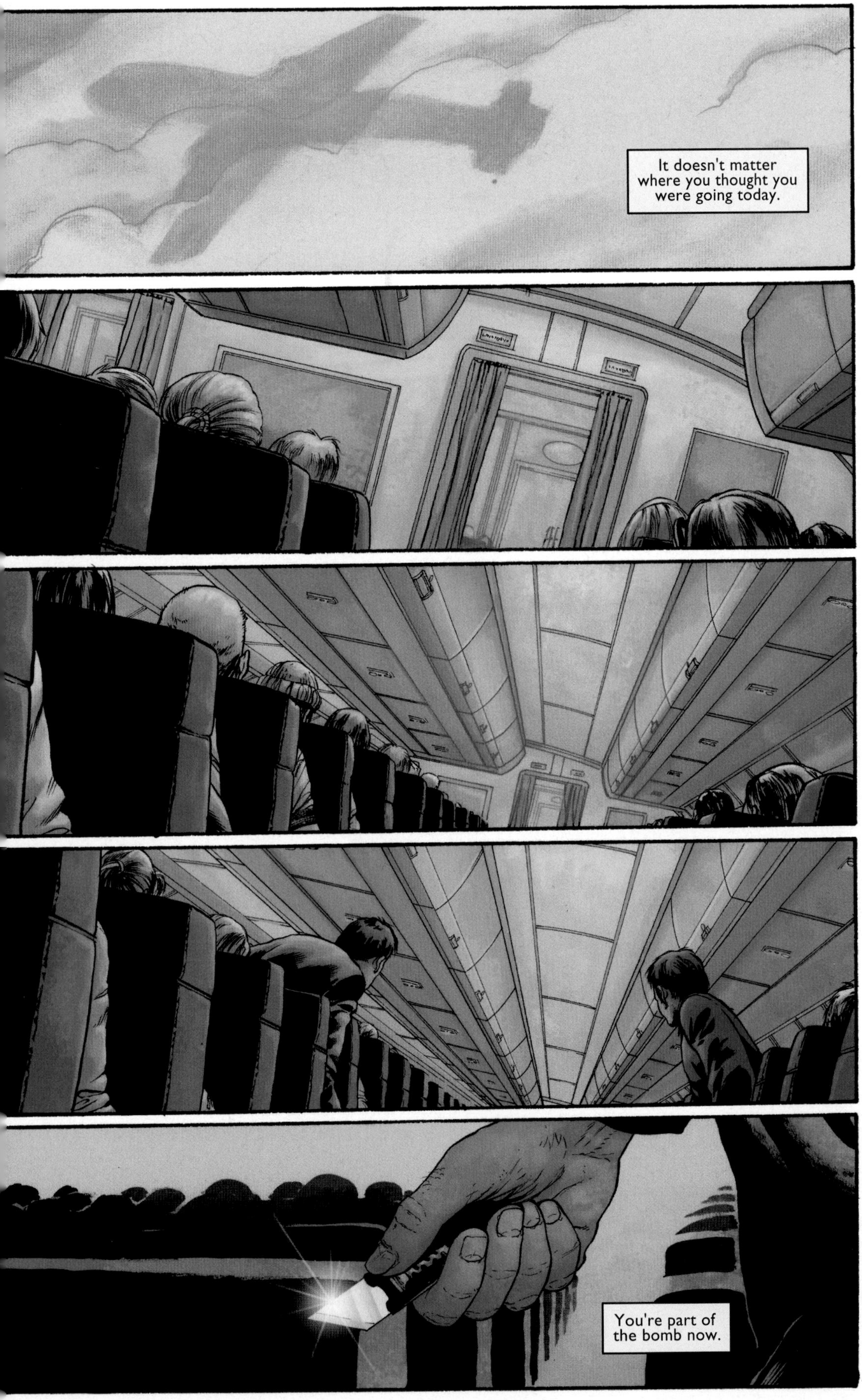
It doesn't matter where you thought you were going today.
You're part of the bomb now.

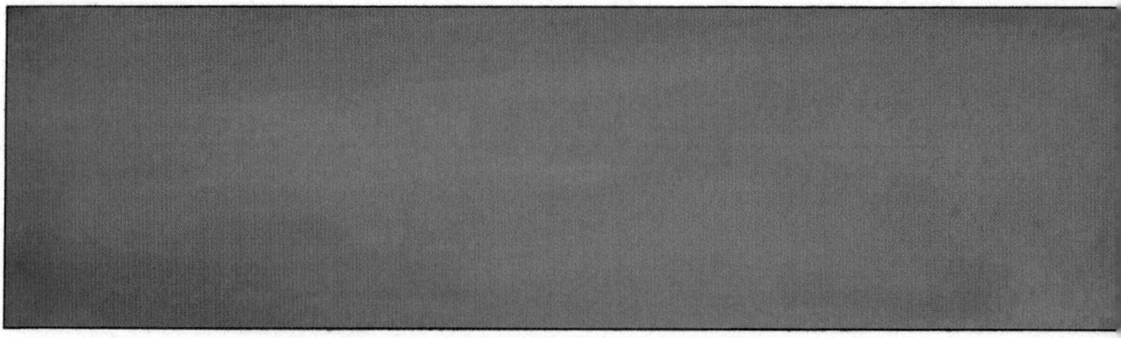

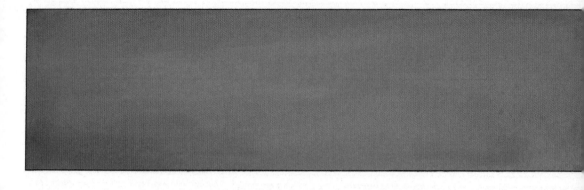

And somewhere in the world --

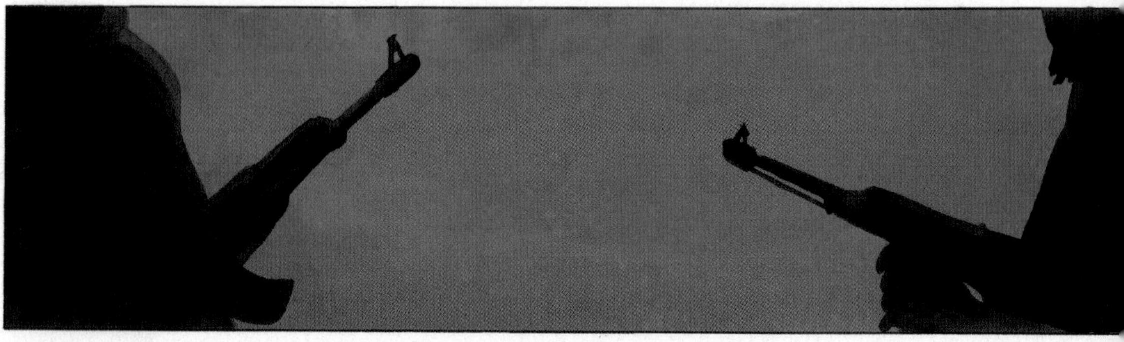

A handful of men with famished eyes sit around a radio --

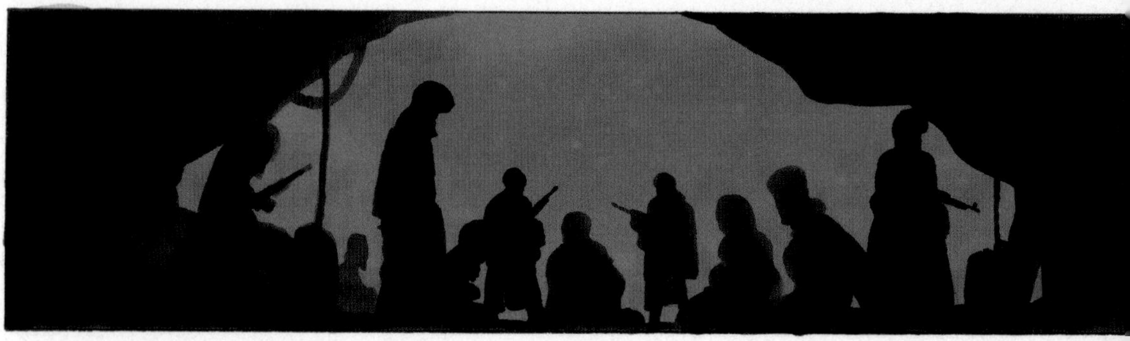

Or a telephone.

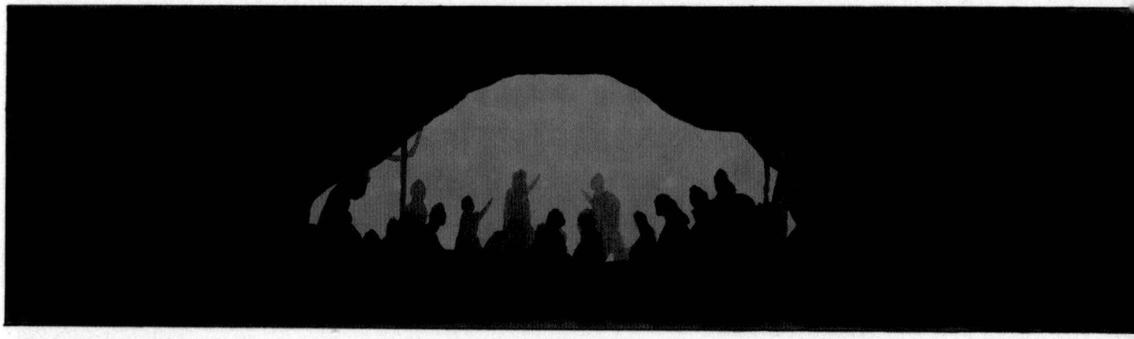

Waiting.

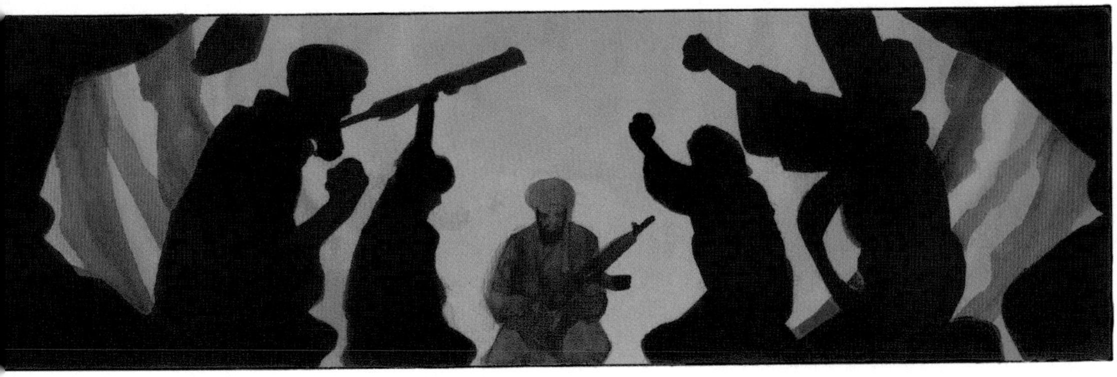

Twenty minutes --

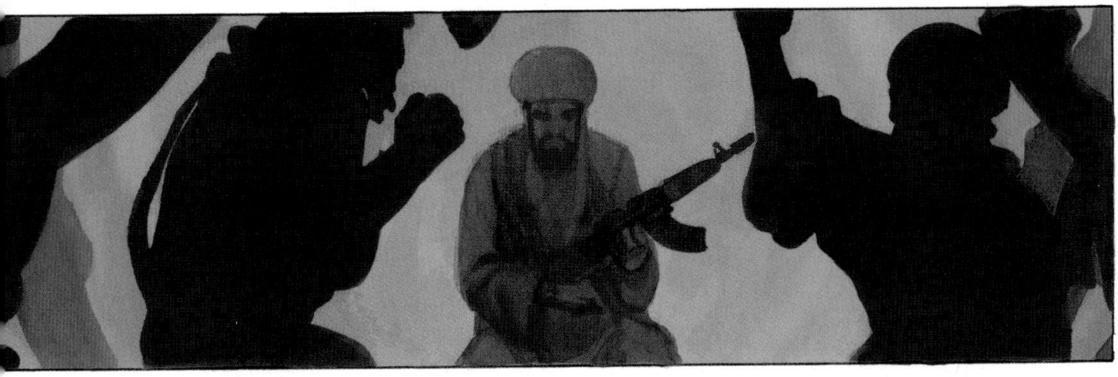

Four thousand murders later --

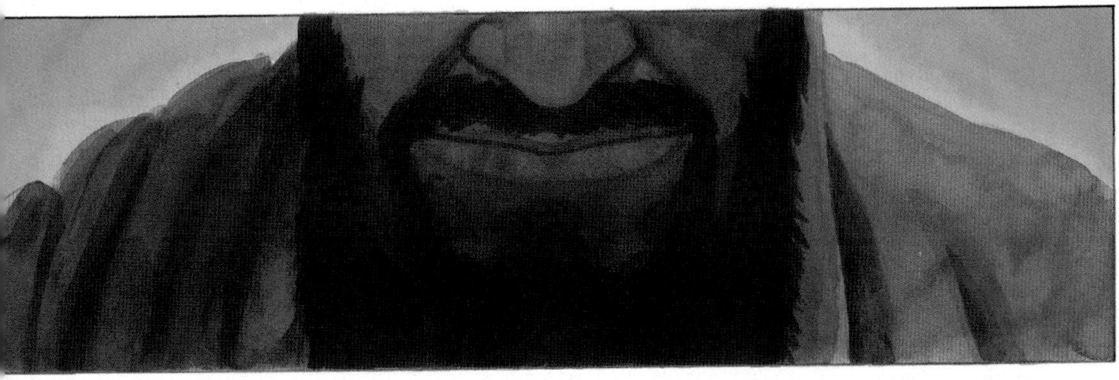

They praise God for the blood that stains their hands.

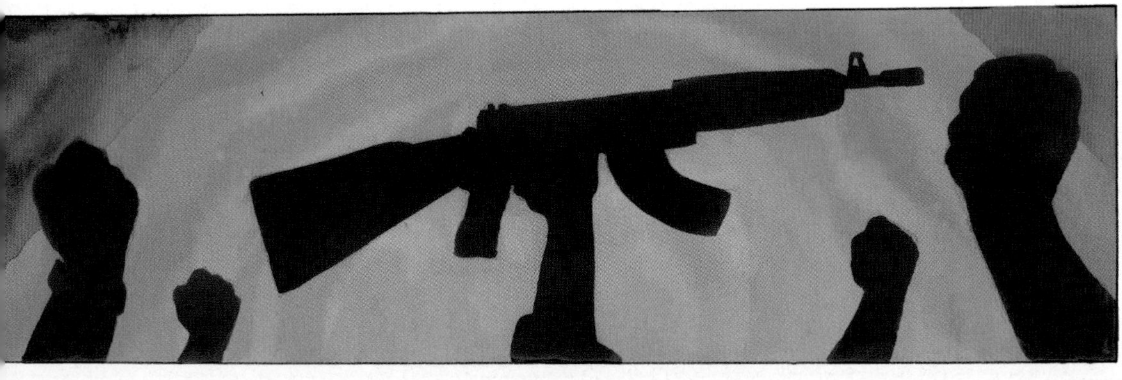

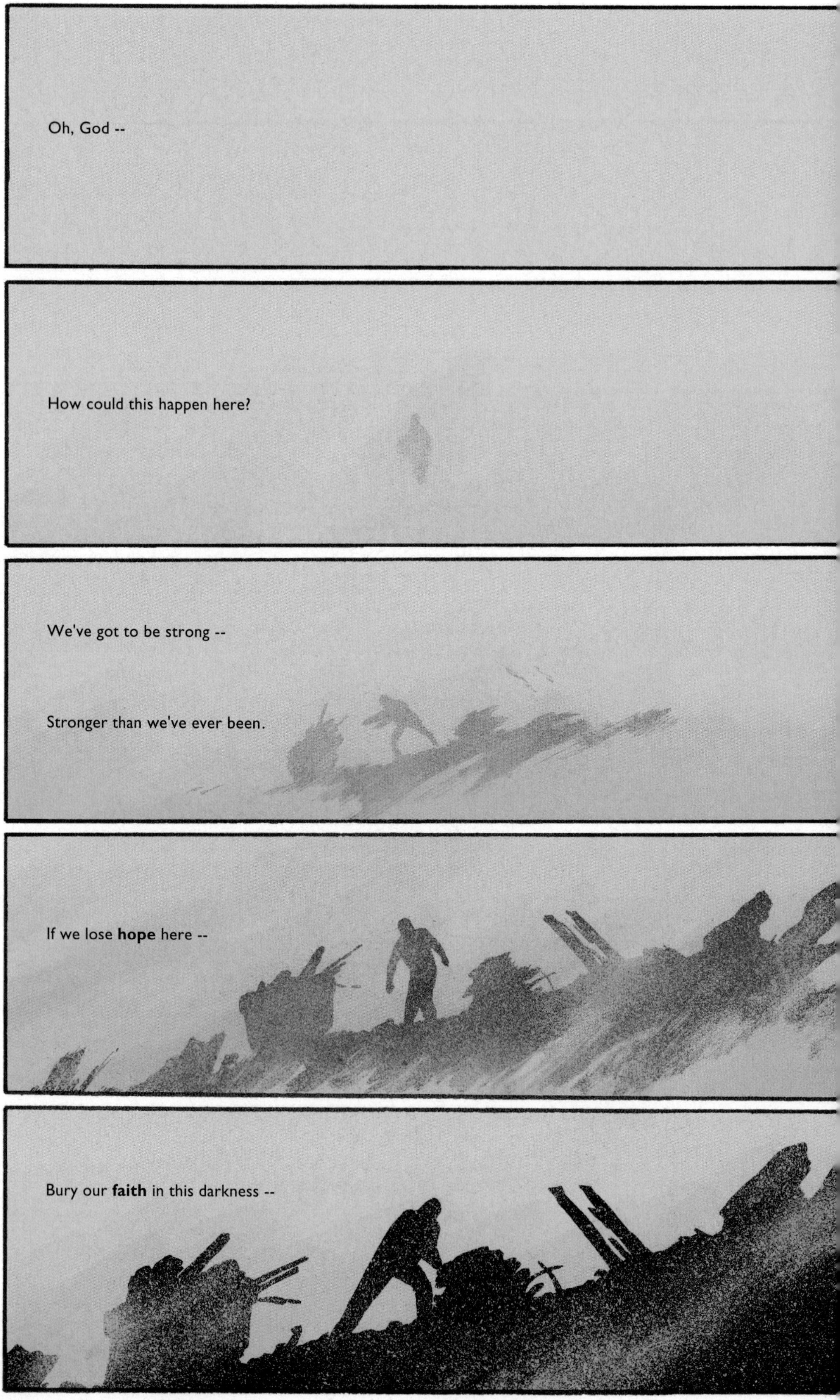
Oh, God --
How could this happen here?
We've got to be strong --
Stronger than we've ever been.
If we lose **hope** here --
Bury our **faith** in this darkness --

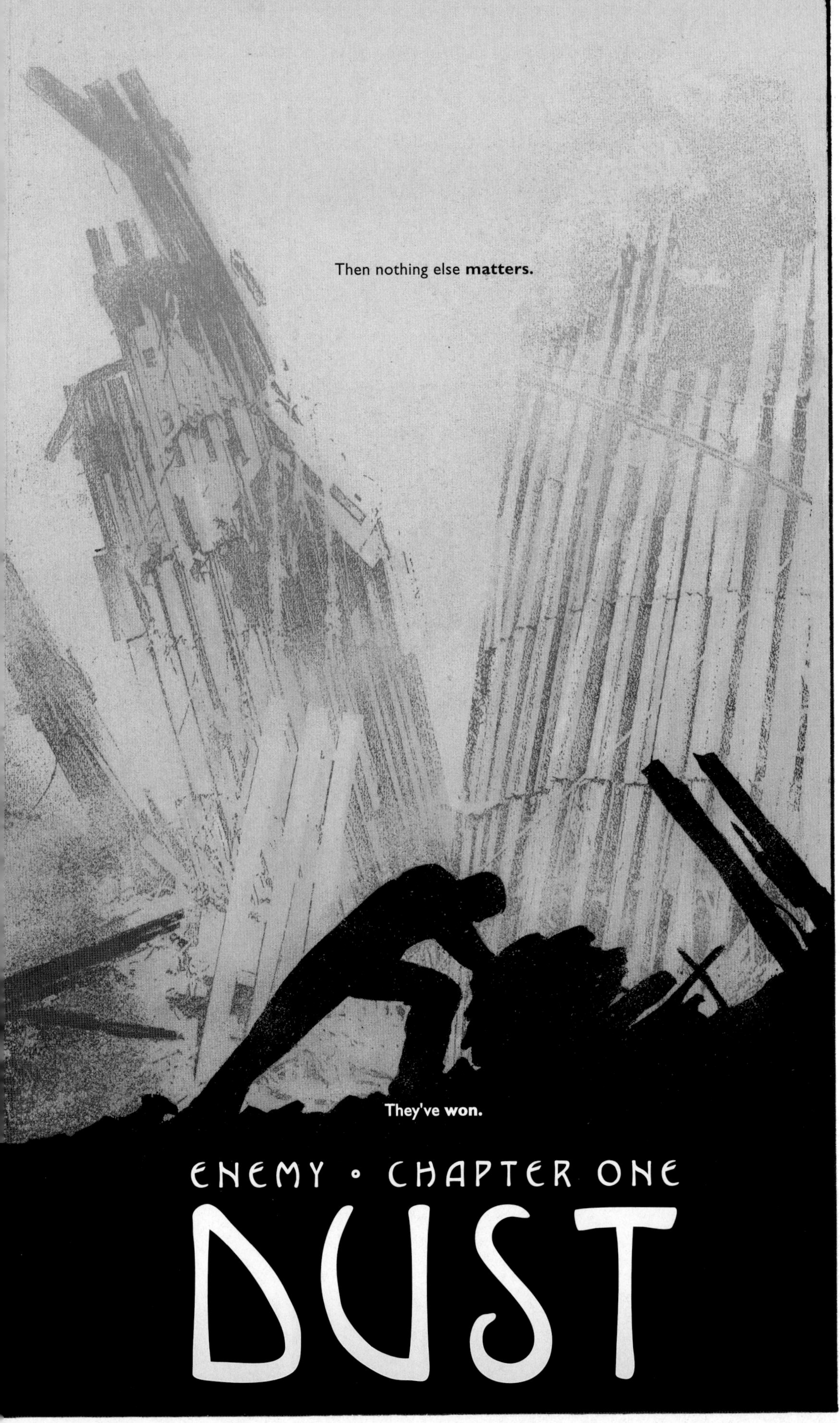
Then nothing else **matters.**
They've won.
ENEMY • CHAPTER ONE
DUST

This
time --

This
time --

Let it not be --

Too late.

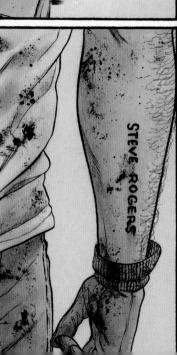

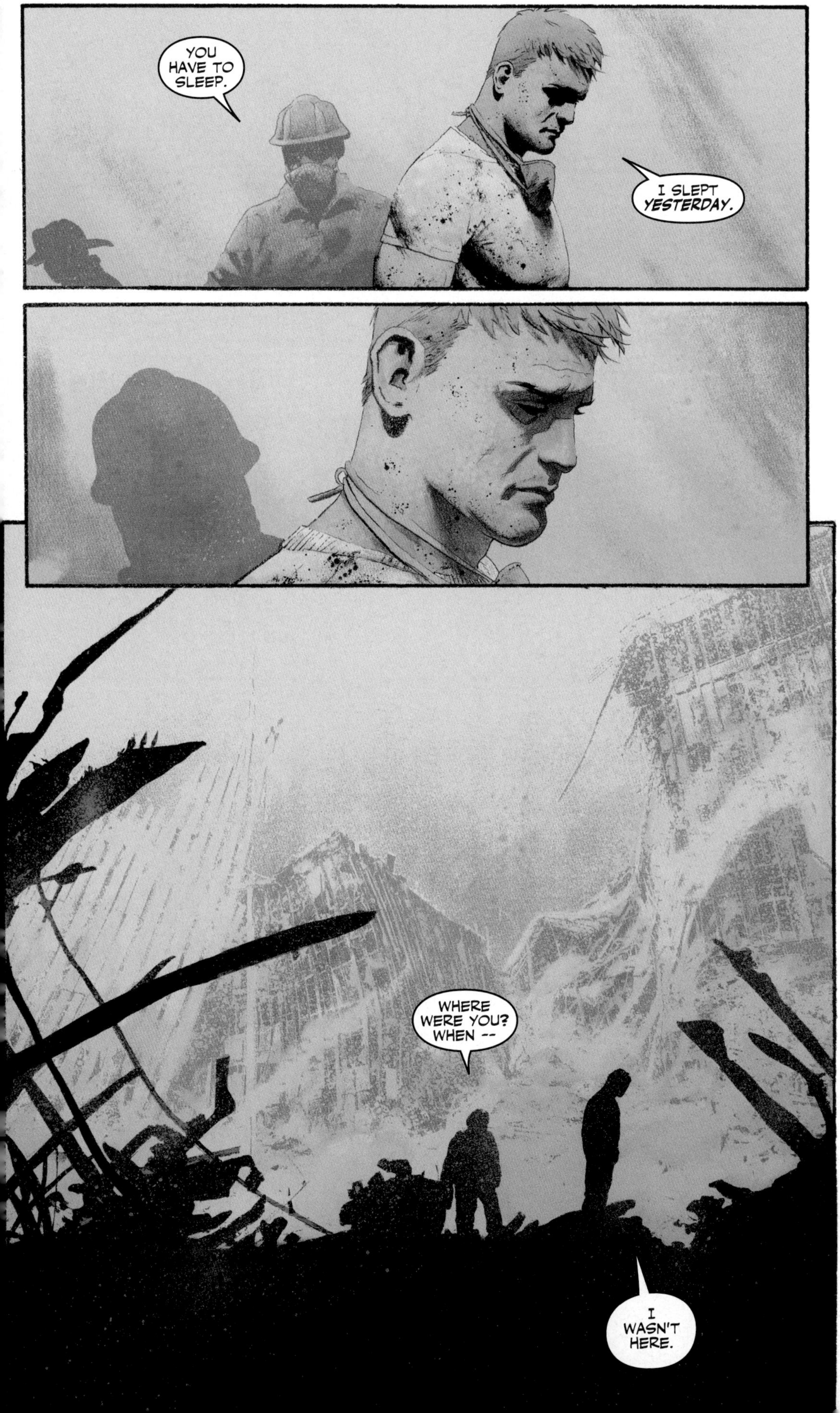

YOU HAVE TO SLEEP.
I SLEPT YESTERDAY.
WHERE WERE YOU? WHEN --
I WASN'T HERE.

I *RUN* IN THE MORNINGS. IT'S A GOOD FEELING -- WHEN *EVERYBODY'S* ON THE STREET, RUNNING TO *WORK* --

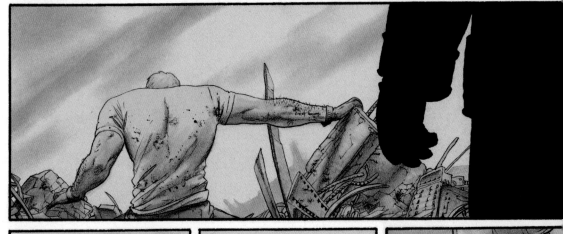

I SAW A MAN AND A WOMAN --

WHEN I'D RUN HERE FROM THE PARK.

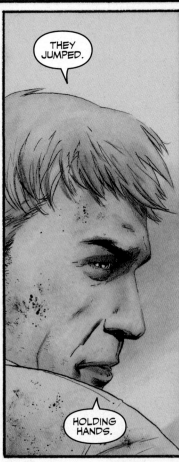

THEY JUMPED.

HOLDING HANDS.

I'LL GET A STRETCHER.

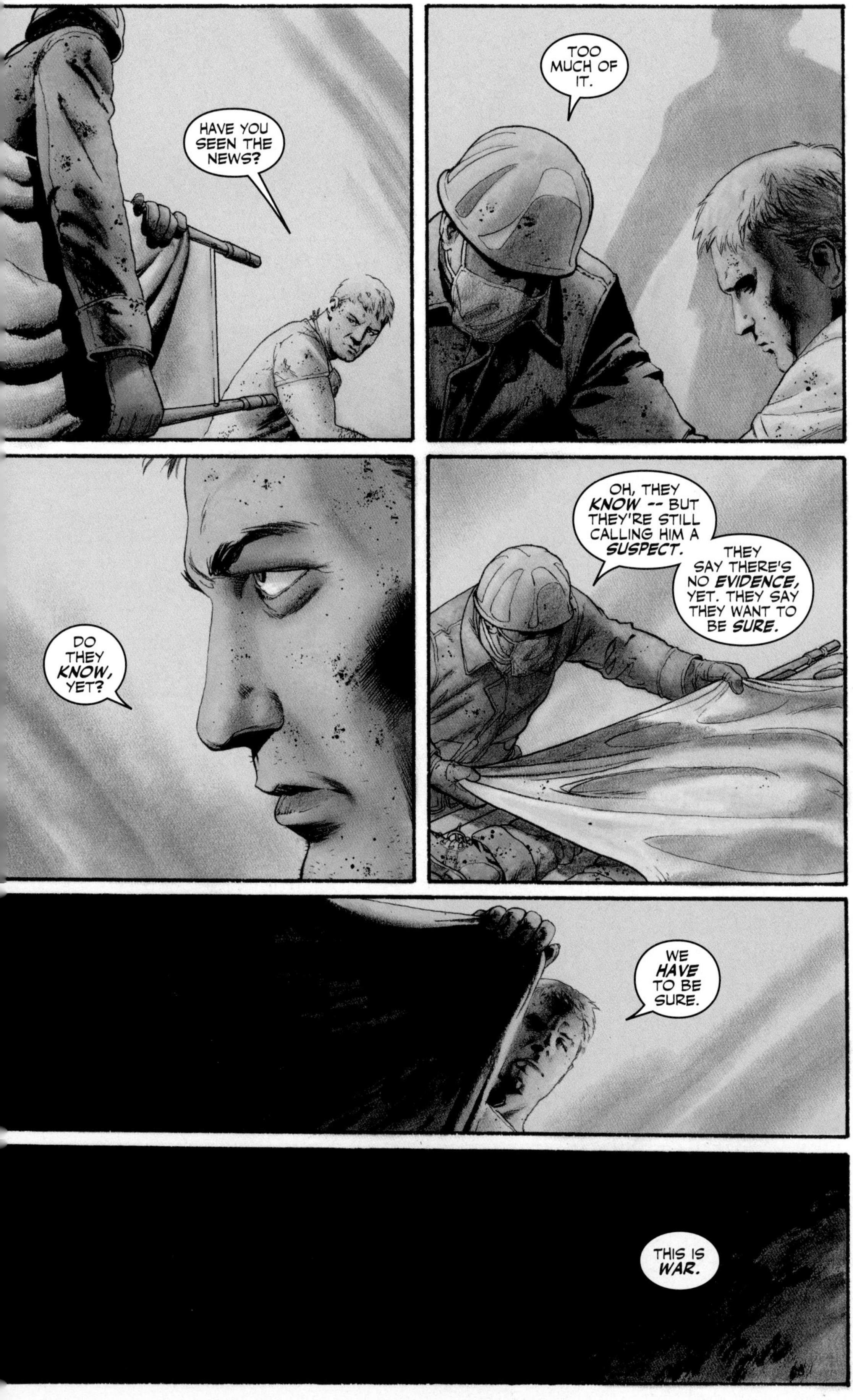
HAVE YOU SEEN THE NEWS?
TOO MUCH OF IT.
DO THEY *KNOW*, YET?
OH, THEY *KNOW* -- BUT THEY'RE STILL CALLING HIM A *SUSPECT*.
THEY SAY THERE'S NO *EVIDENCE*, YET. THEY SAY THEY WANT TO BE *SURE*.
WE *HAVE* TO BE SURE.
THIS IS *WAR*.

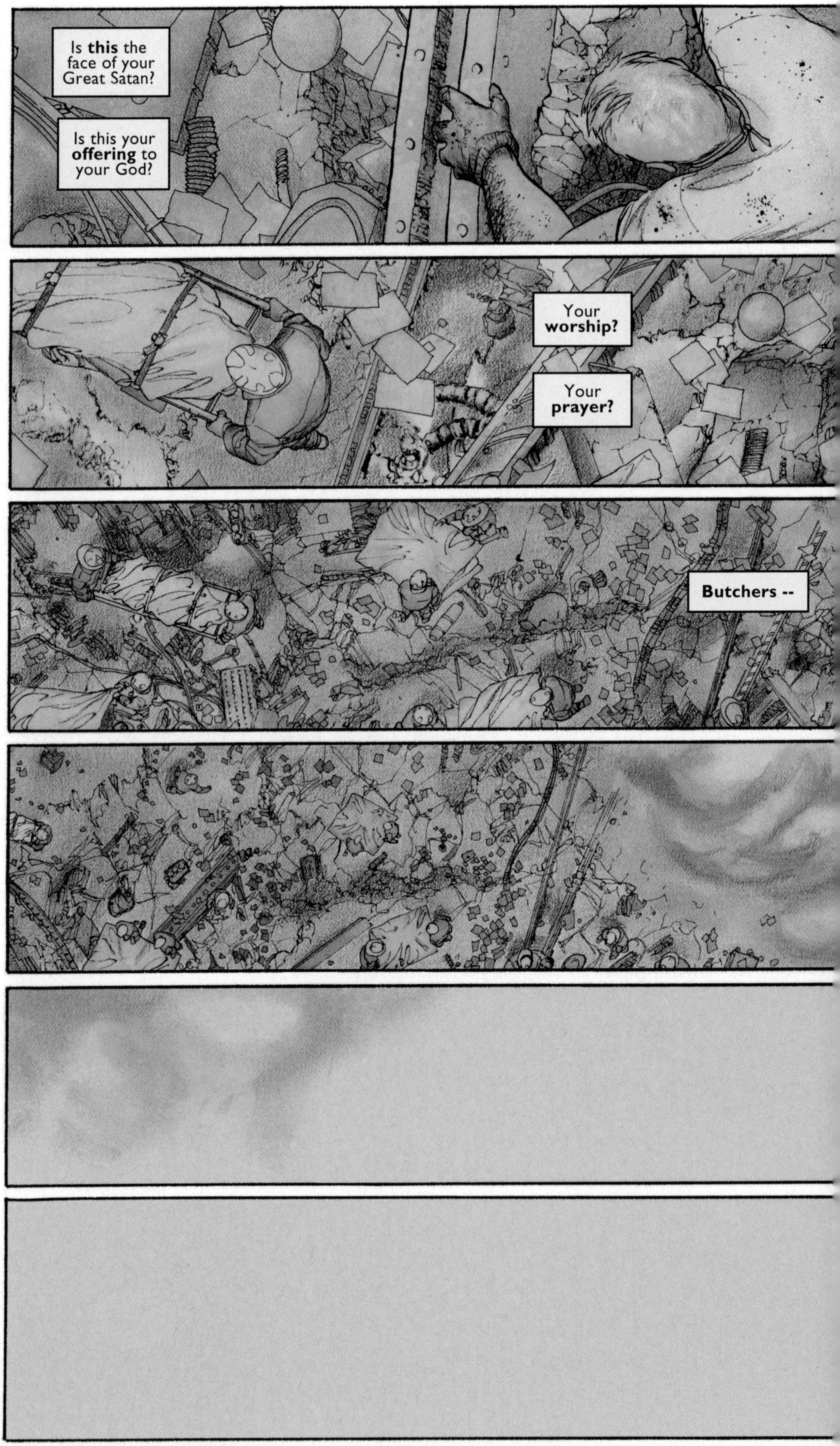
Is **this** the face of your Great Satan?
Is this your **offering** to your God?
Your **worship?**
Your **prayer?**
Butchers --

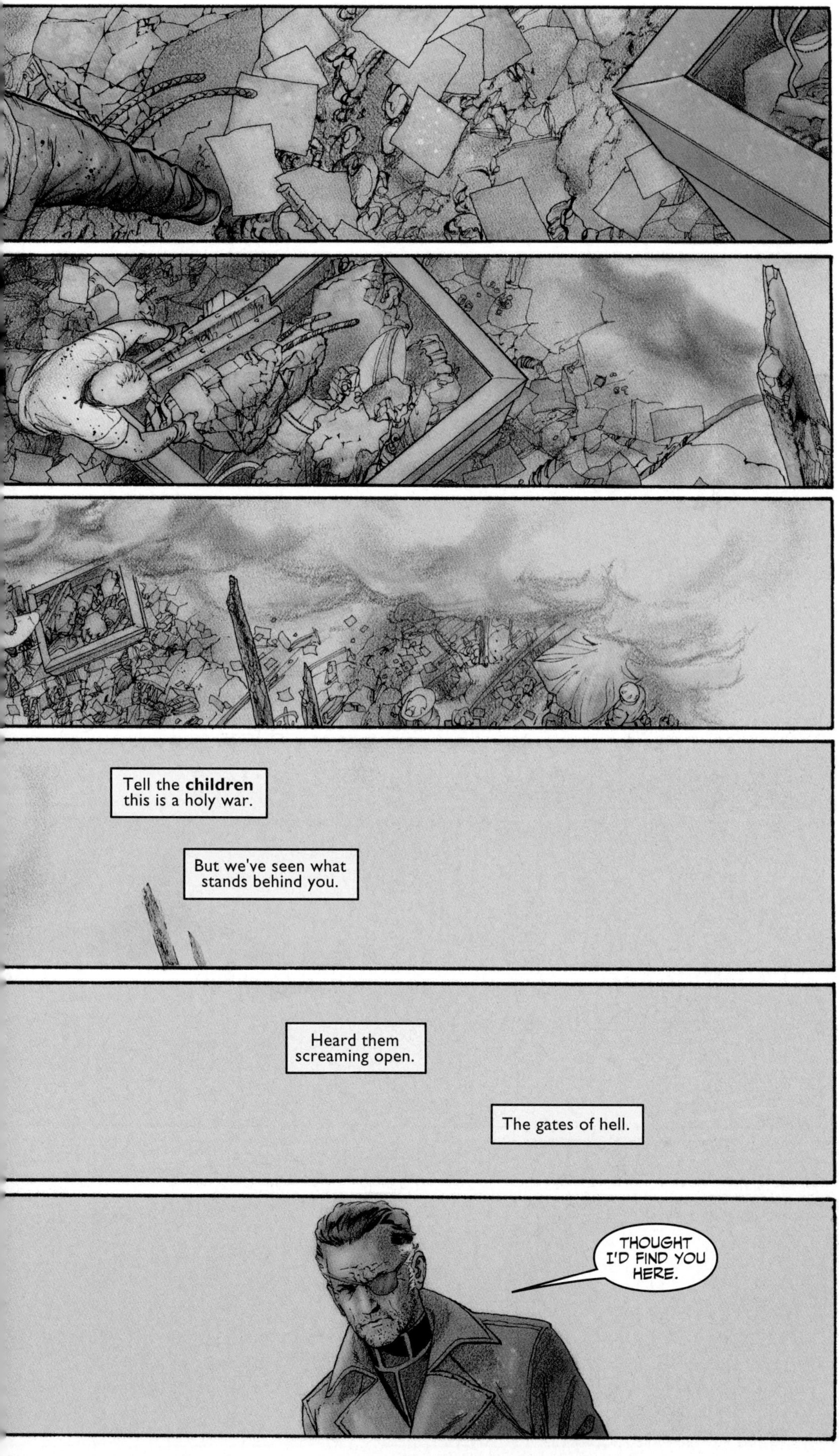
Tell the **children** this is a holy war.
But we've seen what stands behind you.
Heard them screaming open.
The gates of hell.
THOUGHT I'D FIND YOU HERE.

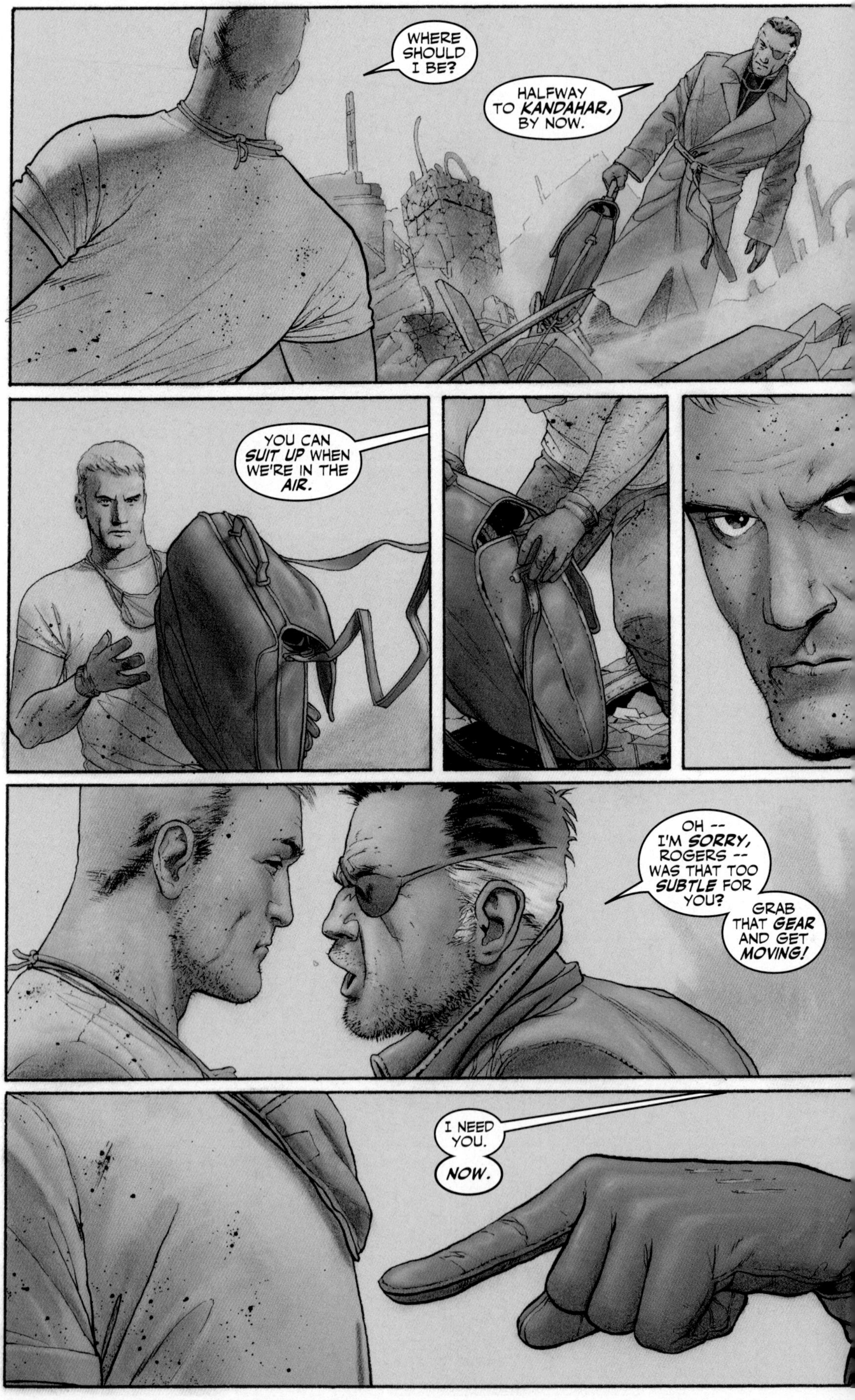
WHERE SHOULD I BE?
HALFWAY TO KANDAHAR, BY NOW.
YOU CAN SUIT UP WHEN WE'RE IN THE AIR.
OH -- I'M SORRY, ROGERS -- WAS THAT TOO SUBTLE FOR YOU?
GRAB THAT GEAR AND GET MOVING!
I NEED YOU.
NOW.

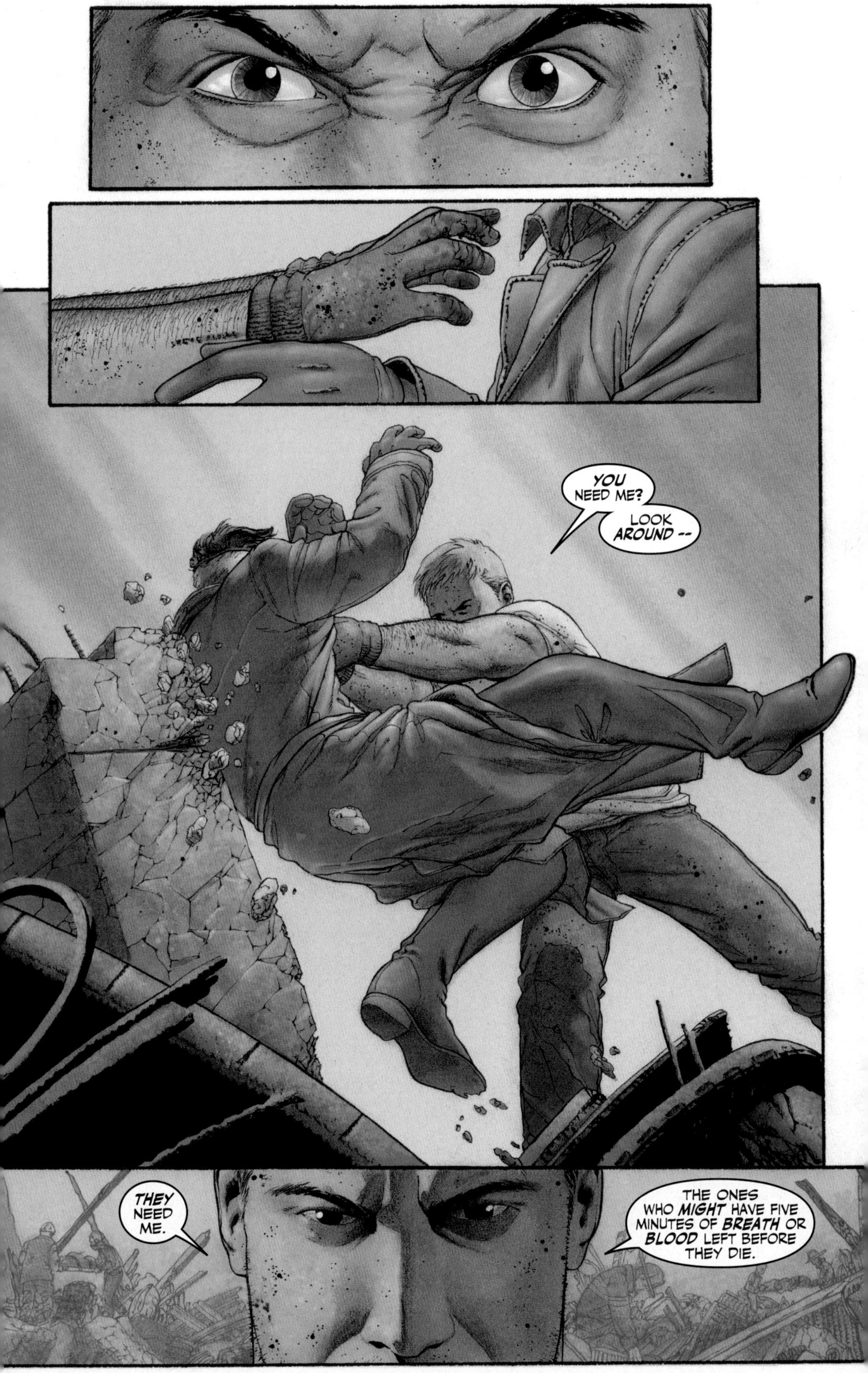
YOU NEED ME? LOOK AROUND --
THEY NEED ME.
THE ONES WHO MIGHT HAVE FIVE MINUTES OF BREATH OR BLOOD LEFT BEFORE THEY DIE.

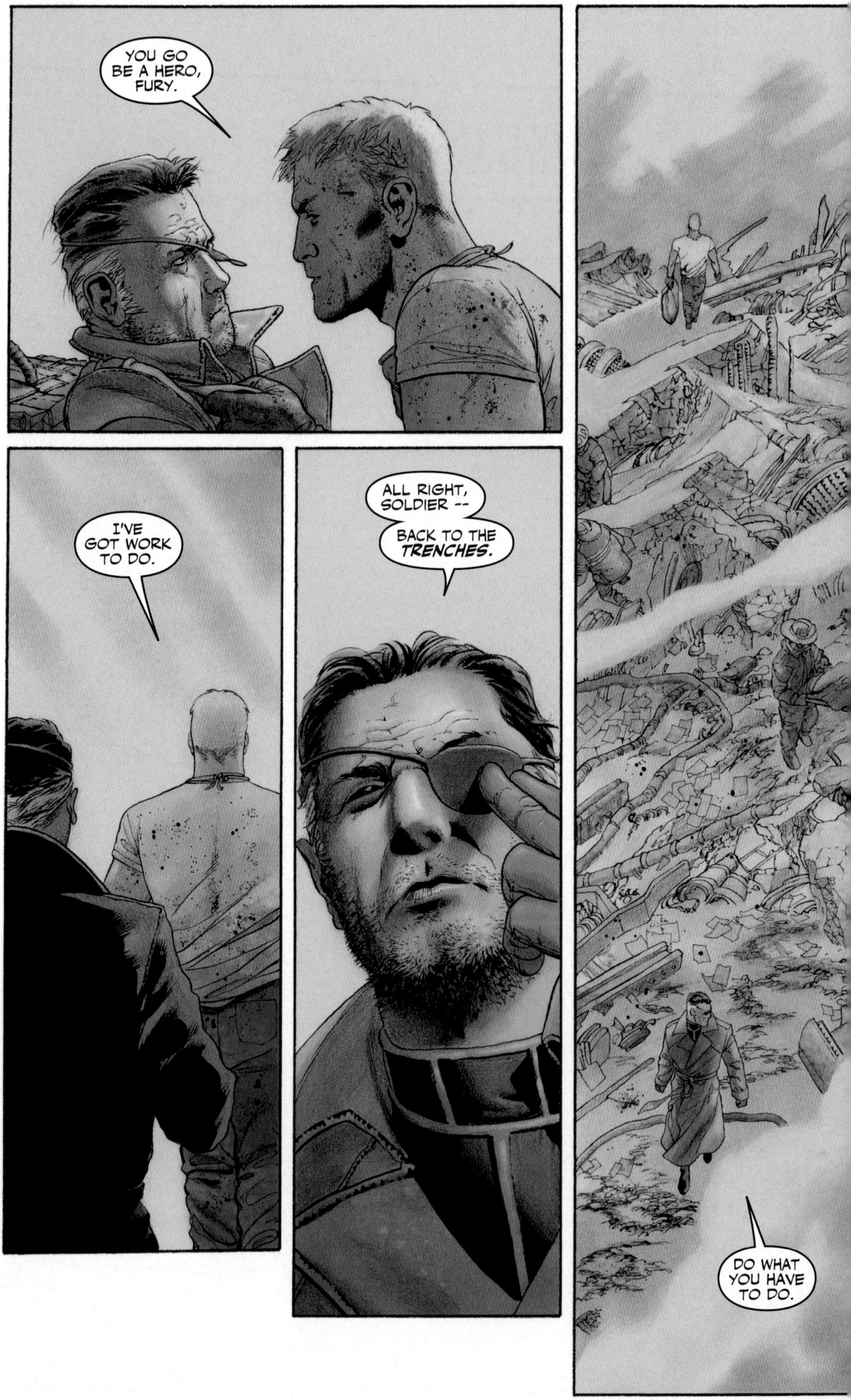
YOU GO BE A HERO, FURY.
I'VE GOT WORK TO DO.
ALL RIGHT, SOLDIER --
BACK TO THE *TRENCHES.*
DO WHAT YOU HAVE TO DO.

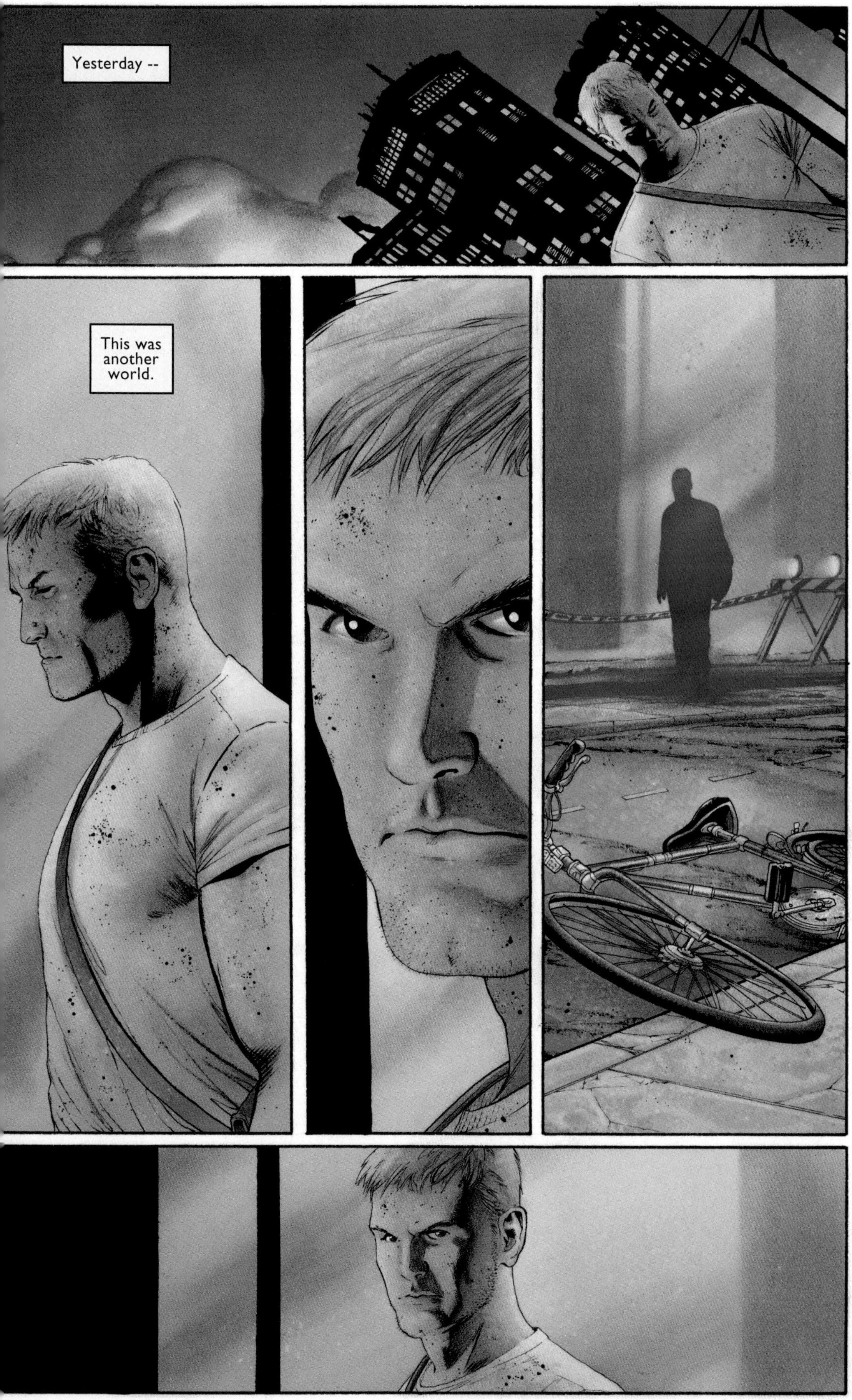
Yesterday --
This was
another
world.

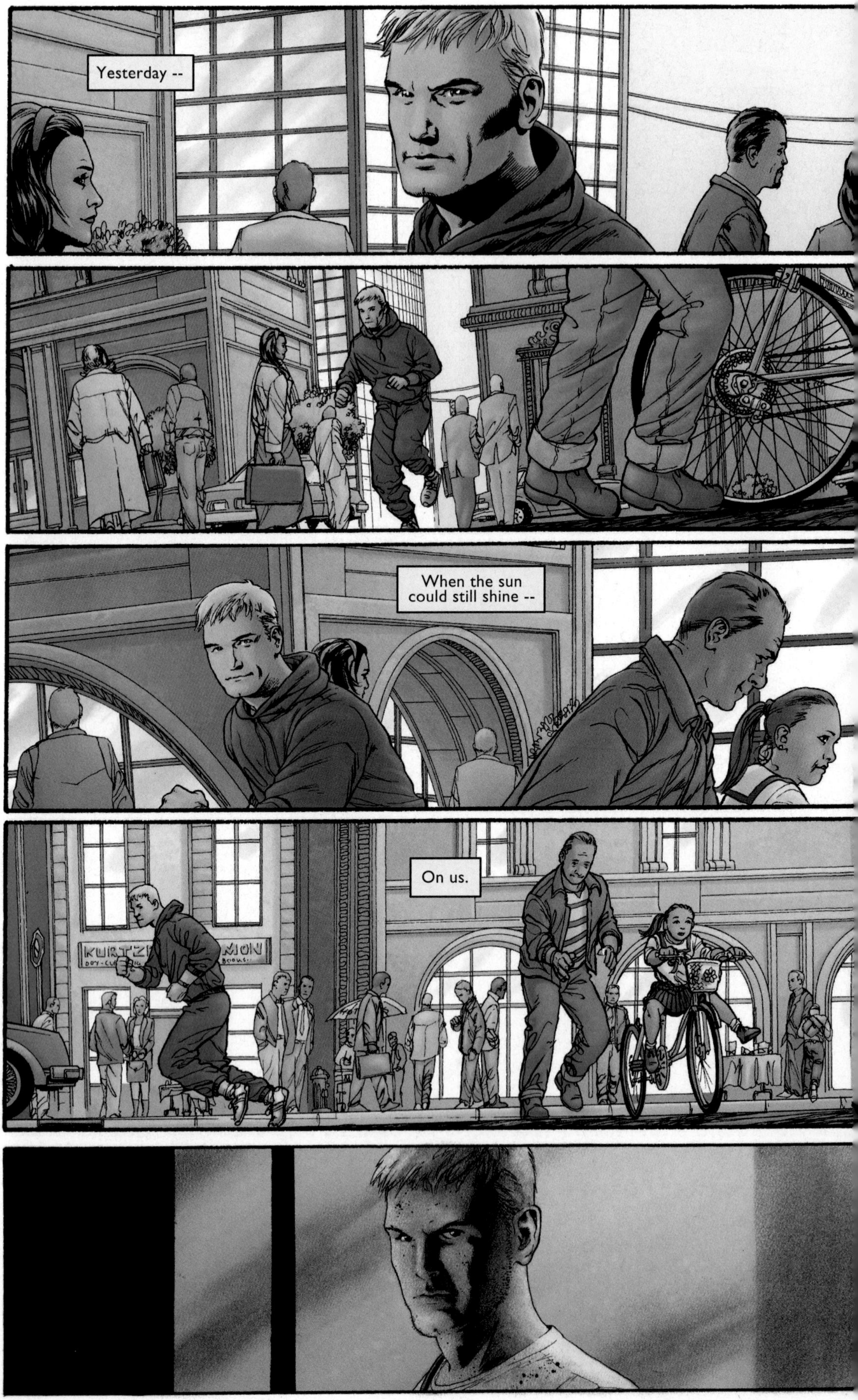

Yesterday --
When the sun could still shine --
On us.

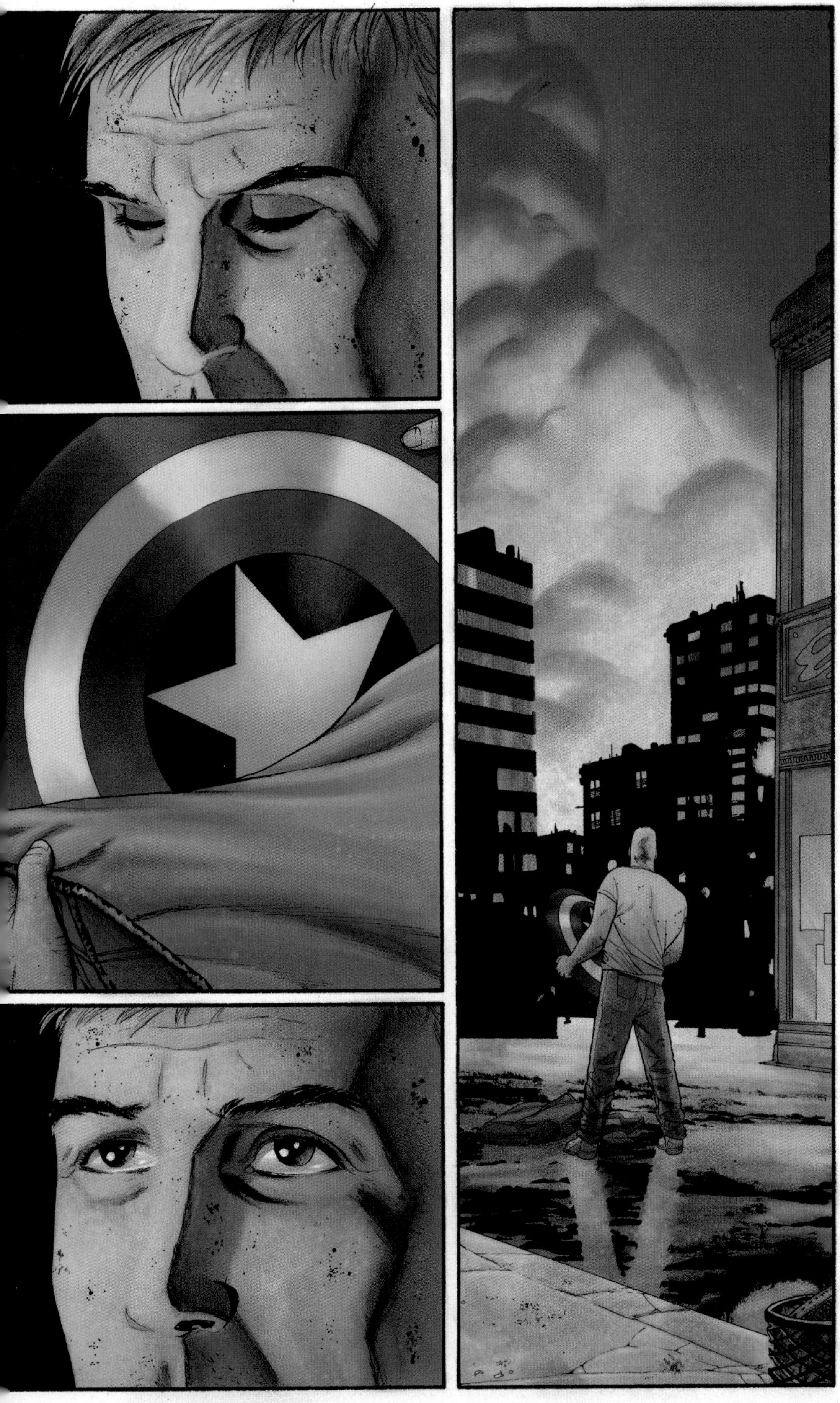

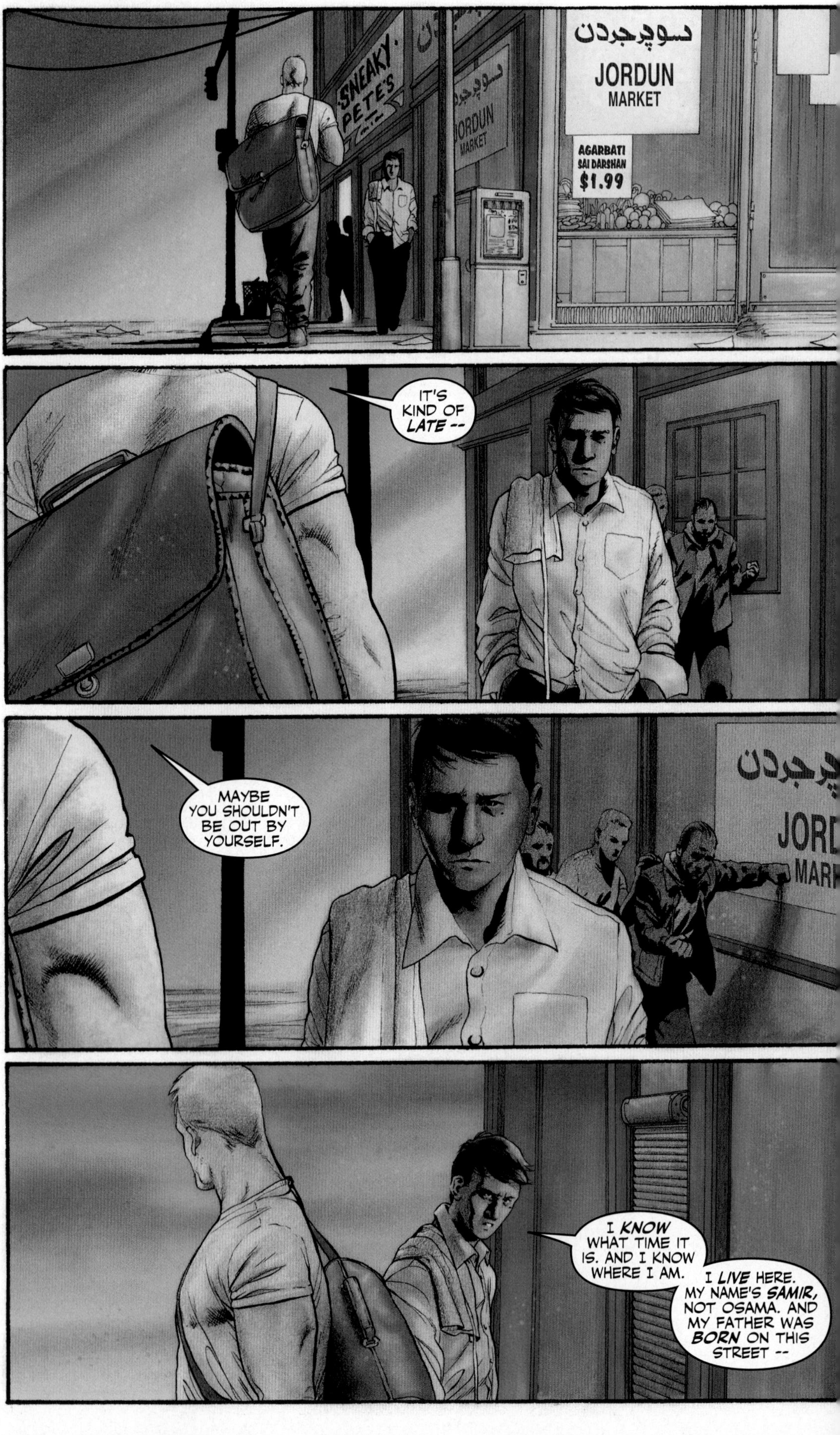

SNEAKY PETE'S
سوپرجردن
JORDUN MARKET
AGARBATI SAI DARSHAN $1.99
IT'S KIND OF *LATE* --
MAYBE YOU SHOULDN'T BE OUT BY YOURSELF.
I *KNOW* WHAT TIME IT IS. AND I KNOW WHERE I AM.
I *LIVE* HERE. MY NAME'S *SAMIR,* NOT OSAMA. AND MY FATHER WAS *BORN* ON THIS STREET --

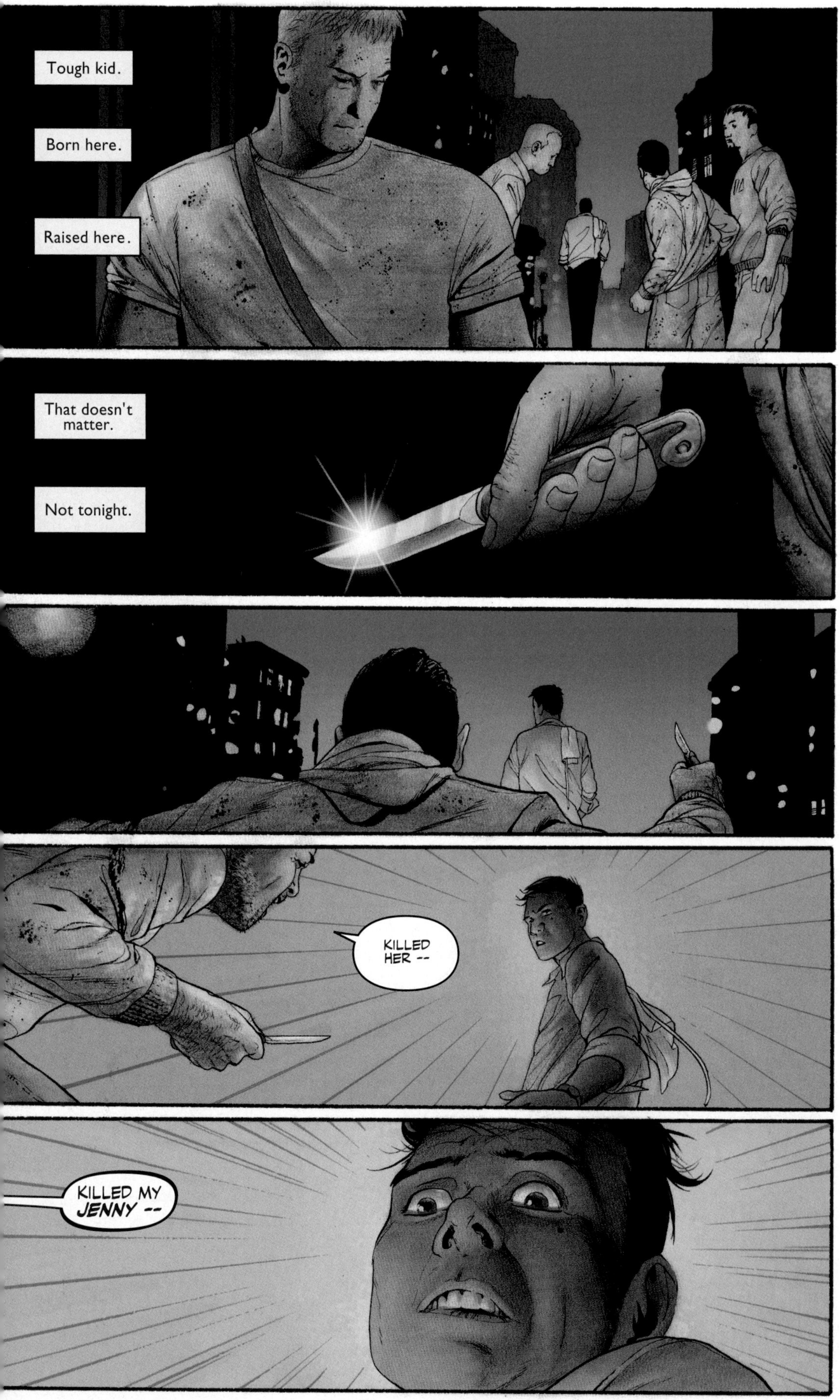
Tough kid.
Born here.
Raised here.
That doesn't matter.
Not tonight.
KILLED HER --
KILLED MY JENNY --

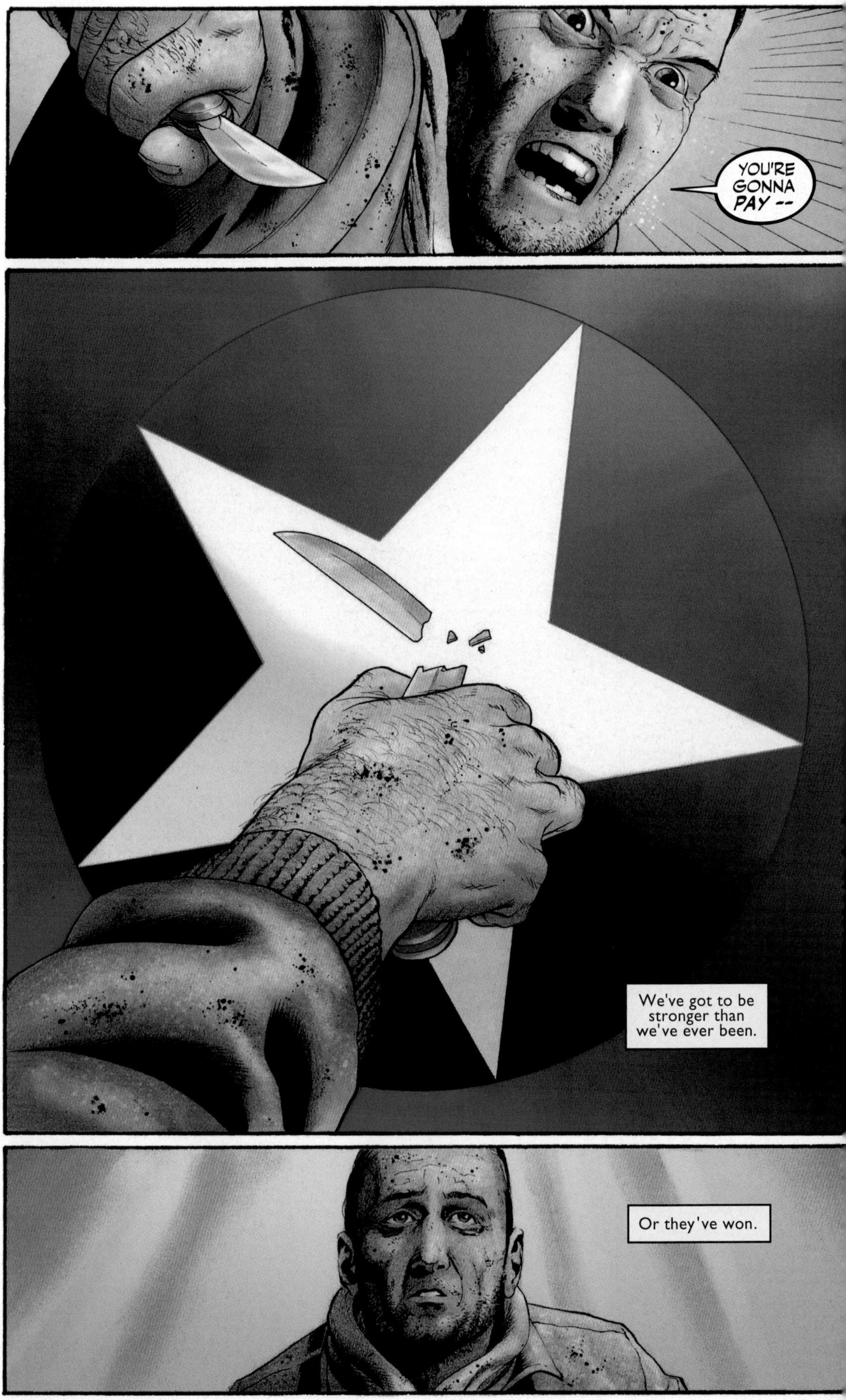
YOU'RE GONNA PAY --
We've got to be stronger than we've ever been.
Or they've won.

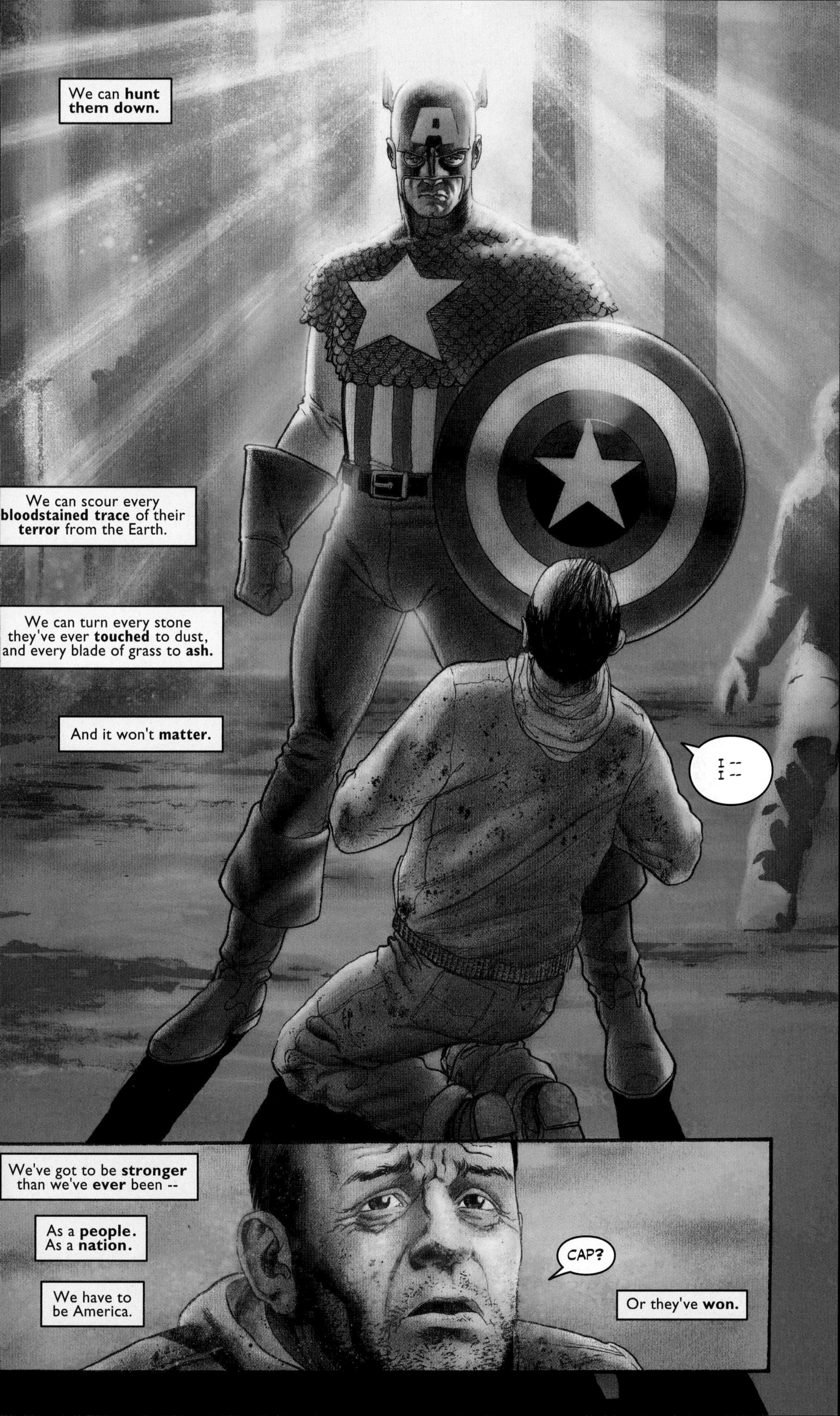
We can **hunt** **them down.**
We can scour every **bloodstained trace** of their **terror** from the Earth.
We can turn every stone they've ever **touched** to dust, and every blade of grass to **ash.**
And it won't **matter.**
I -- I --
We've got to be **stronger** than we've **ever** been --
As a **people.** As a **nation.**
We have to be America.
CAP?
Or they've **won.**

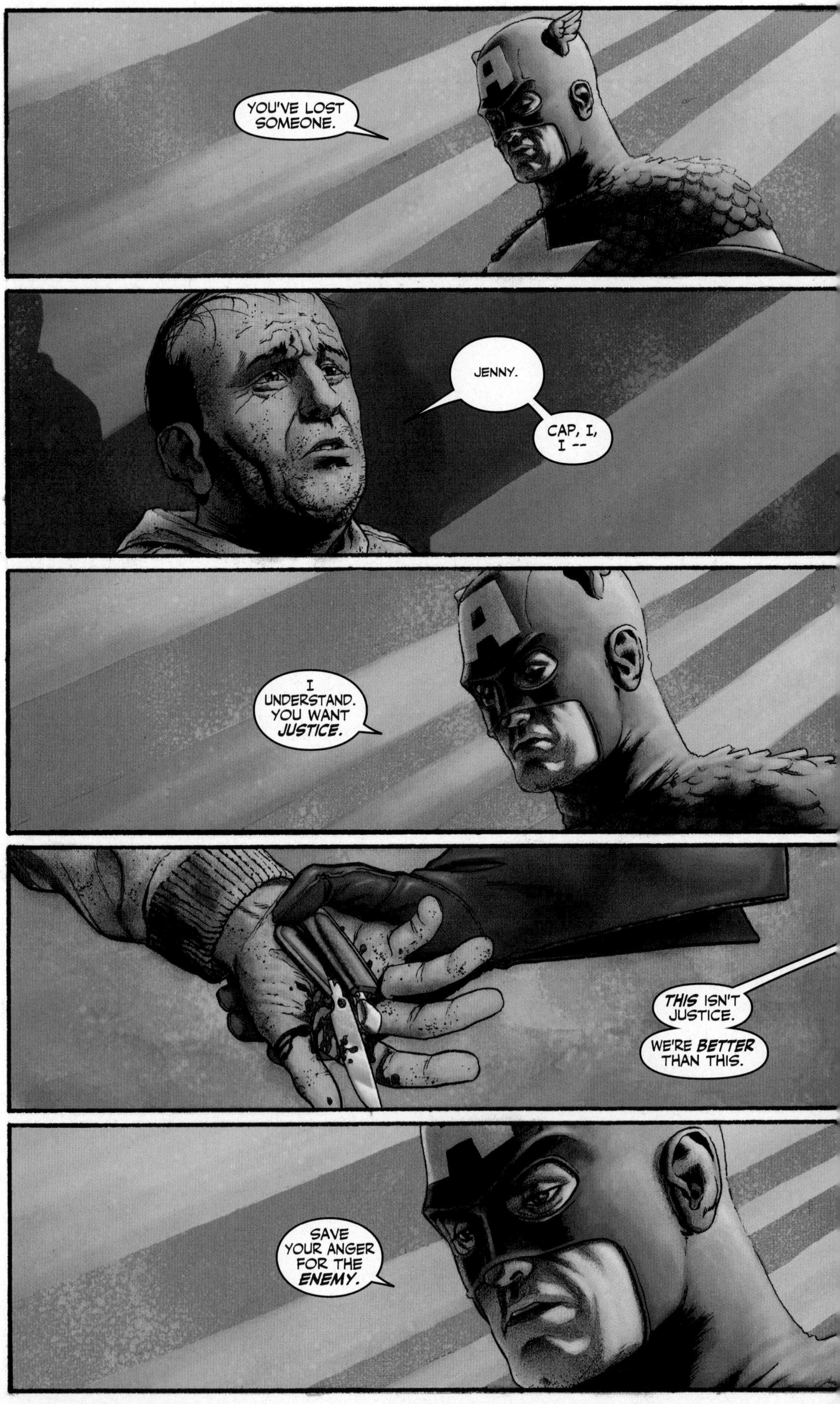

YOU'VE LOST SOMEONE.
JENNY.
CAP, I, I --
I UNDERSTAND. YOU WANT JUSTICE.
THIS ISN'T JUSTICE.
WE'RE BETTER THAN THIS.
SAVE YOUR ANGER FOR THE ENEMY.

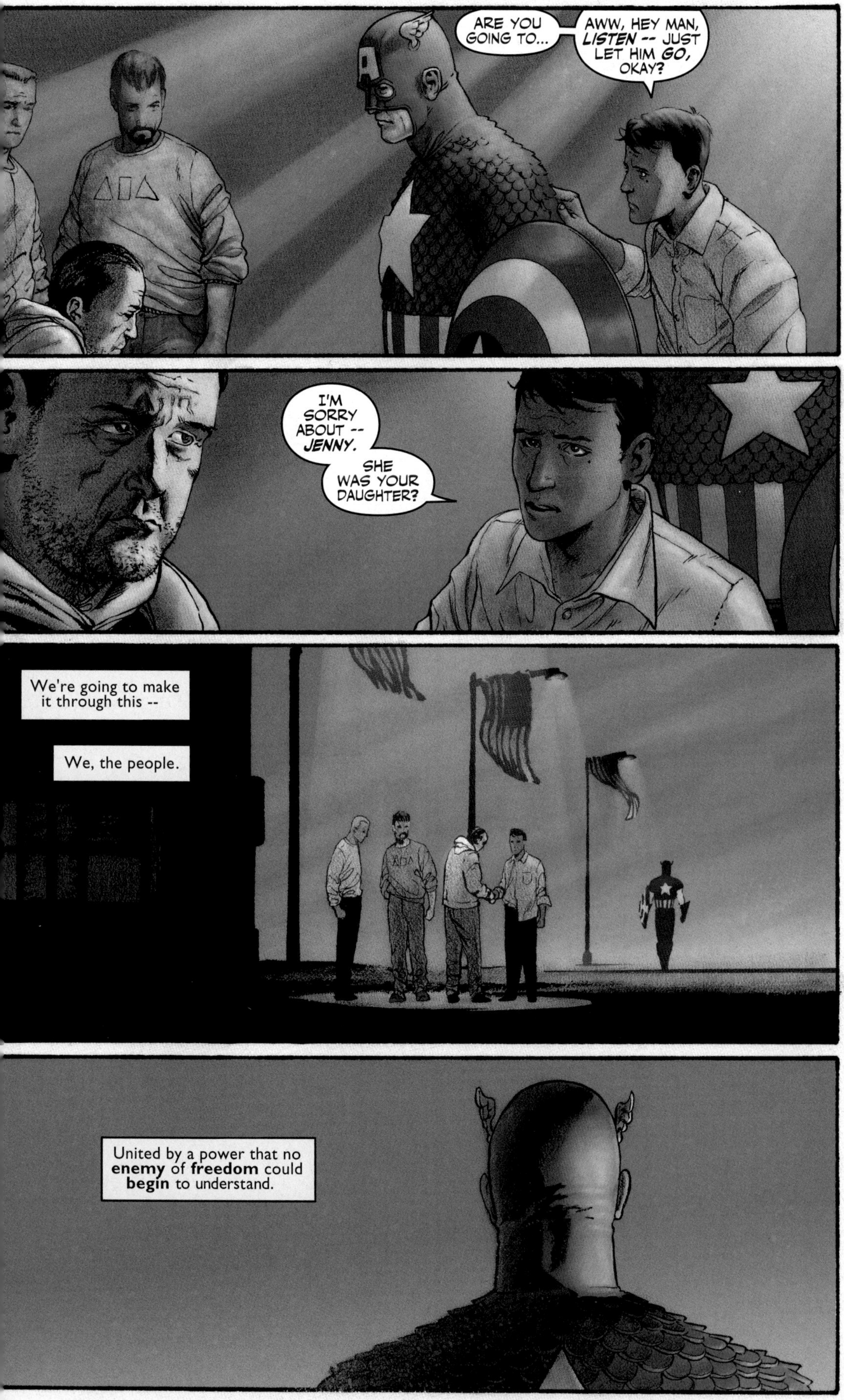
ARE YOU GOING TO...
AWW, HEY MAN, LISTEN -- JUST LET HIM GO, OKAY?
I'M SORRY ABOUT -- JENNY.
SHE WAS YOUR DAUGHTER?
We're going to make it through this --
We, the people.
United by a power that no enemy of freedom could begin to understand.

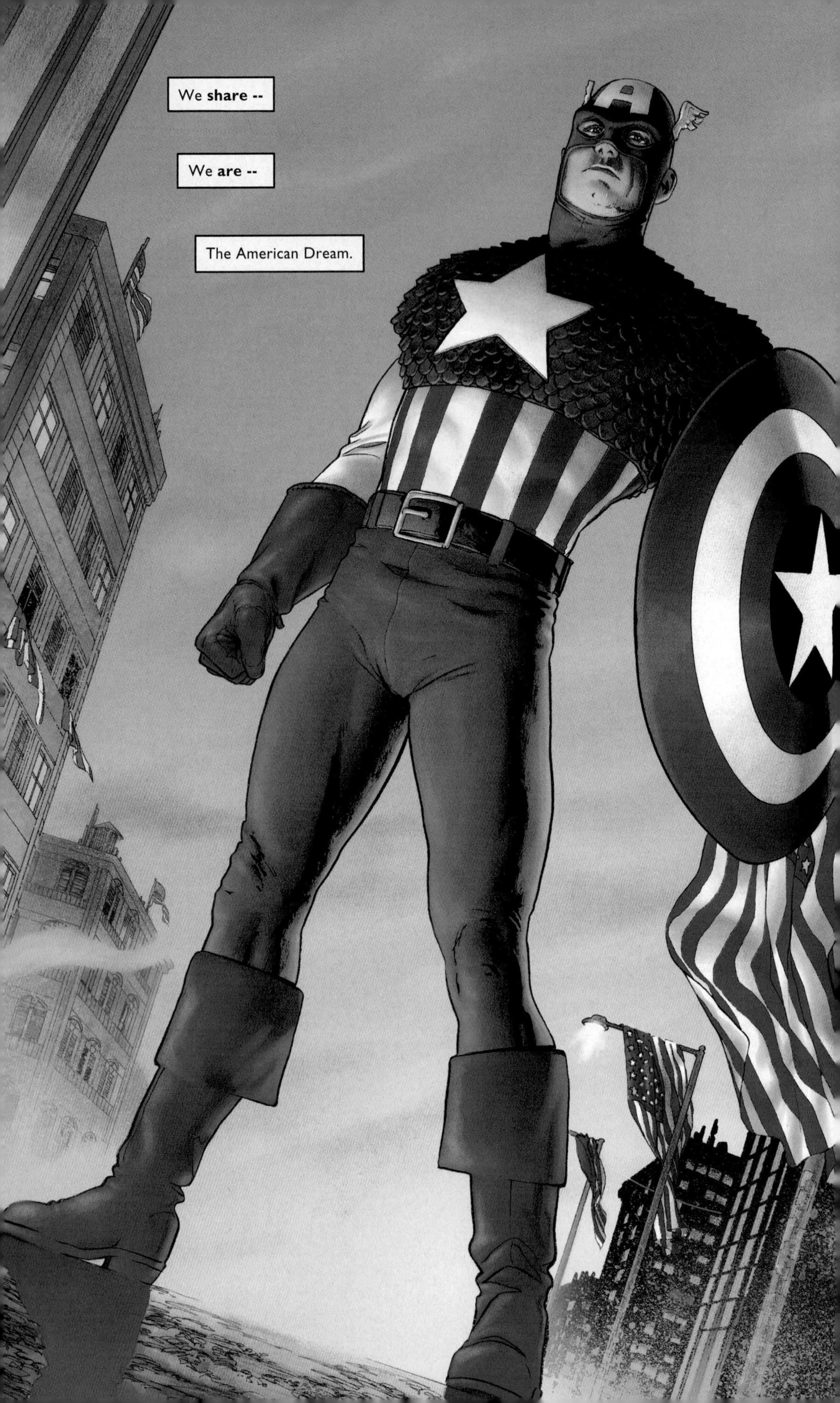

We **share** --
We **are** --
The American Dream.

Seven months later.

Centerville.

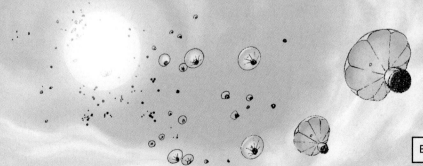

Easter Sunday.

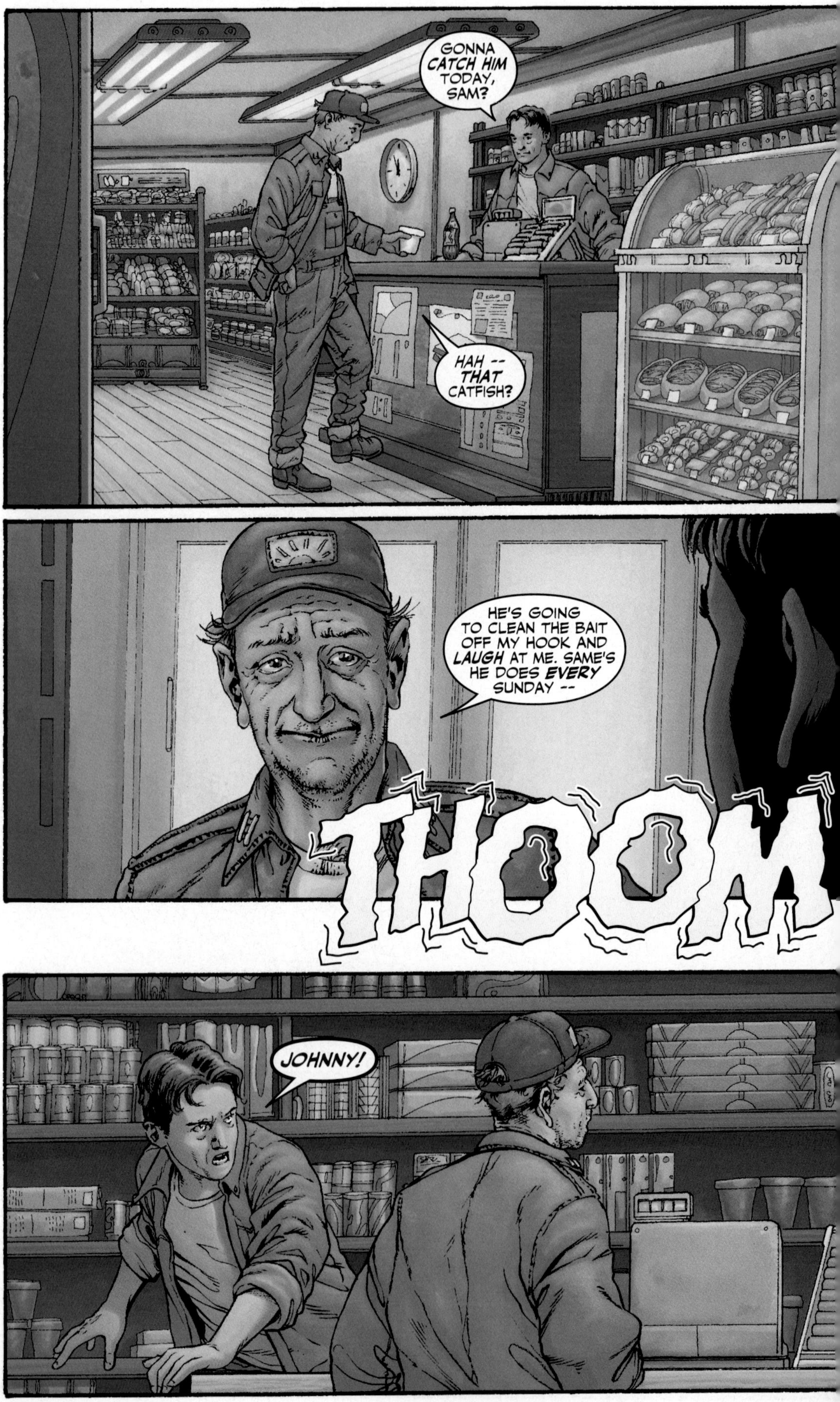
GONNA CATCH HIM TODAY, SAM?
HAH -- THAT CATFISH?
HE'S GOING TO CLEAN THE BAIT OFF MY HOOK AND LAUGH AT ME. SAME'S HE DOES EVERY SUNDAY --
THOOM
JOHNNY!

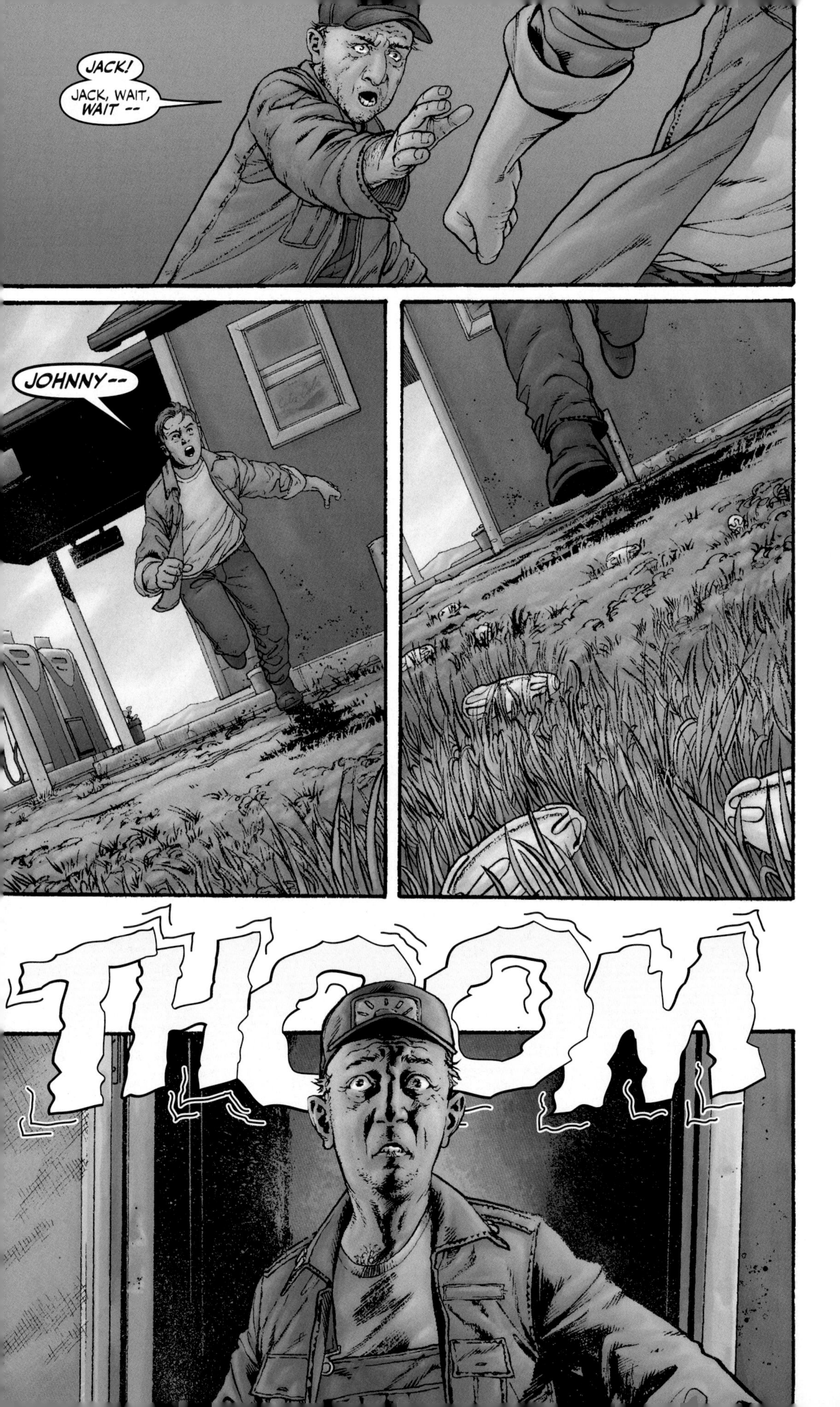
JACK!
JACK, WAIT, WAIT --
JOHNNY --
THOOM

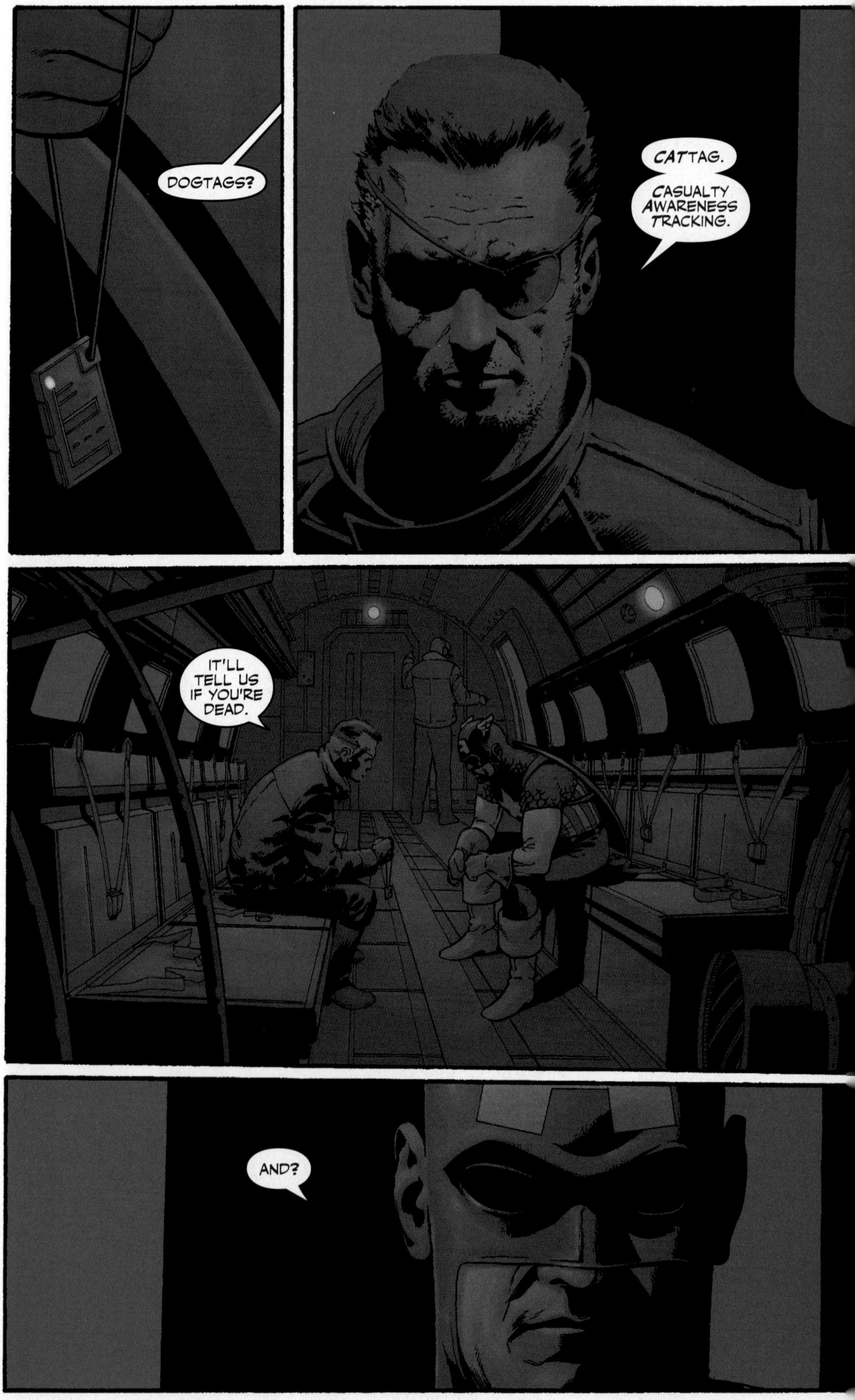
DOGTAGS?
CATTAG.
CASUALTY AWARENESS TRACKING.
IT'LL TELL US IF YOU'RE DEAD.
AND?

THEN THIS FREAK'S GAME IS *OVER*. NO *US* RUNNING *HIS* GAUNTLET -- CRAWLING THROUGH THOSE LAND MINES.

WE GO TO *DELTA FORCE*.

AND?

THEY'LL SAVE AS MANY HOSTAGES AS THEY *CAN*. BUT THEY *WON'T* GET THEM ALL.

THEY'RE *GOOD*. BUT THIS *AL-TARIQ*...

HE'S A *MONSTER*.

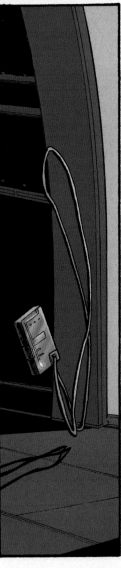

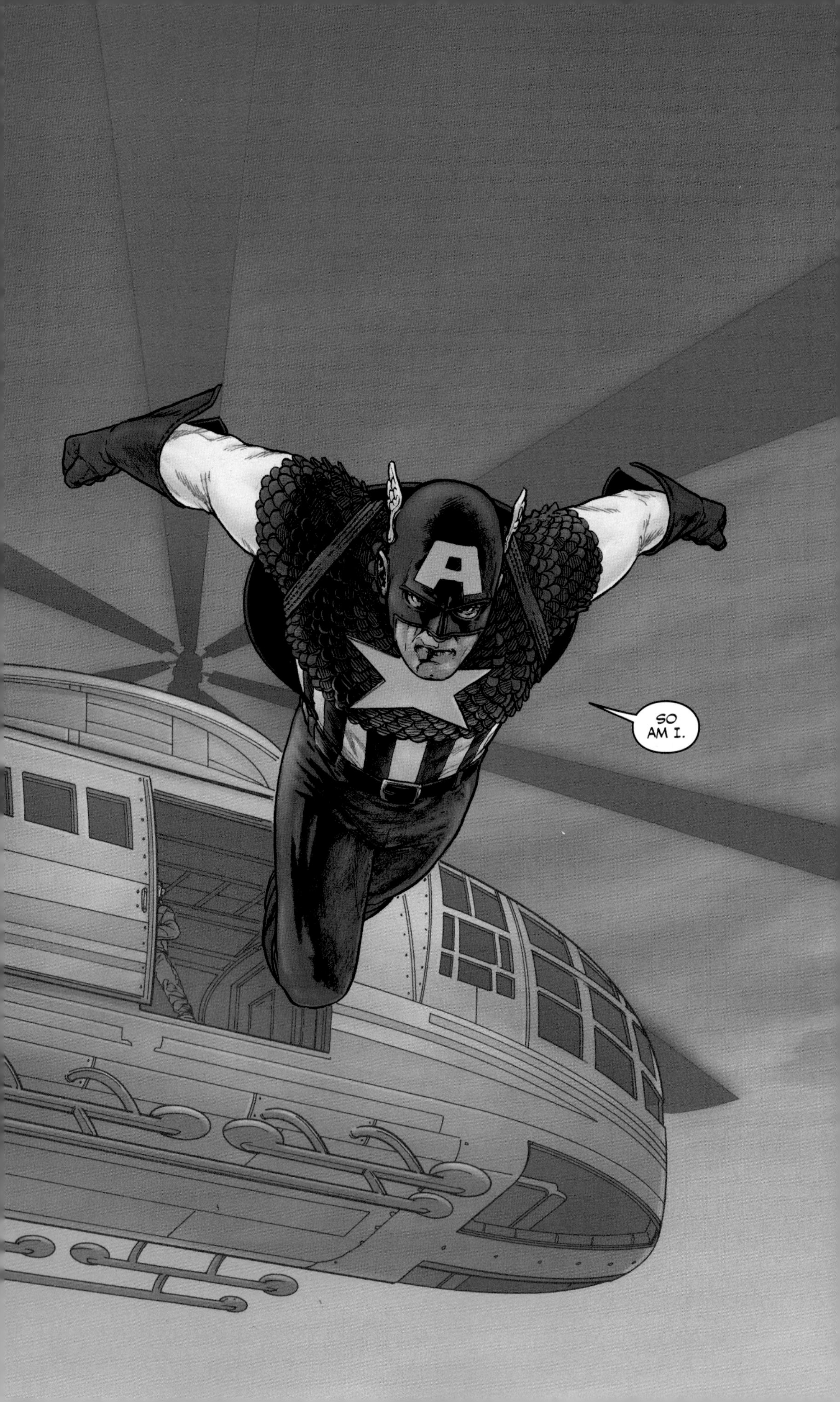
SO
AM I.

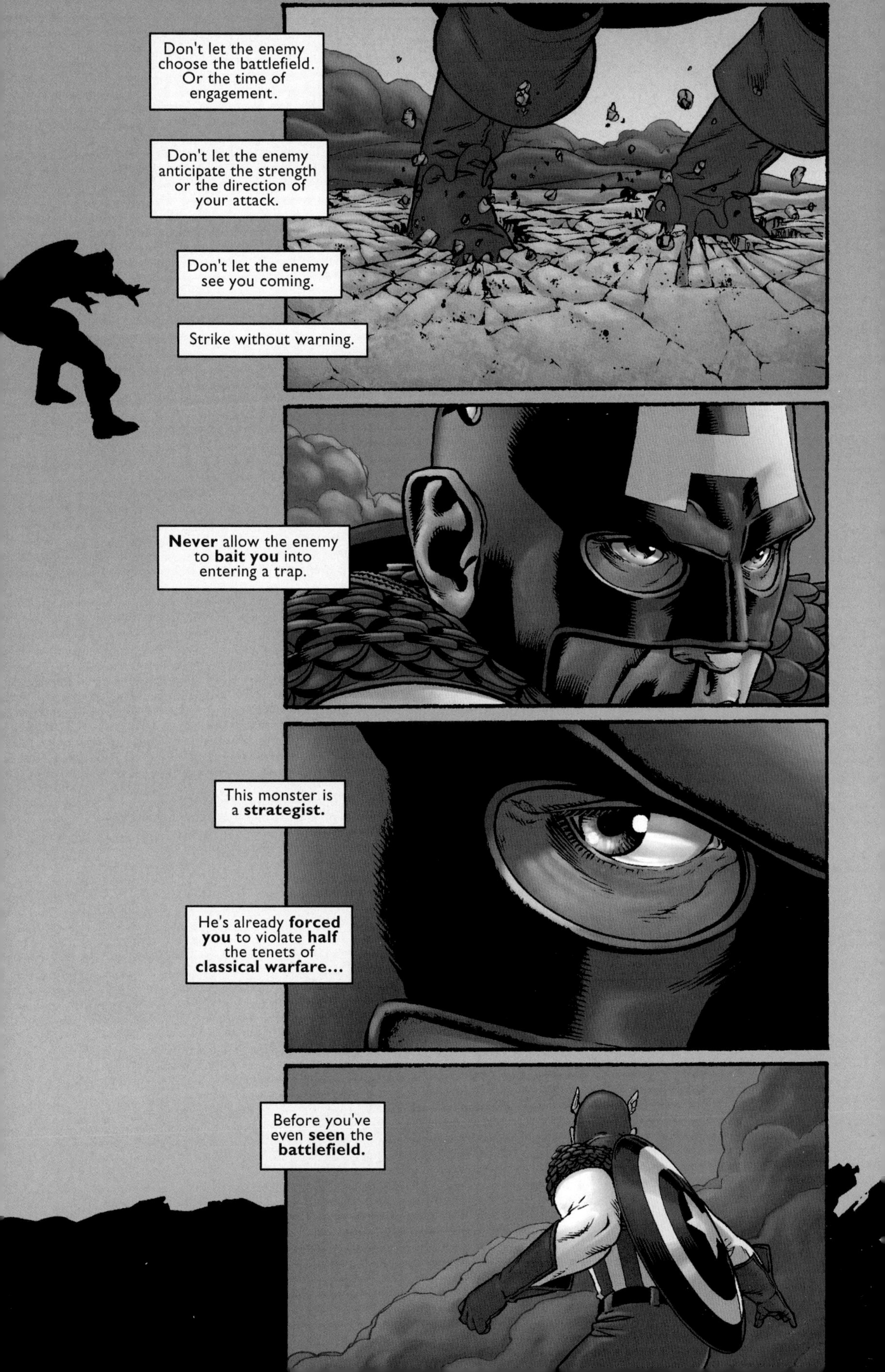

Don't let the enemy choose the battlefield. Or the time of engagement.
Don't let the enemy anticipate the strength or the direction of your attack.
Don't let the enemy see you coming.
Strike without warning.
Never allow the enemy to **bait you** into entering a trap.
This monster is a **strategist.**
He's already **forced you** to violate **half** the tenets of **classical warfare...**
Before you've even **seen** the **battlefield.**

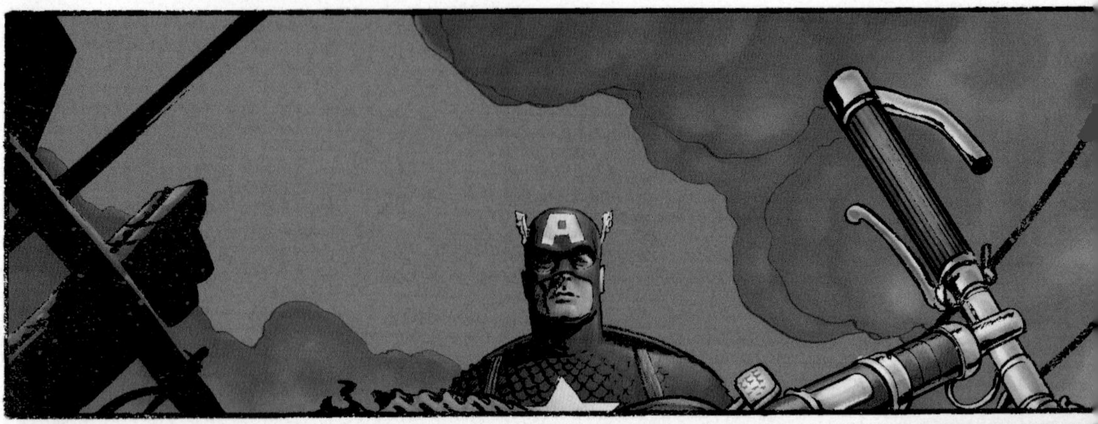

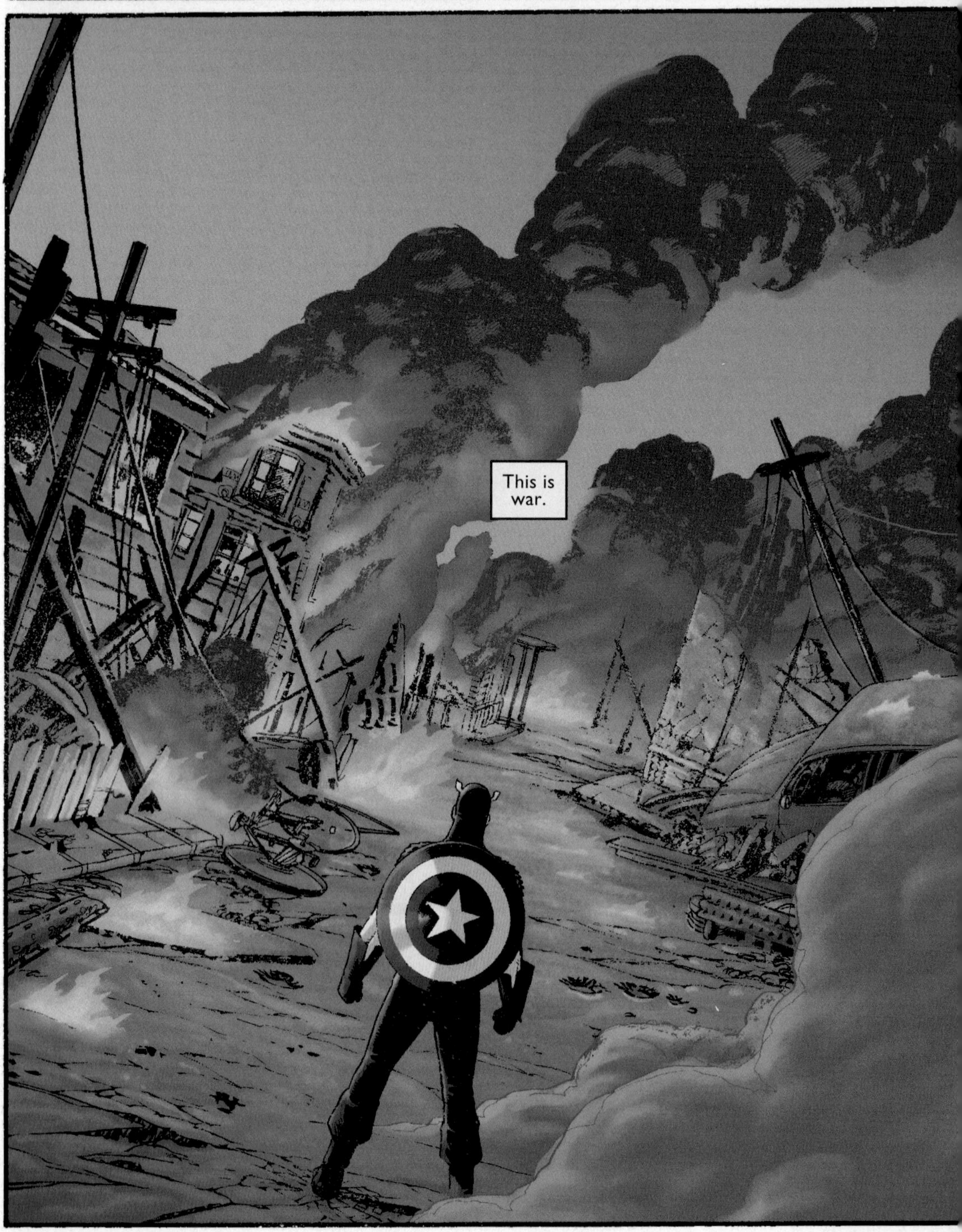
This is war.

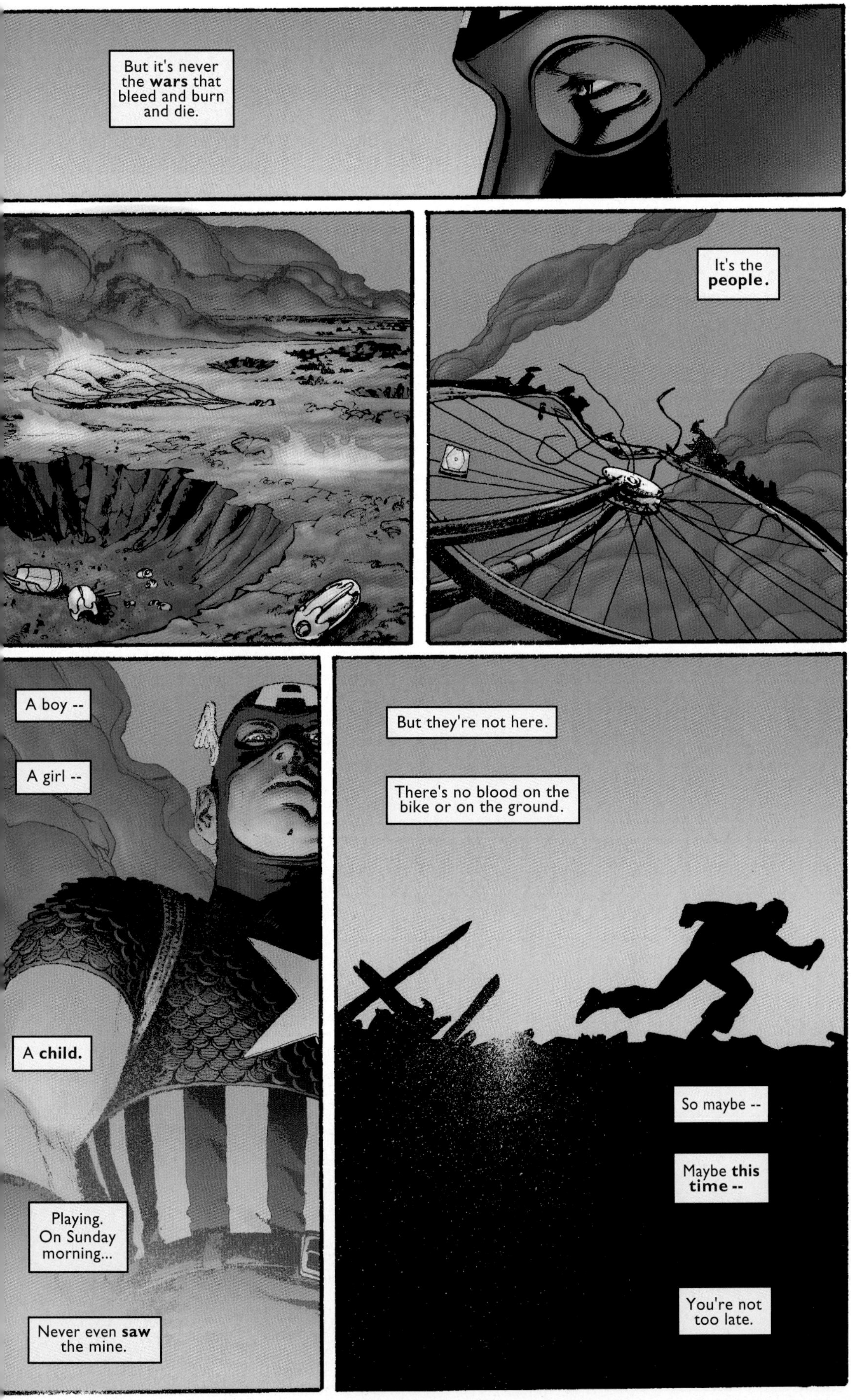

But it's never the **wars** that bleed and burn and die.
It's the **people.**
A boy --
A girl --
A **child.**
Playing. On Sunday morning...
Never even **saw** the mine.
But they're not here.
There's no blood on the bike or on the ground.
So maybe --
Maybe **this time** --
You're not too late.

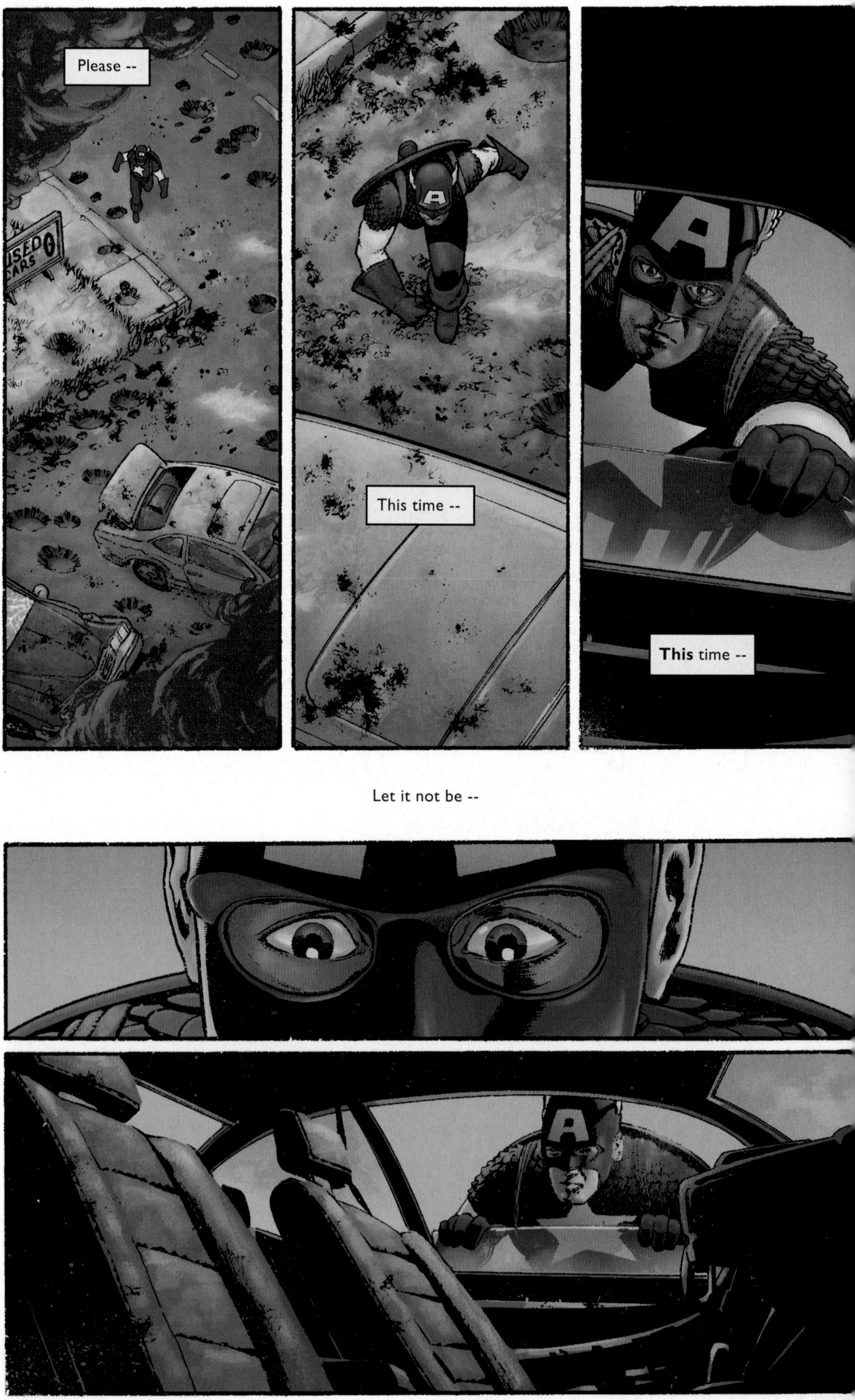
Please --
USED CARS
This time --
This time --
Let it not be --

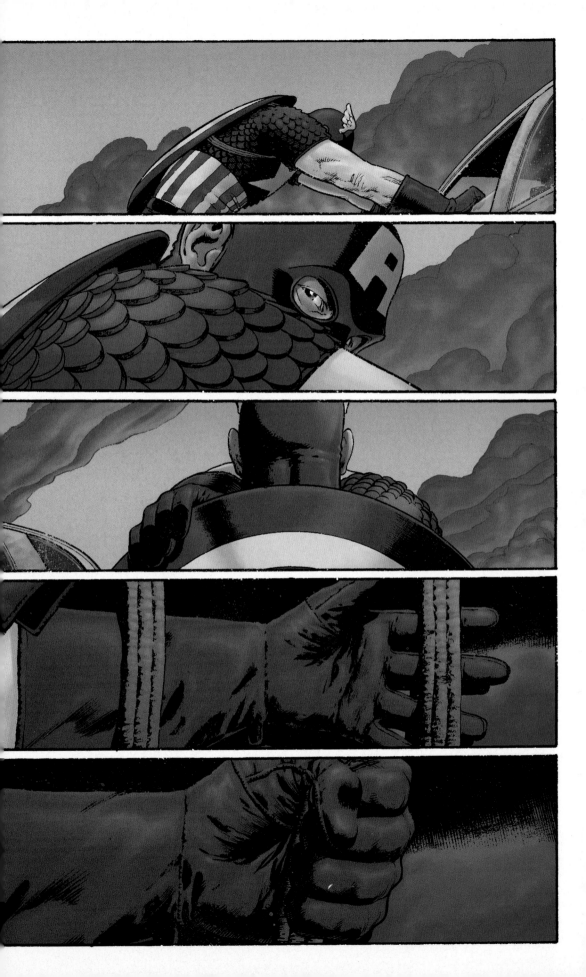

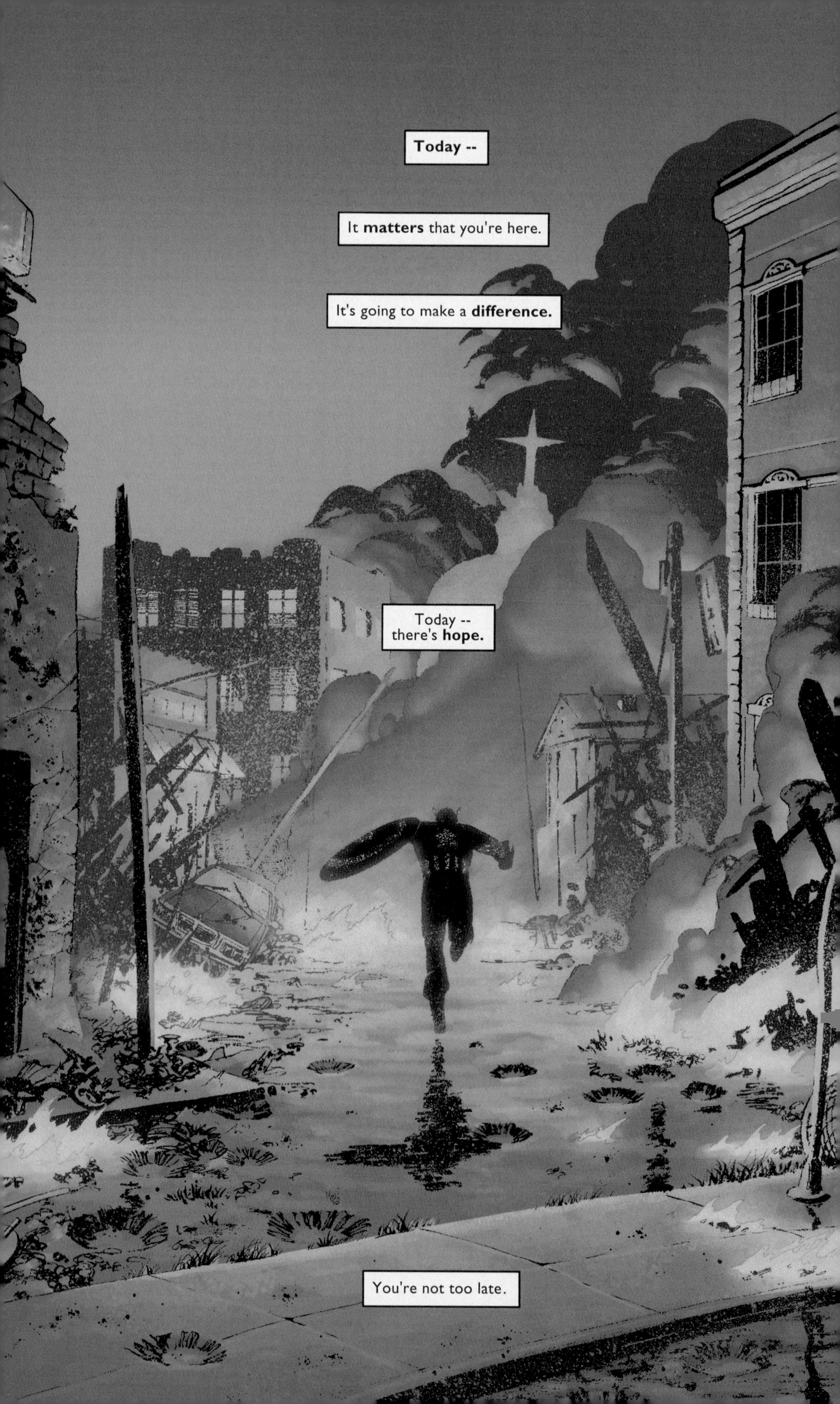
Today --
It matters that you're here.
It's going to make a difference.
Today -- there's hope.
You're not too late.

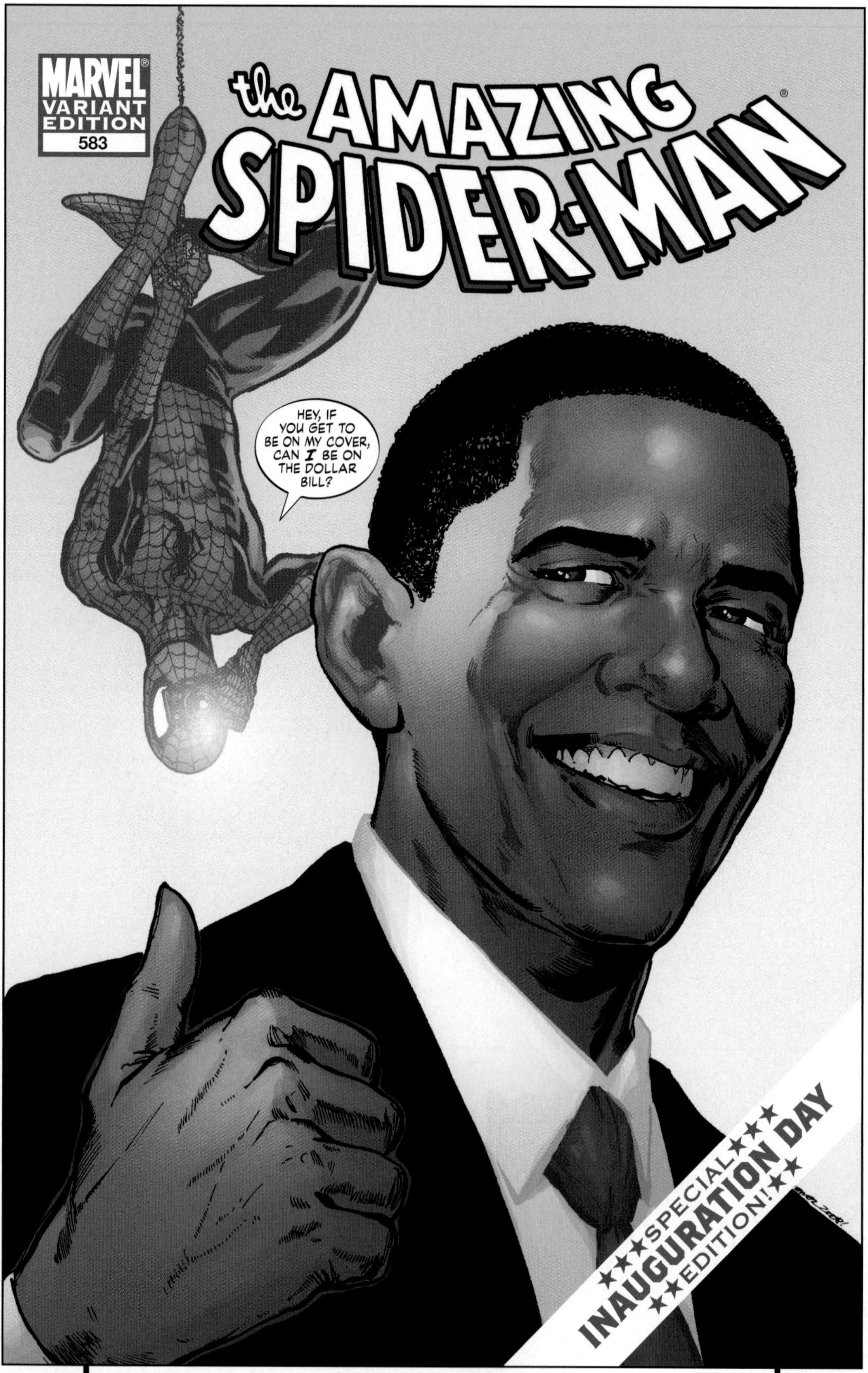
MARVEL
VARIANT EDITION
583
the AMAZING SPIDER-MAN
HEY, IF YOU GET TO BE ON MY COVER, CAN I BE ON THE DOLLAR BILL?
SPECIAL INAUGURATION DAY EDITION!

"SPIDEY MEETS THE PRESIDENT!"
[Extended edition from *SPIDER-MAN: PRESIDENTS' DAY CELEBRATION*]

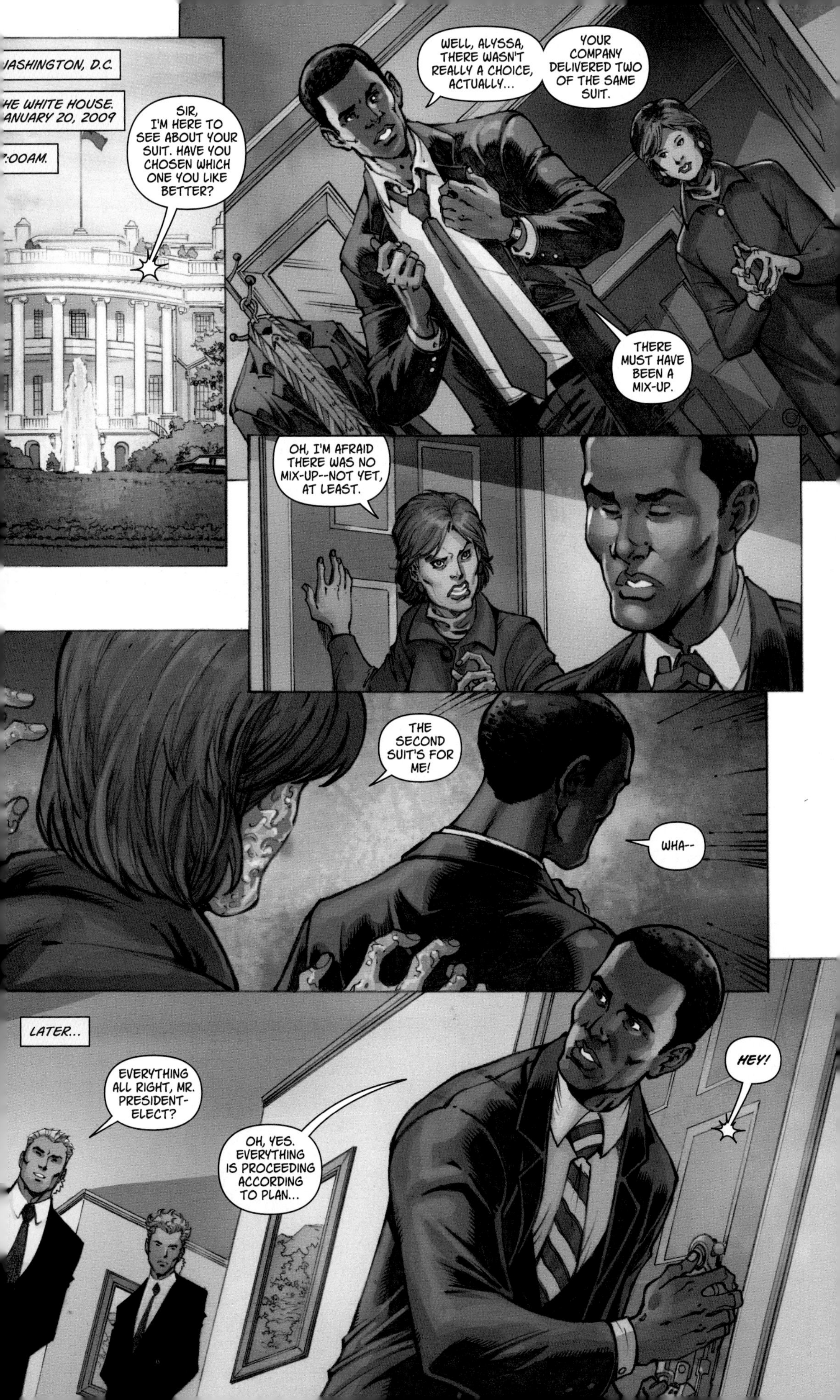

IASHINGTON, D.C.
HE WHITE HOUSE. ANUARY 20, 2009
:00AM.
SIR, I'M HERE TO SEE ABOUT YOUR SUIT. HAVE YOU CHOSEN WHICH ONE YOU LIKE BETTER?
WELL, ALYSSA, THERE WASN'T REALLY A CHOICE, ACTUALLY...
YOUR COMPANY DELIVERED TWO OF THE SAME SUIT.
THERE MUST HAVE BEEN A MIX-UP.
OH, I'M AFRAID THERE WAS NO MIX-UP--NOT YET, AT LEAST.
THE SECOND SUIT'S FOR ME!
WHA--
LATER...
EVERYTHING ALL RIGHT, MR. PRESIDENT-ELECT?
OH, YES. EVERYTHING IS PROCEEDING ACCORDING TO PLAN...
HEY!

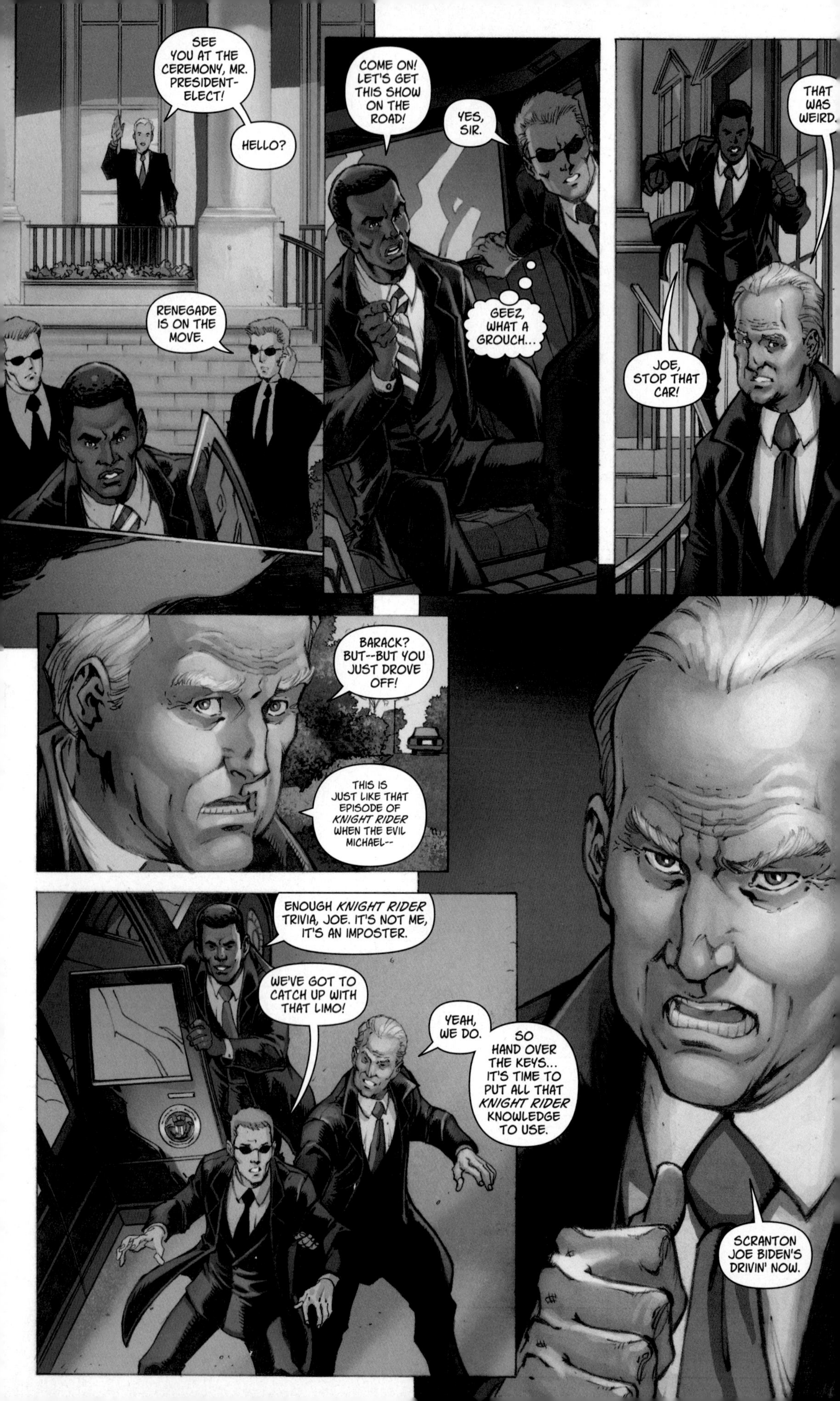

SEE YOU AT THE CEREMONY, MR. PRESIDENT-ELECT!
HELLO?
RENEGADE IS ON THE MOVE.
COME ON! LET'S GET THIS SHOW ON THE ROAD!
YES, SIR.
GEEZ, WHAT A GROUCH...
THAT WAS WEIRD.
JOE, STOP THAT CAR!
BARACK? BUT--BUT YOU JUST DROVE OFF!
THIS IS JUST LIKE THAT EPISODE OF *KNIGHT RIDER* WHEN THE EVIL MICHAEL--
ENOUGH *KNIGHT RIDER* TRIVIA, JOE. IT'S NOT ME, IT'S AN IMPOSTER.
WE'VE GOT TO CATCH UP WITH THAT LIMO!
YEAH, WE DO.
SO HAND OVER THE KEYS... IT'S TIME TO PUT ALL THAT *KNIGHT RIDER* KNOWLEDGE TO USE.
SCRANTON JOE BIDEN'S DRIVIN' NOW.

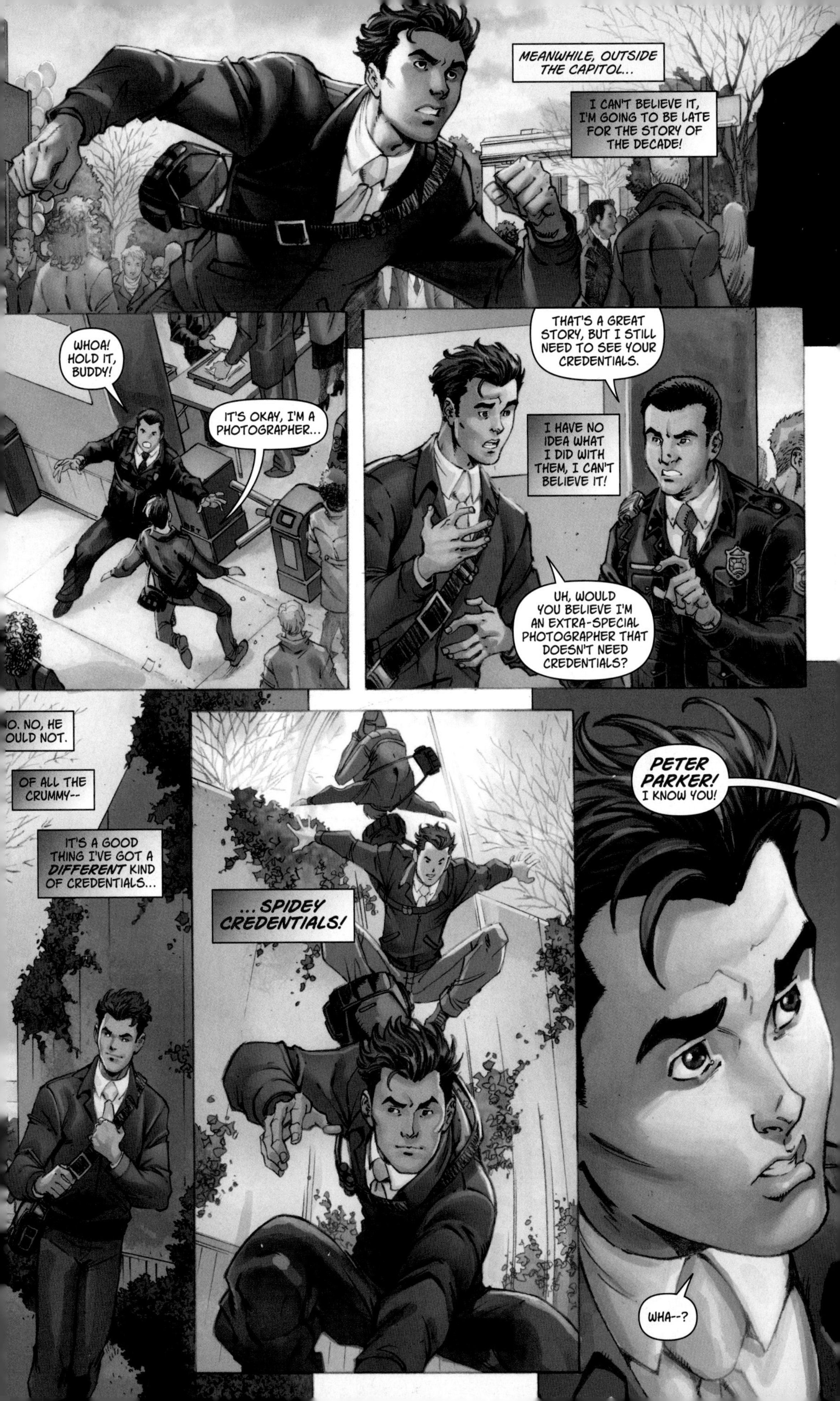

MEANWHILE, OUTSIDE THE CAPITOL...
I CAN'T BELIEVE IT, I'M GOING TO BE LATE FOR THE STORY OF THE DECADE!
WHOA! HOLD IT, BUDDY!
IT'S OKAY, I'M A PHOTOGRAPHER...
THAT'S A GREAT STORY, BUT I STILL NEED TO SEE YOUR CREDENTIALS.
I HAVE NO IDEA WHAT I DID WITH THEM, I CAN'T BELIEVE IT!
UH, WOULD YOU BELIEVE I'M AN EXTRA-SPECIAL PHOTOGRAPHER THAT DOESN'T NEED CREDENTIALS?
O. NO, HE OULD NOT.
OF ALL THE CRUMMY--
IT'S A GOOD THING I'VE GOT A DIFFERENT KIND OF CREDENTIALS...
...SPIDEY CREDENTIALS!
PETER PARKER! I KNOW YOU!
WHA--?

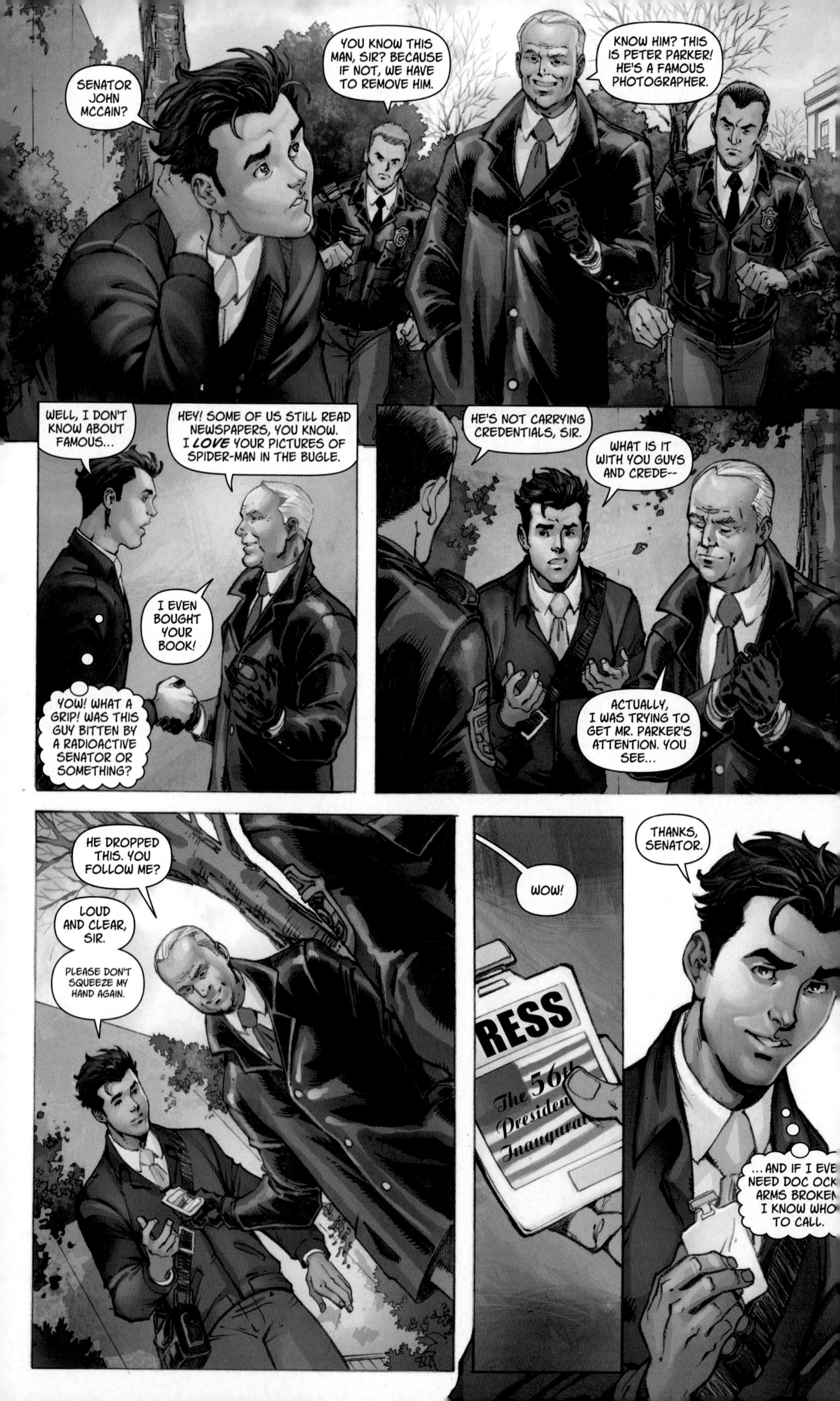

SENATOR JOHN MCCAIN?
YOU KNOW THIS MAN, SIR? BECAUSE IF NOT, WE HAVE TO REMOVE HIM.
KNOW HIM? THIS IS PETER PARKER! HE'S A FAMOUS PHOTOGRAPHER.
WELL, I DON'T KNOW ABOUT FAMOUS...
HEY! SOME OF US STILL READ NEWSPAPERS, YOU KNOW. I LOVE YOUR PICTURES OF SPIDER-MAN IN THE BUGLE.
I EVEN BOUGHT YOUR BOOK!
YOW! WHAT A GRIP! WAS THIS GUY BITTEN BY A RADIOACTIVE SENATOR OR SOMETHING?
HE'S NOT CARRYING CREDENTIALS, SIR.
WHAT IS IT WITH YOU GUYS AND CREDE--
ACTUALLY, I WAS TRYING TO GET MR. PARKER'S ATTENTION. YOU SEE...
HE DROPPED THIS. YOU FOLLOW ME?
LOUD AND CLEAR, SIR.
PLEASE DON'T SQUEEZE MY HAND AGAIN.
WOW!
RESS
The 56th President Inaugural
THANKS, SENATOR.
...AND IF I EVE NEED DOC OCK ARMS BROKEN I KNOW WHO TO CALL.

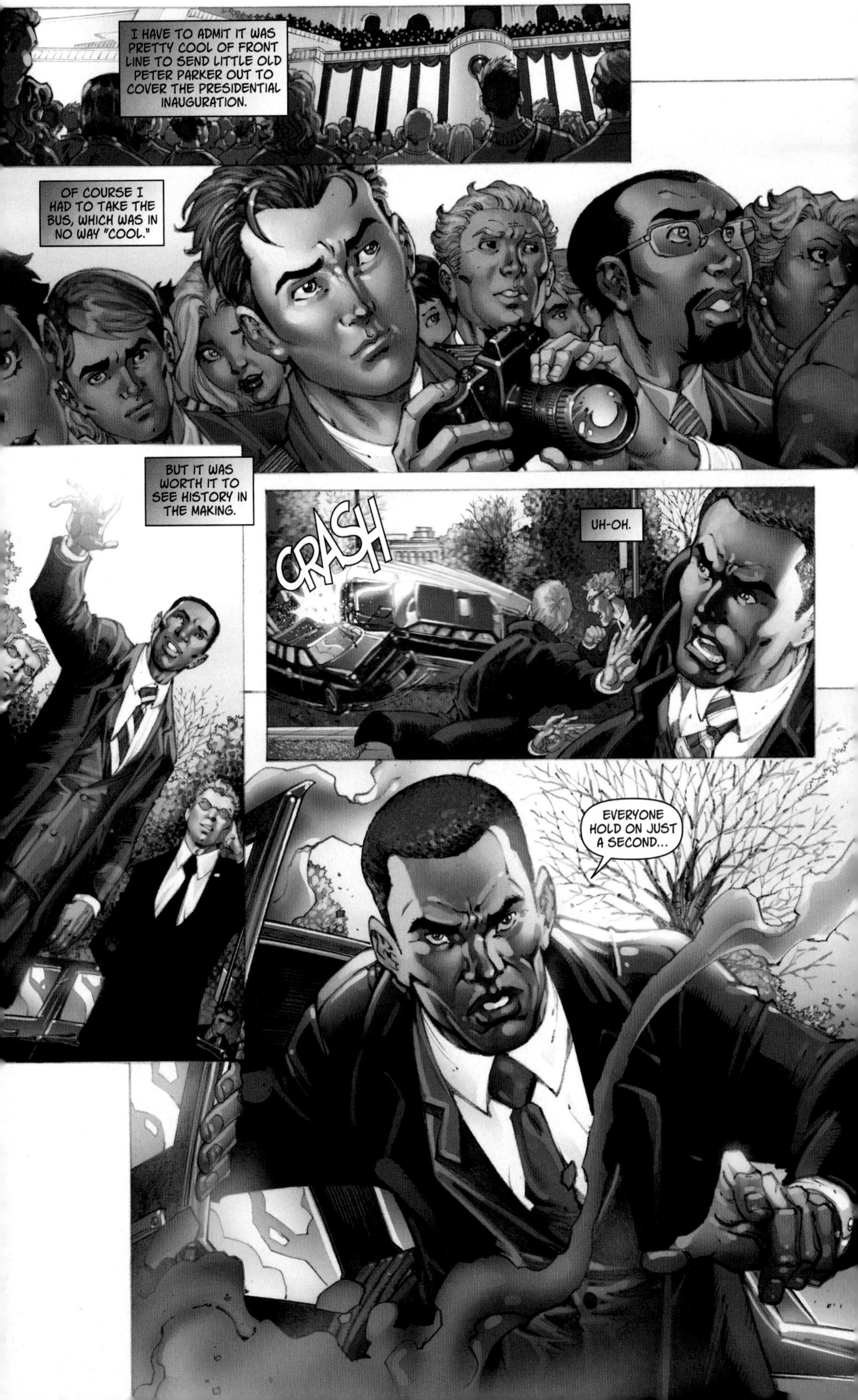

I HAVE TO ADMIT IT WAS PRETTY COOL OF FRONT LINE TO SEND LITTLE OLD PETER PARKER OUT TO COVER THE PRESIDENTIAL INAUGURATION.
OF COURSE I HAD TO TAKE THE BUS, WHICH WAS IN NO WAY "COOL."
BUT IT WAS WORTH IT TO SEE HISTORY IN THE MAKING.
CRASH
UH-OH.
EVERYONE HOLD ON JUST A SECOND...

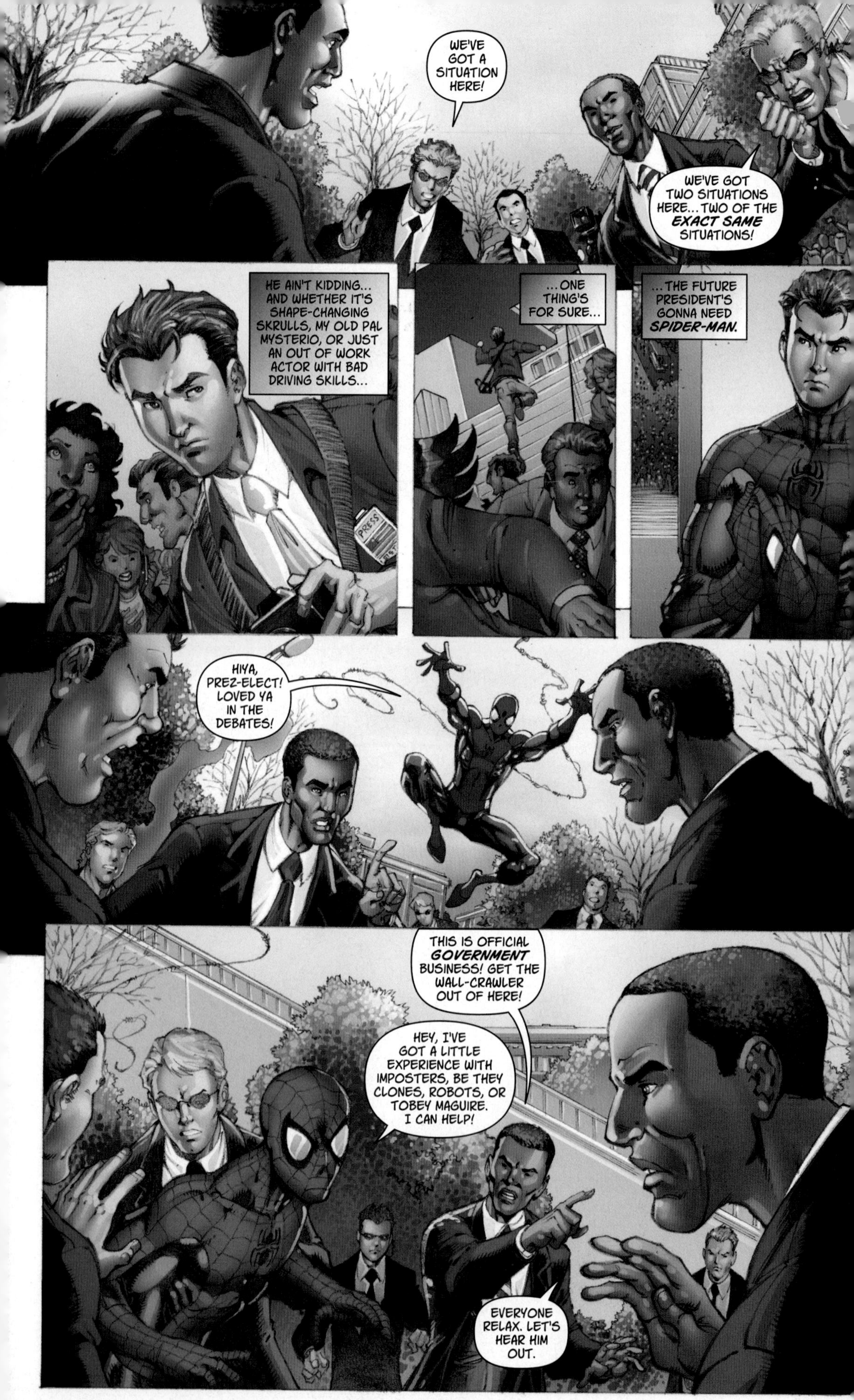
WE'VE GOT A SITUATION HERE!
WE'VE GOT TWO SITUATIONS HERE... TWO OF THE *EXACT SAME* SITUATIONS!
HE AIN'T KIDDING... AND WHETHER IT'S SHAPE-CHANGING SKRULLS, MY OLD PAL MYSTERIO, OR JUST AN OUT OF WORK ACTOR WITH BAD DRIVING SKILLS...
PRESS
...ONE THING'S FOR SURE...
...THE FUTURE PRESIDENT'S GONNA NEED *SPIDER-MAN.*
HIYA, PREZ-ELECT! LOVED YA IN THE DEBATES!
THIS IS OFFICIAL *GOVERNMENT* BUSINESS! GET THE WALL-CRAWLER OUT OF HERE!
HEY, I'VE GOT A LITTLE EXPERIENCE WITH IMPOSTERS, BE THEY CLONES, ROBOTS, OR TOBEY MAGUIRE. I CAN HELP!
EVERYONE RELAX. LET'S HEAR HIM OUT.

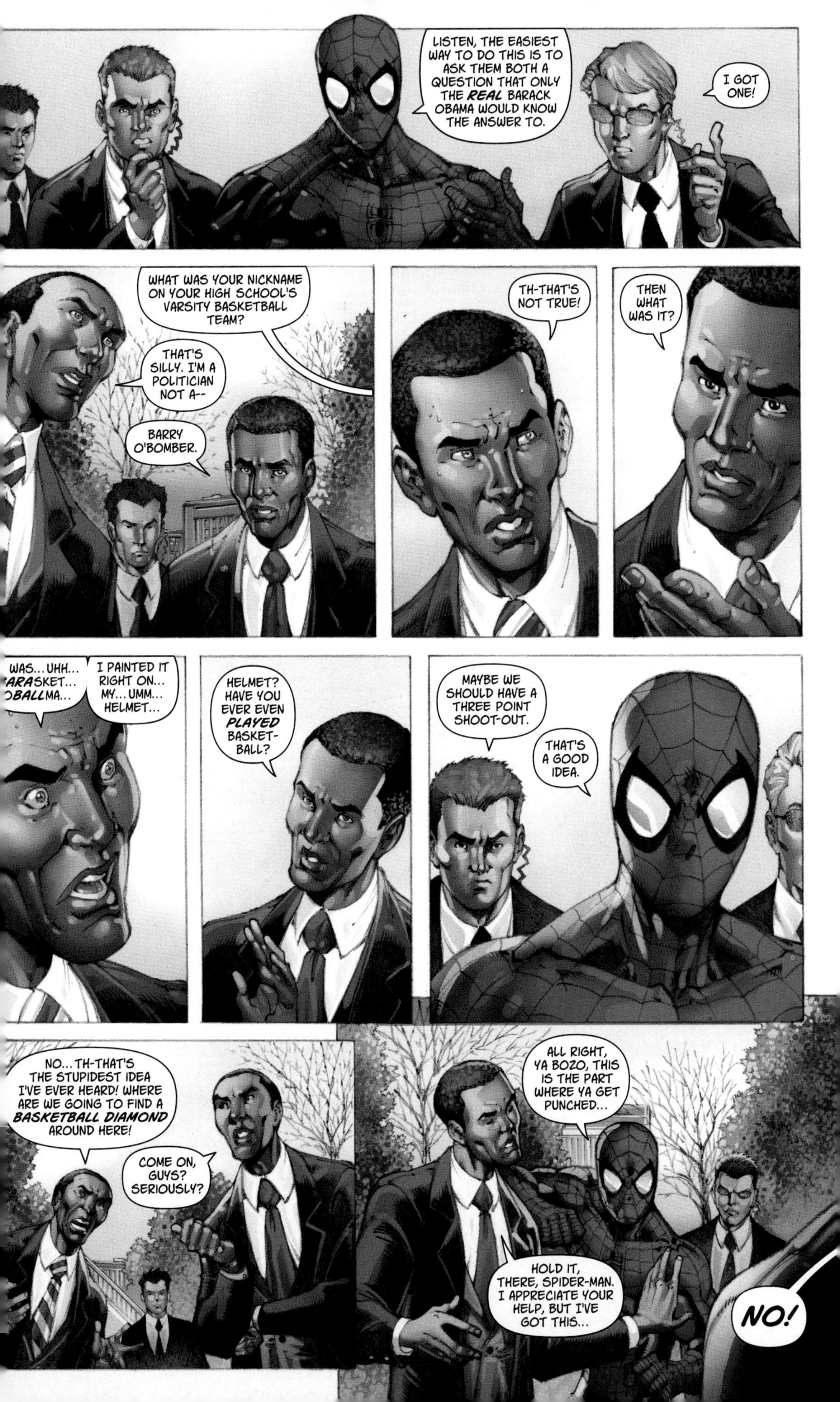

LISTEN, THE EASIEST WAY TO DO THIS IS TO ASK THEM BOTH A QUESTION THAT ONLY THE ***REAL*** BARACK OBAMA WOULD KNOW THE ANSWER TO.
I GOT ONE!
WHAT WAS YOUR NICKNAME ON YOUR HIGH SCHOOL'S VARSITY BASKETBALL TEAM?
THAT'S SILLY. I'M A POLITICIAN NOT A--
BARRY O'BOMBER.
TH-THAT'S NOT TRUE!
THEN WHAT WAS IT?
WAS... UHH... ***ARA***SKET... ***BALL***MA...
I PAINTED IT RIGHT ON... MY... UMM... HELMET...
HELMET? HAVE YOU EVER EVEN ***PLAYED*** BASKET-BALL?
MAYBE WE SHOULD HAVE A THREE POINT SHOOT-OUT.
THAT'S A GOOD IDEA.
NO... TH-THAT'S THE STUPIDEST IDEA I'VE EVER HEARD! WHERE ARE WE GOING TO FIND A ***BASKETBALL DIAMOND*** AROUND HERE!
COME ON, GUYS? SERIOUSLY?
ALL RIGHT, YA BOZO, THIS IS THE PART WHERE YA GET PUNCHED...
HOLD IT, THERE, SPIDER-MAN. I APPRECIATE YOUR HELP, BUT I'VE GOT THIS...
NO!

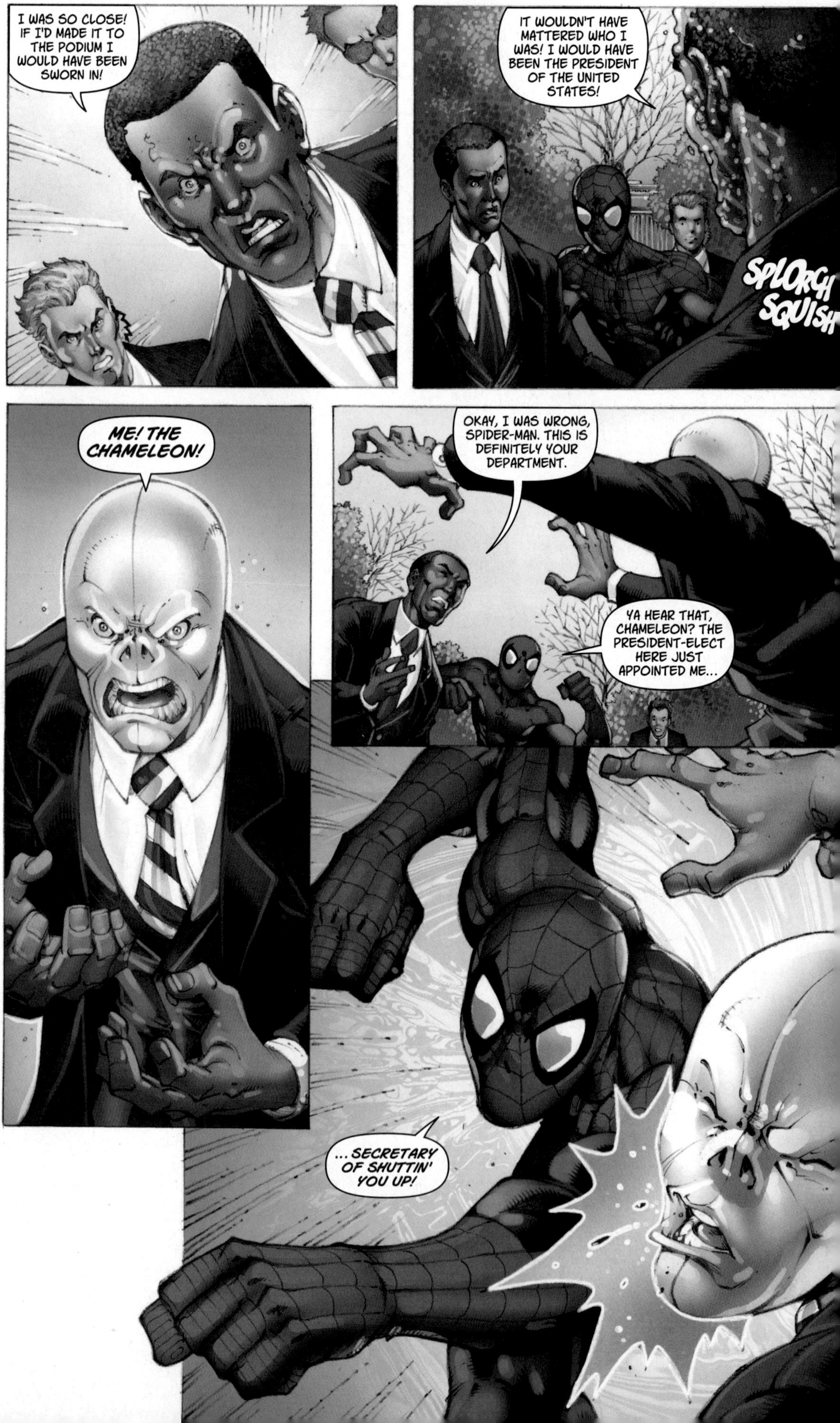
I WAS SO CLOSE! IF I'D MADE IT TO THE PODIUM I WOULD HAVE BEEN SWORN IN!
IT WOULDN'T HAVE MATTERED WHO I WAS! I WOULD HAVE BEEN THE PRESIDENT OF THE UNITED STATES!
SPLORCH
SQUISH
ME! THE CHAMELEON!
OKAY, I WAS WRONG, SPIDER-MAN. THIS IS DEFINITELY YOUR DEPARTMENT.
YA HEAR THAT, CHAMELEON? THE PRESIDENT-ELECT HERE JUST APPOINTED ME...
...SECRETARY OF SHUTTIN' YOU UP!

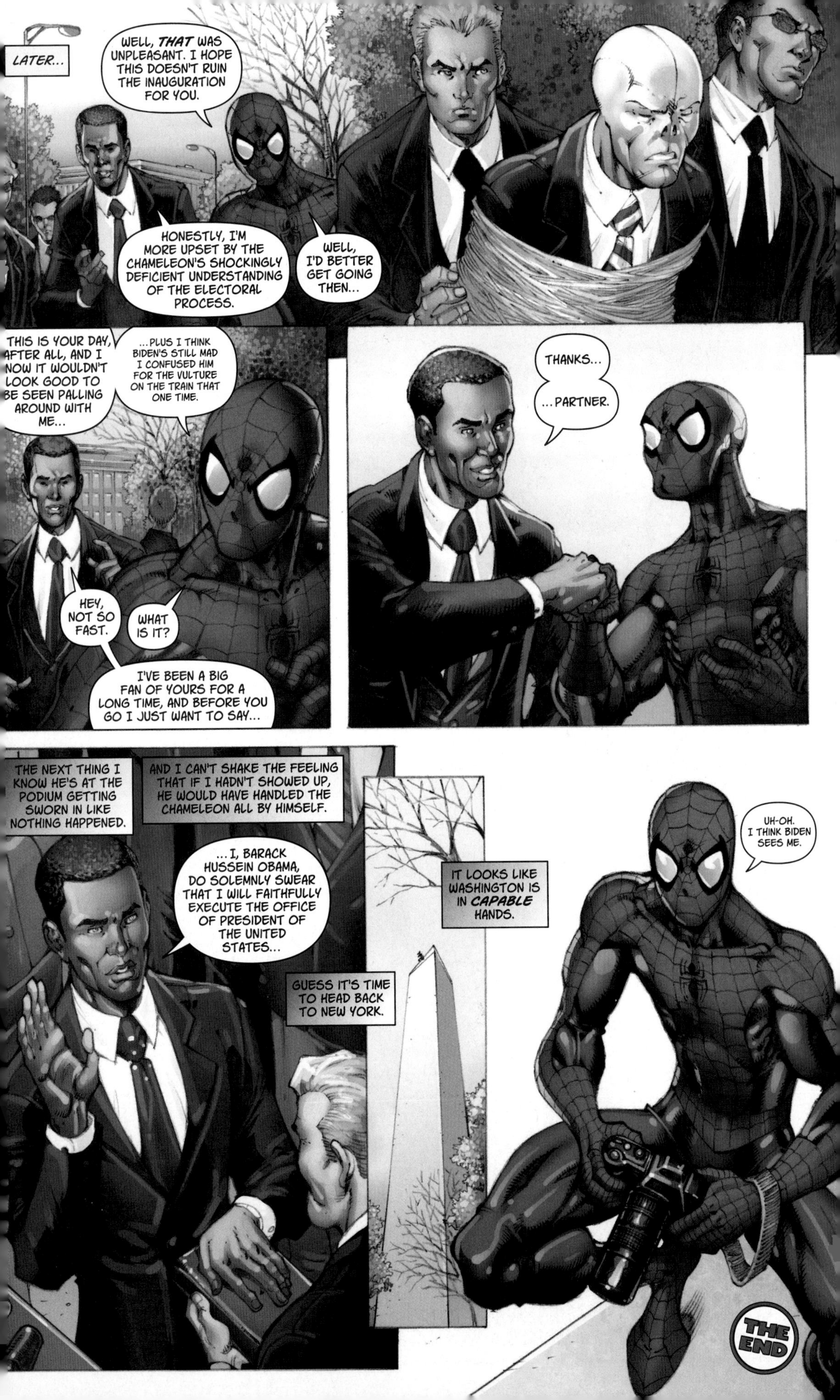
LATER...
WELL, *THAT* WAS UNPLEASANT. I HOPE THIS DOESN'T RUIN THE INAUGURATION FOR YOU.
HONESTLY, I'M MORE UPSET BY THE CHAMELEON'S SHOCKINGLY DEFICIENT UNDERSTANDING OF THE ELECTORAL PROCESS.
WELL, I'D BETTER GET GOING THEN...
THIS IS YOUR DAY, AFTER ALL, AND I NOW IT WOULDN'T LOOK GOOD TO BE SEEN PALLING AROUND WITH ME...
...PLUS I THINK BIDEN'S STILL MAD I CONFUSED HIM FOR THE VULTURE ON THE TRAIN THAT ONE TIME.
HEY, NOT SO FAST.
WHAT IS IT?
I'VE BEEN A BIG FAN OF YOURS FOR A LONG TIME, AND BEFORE YOU GO I JUST WANT TO SAY...
THANKS...
...PARTNER.
THE NEXT THING I KNOW HE'S AT THE PODIUM GETTING SWORN IN LIKE NOTHING HAPPENED.
AND I CAN'T SHAKE THE FEELING THAT IF I HADN'T SHOWED UP, HE WOULD HAVE HANDLED THE CHAMELEON ALL BY HIMSELF.
...I, BARACK HUSSEIN OBAMA, DO SOLEMNLY SWEAR THAT I WILL FAITHFULLY EXECUTE THE OFFICE OF PRESIDENT OF THE UNITED STATES...
IT LOOKS LIKE WASHINGTON IS IN *CAPABLE* HANDS.
GUESS IT'S TIME TO HEAD BACK TO NEW YORK.
UH-OH. I THINK BIDEN SEES ME.
THE END

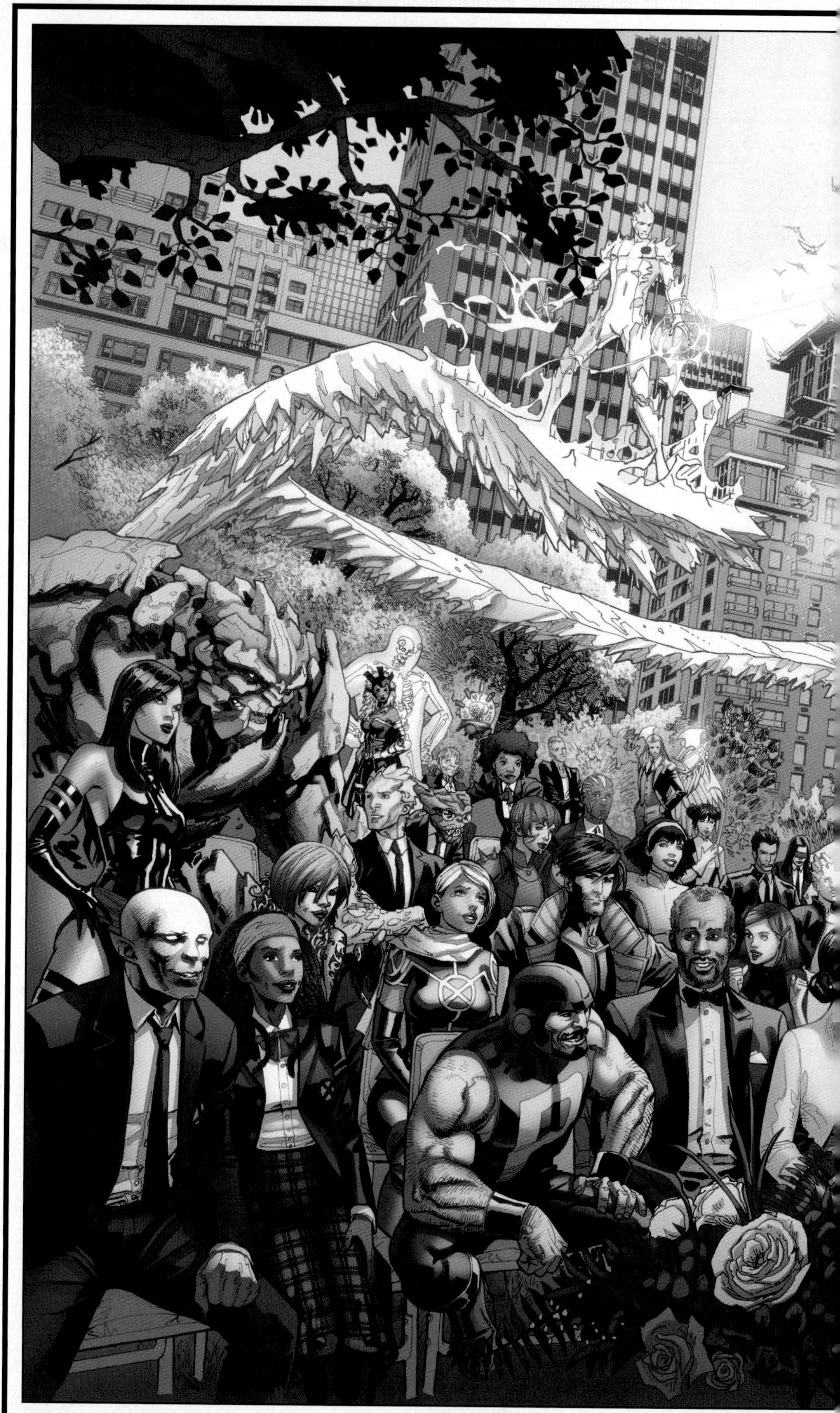

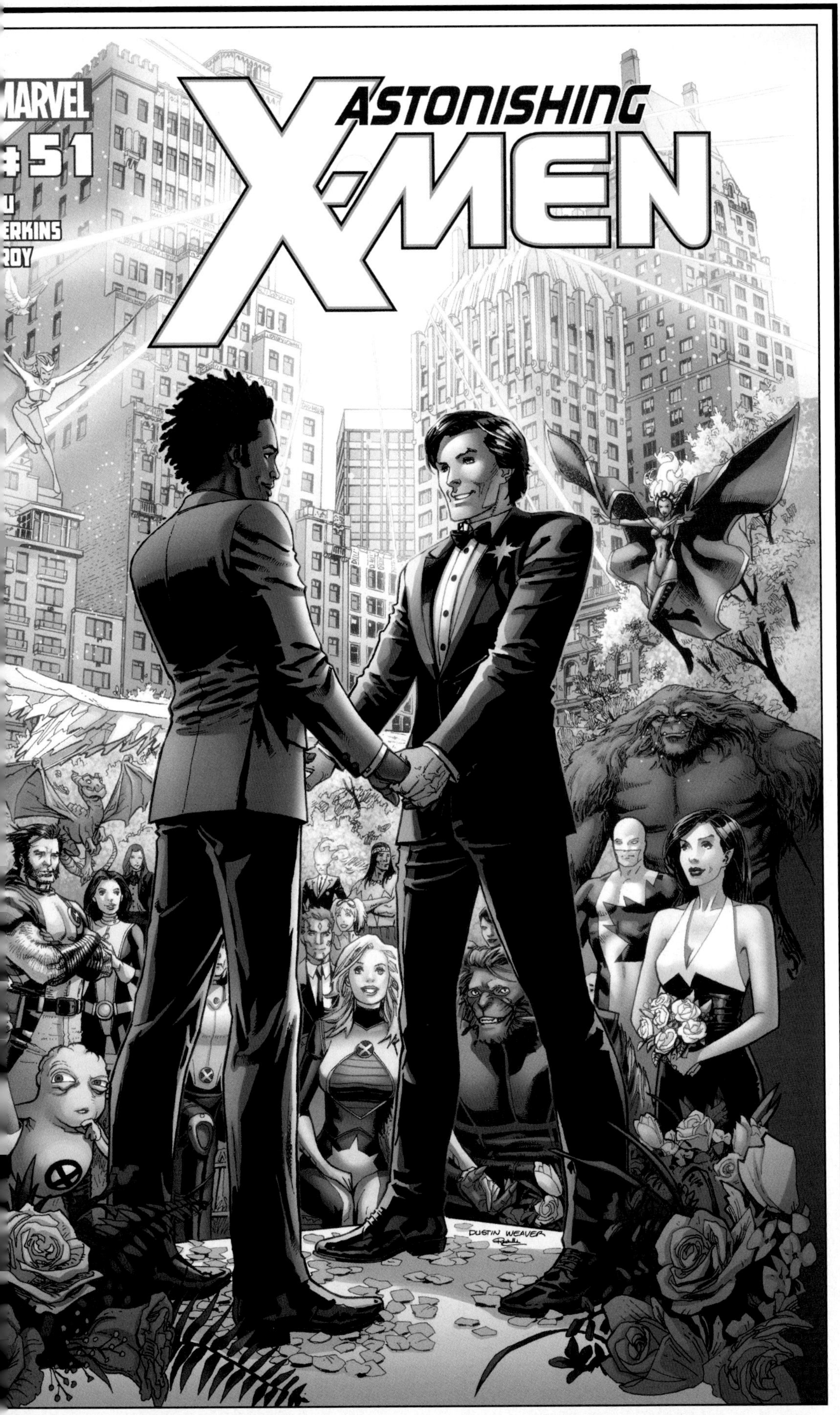
MARVEL
#51
ASTONISHING
X-MEN
U
ERKINS
ROY
DUSTIN WEAVER

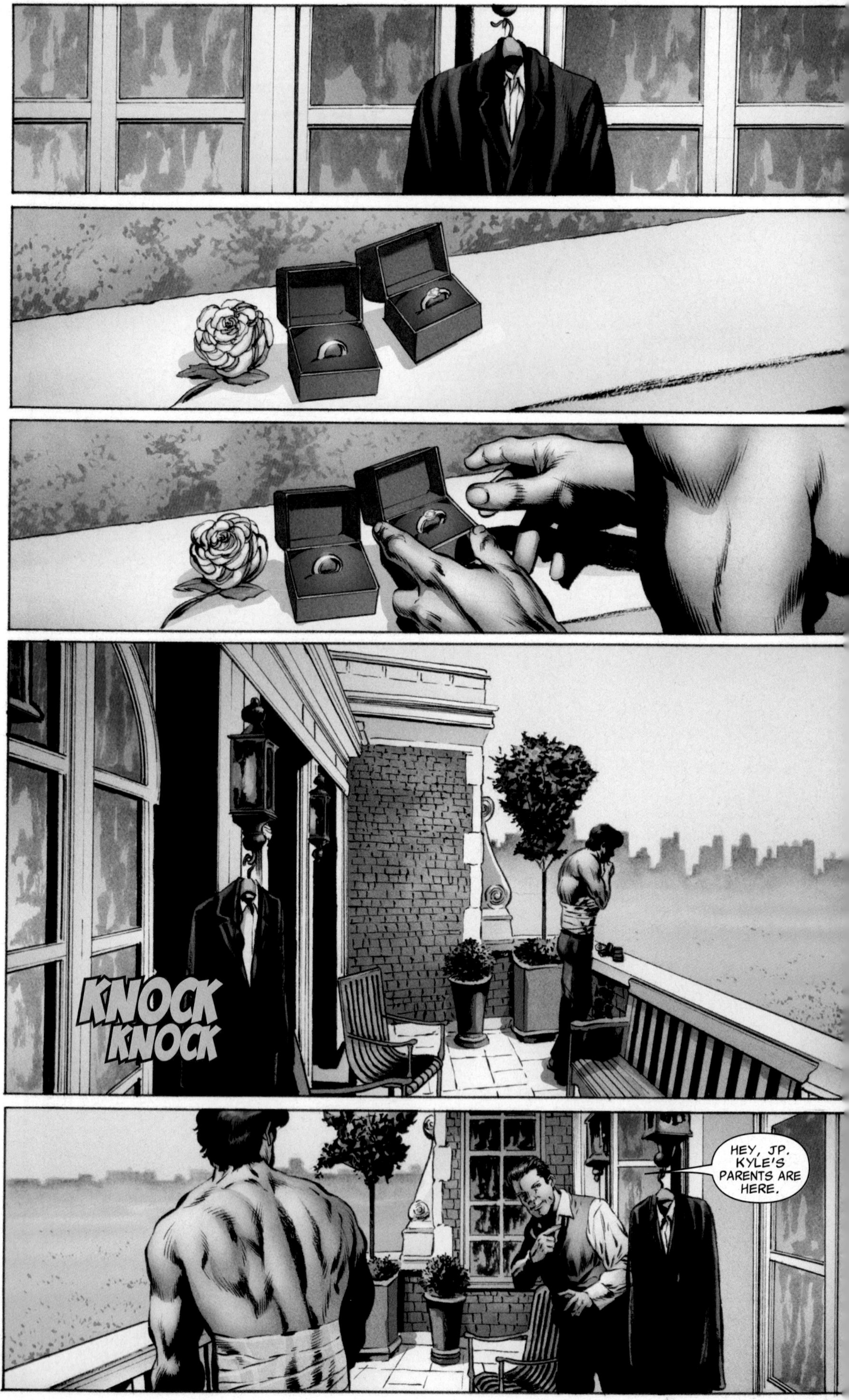
KNOCK KNOCK
HEY, JP. KYLE'S PARENTS ARE HERE.

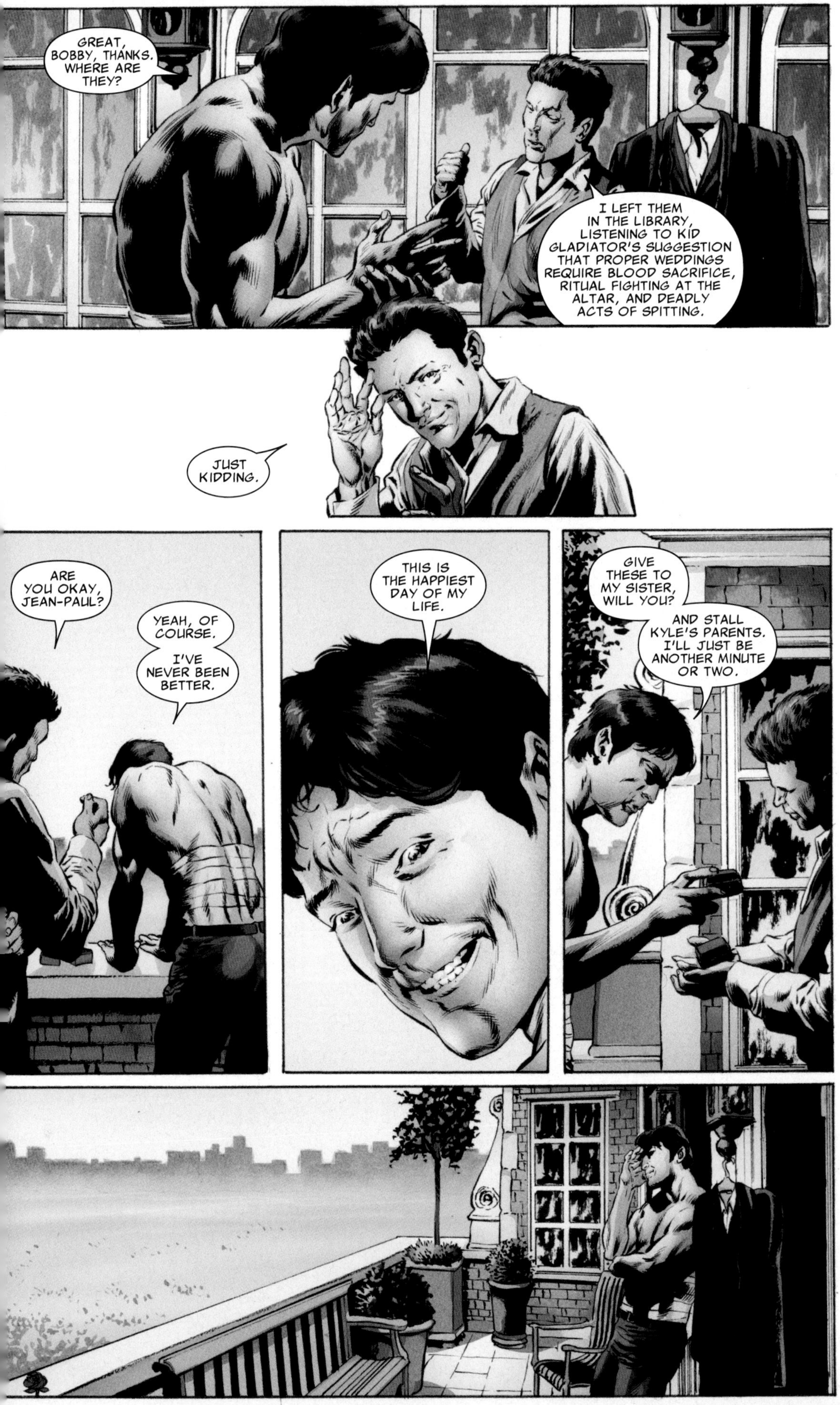
GREAT, BOBBY, THANKS. WHERE ARE THEY?
I LEFT THEM IN THE LIBRARY, LISTENING TO KID GLADIATOR'S SUGGESTION THAT PROPER WEDDINGS REQUIRE BLOOD SACRIFICE, RITUAL FIGHTING AT THE ALTAR, AND DEADLY ACTS OF SPITTING.
JUST KIDDING.
ARE YOU OKAY, JEAN-PAUL?
YEAH, OF COURSE.
I'VE NEVER BEEN BETTER.
THIS IS THE HAPPIEST DAY OF MY LIFE.
GIVE THESE TO MY SISTER, WILL YOU?
AND STALL KYLE'S PARENTS. I'LL JUST BE ANOTHER MINUTE OR TWO.

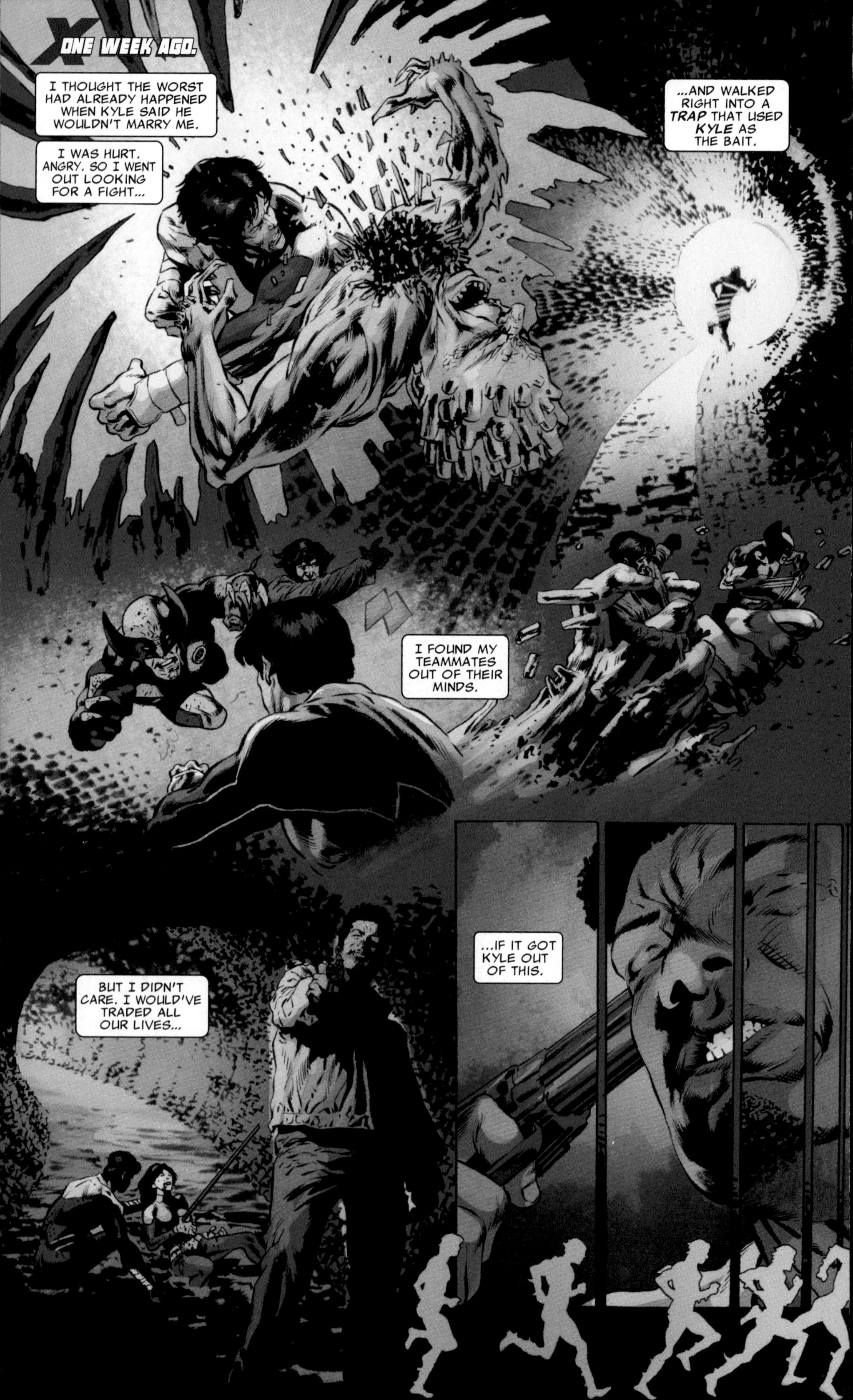
ONE WEEK AGO.
I THOUGHT THE WORST HAD ALREADY HAPPENED WHEN KYLE SAID HE WOULDN'T MARRY ME.
I WAS HURT. ANGRY. SO I WENT OUT LOOKING FOR A FIGHT...
...AND WALKED RIGHT INTO A TRAP THAT USED KYLE AS THE BAIT.
I FOUND MY TEAMMATES OUT OF THEIR MINDS.
BUT I DIDN'T CARE. I WOULD'VE TRADED ALL OUR LIVES...
...IF IT GOT KYLE OUT OF THIS.

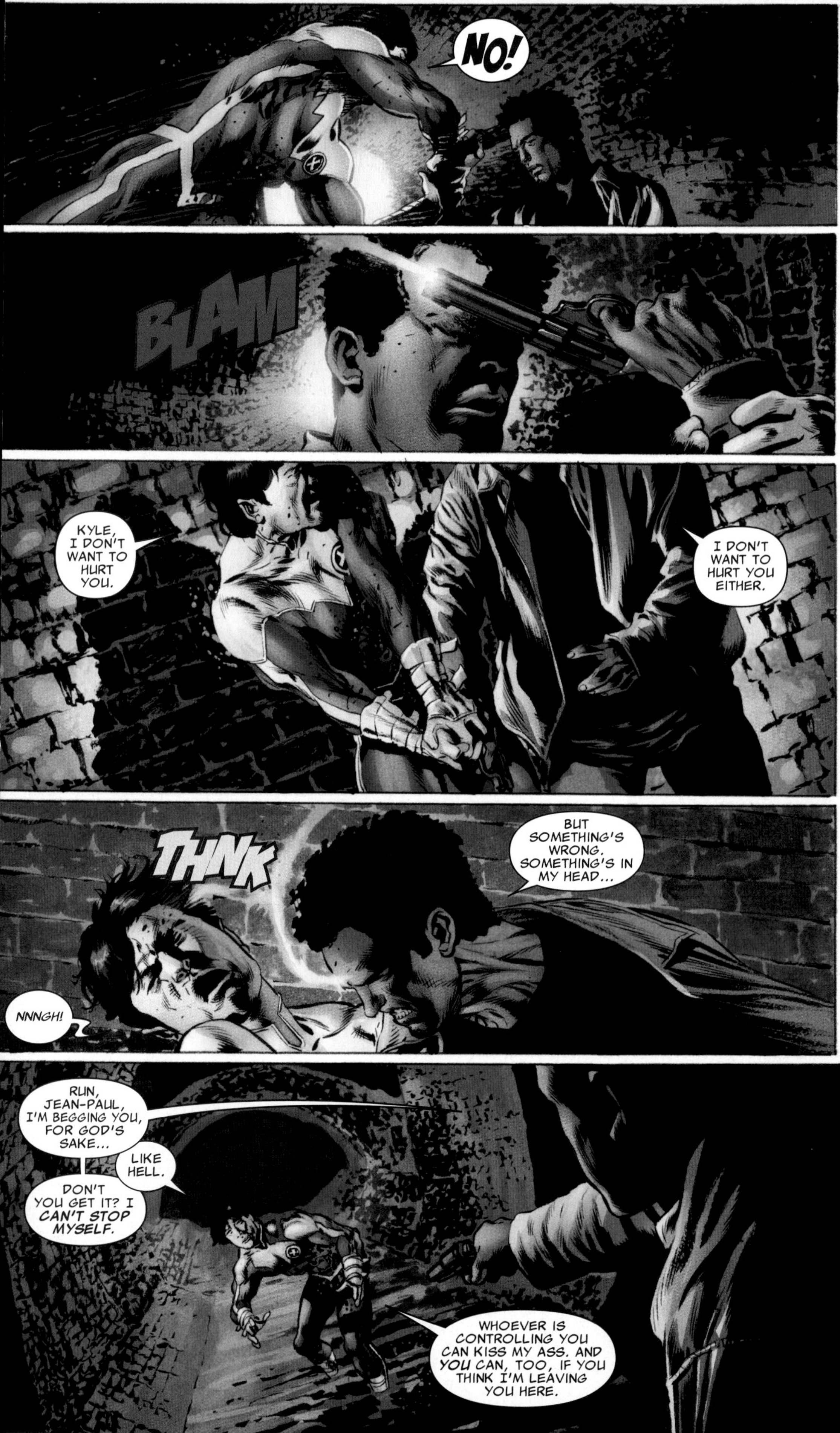

NO!
BLAM
KYLE, I DON'T WANT TO HURT YOU.
I DON'T WANT TO HURT YOU EITHER.
THNK
BUT SOMETHING'S WRONG. SOMETHING'S IN MY HEAD...
NNNGH!
RUN, JEAN-PAUL, I'M BEGGING YOU, FOR GOD'S SAKE...
DON'T YOU GET IT? I CAN'T STOP MYSELF.
LIKE HELL.
WHOEVER IS CONTROLLING YOU CAN KISS MY ASS. AND YOU CAN, TOO, IF YOU THINK I'M LEAVING YOU HERE.

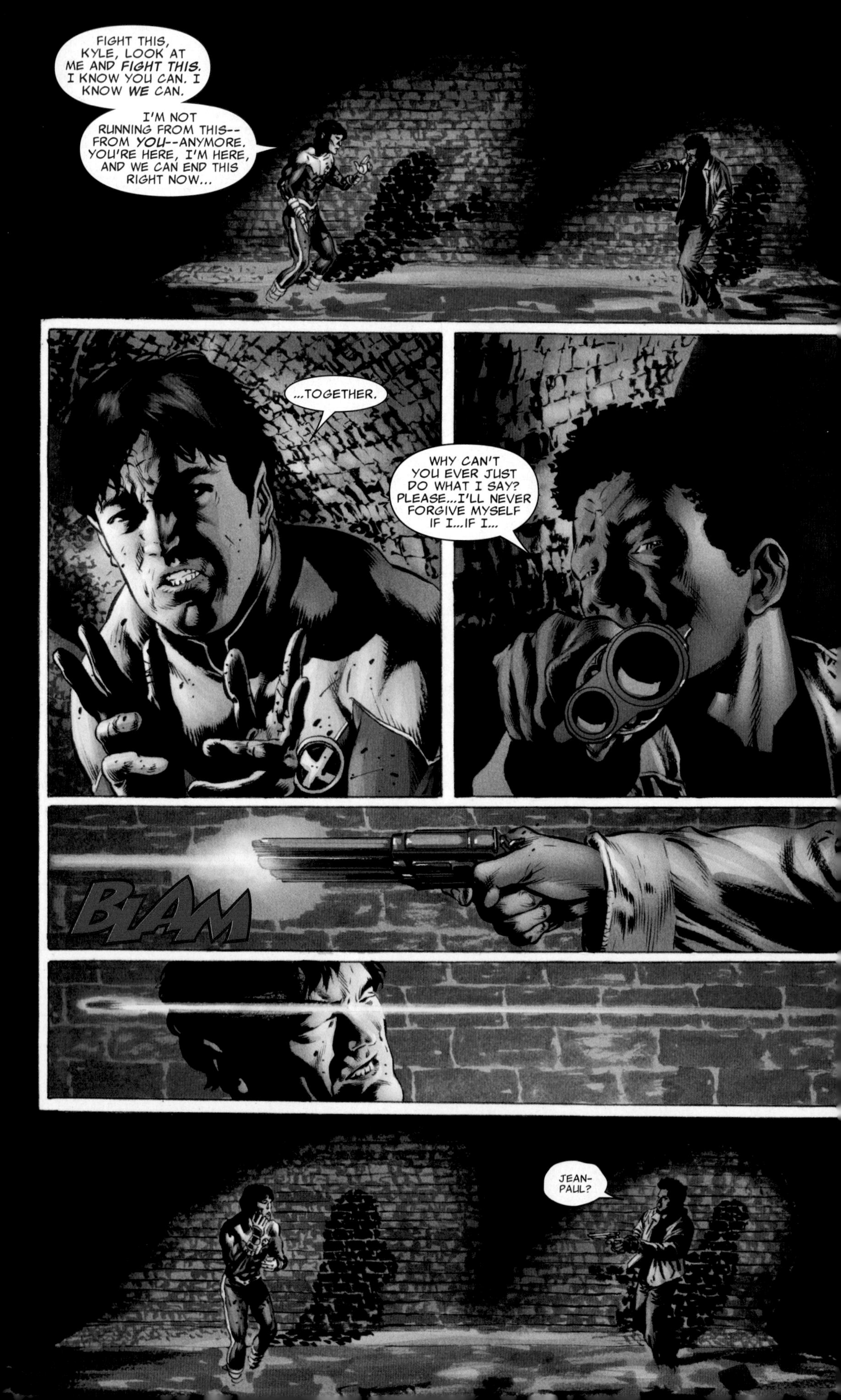
FIGHT THIS, KYLE, LOOK AT ME AND FIGHT THIS. I KNOW YOU CAN. I KNOW WE CAN.
I'M NOT RUNNING FROM THIS-- FROM YOU--ANYMORE. YOU'RE HERE, I'M HERE, AND WE CAN END THIS RIGHT NOW...
...TOGETHER.
WHY CAN'T YOU EVER JUST DO WHAT I SAY? PLEASE...I'LL NEVER FORGIVE MYSELF IF I...IF I...
BLAM
JEAN-PAUL?

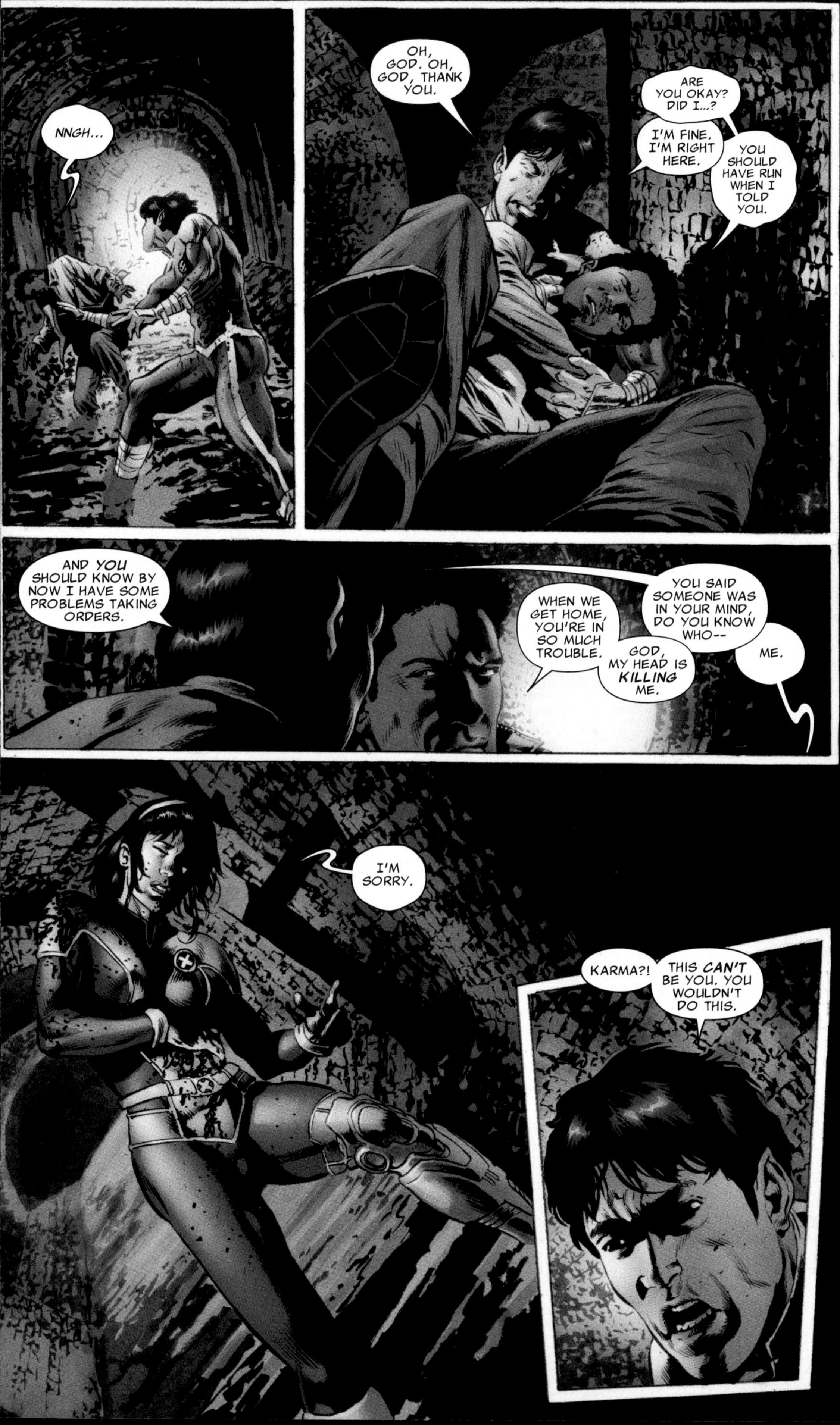
NNGH...
OH, GOD. OH, GOD, THANK YOU.
ARE YOU OKAY? DID I...?
I'M FINE. I'M RIGHT HERE.
YOU SHOULD HAVE RUN WHEN I TOLD YOU.
AND YOU SHOULD KNOW BY NOW I HAVE SOME PROBLEMS TAKING ORDERS.
WHEN WE GET HOME, YOU'RE IN SO MUCH TROUBLE.
GOD, MY HEAD IS KILLING ME.
YOU SAID SOMEONE WAS IN YOUR MIND, DO YOU KNOW WHO--
ME.
I'M SORRY.
KARMA?!
THIS CAN'T BE YOU. YOU WOULDN'T DO THIS.

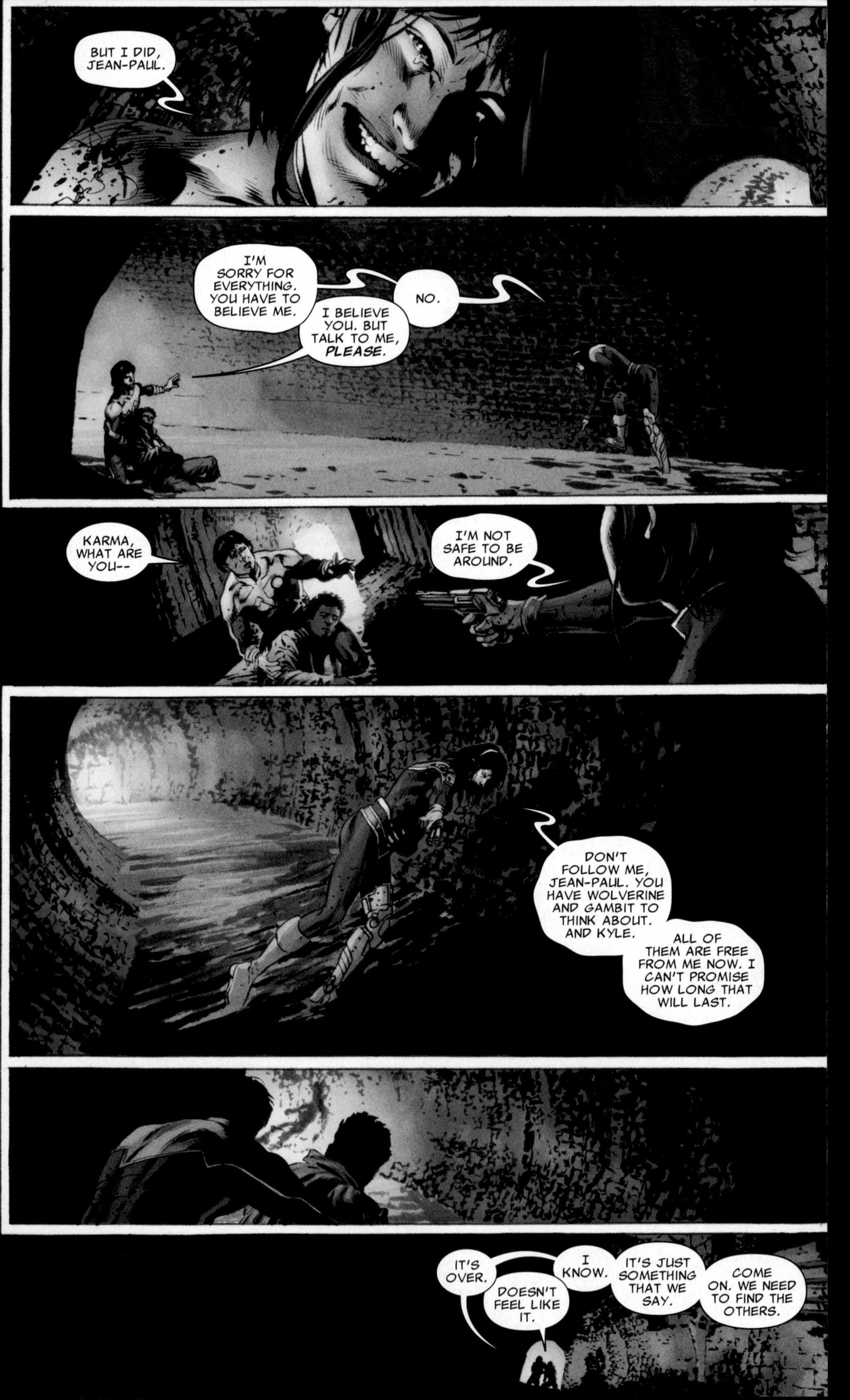

BUT I DID, JEAN-PAUL.
I'M SORRY FOR EVERYTHING. YOU HAVE TO BELIEVE ME.
NO.
I BELIEVE YOU. BUT TALK TO ME, PLEASE.
KARMA, WHAT ARE YOU--
I'M NOT SAFE TO BE AROUND.
DON'T FOLLOW ME, JEAN-PAUL. YOU HAVE WOLVERINE AND GAMBIT TO THINK ABOUT. AND KYLE.
ALL OF THEM ARE FREE FROM ME NOW. I CAN'T PROMISE HOW LONG THAT WILL LAST.
IT'S OVER.
DOESN'T FEEL LIKE IT.
I KNOW.
IT'S JUST SOMETHING THAT WE SAY.
COME ON. WE NEED TO FIND THE OTHERS.

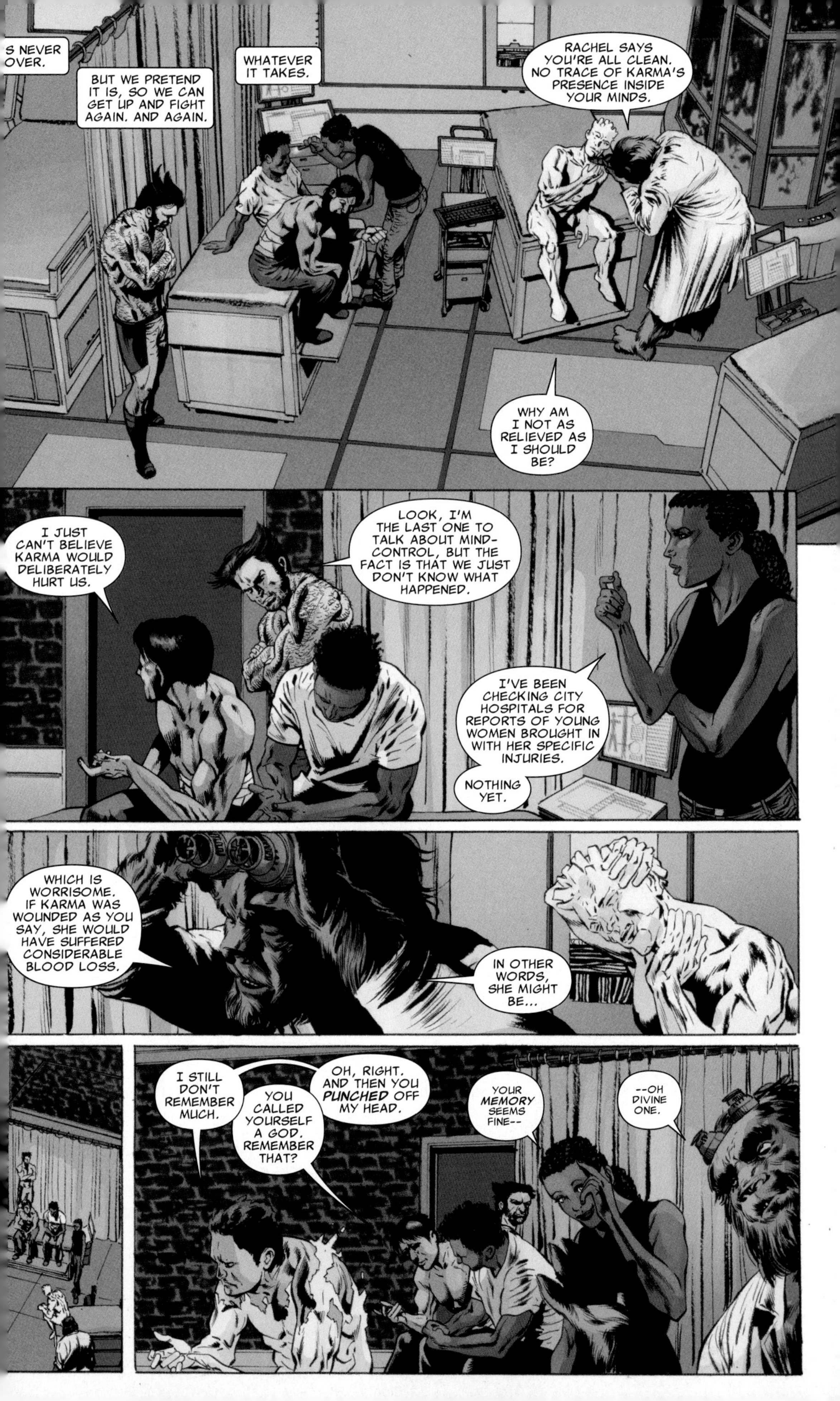

S NEVER OVER.
BUT WE PRETEND IT IS, SO WE CAN GET UP AND FIGHT AGAIN. AND AGAIN.
WHATEVER IT TAKES.
RACHEL SAYS YOU'RE ALL CLEAN. NO TRACE OF KARMA'S PRESENCE INSIDE YOUR MINDS.
WHY AM I NOT AS RELIEVED AS I SHOULD BE?
I JUST CAN'T BELIEVE KARMA WOULD DELIBERATELY HURT US.
LOOK, I'M THE LAST ONE TO TALK ABOUT MIND-CONTROL, BUT THE FACT IS THAT WE JUST DON'T KNOW WHAT HAPPENED.
I'VE BEEN CHECKING CITY HOSPITALS FOR REPORTS OF YOUNG WOMEN BROUGHT IN WITH HER SPECIFIC INJURIES.
NOTHING YET.
WHICH IS WORRISOME. IF KARMA WAS WOUNDED AS YOU SAY, SHE WOULD HAVE SUFFERED CONSIDERABLE BLOOD LOSS.
IN OTHER WORDS, SHE MIGHT BE...
I STILL DON'T REMEMBER MUCH.
YOU CALLED YOURSELF A GOD. REMEMBER THAT?
OH, RIGHT. AND THEN YOU PUNCHED OFF MY HEAD.
YOUR MEMORY SEEMS FINE--
--OH DIVINE ONE.

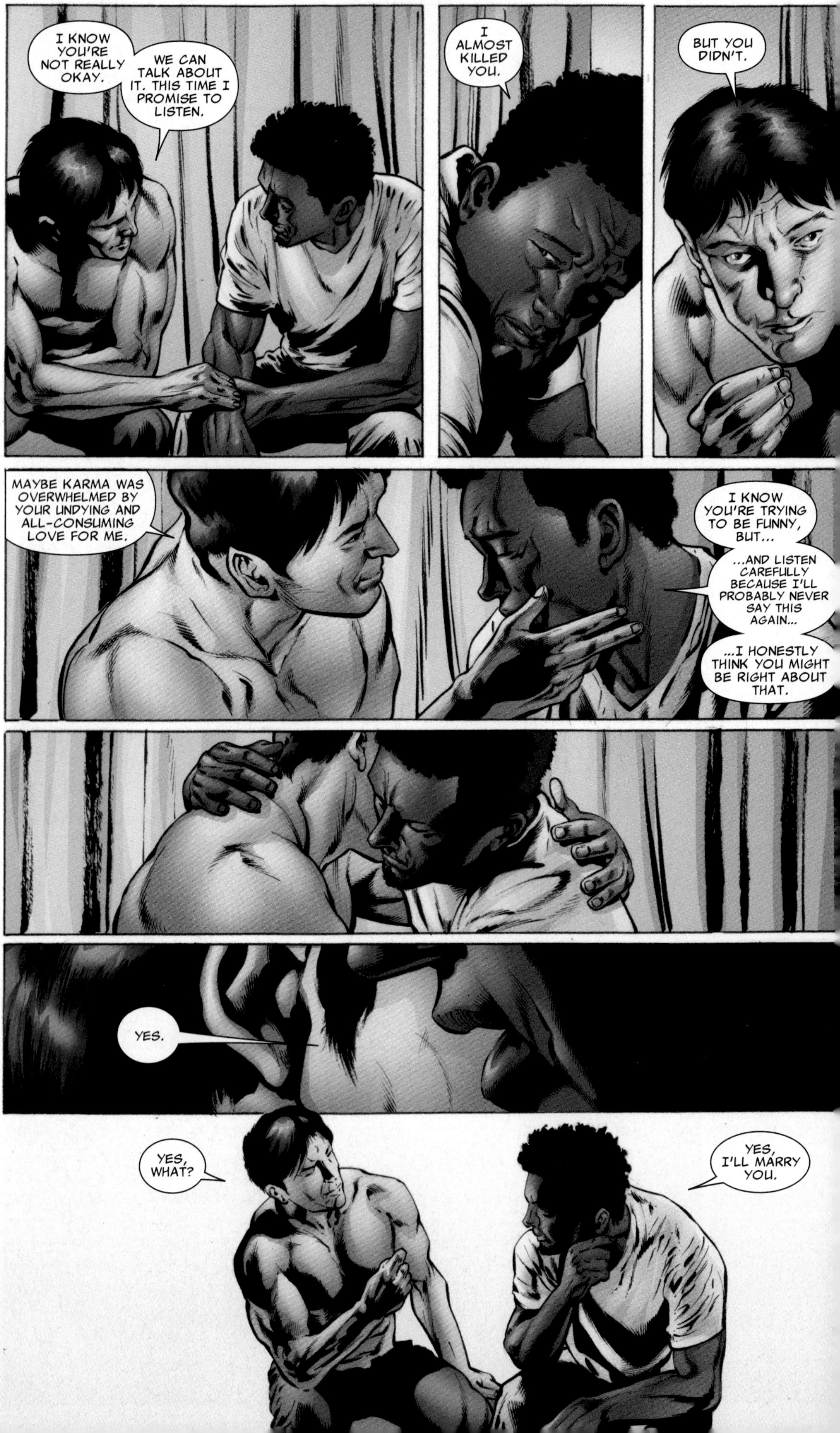
I KNOW YOU'RE NOT REALLY OKAY.
WE CAN TALK ABOUT IT. THIS TIME I PROMISE TO LISTEN.
I ALMOST KILLED YOU.
BUT YOU DIDN'T.
MAYBE KARMA WAS OVERWHELMED BY YOUR UNDYING AND ALL-CONSUMING LOVE FOR ME.
I KNOW YOU'RE TRYING TO BE FUNNY, BUT...
...AND LISTEN CAREFULLY BECAUSE I'LL PROBABLY NEVER SAY THIS AGAIN...
...I HONESTLY THINK YOU MIGHT BE RIGHT ABOUT THAT.
YES.
YES, WHAT?
YES, I'LL MARRY YOU.

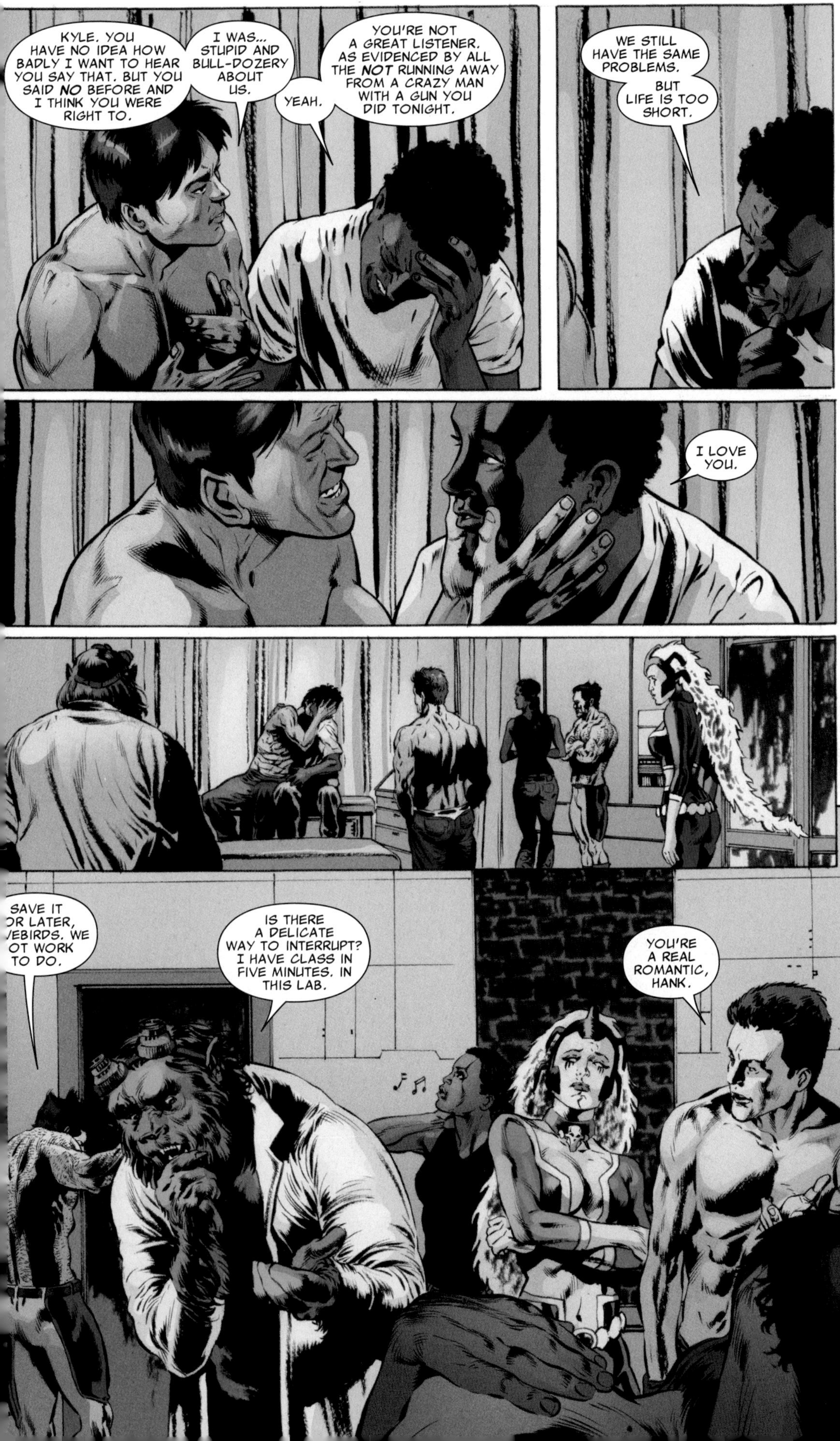

KYLE. YOU HAVE NO IDEA HOW BADLY I WANT TO HEAR YOU SAY THAT. BUT YOU SAID NO BEFORE AND I THINK YOU WERE RIGHT TO.
I WAS... STUPID AND BULL-DOZERY ABOUT US.
YEAH.
YOU'RE NOT A GREAT LISTENER. AS EVIDENCED BY ALL THE NOT RUNNING AWAY FROM A CRAZY MAN WITH A GUN YOU DID TONIGHT.
WE STILL HAVE THE SAME PROBLEMS.
BUT LIFE IS TOO SHORT.
I LOVE YOU.
SAVE IT OR LATER, VEBIRDS. WE OT WORK TO DO.
IS THERE A DELICATE WAY TO INTERRUPT? I HAVE CLASS IN FIVE MINUTES. IN THIS LAB.
YOU'RE A REAL ROMANTIC, HANK.

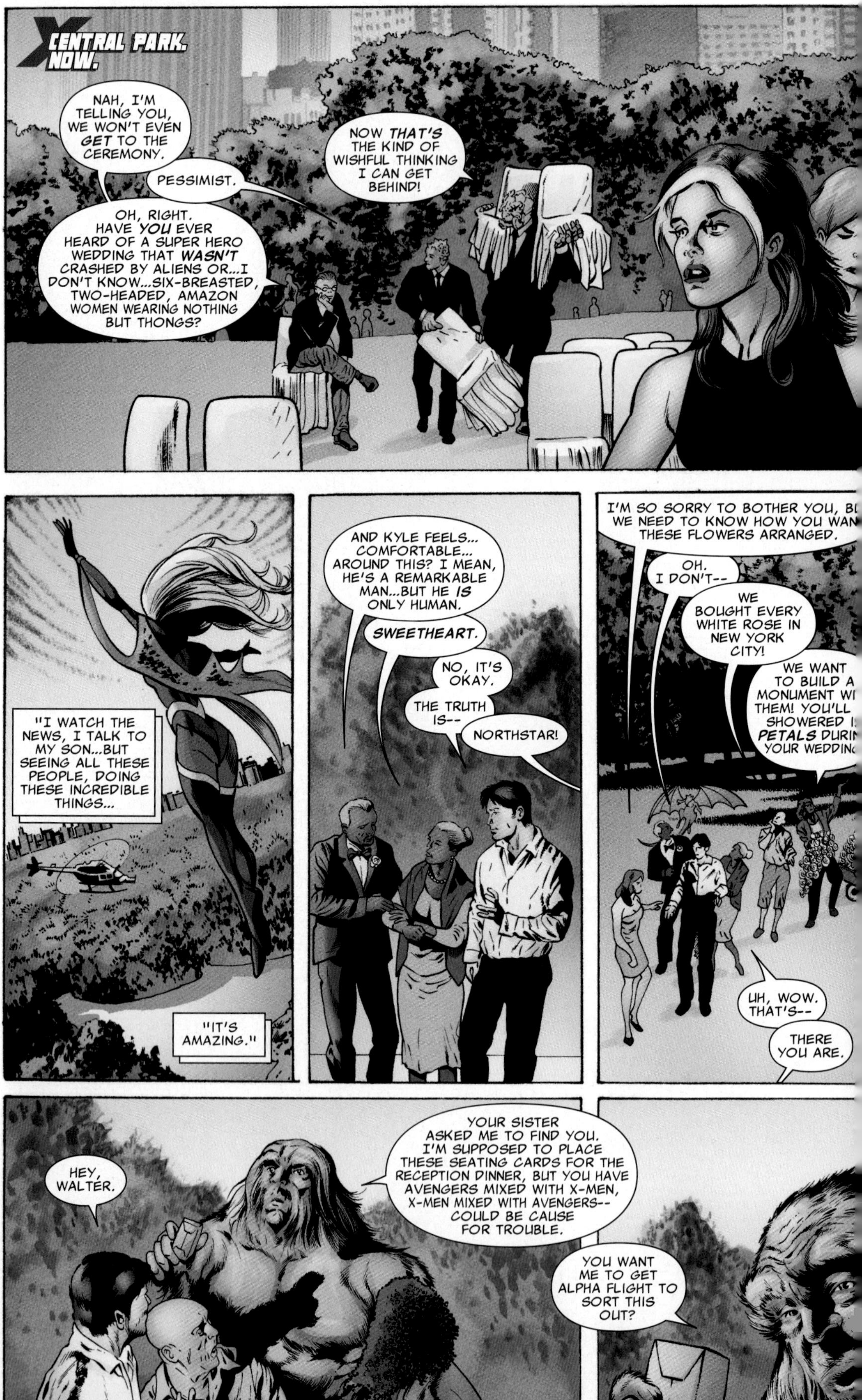
CENTRAL PARK. NOW.
NAH, I'M TELLING YOU, WE WON'T EVEN GET TO THE CEREMONY.
PESSIMIST.
OH, RIGHT. HAVE YOU EVER HEARD OF A SUPER HERO WEDDING THAT WASN'T CRASHED BY ALIENS OR...I DON'T KNOW...SIX-BREASTED, TWO-HEADED, AMAZON WOMEN WEARING NOTHING BUT THONGS?
NOW THAT'S THE KIND OF WISHFUL THINKING I CAN GET BEHIND!
"I WATCH THE NEWS, I TALK TO MY SON...BUT SEEING ALL THESE PEOPLE, DOING THESE INCREDIBLE THINGS...
"IT'S AMAZING."
AND KYLE FEELS... COMFORTABLE... AROUND THIS? I MEAN, HE'S A REMARKABLE MAN...BUT HE IS ONLY HUMAN.
SWEETHEART.
NO, IT'S OKAY.
THE TRUTH IS--
NORTHSTAR!
I'M SO SORRY TO BOTHER YOU, BU
WE NEED TO KNOW HOW YOU WAN
THESE FLOWERS ARRANGED.
OH. I DON'T--
WE BOUGHT EVERY WHITE ROSE IN NEW YORK CITY!
WE WANT TO BUILD A MONUMENT WI THEM! YOU'LL SHOWERED I PETALS DURIN YOUR WEDDING
UH, WOW. THAT'S--
THERE YOU ARE.
HEY, WALTER.
YOUR SISTER ASKED ME TO FIND YOU. I'M SUPPOSED TO PLACE THESE SEATING CARDS FOR THE RECEPTION DINNER, BUT YOU HAVE AVENGERS MIXED WITH X-MEN, X-MEN MIXED WITH AVENGERS--COULD BE CAUSE FOR TROUBLE.
YOU WANT ME TO GET ALPHA FLIGHT TO SORT THIS OUT?

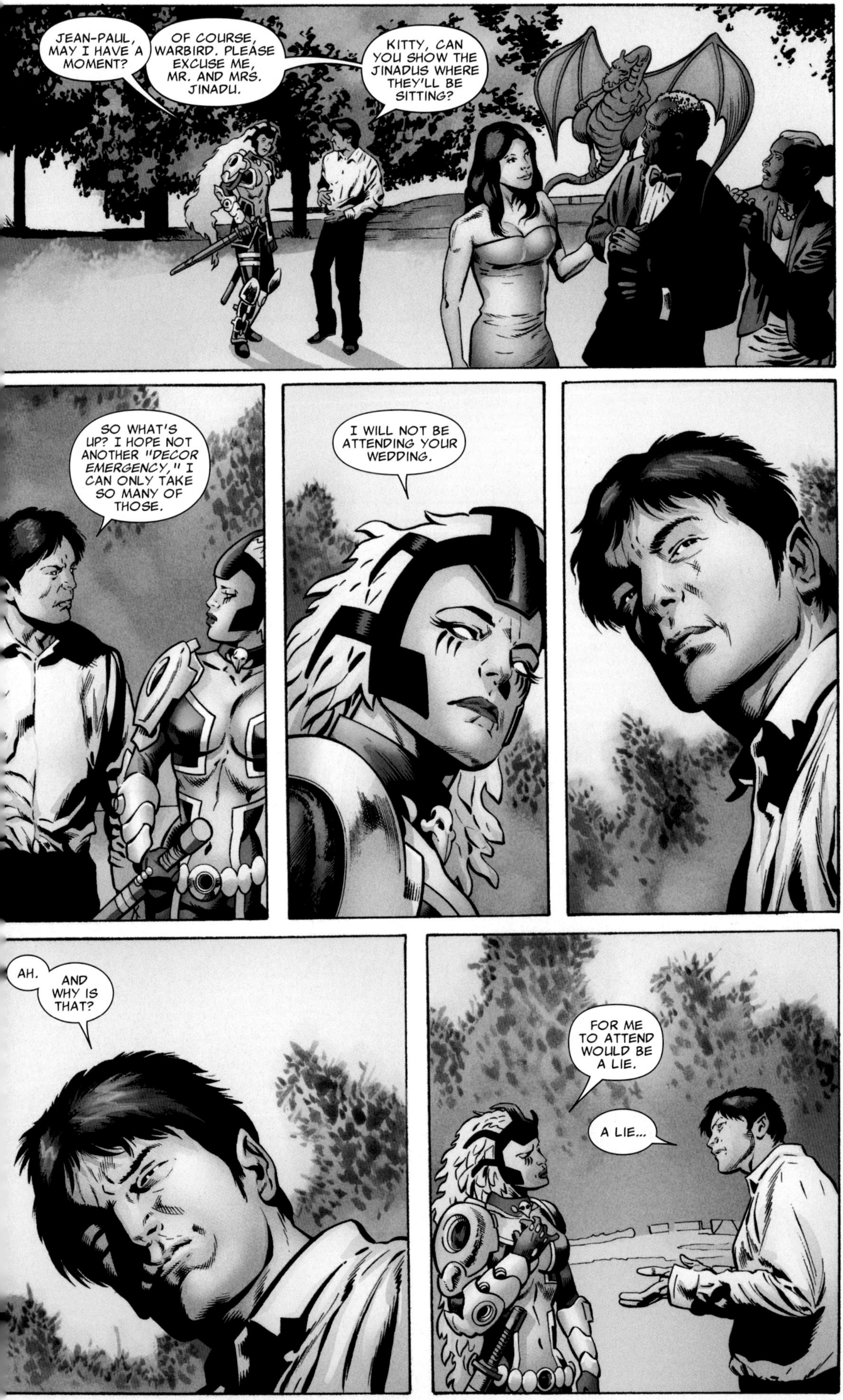

JEAN-PAUL, MAY I HAVE A MOMENT?
OF COURSE, WARBIRD. PLEASE EXCUSE ME, MR. AND MRS. JINADU.
KITTY, CAN YOU SHOW THE JINADUS WHERE THEY'LL BE SITTING?
SO WHAT'S UP? I HOPE NOT ANOTHER "DECOR EMERGENCY," I CAN ONLY TAKE SO MANY OF THOSE.
I WILL NOT BE ATTENDING YOUR WEDDING.
AH.
AND WHY IS THAT?
FOR ME TO ATTEND WOULD BE A LIE.
A LIE...

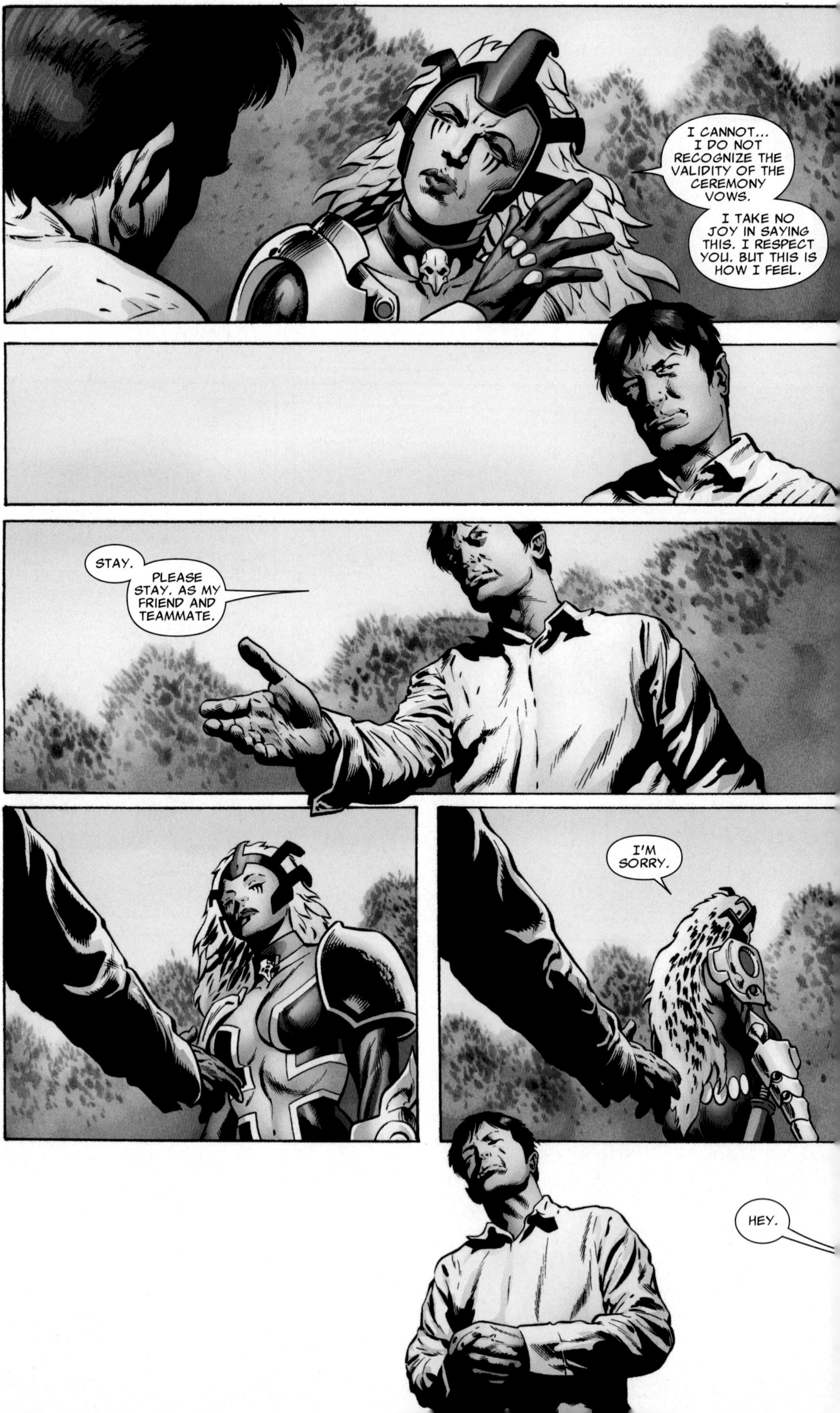

I CANNOT... I DO NOT RECOGNIZE THE VALIDITY OF THE CEREMONY VOWS.
I TAKE NO JOY IN SAYING THIS. I RESPECT YOU. BUT THIS IS HOW I FEEL.
STAY.
PLEASE STAY. AS MY FRIEND AND TEAMMATE.
I'M SORRY.
HEY.

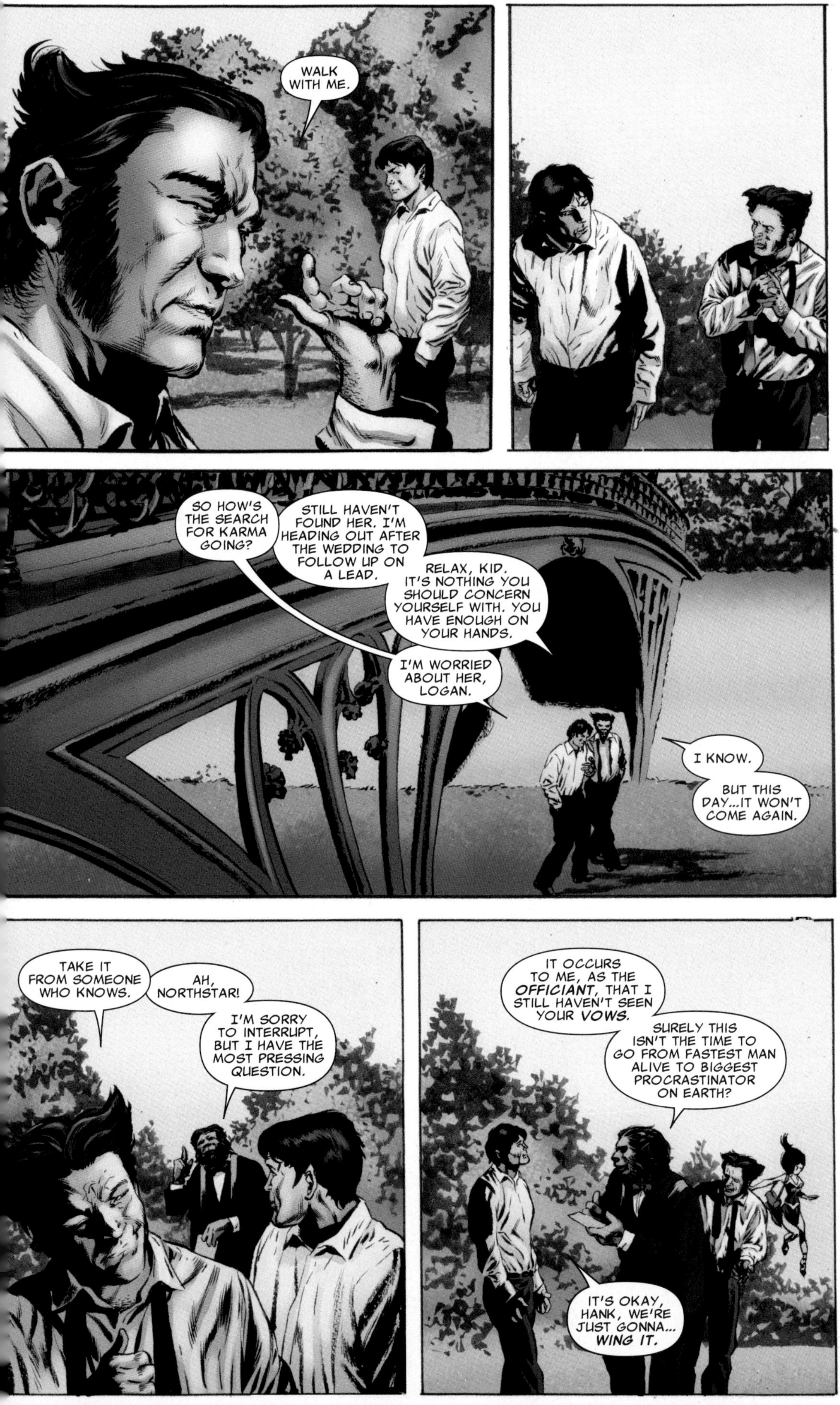
WALK WITH ME.
SO HOW'S THE SEARCH FOR KARMA GOING?
STILL HAVEN'T FOUND HER. I'M HEADING OUT AFTER THE WEDDING TO FOLLOW UP ON A LEAD.
RELAX, KID. IT'S NOTHING YOU SHOULD CONCERN YOURSELF WITH. YOU HAVE ENOUGH ON YOUR HANDS.
I'M WORRIED ABOUT HER, LOGAN.
I KNOW.
BUT THIS DAY...IT WON'T COME AGAIN.
TAKE IT FROM SOMEONE WHO KNOWS.
AH, NORTHSTAR!
I'M SORRY TO INTERRUPT, BUT I HAVE THE MOST PRESSING QUESTION.
IT OCCURS TO ME, AS THE OFFICIANT, THAT I STILL HAVEN'T SEEN YOUR VOWS.
SURELY THIS ISN'T THE TIME TO GO FROM FASTEST MAN ALIVE TO BIGGEST PROCRASTINATOR ON EARTH?
IT'S OKAY, HANK, WE'RE JUST GONNA... WING IT.

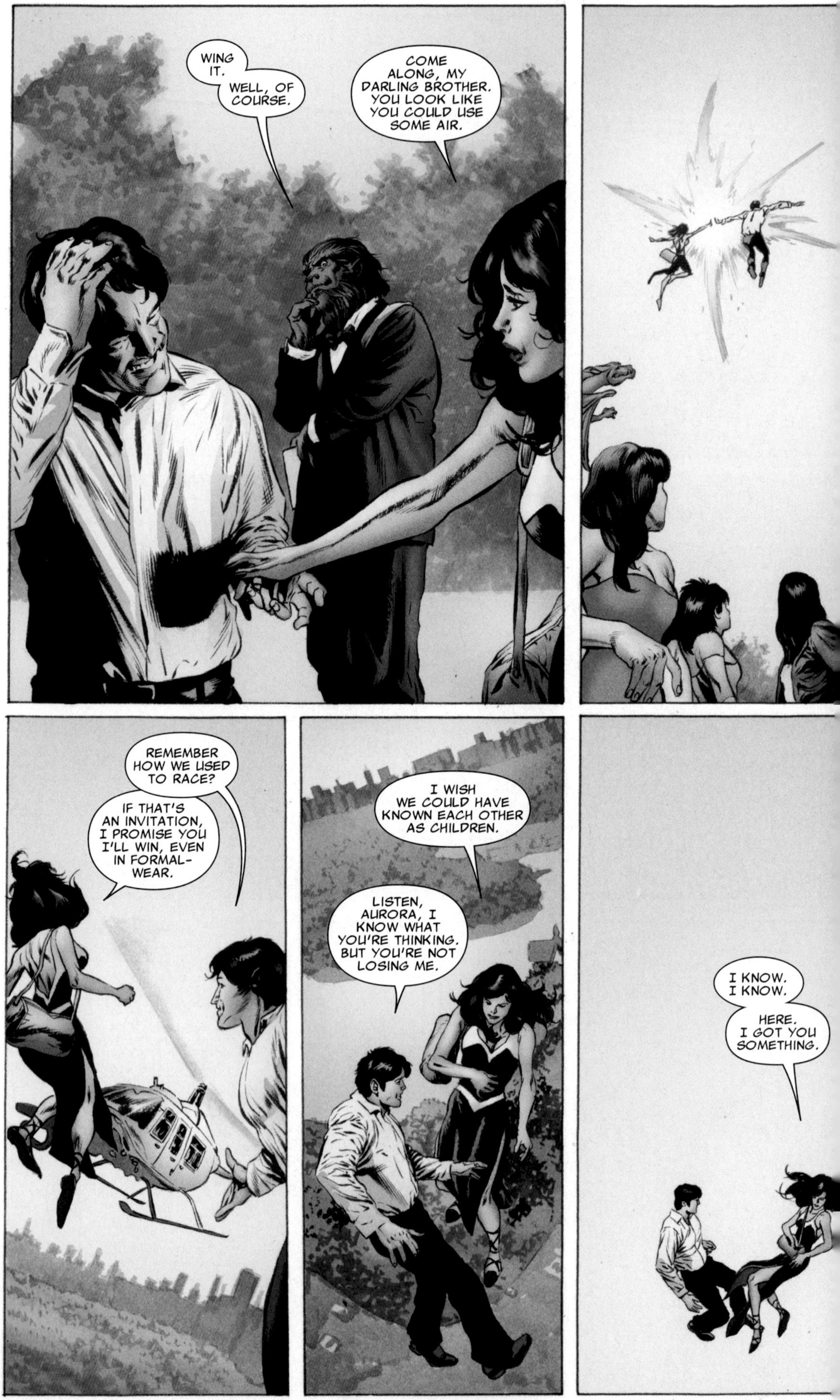

WING IT.
WELL, OF COURSE.
COME ALONG, MY DARLING BROTHER. YOU LOOK LIKE YOU COULD USE SOME AIR.
REMEMBER HOW WE USED TO RACE?
IF THAT'S AN INVITATION, I PROMISE YOU I'LL WIN, EVEN IN FORMAL-WEAR.
I WISH WE COULD HAVE KNOWN EACH OTHER AS CHILDREN.
LISTEN, AURORA, I KNOW WHAT YOU'RE THINKING. BUT YOU'RE NOT LOSING ME.
I KNOW. I KNOW.
HERE. I GOT YOU SOMETHING.

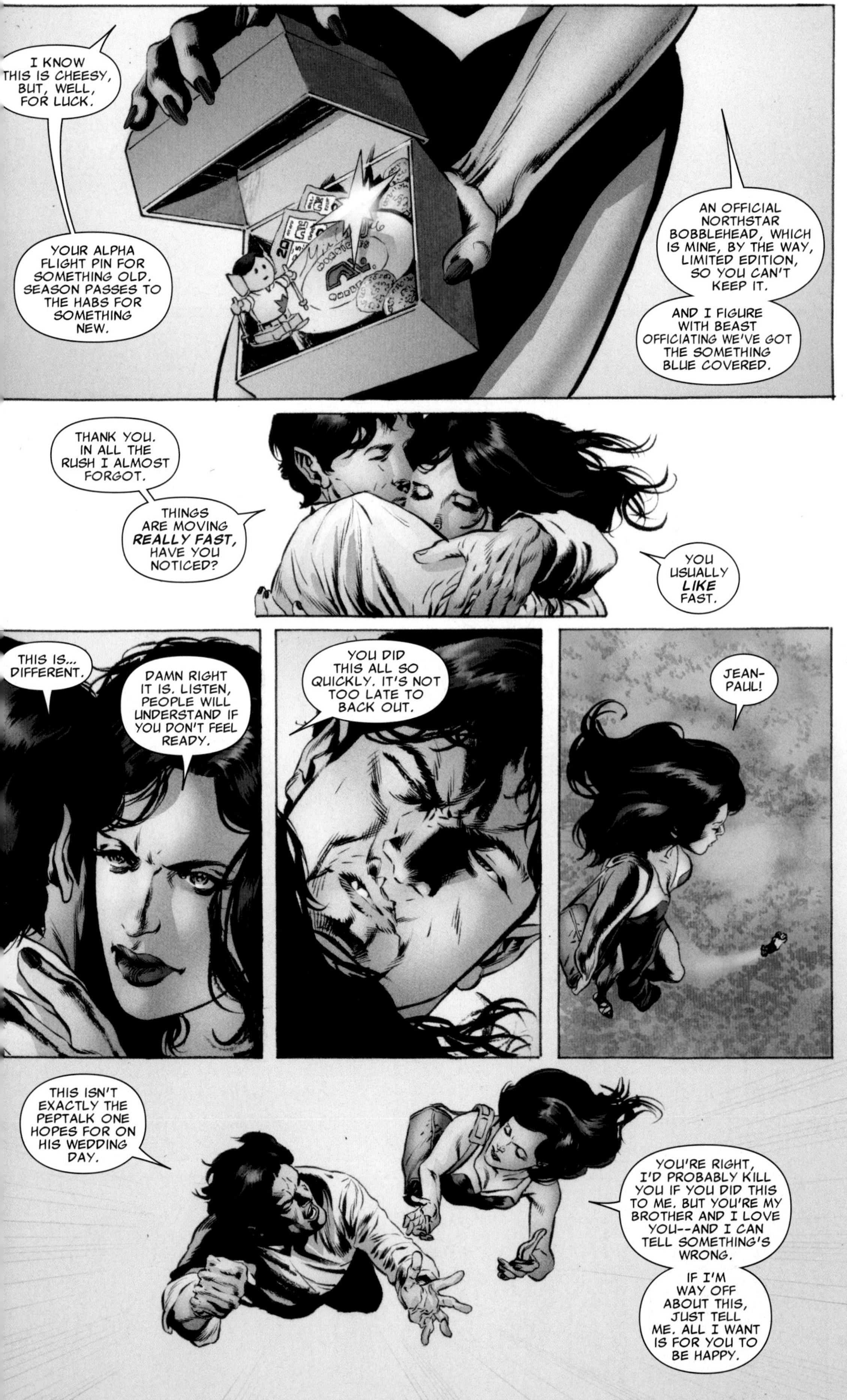
I KNOW THIS IS CHEESY, BUT, WELL, FOR LUCK.
YOUR ALPHA FLIGHT PIN FOR SOMETHING OLD. SEASON PASSES TO THE HABS FOR SOMETHING NEW.
AN OFFICIAL NORTHSTAR BOBBLEHEAD, WHICH IS MINE, BY THE WAY, LIMITED EDITION, SO YOU CAN'T KEEP IT.
AND I FIGURE WITH BEAST OFFICIATING WE'VE GOT THE SOMETHING BLUE COVERED.
THANK YOU. IN ALL THE RUSH I ALMOST FORGOT.
THINGS ARE MOVING *REALLY FAST,* HAVE YOU NOTICED?
YOU USUALLY *LIKE* FAST.
THIS IS... DIFFERENT.
DAMN RIGHT IT IS. LISTEN, PEOPLE WILL UNDERSTAND IF YOU DON'T FEEL READY.
YOU DID THIS ALL SO QUICKLY. IT'S NOT TOO LATE TO BACK OUT.
JEAN-PAUL!
THIS ISN'T EXACTLY THE PEPTALK ONE HOPES FOR ON HIS WEDDING DAY.
YOU'RE RIGHT, I'D PROBABLY KILL YOU IF YOU DID THIS TO ME. BUT YOU'RE MY BROTHER AND I LOVE YOU--AND I CAN TELL SOMETHING'S WRONG.
IF I'M WAY OFF ABOUT THIS, JUST TELL ME. ALL I WANT IS FOR YOU TO BE HAPPY.

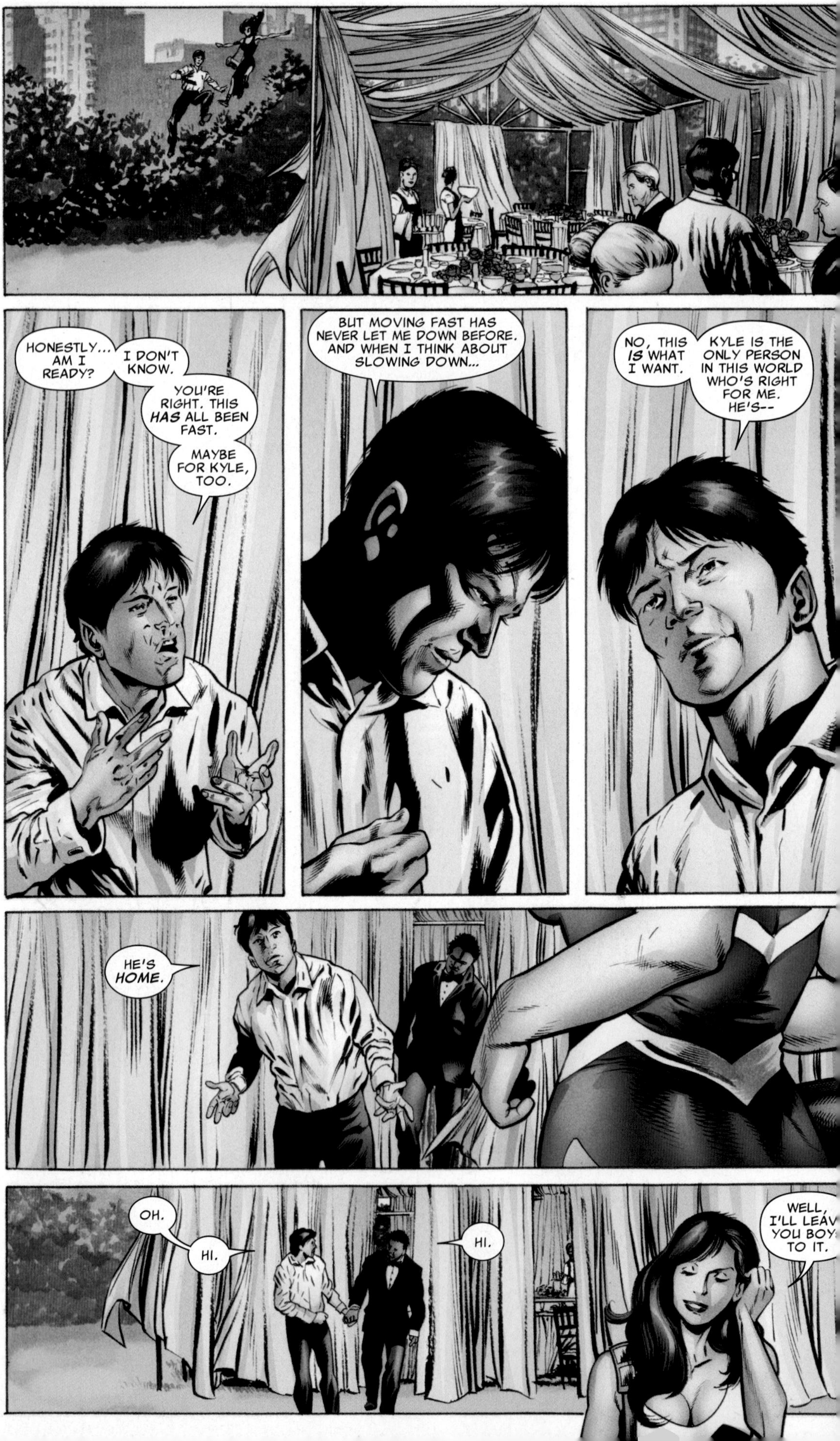
HONESTLY... AM I READY?
I DON'T KNOW.
YOU'RE RIGHT. THIS HAS ALL BEEN FAST.
MAYBE FOR KYLE, TOO.
BUT MOVING FAST HAS NEVER LET ME DOWN BEFORE. AND WHEN I THINK ABOUT SLOWING DOWN...
NO, THIS IS WHAT I WANT.
KYLE IS THE ONLY PERSON IN THIS WORLD WHO'S RIGHT FOR ME. HE'S--
HE'S HOME.
OH.
HI.
HI.
WELL, I'LL LEAV YOU BOY TO IT.

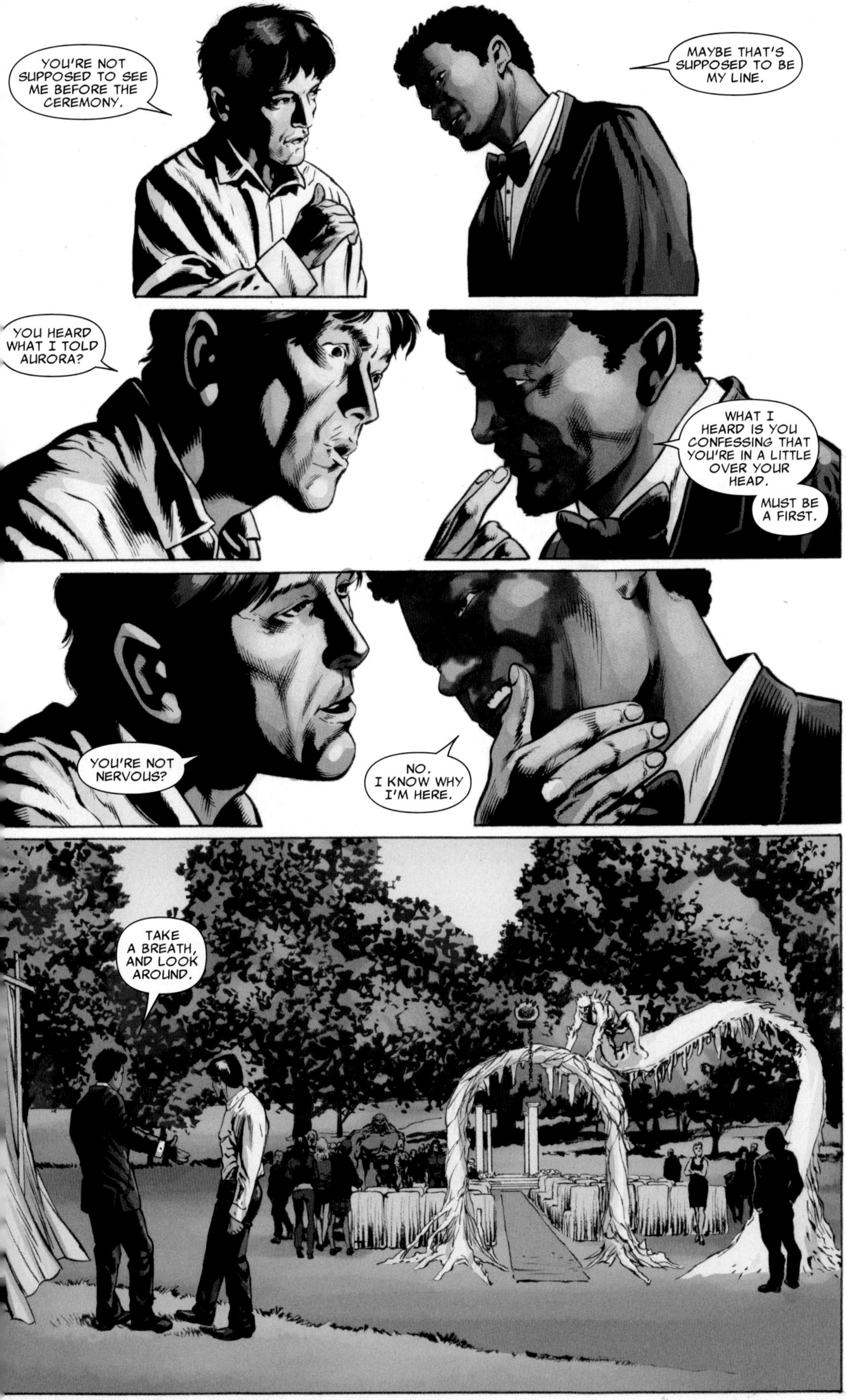
YOU'RE NOT SUPPOSED TO SEE ME BEFORE THE CEREMONY.
MAYBE THAT'S SUPPOSED TO BE MY LINE.
YOU HEARD WHAT I TOLD AURORA?
WHAT I HEARD IS YOU CONFESSING THAT YOU'RE IN A LITTLE OVER YOUR HEAD.
MUST BE A FIRST.
YOU'RE NOT NERVOUS?
NO. I KNOW WHY I'M HERE.
TAKE A BREATH, AND LOOK AROUND.

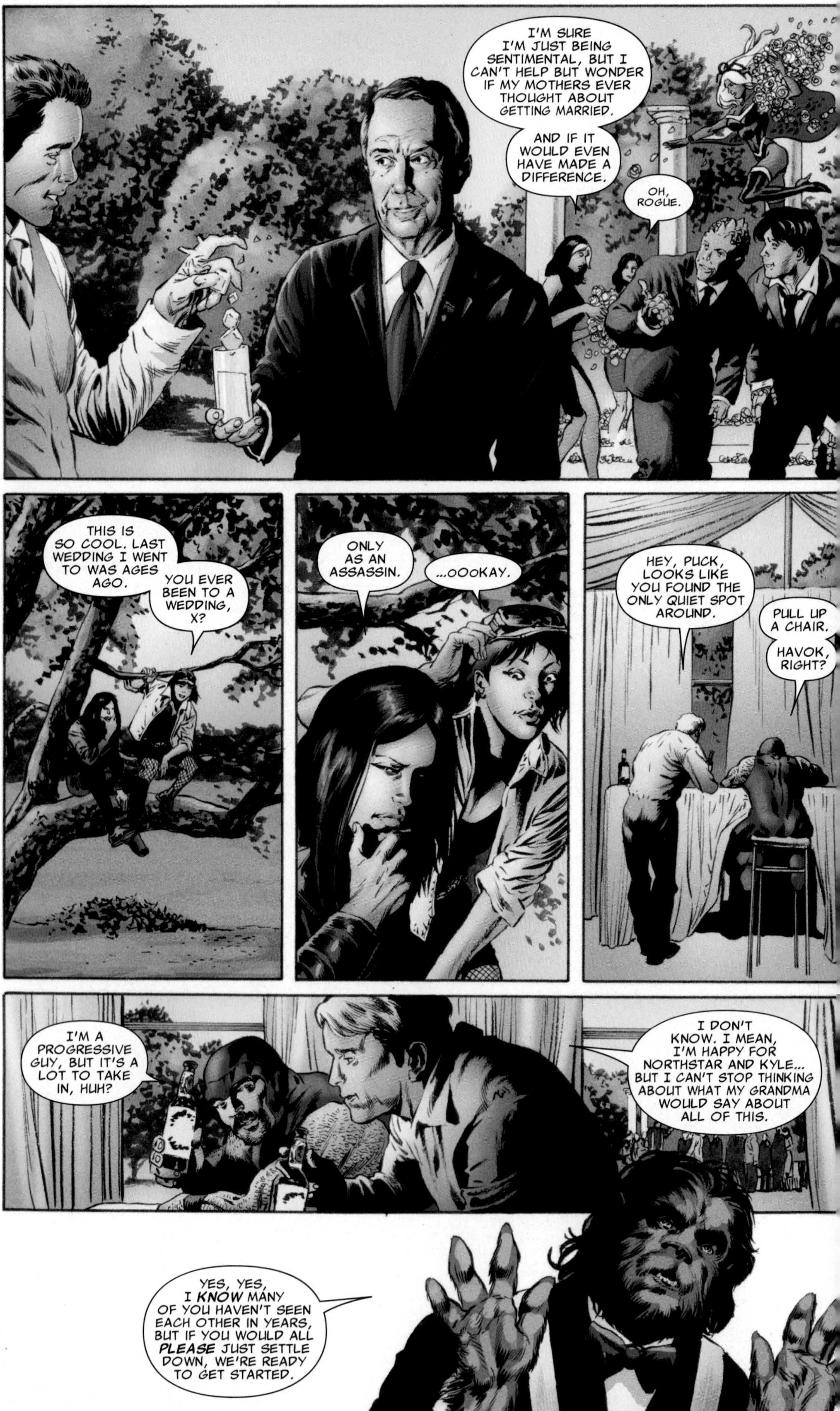

I'M SURE I'M JUST BEING SENTIMENTAL, BUT I CAN'T HELP BUT WONDER IF MY MOTHERS EVER THOUGHT ABOUT GETTING MARRIED.
AND IF IT WOULD EVEN HAVE MADE A DIFFERENCE.
OH, ROGUE.
THIS IS SO COOL. LAST WEDDING I WENT TO WAS AGES AGO.
YOU EVER BEEN TO A WEDDING, X?
ONLY AS AN ASSASSIN.
...OOOKAY.
HEY, PUCK, LOOKS LIKE YOU FOUND THE ONLY QUIET SPOT AROUND.
PULL UP A CHAIR.
HAVOK, RIGHT?
I'M A PROGRESSIVE GUY, BUT IT'S A LOT TO TAKE IN, HUH?
I DON'T KNOW. I MEAN, I'M HAPPY FOR NORTHSTAR AND KYLE... BUT I CAN'T STOP THINKING ABOUT WHAT MY GRANDMA WOULD SAY ABOUT ALL OF THIS.
YES, YES, I *KNOW* MANY OF YOU HAVEN'T SEEN EACH OTHER IN YEARS, BUT IF YOU WOULD ALL *PLEASE* JUST SETTLE DOWN, WE'RE READY TO GET STARTED.

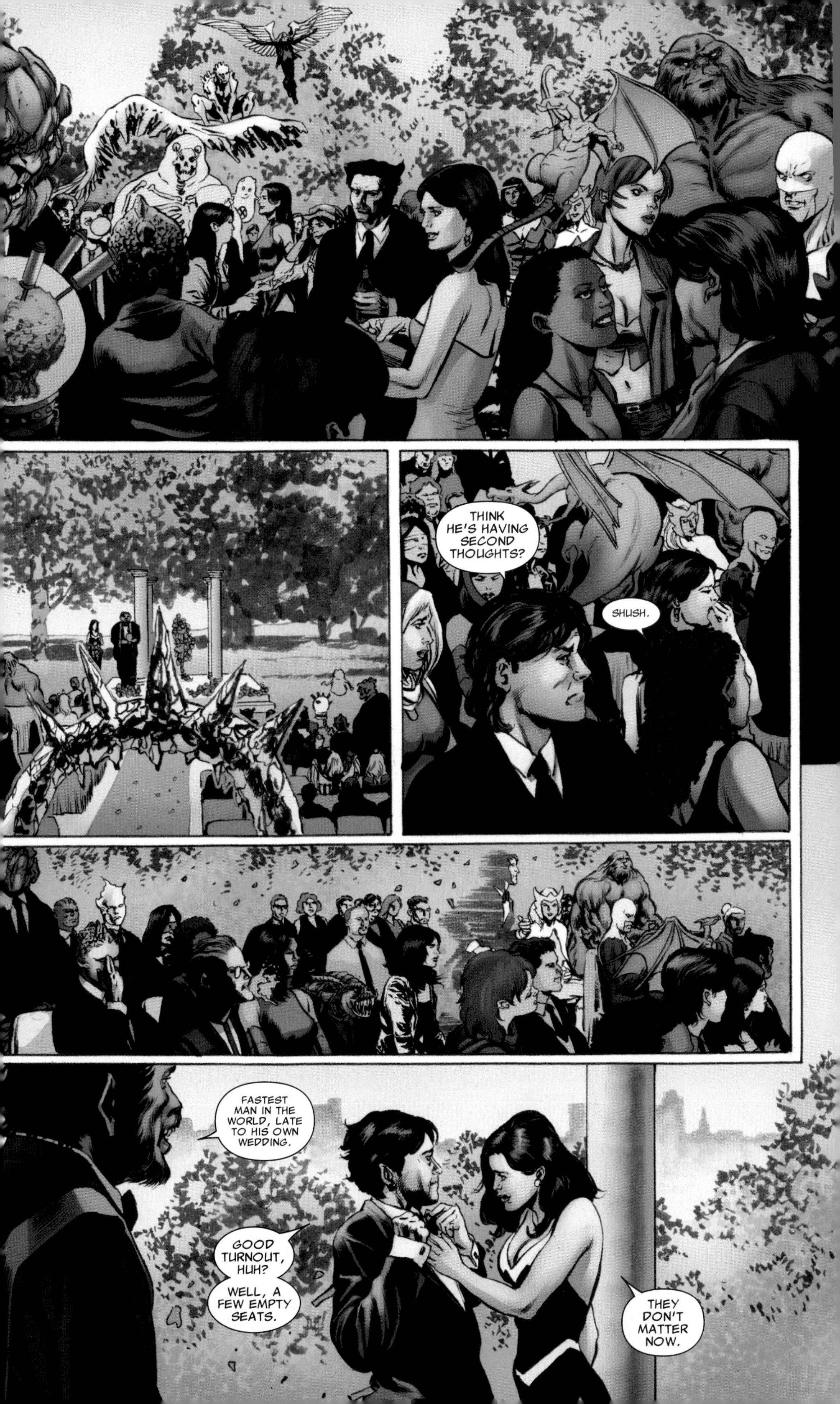
THINK HE'S HAVING SECOND THOUGHTS?
SHUSH.
FASTEST MAN IN THE WORLD, LATE TO HIS OWN WEDDING.
GOOD TURNOUT, HUH?
WELL, A FEW EMPTY SEATS.
THEY DON'T MATTER NOW.

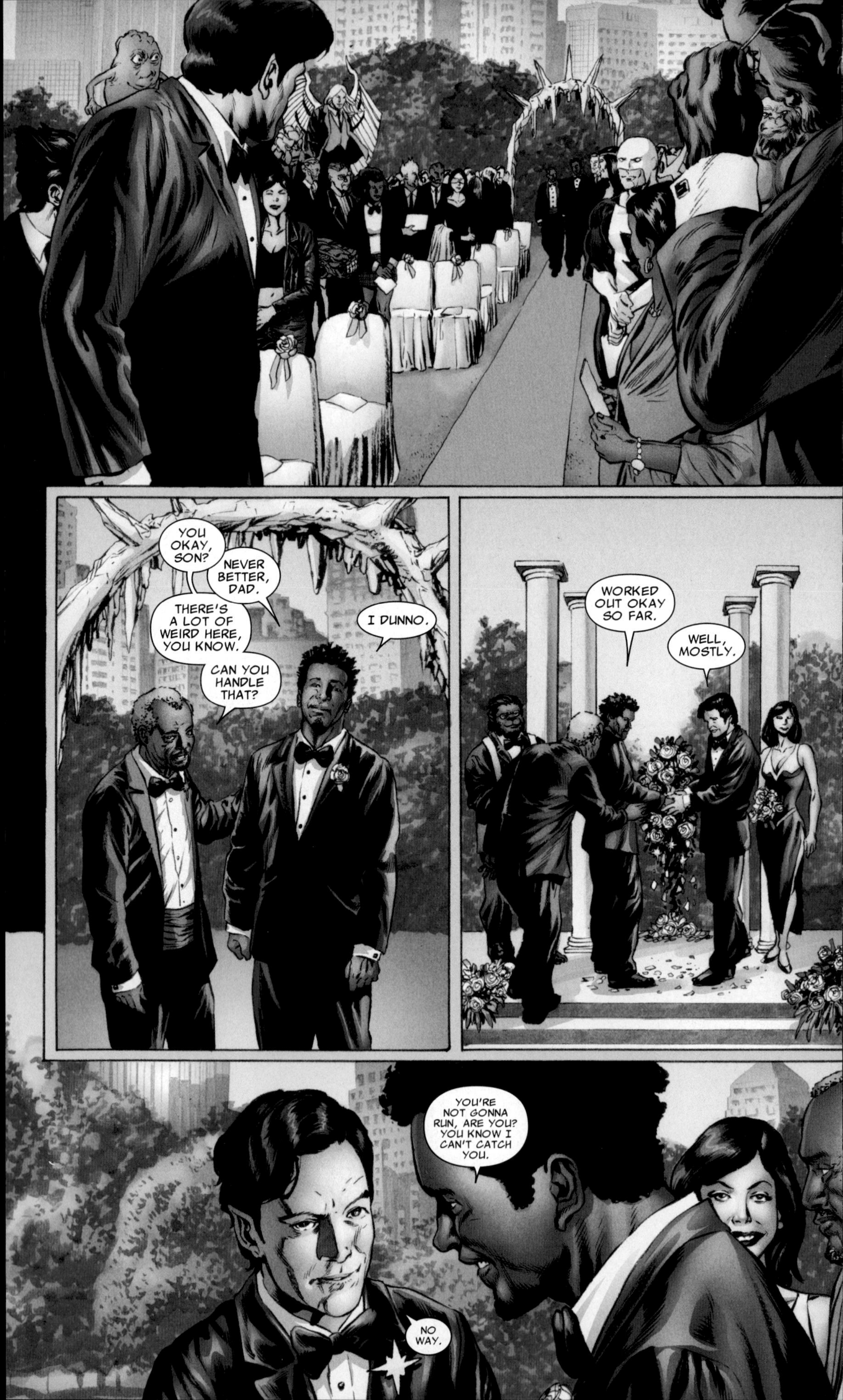
YOU OKAY, SON?
NEVER BETTER, DAD.
THERE'S A LOT OF WEIRD HERE, YOU KNOW.
CAN YOU HANDLE THAT?
I DUNNO.
WORKED OUT OKAY SO FAR.
WELL, MOSTLY.
YOU'RE NOT GONNA RUN, ARE YOU? YOU KNOW I CAN'T CATCH YOU.
NO WAY.

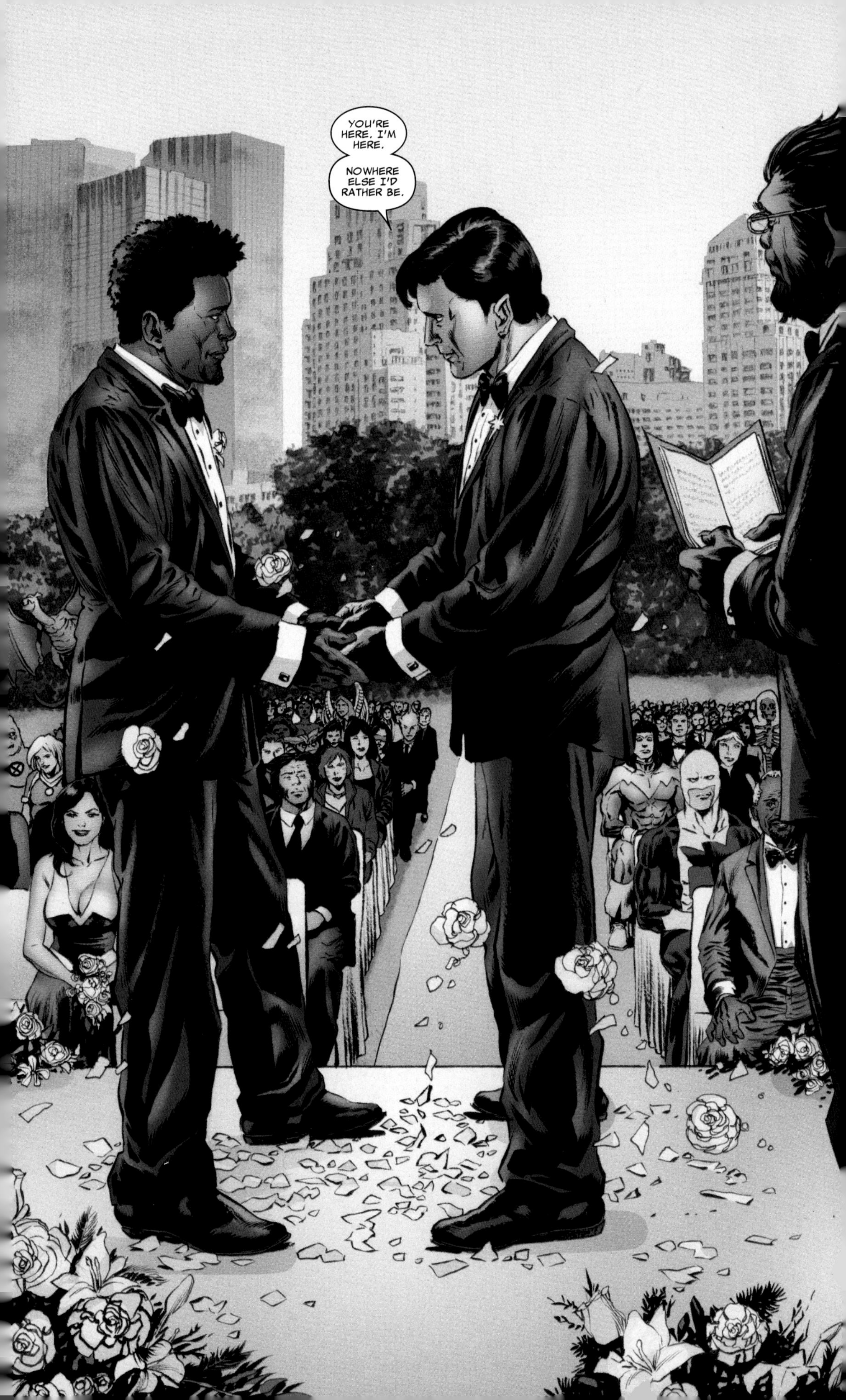
YOU'RE HERE. I'M HERE.
NOWHERE ELSE I'D RATHER BE.

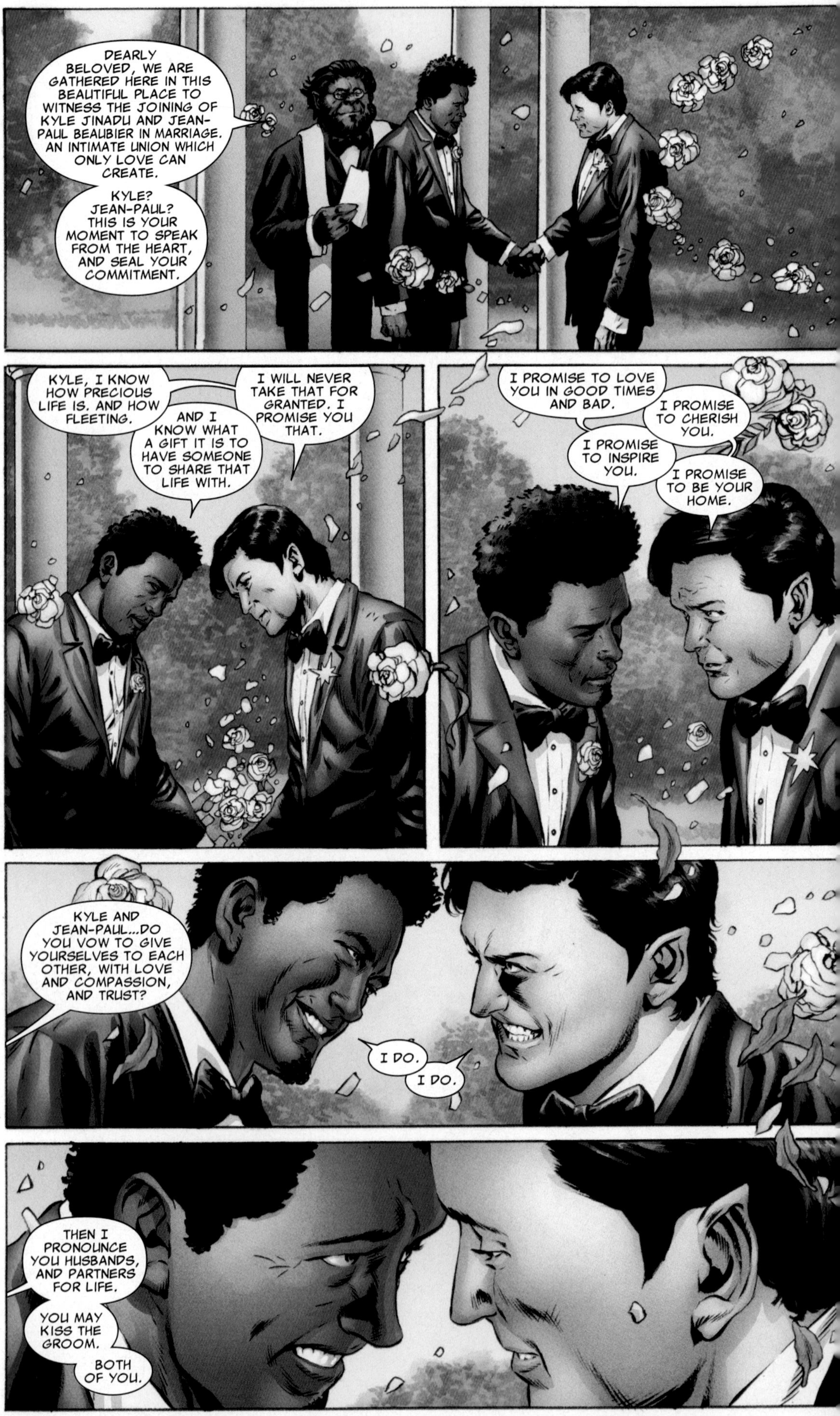
DEARLY BELOVED, WE ARE GATHERED HERE IN THIS BEAUTIFUL PLACE TO WITNESS THE JOINING OF KYLE JINADU AND JEAN-PAUL BEAUBIER IN MARRIAGE. AN INTIMATE UNION WHICH ONLY LOVE CAN CREATE.
KYLE? JEAN-PAUL? THIS IS YOUR MOMENT TO SPEAK FROM THE HEART, AND SEAL YOUR COMMITMENT.
KYLE, I KNOW HOW PRECIOUS LIFE IS. AND HOW FLEETING.
I WILL NEVER TAKE THAT FOR GRANTED. I PROMISE YOU THAT.
AND I KNOW WHAT A GIFT IT IS TO HAVE SOMEONE TO SHARE THAT LIFE WITH.
I PROMISE TO LOVE YOU IN GOOD TIMES AND BAD.
I PROMISE TO CHERISH YOU.
I PROMISE TO INSPIRE YOU.
I PROMISE TO BE YOUR HOME.
KYLE AND JEAN-PAUL...DO YOU VOW TO GIVE YOURSELVES TO EACH OTHER, WITH LOVE AND COMPASSION, AND TRUST?
I DO.
I DO.
THEN I PRONOUNCE YOU HUSBANDS, AND PARTNERS FOR LIFE.
YOU MAY KISS THE GROOM.
BOTH OF YOU.

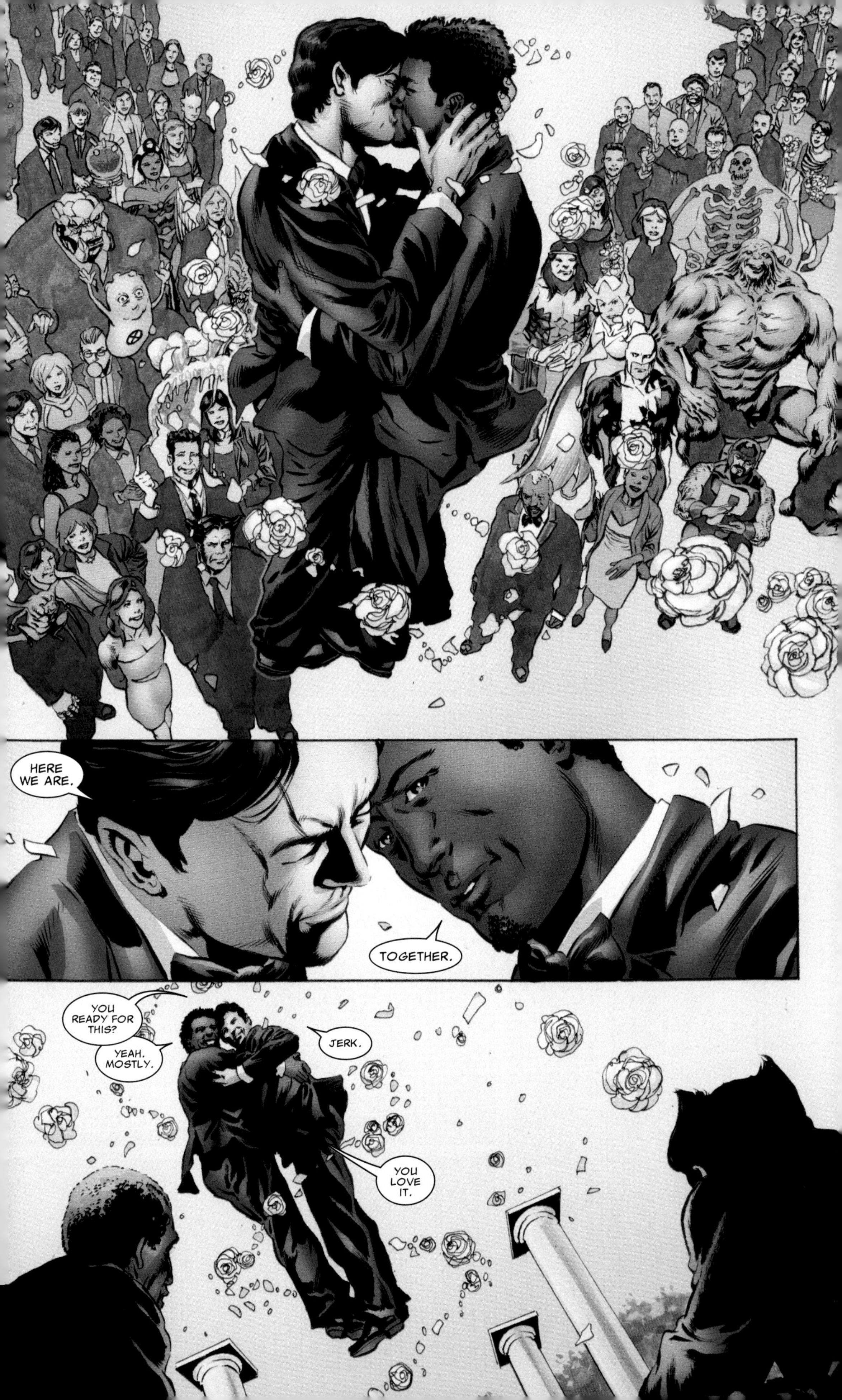
HERE WE ARE.
TOGETHER.
YOU READY FOR THIS?
YEAH. MOSTLY.
JERK.
YOU LOVE IT.

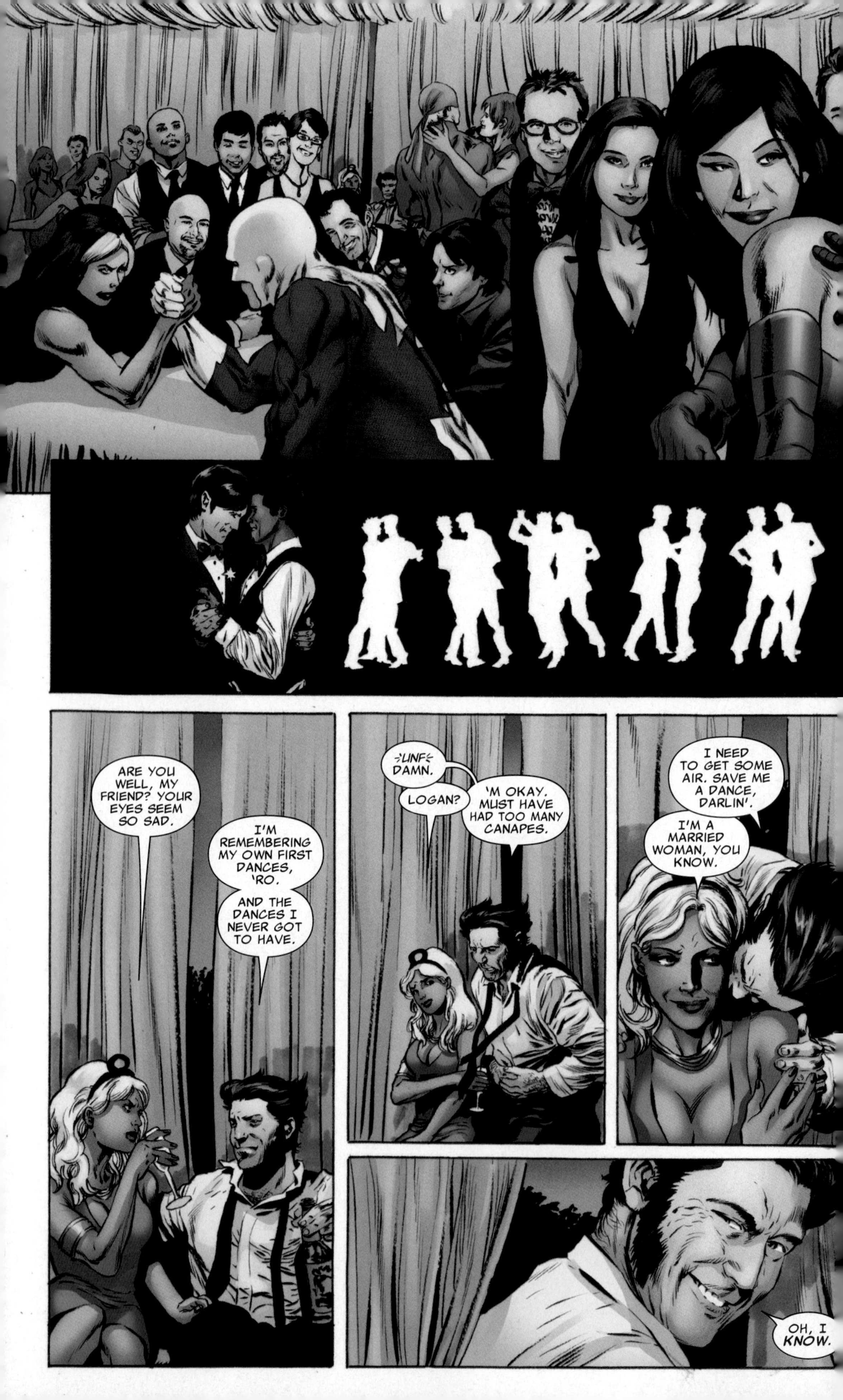
ARE YOU WELL, MY FRIEND? YOUR EYES SEEM SO SAD.
I'M REMEMBERING MY OWN FIRST DANCES, 'RO.
AND THE DANCES I NEVER GOT TO HAVE.
UNF DAMN.
LOGAN?
'M OKAY. MUST HAVE HAD TOO MANY CANAPES.
I NEED TO GET SOME AIR. SAVE ME A DANCE, DARLIN'.
I'M A MARRIED WOMAN, YOU KNOW.
OH, I KNOW.

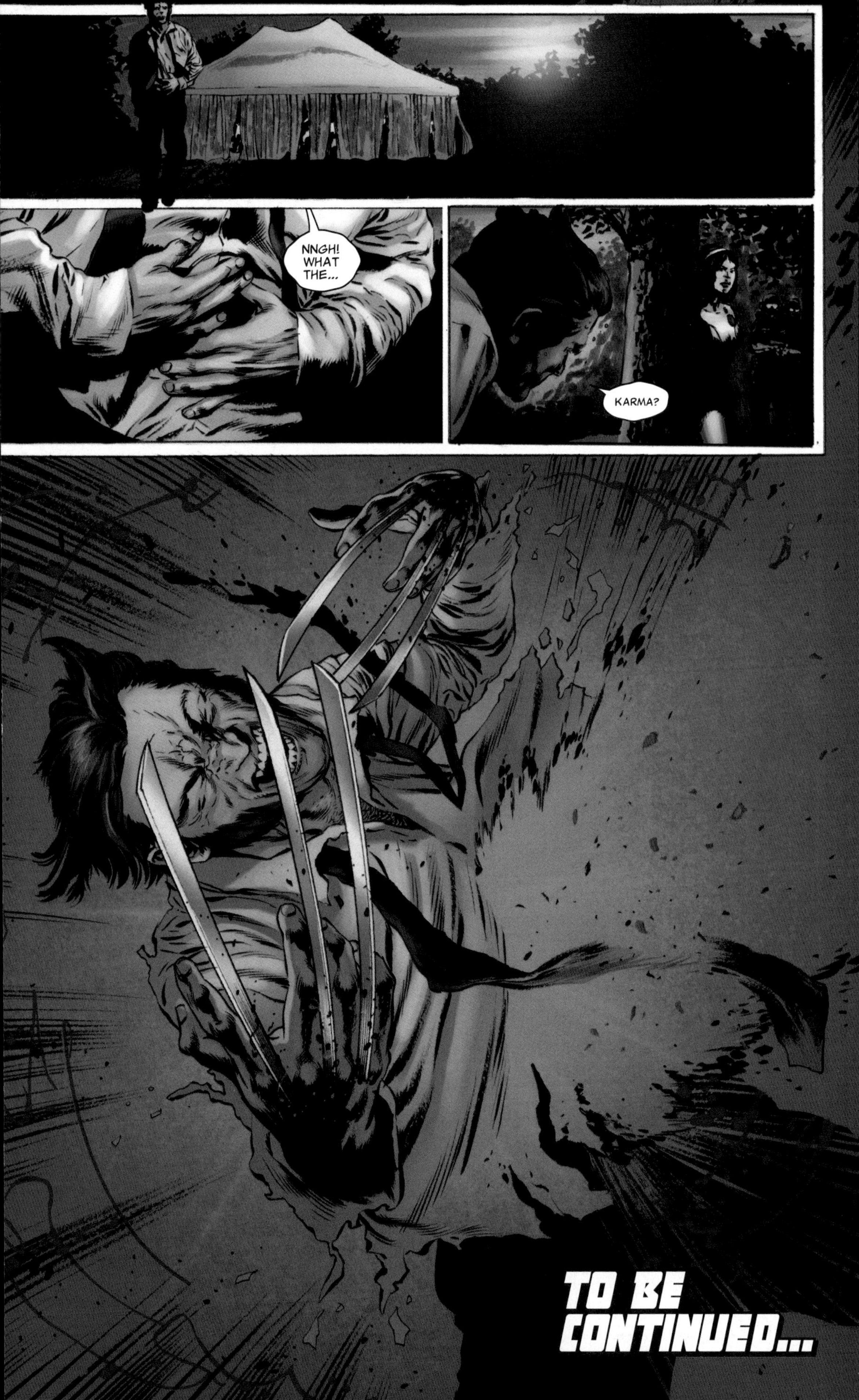
NNGH! WHAT THE...
KARMA?
TO BE CONTINUED...

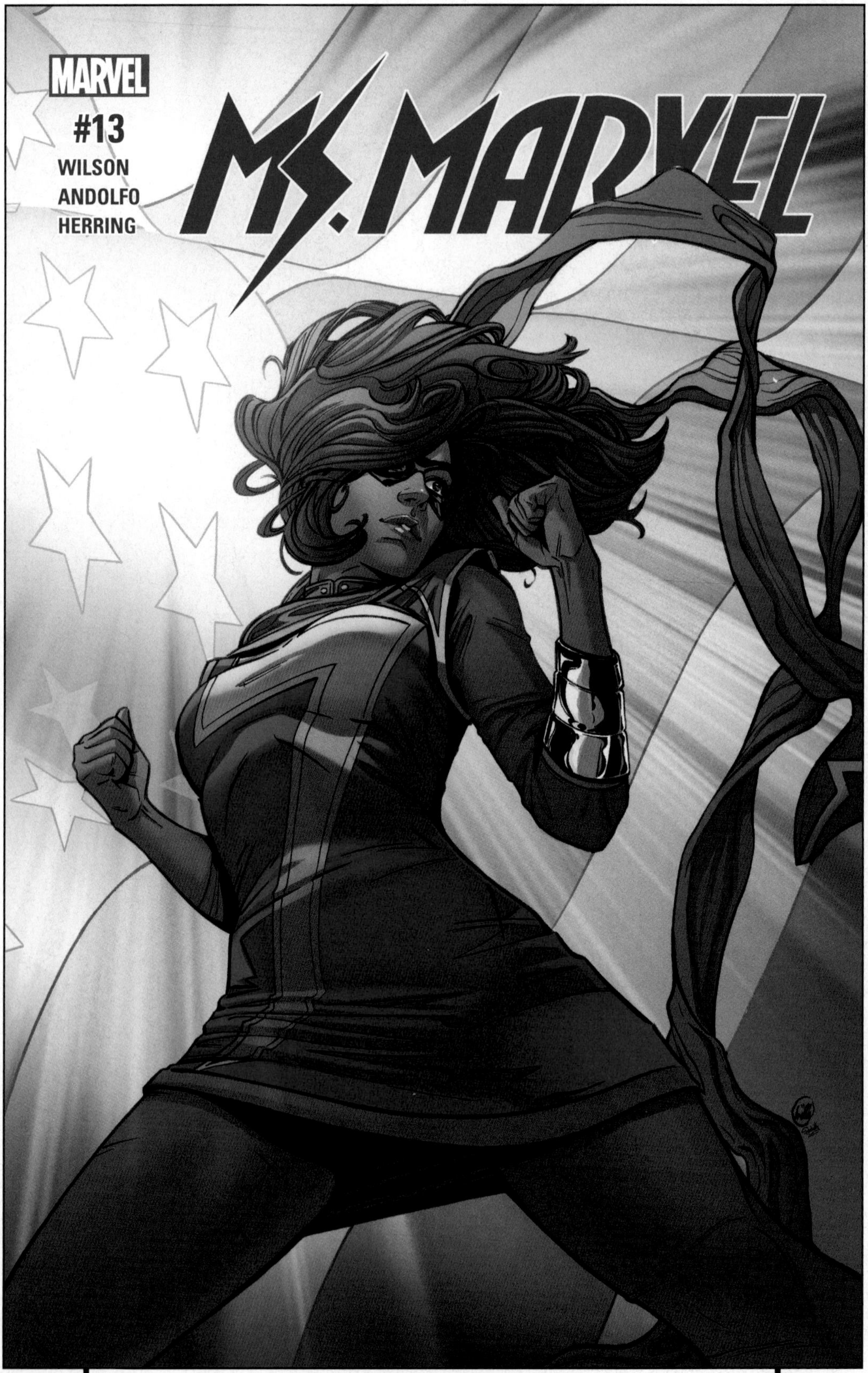

MARVEL
#13
WILSON
ANDOLFO
HERRING
MS. MARVEL

"ELECTION DAY"

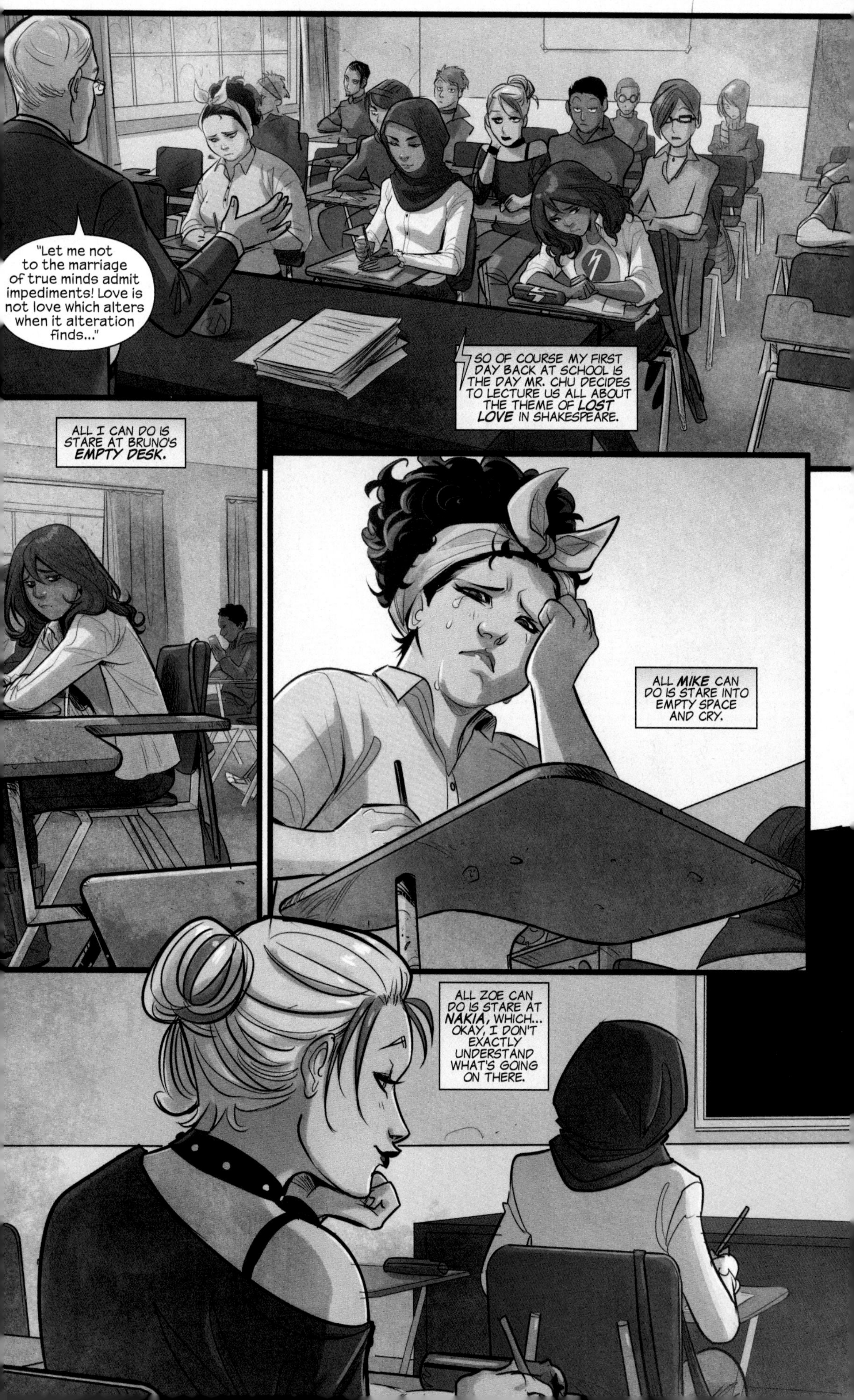
"Let me not to the marriage of true minds admit impediments! Love is not love which alters when it alteration finds..."
SO OF COURSE MY FIRST DAY BACK AT SCHOOL IS THE DAY MR. CHU DECIDES TO LECTURE US ALL ABOUT THE THEME OF LOST LOVE IN SHAKESPEARE.
ALL I CAN DO IS STARE AT BRUNO'S EMPTY DESK.
ALL MIKE CAN DO IS STARE INTO EMPTY SPACE AND CRY.
ALL ZOE CAN DO IS STARE AT NAKIA, WHICH... OKAY, I DON'T EXACTLY UNDERSTAND WHAT'S GOING ON THERE.

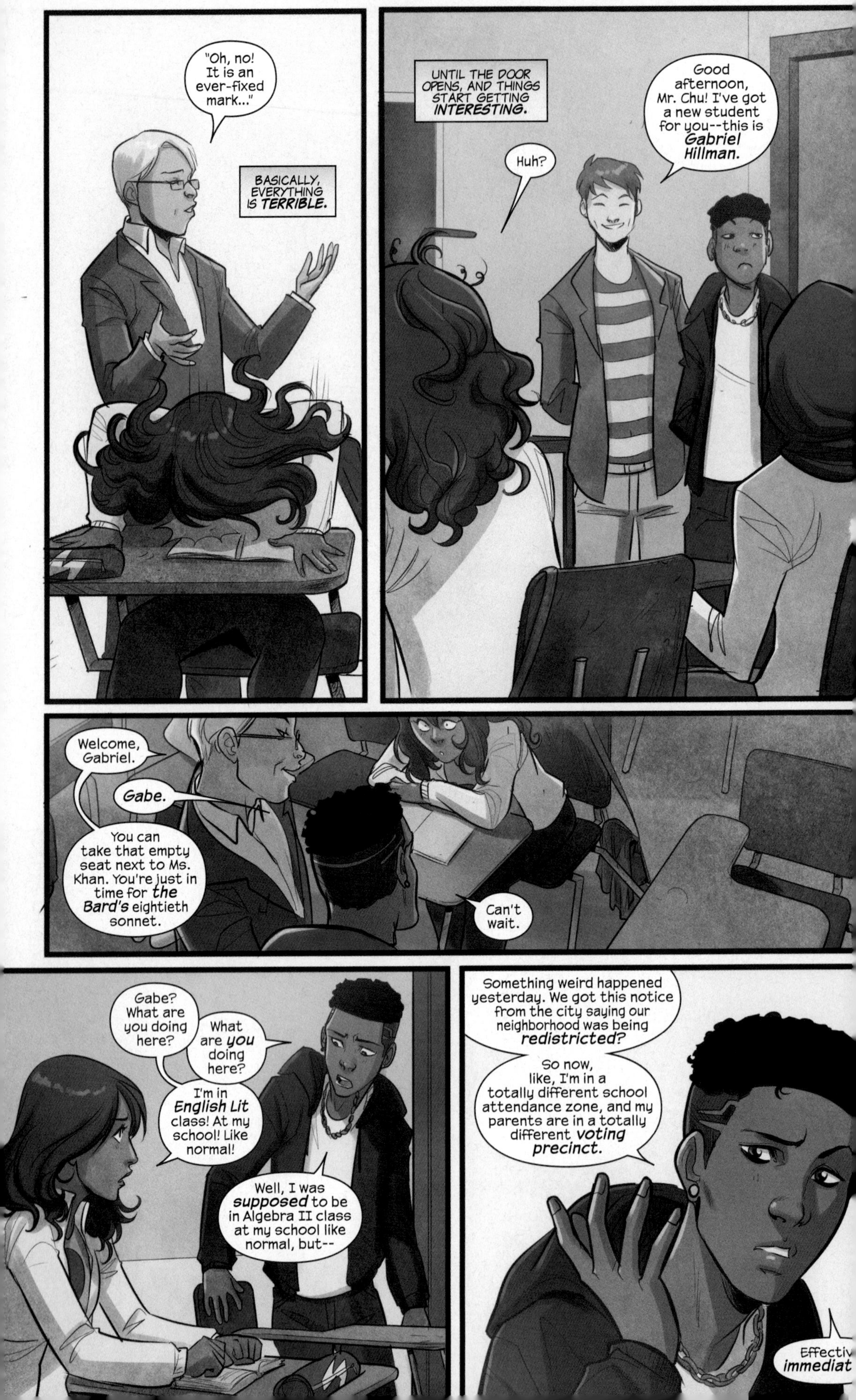
"Oh, no! It is an ever-fixed mark..."
BASICALLY, EVERYTHING IS TERRIBLE.
UNTIL THE DOOR OPENS, AND THINGS START GETTING INTERESTING.
Huh?
Good afternoon, Mr. Chu! I've got a new student for you--this is Gabriel Hillman.
Welcome, Gabriel.
Gabe.
You can take that empty seat next to Ms. Khan. You're just in time for the Bard's eightieth sonnet.
Can't wait.
Gabe? What are you doing here?
What are you doing here?
I'm in English Lit class! At my school! Like normal!
Well, I was supposed to be in Algebra II class at my school like normal, but--
Something weird happened yesterday. We got this notice from the city saying our neighborhood was being redistricted?
So now, like, I'm in a totally different school attendance zone, and my parents are in a totally different voting precinct.

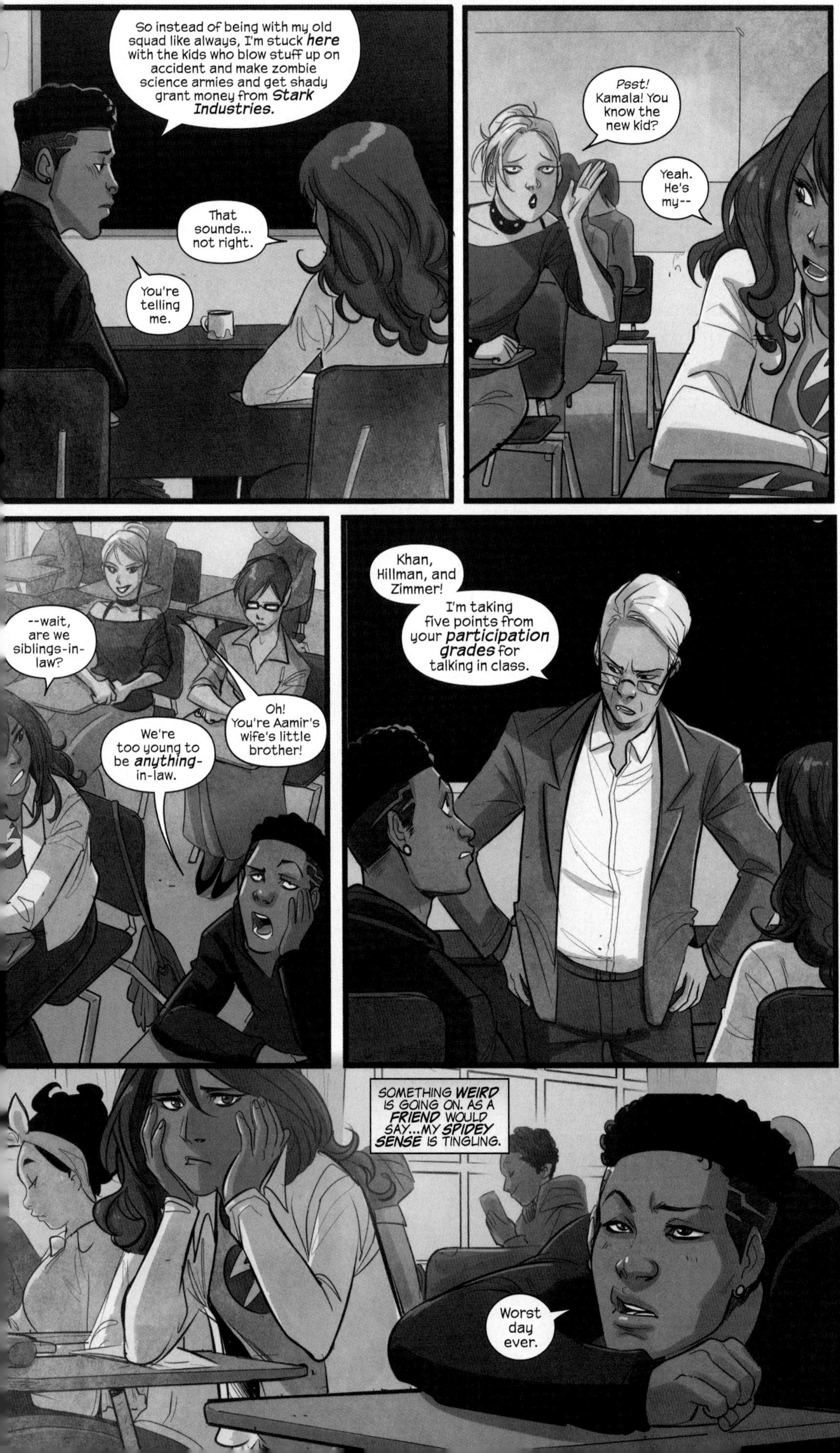
So instead of being with my old squad like always, I'm stuck here with the kids who blow stuff up on accident and make zombie science armies and get shady grant money from Stark Industries.
That sounds... not right.
You're telling me.
Psst! Kamala! You know the new kid?
Yeah. He's my--
--wait, are we siblings-in-law?
Oh! You're Aamir's wife's little brother!
We're too young to be anything-in-law.
Khan, Hillman, and Zimmer!
I'm taking five points from your participation grades for talking in class.
SOMETHING WEIRD IS GOING ON. AS A FRIEND WOULD SAY...MY SPIDEY SENSE IS TINGLING.
Worst day ever.

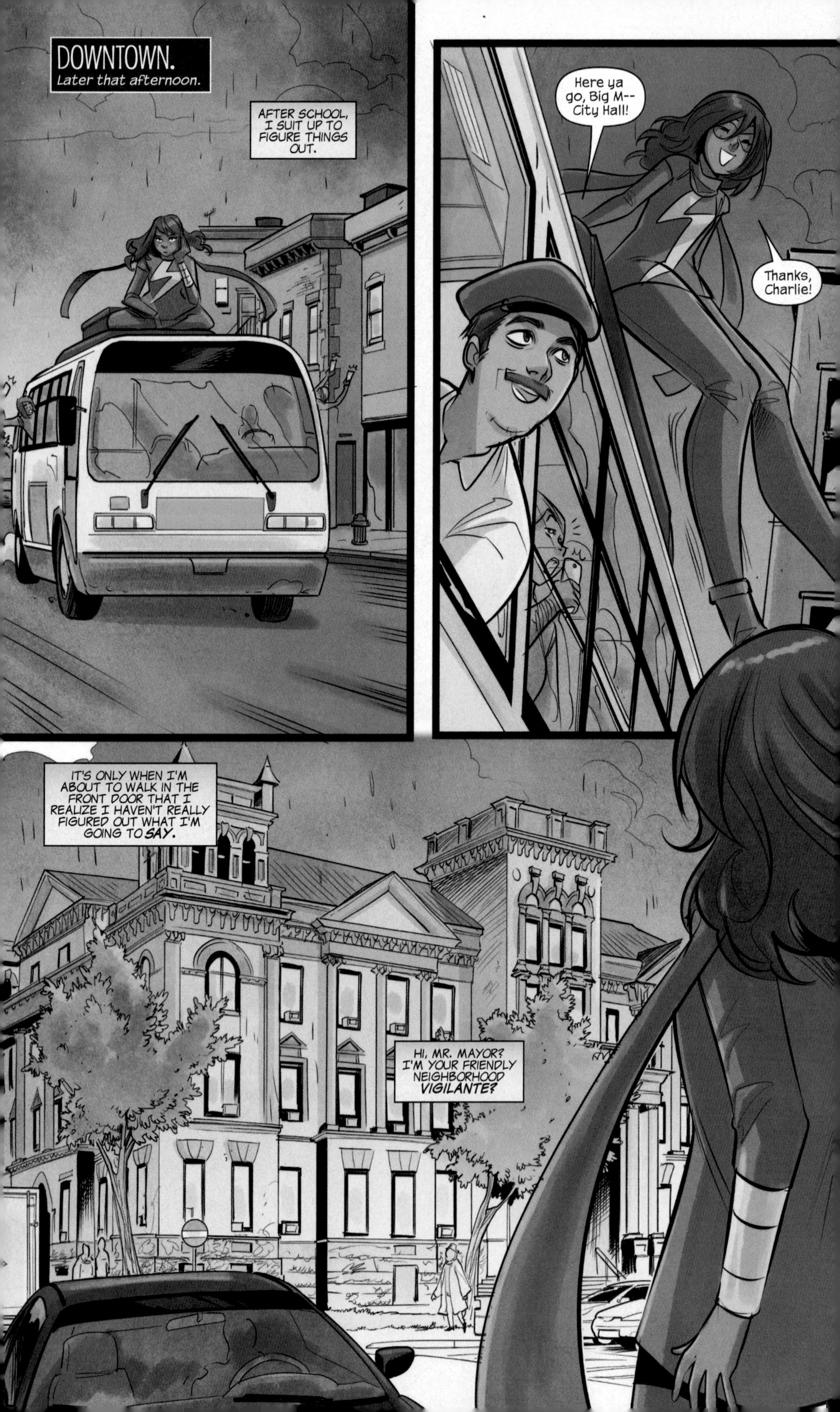
DOWNTOWN.
Later that afternoon.
AFTER SCHOOL, I SUIT UP TO FIGURE THINGS OUT.
Here ya go, Big M-- City Hall!
Thanks, Charlie!
IT'S ONLY WHEN I'M ABOUT TO WALK IN THE FRONT DOOR THAT I REALIZE I HAVEN'T REALLY FIGURED OUT WHAT I'M GOING TO SAY.
HI, MR. MAYOR? I'M YOUR FRIENDLY NEIGHBORHOOD VIGILANTE?

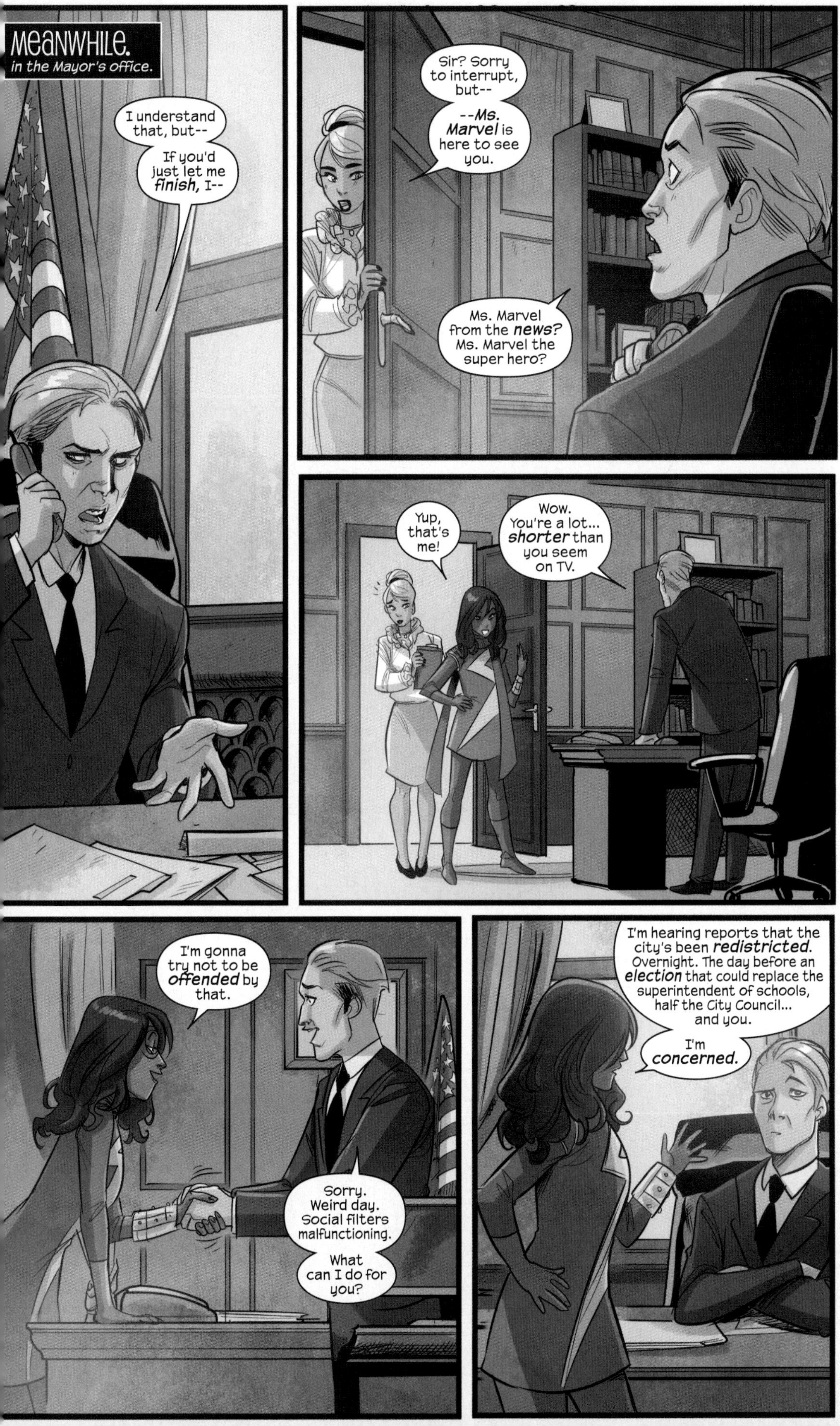
MEANWHILE.
in the Mayor's office.
I understand that, but--
If you'd just let me *finish,* I--
Sir? Sorry to interrupt, but--
--*Ms. Marvel* is here to see you.
Ms. Marvel from the *news?* Ms. Marvel the super hero?
Yup, that's me!
Wow. You're a lot... *shorter* than you seem on TV.
I'm gonna try not to be *offended* by that.
Sorry. Weird day. Social filters malfunctioning.
What can I do for you?
I'm hearing reports that the city's been *redistricted.* Overnight. The day before an *election* that could replace the superintendent of schools, half the City Council... and you.
I'm *concerned.*

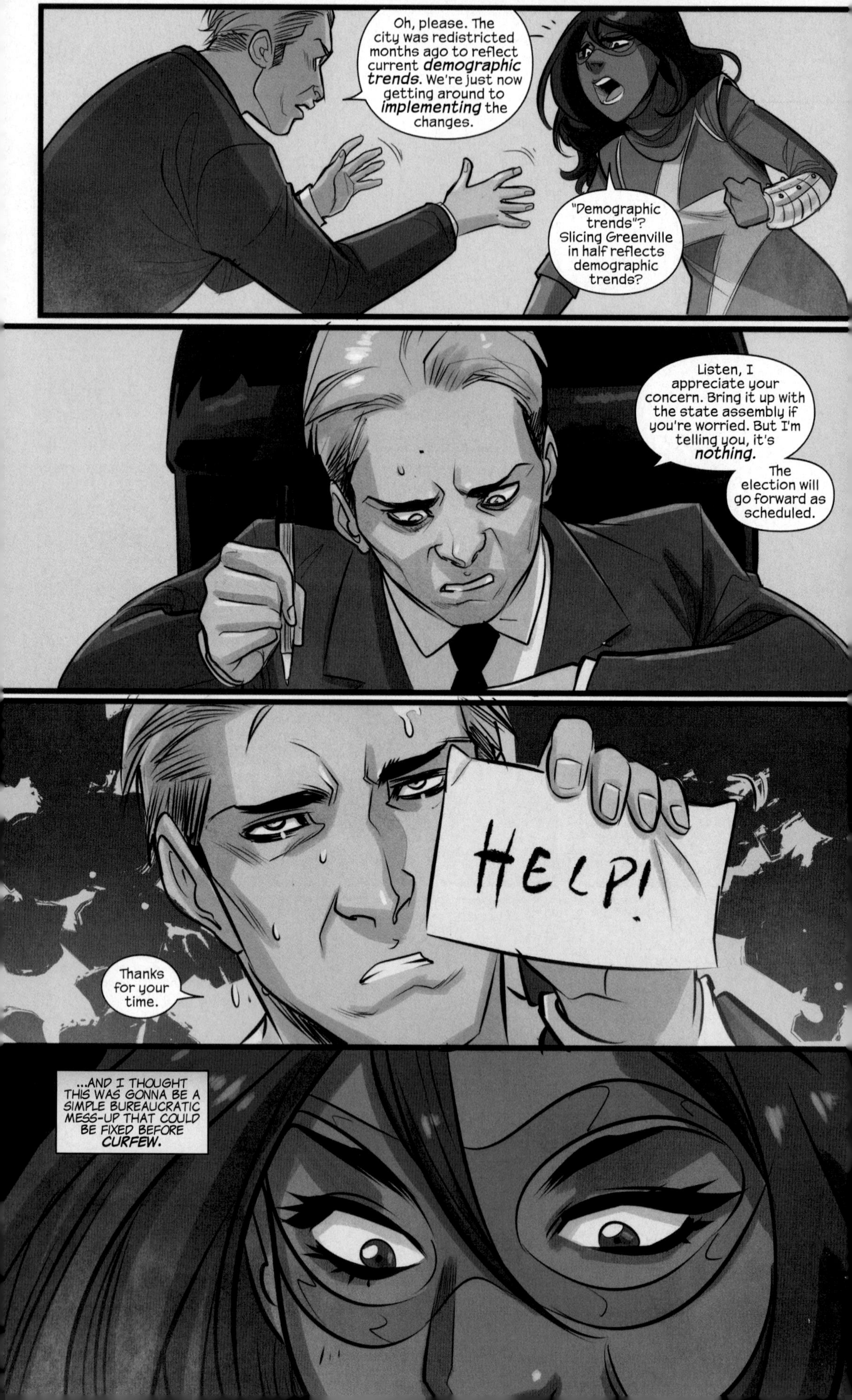
Oh, please. The city was redistricted months ago to reflect current *demographic trends*. We're just now getting around to *implementing* the changes.
"Demographic trends"? Slicing Greenville in half reflects demographic trends?
Listen, I appreciate your concern. Bring it up with the state assembly if you're worried. But I'm telling you, it's *nothing*.
The election will go forward as scheduled.
HELP!
Thanks for your time.
...AND I THOUGHT THIS WAS GONNA BE A SIMPLE BUREAUCRATIC MESS-UP THAT COULD BE FIXED BEFORE *CURFEW*.

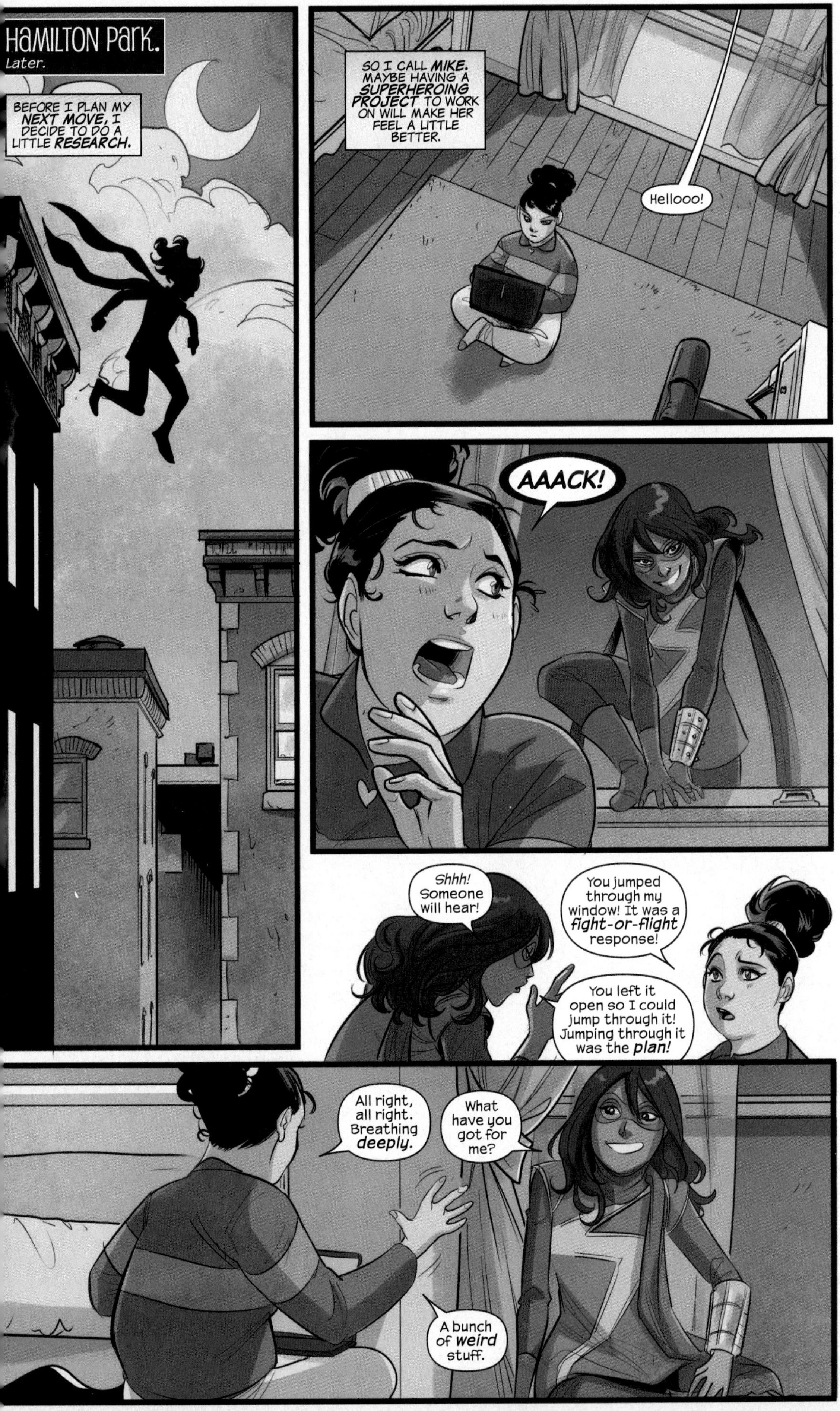

HAMILTON PARK.
Later.
BEFORE I PLAN MY NEXT MOVE, I DECIDE TO DO A LITTLE RESEARCH.
SO I CALL MIKE. MAYBE HAVING A SUPERHEROING PROJECT TO WORK ON WILL MAKE HER FEEL A LITTLE BETTER.
Hellooo!
AAACK!
Shhh! Someone will hear!
You jumped through my window! It was a fight-or-flight response!
You left it open so I could jump through it! Jumping through it was the plan!
All right, all right. Breathing deeply.
What have you got for me?
A bunch of weird stuff.

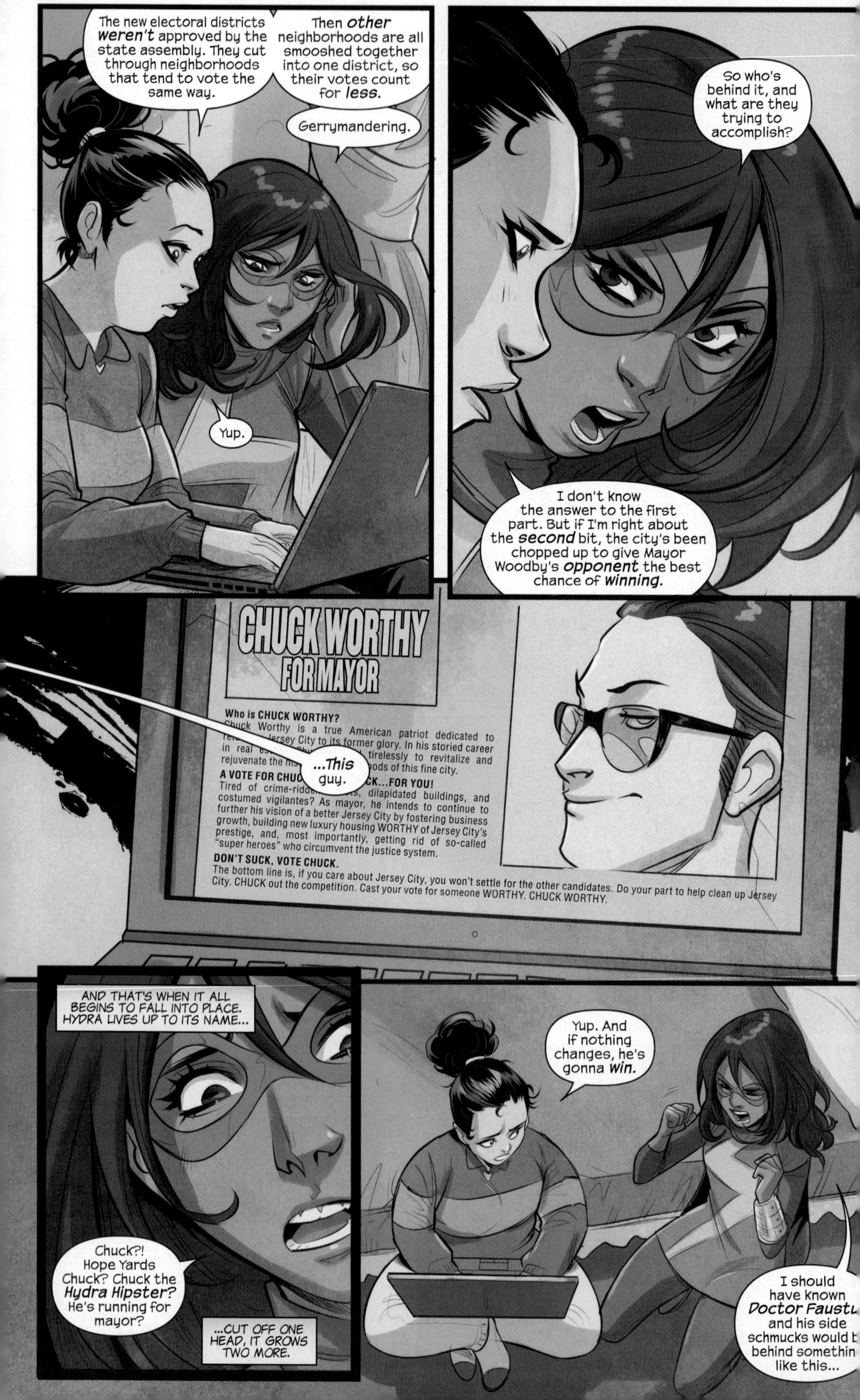
The new electoral districts weren't approved by the state assembly. They cut through neighborhoods that tend to vote the same way.
Then other neighborhoods are all smooshed together into one district, so their votes count for less.
Gerrymandering.
Yup.
So who's behind it, and what are they trying to accomplish?
I don't know the answer to the first part. But if I'm right about the second bit, the city's been chopped up to give Mayor Woodby's opponent the best chance of winning.
CHUCK WORTHY FOR MAYOR
Who is CHUCK WORTHY?
Chuck Worthy is a true American patriot dedicated to
Jersey City to its former glory. In his storied career
in real
tirelessly to revitalize and
rejuvenate the
oods of this fine city.
A VOTE FOR CHUC
CK...FOR YOU!
Tired of crime-ridd
dilapidated buildings, and costumed vigilantes? As mayor, he intends to continue to further his vision of a better Jersey City by fostering business growth, building new luxury housing WORTHY of Jersey City's prestige, and, most importantly, getting rid of so-called "super heroes" who circumvent the justice system.
DON'T SUCK, VOTE CHUCK.
The bottom line is, if you care about Jersey City, you won't settle for the other candidates. Do your part to help clean up Jersey City. CHUCK out the competition. Cast your vote for someone WORTHY. CHUCK WORTHY.
...This guy.
AND THAT'S WHEN IT ALL BEGINS TO FALL INTO PLACE. HYDRA LIVES UP TO ITS NAME...
Chuck?! Hope Yards Chuck? Chuck the Hydra Hipster? He's running for mayor?
...CUT OFF ONE HEAD, IT GROWS TWO MORE.
Yup. And if nothing changes, he's gonna win.
I should have known Doctor Faustu and his side schmucks would b behind somethin like this...

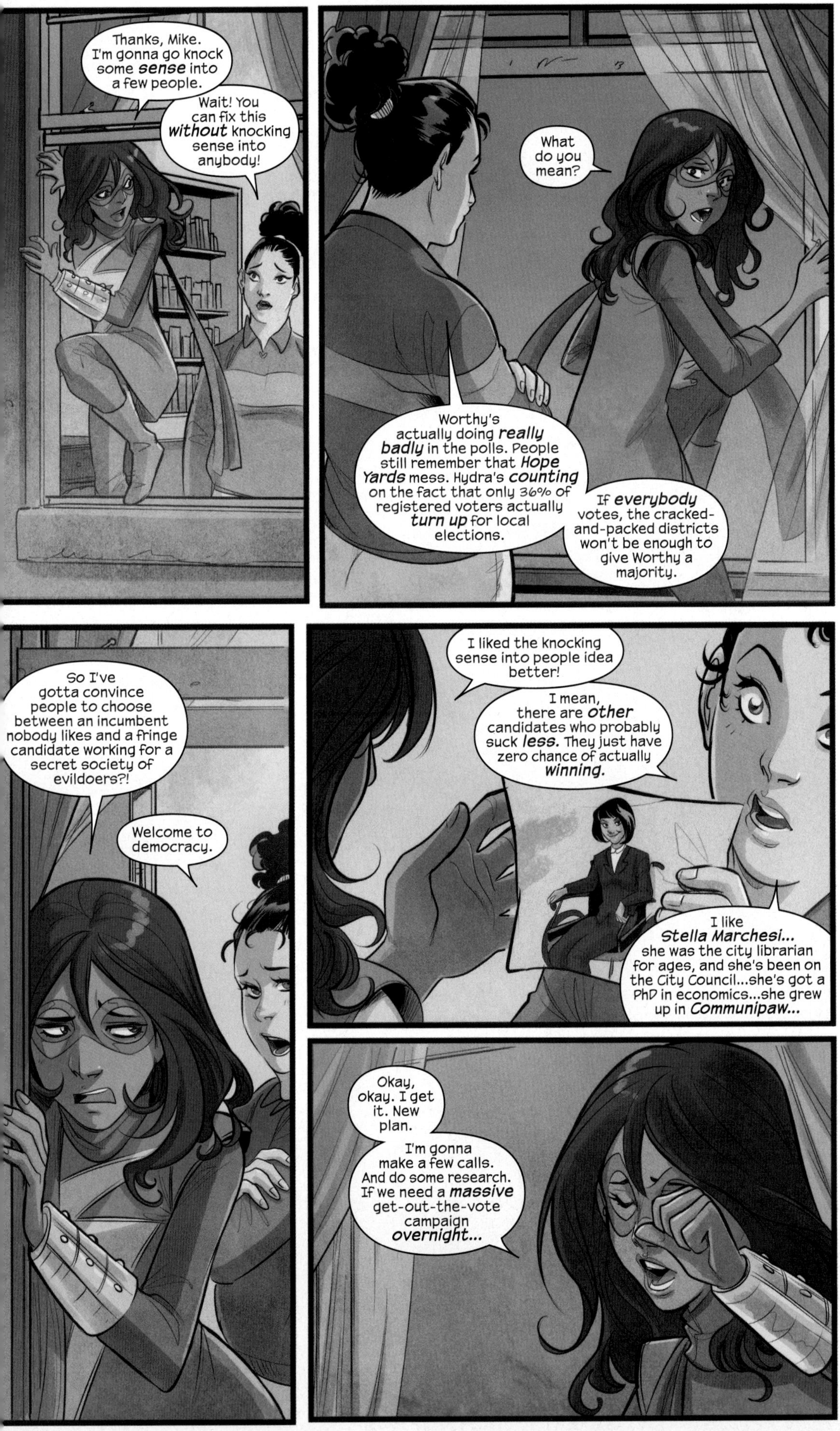

Thanks, Mike. I'm gonna go knock some *sense* into a few people.
Wait! You can fix this *without* knocking sense into anybody!
What do you mean?
Worthy's actually doing *really badly* in the polls. People still remember that *Hope Yards* mess. Hydra's *counting* on the fact that only 36% of registered voters actually *turn up* for local elections.
If *everybody* votes, the cracked-and-packed districts won't be enough to give Worthy a majority.
So I've gotta convince people to choose between an incumbent nobody likes and a fringe candidate working for a secret society of evildoers?!
Welcome to democracy.
I liked the knocking sense into people idea better!
I mean, there are *other* candidates who probably suck *less.* They just have zero chance of actually *winning.*
I like *Stella Marchesi...* she was the city librarian for ages, and she's been on the City Council...she's got a PhD in economics...she grew up in *Communipaw...*
Okay, okay. I get it. New plan.
I'm gonna make a few calls. And do some research. If we need a *massive* get-out-the-vote campaign *overnight...*

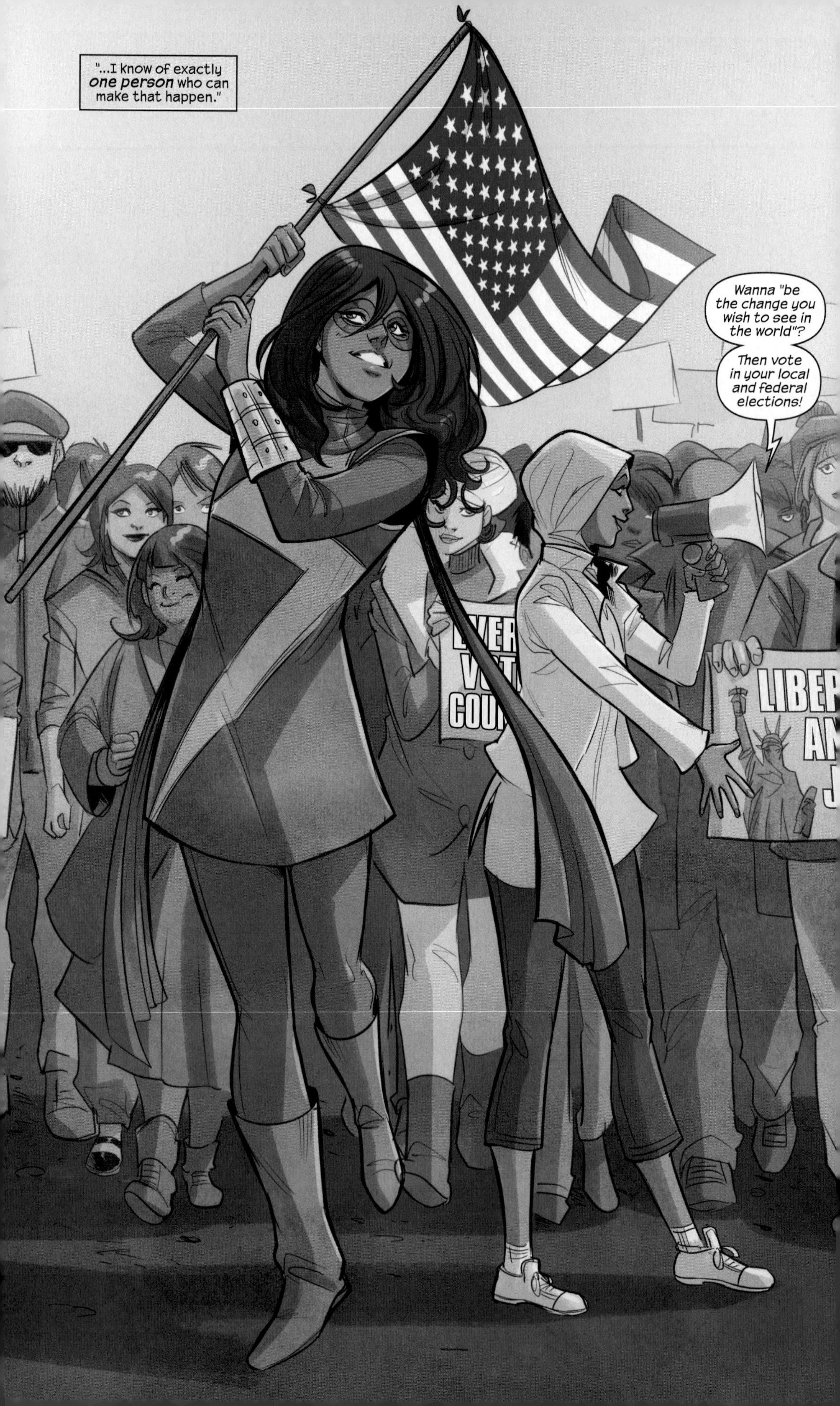
"...I know of exactly *one person* who can make that happen."
Wanna "be the change you wish to see in the world"?
Then vote in your local and federal elections!

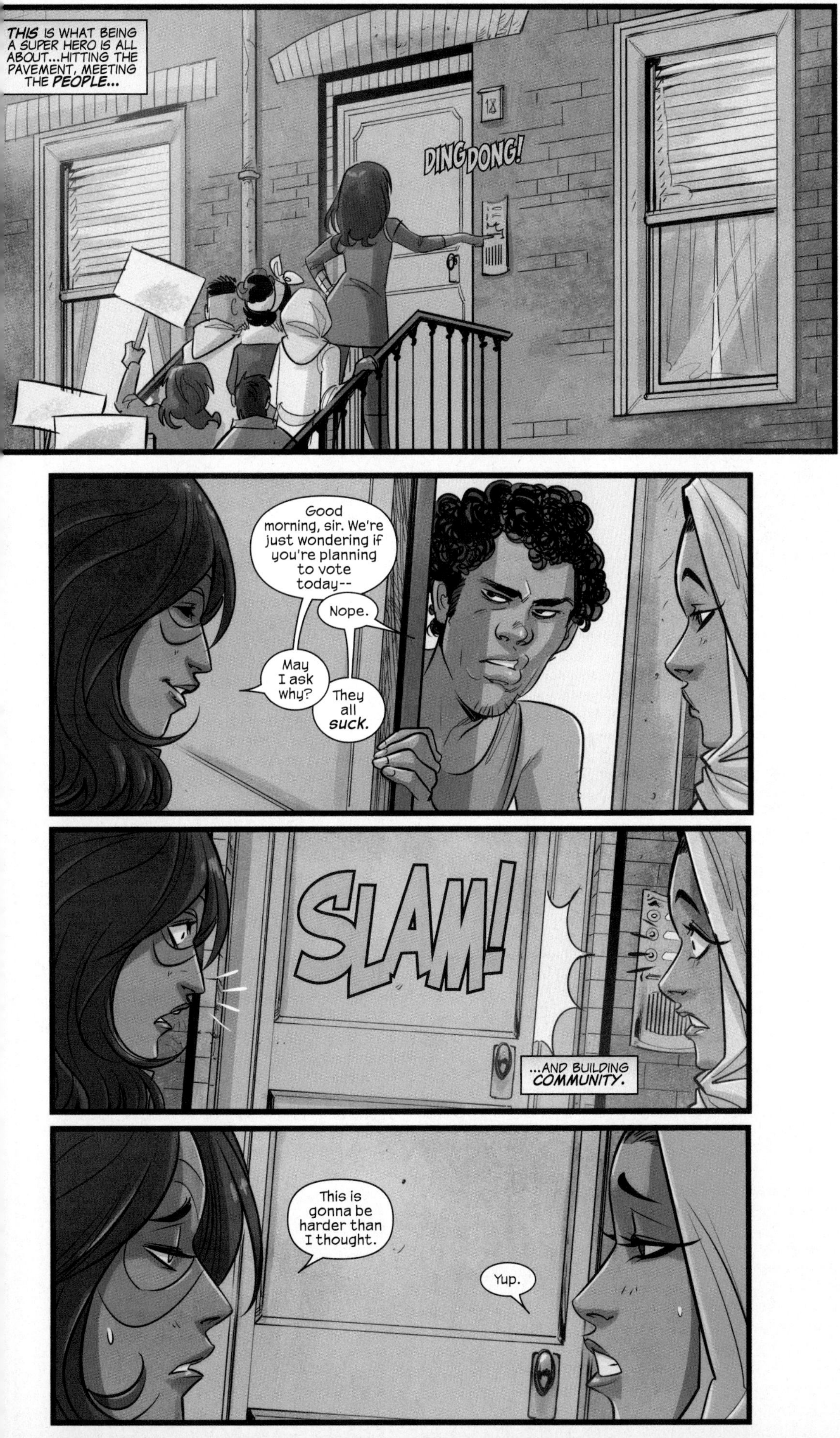
THIS IS WHAT BEING A SUPER HERO IS ALL ABOUT...HITTING THE PAVEMENT, MEETING THE PEOPLE...
DING DONG!
Good morning, sir. We're just wondering if you're planning to vote today--
Nope.
May I ask why?
They all suck.
SLAM!
...AND BUILDING COMMUNITY.
This is gonna be harder than I thought.
Yup.

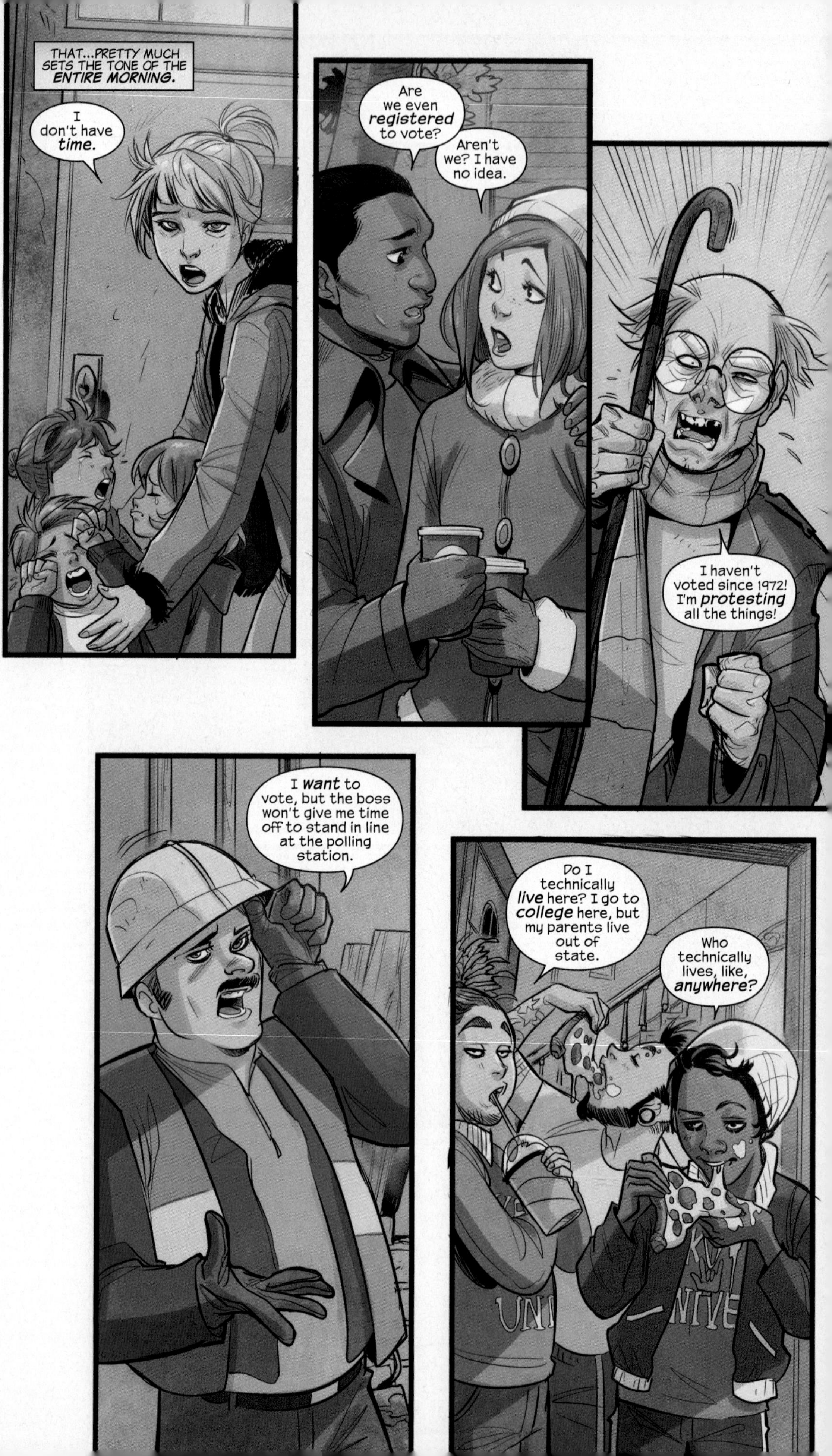
THAT...PRETTY MUCH SETS THE TONE OF THE ENTIRE MORNING.
I don't have time.
Are we even registered to vote?
Aren't we? I have no idea.
I haven't voted since 1972! I'm protesting all the things!
I want to vote, but the boss won't give me time off to stand in line at the polling station.
Do I technically live here? I go to college here, but my parents live out of state.
Who technically lives, like, anywhere?

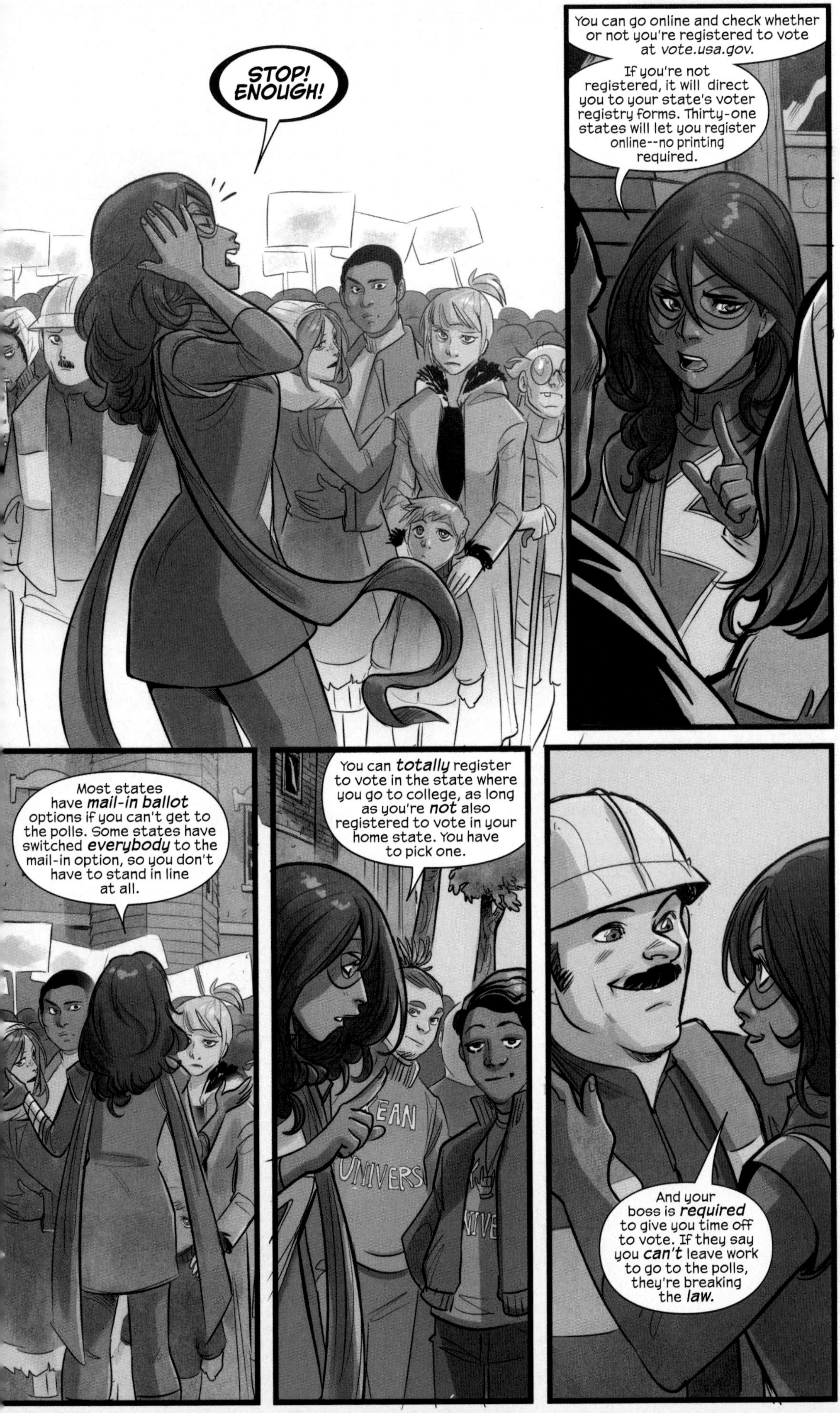

STOP! ENOUGH!
You can go online and check whether or not you're registered to vote at vote.usa.gov.
If you're not registered, it will direct you to your state's voter registry forms. Thirty-one states will let you register online--no printing required.
Most states have mail-in ballot options if you can't get to the polls. Some states have switched everybody to the mail-in option, so you don't have to stand in line at all.
You can totally register to vote in the state where you go to college, as long as you're not also registered to vote in your home state. You have to pick one.
And your boss is required to give you time off to vote. If they say you can't leave work to go to the polls, they're breaking the law.

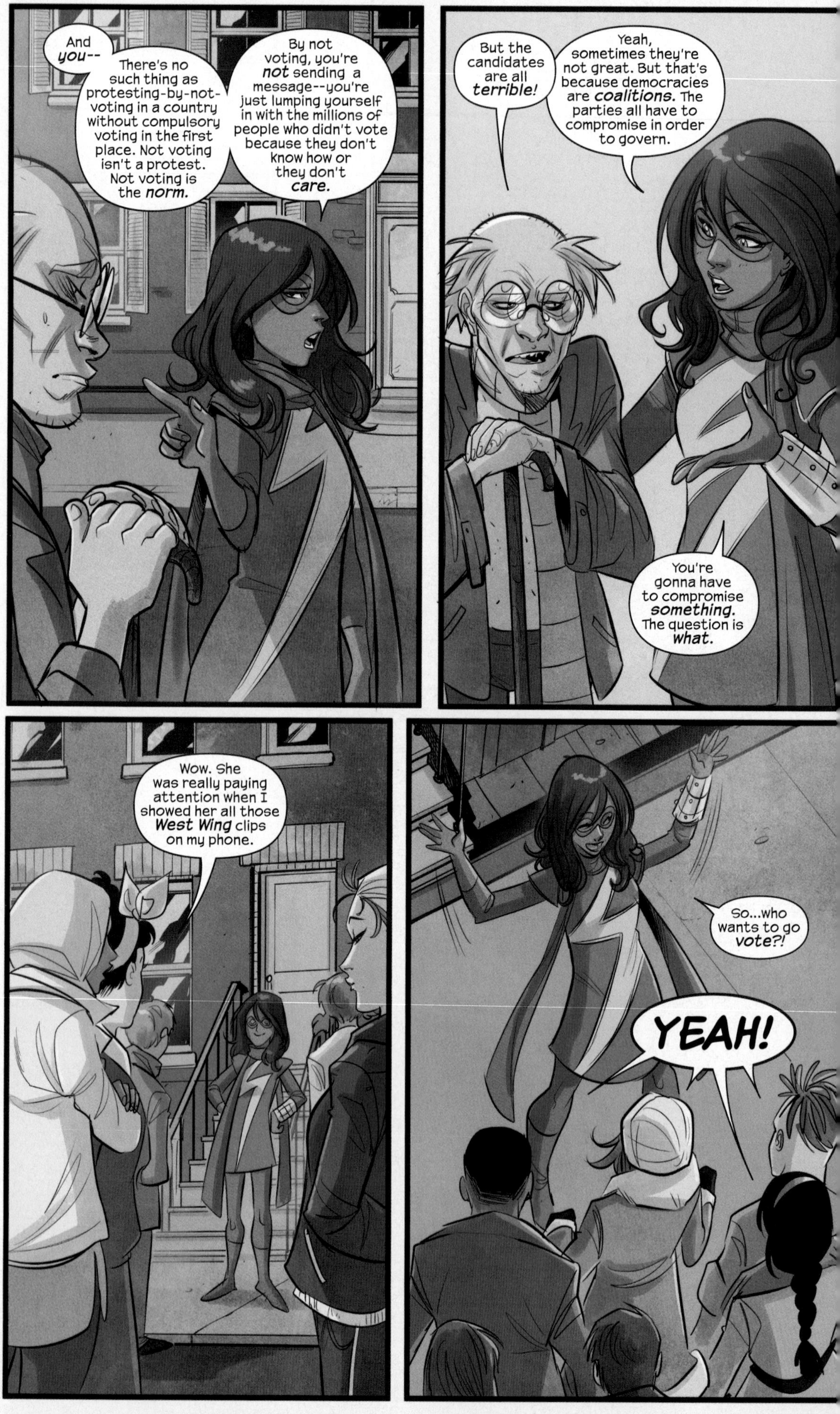
And you--
There's no such thing as protesting-by-not-voting in a country without compulsory voting in the first place. Not voting isn't a protest. Not voting is the norm.
By not voting, you're not sending a message--you're just lumping yourself in with the millions of people who didn't vote because they don't know how or they don't care.
But the candidates are all terrible!
Yeah, sometimes they're not great. But that's because democracies are coalitions. The parties all have to compromise in order to govern.
You're gonna have to compromise something. The question is what.
Wow. She was really paying attention when I showed her all those West Wing clips on my phone.
So...who wants to go vote?!
YEAH!

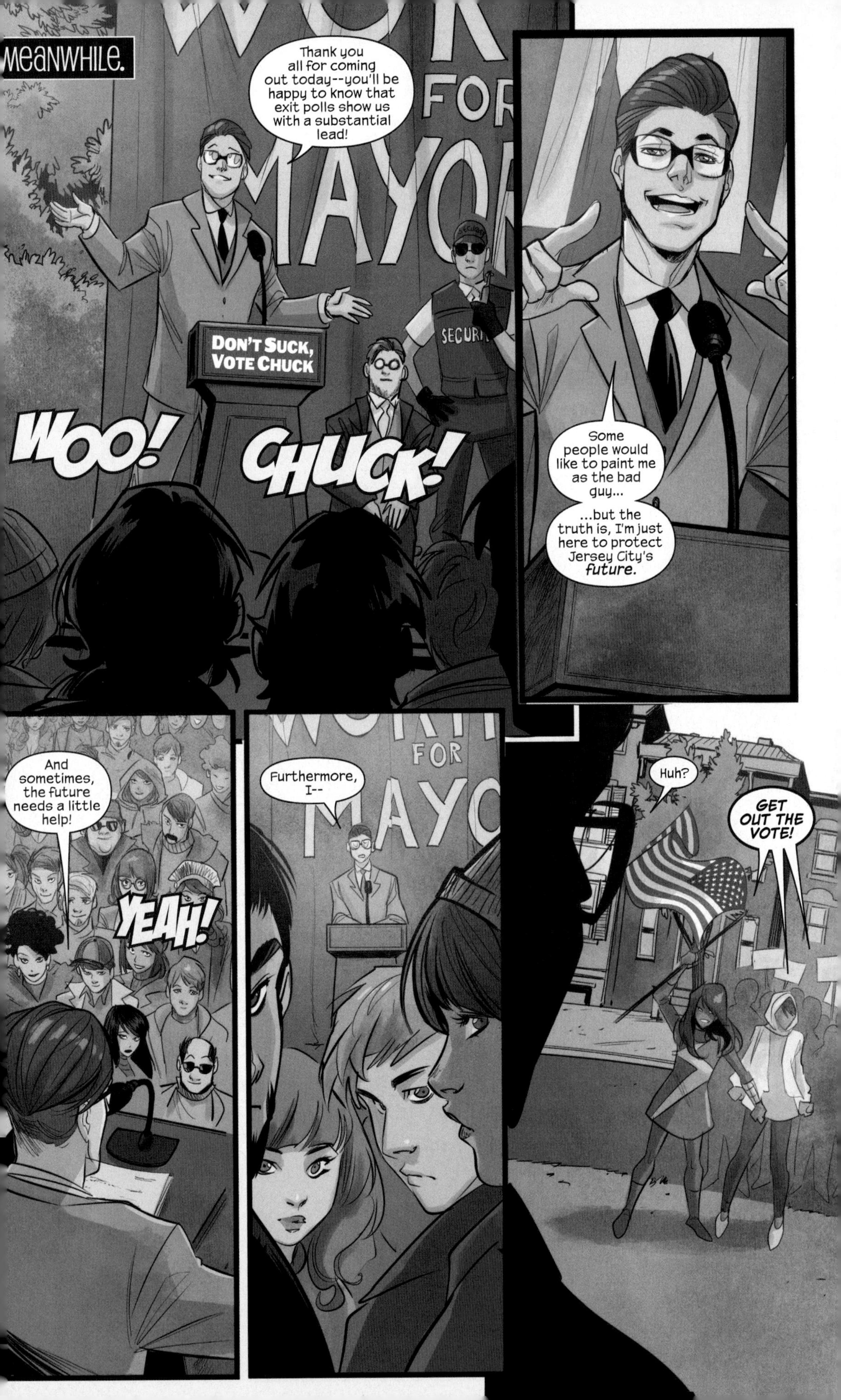

MEANWHILE.
Thank you all for coming out today--you'll be happy to know that exit polls show us with a substantial lead!
DON'T SUCK, VOTE CHUCK
SECURITY
WOO!
CHUCK!
Some people would like to paint me as the bad guy...
...but the truth is, I'm just here to protect Jersey City's *future.*
And sometimes, the future needs a little help!
YEAH!
Furthermore, I--
Huh?
GET OUT THE VOTE!

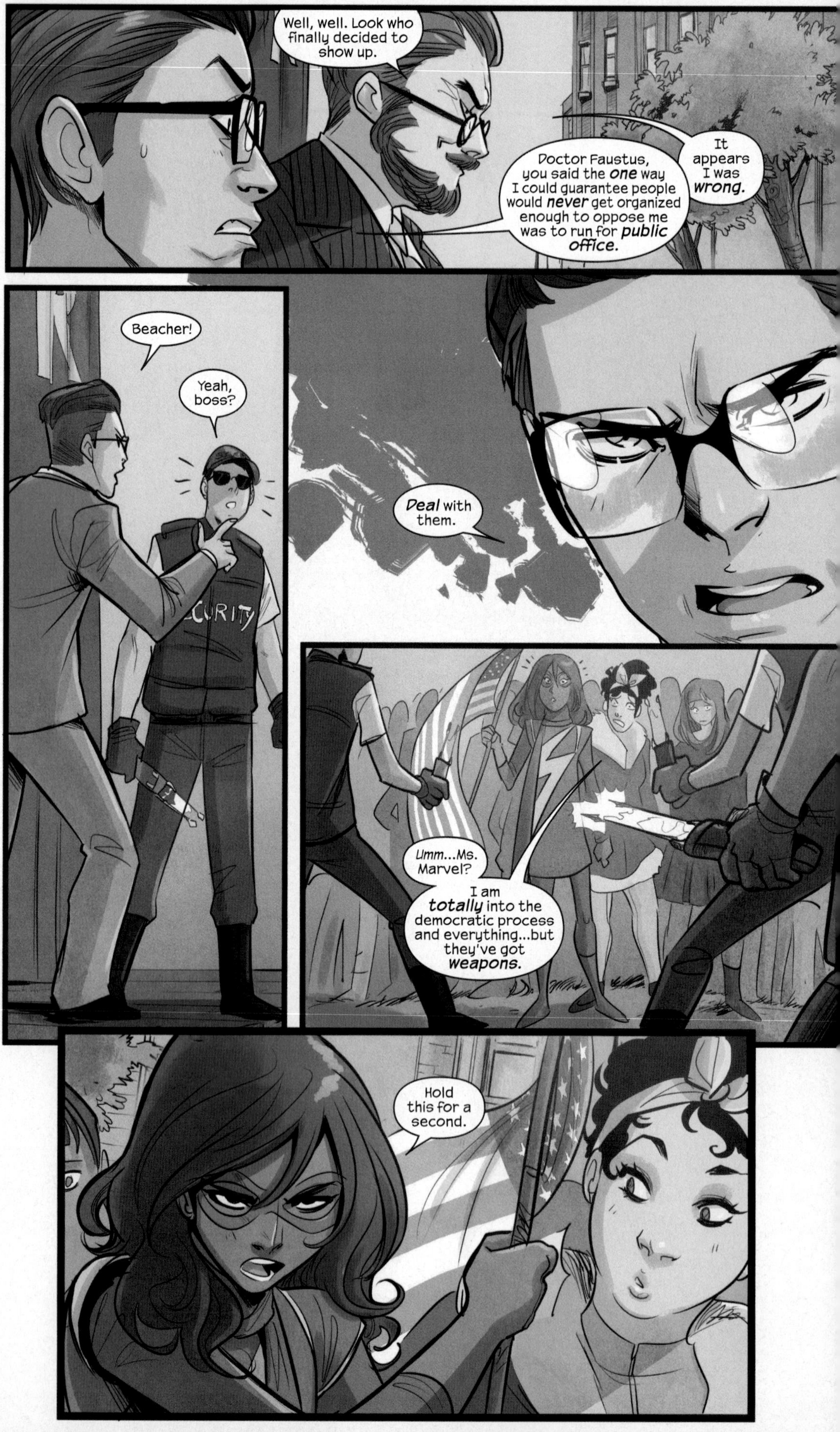

Well, well. Look who finally decided to show up.
It appears I was wrong.
Doctor Faustus, you said the one way I could guarantee people would never get organized enough to oppose me was to run for public office.
Beacher!
Yeah, boss?
Deal with them.
SECURITY
Umm...Ms. Marvel?
I am totally into the democratic process and everything...but they've got weapons.
Hold this for a second.

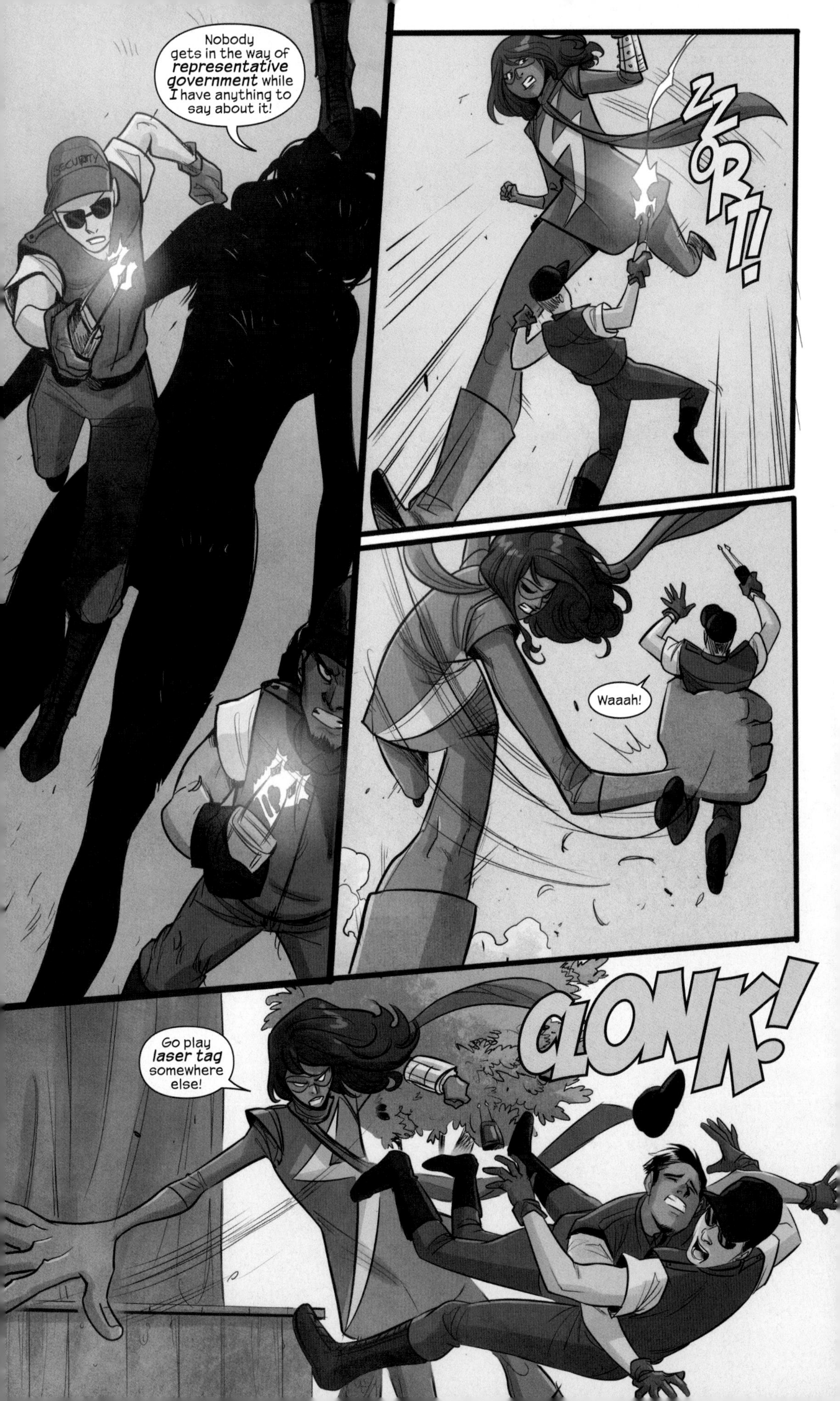
Nobody gets in the way of *representative government* while *I* have anything to say about it!
ZZORT!!
Waaah!
CLONK!
Go play *laser tag* somewhere else!

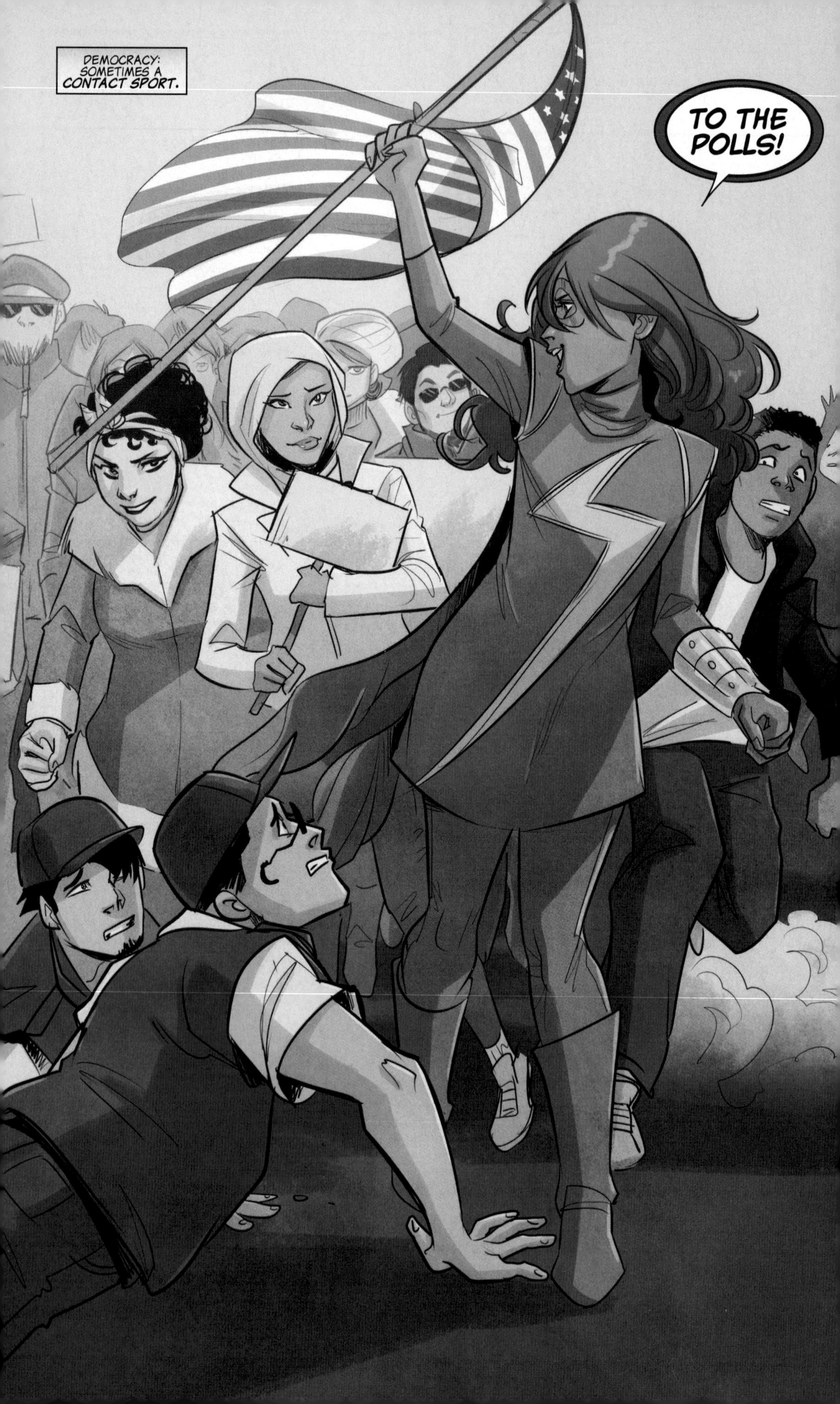
DEMOCRACY: SOMETIMES A CONTACT SPORT.
TO THE POLLS!

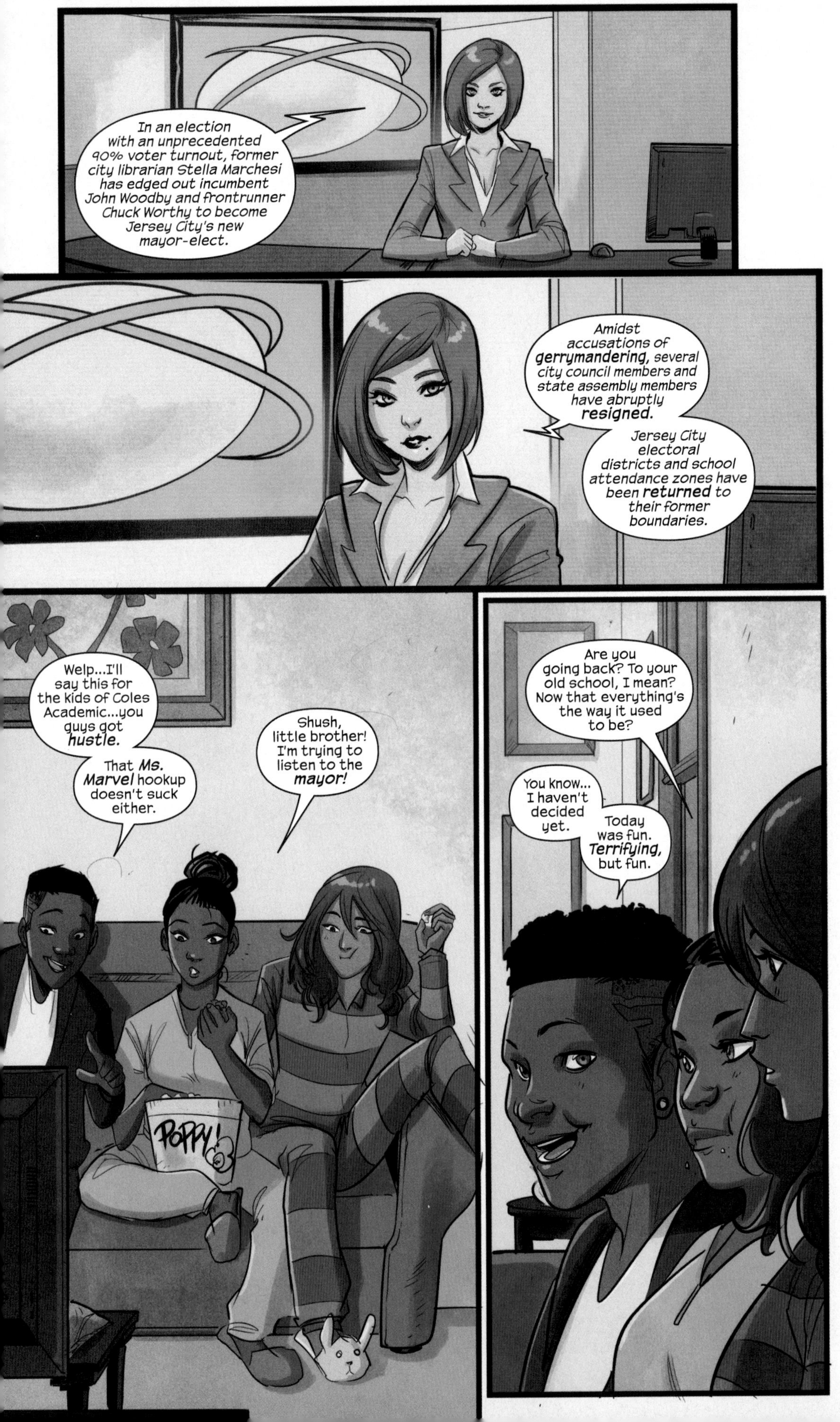

In an election with an unprecedented 90% voter turnout, former city librarian Stella Marchesi has edged out incumbent John Woodby and frontrunner Chuck Worthy to become Jersey City's new mayor-elect.
Amidst accusations of **gerrymandering,** several city council members and state assembly members have abruptly **resigned.**
Jersey City electoral districts and school attendance zones have been **returned** to their former boundaries.
Welp...I'll say this for the kids of Coles Academic...you guys got *hustle.*
That *Ms. Marvel* hookup doesn't suck either.
Shush, little brother! I'm trying to listen to the *mayor!*
POPPY!
Are you going back? To your old school, I mean? Now that everything's the way it used to be?
You know... I haven't decided yet.
Today was fun. *Terrifying,* but fun.

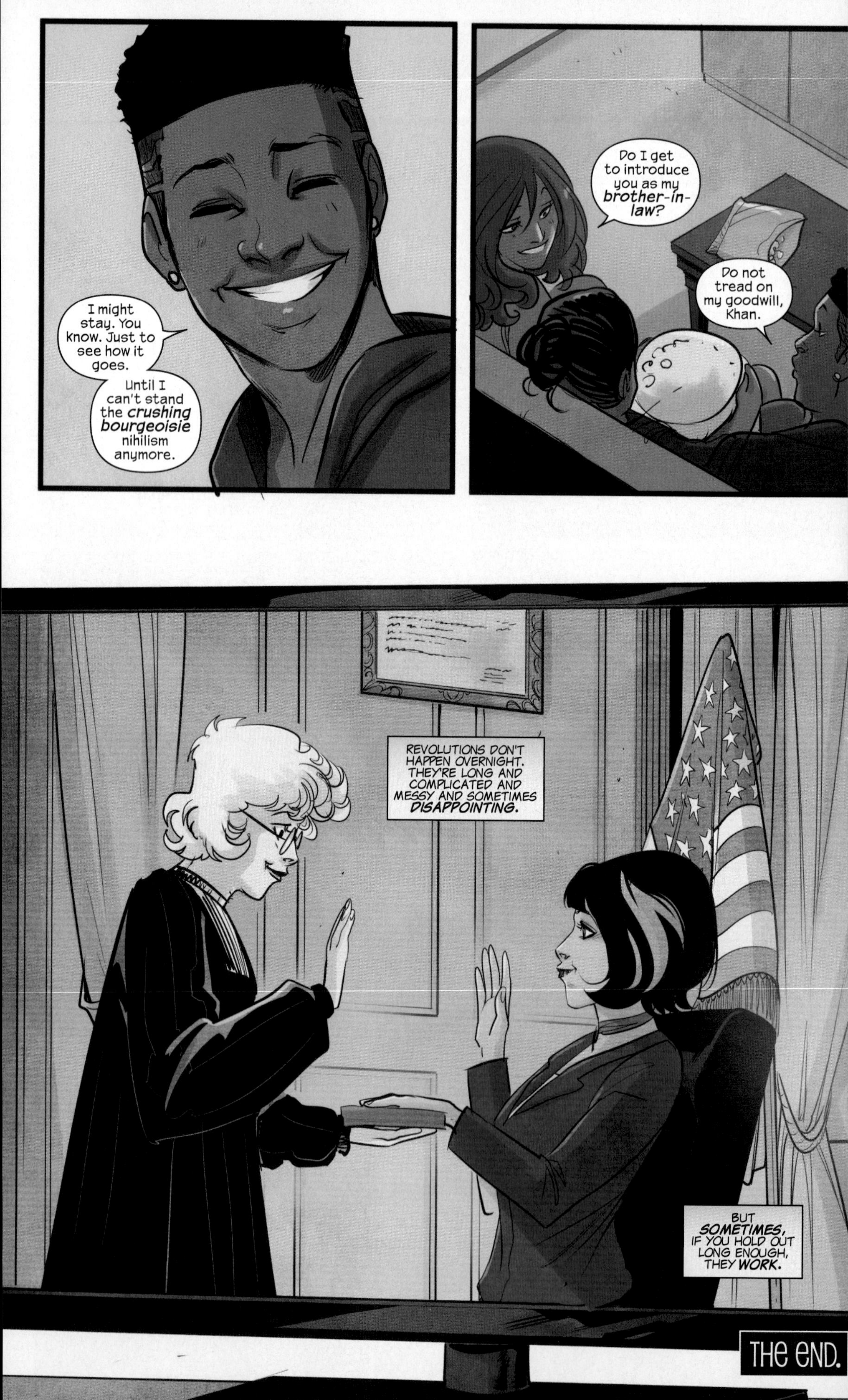
I might stay. You know. Just to see how it goes.
Until I can't stand the *crushing bourgeoisie* nihilism anymore.
Do I get to introduce you as my *brother-in-law?*
Do not tread on my goodwill, Khan.
REVOLUTIONS DON'T HAPPEN OVERNIGHT. THEY'RE LONG AND COMPLICATED AND MESSY AND SOMETIMES *DISAPPOINTING.*
BUT *SOMETIMES,* IF YOU HOLD OUT LONG ENOUGH, THEY *WORK.*
THE END.

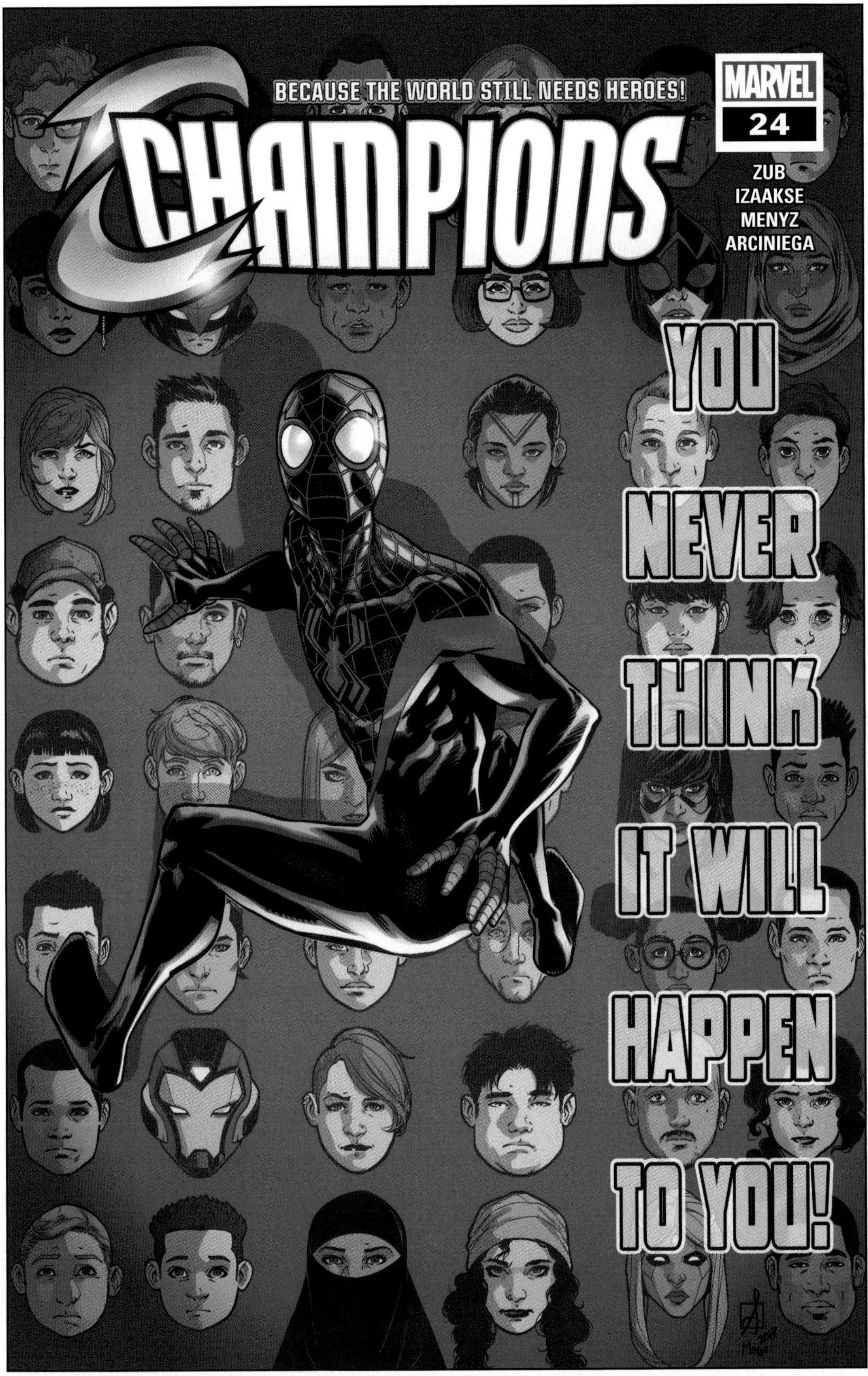
BECAUSE THE WORLD STILL NEEDS HEROES!
CHAMPIONS
MARVEL
24
ZUB
IZAAKSE
MENYZ
ARCINIEGA
YOU
NEVER
THINK
IT WILL
HAPPEN
TO YOU!

We interrupt our regularly scheduled
program to bring you the following
Special Bulletin.

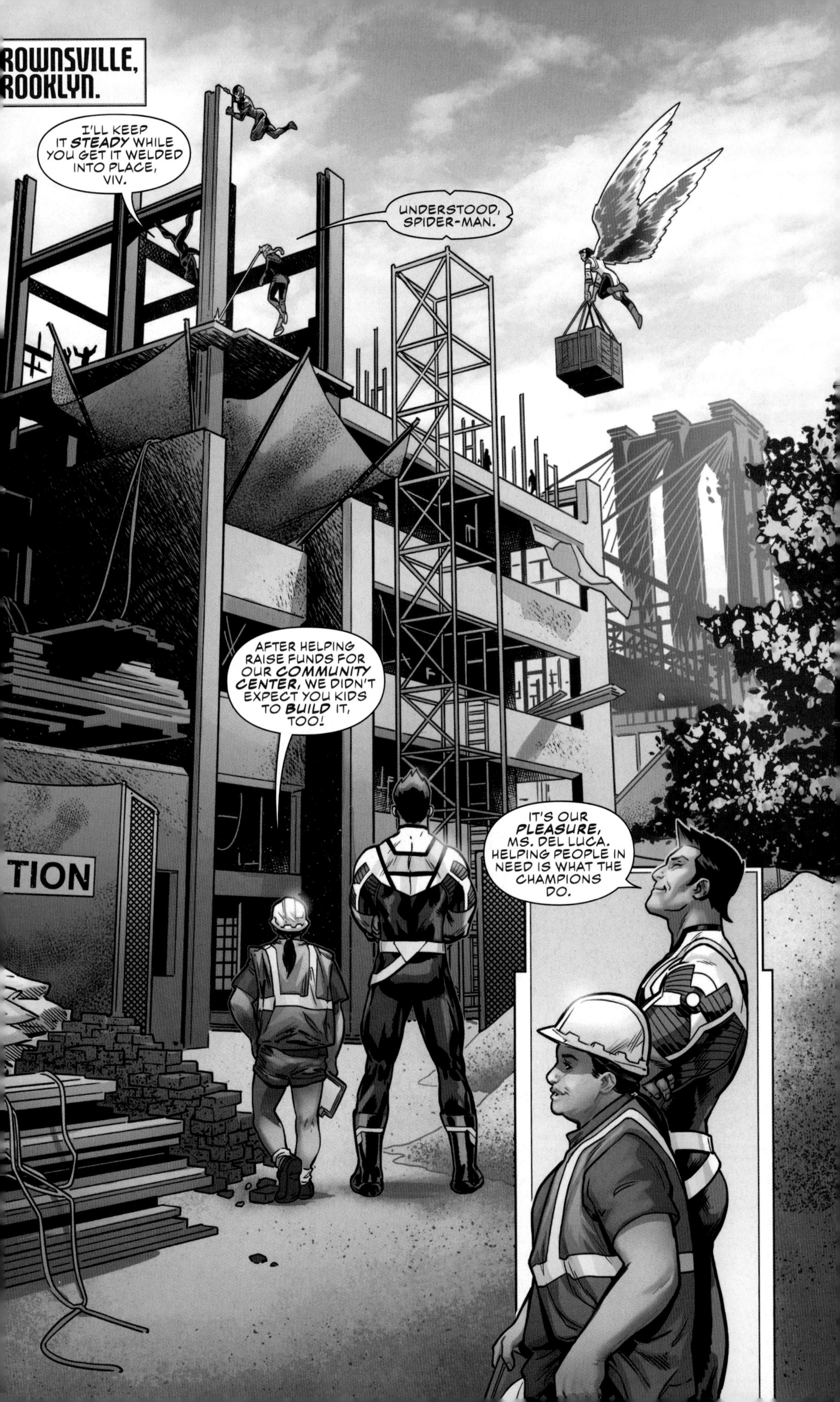
ROWNSVILLE, ROOKLYN.
I'LL KEEP IT STEADY WHILE YOU GET IT WELDED INTO PLACE, VIV.
UNDERSTOOD, SPIDER-MAN.
AFTER HELPING RAISE FUNDS FOR OUR COMMUNITY CENTER, WE DIDN'T EXPECT YOU KIDS TO BUILD IT, TOO!
TION
IT'S OUR PLEASURE, MS. DEL LUCA. HELPING PEOPLE IN NEED IS WHAT THE CHAMPIONS DO.

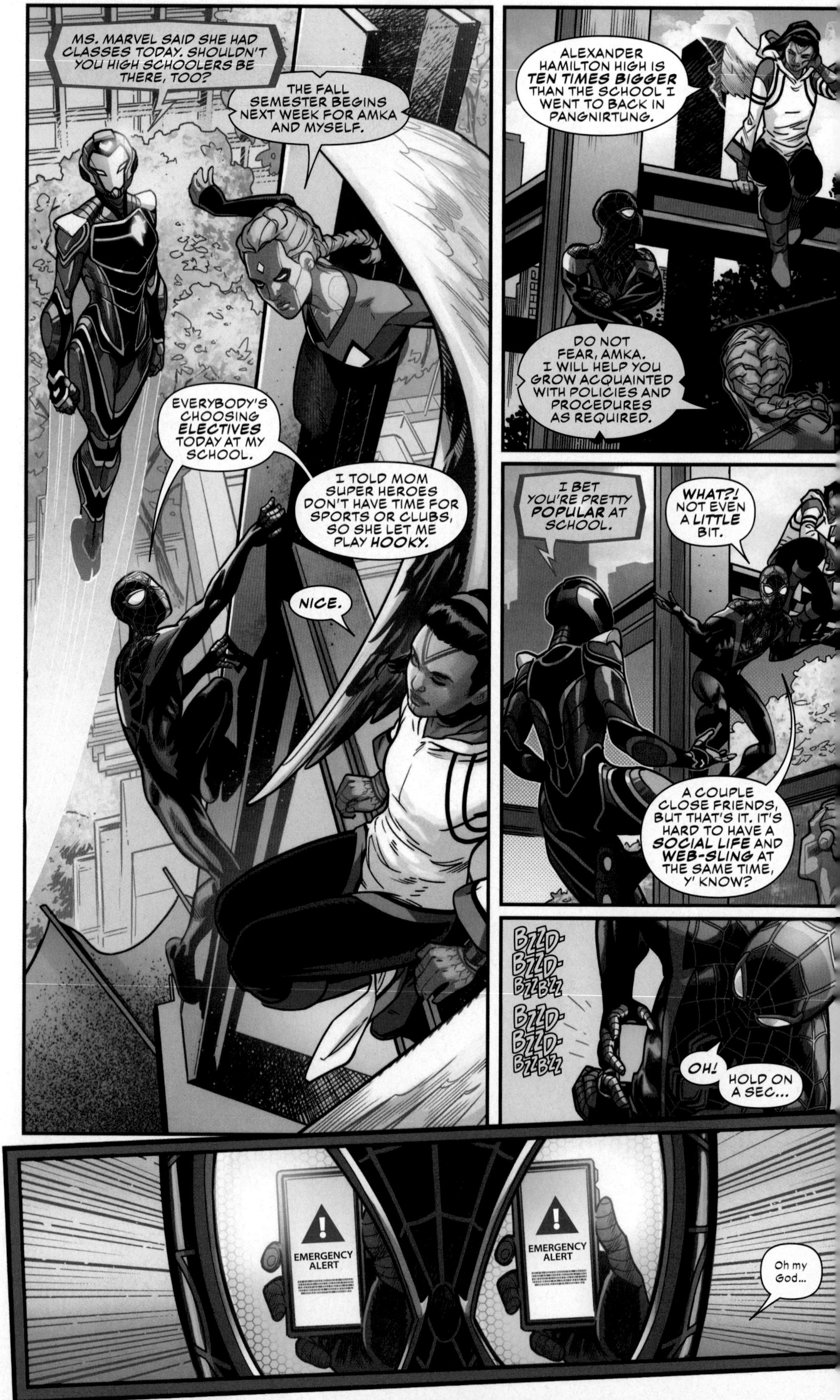
MS. MARVEL SAID SHE HAD CLASSES TODAY. SHOULDN'T YOU HIGH SCHOOLERS BE THERE, TOO?
THE FALL SEMESTER BEGINS NEXT WEEK FOR AMKA AND MYSELF.
EVERYBODY'S CHOOSING ELECTIVES TODAY AT MY SCHOOL.
I TOLD MOM SUPER HEROES DON'T HAVE TIME FOR SPORTS OR CLUBS, SO SHE LET ME PLAY HOOKY.
NICE.
ALEXANDER HAMILTON HIGH IS TEN TIMES BIGGER THAN THE SCHOOL I WENT TO BACK IN PANGNIRTUNG.
DO NOT FEAR, AMKA. I WILL HELP YOU GROW ACQUAINTED WITH POLICIES AND PROCEDURES AS REQUIRED.
I BET YOU'RE PRETTY POPULAR AT SCHOOL.
WHAT?! NOT EVEN A LITTLE BIT.
A COUPLE CLOSE FRIENDS, BUT THAT'S IT. IT'S HARD TO HAVE A SOCIAL LIFE AND WEB-SLING AT THE SAME TIME, Y' KNOW?
BZZD-BZZD-BZZBZZ
BZZD-BZZD-BZZBZZ
OH!
HOLD ON A SEC...
EMERGENCY ALERT
EMERGENCY ALERT
Oh my God...

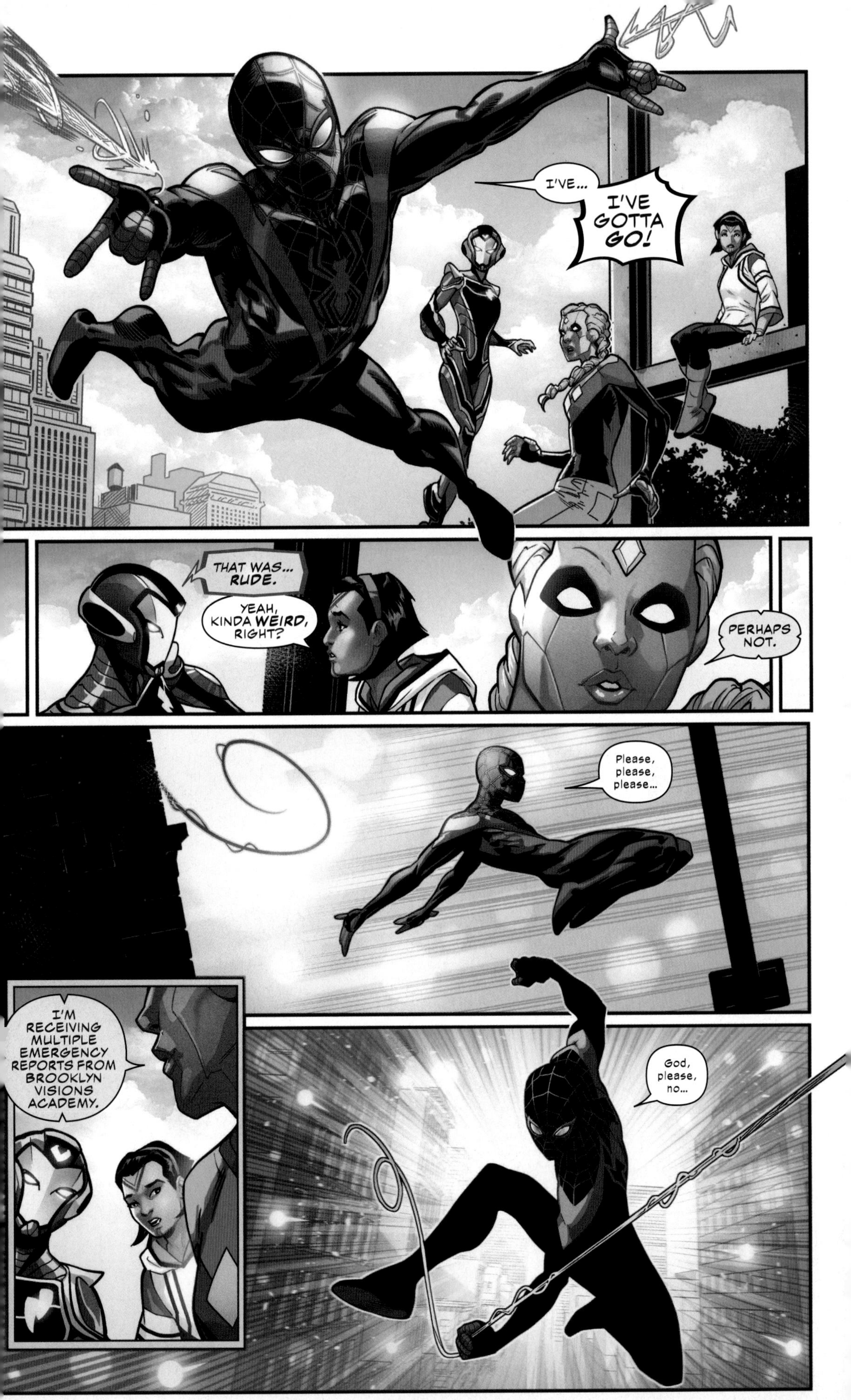
I'VE...
I'VE GOTTA GO!
THAT WAS... RUDE.
YEAH, KINDA WEIRD, RIGHT?
PERHAPS NOT.
Please, please, please...
I'M RECEIVING MULTIPLE EMERGENCY REPORTS FROM BROOKLYN VISIONS ACADEMY.
God, please, no...

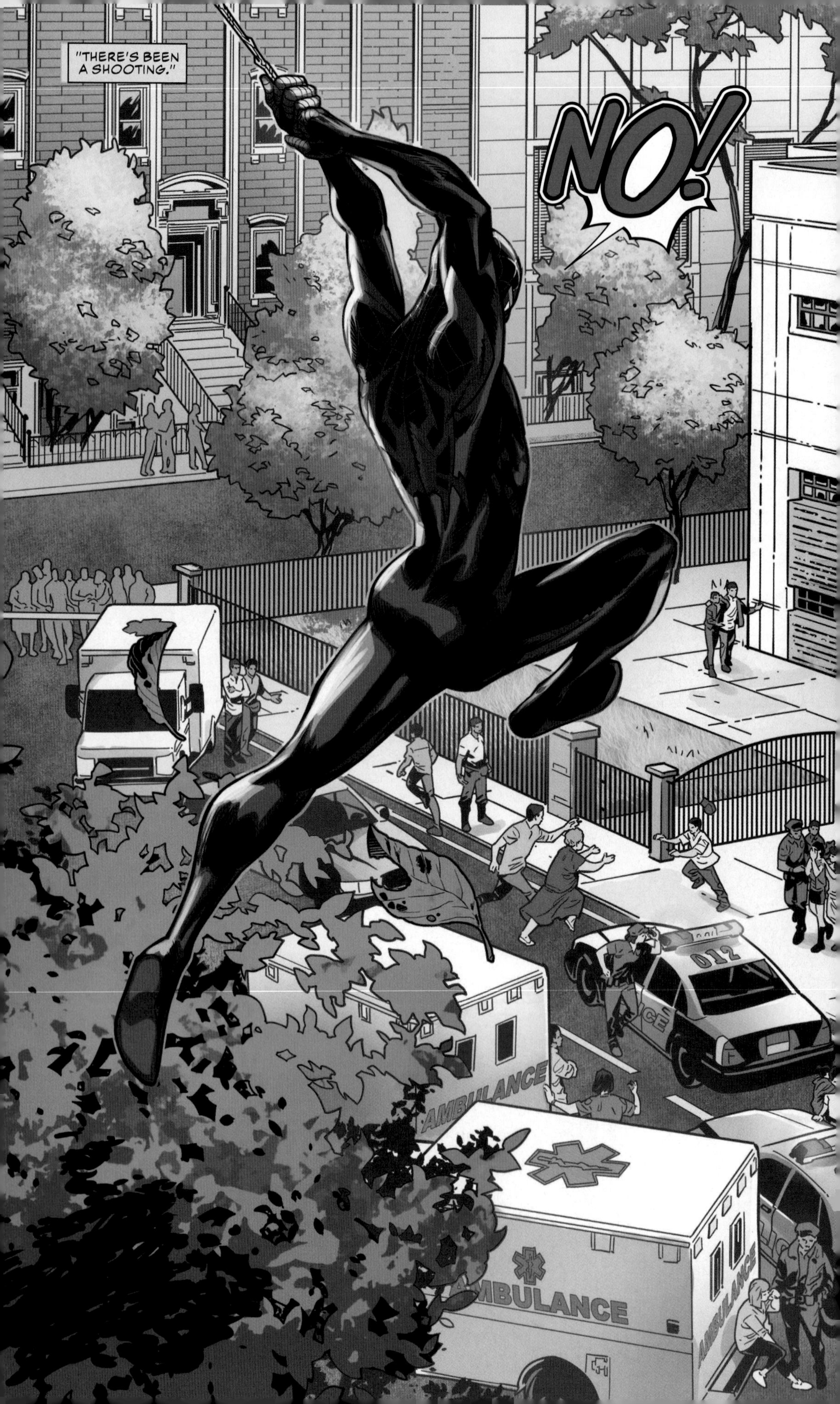
"THERE'S BEEN A SHOOTING."
NO!
AMBULANCE
AMBULANCE
AMBULANCE
012

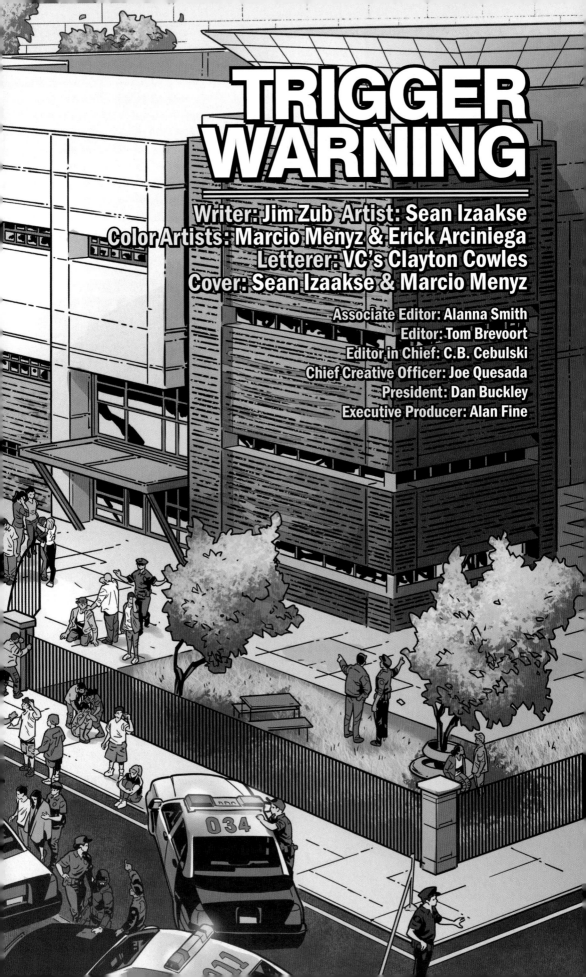

TRIGGER WARNING

Writer: Jim Zub Artist: Sean Izaakse
Color Artists: Marcio Menyz & Erick Arciniega
Letterer: VC's Clayton Cowles
Cover: Sean Izaakse & Marcio Menyz

Associate Editor: Alanna Smith
Editor: Tom Brevoort
Editor in Chief: C.B. Cebulski
Chief Creative Officer: Joe Quesada
President: Dan Buckley
Executive Producer: Alan Fine

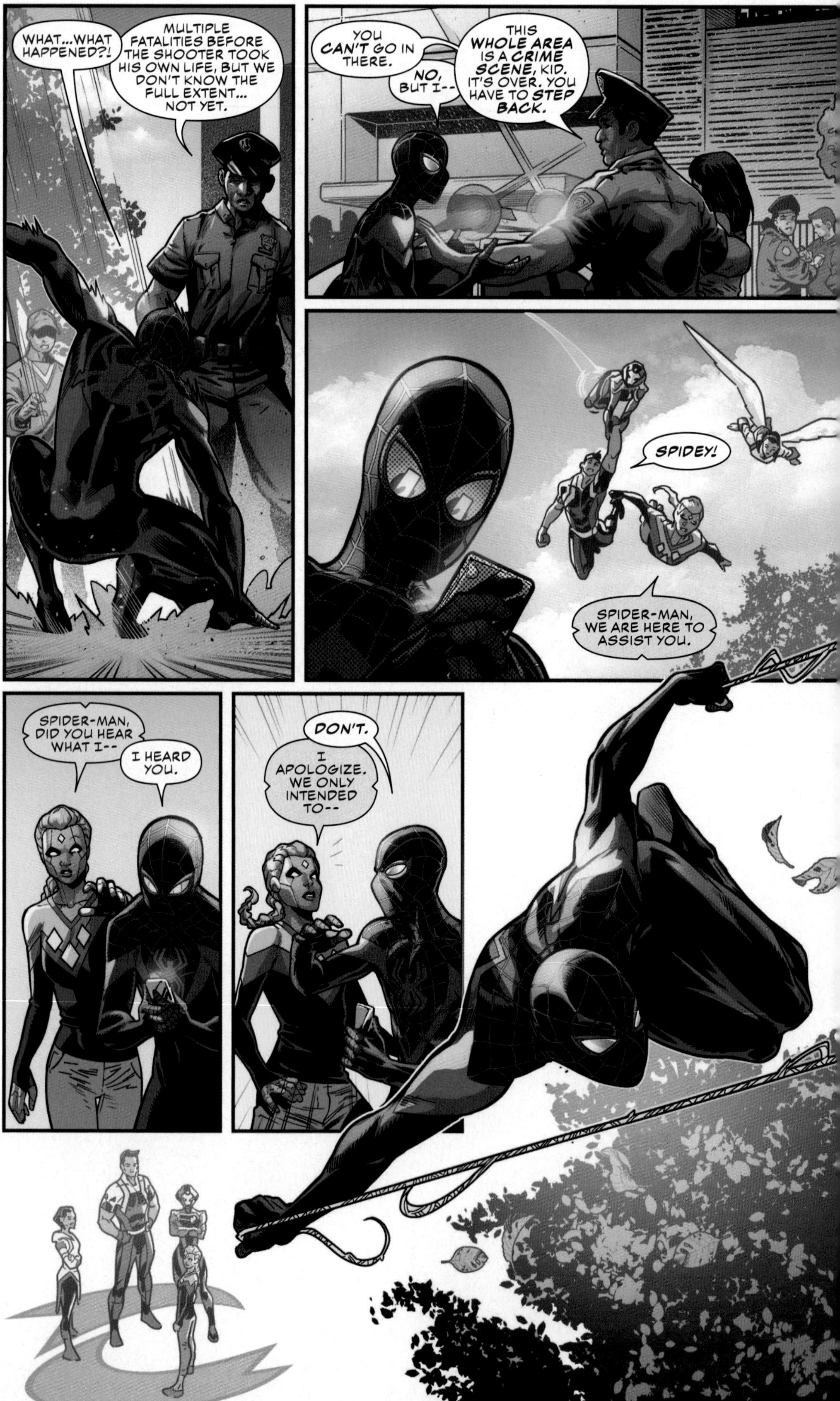

WHAT...WHAT HAPPENED?!
MULTIPLE FATALITIES BEFORE THE SHOOTER TOOK HIS OWN LIFE, BUT WE DON'T KNOW THE FULL EXTENT... NOT YET.
YOU CAN'T GO IN THERE.
THIS WHOLE AREA IS A CRIME SCENE, KID. IT'S OVER. YOU HAVE TO STEP BACK.
NO, BUT I--
SPIDEY!
SPIDER-MAN, WE ARE HERE TO ASSIST YOU.
SPIDER-MAN, DID YOU HEAR WHAT I--
I HEARD YOU.
DON'T.
I APOLOGIZE. WE ONLY INTENDED TO--

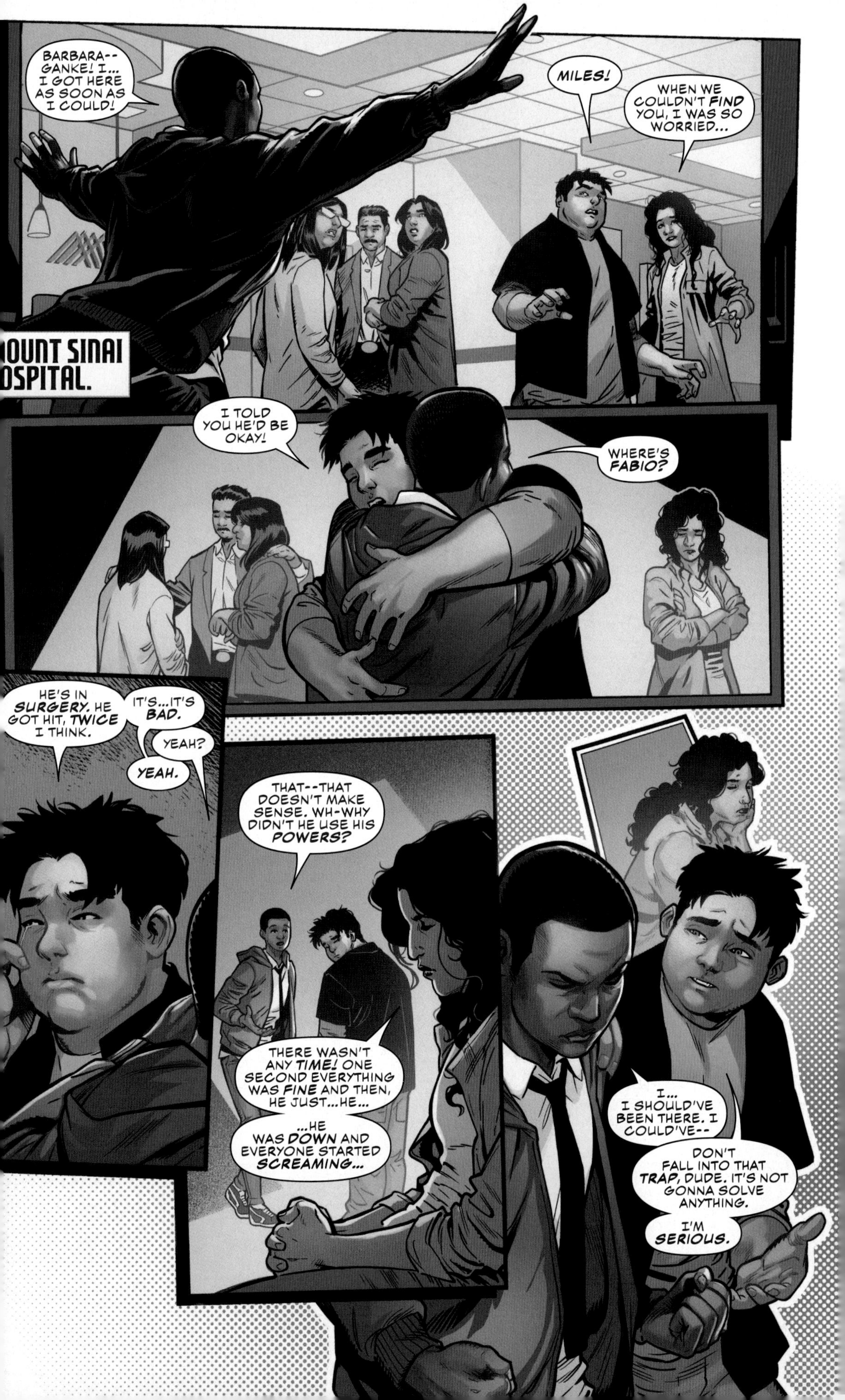
BARBARA--
GANKE! I... I GOT HERE AS SOON AS I COULD!
MILES!
WHEN WE COULDN'T FIND YOU, I WAS SO WORRIED...
MOUNT SINAI HOSPITAL.
I TOLD YOU HE'D BE OKAY!
WHERE'S FABIO?
HE'S IN SURGERY. HE GOT HIT, TWICE I THINK.
IT'S...IT'S BAD.
YEAH?
YEAH.
THAT--THAT DOESN'T MAKE SENSE. WH-WHY DIDN'T HE USE HIS POWERS?
THERE WASN'T ANY TIME! ONE SECOND EVERYTHING WAS FINE AND THEN, HE JUST...HE...
...HE WAS DOWN AND EVERYONE STARTED SCREAMING...
I... I SHOULD'VE BEEN THERE. I COULD'VE--
DON'T FALL INTO THAT TRAP, DUDE. IT'S NOT GONNA SOLVE ANYTHING.
I'M SERIOUS.

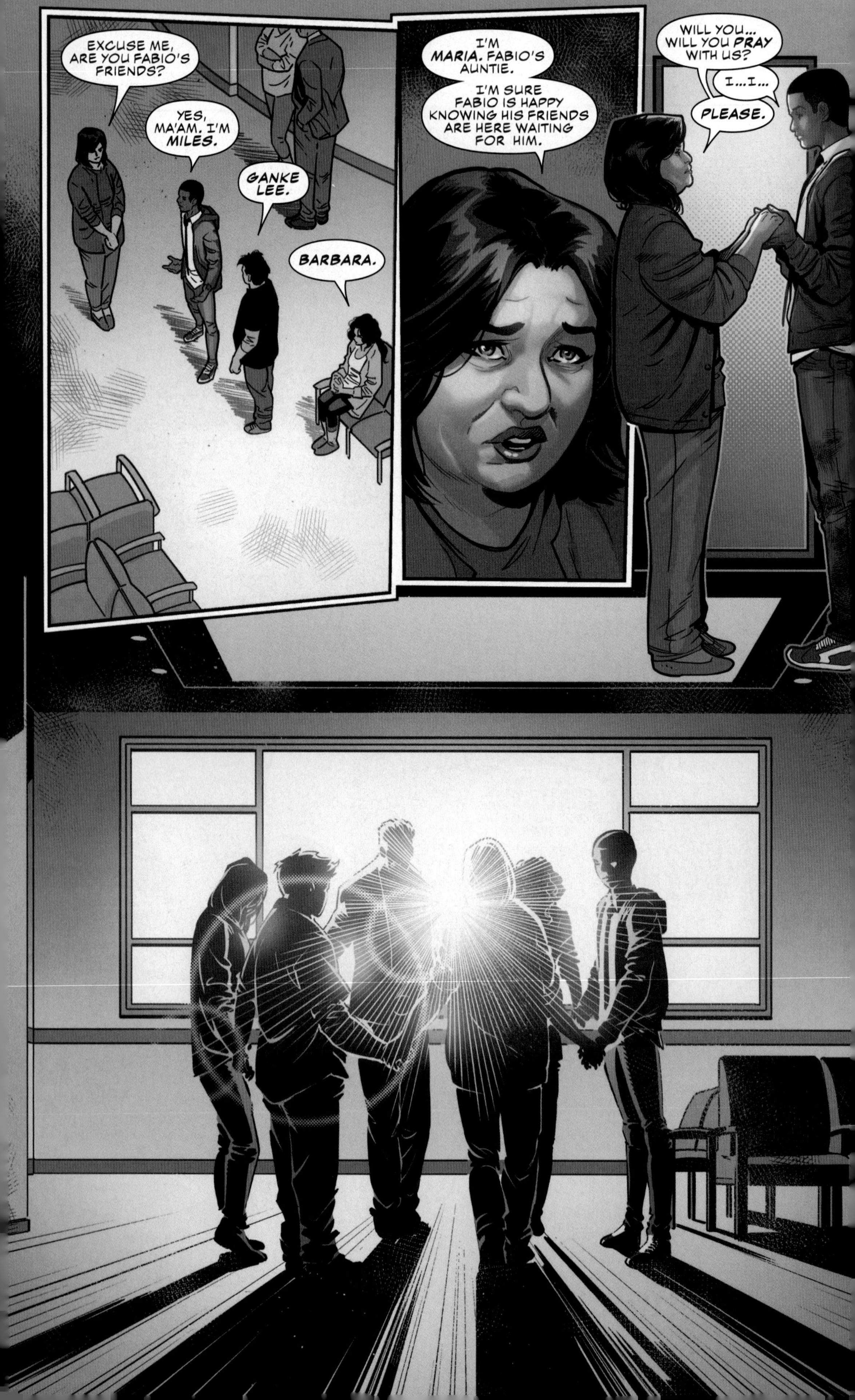
EXCUSE ME, ARE YOU FABIO'S FRIENDS?
YES, MA'AM. I'M MILES.
GANKE LEE.
BARBARA.
I'M MARIA. FABIO'S AUNTIE.
I'M SURE FABIO IS HAPPY KNOWING HIS FRIENDS ARE HERE WAITING FOR HIM.
WILL YOU... WILL YOU PRAY WITH US?
I...I...
PLEASE.

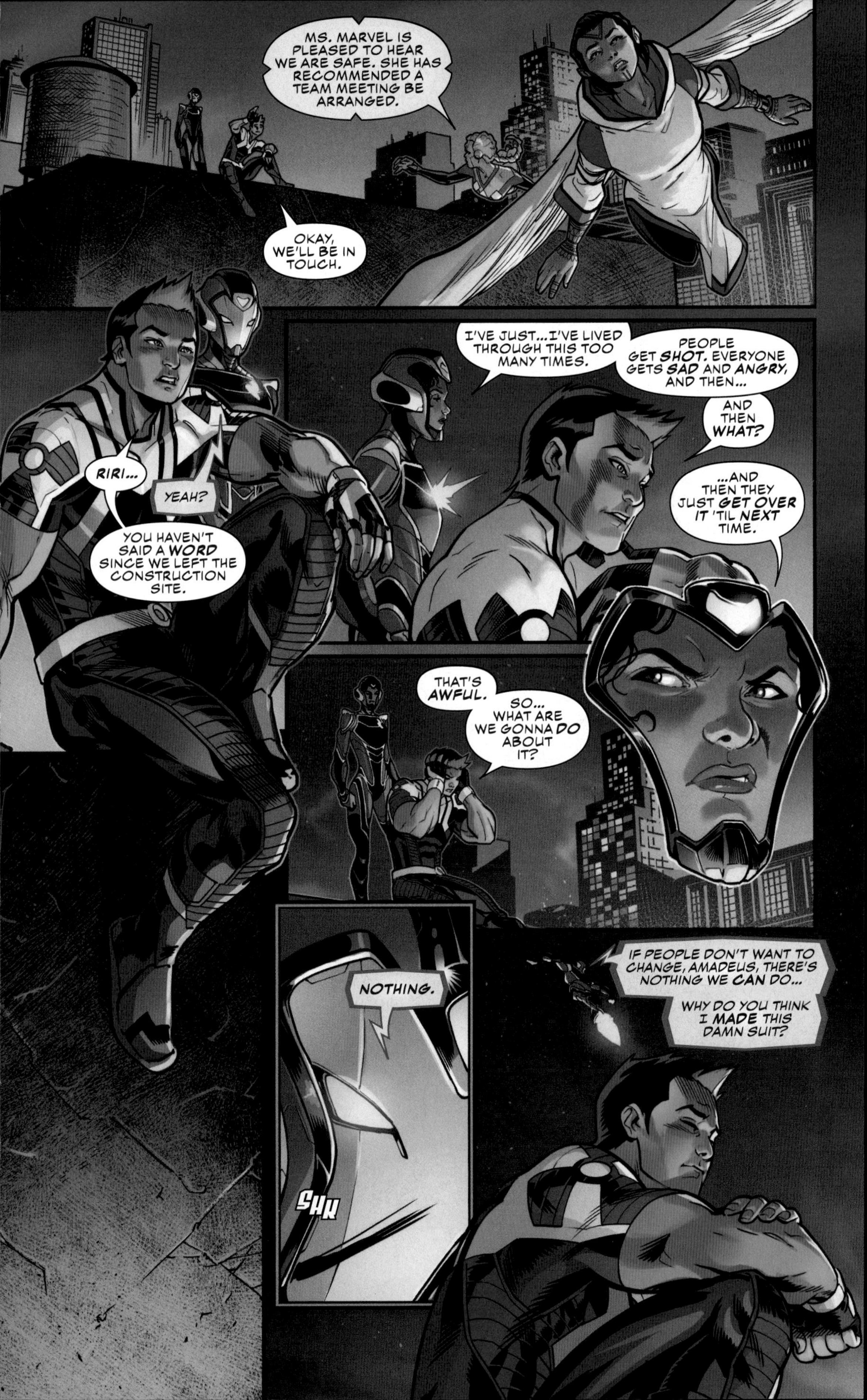
MS. MARVEL IS PLEASED TO HEAR WE ARE SAFE. SHE HAS RECOMMENDED A TEAM MEETING BE ARRANGED.
OKAY, WE'LL BE IN TOUCH.
RIRI...
YEAH?
YOU HAVEN'T SAID A WORD SINCE WE LEFT THE CONSTRUCTION SITE.
I'VE JUST...I'VE LIVED THROUGH THIS TOO MANY TIMES.
PEOPLE GET SHOT. EVERYONE GETS SAD AND ANGRY, AND THEN...
AND THEN WHAT?
...AND THEN THEY JUST GET OVER IT 'TIL NEXT TIME.
THAT'S AWFUL.
SO... WHAT ARE WE GONNA DO ABOUT IT?
NOTHING.
SHK
IF PEOPLE DON'T WANT TO CHANGE, AMADEUS, THERE'S NOTHING WE CAN DO...
WHY DO YOU THINK I MADE THIS DAMN SUIT?

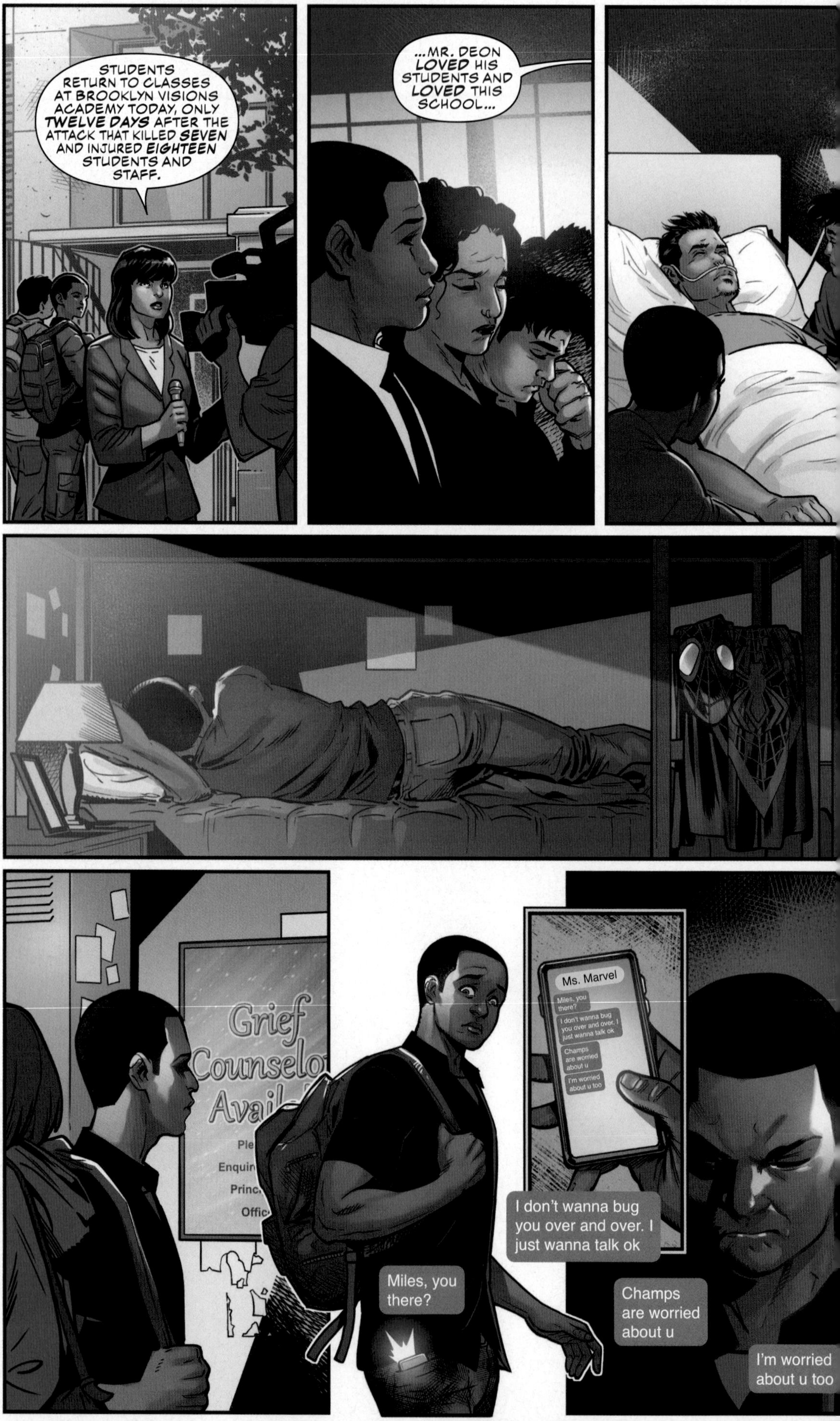
STUDENTS RETURN TO CLASSES AT BROOKLYN VISIONS ACADEMY TODAY, ONLY TWELVE DAYS AFTER THE ATTACK THAT KILLED SEVEN AND INJURED EIGHTEEN STUDENTS AND STAFF.
...MR. DEON LOVED HIS STUDENTS AND LOVED THIS SCHOOL...
Grief Counselo[r]s Availa[ble]
Ple
Enquir
Princ
Offic
Ms. Marvel
Miles, you there?
I don't wanna bug you over and over. I just wanna talk ok
Champs are worried about u
I'm worried about u too
I don't wanna bug you over and over. I just wanna talk ok
Miles, you there?
Champs are worried about u
I'm worried about u too

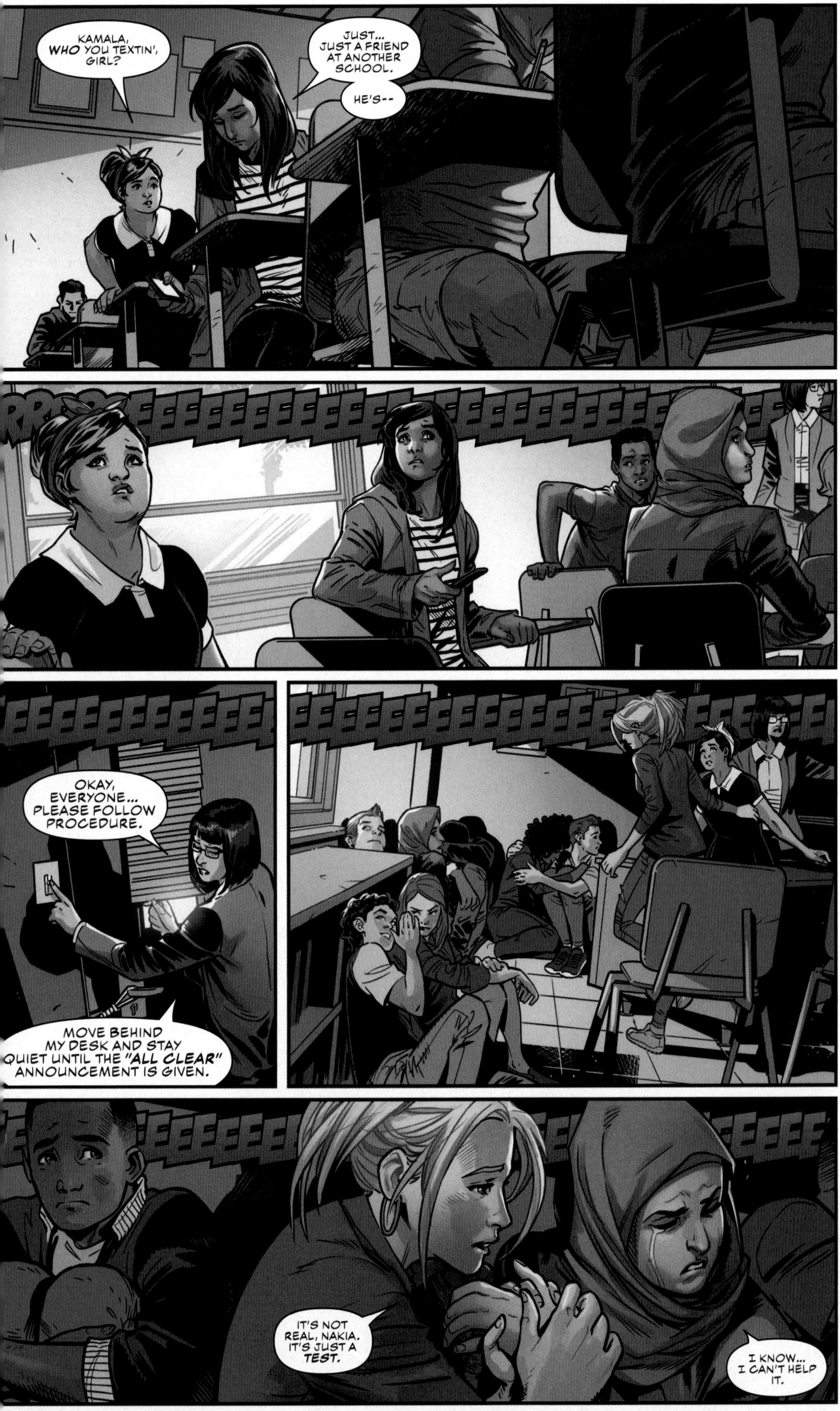

KAMALA, WHO YOU TEXTIN', GIRL?
JUST... JUST A FRIEND AT ANOTHER SCHOOL.
HE'S--
OKAY, EVERYONE... PLEASE FOLLOW PROCEDURE.
MOVE BEHIND MY DESK AND STAY QUIET UNTIL THE "ALL CLEAR" ANNOUNCEMENT IS GIVEN.
IT'S NOT REAL, NAKIA. IT'S JUST A TEST.
I KNOW... I CAN'T HELP IT.

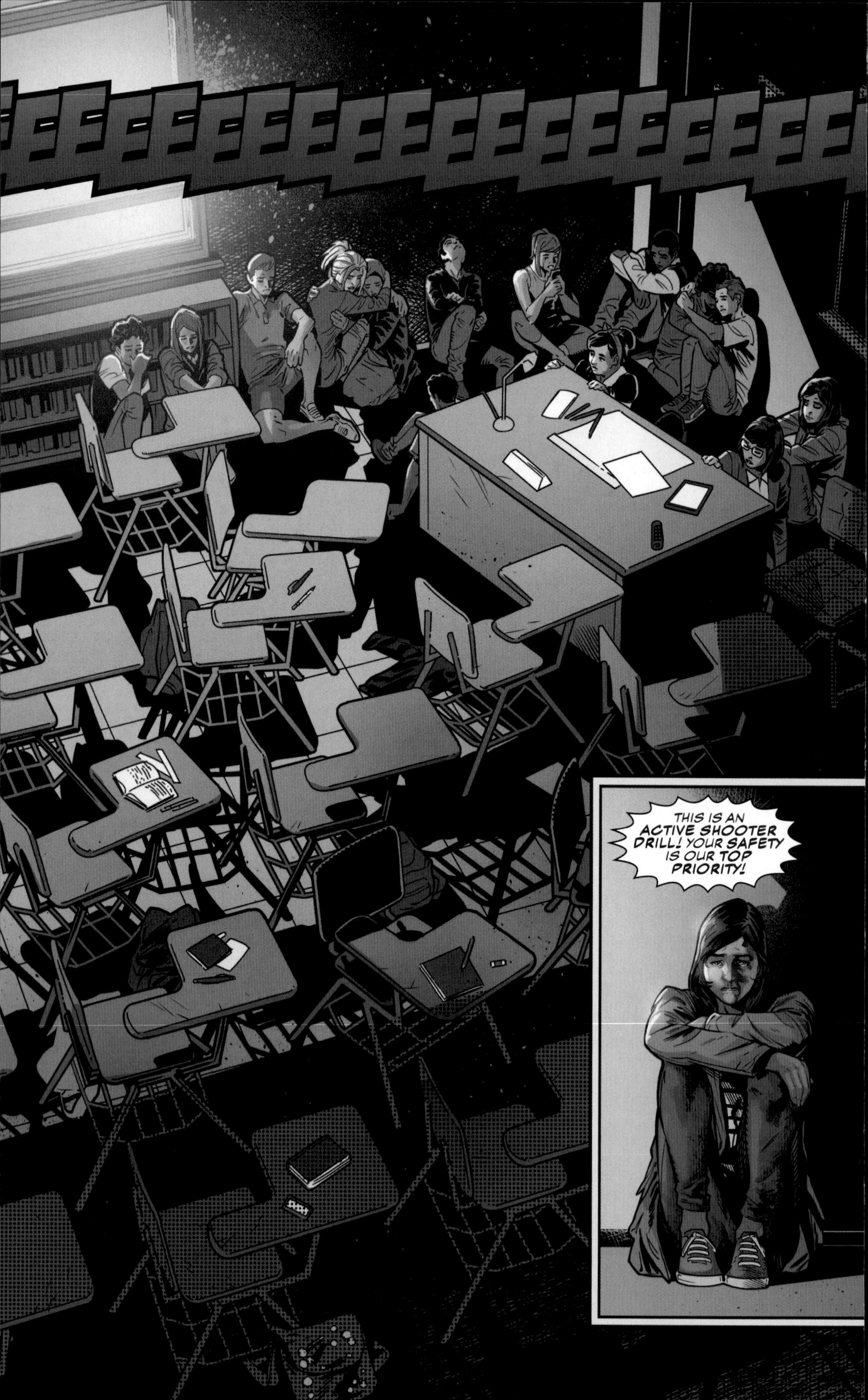
EEEEEEEEEEEEEEEEEEEE
THIS IS AN ACTIVE SHOOTER DRILL! YOUR SAFETY IS OUR TOP PRIORITY!

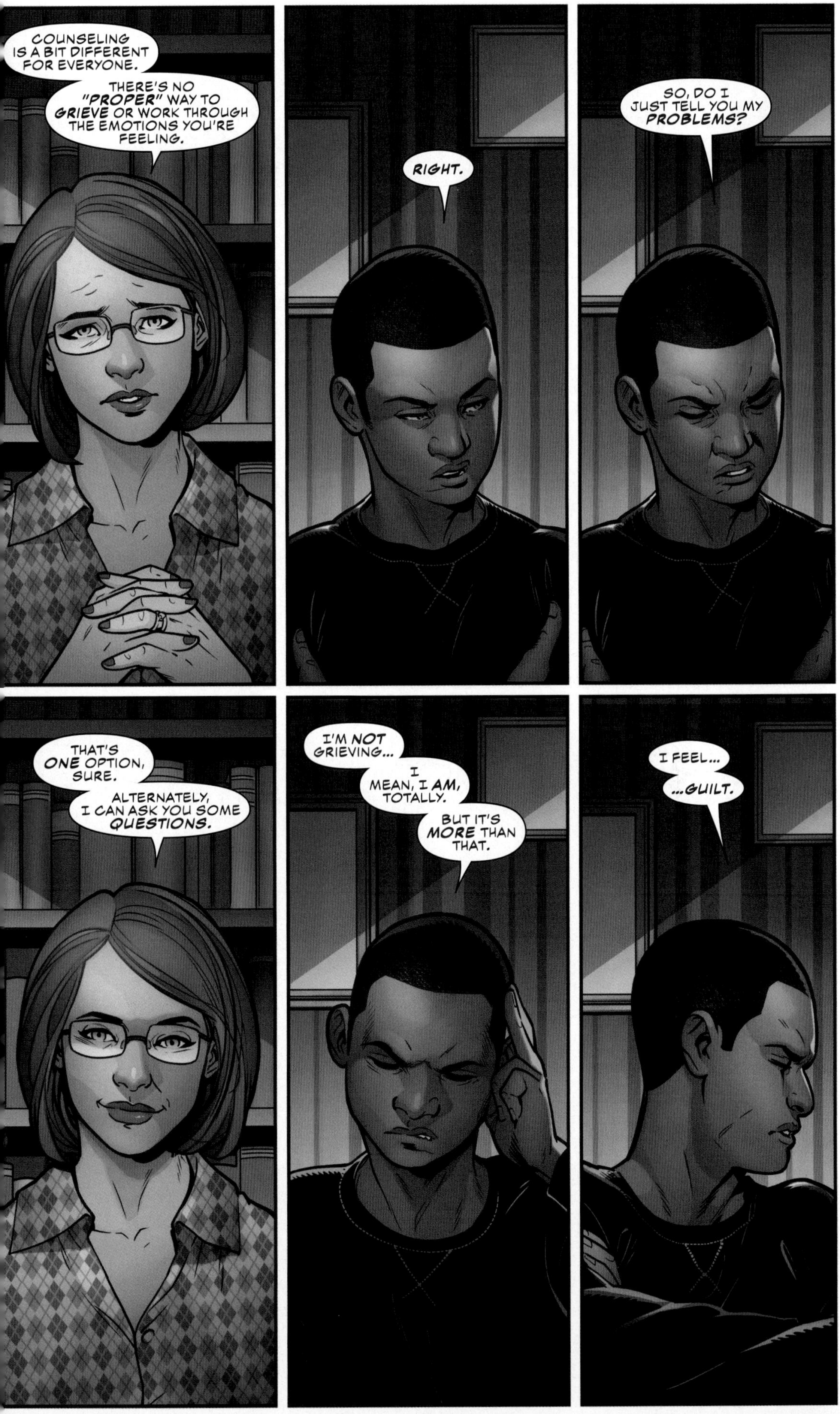
COUNSELING IS A BIT DIFFERENT FOR EVERYONE.
THERE'S NO "PROPER" WAY TO GRIEVE OR WORK THROUGH THE EMOTIONS YOU'RE FEELING.
RIGHT.
SO, DO I JUST TELL YOU MY PROBLEMS?
THAT'S ONE OPTION, SURE.
ALTERNATELY, I CAN ASK YOU SOME QUESTIONS.
I'M NOT GRIEVING...
I MEAN, I AM, TOTALLY.
BUT IT'S MORE THAN THAT.
I FEEL...
...GUILT.

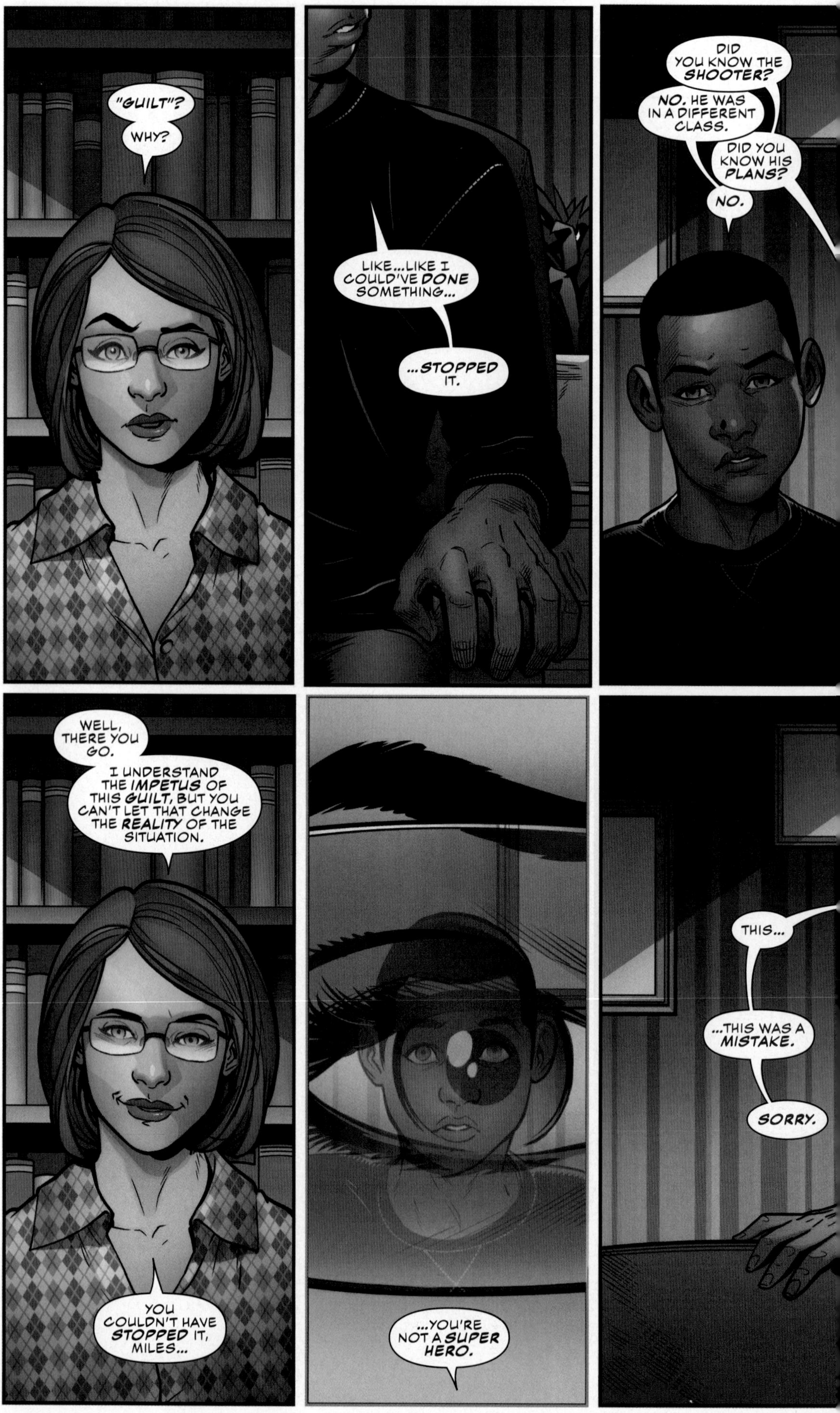
"GUILT"?
WHY?
LIKE...LIKE I COULD'VE DONE SOMETHING...
...STOPPED IT.
DID YOU KNOW THE SHOOTER?
NO. HE WAS IN A DIFFERENT CLASS.
DID YOU KNOW HIS PLANS?
NO.
WELL, THERE YOU GO.
I UNDERSTAND THE IMPETUS OF THIS GUILT, BUT YOU CAN'T LET THAT CHANGE THE REALITY OF THE SITUATION.
YOU COULDN'T HAVE STOPPED IT, MILES...
...YOU'RE NOT A SUPER HERO.
THIS...
...THIS WAS A MISTAKE.
SORRY.

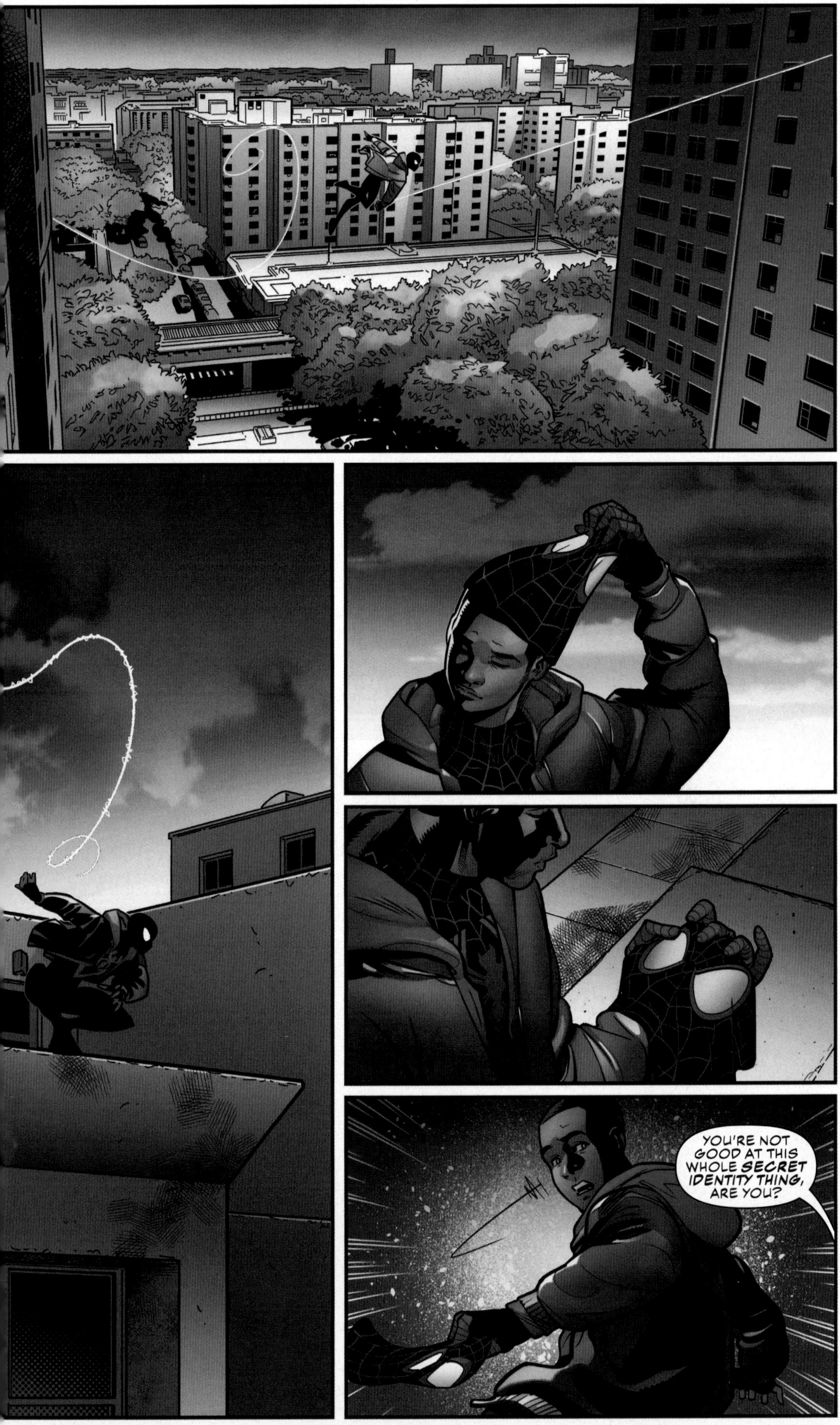
YOU'RE NOT GOOD AT THIS WHOLE SECRET IDENTITY THING, ARE YOU?

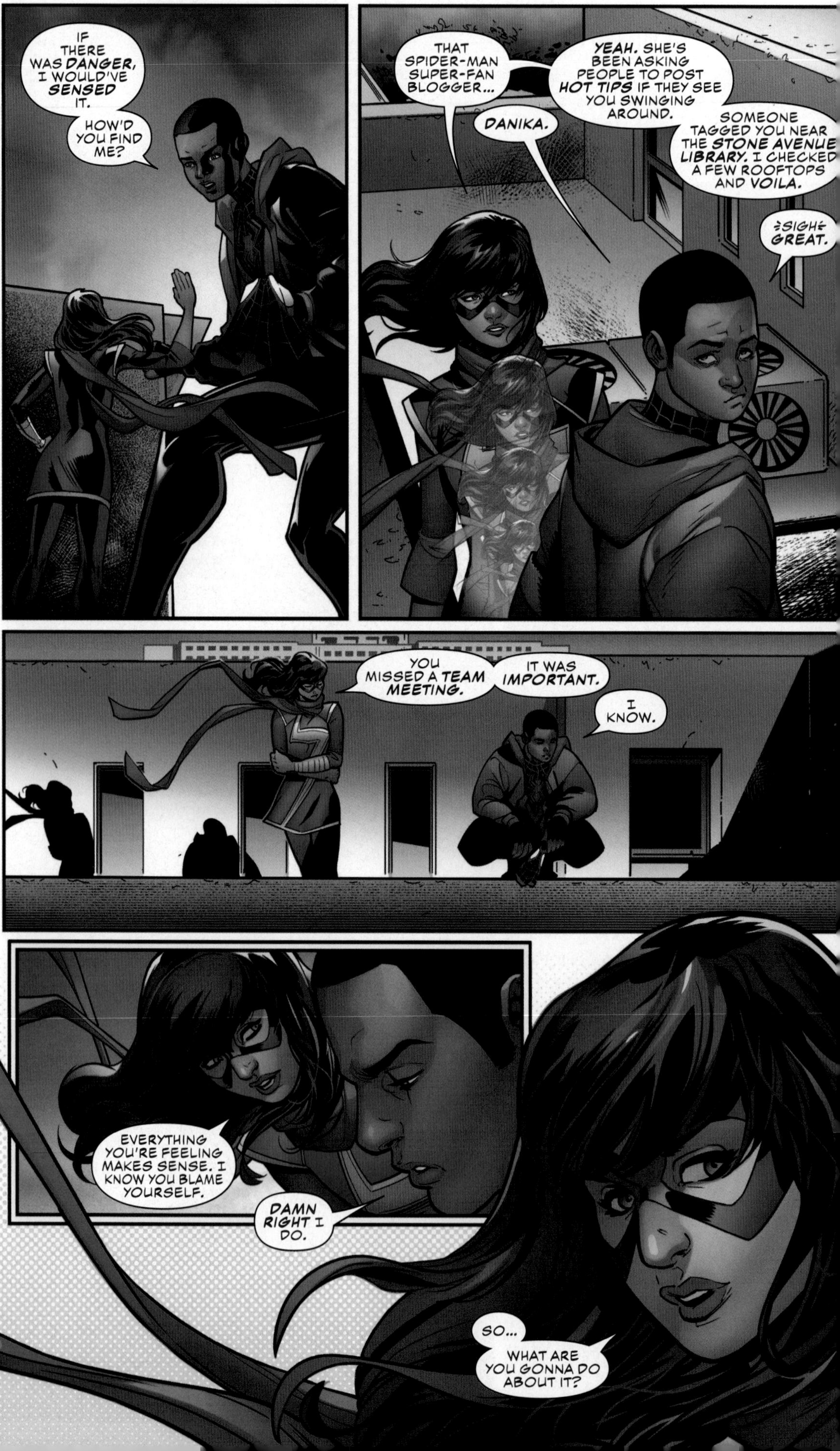
IF THERE WAS DANGER, I WOULD'VE SENSED IT.
HOW'D YOU FIND ME?
THAT SPIDER-MAN SUPER-FAN BLOGGER...
DANIKA.
YEAH. SHE'S BEEN ASKING PEOPLE TO POST HOT TIPS IF THEY SEE YOU SWINGING AROUND.
SOMEONE TAGGED YOU NEAR THE STONE AVENUE LIBRARY. I CHECKED A FEW ROOFTOPS AND VOILA.
SIGH GREAT.
YOU MISSED A TEAM MEETING.
IT WAS IMPORTANT.
I KNOW.
EVERYTHING YOU'RE FEELING MAKES SENSE. I KNOW YOU BLAME YOURSELF.
DAMN RIGHT I DO.
SO...
WHAT ARE YOU GONNA DO ABOUT IT?

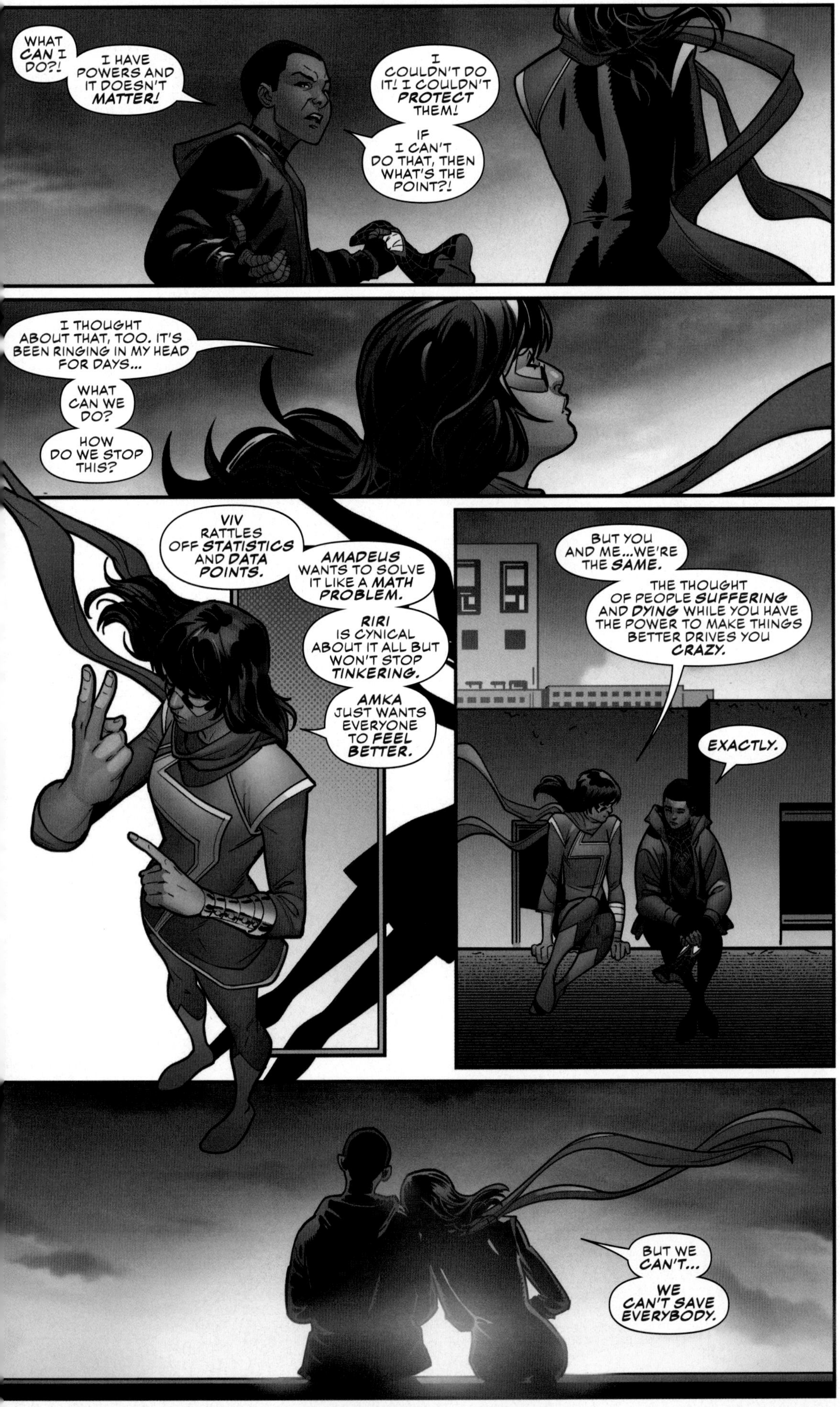

WHAT CAN I DO?!
I HAVE POWERS AND IT DOESN'T MATTER!
I COULDN'T DO IT! I COULDN'T PROTECT THEM!
IF I CAN'T DO THAT, THEN WHAT'S THE POINT?!
I THOUGHT ABOUT THAT, TOO. IT'S BEEN RINGING IN MY HEAD FOR DAYS...
WHAT CAN WE DO?
HOW DO WE STOP THIS?
VIV RATTLES OFF STATISTICS AND DATA POINTS.
AMADEUS WANTS TO SOLVE IT LIKE A MATH PROBLEM.
RIRI IS CYNICAL ABOUT IT ALL BUT WON'T STOP TINKERING.
AMKA JUST WANTS EVERYONE TO FEEL BETTER.
BUT YOU AND ME...WE'RE THE SAME.
THE THOUGHT OF PEOPLE SUFFERING AND DYING WHILE YOU HAVE THE POWER TO MAKE THINGS BETTER DRIVES YOU CRAZY.
EXACTLY.
BUT WE CAN'T...
WE CAN'T SAVE EVERYBODY.

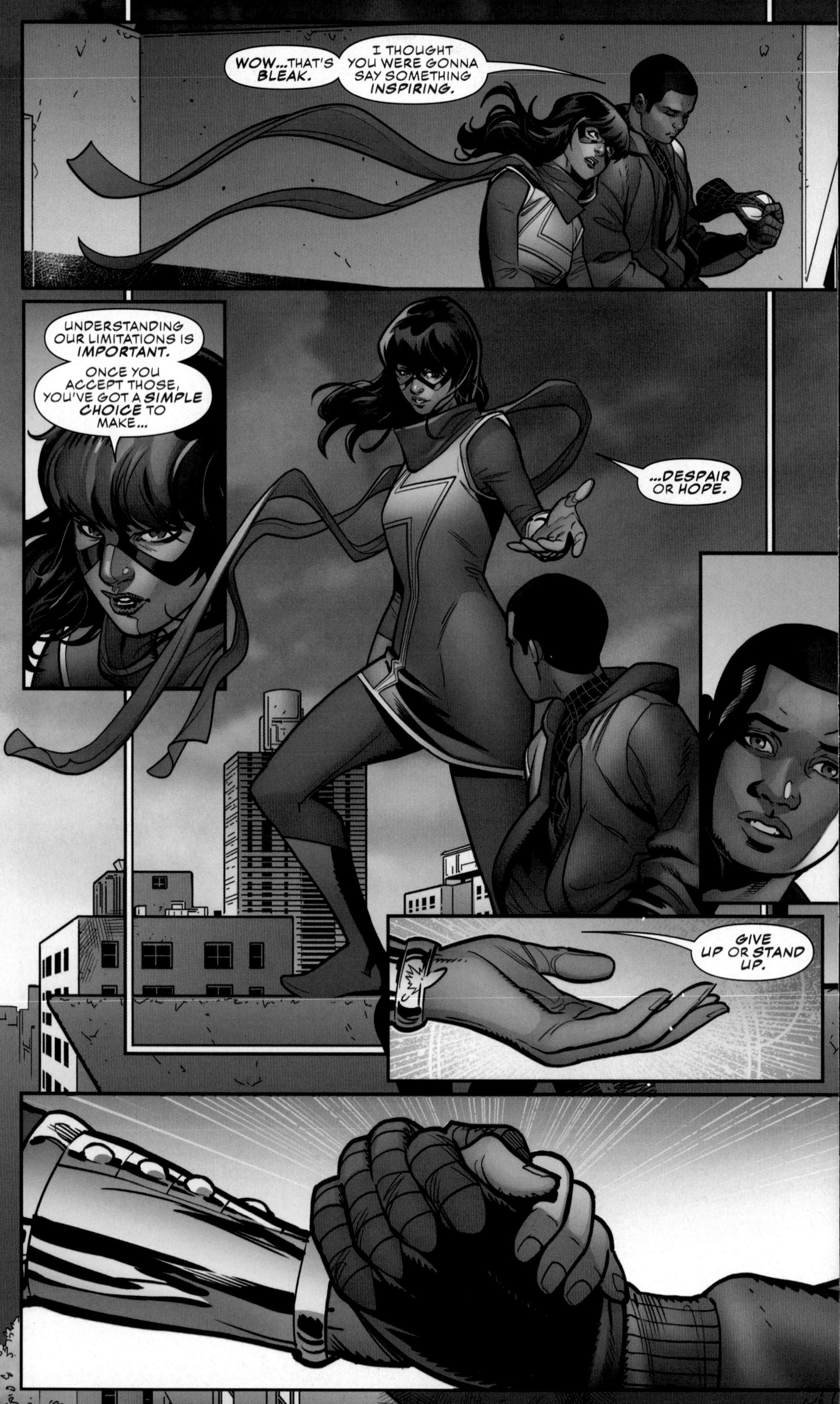
WOW...THAT'S BLEAK.
I THOUGHT YOU WERE GONNA SAY SOMETHING INSPIRING.
UNDERSTANDING OUR LIMITATIONS IS IMPORTANT.
ONCE YOU ACCEPT THOSE, YOU'VE GOT A SIMPLE CHOICE TO MAKE...
...DESPAIR OR HOPE.
GIVE UP OR STAND UP.

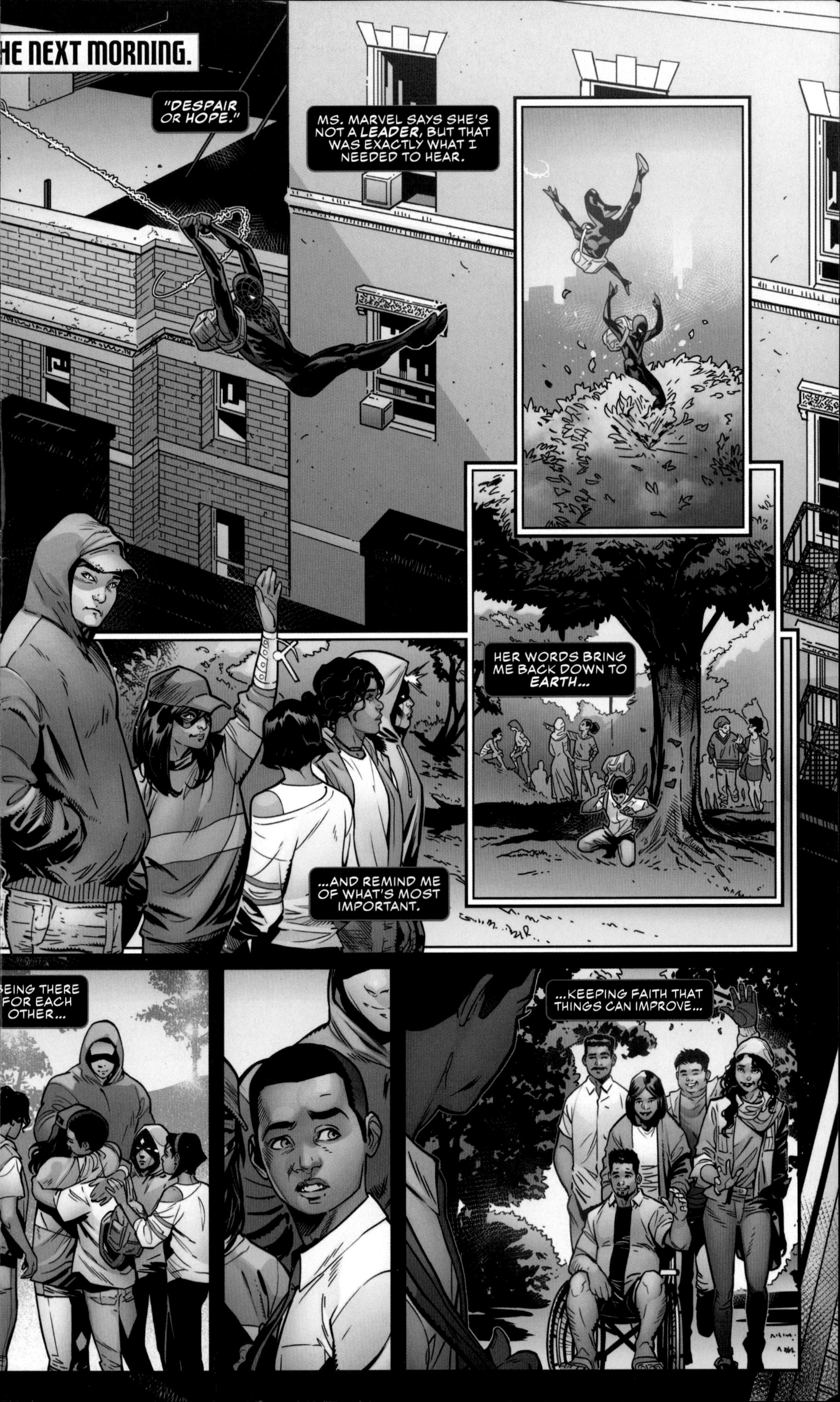
HE NEXT MORNING.
"DESPAIR OR HOPE."
MS. MARVEL SAYS SHE'S NOT A LEADER, BUT THAT WAS EXACTLY WHAT I NEEDED TO HEAR.
HER WORDS BRING ME BACK DOWN TO EARTH...
...AND REMIND ME OF WHAT'S MOST IMPORTANT.
EING THERE FOR EACH OTHER...
...KEEPING FAITH THAT THINGS CAN IMPROVE...

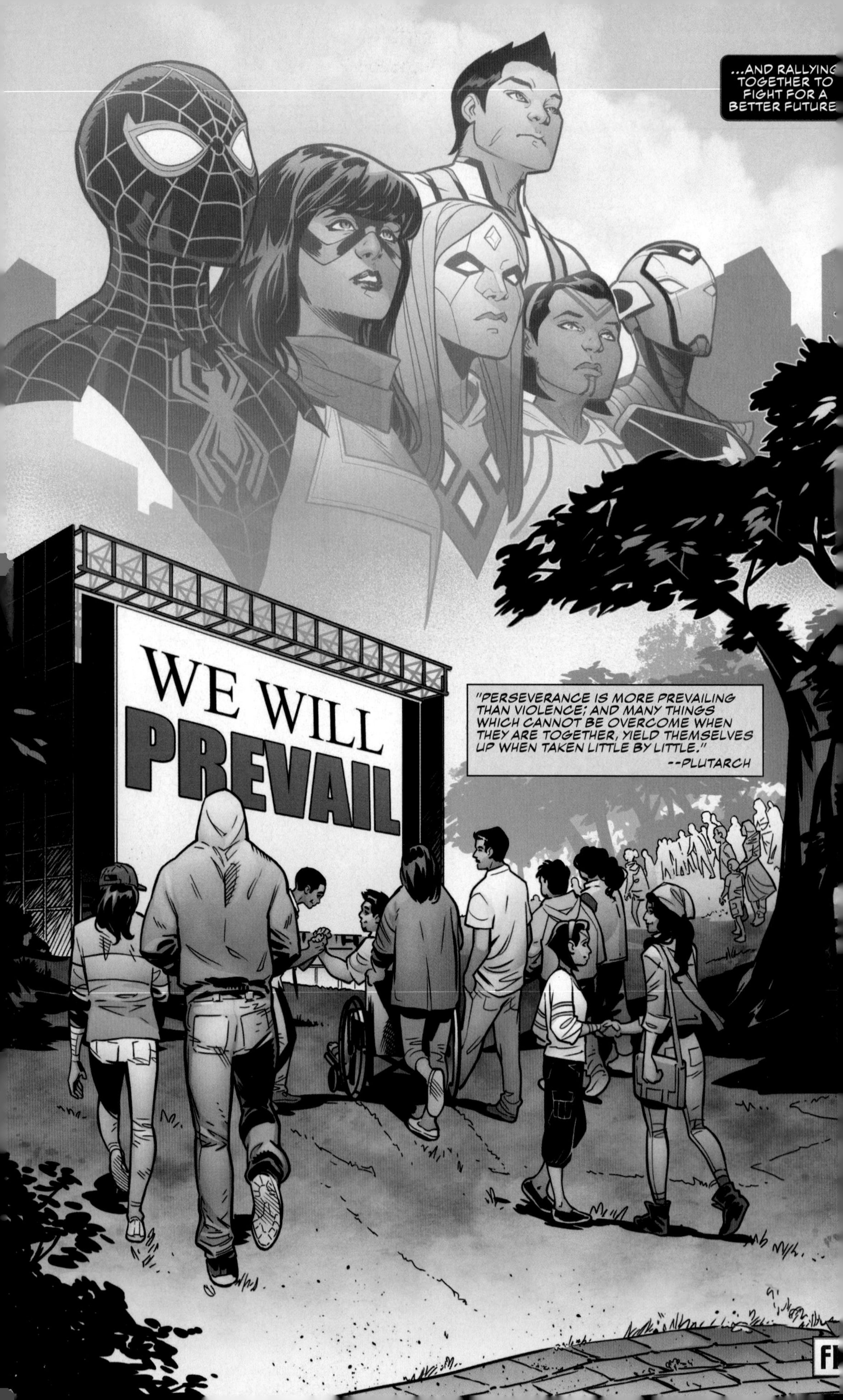
...AND RALLYING TOGETHER TO FIGHT FOR A BETTER FUTURE
WE WILL PREVAIL
"PERSEVERANCE IS MORE PREVAILING THAN VIOLENCE; AND MANY THINGS WHICH CANNOT BE OVERCOME WHEN THEY ARE TOGETHER, YIELD THEMSELVES UP WHEN TAKEN LITTLE BY LITTLE."
--PLUTARCH